Thomas Burri

The Greatest Possible Freedom

Interpretive formulas and their spin in free movement case law

Nomos Verlagsgesellschaft

Thomas Burri is an assistant professor of international and European law at the University of St. Gallen (HSG) in Switzerland. He received his education as a lawyer at the Universities of Basel and Zurich, as well as at the College of Europe in Bruges. This book was written while on research stays at Harvard University and the Ludwig-Maximilians-University in Munich. Thomas Burri previously published a book on the rights of minorities ('Models of Autonomy? Case-Studies of Minority Regimes in Hungary and French Polynesia') as well as articles in various international and European law journals and books. Webpage: www.thomas-burri.com.

Die Deutsche Nationalbibliothek lists this publication in the
Deutsche Nationalbibliografie; detailed bibliographic data
is available in the Internet at http://dnb.d-nb.de

a.t.: St. Gallen, Univ., Habil., 2015

ISBN 978-3-8487-2391-1 (Print)
978-3-8452-6549-0 (ePDF)

British Library Cataloguing-in-Publication Data
A catalogue record for this book is available from the British Library.

ISBN 978-3-8487-2391-1 (Print)
978-3-8452-6549-0 (ePDF)

Library of Congress Cataloging-in-Publication Data
Burri, Thomas
The Greatest Possible Freedom
Interpretive formulas and their spin in free movement case law
Thomas Burri
606 p.
Includes bibliographic references and index.

ISBN 978-3-8487-2391-1 (Print)
978-3-8452-6549-0 (ePDF)

1. Edition 2015

Für Lotti und Kaspar

Table of Contents

A Introduction: The way to the greatest possible freedom

'The greatest possible freedom' is a formula which originated in the very first preliminary ruling of the Court of Justice of the European Union in social security, the judgment in *Hoekstra, 1964*. Ever since then, the Court has regularly relied on this formula, most recently in *Dumont, 2013*. The evolution and the power of formulas like 'the greatest possible freedom' are the topic of this book: Under which circumstances does the Court use them? When do they spin the Court's decisions?

Three types of formula are examined, namely formulas that embody either broad interpretation, like 'the greatest possible freedom', a coordinative interpretation, or a fundamental interpretation. Simply put, the book thus examines certain aspects of the Court's activism, structuralism, and fundamentalism. This is done in the second part entitled 'the evolution of interpretive formulas'.

The object of analysis is the internal market case-law of the Court on natural persons, i. e. on citizens, workers, establishment, services, diplomas, and social security. This body of case-law, roughly 1400 decisions, is presented in the first part named 'the case-law'. Practitioners will be pleased to find that the book is complete: It includes all the decisions the Court has ever handed down concerning natural persons as citizens, workers, established persons, diploma awarders/-ees, service providers/receivers, or persons involved with social security. It includes decisions based on primary as well as secondary law. To uncover this case-law each volume of the European Court Reports was perused manually, from cover to cover. The case-law is included up to 16 April 2013.

I Free movement of persons and services: 1400 decisions

This is a book about the rights of natural persons in the internal market. The book unearths all the decisions the Court of Justice of the European Union has ever handed down concerning free movement of persons and services. This means that the book includes the free movement of workers, the freedom of establishment, the coordination of social security, the recognition of diplomas, and the freedom of Union citizens; it also includes the free movement of services, i. e. the freedoms to provide as well as to receive services. The entire case-law as to *secondary* legislation which implements these freedoms and diplomas/social security is included, too. The book includes judgments and orders.

All in all, this body of case-law includes roughly 1400 decisions that the Court handed down over the course of almost 60 years. These decisions were found first by searching the official data base. Since the data base has no memory – search sessions rapidly expire, decisions cannot be flagged or annotated – it was necessary to peruse all the volumes of the European Court Reports manually. This took the author almost three years to complete. Because of the delay in publishing the European Court Reports books, the last of them scrutinized was volume two of the year 2011. From then on, the online database had to suffice. Decisions therein were perused until 16 April 2013.

The borders of the case-law examined are fuzzy. The freedom of establishment overlaps with the free movement of capital; the way the freedom of establishment of legal persons is interpreted has effects on the freedom of natural persons to establish themselves; a ground justifying a restriction of the free movement of goods – a freedom that is not included in this study – is also relevant for restrictions of the free movement of persons and services. Hence, some hard decisions had to be taken on what is included in this book and what is excluded. They are as follows. The basic rule of thumb is that decisions concerning natural persons are included while those concerning legal persons are excluded. Judgments based on the secondary rules on taxation of intra-group dividends, for instance, are not included, although these rules implement the freedom of establishment; decisions interpreting the secondary rules governing public procurement are not included, either; decisions on the company law directives are not discussed in detail, but mentioned briefly. However, if the *primary* freedom of establishment is treated in any of these decisions, it is necessarily included, regardless of whether it concerns natural persons or companies. The reason for this inclusion is that the primary rules on the establishment of natural persons are too intricately entwined with those on companies to be separated. As a compromise, the decisions concerning the primary freedom of establishment of companies are dealt with less extensively in the first part of this book on 'the case-law'. The same approach is followed for the free movement of services and the secondary norms implementing it for legal persons. Only one line of authority of the primary freedom of establishment of companies is fully excluded, namely the golden share decisions that are handed down on the basis of the freedom of establishment. The free movement of capital is entirely excluded. Decisions concerning social policy, i. e. discrimination on the basis of sex, age, etc., are not included, either. Decisions of the Court of First Instance, now called the General Court, are left aside entirely. Decisions concerning agreements extending the rights of natural persons in the internal market to third states – i. e. decisions on the Agreement on the European Economic Area, the Europe Agreements, and the Agreements with Turkey, the Maghreb countries, Russia, and Switzerland – are included. Decisions concerning the Schengen or Dublin frameworks, in turn, are not included. The opinions of the Advocate Generals are generally excluded. So the occasional hint at an opinion in the first part on 'the case-law' is random.

For those who prefer the jargon of case-law what is included in this book can be described as follows. Are included all lines of authority that, respectively, began with *Ugliola, 1969*; *Costa v. ENEL, 1964* (re freedom of establishment, not primacy); *Hoekstra, 1964*; *Thieffry, 1977*; *Van Binsbergen, 1974* (or *Sacchi, 1974*); and with *Martínez Sala, 1998* (or *Skanavi, 1996*). The series beginning with *Coname, 2005* or arguably *Parking Brixen, 2005* is included, so is the strand initiated by *Commission v. France (tax credit), 1986*. The series that the three judgments *Commission v. Portugal (golden share), 2002*; *Commission v. France (golden share), 2002*; and *Commission v. Belgium (golden share), 2002* began is excluded, as is the thread that began with *Bordessa, 1995*. The likes of *Defrenne II, 1976* and *Mangold, 2005* are not included, either. However, the series beginning, respectively, with *Demirel, 1987*; *Kziber, 1991*; *Krid, 1995*; *Kondova, 2001*; *Simutenkov, 2005*; and *Stamm, 2008* are all included.

II The structure of the book

The first part of the book, 'the case-law', is devoted to a thick description of the case-law within the framework noted above. Each chapter in this first part encompasses a decade of case-law. Each decade is further broken down into 'workers' – or 'workers and citizens' – 'establishment' including diplomas, 'social security', and 'services'. The description within each section sometimes follows a chronological sometimes a content-based order, depending on various factors. The few decisions of the early days are grouped according to substance. Their implications for other decisions are rather evident. Later on, as the case-law developed, decisions became typically more complex and addressed various points while having multiple cross-implications. So a chronological description is more suitable for this time period. Within social security, decisions are easily categorized according to topics – namely aggregation, family benefits, unemployment benefits, etc. – owing to the rather homogenous and self-referential nature of social security. Within the freedom of services judgments are generally more heterogeneous. Services cover a vast array of topics and have multiple links to establishment. Hence, a chronological order combined with categorization according to substance is applied for services. Overall, this structure should make it easy for practitioners to navigate the case-law and to tap into the context of decisions they previously identified as interesting. In general, the presentation in the part on 'the case-law' is as neutral as possible. Opinionated qualification, e. g. through the use of adjectives, is avoided as is analysis more generally.

The second part, 'the evolution of interpretive formulas', takes the body of case-law identified in the first part and traces how certain interpretive formulas evolve. Some interpretive formulas are thus mapped out through the entire case-law of persons and services, from the beginning to the present. It is examined where certain formulas originate, when they appear, and how they influence the Court's decisions. More succinctly, the questions are answered where the formulas are from, when they are used, and how powerful they are. The power of a formula is examined and qualitatively assessed in each decision where it occurs. 'Power' in this context is represented by the 'spin' a formula exerts within a decision. This 'spin' is gradual. In casual parliance, 'spin' occurs when one reads a judgment, arrives at an interpretive formula which raises a certain expectation of the way the decision will go – and the decision then indeed goes this expected way and ends there.

Three sets of interpretive 'formulas' are examined. First, in the chapter entitled 'broad', formulas are examined that embody either broad or restrictive interpretation. Which formulas exist in the body of case-law examined that embody a broad or restrictive approach? In which circumstances are they typically used? How do they evolve? When are they decisive for the Court's decision, when do they provide impetus, exert 'spin'? These are the questions that are answered first for 'broad' interpretation. The chapter on 'broad' interpretive formulas is different from the other two chapters on interpretive formulas in that it may contain aspects that are relevant beyond the law of the Union and the Court of Justice. Broad or restrictive interpretation is common in other legal orders, too, like in international and domestic law. Yet, these broader implications and possible cross-connections are not addressed in this book, because it is about the case-law of the Court of Justice. In the next chapter the above questions are pondered for interpretive formulas in which the Court relied on the idea that parts of Union law merely coordinated national law, as an alternative to harmonizing it. This is the chapter entitled 'coordinated'. This interpretation is highly specific for the law of the Union and the case-law of the Court. Coordination of legal systems is – at least in this terminology and as far as can be judged – unique to the law of the Union. Within this law, social security is of primary importance. The final chapter labelled 'fundamental' ponders the above questions for formulas drawing on the idea that some notions are fundamental, while others are not. Like broad interpretation, interpretation relying on hierarchy, such as a notion being fundamental, is not unique to the law of the Union. Most legal orders, perhaps even all, at one point or another prioritize some notions over others. However, this chapter is uniquely tied to the law of the Union in that it primarily deals with Union citizenship and an intepretive formula used exclusively with regard to it ('the fundamental status').

III Why is the first part on 'the case-law' necessary? Why not cover more interpretive formulas?

Why not drop the voluminous first part on 'the case-law' and cover more interpretive formulas? And why are three interpretive formulas investigated and others left aside? Answers to these questions are not easy to give. They to some degree concern scientific honesty and, in addition, require a deep understanding of the case-law that is the subject of the first part of this book. Admittedly, the evolution of further interpretive formulas could be traced. For instance, the formula used to argue that social security rights based solely on national law must not be lost after the right of free movement has been exercised would have been an alternative; or the formula relying on the need for cohesion of the tax system.

However, several points are important in this regard. First, to live up to scientific rigour the first part on 'the case-law' is indispensable. The body to be investigated must first be established – the facts, the data must first be collected and described, so to speak – before it can be discussed. A crucial step would be missed, if discussion and interpretation were begun right away. Uncertainty about the framework and the limits of the interpretation would result, ultimately rendering the study useless. Second, it cannot be avoided to be selective when it comes to interpretive formulas. Dozens of interpretive formulas are used in the body of case-law under scrutiny, a body of case-law that is, moreover, exceptionally large. It would fill many more volumes, if all of those formulas were to be traced. Third, given the need to select, variety is important. Hence, interpretive formulas are chosen that shed light on as many different aspects of the case-law as possible. The broad as well as the restrictive formulas discussed first in the second part elucidate the Court's activism to some extent and are potentially important beyond the law of the Union; the formula of coordination, which comes next, illuminates a possibly unique structural element in the Court's case-law; and the fundamental formula(s) partly reveal(s) how the case-law relies on hierarchy, in particular with regard to an 'institution' that is central to the Union, i. e. Union citizenship. The examination of this set of formulas, hopefully, allows us to achieve at least a better understanding of the Court's case-law in persons and services and of the way it evolves. Fourth, quite plainly, those interpretive formulas are traced in the case-law which, after years of careful study of the case-law, turned out to be most interesting. A personal element is, obviously, involved in this choice. But it is an informed choice and one the reader hopefully finds plausible.

IV A text-based approach

For all three interpretive formulas the analysis is based on the text of the decisions of the Court. This has two consequences. First, it is possible that some decisions escape scrutiny which, generally speaking, turn out to have a broad, sweeping character or implicitly rely on a coordinative or fundamental approach without that this is reflected in the wording of the decisions. Second, this book is not capable of fully answering the question *why* a specific formula is used in a decision. Factors outside the text of a decision influence the answer to the question 'why'. These factors include the composition of the Court, the opinion of the Advocate General, or the person who writes the decision. Such factors are not taken into account in this book because of the text-based approach. The book rather explains the 'when', the 'how', and to a certain extent the 'wherefore' for the relevant formulas. Yet, although the 'why' is ignored, the contribution this book makes is significant. As indicated above, the analysis of 'broad' formulas clarifies an aspect of the Court's activism, at least implicitly; the engagement with formulas of coordination sheds light on the structural nature of the Court's case-law; and the examination of 'fundamental' formulas helps us understand the hierarchy the Court injected into the law and its constitutional nature.

V Why is this book useful and novel?

The book for the first time gathers *all* the case-law of the Court on workers, citizens, establishment, services, diplomas, and social security. It does not just assemble the 'important' decisions, but *all of them*.[1] This completeness is useful for the practitioner who is relieved of the worry that a relevant judgment escapes attention. The usefulness is not limited to this practical aspect though. The Union's law of social security has so far been a technical domain that has been left to the specialists. Consequently, there are mainly handbooks that are confined to explaining the basics of the Union's law of social security.[2] Such handbooks sometimes also include international social security law; and they deal with the implications of international and Union law for a specific (member) state.[3] Other items address just one aspect of social security.[4] Shorter pieces regularly discuss the latest social security case-law of the Court.[5] More profound contributions remain the exception.[6] In scholarship the market freedoms of workers, service providers, and established persons exist entirely apart from social security.[7] In

1 The book avoids drawing a distinction from the outset between 'important' and 'unimportant' decisions. Such a distinction would typically be drawn on the basis of the number of judges assigned to a case, thus distinguishing between grand and small chamber cases. However, the size of the chamber is plain data which is accessible through the Court's decision database. Given that, it seems exaggerated to add a further layer of complication to an already quite complex analysis. Quite apart from that, though, a distinction between 'important' and 'unimportant' decisions would be at odds with the aim of this book, which is to trace fully the evolution of certain interpretive formulas in the whole case-law examined. This aim basically implies that all cases are treated on an equal footing from the outset. An interpretive formula can then play a key role in a decision that is 'unimportant' in the greater scheme of things (and was e. g. assigned to a small chamber). In other words, from the perspective of interpretive formulas such a decision is indeed truly 'important', although it was decided by a small chamber. In brief, whether a decision is important or not for the evolution of interpretive formulas is to be decided in the light of the role an interpretive formula plays in this decision; 'importance' is an output of the investigation this book undertakes, rather than an input to it.

2 Robin C. A. White, *EC Social Security Law* (Harlow: Longman, 1999); Frans Pennings, *European Social Security Law* (Antwerpen: Intersentia, 2010); Eberhard Eichenhofer, *Sozialrecht der Europäischen Union*, 5. ed. (Berlin: Schmidt, 2013).

3 Bettina Kahil-Wolff and Pierre-Yves Greber, *Sécurité sociale: aspects de droit national, international et européen* (Basel: Helbing, 2006).

4 Yves Jorens and Bernd Schulte (eds), *European Social Security Law and Third Country Nationals* (Bruxelles: La Charte, 1998).

5 Vicki Paskalia, 'Co-ordination of Social Security in the European Union: An Overview of Recent Case Law', 46 *Common Market Law Review* (4) (2009), pp. 1177-1218.

6 One early exception was R. Lecourt, *L'Europe des Juges* (Brussels: Bruylant, 1976); later on, Robin C. A. White, *Workers, Establishment, and Services in the European Union* (Oxford: Oxford University Press, 2004); and Robin C. A. White, 'Social Solidarity and Social Security', in Anthony Arnull, Catherine Barnard, Michael Dougan and Eleanor Spaventa (eds), *A Constitutional Order of States?* (Oxford: Hart, 2011), pp. 301-319, are to be noted.

7 Take the edited volume Henry G. Schermers, Cees Flinterman, Alfred E. Kellermann, Johan C. von Haersolte and Gert-Wim A. van de Meent (eds), *Free Movement of Persons in Europe* (Dordrecht: Ni-

contrast to social security, scholarship has very actively engaged with those freedoms and dealt extensively with them.[8] Union citizenship has drawn most of the attention in recent years.[9] There is thus a gap in scholarship between social security and the market freedoms. This book bridges this gap and for the first time

jhoff, 1993), as an example. Joseph Weiler's well-known article "Thou Shalt Not Oppress A Stranger (Ex. 23 : 9): On the Judicial Protection of the Human Rights of Non-EC Nationals" (pp. 248-271) is in it. It is often quoted. The volume does not contain a section on the coordination of social security, although the Court by the time the book was published had handed down more than 200 judgments on social security, while hardly half as many on the free movement of workers. A more recent example is Anne Pieter Van der Mei, *Free Movement of Persons Within the European Community – Cross-border Access to Public Benefits* (Oxford: Hart, 2003). Despite the impression created by the title, the book only briefly deals with social security. Anthony Arnull, *The European Union and its Court of Justice* (Oxford: OUP, 2006), strongly relies on free movement of workers, establishment, services, and citizens, but does not address social security. Further back, the 'Integration Through Law'-series contained a section about migrant workers, but the author of the section notes: 'In part my purpose is to avoid repeating a story that is now very familiar and, especially with regard to social security, [footnote omitted] full of technical details that would overwhelm a comparative discussion.' (Bryan G. Garth, 'Migrant Workers and Rights of Mobility in the European Community and the United States: A Study of Law, Community, and Citizenship in the Welfare State', in Mauro Cappelletti, Monica Seccombe and Joseph Weiler (eds), *Integration Through Law: Europe and the American Federal Experience*, vol. 3 (Berlin: De Gruyter, 1985), pp. 85-163, p. 98.).

8 Nicola Rogers and Rick Scannell, *Free Movement of Persons in the Enlarged European Union* (London: Sweet & Maxwell, 2005); Andrea Biondi, 'Recurring Cycles in the Internal Market: Some Reflections on the Free Movement of Services', in Anthony Arnull, Piet Eeckhout and Takis Tridimas (eds), *Continuity and Change in EU Law* (Oxford: OUP, 2006), pp. 228-259; Friedl Weiss and Frank Wooldridge, *Free Movement of Persons within the European Community*, 2. ed. (Kluwer: Alphenn aan den Rijn, 2007); Eleanor Spaventa, *Free Movement of Persons in the European Union – Barriers to Movement in their Constitutional Context* (Kluwer: Alphenn aan den Rijn, 2007); Alina Tryfonidou, 'In Search of the Aim of the EC Free Movement of Persons Provisions: Has the Court of Justice Missed the Point?', 46 *Common Market Law Review* (5) (2009), pp. 1591-1620; Siofra O'Leary, 'Free Movement of Persons and Services', in Paul Craig and Gráinne de Búrca (eds), *The Evolution of EU Law*, 2nd. ed. (Oxford: Oxford University Press, 2011), pp. 499-545. Much work has also been invested in non-discrimination: Astrid Epiney, *Umgekehrte Diskriminierungen* (Köln: Heymanns, 1995); Christa Tobler, *Indirect Discrimination: A Case Study into the Development of the Legal Concept of Indirect Discrimination under EC Law* (Antwerpen: Intersentia, 2005).

9 The earliest item on this topic (the market citizen) was Hans Peter Ipsen and Gert Nicolaysen, 'Haager Kongress für Europarecht und Bericht über die aktuelle Entwicklung des Gemeinschaftsrechts', 17 *Neue Juristische Wochenschrift* (8) (1964), pp. 339-344. Newer pieces include Michelle Everson, 'The Legacy of the Market Citizen', in Jo Shaw and Gillian More (eds), *New Legal Dynamics of European Union* (Oxford: Clarendon, 1995), pp. 73-90; Joseph Weiler, *The Constitution of Europe* (Cambridge: Cambridge University Press, 1999), in particular pp. 324-357; Dominik Hanf, 'Le développement de la citoyenneté de l'Union européenne', in Dominik Hanf and Rodolphe Muñoz (eds), *La libre circulation des personnes – Etats des lieux et perspectives* (Brussels: Peter Lang, 2007), pp. 15-28; Ferdinand Wollenschläger, *Grundfreiheit ohne Markt* (Tübingen: Mohr Siebeck, 2007); Helmut Philipp Aust, 'Von Unionsbürgern und anderen Wählern – Der Europäische Gerichtshof und das Wahlrecht zum Europäischen Parlament', 11 *Zeitschrift für europarechtliche Studien* (2) (2008), pp. 221-242; Jo Shaw, 'A View of the Citizenship Classics: Martínez Sala and Subsequent Cases on Citizenship of the Union', in Miguel Poiares Maduro and Loïc Azoulai (eds), *The Past and Future of EU Law – The Classics of EU Law Revisited on the 50th Anniversary of the Rome Treaty* (Oxford: Hart, 2010), pp. 356-362; Ulrich Hufeld, 'Vom Wesen der Verfassung Europas – die Freiheit der Unionsbürger als europäisches Legitimationsfundament', 59 *Jahrbuch des öffentlichen Rechts der Gegenwart* (2011), pp. 457-475; Jürgen Habermas, 'Bringing the Integration of Citizens into Line with the Integration of States', 18 *European Law Journal* (4) (2012), pp. 485-488; Christian Calliess, 'The Dynamics of European Citizenship: From Bourgeois to Citoyen', in ECJ (ed.), *The Court of Justice and the Construction of Europe: Analyses and Perspectives on Sixty Years of Case-law* (The Hague: Asser, 2013), pp. 425-441; Daniel Thym, 'Toward 'Real' Citizenship? The Judicial Construction of Union Citizenship and Its Limits', in Maurice Adams, Henri de Waele, Johan Meeusen and Gert Straetmans (eds), *Judging Europe's Judges* (Oxford: Hart, 2013), pp. 155-174.

builds an argument on the basis of the whole case-law concerning natural persons in the internal market.

The study also seeks to contribute to the understanding of the Court and its decisions. The Court's methods of interpretation have been studied and debated intensely.[10] Its activism and its political nature have stirred controversy at the latest since Rasmussen's *On Law and Policy*.[11] The way the Court's decisions and its approach to interpretation have changed from the beginning up to the present is well established.[12] The nature of the Court's decisions, including whether they create precedent,[13] and the nature of the Court itself are well understood by now.[14] This book adds to this scholarship. It is a deep study of in-

10 The early authorities in this regard are Roger-Michel Chevalier, 'Methods and Reasoning of the European Court in Its Interpretations of Community Law', 2 *Common Market Law Review* (1964), pp. 21-35; C. J. Mann, *The Function of Judicial Decision in European Economic Integration* (The Hague: Nijhoff, 1972); and Hans Kutscher, 'Methods of Interpretation as Seen by a Judge at the Court of Justice', in European Court of Justice (ed.), *Judicial and Academic Conference* (Luxembourg, 1976), pp. I-1-51. Later came Anna Bredimas, *Methods of Interpretation and Community Law* (Amsterdam: North Holland, 1978); Richard Plender, 'The Interpretation of Community Acts by Reference to the Intentions of the Authors', 2 *Yearbook of European Law* (1982), pp. 57-105; J. Mertens de Wilmar, 'Reflexions sur les méthodes d'interprétation de la Cour de Justice des Communautés Européennes', 22 *Cahiers du Droit Européen* (1) (1986), pp. 5-20; Joxerramon Bengoetxea, *The Legal Reasoning of the European Court of Justice: Towards a European Jurisprudence* (Oxford: Clarendon, 1993).

11 Hjalte Rasmussen, *On Law and Policy in the European Court of Justice* (Dordrecht: Martinus Nijhoff, 1986); followed in particular by Mauro Cappelletti, *The Judicial Process in Comparative Perspective* (Oxford: Clarendon, 1989). The discussion is not over: Lüder Gerken, Volker Rieble, Günter H. Roth, Torsten Stein and Rudolf Streinz, "*Mangold*" *als ausbrechender Rechtsakt* (München: Sellier, 2009); Andreas Grimmel, 'Judicial Interpretation or Judicial Activism? The Legacy of Rationalism in the Studies of the European Court of Justice', 18 *European Law Journal* (4) (2012), pp. 518-535; Ulrich Haltern and Andreas Bergmann (eds), *Der EuGH in der Kritik* (Tübingen: Mohr Siebeck, 2012); Mark Dawson, Bruno De Witte and Elise Muir (eds), *Judicial Activism at the European Court of Justice* (Cheltenham: Edward Elgar, 2013). For a broader perspective: Antoine Vauchez, 'The transnational politics of judicialization. Van Gend en Loos and the making of EU polity', 16 *European Law Journal* (1) (2010), pp. 1-28.

12 The historical groundwork was done by Jack Dawson, *The Oracles of the Law* (Ann Arbor: University of Michigan Press, 1968), though not specifically with regard to the Court; later on came Michel Waelbroeck, 'Le Rôle de la Cour de justice dans la mise en oeuvre du Traité CEE', 18 *Cahiers du Droit Européen* (4) (1982), pp. 347-380. With a broader approach: Joseph H. H. Weiler, 'The Transformation of Europe', 100 *The Yale Law Journal* (1990-1991) (1991), pp. 2403-2484; also more recently, Francis Snyder, *New Directions in European Community Law* (London: Weidenfeld, 1990); Neville March Hunnings, *The European Courts* (London: Cartermill, 1996); Miguel Poiares Maduro, *We, the Court* (Oxford: Hart, 1998); Gráinne de Búrca and Joseph Weiler (eds), *The European Court of Justice* (Oxford: Oxford University Press, 2001); Gunnar Beck, *The Legal Reasoning of the Court of Justice of the EU* (Oxford: Hart, 2012); Suvi Sankari, *European Court of Justice Legal Reasoning in Context* (Groningen: Europa Law Publishing, 2013); or from a comparative perspective, Mitchel de S.-O.-L.'E. Lasser, *Judicial Deliberations – A Comparative Analysis of Judicial Transparency and Legitimacy* (Oxford: Oxford University Press, 2009). For a history in broad strokes consider Waltraud Hakenberg, 'Der Europäische Gerichtshof – 59 Jahre Gestaltung von Europa durch Recht', in Werner Meng, Georg Ress and Torsten Stein (eds), *Europäische Integration und Globalisierung* (Baden-Baden: Nomos, 2011), pp. 233-247.

13 The authority in this regard is John J. Barceló, 'Precedent in European Community Law', in Neil Maccormick and Robert Summers (eds), *Interpreting Precedents – A Comparative Study* (Aldershot: Dartmouth, 1997), pp. 407-422. More recently: Maurice Adams, Henri de Waele, Johan Meeusen and Gert Straetmans (eds), *Judging Europe's Judges – The Legitimacy of the Case Law of the European Court of Justice* (Oxford: Hart, 2013).

14 Alec Stone Sweet, *Governing with Judges – Constitutional Politics in Europe* (Oxford: Oxford University Press, 2000); Alec Stone Sweet, 'The European Court of Justice', in Paul Craig and Gráinne de Búrca (eds), *The Evolution of EU Law*, 2nd ed. (Oxford: Oxford University Press, 2011), pp. 121-153; Ninon Colneric, 'Entwicklungslinien in der Rechtsprechung des Gerichtshofes der Europäischen Gemeinschaften zum Status von Ausländern', in Klaus Barwig, Stephan Beichel-Benedetti and

terpretation in a specific, though large, body of case-law. It thereby tries to make up for the deficiencies of previous methodological works, which were typically over-arching, focussing on what they identified as the 'most important' cases in the entire case-law. Those studies could therefore only reach very broad conclusions, such as that the Court relies on *effet utile*, uses the four or five traditional methods of interpretation, or applies other interpretive approaches such as *lex specialis* or *e contrario* arguments. In contrast, this book pinpoints certain interpretive formulas in the case-law, traces them through the entire story of the case-law under scrutiny, and assesses their power. These interpretive formulas have so far not received sufficient attention.

VI An illustration of how this book is different from other works

As an illustration of the usefulness and novelty of this book, let us consider four examples of scholarship discussing broad and restrictive interpretation, an interpretation that is, among other interpretations, dealt with in the part of this book on 'the evolution of interpretive formulas'. A classic passage in Hans Kutscher's influential contribution of 1976 notes: The 'Community Treaties, as the constitution of the Community, are to be interpreted broadly rather than restrictively, according to the methods of interpretation applicable to constitutional jurisdiction, and thus like national constitutional law'[15]. It continues: 'The exception which the Treaty makes to the basic rules of equality of treatment, freedom of movement and freedom to provide services have been consistently given a narrow interpretation by the Court' (p. I-37), citing as examples *Van Duyn, 1974*, and *Rutili, 1975*.[16] A passage from a book of 1978 by another prominent author, Anna Bredimas, reads: '[T]he Court has adopted the principle that exceptions to general Community rules and derogations to Treaty obligations must be restrictively interpreted. This is the case where a narrow construction has been applied in order to promote the purposes of the Treaty and reinforce Community efficacy. Its application is so consistent that the case law bristles with examples of it.'[17] This statement is supported with passages from seven judgments stemming from the whole spectrum of the Court's case-law. In 1993, a third leading author, Joxerramon Bengoetxea, in his book quotes the above passage

Gisbert Brinkmann (eds), *Perspektivwechsel im Ausländerrecht* (Baden-Baden: Nomos, 2007), pp. 49-60, in particular p. 60. On the way scholarship has changed: Anthony Arnull, 'The Americanization of EU Law Scholarship', in Anthony Arnull, Piet Eeckhout and Takis Tridimas (eds), *Continuity and Change in EU Law* (Oxford: OUP, 2006), pp. 415-431; and more broadly on judges: Daniel Thürer, 'Die Worte des Richters – Gedanken rund um die Verfassungsgerichtsbarkeit', in Stefan Hammer, Alexander Somek, Manfred Stelzer and Barbara Weichselbaum (eds), *Demokratie und sozialer Rechtsstaat in Europa – Festschrift für Theo Öhlinger* (Wien: WUV, 2004), pp. 272-297.

15 Kutscher, 'Methods of Interpretation as Seen by a Judge at the Court of Justice', p. I-31.

16 That Kutscher does not cite any services cases to support this statement is not surprising given that the three cases with a services dimension which had been decided up to that point – *Sacchi, 1974*; *Van Binsbergen, 1974*; and *Coenen, 1975* – did not contain any evident passage to that effect.

17 Anna Bredimas, *Methods of Interpretation and Community Law*, p. 109-110 (footnote omitted).

on the broad interpretation of the constitutional treaties by Kutscher and adds a 'corollary criterion, i. e. that exceptions to fundamental Community principles are to be narrowly interpreted (see, in general, jurisprudence on article 36)'[18]. Later in his book he identifies 'the directive that „exceptions to fundamental rules (principles) found in the Treaties are to be interpreted strictly"' (p. 246) as a conceptual argument, a systemic criterion. Finally, in a most recent book of 2012, Gunnar Beck examines 'topoi' of interpretation and states as to the restrictive interpretation mentioned in the above passages: 'The principle of the restrictive interpretation of derogations, exceptions, exemptions and exclusions has been well established since the 1970s.'[19] He cites *Commission v. France (maritime worker quota), 1974* as proof and goes on: '[...] [T]he distinction between a broad and a restrictive interpretation, the former designed to give maximum effect to general principles and fundamental rights and the latter ensuring that legitimate national policy prerogatives cannot be used to avoid treaty obligations, is somewhat artificial, not always easy to apply in practice, and in reality the judicial interpretation of a principle or right is determined by a congery of factors which include the area of law concerned as well 'extra-legal' motivational factors' (p. 204).

These are passages from four of the most authoritative works on the Court's methods of interpretation. The above statements are basically all these works say about the notion that some terms are subject to broad while others to restrictive interpretation (while they, of course, say much more than this book about other aspects of interpretation). These statements all suffer from three deficiencies which this book attempts to remedy. (i) They all rely on a selective, anecdoctal range of cases, namely one, two, seven or an undefined range of cases. In contrast, the evidence this book relies on is comprehensive. *All* occurrences of the idea, which is mentioned in the above statements, in the body of case-law identified in the first part are documented. The conclusions this book is able to draw are thus firm and reliable. The conclusions of this book rely on evidence, not eminence. (ii) The ambition of all of the above statements is strong. They all extrapolate and claim to apply to the entire case-law of the Court. In contrast, this book is more modest. It does not work with inference. Its conclusions only relate to a clearly identified body of case-law, the case-law on free movement of persons and services. (iii) The content of the above statements is weak. They only say that interpretation is consistently narrow, that a principle is consistently applied, that there is a directive to interpret exceptions strictly, or that this directive is somewhat artifical, not always easy to apply, and subject to influence by extra-legal factors (see the above statements). In contrast, this book attempts to come to firmer conclusions with regard to such 'directives'. Its thick description offers more context and allows the reader to identify the circumstances in which the 'directives' are deployed. This book is thus not satisfied with plain conclu-

18 Joxerramon Bengoetxea, *The Legal Reasoning of the European Court of Justice*, p. 233.
19 Beck, *The Legal Reasoning of the Court of Justice of the EU*, p. 204 (italics removed).

sions such as that a specific interpretation is not easy to apply in practice and subject to extra-legal factors. Rather, it combines methods and substantive law to reach more solid conclusions.

What distinguishes this book most clearly from the above works, though, is an element that seems to be foreign to those works, partly because of the three points identified above, namely that the broad/restrictive interpretation they identify might constitute an interpretive *formula*, a formula that evolves over the years, one that exercises a certain function within decisions and exerts a certain power – ‚spin' – that is of interest. It is in these regards that this book breaks fresh academic ground. This, in turn, again generates practical value. The book enables practitioners representing natural persons in the internal market to predict more accurately whether certain notions in persons and services will be interpreted broadly or restrictively by the courts, to name just one formula examined in this book. Thus, ideally, the book, owing to its depth, should allow lawyers to strengthen their cases and bind the Court to its own logic. Underlying the approach of this book is obviously the belief that it matters what the Court writes in its decisions. The idea that the grounds of a judgment constitute merely *ex post* justification for majoritarianism or for other unmentioned 'exogenous' factors is too simple. Moreover, a Court that speaks to several hundreds of millions of people does not mention passages, formulas, and even single words by accident. Formulas do not just slip in. We have to take every word the Court writes seriously.

VII What this book is not

Why is there so little discussion of academic writings in this book, in particular in the part on 'the case-law'? Why are there not more footnotes quoting scholarship to underpin a statement made in the text? The terseness in terms of footnotes and quoting is owed to the rigorously scientific approach applied in this book.[20] The body investigated is not academia's publications, but a certain, clearly delineated body of case-law established by the Court of Justice – see the description above. This large body of case-law is the data the book uses and relies on. Consequently, this book can only make reliable statements with regard to this case-law, and not with regard to academic writings. A full investigation of academic writings – and in order to live up to scientific rigour it would necessarily have to be full – would be a different project, one that would for instance investigate the evolution of interpretive formulas or their reception in academic writing. Hence, this book uses academic writings for one purpose only, namely

20 Note also that in-text citations rather than footnotes are used for references to case-law.

to show that the study it undertakes has not been done before and to justify why it should be done. This is done above.[21]

21 When a legislative act is mentioned in this book the publication in the Official Journal is not cited. Citing the details of legislative acts would have overburdened the text. Some acts, like Regulation 1408/71, were changed repeatedly. Hence, the official publication would have to be cited over and over again, in particular when during one and the same year one version was applicable in one judgment, while another was applicable in another judgment. The version relevant in a specific judgment can easily be found out by looking up the case in the official database and verifying it in the text of the judgment. It is usually mentioned right at the beginning of the judgment.

B The case-law

This first part of the book is about the case-law only. It contains a thick, roughly chronological description of the case-law in free movement of persons and services. The second part on 'the evolution of interpretive formulas' then traces how certain interpretive formulas have developed in this body of case-law.

I The 1960s

The famous *Van Gend en Loos, 1963* and *Costa v. ENEL, 1964* overshadowed everything the Court delivered up to the 1970s. However, in the shadow of direct effect and primacy other less obvious developments took place. *Costa v. ENEL, 1964* did not just establish the primacy of Community law, but also instilled article 53 Treaty with direct effect, thus precluding a member state from adopting new measures hindering predominantly the establishment of nationals of other member states (p. 596). In 1969, the Court handed down the first judgment in free movement of workers, *Ugliola, 1969*. In that judgment the Court found that the time period completed in the military service of one member state had to be taken into account on an equal basis in another member state when seniority in an undertaking was determined (paras 6 and 7).

By the time the Court had handed down these two judgments, however, it had already decided more than twenty cases in social security. This social security case-law had begun with *Hoekstra, 1964* in which the Court gave the concept of a worker within the sense of both Regulation 3 concerning social security of migrant workers, i. e. a wage-earner or an assimilated worker, and articles 48 and 51 of the Treaty a Community meaning. It thus removed the term 'worker' from the grasp of the member states. The term 'worker' covered persons who were subject to social security under the various national systems. More specifically, a 'worker' was a person who had been employed and could be employed again and was subject to voluntary continued insurance for workers, regardless of any temporary residence abroad. In the second judgment in social security, *Nonnenmacher, 1964*, the ECJ ruled that the principle that the law of the state of employment was mandatorily applicable pursuant to article 12 Regulation no. 3 did not preclude the state of residence from applying its own law simultaneously, when it afforded additional protection to the migrant worker (para. 1b). The next case was *Kalsbeek, 1964*. In this case the Court first clarified that 'legislation' under Regulation 3 included present and future legislation; the Regulation was applicable regardless of whether a member state had notified the amendment of an act. The Court then dealt for the first time with the aggregation of insurance periods. It decided that the apportionment in article 28(1)(b) Regulation 3 need not have been applied if periods had not previously been aggregated pursuant to article 27 in order to acquire, retain or recover a right to benefits, viz. when a benefit calculated solely on the basis of national law was more advantageous. Moreover, apportionment also had to be applied in systems that relied on the materialization of risks rather than the duration of insurance. (The Court also dealt with some transitional problems in this judgment.) In the fourth social security case, *Dingemans, 1964*, the Court categorized a benefit in Dutch legislation as an invalidity benefit under Regulation 3, and more specifically as a type B benefit. It is noteworthy that all four judgments in social security were handed down upon requests from the same court in the Netherlands, the Centrale Raad van Beroep.

The first two cases in 1965 again originated in the Netherlands. *Bertholet, 1965* opened the line of case-law on insurance subrogation in case of accidents. The Court ruled that the application of the subrogation clause in article 52 Regulation 3 did not depend on any implementing convention between the member states (p. 86); and that there was no reason to restrict the scope *ratione personae* of the Regulation to those who resided in one state while working in another (p. 87). Moreover, the Dutch benefit at issue was within the scope *ratione materiae*. The reference in *Van Dijk, 1965*[22] concerned a frontier worker to whom article 52 Regulation 3 was also deemed applicable. The Court answered in almost the same terms as in *Bertholet, 1965*. Seized once more in the context of insurance subrogation the Court in *Singer, 1965* again refused a restrictive reading of the scope *ratione personae* of Regulation 3 and article 51 ECT and found a German holidaymaker in France who had suffered a traffic accident to be within the ambit of the Regulation (p. 970). Moreover, the Regulation applied to claims based on accidents that had occurred before the entry into force of the Regulation (p. 971). *Singer, 1965* was the first judgment that was handed down upon a reference from France. Eight days before that the ECJ had handed down the first social security case originating in Germany in *Dekker, 1965*. The Court in this case began the line of authority on 'benefits in kind' in sickness insurance. In the case at issue a supplementary contribution to a pension for the purpose of financing sickness insurance was considered not to be a benefit in kind under article 22 Regulation 3.

In *Vaassen, 1966*, the first of two social security judgments of the year 1966, the Court included social security schemes that were run by private law bodies in the legislation covered by Regulation 3; more specifically, the sickness insurance managed by a Dutch pension fund for civil servants was included, although it was optional in the case at issue (p. 274).[23] Moreover, after having dealt with an annex problem, the Court ruled that sickness insurance could not be terminated on the sole ground that the insured person – a pensioner who had survived a worker – had moved to reside in another member state, even though her insurance was optional (p. 277). Thus began the long line of authority on residence clauses in social security. Also in *Vaassen, 1966* the Court added to *Dekker,*

22 The case is sometimes also called *Koster* or *Koster (née van Dijk)*.
23 The second part of the judgment interpreted the annex to Regulation 3 concerning the Netherlands.

1965 that 'benefits in kind' also included reimbursements of costs incurred by the insured because of sickness, in other words indirect benefits in kind, and that 'cash benefits' essentially consisted of payments made to compensate for loss of earnings through illness (p. 278). In *Hagenbeek, 1966* – like *Vaassen, 1966* a reference from the Netherlands – the Court dealt with a change in legislation in the Netherlands and the consequent repercussions on a widow of a migrant worker. The Court essentially ruled that the insurance periods completed before moving abroad were not to be lost and had to be aggregated not just for the purpose of calculating but also for acquiring and recovering a benefit, although the pertinent annex to Regulation 3 concerning the transitional regime in the Netherlands (G(III)(B)(b)) only mentioned 'the purpose of ascertaining the amount of the benefit' (p. 429).

The year 1967 was a key year. The Court decided ten social security cases, as many as in three previous years together. While Advocate-General Gand (in *Ciechelski, 1967*) was 'happy' to see seven cases relating to aggregation pending before the Court, because the preliminary ruling procedure was obviously working, he also 'express[ed] a certain amount of anxiety at the number of questions of law and practice raised [...]' (p. 192). The many issues raised by the need to aggregate insurance periods became evident. Six of the judgments of 1967 related to aggregation: *Ciechelski, 1967*; *De Moor, 1967*; *Goffart, 1967*; *Welchner, 1967*; *Couture, 1967*; and *Guissart, 1967*. The Court established that the Community rules regarding aggregation were not to replace, but to supplement the national rules on awarding pensions, notably where national law on its own excluded the acquisition of benefits when the insurance periods completed under national law were insufficient and periods had also been completed in other member states (*Ciechelski, 1967*, p. 188; *Couture, 1967*, pp. 388-9). Community rules had to be applied in their entirety. Aggregation had to go hand in hand with apportionment which (apportionment) could not be applied if aggregation had not been applied previously (*Ciechelski, 1967*, p. 188; *De Moor, 1967*, pp. 206-7). The cumulation of pensions awarded by different member states – be it an award on the basis of national law alone or on the basis of the Community rules on aggregation – to a single migrant worker was not excluded, but the very idea of Community law (*De Moor, 1967*, p. 207). A national authority could not rely on aggregation/apportionment to bring the overall benefits of a migrant worker, viz. the benefits due in all member states together, down to the ceiling applicable pursuant to national law (*Ciechelski, 1967*, p. 189). Cumulating benefits in two states for one and the same insurance period was not possible though (*Ciechelski, 1967*, p. 189). *Guissart, 1967* added that periods completed in one state where they were taken into account to calculate a benefit need not have been treated as notional periods pursuant to the national law of another member state (p. 434). The Court also ruled in *Goffart, 1967* that the suspension of the payment of a pension in one state meant that the person concerned did not meet the 'conditions required by all the legislative systems applicable' pursuant to article 28(1)(f) Regulation 3. Hence, calculation pursuant to national law alone was applicable in the case at issue. In *Welchner, 1967* the Court refused to oblige Germany to recognize periods of captivity during World War II followed by work in France as substitute periods under article 1(r) Regulation 3 ('assimilated periods'). Germany therefore did not have to factor in such periods of captivity into the calculation of an invalidity benefit. *Couture, 1967* and *Guissart, 1967* made it plain that migrant workers did not in general have the option to chose between the application of national law alone and aggregation/apportionment pursuant to Community law (pp. 388 and 433, respectively). Aggregation and apportionment were not applicable, if national law alone achieved the aims the Community approach pursued (*Couture, 1967*, p. 388). Moreover, even if aggregation was applicable, it did not imply that pensions necessarily had to be determined simultaneously in all member states (*Couture, 1967*, p. 389).

In 1967, the Court in *Colditz, 1967* was also confronted with the following question: Did an application for an old-age pension in Germany mean that the French authorities could 'liquidate' a pension due under the French system or was successive payment of pensions possible, thus giving the person concerned the option to continue to pay contributions in France accruing further rights, while a pension in Germany was already being paid? The Court opted for the possibility of successive payment under article 28 Regulation 3, emphasizing that separate social security systems continued to exist in the member states and that the rules of the Community were not to be applied in a way that a migrant worker was deprived of the benefit of national law. In *Van der Vecht, 1967*, the Court ruled that in general one single national legislation was applicable, so as 'to avoid any plurality or purposeless confusion of contributions and liabilities' (p. 352). In the case of a worker who commuted daily from one state where he resided and where his employer was established to another state where he actually worked the latter state was competent, save when the duration of the work in that latter state did not exceed twelve months (article 13(a) Regulation 3). The state of residence could not levy any additional charges from the employee or the employer, in particular when those charges yielded no additional social security protection (p. 354). Apart from that, the Court clarified that the decisions adopted by the administrative commission under Regulation 3 were not binding; and that the probable duration of employment mentioned in article 13(a) of the said Regulation referred to the duration of the employment of the individual worker (p. 355). Finally, the Court dealt with some of the more intricate details of social security: Courts as authorities had to accept documents submitted in the languages of other member states based on Regulation 3 (*Guerra, 1967*); in the situation when one member state calculated pensions in units of years while another calculated them in units of months, the smaller unit had to be applied in both cases in order to avoid granting two benefits for one and the same period of insurance (*Cossutta, 1967*).

The rest of the decade saw the ECJ handing down four more judgments in social security. Three of them concerned aggregation under Regulation 3. In *De Cicco, 1968* the Court broadened the scope of aggregation to cover a 'mixed career' (Advocate General Gand, p. 483), i. e. the career of a person who had pursued a self-employed activity in one state and then worked as an employee in another state. The reason for this broadening was that the self-employed person concerned had been affiliated under national law to a special social security scheme which was treated as an extension of the general social security scheme applicable to wage-earners (p. 481). More generally, the Court noted the tendency of member states 'to extend the benefits of social security in favour of new categories of persons by reason of identical risks', while it was for national law to determine the extent of such extensions (p. 480). In *Torrekens, 1969* the ECJ brought a particular French non-contributory benefit scheme for workers of more than 50 years of age within the scope of aggregation. Despite the applicability of Regulation 3, the Court cautioned that any previously existing social security convention mentioned in the annex was to be applied. In *Duffy, 1969* it was again made clear that the Community rules had to be applied in their entirety. The provisions for the reduction and suspension of benefits referred to in article 11(2) Regulation 3 were only applicable to benefits acquired on the basis of the Community rules on aggregation and apportionment, but not to benefits acquired solely based on national law. Finally, *Compagnie belge, 1969* was another insurance subrogation case in which the Court in a similar way as in *Singer, 1965* decided that for the subrogation in article 52 Regulation 3 to be applicable a link between the professional activity of a wage-earner and the injury he or she had sustained was not required (paras 6-7). Moreover, the subrogation article in Regulation 3 did not alter the jurisdiction of courts, i. e. the place where a claim could be brought (paras 10-1). Finally, the Court reiterated the ruling in *Bertholet, 1965*, namely that the article had direct effect.

The 'constitutional' principles of direct effect and primacy were the beacons of the first years of the Court's case-law. Yet at least quantitatively speaking social security rather than free movement of workers or freedom of establishment dominated the Court's work. Many developments in the social security case-law began in these first years, in particular in the field of aggregation and apportionment of periods of insurance. However, they were in many ways years of uncertainty. Regulation 3 was hard to read – and so was the case-law, not least because the Court during that time never expressly referred to previous judgments. The implications of the rulings remained somewhat uncertain. They related to very specific provisions, but at the same time seemed to include wider principles. The Commission, for instance, repeatedly argued a principle of interpretation in favour of migrant workers based on *Nonnenmacher, 1964*, but never managed to obtain the Court's express backing.[24] Besides that, *Nonnenmacher, 1964* created confusion until as late as *Ten Holder, 1986*, because the Court had been ambiguous in 1964 as to whether more than one legislation could apply to one and the same person. However, aggregation of insurance periods proved the thorniest issue of social security. It became evident during the 1960s that many

24 So argued in *Guerra, 1967*, p. 222 and *Merola, 1972*, p. 1259.

kinds of periods were potentially concerned by aggregation. The interplay in aggregation between national law and Community law, and between different provisions of Community law, such as articles 11, 27, and 28 Regulation 3, also proved challenging.

II The 1970s

In the 1970s the case-law exploded. The Court handed down more than 120 judgments in free movement of persons, services, and social security, the vast majority being social security judgments. 95 judgments were given in social security and half a dozen more concerned mainly free movement of workers but in addition social security (section 0). Free movement of workers contributed with 18 judgments (section 0), while a few more social security cases also dealt with the worker freedom. In contrast, freedom of establishment (section 0) and services (section 0) remained relatively quiet with seven judgments in establishment and nine judgments in services five of which overlapped with the freedom of workers or establishments.

1 Workers

In free movement of workers, *Marsman, 1972* took up the thread of *Ugliola, 1969*. *Marsman, 1972* concerned discrimination based on residence and nationality. The Court held that a rule which required the consent of an authority to dismiss a foreign worker only when the foreigner was resident in Germany amounted to discrimination prohibited by free movement of workers. The residence requirement had only applied to foreign nationals but not German nationals. In *Michel S, 1973* the Court read article 12 Regulation 1612/68 so that a handicapped child of a migrant worker could claim benefits intended to improve the capacity to work. In contrast, article 7 of the same Regulation applied only to benefits for workers themselves but not for their families (paras 13-5 and 8-10).

A first wave of cases

In the year 1975 a first true wave of worker cases was tackled by the Court. The Court handed down five judgments: *Sotgiu, 1974*; *Commission v. France (maritime worker quota), 1974*; *Casagrande, 1974*; *Van Duyn, 1974*; and *Walrave, 1974*. *Sotgiu, 1974* concerned the refusal to increase the separation allowance for an Italian employee of the German postal service on the ground that his wife did not reside in Germany but in Italy. The Court found this approach to amount to indirect, covert discrimination (para. 11). The public service exception did not apply, because it only concerned access to employment in the public service. Once a worker was admitted to public service, discriminatory treatment was no longer an option (para. 4). Moreover, whether national law categorized the employment as public or private was irrelevant (paras 5). Whether the separation allowance was mandatory or optional was also immaterial. Either way, it came within the concept of 'conditions of employment' in article 7 Regulation 1612/68 (para. 8).

Commission v. France (maritime worker quota), 1974 was the first infringement procedure in persons and the first of a series of cases that occupied the Court with ship crews. It established that the Treaty freedoms also applied in the sea transport sector, in particular the directly effective article 48 and Regulation 1612/68. Measures that violated those provisions had to be formally abolished, else a state of uncertainty continued to exist. That in itself amounted to an unlawful obstacle to free movement regardless of the secondary importance of that obstacle (paras 46-7). In *Casagrande, 1974* the Court implicitly built on *Michel S, 1973* to find that educational grants had to be awarded on an equal basis to the children of migrant workers, as with all 'general measures intended to facilitate educational attendance' under article 12 Regulation 1612/68 (para. 9). Moreover, the member states' educational policies were not removed from the influence of the Treaty freedoms, regardless of whether they had been adopted on the regional or the national level of a state (para. 12).

Van Duyn, 1974 was the first preliminary ruling in free movement of persons and services asked by a court in the United Kingdom. Faced with the situation of a migrant worker who had been refused leave to enter the United Kingdom because she had intended to work for a religious organization, the Court confirmed the direct effect of free movement of workers and dealt with the public policy derogation for the first time. The Court held that the provisions of a directive such as Directive 64/221 were in principle capable of having direct effect. Although the public policy derogation had to be interpreted narrowly, the member states had some discretion in public policy, since it could vary in time and space (para. 18). As long as a state had adopted certain measures to counter socially harmful behaviour, it was not required for the public policy derogation to apply that the behaviour was unlawful in the state (para. 23). A state could not adopt some measures, such as expulsion, against its own nationals. Nonetheless it could adopt such measures against nationals of other member states (para. 20-2).

In *Walrave, 1974*, a judgment that concerned free movement of workers as well as services, the Court then dealt with sport as an economic activity for the first time. The Court refused to remove sport from the grasp of Community law. According to the Court, the rules of sporting associations, like all 'rules of any nature aimed at regulating in a collective manner gainful employment and the provision of services' (para. 17), had to refrain from discrimination based on nationality. However, the sporting activity in national teams was not, according to the Court, an economic activity (paras 8-9). Worldwide sporting activities were caught by non-discrimination, if they were connected to the Community either through the place where the legal relationship had been established or where it took effect (para. 28).

The year 1975

The Court began the year 1975 by expressly confirming *Casagrande, 1974* in *Alaimo, 1975*. The Court then ruled in *Bonsignore, 1975* that grounds of a general preventive nature were not capable of justifying the expulsion of a national of a member state under the public policy and security exception; only the personal conduct of an individual in a specific case could be a ground of justification (para. 7). In *Cristini, 1975* the Court interpreted the term social advantages in article 7(2) Regulation 1612/68 so as to include a family card issued to the widow of migrant worker by the French national transport company, even though the benefit was not in any way connected to an employment contract. In *Rutili, 1975* the Court added to *Bonsignore, 1975* that for the public policy exception to be applicable a genuine and sufficiently serious threat was required (para. 28). The freedom to move had to be respected by individual decisions, too. Such decisions had to comply with fundamental rights as laid down in the European Convention of Human Rights. The right to notification, statement of grounds, and appeal had to be respected (paras 37-8). Moreover, public security measures could only be applied with regard to the entire territory of a member state, when 'regional' measures could not be imposed on nationals of the member state concerned (paras 48-9).

The remaining years of the decade

The remaining years of the decade added seven more cases in free movement of workers. All three judgments of the year 1976 were based on free movement of persons as well as services. In *Royer, 1976* the Court again dealt with expulsion on grounds of public policy and security. The Court confirmed the direct effect of articles 48, 52, and 59 Treaty, despite the possibility to derogate from them (para. 23). National residence permits were merely of declaratory nature (paras 32-3). Consequently, the failure to comply with administrative formalities did not justify expulsion (para. 38-9). Other suitable sanctions remained possible, though (para. 42), while a foreigner could only be deprived of her or his liberty, if expulsion was lawful under Community law (para. 44). An expulsion decision could have immediate effect only under very restrictive conditions (para. 53-62). The standstill clauses in articles 53 and 62 Treaty prevented the member states from adopting less liberal measures than those in force when the Treaty became effective, when they implemented Community law. Implementation, in turn, had to be effectuated by means of the most appropriate forms and methods (paras 65-73). Next, the Court in *Watson and Belmann, 1976* dealt with the obligation to report the presence of nationals of other member states. A reasonable time period had to be granted for this purpose and sanctions in case of failure to do so needed to be proportionate (paras 19-21). The judgment in *Donà, 1976* validated the Court's ruling in *Walrave, 1974* for professional football players. It was unlawful to discriminate against them on the basis of nationality.

Sagulo 1977 again dealt with the formal requirements of residence. A general residence permit beyond the permit provided by Directive 68/360 could not be required. Valid identification was necessary though, and failure to produce it could be sanctioned appropriately even though a state could not impose such sanctions on its own nationals. In the judgment in *Bouchereau, 1977* the Court implicitly elaborated on *Bonsignore, 1975* and expulsion on grounds of public policy. A recommendation to expel a national of a member state was subject to the requirements of Community law, even though a recommendation might not be binding (paras 17-23). Prior criminal convictions could be factored into the expulsion decision in each specific case, but only insofar as they constituted a present threat evidenced by a propensity to act in the same way in the future (paras 27-30). For the public policy derogation to bite, the normal perturbation involved with any criminal act was not sufficient; rather, the fundamental interests of society had to be seriously and genuinely threatened (para. 35).

The decade ended in free movement of persons with two decisions. First, *Choquet, 1978* tabled driving licences for the first time. The decision watered down the conditions for the recognition of licences issued abroad in other member states. While a state could impose requirements to ensure road safety as long as harmonization had not taken place, charges were not to be excessive, linguistic barriers had to be taken account of, and tests could not simply be duplicated, else obstacles to the worker, service, and establishment freedom would arise (para. 8). Second, in *Saunders, 1979*, the Court refused to address the worker freedom, because the case concerned a situation wholly internal to the United Kingdom (paras 11-2).

Finally, two more judgments concerned free movement of workers, although both, strictly speaking, belong to social security (i. e. Regulation 1408/71). On the one hand, *Inzirillo, 1976* included benefits for the handicapped son of a migrant worker in article 7(2) Regulation 1612/68 (para. 19). With *Inzirillo, 1976* – and *Cristini, 1975* – thus began the line of authority which allowed the family members of migrant workers to claim benefits by reason of article 7(2) Regulation 1612/68. Previously, their rights had been assessed under article 12 Regulation 1612/68, notably in *Michel S, 1973*; *Casagrande, 1974*; and *Alaimo, 1975*. On the other hand, *Even, 1979* completed the definition begun in *Inzirillo, 1976* of social advantages in article 7(2) Regulation 1612/68: '[...] all those which, whether or not linked to a contract of employment, are generally granted to national workers primarily because of their objective status as workers or by virtue of the mere fact of their residence on the national territory and the extension of which to workers who are nationals of other member state therefore seems suitable to facilitate their mobility within the Community' (*Even, 1979*, para. 22). Yet the Court found in *Even, 1979* that benefit for victims of war did not come within this definition.

2 Establishment

The Court handed down only a handful of judgments in freedom of establishment during the 1970s. *Reyners, 1974* established the direct effect of equal treatment for those who had exercised the freedom of establishment (para. 25). Direct effect could be invoked, although the implementing provisions mentioned in the Treaty had not yet been adopted. The judgment also restricted the scope of the public service exception to activities that were directly and specifically connected to the exercise of public authority. The derogation had to be examined for each member state separately. A whole profession could only be excluded from the freedom, if otherwise a member state would have to tolerate the exercise, even though only occasionally, of public authority. If possible the exercise of public authority had to be separated from the rest of the activities of the profession (paras 45-9). The exception did not cover the activities of lawyers, even though they were in contact with courts (paras 51-3).

In *Thieffry, 1977* the Court ruled that the admission to practice as a lawyer could not be refused when a foreign diploma had been recognised as equivalent to a domestic university degree and the local bar exam had been passed. The Court also acknowledged to some extent a distinction between an academic and a civil effect of the recognition of a qualification, but left this distinction to the national court for assessment (para. 24). *Patrick, 1977* followed up by ruling that the requirement to possess certain qualifications to be allowed to exercise a profession constituted a restriction of freedom of establishment (para. 16). Though the implementing directives had not yet been adopted as required by the Treaty, the admission to a profession could not be made subject to an exceptional authorization once the national conditions to become established were satisfied. Hence, French law could not make recognition of the British qualification as an architect dependent on a convention establishing reciprocity (paras. 10-7). In *Razanatsimba, 1977* the Court made it plain that the ruling in *Reyners, 1974* as to equal treatment did not apply to third country nationals. The Lomé Convention was not to be read in a similar way as the Treaty pursuant to *Reyners, 1974* (para. 14), nor did the Treaty require a member state to apply a most favoured nation rule to nationals of third countries (para. 19).

Auer, 1979 and *Knoors, 1979* were handed down on the same day. Both concerned diploma recognition. In *Knoors, 1979* the Court decided that a national returning to his 'home' state after having practised a profession in another member state remained within the scope of the diploma directive (Directive 64/427 on certain industries and small craft industries), because he had exercised his freedom of establishment (paras 18-20). However, the Court also acknowledged as legitimate the interest of a member state to prevent abuse of rights through Community law. Under the Directive such abuse was not conceivable though (paras 25-7). In *Auer, 1979* the Court also held that a national returning to his home state with a diploma in veterinary medicine awarded abroad was within the scope of freedom of establishment (paras 20-6). Moreover, the point in time at which the nationality of the member state concerned had been acquired was irrelevant, provided that the person concerned had it at the point in time when he relied on Community law (para. 28-9). However, the recognition of a diploma acquired abroad could not be effected on the basis of article 52 ECT alone. The national provisions had to be complied with until the provisions of Community law which regulated the matter were transposed into national law. Finally, *Van Ameyde, 1977* was a highly specific case which concerned the so-called green card system for accident insurance of motor vehicles. The Court in essence found that the national measures adopted to implement the system established by various Community instruments did not violate freedom of establishment or services, although those measures reserved certain functions to certain bodies (paras 29-30). In a similar way as in *Walrave, 1974* the Court found that freedom of establishment applied to any 'rules of whatever kind which [sought] to govern collectively the carrying on of the business in question' (para. 28). (The judgment also dealt with competition law.)

3 Social security

In the 1970s, the Court first handed down the first ruling concerning posted workers, *Manpower, 1970*. In this judgment the Court applied the exception to article 12 Regulation 3 in article 13(a) resulting in the application of French law to workers posted to Germany by a company established in France. According to the Court, this rule prevented the company posting workers abroad and the worker being posted from suffering disadvantages by reason of the host state's law becoming applicable. It was irrelevant that the company employed the workers for the sole reason of posting them abroad. Since the company was established in France and conducted business there, it was also irrelevant that its only business consisted in offering the temporary service of workers. Moreover, the posted workers only had a contract with the company posting them, they only answered to that company, and they received their salary from it (paras 10-9).

Aggregation and apportionment

The Court then became deeply involved again in aggregation and apportionment. In *La Marca, 1970* the Court limited the possibility for the authorities to disregard short periods of insurance pursuant to article 28(2) Regulation 4, which implemented Regulation 3. The authorities could only disregard periods of insurance of less than six months completed under 'their' social security scheme, if there was another member state to take account of them. If that was not the case because no sufficient period had been completed abroad, the administration had to apply the regular rules of articles 26 to 28 Regulation 3 (paras 11-3). Three aggregation judgments handed down on the same day, 10 November 1972, concerned similar constellations under Regulation 3. In *Gross, 1971* and the identical judgment in *Höhn, 1971* the Court dealt with different categories of old-age pensions pursuant to French law that depended on the length of insurance periods completed; moreover the ceiling for insurance periods completed under French law which (the ceiling) was set at 120 months was at issue. *Keller, 1971* concerned the same rules though in somewhat different factual circumstances. The Court essentially explained what it meant for the French rules that migrant workers had to be granted the benefit that was most favourable after a comparison of calculations solely under national law on the one hand and under the Community rules on the other. In essence, aggregation had to be applied to bring the migrant worker concerned within the most favourable group of benefits pursuant to national law (*Gross, 1971*, para. 9); the apportioned benefit was to be calculated by reference to the aggregated periods completed in all member states involved, rather than the maximum period provided by the law of the member state under which the benefit was calculated, i. e. the ceiling under French law (*Gross, 1971*, para. 11-2). In *Keller, 1971* the Court clarified that a pension was not to be awarded on the basis of aggregation and apportionment, if the calculation of the benefit based on national law alone and the periods completed exclusively in the state concerned was more favourable (para. 12).

Another triplet followed in 1972: *Heinze, 1972; Land Niedersachsen, 1972; Ortskrankenkasse Hamburg, 1972.* All of them concerned the same benefit in Germany aiming at prevention of tuberculosis. Aggregation was at issue only implicitly, since German law required completion of a minimum insurance period of 60 months for entitlement to the benefit. The main concern of the judgments was classification of the benefit as a social security benefit rather than social assistance outside the scope of Regulation 3 and as a sickness benefit rather than an invalidity benefit since it did not concern earning capacity. In addition, the Court also rejected under Regulation 3 the obligation of Germany to aggregate periods completed in Switzerland, although Italy was bound to take such periods into account due to a convention it had concluded with Switzerland (*Ortskrankenkasse Hamburg, 1972*, paras 10-1).

Mancuso, 1973 established that aggregation and apportionment were not just linked necessarily for old-age pensions, but also for invalidity pensions. To the latter pensions aggregation and apportionment applied by reason of article 26 Regulation 3 as soon as one type B legislation was involved, i. e. legislation that made the acquisition of benefits dependent on the completion of insurance periods. In other words, if no need arose to aggregate periods of invalidity insurance, the resulting invalidity benefit was not to be apportioned. *Kaufmann, 1974* next threw light on article 11 Regulation 3 which dealt with rules against the overlapping of benefits. Article 11(2) covered all national provisions for suspension or reduction of benefits, irrespective of whether they concerned entitlement to or provision of a benefit (para. 4). That article became applicable as soon as benefits were awarded on the basis of the Regulation; it was the counterpart to the advantages migrant workers drew from the Regulation, e. g. from the aggregation of periods. It was only necessary that the benefits from two states that (the benefits) overlapped were genuinely comparable for the article to apply (para.

15). In case of provisions reducing benefits the correct amount to be taken account of was the amount of the benefits awarded abroad as it was actually paid; the amount awarded abroad before reduction was irrelevant (paras 19-21).

Niemann and Petroni

Niemann, 1974 then foreshadowed the *Petroni, 1975*-judgment, for the Court ruled in a similar vein for Regulation 3 as later on in *Petroni, 1975* with regard to Regulation 1408/71, the Regulation succeeding Regulation 3. The Court in *Niemann, 1974* declared article 28(3) Regulation 3 partly invalid in light of article 51 Treaty. The article enabled national authorities that had calculated a benefit solely on the basis of *national* law to reduce the benefit that resulted from this calculation (paras 6-8). In the case at issue national law allowed extra affiliation to a voluntary insurance scheme and required the national authority to take periods completed under such a scheme into account. The national authorities had then reduced the benefit on the basis of article 28(3) Regulation 3, because it had been higher than the benefit the calculation based on aggregation and apportionment had yielded. In *Petroni, 1975* the Court followed up and declared article 46(3) Regulation 1408/71 invalid in light of article 51 Treaty insofar as it imposed the reduction of a benefit acquired solely on the basis of the national law of a single member state. In both cases the reason for the Court's ruling was that migrant workers were not to lose benefits that were due solely on the basis of national law.

The development of aggregation continued with *Massonet, 1975*. The case under Regulation 3 clarified the need to safeguard benefits due solely pursuant to national law when a benefit was granted in a second member state based on the rules of the Community on aggregation. The judgment namely refused Luxembourg the possibility to rely on Community law to reduce a widow's benefit. That benefit had been increased, because certain periods of child-raising had been factored in, but it had been due solely on the basis of national law. At the same time a widow's benefit had been due in Germany and it had been increased based on those periods of child-raising (para. 3). The Court found that insurance periods were not duplicated; Luxembourg was precluded from applying Community law to reduce 'its' benefit, (para. 25). Apart from that, the Court also made it plain that article 12 Regulation 3 merely determined the applicable legislation. It did not lend itself as a basis to interpret a national provision so as to reduce a benefit due under national law (paras 16-7). *Plaquevent, 1975* next concerned a specific point of aggregation in type A invalidity schemes, i. e. article 28(1)(c) Regulation 3 governing the average wage used to calculate benefits. The judgment made it clear that pro rata calculation/apportionment applied even under schemes where the benefit did not depend on the completion of insurance periods (type A); the article only referred to the way the average wage was to be determined (paras 18-9).

In 1977, a number of cases mainly confirmed the *Petroni, 1975*-ruling. *Strehl, 1977*, three judgments of 13 October 1977 – *Greco, 1977; Manzoni, 1977; Mu-*

ra, 1977 – and just one week later *Giuliani, 1977* did so. *Greco, 1977* added that the obligation of a member state to apply 'its' national rules to calculate a benefit also included the possibility to apply national rules against the overlapping of benefits. In other words, national law was to be applied in its entirety, if it was more favourable than the Community rules. *Mura, 1977*, made it plain that it did not amount to discrimination when migrant workers were better off than non-migrant workers after the *Petroni, 1975*-ruling, because the situations those two types of workers found themselves in were not comparable (paras 9-10). *Giuliani, 1977* spelled out that, when a residence requirement in national law had to be set aside pursuant to article 10 Regulation 1408/71 and a benefit was then granted based on the 'corrected' national law, the calculation of that benefit was still based solely on national law within the sense of *Petroni, 1975*. *Strehl, 1977* added that the invalidity of article 46(3) Regulation 1408/71 also affected decision no. 91 of the administrative commission under Regulation 1408/71.

Thereafter, the judgment in *Schaap, 1978* again confirmed the *Petroni, 1975*-ruling as it had been clarified in *Greco, 1977*. It added that retroactively buying into a German insurance scheme for the periods during which the nazi regime had been in power in Germany equalled voluntary insurance; as such it was to be left out of account when applying article 46(3) Regulation 1408/71 in the calculation of the benefit pursuant to Community law. The Court further elaborated this point in *Schaap II, 1979*. The Court ruled that article 46 Regulation 574/72, which implemented Regulation 1408/71, was pertinent not just when two type B legislations were applicable, but also when one type B and one type A legislation applied. Thus, in both situations the benefit of an insurance period completed voluntarily was maintained. *Boerboom, 1978* again reiterated *Petroni, 1975* and the interpretation given in *Greco, 1977*. *Naselli, 1978* was handed down on the same day as *Schaap, 1978* and *Boerboom, 1978*. *Naselli, 1978* established that the ruling in *Greco, 1977* – that national law had to be applied in its entirety including rules against overlapping – was also applicable to articles 27 and 28 Regulation 3. *Viola, 1978* merely extended this ruling to invalidity benefits to which aggregation and apportionment applied by analogy pursuant to Regulation 3. The same was valid for Regulation 1408/71 according to *Brouwer-Kaune, 1979*. That judgment also dealt with the situation where an invalidity benefit was awarded and converted into an old-age benefit in one state, before an invalidity benefit was awarded in another state. Although articles 40(1) and 43 Regulation 1408/71 did not technically cover this situation, the principles developed in the case-law, i. e. application of national law in its entirety and aggregation/apportionment, applied nonetheless (para. 8). *Mura II, 1979* then attempted to explain the whole calculation to be made pursuant to Regulation 1408/71 and the case-law; essentially it only clarified a point as to which *Mura, 1977* and *Schaap, 1978* had been ambiguous, namely that article 46 Regulation 1408/71 had to be applied in its entirety in the calculation according to the Community rules.

Other aggregation

Not all aggregation cases of the 1970s dealt with questions related to the *Petroni, 1975*-judgment. In *D'Amico, 1975* the Court set some limits to the need to take account of periods completed abroad under Regulation 1408/71. When one condition for receiving early retirement benefits under national law was that the person concerned had been unemployed for a year, periods of unemployment spent in another member state need not have been taken into account. The reason was that the year of unemployment was merely a 'separate additional condition' (para. 11) for the award of the benefit, not a factor influencing the calculation of the benefit; pursuant to national law the benefit was not included in the period of membership with the social security scheme concerned, either. In a similar vein, the Court decided in *Brunori, 1979* that a period of compulsory insurance with a specific old-age insurance scheme was a condition of affiliation to such a scheme, rather than a condition for the acquisition, retention or recovery of rights with which article 45 Regulation 1408/71 was solely concerned. That was why a period of insurance completed in another member state did not count towards that period. Before the judgment in *Brunori, 1979* – and in some contrast to it – the Court in *Warry, 1977* decided that pursuant to Regulation 1408/71 insurance periods completed in Germany had to be taken into account in the United Kingdom. A specific period of sickness insurance was required in the United Kingdom for entitlement to sickness benefits and, as a consequence, to invalidity benefits. In such circumstances, the British authorities were required to take account of periods of sickness insurance completed in Germany when deciding whether to award an invalidity benefit (paras 24-5). Apart from that, the British authorities had to accept a claim for invalidity benefits filed in Germany as a claim for sickness benefits in the United Kingdom (paras 27-9).

A series of further cases dealt with some technical aspects of aggregation. In *Galati, 1975* the Court decided how to bring an incomplete month of insurance to a round figure – essentially by rounding it up (see article 15(3) Regulation 574/72). According to *Borella, 1975* a short period of insurance could not be left out of account based on article 48 Regulation 1408/71, because German law on its own granted a benefit for the short period. *Torri, 1977* concerned the minimum benefit guaranteed pursuant to article 50 Regulation 1408/71. Such a benefit was only available if and to the extent a member state had declared a minimum benefit.

Aggregation and third states

A number of further cases also involved issues of aggregation in a broad sense. However, the questions raised involved third countries which the insurance careers of the claimants touched at one point or another. Algeria figured prominently among those third countries, because it had gained independent from France while Regulation 3 was in force. *Fiege, 1973* was the first such case. The Court in essence ruled that France was obliged to honour pensions rights acquired before Algeria was deleted from the annex to Regulation 3. Besides, the

Court ruled that an invalidity pension could not be transferred (paras 5-7). In *Horst, 1975* the Court added that it was irrelevant that the risk had materialized after Algeria had been deleted from the annex or that the claim had been filed thereafter. Thus periods completed in Algeria had to be taken into account in the calculation of benefits in the member states (paras 7-8). *Hirardin, 1976* continued this line of authority. A Belgian national who had completed periods in Algeria could not be subjected to less advantageous conditions than a French national when both applied for a pension in France (paras 15-9). In *Belbouab, 1978*, moreover, the Court ruled that the condition of having the nationality of a member state for Regulation 1408/71 to apply was to be assessed at the time the relevant insurance periods were completed. An Algerian national who had been a French national at the time he completed an insurance period could therefore rely on the Regulation. *Kaucic, 1977* did not concern Algeria but Austria. In this case, the Court held that periods completed in third states, in this case Austria, need not have been taken into account. Regulation 3, in particular article 11(2), did not apply to periods completed in third states. Hence, Belgium was justified in reducing a benefit by an amount previously awarded in Austria as a benefit. Before *Kaucic, 1977* the judgment in *Merluzzi, 1972* had already in a certain sense concerned insurance in a member state for work in a third state. However, the Court in *Merluzzi, 1972* merely reiterated the conditions included in annex G to Regulation 3, i. e. that nationals of member states other than France could claim affiliation to a specific French scheme only if they worked in a third state, after having at least been affiliated to a French insurance scheme or resided in France for a decade. The Court then left it to the national court to apply that set of rules. *Bozzone, 1977* then concerned an Italian worker whose claim for benefits in Belgium based on insurance periods completed in the former Belgian Congo was rejected for lack of residence in Belgium. However, the Court included the Belgian scheme within 'legislation' pursuant to article 1(j) Regulation 1408/71 and applied article 10 of that Regulation to strike down the residence requirement.

Social security v. social assistance

Aggregation and apportionment was not the only social security topic the Court dealt with. Numerous questions referred to the Court concerned the scope of Regulations 3 and 1408/71. *Frilli, 1972* began the long line of authority that distinguished between social security benefits and social assistance. Benefits of social security usually required 'periods of employment, membership, or contribution' and conferred a 'legally defined position' with a 'right to a benefit'. They were subject to Community rules. In contrast, in case of social assistance the authorities considered each case individually based on criteria such as the needs of the person concerned. Social assistance was *not* subject to Community law (all in para. 14). Yet the Court also recognized the difficulties in drawing the distinction. Therefore, benefits addressing both social security and assistance could be subject to the social security rules of the Community (paras 13-4). *Frilli, 1972* concerned the guaranteed income of persons of old age under Regulation 3. Three judgments of the same year concerning prevention against tuberculosis, *Heinze, 1972*; *Land Niedersachsen, 1972* and *Ortskrankenkasse Hamburg, 1972* then made it clear that sickness benefits of preventive character could also be considered as social security benefits rather than social assistance. *Mazzier, 1974*; *Callemeyn, 1974* and *F., 1975* then applied the same criteria distinguishing social security from social assistance to a Belgian supplementary benefit for handicapped persons under Regulations 3 and 1408/71. The consequence was that the benefit came within the scope of the Community rules. *Callemeyn, 1974* in addition clarified that Regulation 1408/71 only took precedence over the preceding European interim agreement, if it was more favourable for the migrant worker. *Biason, 1974* again distinguished social security from assistance under Regulation 3 for a French supplementary allowance to an invalidity pension. The allowance was classed as social security. *Inzirillo, 1976* confirmed *Mazzier, 1974* for Regulation 1408/71: the French allowance for handicapped adults was part of social security.

Definitions and scope

With *Fossi, 1977* the Court excluded some discretionary benefits awarded to alleviate certain predicaments stemming from World War II and the nazi regime from the scope of the social security rules of the Community. *Tinelli, 1979* confirmed this decision. Similarly, a French benefit awarded in recognition of the hardships endured during World War II as a 'testimony of national gratitude' was considered to be outside the scope of social security in *Gillard, 1978* (para. 13). Article 4(4) excluded such benefits from the scope of Regulation 1408/71. The Court confirmed this approach in *Even, 1979*. In *Lohmann, 1979* the Court applied the exclusion of special schemes for civil servants in article 4(4) Regulation 1408/71 for the first time. It ruled that such schemes did not come within the term 'legislation' pursuant to article 1(j) Regulation 1408/71 and were therefore outside the scope of the Regulation.

The Court also settled some other definition issues in the 1970s. *Murru, 1972* explained that the national law under which a period was completed determined whether that period constituted a period assimilated to a period of insurance within the sense of article 1(r) Regulation 3. In *Vandeweghe, 1973* the Court qualified a settlement grant as a 'pension' under article 1(t) Regulation 1408/71. In contrast, a death grant did not qualify as a 'pension'. *Blottner, 1977* gave the Court the occasion to interpret the term 'present or future' legislation in article 1(j) Regulation 1408/71 so as to include legislation that had existed in the past (para. 13).

Personal scope

The Court came back to the personal scope of the social security rules in *Janssen, 1971*. The Court revisited *De Cicco, 1968* to find that the Community terms 'wage earners' or 'assimilated workers' in article 4 Regulation 3 were capable of covering persons whom national law regarded as self-employed persons, although the rules of the Community in principle did not apply to self-employed persons. This body of case-law was further differentiated in *Brack, 1976* because of the transition from Regulation 3 to Regulation 1408/71 and some modifications in annex V to Regulation 1408/71 which applied exclusively to the United Kingdom. The Court in *Brack, 1976* ruled very much on the specifics of the case. It limited the possibility for national law to exclude self-employed persons from having the status of workers within the sense of article 1(a) Regulation 1408/71 who (the workers) were entitled to sickness benefits. Moreover, the Court held in *Brack, 1976* that some persons could still be considered as employed persons, although their employment had ended, because they remained compulsorily insured under the insurance scheme that had covered them while they had been employed (para. 24). *Recq, 1978* again concerned the status of a person under the sickness insurance scheme in the United Kingdom, this time an au pair girl. It was up to the national court to determine whether an au pair girl was obliged to pay sickness insurance contributions as an employed person in the United Kingdom and thus qualified as a worker under Regulation 1408/71 (paras 13-4). Before the judgment in *Recq, 1978* the Court in *Mouthaan, 1976* had stated clearly in a case concerning the Dutch system that the status of a worker under Regulation 1408/71 was not lost just because the person concerned had failed to comply with administrative formalities (paras. 8-10).

In *F., 1975* the Court included a dependent descendant in the members of the family of a worker pursuant to article 2 Regulation 1408/71 when such a descendant, even though he was an adult, did not have any chance whatsoever of entering the employment market given his or her handicap. The Court thus opened up entitlement of family members of workers to benefits for handicapped persons based on non-discrimination in Regulation 1408/71. That move was consequential since the Court's case-law on the social benefits of family members under Regulation 1612/68 converged towards a similar point, notably in *Michel S, 1973*; *Casagrande, 1974*; and *Cristini, 1975*. The approach taken in *F., 1975* was confirmed in *Inzirillo, 1976*. In a similar vein, *Laumann, 1978* broadened the personal scope of Regulation 1408/71. It established that it was sufficient for Regulation 1408/71 to apply that the survivors of a worker moved to reside abroad, even if the worker himself had never made use of his freedom of movement.

Family

The Court did not just address family benefits incidentally, under definitions and scope of the social security rules. It also ruled on the provisions of the Community on family benefits. In *Di Bella, 1970* the Court devoted itself to these rules for the first time. Article 42 Regulation 3 had been amended regarding benefits for orphans. The Court found that the phrase 'came under the legislation' of a member state did not include legislation the application of which was not capable of leading to the acquisition of a right to benefits (para. 14). The Court came back to the same article 42 Regulation 3 in *Anselmetti, 1975* ruling that it applied to a Belgian invalidity allowance as a 'pension' within the meaning of that article. Moreover, the Court in *Triches, 1976* held that article 42 Regulation 3 did not violate article 51 ECT, although the article did not remove all possible inequalities. In *Saieva, 1976*, the Court ruled that article 42(5) Regulation 3 merely determined the applicable legislation and applied to any family allowance payable by reason of the death of a worker.

Owing to *Laumann, 1978* family benefits in Regulation 1408/71 attracted the Court's attention for the first time. The Court ruled that the suspensory rule against overlapping of benefits in 79(3) Regulation 1408/71 applied only when benefits of the same kind were received by the same person. The benefit of an orphan had to be distinguished from the benefits acquired by others for the purpose of article 79(3). *Ragazzoni, 1978* also concerned a suspensory rule for overlapping entitlements, but this time article 76 Regulation 1408/71. The judgment made clear that entitlements to family allowances in two states only overlapped when all the requirements for the award of the benefit were met in the state where the family resided. In other words, a family benefit was not 'payable' pursuant to article 76 when a mother was not capable of receiving a family benefit because national law did not consider her to be the head of household (paras 9-11). *Rossi, 1979* transposed this ruling to the rule against overlapping of benefits of pensioners in article 79(3) Regulation 1408/71. However, *Rossi, 1979* had an important further dimension. The suspension of benefits according to article 79(3) could apply partially; if the benefits granted originally by a state exceeded the benefits to be paid by another state, the first state had to continue to pay the amount in excess as a supplement.

Unemployment

Kermaschek, 1976 also concerned the members of the family of migrant workers, though with regard to unemployment benefits. The Court in *Kermaschek, 1976* rejected the view that members of the family could claim unemployment benefits under Regulation 1408/71 based solely on their link to the migrant worker. The members of the family of a worker therefore only benefitted from 'derived rights' (para. 7), i. e. they could exclusively claim benefits that national law provided for the members of the family of an unemployed worker. Those benefits provided for the worker him- or herself remained out of reach for them. Moreover, the scheme established by Regulation 1408/71 for unemployment benefits was only available to nationals of the member states. Yet the benefits that were available to family members – 'derived rights' – did not depend on nationality, i. e. third country nationals could also lay claim to them.

Seven more judgments of the ECJ dealt with unemployment benefits in the 1970s. *Bonaffini, 1975* was the first judgment to deal with the exportability of unemployment benefits under article 69 Regulation 1408/71. It made clear that article 69 established a limited possibility for migrant workers to continue to receive unemployment benefits from the state where they last worked while they sought employment in another state; but that article did not offer any grounds for national authorities to refuse unemployment benefits normally due to 'incoming' migrant workers under domestic law. Yet national authorities were allowed to factor in benefits received in actual fact under the unemployment scheme of another member state. Next, *Mouthaan, 1976* confirmed the right to unemployment benefits of a frontier worker in the state where he or she resided in accordance with that state's legislation pursuant to article 71(1)(b)(II) Regulation 1408/71. The judgment, however, excluded the guarantee of salary arrears due to the employee by a third body in case of insolvency of the employer from the unemployment benefits covered by Regulation 1408/71. Such a guarantee did not correspond to contributions made by the worker during his employment. *Di Paolo, 1977* explained in detail the concept of residence in the situations covered by article 71 Regulation 1408/71. Essentially, the Court required an examination of all the circumstances to establish whether a worker came within the exceptional situation of having residence in a state other than where she or he was employed. Those circumstances included the family situation, the reasons for him or her to move, the character of the work, the duration of the stay, etc. A presumption in favour of residence where the worker was employed applied though (paras 19-20). Basically, it was required for the exceptional situation requirement that the worker retained close ties with the country where she or he had settled and retained habitual residence (para. 12).

In *Beerens, 1977* the Court accepted that the mentioning of a benefit in the declaration required by article 5 Regulation 1408/71 was sufficient proof that it was an unemployment benefit within the ambit of the Regulation. However, a declaration was not indispensable for a benefit to constitute an unemployment benefit. In *Kuyken, 1977* the Court ruled that the unemployment rules were only applicable to those who had been subject to unemployment insurance at some point. A Belgian national who had studied at a university in another member state could therefore not come back to Belgium and claim an unemployment allowance – Belgium's tideover allowance – based on Regulation 1408/71. (The Court also ruled that such a student was outside the scope of free movement of workers and thus the principle of non-discrimination; para. 22.) In *Frangiamore, 1978* the Court held that employment periods completed abroad had to be aggregated for the purpose of fulfilling the reference period of an unemployment benefit in two cases, either when the employment period would have constituted an insurance period had it been completed in the member state where the benefit was claimed, or when the employment period constituted an insurance period under the legislation of the state where it had been completed. *Coccioli, 1979* finally concerned the exceptional situation where the three months exportability period for unemployment benefits could be extended according to article 69(2) Regulation 1408/71. The Court ruled that the application for such an extension need not have been made within the period of three months. But the Court also emphasised that it was up to the national authorities to ensure that proper use was made of the possibility offered by article 69 Regulation 1408/71 (paras 7-8).

Sickness

In the 1970s, the Court also dealt with a number of sickness insurance cases. In *Kunz, 1973* the transition from Regulation 3 to Regulation 1408/71 raised a problem. The Court ruled that article 22(1) Regulation 3 could not be read so as to entitle a pensioner to sickness benefits in the state where he resided, if national law did not grant such a right, although article 28 Regulation 1408/71 had to be understood in this way. The reason was that article 28 Regulation 1408/71 had extended the social security law of the Community (para. 5). However, in the judgment *Aulich, 1976* the Court came back to the allowance that had been at stake in *Kunz, 1973*. The Court held that an allowance which supplemented the sickness contributions paid by the insured person constituted a share in the contributions to sickness insurance which gave rise to the right to benefits, rather than a benefit in its own right under article 27 Regulation 1408/71. That article assumed that a right to benefits already existed and that the risk had already materialized (para. 7).

Pierik I, 1978 was the first case dealing with the authorization to seek treatment abroad. *Pierik I, 1978* established that article 22 Regulation 1408/71 concerned all treatment that was effective against the sickness the person concerned suffered from (para. 15). It also concerned treatment that was more appropriate than the treatment provided in the state normally competent (para. 16). In the latter case, the authorization could not be refused (para. 18). Finally, the provider of the benefits in the host state was allowed under article 22 Regulation 1408/71 to provide all benefits that it was entitled to provide under host state legislation. *Pierik II, 1979* in turn clarified that the competent authority was bound to grant the authorization, once it had been established in the light of objective medical requirements that treatment abroad was effective and necessary. *Pierik II, 1979* also made it clear that article 22 Regulation 1408/71 applied to pensioners; and that once the authorization had been given, the institution in the host state had to provide all benefits it had the power, rather than the duty, to provide. *Kenny, 1978* then clarified in relation to article 22 Regulation 1408/71 that the conditions for the acquisition, retention, loss, or suspension of sickness benefits were laid down by national law; national law had to refrain from discriminating on the basis of nationality though.

Non-discrimination and residence

The principle of non-discrimination was also involved in *Smieja, 1973*. A residence condition had been established in the Netherlands for certain increases in old-age pensions. The Court ruled that non-discrimination did not per se preclude a residence requirement. Yet certain other provisions of Regulations 3 and 1408/71 did, like article 10(1) of each of the Regulations. Owing to those provisions the Dutch pension increase could not be refused to persons residing abroad. A residence requirement was also rejected in *Biason, 1974* for a French supplementary allowance to an invalidity pension under Regulation 3. *Jansen, 1977* concerned the effects of a change of residence on the reimbursement of contributions paid under an old-age insurance scheme. Article 10(2) Regulation 1408/71 established that contributions paid could not be reimbursed merely because of a cessation of compulsory affiliation to a scheme when a person had changed residence and consequently become compulsorily affiliated to a scheme in another member state. However, a corresponding provision did not exist in Regulation 3. The reimbursement of contributions which was established by national law in case compulsory insurance ceased could therefore not be refused on the basis of Regulation 3. This was valid even though contributions would technically not be lost when reimbursement was refused given that insurance periods completed would later have to be aggregated (para. 12). The Court finally struck down a nationality criterion in *Toia, 1979*. The requirement in French law that an allowance for women with children was only granted, if the children had French nationality, amounted to disguised discrimination which was not properly justified in the specific case.

One legislation

Another principle was at issue in a number of cases in the 1970s, namely the principle that only one legislation can be applicable at a given point in time. The confusion that would be caused, if several legislations were applicable at the same time, made the Court decide in *Bentzinger, 1973* that article 13(1)(c) Regulation 3 did indeed apply when a person was employed by several, instead of just one single employer. Consequently, the legislation of the state where the person concerned was employed and resident was applicable. *Angenieux, 1973* laid down some details of the notion that the legislation of the state where a person was employed was the only legislation applicable. The decisive employment relationship was to be determined by the 'predominant connection' when a person worked in several member states (para. 19). After the amendment of article 13 Regulation 3, which dealt with workers who performed their activities in several member states and resided in one of them, the case was clearer. From then on, the place of permanent residence was decisive for the applicable legislation. The term 'permanent residence' implied that all circumstances were taken account of, namely work, permanent address, centre of interests, and nationality of the person concerned (paras 29-31). *Andlau, 1975* confirmed this interpretation of article 13 Regulation 3. The Court added that German legislation was applicable to musicians residing in Germany if they performed occasionally, rather than habitually, in France, provided that they were affiliated to a German scheme. The employer in France, as a consequence, had to pay the contributions in Germany relating to the occasional work in France (paras 15-7). In case of an accident in France, the French institutions provided benefits in kind under their French legislation at the expense of the German institutions (paras 19-23). In *Perenboom, 1977* the Court finally held that the fact that only one single legislation was to be applied during a certain period of time also excluded the levying of contributions twice over the same period of time. Mr Perenboom had earned income that had been subject to contributions in Germany and when he ceased work in Germany was again made subject to contributions in the Netherlands where he resided, although he had only been insured under one scheme at a time.

Transition and technicalities

The rest of the social security cases of the 1970s either concerned issues of transitional application or technicalities. *Brock, 1970* established that, bar explicit exceptions, amended legislation applied to events that had taken place before the amendment in so far as the continuing effects of such events were concerned (para. 7). The Court also ruled that benefits awarded previously could basically be reconsidered automatically in the light of amendments of Community rules if the outcome of such reconsideration was more favourable for the recipient of the benefit (paras 13-5). *Saieva, 1976* confirmed this ruling for the transition from Regulation 3 to Regulation 1408/71 (paras 15-7). *Walder, 1973* confirmed that articles 5 and 6 Regulation 3 and articles 6 and 7 Regulation 1408/71 had replaced existing social security conventions between member states – except when the annexes provided otherwise – even if their application would have been more advantageous for the persons concerned than the Community rules.

In *Merola, 1972* the Court decided that the ruling in *Guerra, 1967* regarding the language of documents submitted to administrative courts also applied to other courts. *Maris, 1977* continued that social security claims under the Community rules – and only such claims – could be submitted in any official language of a member state, even if domestic law required them to be drafted in a national language, in this case Flemish.

The judgment in *de Waal, 1973* added to the subrogation case-law, which had begun with *Bertholet, 1965*. It ruled that the substance of the claim into which an insurer was subrogated was determined by the national law governing the rights of the victim to compensation. *Töpfer, 1977*, however, limited the subrogation in light of the wording of article 52 Regulation 3 to the injury, i. e. to the damage caused by the accident. It thus excluded any other compensation for (non-)material or personal damage from subrogation.

Rzepa, 1974 clarified that national social security law rather than Community law laid down the statute of limitation for claims aiming at repayment of benefits that had been advanced (paras 12-3). *Costers, 1974* elaborated on the submission of documents to national authorities other than those for whom they were destined. The possibility pursuant to article 47 Regulation 3 to submit documents to the authorities of another member state also applied to the filing of an appeal. *Farrauto, 1975* allowed the direct notification of a social security decision via postal or telecommunication services to the recipient. However, the Court reminded the national authorities that they had to take care that the recipient understood the language of the decision (para. 6). *Balsamo, 1976* pertained to the formal submission of claims for benefits in several jurisdictions. Once a claim was submitted correctly in the member state of residence, the authorities of another member state were precluded from applying further formal conditions. However, material conditions, such as the cessation of work, had to be satisfied at the time the decision was adopted. *Koschniske, 1979* dealt with the interpretation of the notion of a female spouse in article 10(1)(b) Regulation 574/72 in the Dutch version in the light of the other official language versions of the Regulation. The Court concluded that the notion included male spouses as well.

Three more social security judgments were handed down in the 1970s. *Pennartz, 1979* was about the average salary that had to be applied according to article 18(1) Regulation 3. According to the Court, the French authorities were right to focus exclusively on the salary received in France. *Liegeois, 1977* dealt with an option to buy-in retroactively study periods. Such an option amounted to continued voluntary or optional insurance within the meaning of article 9(2) Regulation 1408/71. In *Villano, 1979* the Court ruled that the concept of previous accidents in article 30(1) Regulation 3 and article 61(5) Regulation 1408/71 was not amenable to an interpretation that included subsequent accidents.

4 Services

It took the Court until 1974 to hand down the first judgments in freedom of services. *Van Binsbergen, 1974* was the first true services judgement. Previously, *Sacchi, 1974* had concerned services only to some limited extent, while the focus was on competition and goods. The Court ruled with regard to services only in eight other judgments in the 1970s: on the one hand, *Coenen, 1975; Koestler, 1978; Van Wesemael, 1979*, and on the other hand the judgments that were already mentioned, *Walrave, 1974*; *Royer, 1976*; *Watson and Belmann, 1976*; *Donà, 1976* and *Van Ameyde, 1977*. In the latter cases the rulings regarding the free movement of workers or establishment, as the case may be, also applied to services.

Sacchi, 1974 dealt with the monopoly of the national television broadcaster in Italy. The Court held that TV broadcasting including advertisements constituted services. It was thus subject to the freedom of services rather than the free movement of goods (para. 6). In contrast, trade in films, sound recordings, etc. was subject to free movement of goods (para. 7). Since broadcasting constituted a service, Article 37 ECT on the adjustment of monopolies was not applicable to the broadcasting monopoly in Italy (para. 10). (The monopoly did not fall foul of the rules on goods or competition. However, owing to non-discrimination the Italian TV broadcaster was not allowed to discriminate against nationals of other member states; para. 20.)

In *Van Binsbergen, 1974*, the first pure services case, the Court recognized the direct effect of the freedom of services in the Treaty as regarded discrimination based on nationality and residence (paras 20-7). Furthermore, the Court differentiated with regard to a residence requirement for lawyers. While such a requirement generally failed to comply with the freedom of services, the professional rules of the host state had to be observed. Any lawyer could be required to comply with such rules, i. e. including those residing abroad; compliance could be monitored; and lawyers could lawfully be required to reside in the vicinity of the courts they served. However, a service address at the relevant place equally sufficed to guarantee compliance with the professional rules. Finally, the Court held that a host state could take measures against providers that were established abroad and principally directed services at its territory, and thus intended to avoid the professional rules of the host state from being applied to them. *Coenen, 1975* essentially confirmed this approach. Where the person concerned, *in casu* an insurance intermediary, had a place of business in the state where the service was provided, it was unlawful to require residence in addition.

Van Wesemael, 1979 dealt with employment agencies for entertainers. The Court added the aspect of the dual burden. While the need for supervisory rules could justify certain measures, as held in *Van Binsbergen, 1974* and *Coenen, 1975*, the state where the service was provided would have to take two elements into account, namely, on the one hand, a licence that had been issued by another member state under comparable circumstances; and, on the other hand, proper mechanisms of supervision in other member states (para. 30). The Court also rejected Belgium's argument that a previous International Labour Organization Convention justified more restrictive requirements than those allowed under the free movement of services (paras 31-8). In *Koestler, 1978*, finally, the Court ruled that the free movement of services was not violated when debts arising out of a contract akin to a wagering contract which (the debts) were enforceable in the state where they had arisen could not lawfully be enforced in another state. That applied, however, only in so far as debts of that kind were unenforceable as a matter of principle in the latter state.

III The 1980s

During the 1980s the net of case-law in social security was knit tighter. The Court handed down 90 judgments in social security and half a dozen judgments in the free movement of workers in which social security was also addressed. However, in the course of this decade the freedom of workers significantly expanded, too, numbering 55 judgments and a handful of decisions in which the freedom of establishment and services overlapped with the freedom of workers. Establishment and services still maintained a relatively low profile with 21 and 18 cases, respectively, again with some decisions overlapping.

1 Workers

In the judgment in *Levin, 1982* the Court for the first time addressed the concept of a 'worker' in article 48 Treaty and Regulation 1612/68. The Court decided, in line with what *Hoekstra, 1964* had laid down for the definition of a 'worker' in social security, that 'worker' was a concept that needed to be interpreted uniformly throughout the Community. Part-time work was also 'work', provided it was a genuine and effective economic activity of more than purely ancillary and marginal scale (para. 17). Moreover, the motives of the person for making use of the freedom to move were irrelevant. In *Kempf, 1986* the Court built on *Levin, 1982*. The part-time work of Ms Levin had generated income below the minimum means of subsistence, but she had been able to supplement it with income from her husband and real property. *Kempf, 1986* added that a low income based on 12 lessons given per week, but supplemented in accordance with domestic law by contributions from public sources of the host state still fulfilled the requirements of 'work' in article 48 Treaty. In *Lawrie-Blum, 1986* the Court included teacher trainees in the scope of the worker definition. It clarified that a person was a worker, if she or he 'perform[ed] services for and under the direction of another person in return for which [she or] he receive[d] remuneration' (para. 17). *Lair, 1988* clarified that the status of a worker and the rights flowing from it could be maintained even after the employment had ended (paras. 33 et seq.). The Court in *Steymann, 1988* added that the activities within a Bhagwan community, which (the activities) were typically not directly remunerated but for which the community provided an 'indirect quid pro quo' (para. 12), could constitute work under article 48 Treaty provided that the activity was effective and genuine. *Bettray, 1989* excluded from the scope of 'work' in article 48 Treaty activities in a drug rehabilitation programme, because they were mainly designed to allow the person concerned to recover the ability to take part in the employment market (para. 17). Yet neither the public origin of the funds to pay for the activities nor the level of productivity of the persons concerned were relevant for the categorization of an activity as 'work' (para. 15). *Agegate, 1989* clarified that fishermen who received remuneration in the form of a share of the fish they caught could be 'workers'. The definition of 'worker' in article 55 of the Act of Accession of Spain and article 48 Treaty were congruent. An assessment was needed case by case, factoring in the distribution of risks, working hours, and the degree of liberty. That payment consisted in a 'share' and that remuneration was calculated on a collective basis was not decisive (para. 36). Finally, in *Danmols, 1985* the Court refused to apply the above definition of a 'worker' in social policy where only partial harmonization had been achieved by a Directive on safeguarding employees' rights in case of transfers of undertakings (Directive 77/187) (paras 24-6).

'Work' could also occur outside the Community, as had already been indicated in *Walrave, 1974* (paras 28-9). In *Prodest, 1984* the Court held that an employment contract by a Belgian national with a French company created a sufficiently close link to the territory of a member state so that the requirements of 'work' were met, although a part of the activities under the contract was performed outside the Community. In *Lopes da Veiga, 1989* the Court found with reference to *Commission v. France (maritime worker quota), 1974* that employment of a national of a member state aboard a ship registered in another member state constituted 'work' for the purpose of Regulation 1612/68, even though some work might be carried out outside the territory of the Community. There was a link within the meaning of *Prodest, 1984* to the territory of a member state.

Advantages

Most of the judgments of the 1980s in free movement of workers dealt with article 7(2) Regulation 1612/68. *Reina, 1982* was the first of the decade to deal with that article. The Court ruled on the basis of the definition of social advantages in *Even, 1979* that a childbirth loan was a social advantage, although the benefit pursued a demographic aim and was granted on a discretionary basis. In *Castelli, 1984* the Court decided that the minimum income guaranteed to the elderly was a social advantage under article 7(2) Regulation 1612/68. Hence it had to be granted to the dependent mother of a migrant worker who had retired. More specifically, a convention establishing reciprocity could not be required as a prerequisite. This judgment was confirmed in *Frascogna, 1985* for the mother of an active migrant worker and re-confirmed in *Frascogna II, 1987*. *Frascogna, 1985*, moreover, rejected a residence requirement that did not apply on an equal basis to a state's own nationals, or more precisely their relatives in the ascending line (para. 24). In *Scrivner, 1985* and *Hoeckx, 1985* – judgments that were both delivered on the same day – the Court included Belgium's minimex, a benefit guaranteeing minimum means of subsistence, in the benefits covered by article 7(2) Regulation 1612/68, though not in the benefits covered by Regulation 1408/71 (as to the latter, see below). In *Hoeckx, 1985* the Court additionally made it clear that a discriminatory residence requirement was not lawful. *Deak, 1985* added that article 7(2) Regulation 1612/68 comprised the benefit a migrant worker enjoyed when her dependent descendant could claim a tideover unemployment benefit. Moreover, the nationality of the descendant was irrelevant. *Mutsch, 1985* added a further aspect to article 7(2) Regulation 1612/68. According to *Mutsch, 1985* it amounted to a social advantage for the residents of a region of a member state to be able to conduct legal proceedings in the language that was one of the official languages of that member state. This privilege therefore had to be extended to the speakers of the same language from other member states. In *Reed, 1986* the Court decided that the fact that one was able to be accompanied by an unmarried partner also constituted a social advantage under article 7(2) Regulation 1612/68. If reunion with partners was possible in a member state, that possibility had to be open to migrant workers as well.

Educational advantages

One of the branches of the case-law on article 7(2) Regulation 1612/68 dealt with educational advantages. The first case in point was *Forcheri, 1983* where the Court after having given a first indication in *Casagrande, 1974* brought education into the focus of Community law. To levy higher enrolment fees for vocational studies from the wife of a worker was discriminatory.[25] The Court detached this approach from the free movement of workers and article 7(2) Regulation 1612/68 in *Gravier, 1985* and expanded it on the basis of article 7 Treaty to students who did not work and did not have any link whatsoever to a migrant worker. The Court moreover sent a very broad definition of 'vocational training' (para. 30), including courses in strip cartoon art. *Gravier, 1985* was followed up by *Commission v. Belgium (vocational training, interim), 1985* in which the Court granted interim measures, because Belgium did not apply the *Gravier, 1985*-ruling to the enrolment fees at universities. The so-called 'minerval' was charged as a supplementary fee from foreign students (para. 2). However, the infringement procedure was later declared inadmissible in *Commission v. Belgium (vocational training), 1988*, because the periods set by the Commission to reply to the letter of formal notice and the reasoned opinion were too short. On the very same day that the inadmissibility ruling in *Commission v. Belgium (vocational training), 1988* was handed down, *Blaizot, 1988*, however, clarified the point. According to *Blaizot, 1988* university studies in general were included in 'vocational training' within the sense of *Gravier, 1985*. Exception was made though for courses intended to improve 'general knowledge' (para. 20). Moreover, while the Court in *Barra, 1988* had refused to limit the application of *Gravier, 1985* in time, in *Blaizot, 1988* the Court decided that *Gravier, 1985* applied only *ex nunc* as far as university education was concerned, except for those applicants who had already brought proceedings (paras 25 et seq.). *Humbel, 1988* soon thereafter explained that a programme of studies followed by a student at university would have to be assessed as a whole and in the light of its purpose (para. 11) to determine whether it constituted vocational training. The assessment was, however, not to be made on the basis of the individual years of the programme, if the 'programme form[ed] a coherent single entity' (para. 12) which could not be divided into parts. *Commission v. Belgium (students), 1988* was another follow-up case to *Gravier, 1985*. Belgium still applied a distinction based on the nationality of students in the financing of higher education establishments other than universities. More specifically, only a limited number of students of nationality of member states other than Belgium had been factored in to determine the amount of state financing provided for such establishments. The Court rejected this approach under the *Gravier, 1985* line of authority (para. 8).

Maintenance grants

The judgment in *Lair, 1988* refused to extend this autonomous approach based on article 7 Treaty to maintenance and training grants. Such grants were outside the scope of Community policy. Only workers could therefore claim maintenance grants on a non-discriminatory basis pursuant to article 7(2) Regulation

25 The judgment considered officials employed by the European Community to have the status of migrant workers, see para. 9.

1612/68. The Court, however, made sure that even those who had ceased work were considered as 'workers' and could thus validly claim maintenance grants, provided that there was 'some continuity between the previous occupational activity and the course of study' (para. 37). In short, the purposes of the previous work and the studies had to be related. Persons who had become unemployed involuntarily and were required to retrain were in addition exempt from this condition of continuity. However, in a judgment of the same day as *Lair, 1988* – *Brown, 1988* – the Court held that a future student who bridged the gap-year before beginning studies by working in a company, undertaking so-called 'pre-university industrial training' (para. 3), in the state where he was going to study could not rely on article 7(2) Regulation 1612/68 to lay claim to a maintenance grant in the host state, despite being a 'worker'. The reason was that his work was only ancillary to the studies to be financed by the grant (para. 27). In *Matteucci, 1988* the Court followed up on the ruling in *Lair, 1988* as to the right of migrant workers to claim maintenance grants under article 7(2) Regulation 1612/68. The Court held that maintenance grants in application of a cultural agreement between two member states had to be opened up for migrant workers.

Family members

The Court also dealt with various matters concerning families under the free movement of workers. In the judgments already discussed in *Forcheri, 1983*; *Castelli, 1984*; *Frascogna, 1985*; and *Deak, 1985* the Court granted family members – in accordance with *Cristini, 1975* and *Inzirillo, 1976* – the benefit of article 7(2), essentially by channelling it through the migrant worker. Yet other judgments also concerned the family members of migrant workers. *Diatta, 1985* concerned a third country national who was married to a migrant worker. However, the two spouses no longer lived together. The Court ruled that article 10 Regulation 1612/68 did not require spouses to live under the same roof and that a marriage had to be considered to last, until it was formally dissolved. Moreover, the right of residence of the third country national spouse derived from article 10, rather than article 11 Regulation 1612/68. The latter merely regulated the right of spouses to be employed in the host state. The Court further elaborated on article 10 in *Commission v. Germany (adequate housing), 1989*. The Court decided that the requirement to have adequate housing for family members in article 10(3) Regulation 1612/68 applied at the time the family joined the worker, but not throughout the entire stay in the host state. Apart from cases of abuse of rights, a member state could therefore only apply housing requirements which it also applied to its own nationals (para. 12).

In *Gül, 1986* the Court recognized that a spouse who was a third country national had access to *any* activity as an employed person pursuant to article 11 Regulation 1612/68 (para. 11). That included even activities that were subject to authorization, provided the ordinary requirements to be met by all applicants were fulfilled. The rights of spouses pursuant to articles 10 and 11 Regulation

1612/68 were secondary rights which flowed from the original rights of their spouses who were migrant workers. Such spouses could thus rely on article 11 to benefit indirectly from article 3 Regulation 1612/68 and be treated in a non-discriminatory fashion like all migrant workers having the nationality of a member state (para. 20). *Lebon, 1987* continued this line of authority by ruling that members of the family of migrant workers benefitted only indirectly from non-discrimination under article 7(2) Regulation 1612/68, that is when there was a social advantage for the migrant worker himself. Such an advantage did not accrue to the migrant worker when his descendant drew a guaranteed minimum income (minimex) while she (the descendant) was no longer dependent on him (the worker; paras 12-3). Moreover, whether a person was 'dependent' within the meaning of article 10 Regulation 1612/68 had to be decided in the light of the factual circumstances, without regard to the reasons for the support granted or the ability to take up paid employment. Finally, those who moved to seek employment could not benefit from equal treatment in the sense that they enjoyed the full benefit of article 7(2) Regulation 1612/68; rather they only enjoyed equal treatment access to employment.

The indirect approach to non-discrimination of family members of migrant workers was also confirmed in *Matteucci, 1988* (para. 8). In *Brown, 1988* the Court spelled out another limit to the rights of family members of migrant workers, namely that the descendant of a national of a member state could not rely on the rights in Regulation 1612/68 as a family member of a migrant worker when the parent who had been a migrant worker in the host state had left the host state for good, viz. the parent no longer resided or had any employment there. However, this applied only when the parent had left the host state *before* the birth of the descendant (para. 30). In a similar vein the Court held in *Humbel, 1988* that the child of migrant workers could not rely on article 12 Regulation 1612/68 when it sought education – outside the scope of *Gravier, 1985* – in a third member state, i. e. a member state other than where the parents worked and resided. However, *Echternach, 1989* carved out a special situation in this regard. When the parents who had worked in the host state migrated back to their country of origin and their child's education in the host state was not recognised in the country of origin, the child could go back to the host state alone and rely on article 12 Regulation 1612/68. Besides, that article covered 'all forms of education' (para. 29). The interpretation given by the Court to article 7(2) Regulation 1612/68 regarding maintenance grants in *Lair, 1988* also applied to the child covered by article 12 Regulation 1612/68.

Derogations

The Court also expanded the derogation case-law in the 1980s. In *Adoui, 1982* the Court built on *Van Duyn, 1974*. It was faced with the problem that prostitution was not illegal in Belgium, but that the residence permits of prostitutes who were nationals of other member states were not extended. The Court reiterated in keeping with *Van Duyn, 1974* that expulsion on the ground of public order could be ordered against nationals of other member states, while it was not possible for a state to adopt such a measure against its own nationals. The Court added, however, that care had to be taken not to apply arbitrary distinctions to the detriment of nationals of other member states, when it was decided to expel a person (para. 7). That would be the case, if a state did not adopt measures against its own nationals in case of behaviour which would have resulted in the refusal to extend a residence permit had a national of another member state displayed it (para. 8). The remainder of the judgment dealt with the minimum procedural safeguards available to those who were subject to expulsion orders pursuant to articles 8 and 9 Directive 64/221. Previously, *Pecastaing, 1980* and *Santillo, 1980* had already elaborated these procedural safeguards. The gist of this procedural case-law is as follows. The articles had direct effect. They essentially required non-discrimination to be applied in procedural matters. At least the opinion of an absolutely independent authority was required when an expulsion order was only subject to legal review. The procedure before that authority had to respect the full rights of defence. The authority had the power to review facts and expediency fully. The opinion it adopted had to be based on present facts, viz. facts as they stood at the time the opinion was adopted, and it had to be duly notified.

In *Gül, 1986* the Court also ruled on derogations. It held that in the light of the free movement of persons the public health derogation did not serve to exclude access by nationals of other member states to entire sectors of economic activity. Rather, it solely served to prevent specific individuals from having access to the territory or a profession when this access would on its own amount to a danger to public health (para. 17). In *Commission v. Germany (adequate housing), 1989*, the Court was faced with the national requirement for migrant workers to have continuous adequate housing. It reiterated the existing case-law on the public policy and security derogations, implying that the requirement was not justifiable under those derogations (paras 17-20).

The Court repeatedly dealt with the public service exception which it had already addressed in *Sotgiu, 1974* and *Reyners, 1974*. The judgment in *Commission v. Belgium (public service), 1980* established that the term 'public service' in article 48(4) Treaty was a Community term (para. 18). The national authorities were not allowed to interpret it as they saw fit. The Court also refused to remove all employment with the state from the scope of the freedom of workers. Instead, only employment fell under the exception that 'involve[d] direct or indirect participation in the exercise of powers conferred by public law and duties designed to safeguard the general interests of the state', requiring a 'special relationship of allegiance to the state' (para. 10). Thus an assessment of each individual post was required. The Court confirmed this interpretation in the follow-up case *Commission v. Belgium (public service II), 1982*. In *Commission v. France (nurses), 1986* the Court corroborated the approach taken in *Sotgiu, 1974* that the way national law classed certain posts, in particular as belonging to civil servanthood, was irrelevant. The Court also reiterated in keeping with *Commission v. Belgium (public service), 1980* that the public service exception did not generally cover hospital nurses (para. 13). Therefore nurses from other member states had to be employed under the same conditions as French nurses (paras 14 et seq.). Later, the Court added in *Lawrie-Blum, 1986* that the activities of trainee teachers did not come within 'public service' (para. 28); neither did those of researchers working for a national research council according to *Commission v. Italy (research council), 1987*. However, in the latter case the Court included the 'duties of management or advising the state on scientific and technical questions' (para. 9) in 'public service'. It also held that discrimination arose from the facts that foreign researchers were offered employment of merely limited duration and that no career structure was available for them in contrast to Italian nationals (para. 13). In *Commission v. Greece (vocational schools), 1988* the Court implicitly excluded directors and teachers of vocational schools from 'public service' (paras 6 and 19-21). Finally, in *Allué I, 1989* the Court held that foreign language assistants did not come within the scope of 'public service'. Quite apart from that aspect, *Allué I, 1989* marked the beginning of a long series of cases on foreign language assistants. The Court in *Allué I, 1989* ruled that nationals of other member states who were employed as foreign-language assistants at Italian universities were covertly and unjustifiably discriminated when 75 per cent of foreign-language assistants were nationals of other member states and foreign-language assistants in general were only given contracts of limited duration, while other university employees regularly received contracts of infinite duration.

No violation of non-discrimination

In the 1980s, the Court also decided in a number of other cases that the principle of non-discrimination on the basis of nationality was not violated. According to *Haug-Adrion, 1984* non-discrimination was not violated with respect to either the free movement of workers or services when an insurance company refused to grant personal premium reductions (no-claims bonuses) applying to regular contracts on personal liability insurance in case of car accidents, in an insurance contract taken out for a car destined for export and thus given customs registration plates. The reason was that the general tariff conditions of the contract were not in any way based on the nationality or residence of the person insured, but rather on the mere fact that the car had customs registration plates (para. 16). According to *Pesca Valentia, 1988*, non-discrimination was not violated, either, by the requirement of national law that 75 per cent of the crew of fishing boats registered in the member state concerned had to be nationals of a member state of the Community. This ruling was confirmed in *Agegate, 1989*. Yet, in *Agegate, 1989* – a judgment that was handed down in the particular context of the Community fishery policy – a requirement for crew members of ships fishing against the national quota to reside on shore in the United Kingdom was struck down (paras 22-5).

In a similar vein, according to *Commission v. Greece (real estate), 1989*, certain restrictions on the acquisition of real estate in Greece imposed on nationals of other member states but not Greek nationals, contravened article 9 Regulation 1612/68 and article 48 Treaty: 'access to housing and ownership of property, as provided in article 9 of Regulation [...] 1612/68, is the corollary of freedom of movement of workers and is for that reason covered by the prohibition of discrimination [...] laid down in [a]rticle 48' ECT (para. 18). Yet, the act of accession of Greece had the effect that Greece's restriction were only partly precluded in so far as they had an effect on persons who had already been lawfully employed at the time of accession (paras 18-9). In *Groener, 1989* no violation of non-discrimination was found, either. The Court held that the requirement for an art lecturer in Ireland to be fluent in Irish as the first national language which had consistently been promoted was covered by the condition in article 3(1) Regulation 1612/68, namely 'conditions relating to linguistic knowledge required by reason of the nature of the post to be filled'. Hence, the requirement was not precluded.

Diploma recognition

Heylens, 1987 followed up on the diploma recognition judgments in *Thieffry, 1977* and *Patrick, 1977*. It established that the authorities seized with a request for diploma recognition had to assess objectively in the light of the studies and training undertaken whether the person concerned had, 'if not identical, at least equivalent' knowledge and qualifications as those required by national law (para. 13). Some safeguards in the procedure for diploma recognition were also required (judicial remedy and notification of reasons; paras 14-6). The Court also handed down *Commission v. Germany (nurses), 1985* in diploma recognition. The case dealt exclusively with Germany's failure to adopt the legislation to implement the directives regarding diplomas and activities of nurses.

The Ankara Agreement

In the 1980s, the Court initiated a new line of authority. In *Demirel, 1987* the Court dealt with Turkish migrant workers under the Ankara Agreement of 1963 for the first time. The Court acknowledged that the Agreement could potentially have direct effect (para. 14). However, the Court rejected direct effect for article 12. That article only required the parties to be guided by the internal market rules on the free movement of workers in order to establish that freedom with Turkey. It did not have direct effect in the sense of transposing enforceable Community rules on family reunification to the relationship with Turkey. Decision 1/80 which had been adopted within the framework of the Ankara Agreement did not cover family reunification, either (paras 15-25).

Enlargement

A number of transitional problems in the free movement of workers that were caused by the second and third enlargement of the Community, viz. the accession of Greece, Spain and Portugal, were also dealt with during the 1980s. The Court held in *Peskeloglou, 1983* that the Act of Accession of Greece prevented member states during the transitional phase after accession from making their employment conditions for Greek nationals more stringent relative to the conditions in force at the time of accession (para. 13). In *Commission v. Greece (real estate), 1989* the Court ruled that the suspension of parts of Regulation 1612/68 under the transitional regime after accession did not affect the rights of migrant workers who were already working in Greece at the time of accession under article 48 Treaty. The right of those who were lawfully employed for the first time in Greece after accession were not affected, either (para. 15). This finding was confirmed for Portuguese workers who had worked in one of the old member states before accession in *Lopes da Veiga, 1989* (para. 10). *Agegate, 1989* transposed the rulings in *Peskeloglou, 1983* and *Commission v. Greece (real estate), 1989/Lopes da Veiga, 1989* to the Act of Accession of Spain.

Technicalities, purely internal situations

Finally, the Court also dealt with some of the more technical details of the free movement of workers and with the issue of situations being purely internal to one member state. *Pieck, 1980* addressed the traditional formal requirements of immigration in the light of Community law. In brief, a traditional visa could not be required any longer from nationals of the member states, the residence permit under Community law was different from the permit required hitherto, and only proportional sanctions could be taken when these formal requirements were not complied with. Imprisonment or deportation were not proportional sanctions. In *Commission v. Italy (tourism), 1986* the Court held that certain unlawful reciprocity and nationality requirements in Italian law with regard to tourism, journalism, and pharmacies were not sufficiently remedied by mere administrative practices. The free movement of workers as well as establishment and services were therefore violated. *Commission v. Belgium (border control), 1989* accepted sporadic and unsystematic border controls of residence permits of nationals of member states, provided that the production of the permit was not a condition precedent to admission to the territory of a member state. In addition, the authorities were allowed to check compliance with the obligation to carry a resident permit on person at all times, if the obligation to carry an identity card was imposed by a member state on its own nationals. *Messner, 1989* found that, while nationals of other member states could be required to report their presence in the host state pursuant to *Watson and Belmann, 1976*, a three-day period to do so was excessively restrictive.

The Court dealt with purely internal situations in four judgments. In *Morson, 1982* the Court ruled that the freedom of workers was not applicable when no link at all was given to any of the situations governed by Community law (para. 16). That was the case when parents who were third country nationals sought residence in the Netherlands with their children who were Dutch nationals employed in the Netherlands and who had never exercised their freedom to work in other member states. *Moser, 1984* added that the claim that a person might at a later point in time, after having passed the educational training to which he sought access, make use of the treaty freedoms to seek employment abroad was a purely hypothetical prospect (para. 18). That aspect did not suffice to bring a situation within the reach of Community law when the situation was otherwise confined to a single member state. In *Hurd, 1986* the Court confirmed the approach taken in *Morson, 1982*. It held that employment by a European school in a member state did not suffice for a teacher, who was a national of that member state who had never made use of his freedom, to establish a connection to a situation governed by Community law. The tax treatment to which that member state subjected its own nationals and which had the effect that the national concerned was worse off than nationals of other member states in the same situation was therefore lawful under Community law (paras 54-6). (The Court also addressed other aspects of Community law such as the principle of loyal cooperation.) Finally, in *Iorio, 1986* a train journey within Italy by an Italian national was considered to be a situation purely internal to Italy. Yet the Court also noted that the member states were free to regulate access to public transport, if they did so on a non-discriminatory basis and based on the 'needs of rational and economic organization' (para. 16).

2 Establishment

One of the first judgments in freedom of establishment in the 1980s *Klopp, 1984* concerned lawyers again. Mr Klopp wanted to register with the Paris bar while maintaining his registration in Germany. His request was refused though, because lawyers in France were only allowed to have one set of chambers in France, namely at the place where they were registered. The Court ruled that, while a member state was free to regulate the legal profession, the French requirement violated the freedom of establishment. That freedom included the right to have more than one place of work, else nationals of other member states were required to abandon their business in the state where they had already been established (paras 18-19). Compliance with the host state's rules governing the profession was required, but contact with the clients could also be maintained via 'modern methods of transport and telecommunications' (para. 21).

In *Fearon, 1984* the Court dealt with the Irish system under which a commission had the power to acquire rural land to ensure that it was used for certain purposes. An exemption was granted, though, when the owner of the land had resided within three miles of the piece of land concerned. When the land was owned by a company, the residence of the company's owners was relevant. An Irish company owned by British nationals none of whom met the residence requirement contested the acquisition of land. After having rejected the argument that article 222 Treaty removed the ownership system from non-discrimination and the freedom of establishment, the Court ruled that the residence requirement was not precluded by the freedom of establishment, since it applied to Irish nationals and nationals of other member states alike (para. 10). The freedom of establishment of companies in article 58 Treaty, in turn, was not concerned, as the relevant company had been Irish (para. 8).

1985

In *Steinhauser, 1985* the city of Biarritz in France required persons to have French nationality to be allowed to participate in a public tender for the allocation of property owned by the municipality. The Court found that the resulting exclusion of a German artist from a tender violated the freedom of establishment, since the renting of business premises facilitated the pursuit of the freedom. All public authorities, including the local authorities, had to comply with the freedom. The measure was obviously discriminatory and thus precluded (paras 14-6).

1986

In *Commission v. France (doctors), 1986* France's registration requirements had the effect that doctors established abroad could not open a second practice in France or work in France while maintaining a practice abroad. Moreover, cross-border medical care could lawfully be offered to a single patient for only two days. According to the Court, the member states had to respect non-discrimination and abstain from raising unnecessary obstacles when regulating the medical profession with a view to ensure protection of health (para. 11). Non-discrimination was violated in that French doctors were sometimes allowed to have a second practice in a specific region. The rules applied were, moreover, unduly restrictive for too absolute and general to be justified by the need of patients for continuous care or by the ethics of the medical profession. In some medical specialties, a single treatment was sufficient for the needs of the patient. Doctors often worked in group practices and foreign doctors were thus prevented from acting as a *locum tenens* for doctors established in France. In particular, the two days-service rule prevented that and thereby infringed the freedom to provide *services* (paras 12-6). *Bertini, 1986* again concerned the medical profession, though this time the training of doctors. Some Italian doctors had argued that the existence of a *numerus clausus* for medical studies at universities in other member states restricted their medical practice in Italy. Medical students from other member states overflowed to Italian universities, thus increasing pressure on the Italian market. According to them, Italy had to introduce a similar restriction to admission to Italian universities. The Court heard none of those arguments. In the absence of measures adopted by the Council, the member states were not required by Community law to restrict access to universities and introduce a *numerus clausus* (para. 11). The absence of a restriction could not impede free movement (para. 10).

Segers, 1986 was a case in which a company was established in the United Kingdom. It conducted all of its business through a subsidiary in the Netherlands. Mr Segers was one of two owners of the company, with each holding 50 per cent of the shares, and a director of it. Netherlands' law normally granted such company directors sickness insurance benefits. However, in the case of Mr Segers that was refused, because the company was not established in the Netherlands. The Court found that the Dutch refusal violated the freedom of establishment. The refusal to affiliate such a person to Dutch sickness insurance indirectly violated the British company's right to exercise its freedom of establishment by means of a subsidiary (para. 15). While it was possible for member states to apply a difference in treatment in order to combat fraud, the refusal to grant social security benefits was not an appropriate means to do so (para. 16).

1987

In *Commission v. Belgium (bio labs), 1987* the Court found a Belgian rule to be in accordance with the freedom of establishment. The rule had required all directors, partners, or members of private legal persons providing bio-medical laboratory services to be either doctors or pharmacists. The right to pursue a self-employed activity in the host state was subject to the rules of the host state regulating such activity, provided that equal treatment was respected. The Belgian rule applied without distinction. It neither had discriminatory effects, nor was its purpose discriminatory (paras 9-11).

1988 and 1989

In *Commission v. Italy (social housing), 1988* Italy had reserved certain social housing and some reduced-rate mortgage loans to Italian nationals. Relying on the general programmes adopted by the Council to implement establishment, the Court found that housing was of assistance in the pursuit of establishment. The freedom of establishment and, consequently, non-discrimination were applicable to housing legislation. Italy's condition was liable to constitute an obstacle to establishment. Equivalent conditions, including with regard to facilities alleviating the financial burden, had to be granted to nationals of other member states. As providers of services sometimes also had to stay in the host state for a certain time, the Italian approach was also contrary to the freedom of *services* (paras 14-9). The ruling in *Commission v. Italy (social housing), 1988* was confirmed in *Commission v. Greece (real estate), 1989* as far as real estate was needed for the pursuit of the freedom of establishment and services. The nationality conditions Greece applied when it came to real estate acquisition and long-term rental agreements contravened the freedom of establishment and services, since the acquisition of real estate was a corollary of long- and short-term service provision (paras 20-7).

Gullung, 1988 established that a non-discriminatory obligation for lawyers to register with the host state bar was in accordance with the freedom of establishment and services (para. 29). Moreover, Directive 77/249 on lawyers' services did not prevent the host state from applying its own rules on professional ethics, in particular the requirement for lawyers to be in good character (para. 18). Apart from that, a member state could not refuse one of its own nationals who was also a national of another member state the benefits of the Directive (para. 12). In *Commission v. Greece (vocational schools), 1988* the Court scrutinized certain of Greece's requirements related to running a school and teaching in Greece. More specifically, foreign nationals could not set up private vocational schools, act as directors and teachers, and give private lessons at home in Greece. The restriction to set up a school could not be justified by the exercise of official authority pursuant to article 55 Treaty, since it was not connected thereto. Supervision could as well ensure the proper operation of schools. A non-discriminatory requirement to be authorized to establish a school was, however, in accordance with the freedom of establishment. The prohibition to give private lessons at home, in addition, was at odds with the freedom of services, as was the exclusion from teaching with the freedom of workers as far those were concerned who had been employed in Greece already at the time of Greece's accession to the Community (paras 8-21). In *Commission v. Greece (registers), 1988* the Court held that Greece violated the freedom of establishment and services in that the law did not expressly provide that nationals of other member states could equally register as ordinary members of the professional organizations of architects, civil engineers, and surveyors and thereby enjoy the benefits that membership conferred. The freedom of establishment and services was equally violated by the explicit nationality condition for access to the profession of lawyers.

In *Commission v. Italy (data-processing systems), 1989* the Court decided that Italy could not reserve the conclusion of public contracts involving the development of data processing systems for the public authorities to companies in which the Italian state held a controlling stake, else domestic companies were favoured (para. 9). The restriction of the freedom of establishment and services involved was not justified. The confidentiality of data could be ensured by duties of secrecy imposed on the staff of companies entrusted with the task; the tasks assigned were unrelated to the exercise of official authority; and a threat to public policy was not established (paras 11, 13, and 15).

Purely internal situations and remainders

In *Gauchard, 1987* the Court refused to address the merits, for the situation was confined in all aspects to France. A French national who was resident in France managed a supermarket in France. That supermarket was operated by a French company. He was prosecuted for having failed to obtain the necessary authorization to extend the sales area of his supermarket. In a very similar situation in *Bekaert, 1988* the Court also refused to address the merits based on the same ground.

For the sake of completeness, *Conradi, 1987* must be mentioned. In this case, the Court held that the definition of a retail trader in Directive 64/233 – concerning the attainment of the freedom of establishment and the freedom to provide services in respect of activities in wholesale trade – was not to be relied upon outside the field of application of that directive for the purpose of application of national law.

Companies

Two more judgments dealt with aspects of establishment that were related to companies, i. e. article 58 Treaty. In *Commission v. France (tax credit), 1986* the Court found a violation of the freedom of establishment in that France granted a tax credit only to subsidiaries, but not to branches or agencies of companies established in other member states, while domestic companies could always claim the tax credit (paras 20 and 26). According to *Daily Mail, 1988*, the freedom of establishment did not force the United Kingdom to allow a company to transfer its central management and control to the Netherlands, while maintaining its legal personality and status under British law.

Diploma

The Court also dealt with a few cases concerning diploma recognition under the freedom of establishment. In *Broekmeulen, 1981* the Court interpreted Directive 75/362 on doctors' diplomas to the effect that a returning own national who had obtained in another member state a doctor diploma which was to be recognized under the directive could rely on the directive for recognition (paras 19-20). Moreover, the right to recognition as a general practitioner flowed directly from the directive. Hence, in such a case an additional preparatory training period could not be imposed by the 'home' member state, in particular when the completion of such a period was not required from nationals of other member states holding a foreign diploma (paras 24-5). According to *Auer II, 1983*, a veterinarian holding the prerequisite Italian qualification was entitled to rely directly on Directive 78/1026 on diploma recognition in veterinary medicine, because France had failed to implement it (para. 16). Accordingly, even though the French authorities had refused to register him as a veterinarian, he could not be prosecuted (para. 19). That judgment was fully confirmed for Italy in *Rienks, 1983*. In *Commission v. Germany (nurses), 1985* the Court held that Germany's administrative practice and conclusion of the relevant Council of Europe Agreement in itself were not sufficient to implement Directives 77/452 and 77/453 on the activities and recognition of diploma of nurses (paras 28 and 38). In *Van de Bijl, 1989* the Court interpreted Directive 64/427 concerning some activities of self-employed persons in manufacturing and processing industries. It *inter alia* found that, while the member states were generally bound by certificates issued pursuant to that directive, a member state was not bound by a certificate issued by another member state, if it evidenced facts which had taken place in the first member state's territory. Indeed, a member state could prevent circumvention of its own rules (para. 26). Finally, *Commission v. Italy, 1987* is to be mentioned. In this case, Italy admitted that it had failed to transpose an amendment to Directives 75/362 and 75/363 on doctors.

3 Social security

Definitions and scope

During the 1980s, the Court elaborated the case-law on the scope of Regulation 1408/71 and the definitions needed to apply the Regulation in various judgments. In *Walsh, 1980* the Court built on *Brack, 1976*. The Court found that a person could still be considered 'employed' even though her employment had ended, because the insurance scheme still covered her by reason of the contributions she had paid while she had been employed (para. 6). Moreover, the Court reiterated a ruling that had already led to the decision in *Smieja, 1973*, namely that the term 'legislation' used in Regulation 1408/71 generally meant legislation of the member states, while elements of Community law could also be included (paras 8-9). Such was the case with article 8 Regulation 574/72, because the individual derived rights from a combination of national law and Community law. In *Galinsky, 1981* the Court ruled that a person who had worked on a self-employed basis in one member state and as an employed person in another member state came within the scope *ratione personae* of Regulation 1408/71. However, the old-age pension acquired by reason of the self-employed activity and based on national law alone, i. e. not in conjunction with Regulation 1408/71, was outside the scope of that Regulation. Article 77 Regulation 1408/71, which governed family allowances for recipients of old-age pensions, was therefore not applicable to such a pension.

In *Meade, 1984* the Court decided that Regulation 1408/71 did not apply. A national of the United States of America who was self-employed in France could not rely on Regulation 1408/71 to challenge a withdrawal of family benefits on the ground that the second child went to pursue studies abroad; neither could his wife, who was a British national, because she had never worked (para. 7). Their son, also a British national who went to study in the United Kingdom, could not pursuant to *Kuyken, 1977* rely on article 48 Treaty or Regulation 1408/71, either, because he had never been insured under a scheme for employed persons (para. 8). *Frascogna, 1985* also concerned the scope *ratione personae* of Regulation 1408/71. Ms Frascogna was an Italian national living in France with her son who was a worker. She was denied a special old-age allowance for persons who had insufficient income on the ground that she had not resided in France for 15 years. The Court, based on the *Kermaschek, 1976*-line of authority, rejected her claim to have the residence clause set aside on the basis of Regulation 1408/71. She could only claim rights derived from the migrant worker. The French benefit, however, was granted generally to old persons, and not specifically to family members of workers (para. 16). (However, see the assessment under article 7(2) Regulation 1612/68, above.) On the same ground the Court rejected the claim of a descendant of a migrant worker for a tideover unemployment benefit in Belgium in *Deak, 1985*. The tideover allowance was not granted to a person *qua* its status as a family member of an unemployed worker, but on the basis of a person's own inability to find employment (paras 14-5). (See again the ruling under Regulation 1612/68, above.) In *Zaoui, 1987* the Court applied the derived rights-approach again. It found that an Algerian national who was married to a French national could not claim a French supplementary allowance to an invalidity pension based on him being the member of the family of a worker (paras. 11-2). (His claim was equally rejected under Regulation 1612/68, because the situation was purely internal to France; para. 15.)

In *Van Roosmalen, 1986*, the Court interpreted the term 'self-employed person' in Regulation 1408/71 with regard to voluntary social insurance so as to encompass a person that pursued an occupation. That included a missionary priest who did not receive remuneration, but was maintained by parishioners (para. 22). According to the Court, since Regulation 1408/71 had been amended to include 'self-employed persons', this term equally had to be interpreted comprehensively, as it had already been established for the term 'employed person' (para. 20). *Van Roosmalen, 1986* had an additional dimension. The Court in *Bozzone, 1977*, had already dealt with the Belgian social security system for work in the former Belgian Congo. *Bozzone, 1977* had recently been reiterated in *Commission v. Belgium (Congo), 1980*. In the same vein the Court again found it irrelevant for the question whether there was 'legislation' pursuant to article 1(j) Regulation 1408/71 that the self-employed activity was pursued outside the Community, so long as a link to a member state's social security scheme was established. That was the case in *Van Roosmalen, 1986*, for the affiliation to a social security scheme in Belgium, albeit for an activity in the former Belgian Congo, evidenced such a link (paras 29-30). This was later on confirmed in *Laborero, 1987* (paras 24-5). *Laborero, 1987*, moreover, made it clear that it did not matter that the social security scheme which covered work in the Belgian Congo was separate from the general social security system in Belgium and required particular conditions of affiliation to be met (para. 17). In addition, the voluntary nature of the scheme was irrelevant and so was the fact, by nature, that the person was no longer working in the case of an application for a survivor's pension.

Social security v. social assistance

Vigier, 1981 returned to the distinction between social security and social assistance. The Court found Germany's scheme which offered victims of nazi persecution the option to buy retroactively into periods of insurance for the time of the persecution to be a scheme of social security which supplemented the general social security scheme. That Germany had not declared the scheme to be part of social security for the purposes of Regulation 1408/71 was irrelevant (para. 15). The decisive point was that eligibility did not depend on a discretionary assessment of the situation and the need of the individual (paras 13-4). In *Piscitello, 1983* a supplement provided by Italian law for old-age pensioners when their pension was below a minimum amount was at issue. Although the Court acknowledged that the benefit also fulfilled purposes of social assistance, it categorized the benefit as social security, because Italian law established a defined legal position which, once the conditions were met, automatically led to the award of the supplement to the pension. There was no discretionary assessment of the position of the individual (para. 13). After that point was settled, it was clear that the residence clause in Italian law was precluded by article 10 Regulation 1408/71.

In the twin judgments of 27 March 1985, *Scrivner, 1985* and *Hoeckx, 1985*, the question was tabled whether Belgium's minimex benefit was a social security benefit within the meaning of Regulation 1408/71. (For the assessment under Regulation 1612/68, see above). The Court emphasized that, even if a benefit was based on a defined legal position, the decisive question was whether a benefit addressed one of the risks that were exhaustively listed in article 4(1) Regulation 1408/71 (para. 19). With the Belgian minimex this was not the case, since the primary criterion for awarding minimex was the lack of adequate means, that is the need of the person concerned. 'Need', however, was not one of the risks covered by Regulation 1408/71 (paras 20-1). In *Giletti, 1987* the Court then had to classify an allowance granted to the elderly in France to supplement their income. From the fact that article 4(2) Regulation 1408/71 included non-contributory benefits in the scope of the Regulation, it necessarily followed that is was irrelevant that the benefit was financed from public sources. Reiterating that national legislation could at the same time fulfil functions of social assistance and social security, the Court concluded that the French benefit was a social security benefit, because national legislation conferred a *right* to the supplement to a pension which was independent of the need of the person concerned (para. 11). This interpretation was confirmed in *Zaoui, 1987* (para. 8).

Further issues of definition

Campana, 1987 also addressed a definition under Regulation 1408/71. The Court interpreted the term unemployment benefits in article 4(1)(g) Regulation 1408/71. The Court included in this term benefits provided to prevent a person from becoming unemployed, such as Germany's assistance toward vocational training for persons in employment. However, such benefits were only covered by Regulation 1408/71, if the person concerned was at least threatened by unemployment (para. 12).

Derks, 1984 was a case which concerned the amendment of the Netherlands' legislation on incapacity of work which introduced (the amendment) a new type A system, i. e. a system under which the amount of benefits were *not* dependent on the completion of insurance periods, replacing the old type B system, in which the amount of benefits was dependent on periods. More specifically, the case concerned the regime designed to ensure a smooth transition to the new system. In the light of the definitions of 'legislation' and 'period of insurance' in article 1(j) and (r) Regulation 1408/71 as well as the annex relating to the Netherlands the Court, relying on *Blottner, 1977*, ruled that periods completed under the old system were true 'periods of insurance', rather than periods not covered by insurance which are sometimes treated as periods of insurance for the purpose of the provision against overlapping of benefits in article 15 Regulation 574/72 (paras 16-7). In the case at hand the Court thus gave preference, with a view to aggregation, to the period completed under the old Netherlands system over an overlapping period of voluntary insurance completed in Germany.

Aggregation and apportionment

In the 1980s, the Court decided more than 30 cases concerning the aggregation of insurance periods, almost all of them under Regulation 1408/71. Just one of them concerned Regulation 3, namely *Salmon, 1980* in which a pension had been awarded in Belgium for insurance periods completed in Belgium based on aggregation pursuant to article 27 and 28 Regulation 3. At the same time, in Germany a pension was awarded based on national law alone for periods completed in Germany. Belgium then reduced the pension awarded in application of article 28(4) Regulation 3. The Court invalidated that approach by holding that no provision in the Regulation or the Treaty allowed the reduction of a pension awarded on the basis of aggregation on the ground that another member state had awarded a pension based on national law alone, provided that the two pensions were not paid with respect to one and the same period of insurance. The reason was that aggregation and apportionment pursuant to Community law already ensured that a member state paid a pension only with regard to periods actually completed under its own system (para. 11).

In *Menzies, 1980*, the issue came up how a supplementary period which, pursuant to national law, was added to the periods of insurance completed in actual fact was to be dealt with in aggregation and apportionment. The Court held that the supplementary period was to be factored in when calculating the theoretical amount, as this was the amount that would have resulted if *all* occupational activity had been carried out in the member state concerned (para. 10). However, in the next step, apportionment, the supplementary period was to be left out of account, because it would 'unilaterally and artificially upset[...] the balance of the burden of the benefits existing between member states' (para. 11), if a supplementary period which did not correspond to an actual period of insurance or even a period of residence would have to be factored in when apportioning, thus resulting in a benefit. In *Besem, 1982*, the Court next elaborated the calculation of the theoretical amount pursuant to article 46 Regulation 1408/71. The Court held that the rules of aggregation and apportionment were a 'complete set of Community rules' (para. 12). They could not be supplemented by national rules which modified the way the theoretical amount was calculated so as to reduce that amount (para. 13). That amount simply had to be calculated in application of national law as if all insurance periods completed in the member states had been completed in the member state concerned. Was therefore precluded a rule of the Netherlands which applied *exclusively* in the calculation under Community rules and which had the effect that the daily wage which was the basis of calculation of an invalidity benefit was reduced in proportion to periods during which the person concerned had not been insured. *Weber, 1984* concerned the calculation of the theoretical amount for an invalidity benefit under the Netherlands system, which was based on the materialization of the risk (type A), when insurance periods had lastly been completed in Germany where a type B system was in force. The Netherlands system again relied on a 'daily wage' which was based on the last earnings of the insured person. The Court ruled that the theoretical amount needed to be calculated on the basis of national law as always under article 46(2) – which meant in this case that the last earnings in Germany were relevant to determine the 'daily wage'. Article 47 Regulation 1408/71 concerned particular rules to simplify the calculation which did not apply to the approach of the Netherlands system (para. 15).

Benefits of the same kind and rules against overlapping

Remo D'Amico, 1980 raised the question whether Mr D'Amico's Belgian invalidity pension which had been converted into an old-age pension was a 'benefit of the same kind' as his Italian invalidity pension within the meaning of article 12(2) second sentence Regulation 1408/71. The point was raised, because a rule in Belgian law prevented the overlapping of old-age with invalidity pensions. This rule had the effect that pursuant to national law alone Mr D'Amico's Belgian pension at the moment it was converted from an invalidity pension to an old-age pension was reduced to naught. If this rule had been applicable pursuant article 12(2) Regulation 1408/71 in the following calculation under Community law, namely article 46 Regulation 1408/71 by analogy, as well, the Community rules would not have yielded a pension in Belgium, either. Hence the Court, formally applying an *e contrario* argument based on article 43(2) Regulation 1408/71, ruled that an invalidity pension turned old-age pension was of the same kind as an invalidity pension. This ruling was reiterated in *Celestre, 1981* (para. 11). In addition, *Celestre, 1981* also covered an aspect of the calculation under article 46 Regulation 1408/71. The Court made it clear that notional years that were according to Belgian law added to the periods of insurance completed in actual fact – typically in the case of miners – had to be taken into account in the calculation of the pension pursuant to article 46(1) Regulation 1408/71. However, in this calculation a national rule against the overlapping of benefits which reduced the notional periods in the light of periods completed in another member state did not apply pursuant to article 12(2) second sentence Regulation 1408/71 (para. 12). This ruling was confirmed in two judgments of 4 June 1985, *Romano, 1985* and *Ruzzu, 1985*. The fact that the Belgian rule regarding notional periods in *Celestre, 1981* had followed from mere administrative practice, while in *Romano, 1985* and *Ruzzu, 1985* it was applied after having been codified in a legislative act, did not change the assessment made in *Celestre, 1981*. In *Van der Bunt-Craig, 1983* the question was also raised whether two benefits were of the same kind according to article 12(2) Regulation 1408/71 so that national rules against the overlapping of benefits would be excluded in the calculation pursuant to article 46 Regulation 1408/71. In this case a Dutch survivor's pension came together with a British retirement pension which had been increased when the spouse had died. The Court answered that benefits were of the same kind when their 'purpose and basis of calculation' were the same (para. 13). This was the case, if both benefits intended to guarantee some means of subsistence to the surviving spouse who had been deprived of the deceased spouse's income, and both benefits were based on the contributions of the deceased spouse (para. 14). In *Valentini, 1983*, in turn, the Court ruled that a French allowance under the guaranteed income retirement scheme was not of the same kind as an old-age pension. The French benefit scheme had not been established with a view to the typical objective of old-age retirement schemes covered by article 46 Regulation 1408/71 which was to dispense elderly people from work. Rather, it had been established mainly to release elderly employees and to generate employment for younger employees in times of economic crisis (para. 17). Moreover, benefits covered by article 46 Regulation 1408/71 were normally based on a person's own contributions and calculated on the basis of periods of affiliation (para. 14). That was not the case with the French benefit (para. 15).

In *Jerzak, 1983* the Court further elaborated on article 12(2) Regulation 1408/71. Article 12(2), in so far as it allowed the application of national rules against the overlapping of national benefits also where national benefits overlapped with benefits awarded by another member state, was according to the Court the counterpart to the facilities Community law afforded to migrant workers. The article intended to prevent the granting of benefits based on Community law which national law considered excessive (para. 10). However, article 12(2) could only be applied when a benefit was awarded in application of Community law (para. 12). When it had been awarded based on national law alone article 12(2) was not to be applied, even if the division of the cost of financing the benefit had been made pursuant to article 57(3) Regulation 1408/71 (para. 15). In *Van Gastel (Coenen), 1987*, the Court again applied the criteria developed in *Van der Bunt-Craig, 1983* and *Valentini, 1983* to determine whether benefits were 'of the same kind'. The question was whether a Belgian survivor's pension was of the same kind as a Dutch old-age pension. The Court held, like in *Van der Bunt-Craig, 1983*, that the objective and purpose of the benefits were the same, viz. ensuring that an elderly person had sufficient means, although one of them was based on the deceased spouse's periods of insurance (para. 11). Moreover, the basis of calculation and the conditions for the award of the benefit were identical as well (para. 12). Finally, the Court rejected an *e contrario* argument based on the annex relating to benefits of the same kind in Denmark, Ireland, and the United Kingdom.

In *Stefanutti, 1987*, in contrast, two benefits were not of the same kind, namely an Italian invalidity pension of a widow in Italy and her survivor's pension from Belgium, because the benefits were not based on the same insurance record. The invalidity pension relied on the widow's own insurance record in one member state and the survivor's pension on the employment record of the deceased spouse in another member state (para. 13). In *Bakker, 1988*, the Court further clarified article 12(2) Regulation 1408/71. The Netherlands had amended their pension legislation so as to reflect equal treatment of women and men. To be more specific, the Netherlands no longer awarded a household pension when only one spouse was working, but rather separate pensions, one for each of the spouses. In *Bakker, 1988*, this amendment had a ripple effect in Belgium. As Ms Bakker suddenly received her own pension in the Netherlands, Mr Bakker's second pension in Belgium was re-calculated on the basis of the less advantageous single rate, instead of the higher household rate as before. However, the Court ruled that 'benefits of the same kind' were only overlapping within the meaning of article 12(2) Regulation 1408/71, when different benefits which were awarded to one and the same person overlapped, but not when benefits were paid to two persons (para. 14). The Belgian rule which provided that the single rate instead of the household rate was to apply to calculate a pension when the spouse of the person concerned received benefits in her own right – as in this case, due to the amendment in the Netherlands – was therefore not a rule against the overlapping of benefits within the sense of article 12(2).

Di Felice, 1989 again dealt with a rule against the overlapping of benefits. In this case a Belgian early retirement pension was refused, because the worker was receiving an invalidity pension in Italy. The Court categorized this rule as a rule against the overlapping of benefits and, in expanding *Celestre, 1981*, the Belgian early retirement pension as a benefit of the same kind as an invalidity pension, regardless of the facts that the retirement pension had not been converted from an invalidity pension or that it concerned early retirement (paras 14-5).

Further aggregation

In *Coppola, 1983*, the Court clarified *Petroni, 1975*, in which article 46(3) Regulation 1408/71 had been invalidated in so far as it required the reduction of a benefit acquired solely on the basis of national law. Article 40(3) Regulation 1408/71 required national authorities to aggregate periods during which sickness benefits were granted in another member state, if such a period was required by national law for the award of an invalidity benefit. However, when periods were aggregated pursuant to this article then the invalidity benefit concerned was not any longer based solely on national law within the sense of *Petroni, 1975*. Thus article 46(3) Regulation 1408/71 could be applied to such a benefit. In *Collini, 1987* the Court came back to article 46(3) Regulation 1408/71. The Court had to decide how the ceiling in that article was to be applied when Belgium was calculating an old-age benefit based on Community law, while Italy had awarded a pro rata old-age pension. The Advocate General was careful to point out that only the calculation pursuant to Community law was at stake (p. 5497), thus ruling out any implication of the *Petroni, 1975*-line of authority in this case. In Belgium, the independent amount pursuant to article 46(1) Regulation 1408/71 was higher in the case of Mr Collini than the pro rata amount calculated pursuant to 46(2) Regulation 1408/71. Thus only the first amount was relevant. However, article 46(3) Regulation 1408/71 set as an overall ceiling, i. e. an upper limit to the sum of all the benefits awarded in the member states, the highest theoretical amount pursuant to article 46(2)(a) Regulation 1408/71. Given that in the case at hand that ceiling was exceeded when the Italian pro rata pension and the Belgian independent pension under article 46(1) were added up, the question had to be answered how the benefits were to be reduced in application of article 46(3). The Court ruled first that the ceiling in article 46(3) applied in all cases, even if the exceeding of the ceiling was not due to a duplication of insurance periods (paras 11-2). Then the Court supplemented article 46(3) by holding that when an independent pension met with a pro rata pension, as in the case at hand, only the independent pension had to be reduced so far that the ceiling in article 46(3) was no longer exceeded (para. 16).

Before *Collini, 1987* the Court had decided another case that related to insurance periods completed in Belgium and Italy, *Sinatra II, 1986*, a follow-up case to *Sinatra, 1982* (as to this case, see below). In *Sinatra II, 1986*, an invalidity benefit awarded in Belgium under a special scheme for miners came together with an Italian pro rata pension. The amount of the Belgian benefit did not depend on the length of insurance periods. The conditions for its award it were met without that periods of insurance completed abroad had to be taken into account. Under these circumstances, the Court ruled that the Community rules in article 46 Regulation 1408/71 had to be applied as usual, including the determination of the independent amount, the apportioned amount, as well as the comparison of the two, in spite of article 45(2) Regulation 1408/71. Arguably, that article excluded aggregation when periods were completed under a special scheme for a particular occupation in one member state, such as Belgium's miners scheme, and periods were completed in another member state under a scheme that was not comparably special. However, article 46 did not require that all periods were capable of aggregation to determine benefits (para. 20). In this case therefore article 46 had to be applied fully.

Aggregation and third states

In *Borowitz, 1988* aggregation of periods completed in third countries became an issue. Germany had concluded a convention with Poland according to which some insurance periods completed in Poland were assimilated to periods completed in Germany. In the case of a migrant worker who had completed periods in Poland, the Netherlands, and Germany the question arose how the periods completed in Poland were to be dealt with under article 46 Regulation 1408/71. The Court essentially answered that nothing in the Regulation precluded Germany from applying an integrated approach: when Germany calculated the pension pursuant to article 46 Regulation 1408/71 the provisions of the convention together with national law could be applied, in this case to assimilate Polish with German periods or to determine whether a semi-complete insurance record was given in the light of periods completed in Poland, the Netherlands, and Germany (para. 25). However, another member state, like the Netherlands, was not required to apply conventions concluded by other member states (para. 26).

Short periods of insurance and other intricacies

The Court came back to short periods of insurance, i. e. of less duration than a year, in *Vermaut, 1982.* According to article 48 Regulation 1408/71, a member state was not required to award a pension under article 46(2) Regulation 1408/71 for an insurance period of less duration than a year which had been completed under its insurance schemes. However, a member state where a longer period had been completed had to factor in those short periods in the calculation of the theoretical amount under article 46 Regulation 1408/71, while refraining from a *pro rata* calculation. As the calculation of the theoretical amount presupposed that all insurance periods had to be treated as if they had been completed in the member state concerned, the overall effect in *Vermaut, 1982* was that periods spent in the service of the army or as a prisoner of war during World War II had to be taken into account in the calculation of the theoretical amount under Belgium's system, although a short period of insurance abroad had preceded them (para. 11). Moreover, Belgium could not require that the contributions paid during the short periods be transferred to Belgium (para. 15). The Court again dealt with article 48 Regulation 1408/71 in *Malfitano, 1982* in which a worker was insured in Belgium for a short period, then went on to work in other member states, and finally claimed invalidity benefits in Belgium. The Court first ruled that the concept of periods of *residence* in article 48 was only applicable in member states where such periods gave rise to entitlement to benefits. The concept had been introduced into the Regulation when member states acceded to the Community whose insurance systems determined affiliation based on residence. Belgium was not such a state and hence the Belgian authorities were precluded from relying on the concept of periods of residence (para. 6). Second, when applying the alternative condition to be met for disregarding short periods of insurance in article 48(1), i. e. that a right on the basis of national law was not acquired, the point in time was relevant when the insurance periods had actually been completed. In other words, the Belgian authorities' argument was rejected that a right was not acquired under national law on the ground that the legislation that had been in force when the insurance periods had been completed was not any longer in force when the incapacity for work materialized (para. 14).

In *Browning, 1981* the Court dealt with the award of a supplement to a pension pursuant to article 50 Regulation 1408/71. The Court in this case deduced from the declarations made by the member states with regards to supplements covered by article 50 that a supplement to a pension paid by the United Kingdom, a state which had not put forward a declaration, did not come within the scope of article 50. This article only covered special guarantees of minimum incomes (article 11) that were applicable separately from the ordinary calculation of pensions pursuant to article 46 Regulation 1408/71 (para. 13). In particular, the supplement of article 50 was not just the difference between the benefit calculated and the theoretical amount according to article 46(2)(a) Regulation 1408/71 (para. 14).

Recalculation

In *Sinatra, 1982* the Court dealt with a change in personal circumstances and its effects on the calculation under article 46 Regulation 1408/71. A pension had been awarded to a migrant worker in Belgium based on a household rate because the spouse of the pensioner had not worked. When she began to work, the issue arose whether a pension awarded in application of article 46 Regulation 1408/71 had to be recalculated given that in a recalculation the single rate instead of the household rate would have been applicable. The Court decided that article 51 Regulation 1408/71 did require a full re-calculation, i. e. under national law as well as and under Community law, with a 'fresh comparison' (para. 8), whenever the personal circumstances changed. It was only when a pension was adapted in accordance with 'the general evolution of the economic and social situation' (para. 10) that article 51(1) rendered a re-calculation unnecessary. The Court in *Van der Bunt-Craig, 1983* added that no provision of Community law required current benefits awarded in application of Community law to be re-calculated periodically because of fluctuations in currency conversion rates (para. 24). In *Cinciuolo, 1984* the Court extended the scope of article 51. The Court held that the exclusion of re-calculation when a benefit was merely adapted to the changing economic circumstances was also warranted in case of benefits which had not strictly been calculated pursuant to article 46 Regulation 1408/71. More specifically, when an occupational disease benefit which supplemented an invalidity pension granted in Italy and which had originally affected the calculation of an invalidity pension granted in Belgium was periodically adapted in Italy to the economic circumstances, this adaptation did not trigger a re-calculation of the Belgian pension, despite the fact that the supplement was not, strictly speaking, a benefit determined under article 46 (paras 10 and 13). In *Jordan, 1989* the Court again came back to article 51 Regulation 1408/71. According to the Court, a re-calculation of a pension was necessary when the method of determining the benefit was changed (para. 11). However, when the legislation according to which a benefit had been calculated was amended, but the amendment was only applicable to pensions calculated after a specific date, viz. the date of entry into force of the amendment, article 51 Regulation 1408/71 and article 48 Treaty did not require that pensions which had been calculated before that date were re-calculated (paras 13-5).

Aggregation and conditions of affiliation

The Court also dealt with the taking into account of insurance periods completed abroad outside the technical domain of aggregation for the purpose of awarding pensions. *Coonan, 1980* was a case in point. Yet it was a case that was complicated by the high specificity of the law of the United Kingdom and an apparently wrong decision to affiliate Ms Coonan to the British insurance system. The case was so complex that in fact Advocate General Mayras found it 'difficult to formulate meaningful answers to the questions referred' (page 1471). The problem in *Coonan, 1980* was approximately as follows. Ms Coonan had completed insurance periods in Ireland and then, before having reached the Irish pension age of 65 years, left to the United Kingdom where she continued to work as a self-employed person. In the United Kingdom, she was already beyond the regular retirement age of 60 years. When she applied for sickness benefits in cash in the United Kingdom her application was rejected, because the British scheme in question subjected those benefits to the condition that a person had been subject to a pension scheme in the United Kingdom for a certain period of time before reaching retirement age, if that person continued to work after having reached the age of retirement. In these rather specific circumstances, the Court ruled that for the purpose of meeting the British condition the periods of affiliation to an insurance scheme in Ireland did not have to be treated as equivalent to periods of affiliation to the British scheme. The Court held that articles 18 and 46 Regulation 1408/71 did not apply in this case (para. 8). The Court based its decision essentially on *Brunori, 1979* according to which the member states were competent to lay down the conditions of affiliation to their insurance schemes (para. 12). Thus, when affiliation to a specific scheme was subject to previous affiliation to the national social security scheme a member state was not required to treat periods of affiliation to the scheme of another member state as equivalent (para. 13). Moreover, it was not the purpose of Regulation 1612/68 to create rights under the national law of one member state by virtue of insurance periods completed in another member state (para. 6).

Vigier, 1981 was a case in which the Court built on *Coonan, 1980*. Germany had offered the option to victims of nazi persecution to buy in retroactively the periods during which the victims had been persecuted. However, the option was only offered subject to certain conditions, namely the person concerned had to be an insured person, i. e. she must have paid at least one contribution to a German insurance scheme. Based on *Coonan, 1980*, the Court decided that article 9(2) Regulation 1408/71 did not require periods of insurance completed under the scheme of another member state to be taken into account to determine whether that condition was met. Like in *Coonan, 1980* it was a matter of prior affiliation to a scheme of a member state. For that purpose, affiliation to the scheme of another member state need not have been treated as equivalent (para. 19). In *Schmitt, 1989*, a judgment that was only summarily published, the Court again repeated that the member states were competent to lay down the conditions of affiliation to insurance schemes. In *Hartmann Troiani, 1989* the Court also dealt with the conditions of affiliation to insurance schemes, but this time in the context of voluntary continued insurance. The German authorities required that a woman was compulsorily affiliated to a German insurance scheme to be eligible for a retro-active buy-in into insurance, after insurance contributions had been refunded to her before because of marriage. The Court ruled that this was a condition of affiliation to an insurance scheme which was precluded neither by article 48 Treaty nor by article 9 Regulation 1408/71 concerning optional or voluntary continued insurance. Article 9 Regulation 1408/71 merely precluded residence requirements and required that periods of insurance completed abroad were treated as equivalent when national law relied on a minimum period of affiliation.

Finally, an unexpected issue of aggregation arose in *Rebmann, 1988*. It was unclear which member state had to take into account periods of unemployment for the purpose of awarding a pension in the case of a frontier worker. Was it the member state where the worker was last employed or the member state where he resided? In the absence of a provision dealing with the issue, the Court fell back on the 'general spirit and the intendment' of Regulation 1408/71 (para. 11) to consider as competent the member state where the frontier worker had worked last. That approach was in line with the general idea in article 13 Regulation 1408/71 to apply the law of the member state of employment to a frontier worker. The exceptions to this approach for sickness, invalidity, and unemployment benefits lent themselves only to analogous interpretation if a situation was closely connected to one of these exceptions (para. 17). This was not the case for the taking into account of unemployment periods for pension purposes. In most cases, indeed, it was in the member state of employment where a frontier worker had already acquired a right to a pension (para. 19). For the sake of completeness, the case *Vlaeminck, 1982* must be mentioned to conclude aggregation. In this case, the Court answered that the national court had correctly applied the Community rules concerning aggregation and overlapping of benefits in recalculating a survivor's pension awarded in Belgium and that therefore no question of Community law had been raised.

Overlapping benefits, supplements

Periods of insurance and the overlapping of benefits did not just matter in aggregation to determine old-age or invalidity pensions. Cases concerning sickness and family benefits also raised the issue of overlapping of benefits. In *Walsh, 1980* the problem was that maternity benefits in two member states were potentially overlapping. Article 8 Regulation 574/72 addressed the problem by assigning the competence to one member state, viz. the member state where the confinement took place or *eventualiter* the member state to whose legislation the worker was last subject. The Court answered that the aim of article 8 Regulation 574/72 was to grant an allowance to a mother and her child for the time before and after confinement. The article had to be read together with article 12 Regulation 1408/71. According to the Court, maternity benefits only overlapped within the meaning of article 12 when a person's claim for benefits was actually satisfied in the member state of confinement *and* in another member state. Thus, after benefits had been exhausted in the member state of confinement and the legislation of another member state to which the mother had been subject provided further benefits, e. g. a maternity allowance for a longer period, she could go on to claim those benefits (para. 15-7). Shortly after *Walsh, 1980*, the Court was faced with a constellation raising a similar problem with regard to allowances for dependent children in *Laterza, 1980*. Article 77 Regulation 1408/71 assigned the competence for such allowances to the member state where a pensioner resided when the pensioner drew a pension in that state and at the same time a pension in another state. Yet the Court fell back on *Rossi, 1979* to hold that this competence applied only in so far as the allowance in the state of residence was actually payable. When the amount of the allowance potentially payable in the state where the other pension was paid exceeded that of the allowance granted in the state of residence that other state had to pay a supplement to guarantee the greatest benefit (paras 8-9). The Court applied the same reasoning to orphan's pensions under article 78(2) Regulation 1408/71 in *Gravina, 1980*. A change of residence of an orphan in receipt of an orphan's pension based solely on national law had the effect pursuant to article 78(2) Regulation 1408/71 that the member state where the orphan had moved to became competent for the orphan's benefits. However, this article was not to have the effect of depriving an orphan of a benefit based solely on national law. According to the Court, the state where the orphan resided originally had to continue to pay a supplementary benefit to guarantee the greater benefit it had awarded in the first place (para. 8). The Court later on in *D'Amario, 1983* held that this ruling applied regardless of whether the orphan ever moved residence, as long as the orphan resided in a member state where the migrant worker had been subject to a social security scheme (para. 7).

In *Beeck, 1981* the Court developed this line of authority further. In this case family allowances potentially overlapped, because one spouse worked in Denmark where the family lived and the other spouse worked in Germany. Articles 13 and 73 Regulation 1408/71 assigned the competence for family allowances in such a constellation to the member state in which the family resided. Family allowances in the other state, i. e. Germany, were suspended. In this case, German law contained a clause which excluded all benefits, including a potential supplement to bring the foreign benefits up to the amount normally payable in Germany. However, after having confirmed that a frontier worker could rely on article 73 Regulation 1408/71, the Court ruled based on article 51 Treaty that article 73 Regulation 1408/71 and article 10(1)(a) Regulation 574/72, which contained an implementing rule against overlapping, had to be read to the effect that Germany had to grant a benefit to supplement the allowance awarded on the basis of Danish law so as to guarantee the family the higher amount of benefits ordinarily granted in Germany. This was valid, although the national rule excluded the award of a benefit in such cross-border situations (para. 12). Next, *Robards, 1983* established that it was irrelevant for the rules regarding the overlapping of family allowances that the 'family members' had divorced (para. 15).

The entire line of authority regarding the exportability of the supplement was questioned in the light of article 51 Treaty in *Patteri, 1984*. However, the Court ruled that article 51 Treaty had to be interpreted so as to cover all measures that promote the free movement of persons (para. 8). The interpretation laying the foundation for the award of a supplement to the local family allowance was therefore in accordance with article 51 Treaty and the article 77(2)(b)(I) Regulation 1408/71 thus interpreted was valid (para. 10).

In *Salzano, 1984* the Court relied on *Ragazzoni, 1978* and reiterated that a benefit was only payable within the meaning of the suspension rule in article 76 Regulation 1408/71 when all the requirements for the award of the benefit were met. In *Salzano, 1984*, this was not the case. That the family concerned refused to make an application for family benefits in Italy meant that not all conditions of substance and form for the award of the Italian benefit were met. The benefit was thus not payable in Italy. It did not overlap with a family benefit granted in Germany and article 76 Regulation 1408/71 was not applicable (paras 7 and 10). This interpretation was later on fully confirmed in *Ferraioli, 1986*.

In *Kromhout, 1985* again an issue of overlapping of family benefits arose. The Court first decided that it was sufficient that one parent was a worker for the Community rules on family allowances to apply; whether the other parent was also subject to Community rules was irrelevant for the application of the rules against overlapping, as was the question whether the marriage had been divorced. Then the Court addressed the situation that one parent was employed in Germany and received family allowances there, while the other parent resided with the children in the Netherlands where she was eligible by the sole reason of her residence to family allowances on the basis of Dutch law alone. The Court decided that the interpretation given to the rules against overlapping of family allowances requiring the award of a supplementary benefit also applied when an allowance was granted on the basis of national law alone in the member state where one parent resided and when, pursuant to that national law, the award of an allowance was solely subject to residence in the member state concerned. Thus, the Netherlands could suspend the overlapping part of the allowance, but had to guarantee the amount in excess by granting a supplement (paras 22 and 27). The judgment in *Kromhout, 1985* was, however, put into perspective in *Burchell, 1987*, albeit only for the `coincidence' (Advocate General Darmon, p. 3338) that the national legislations of two member states each by itself granted family allowances with respect to the same children and for the same period. This was the case, because Ms Burchell lived in the United Kingdom with the children, while Mr Burchell resided in the Netherlands where he was employed. The Court decided that when the Dutch legislation on its own already granted benefits, although the children were not resident in the Netherlands, article 73 Regulation 1408/71 need not have been applied. Consequently, the British authorities could not rely on article 10(1)(a) Regulation 574/72, either, to exclude the overlapping of benefits and to reduce the British benefit accordingly (para. 18).

Adding to the disparities

Pinna, 1986 also concerned the obligation of the member states under Community law to award family benefits even though the family of a migrant worker did not reside in the member state where the migrant worker was employed. More specifically, the Court held that the exception in article 73 Regulation 1408/71 which exempted France, as the only state, from the general obligation to award benefits even though the family did not reside in the member state concerned was incompatible with articles 48 to 51 Treaty. The Court therefore invalidated article 73 Regulation 1408/71 in so far as it dealt in a different way with benefits awarded in France than with benefits granted in other member states. The reason was that the Community legislature had to refrain from introducing 'unnecessary differences' in the social security rules and from 'adding to the disparities' existing in the social security systems of the member states (para. 21). Exempting France's benefits from exportability, moreover, amounted to covert discrimination of migrant workers in France which was prohibited by article 48 Treaty (para. 24). The French authorities therefore had to apply the regular regime that applied to family benefits in all other member states pursuant to article 73 Regulation 1408/71, as was later confirmed in *Pinna II, 1989*. The approach developed in *Pinna, 1986* served as a basis of argument again in *Lenoir, 1988*. In this case a pensioner who had moved from France to the United Kingdom was refused some benefits supporting his children in going to school, because he no longer resided in France. The Court held that the benefits had to be categorized as family benefits other than family allowances according to article 1(u) Regulation 1408/71, since they were not based exclusively on the number of children or their age. Consequently, under article 77 Regulation 1408/71 they were not exportable. However, article 77 did not thereby add to the existing disparities and it was not discriminatory to refuse the benefits within the sense of *Pinna, 1986*. Article 48 Treaty was not concerned with the disparities of national social security systems, as long as they (the systems) applied on the basis of objective criteria. Article 77 Regulation 1408/71 was applicable to all migrant workers alike. Moreover, the French benefits at stake were tied to the social environment. Hence, they could be made dependent on residence (paras. 13-7).

More supplements

Ventura, 1988 reiterated the obligation of a member state to pay the supplement when orphan's pensions under its legislation were higher in amount than the pensions paid in another member state. The Court, moreover, clarified that, even though article 48(1) Regulation 1408/71 had precluded the award of an old-age pension to the migrant worker in the case at hand because the insurance period he had completed had not amounted to a full year, that article could not be relied upon to exclude the award of an orphan's pension in the same member state, given that the conditions required by national law were met. For lack of an express reference in the rules governing orphan's pensions article 48(1) could not be applied to them (para. 11). In *Baldi, 1989* article 78 Regulation 1408/71 regarding orphans was said not to be relevant, because it was not the worker who had died, but his spouse who had not been working. However, the Court decided that in this case Belgium's increase in family allowances by reason of a spouse having deceased constituted a family allowance. As Mr Baldi drew an invalidity pension – first only in Italy, then also in Belgium – article 77 Regulation 1408/71 applied. Under this article, regardless of whether paragraph 2 letter a re a pension in Italy only or letter b re a pension in Belgium also was applicable, the case-law regarding the supplement to family benefits to guarantee the greater benefit was pertinent (para. 22). In *Georges, 1989* the Court decided that the supplement-case-law also applied when a family member was working in two member states. In this case, Mr Georges was self-employed in Belgium where he resided with his family and at the same time employed in France. The Court decided on the basis of article 76 Regulation 1408/71 that the higher family allowance payable in France had to be guaranteed in this case, too (para. 12). Finally, the Court decided in *Dammer, 1989* that the supplement approach was also valid when each spouse worked in a different member state and they both resided with the children in a third member state. This eventuality was not addressed by the rule against overlapping in article 10(1)(a) Regulation 574/72. In such a case, the highest family benefit awarded by one of the states where one of the spouses was employed had to be guaranteed by providing a supplement (para. 25).

Unemployed frontier workers

In the 1980s, the Court also dealt with unemployment benefits. *Fellinger, 1980* raised the issue of how unemployment benefits were to be calculated for frontier workers. In the case of a frontier worker who had been last employed in Luxembourg, Germany had taken the notional salary, i. e. the salary which that frontier worker would have gained in Germany for the same work, as a basis for the calculation of unemployment benefits in Germany. This approach was literally sanctioned by article 68(1) Regulation 1408/71. This article provided that a state could use the notional salary as a basis of calculation instead of the salary last gained in that state, if a worker had been in employment in that state for less than four weeks. Yet the Court held that the notional salary-approach in article 68(1) Regulation 1408/71 was not to be applied to frontier workers, else they would never receive unemployment benefits based on the last salaries they had in fact gained. Article 68 Regulation 1408/71, in declaring the notional salary as relevant, dealt with an exception to the regular situation where migrant workers received unemployment benefits based on the salary last gained in the member state concerned. That was why the notional salary was not suitable as a basis when it meant to turn the exception into the rule by covering each and every case of frontier work (paras 6-7). As a result, Germany had to calculate the unemployment benefit based on the income last received in Luxembourg.

Aubin, 1982 also dealt with frontier workers. According to this judgment, frontier workers did not have a choice where to claim unemployment benefits according to article 71(1) Regulation 1408/71. They had to claim them in the member state where they resided, save when they were not wholly unemployed. In that case the member state of employment was competent. In contrast, workers other than frontier workers who did not have residence in the state where they worked had a choice, namely they could hold themselves available to the employment offices in the member state either where they worked or where they resided and claim benefits accordingly. Of course, they were not allowed to cumulate benefits (para. 19). In *Guyot, 1984* those cases, in which workers resided in a different state than the state of employment, were further clarified. The Court explained that article 71 Regulation 1408/71 did not cover a person who had resided and been employed in one and the same state when she had become unemployed, even if she then moved residence to another state. The regime for exporting unemployment benefits in Article 69 Regulation 1408/71 rather than article 71 Regulation 1408/71 applied in such a situation.

Atypical frontier workers

In *Miethe, 1986* again a particular situation came before the Court. Mr Miethe and his wife had always resided and worked in Germany. They moved to Belgium, however, thus making it possible for their children to come home every evening from the school they visited in Belgium. Mr Miethe maintained all professional links in Germany and went to work there on a daily basis. When he became unemployed he would have been entitled to benefits in Belgium, for he was a frontier worker. In the light of this designation of the competent state, according to the court, national law could not be applied. Even if German law on its own granted Mr Miethe unemployment benefits, he did not have the option to claim benefits there (para. 11). However, the Court left the national court the possibility to treat Mr Miethe as an 'atypical', 'false frontier worker' (paras 14 and 15). As he should receive benefits in circumstances most conducive to finding new employment and his chances were probably best in Germany given his professional ties, he could be regarded, instead of as a frontier worker, as a worker who resided in another state than the state where he worked (para. 18). This would create the choice for Mr Miethe to claim unemployment benefits in Germany based on article 71(1)(b) Regulation 1408/71. The Court significantly expanded this reasoning applied in *Miethe, 1986* in the judgment in *Bergemann, 1988*. Ms Bergemann had moved from the Netherlands to Germany to reside with her husband whom she had recently married. She had worked in the Netherlands and used her final holiday to move to Germany. As she clearly was not a frontier worker, the question was raised whether she could, like a false frontier worker, benefit from article 71(1)(b) Regulation 1408/71 to acquire a claim to unemployment benefits in Germany. In the light of *Di Paolo, 1977*, in which the close ties to the state of residence were considered pertinent, the Court acceded to that claim because she benefitted from more favourable conditions in Germany to find new employment (para. 21).

Article 71(1)(b) also created another difficulty in *Warmerdam-Steggerda, 1989*. In this case it was doubtful whether insurance periods completed abroad had to be taken into account for the purpose of acquiring unemployment benefits. More specifically, the case concerned the issue of how a period of employment in Scotland was to be treated under article 67 Regulation 1408/71 when such a period was considered under the Scottish system as a period of invalidity insurance, but not as a period of unemployment insurance. Ms Warmerdam-

Steggerda had completed such a period in Scotland and then went back and claimed unemployment benefits in the Netherlands. The Dutch authorities had to decide what was relevant for unemployment benefits provided under the Dutch system, namely a) the fact that the employment periods completed in Scotland did *not* qualify as unemployment insurance periods in Scotland leading to the conclusion that they could be disregarded under the Dutch system; or b) the fact that the employment periods would have qualified as unemployment insurance periods had they only been completed in the Netherlands leading to the conclusion that they had to be taken into account by the Dutch authorities. The Court applied a literal interpretation of article 1(r) and (s) Regulation 1408/71 and opted for variant b) (para. 17, second sentence).

Exporting unemployment benefits

The regime for exporting unemployment benefits was already at stake in *Testa, 1980*. The regime based on article 69 Regulation 1408/71 allowed job seekers to continue to receive unemployment benefits for three months while searching for employment abroad. It was an independent regime of Community law which had to be applied uniformly throughout the Community, the Court held (para. 5). A job seeker could therefore not fall back on national law to continue claiming benefits, if he forfeited the right to unemployment benefits according to article 69(1) for having exceeded the three months period and failed to come back in time (para. 5), save where he could rely on the ground in article 69(2). This regime was, moreover, in accordance with, on the one hand, article 51 Treaty, because it extended the rights of workers and hence could be made subject to certain conditions, and, on the other hand, with the fundamental right to property (paras 14 and 19-21, respectively). However, according to *Cochet, 1985*, the regime in article 69 Regulation 1408/71 was not applicable in a particular situation, namely when a worker who had resided in another state than where he had worked claimed unemployment benefits in the state of residence pursuant to article 71 Regulation 1408/71 and *then* moved residence to the state where he had been employed. In such a situation, the exceptional right to claim benefits in the state of residence became undone and the regular right under article 13 Regulation 1408/71 to claim benefits in the state of the last employment applied (para. 16). More specifically, the state where the worker had been employed last had remained the 'competent state' within the meaning of article 69, although benefits had been granted under article 71 Regulation 1408/71 by the state where the worker had resided. In *Vanhaeren, 1988* the Court again clarified a detail of article 69 Regulation 1408/71. The Court decided that when a person went to seek employment abroad while receiving benefits under article 69 and actually succeeded in finding employment the state where the new employment had been found became the 'competent state' within the sense of article 69. When the person then returned to the original state this state could no longer be the 'competent state', although it had been just that previously (para. 12).

A Kafka novel

In *Baccini, 1982* the Court addressed a case the creation of which 'the Commission's representative justifiably likened to a Kafka novel' (Advocate General Verloren van Themaat, p. 1080). Ms Baccini had received invalidity pensions in Belgium and in Italy, before she became fit for work again. As a result, the Belgian invalidity pension was withdrawn, but unemployment benefits were refused, because she was deemed unfit for work given that she still received an invalidity pension in Italy. In spite of the wording of article 12(2) Regulation 1408/71 the Court decided that where it was clearly established that the person was indeed fit for work unemployment benefits based on national law were not to be refused on the sole ground that national law deemed a person unfit for work because an invalidity pension was being paid to her in another state pursuant to Regulation 1408/71 (para. 15). However, the Court had to address the situation once more in *Baccini II, 1983* and it was still 'little short of absurd' according to the national court in the question referred (p. 594). This time the Court judged that the ensuing Belgian decision that Ms Baccini was not any longer invalid was not covered by article 40(4) Regulation 1408/71. It was not binding on the other member states, since articles 48 and 51 Treaty and Regulations 1408/71 and 574/72 did not regulate the conditions of the withdrawal of benefits (para. 17).

Sickness

The Court also dealt with sickness benefits in a few cases in the 1980s. *Jordens-Vosters, 1980* was one such case. The Court clarified that the chapter on invalidity benefits in Regulation 1408/71 dealt with cash benefits, while medical benefits in kind came within the chapter on sickness benefits, regardless of the terms national legislation used. The Court, moreover, held that the rules to determine the institution obliged to provide sickness benefits in kind did not oust national rules granting beneficiaries additional benefits, i. e. benefits that an institution was not required to provide under the chapter on sickness benefits in Regulation 1408/71 (paras 12-13). More generally the Court held that Regulation 1408/71 was not to be construed so as to prohibit national law from granting broader social security benefits than those a member state was required to provide under the Regulation (para. 11).

Mittelfranken, 1980 was another case that dealt with sickness benefits, though on the basis of Regulation 3. The Court decided that, in case a worker was affiliated to two insurance schemes in one state, each institution that managed one of the two schemes had to be considered the competent institution for the purposes of articles 20(1) and 23(1) and (3) Regulation 3. It was thus up to national law to decide how the costs of providing benefits were ultimately allocated between the two institutions (paras 9 and 10). The Court then also confirmed the infringement brought in *Commission v. Belgium (pension deductions I), 1985*. Belgium had levied sickness insurance contributions on pensions paid in Belgium to pensioners residing abroad, although those pensioners did not have a right to claim sickness benefits in Belgium under article 27 to 32 Regulation 1408/71 (paras 3 and 6).

Applicable legislation

In the 1980s, the Court also dealt with the rules determining the applicable legislation in a number of cases. In *Kuijpers, 1982* the Court ruled that the one and only legislation applicable was determined by Regulation 1408/71. When a person worked in two states, the legislation of the state where he resided was applicable pursuant to article 14(1)(c)(i) Regulation 1408/71, if he also worked there. When a person worked and resided in the Netherlands, while he also worked in Belgium, the Netherlands could therefore not regard his employment in the Netherlands as secondary and on that ground refuse to apply Dutch law. The Regulation did not draw any distinction between primary and secondary work (para. 15). Moreover, although the member states had the power to determine the right or duty to be affiliated to insurance schemes, they could not determine the extent to which their own legislation or that of another state was applicable (para. 14). In contrast, in *Koks, 1982* – which was handed down on the same day as *Kuijpers, 1982* – the power of the member states to determine the right and obligation to become affiliated to their social security systems as well as the conditions of affiliation thereto prevailed. The Dutch way of treating a spouse as uninsured when her husband was insured abroad for retirement purposes was therefore not subject to challenge under Regulation 1408/71 (para. 11). (Directive 79/7 on equal treatment of women and men in social security was not yet applicable at that time.)

In *Coppola, 1983* the Court was faced with a question of aggregation of insurance periods which it solved by means of the provisions on the applicable legislation. When a worker had last been employed in Italy and before that in the United Kingdom, were the British authorities required to aggregate periods of insurance for the purpose of acquisition of a right to sickness benefits in the United Kingdom? The Court replied that only one single legislation was to be applied. That was normally the legislation of the state where the worker was employed pursuant to article 13 Regulation 1408/71. For the purpose of article 18(1) Regulation 1408/71, when a person who was no longer employed sought sickness benefits, the legislation of the member state where the person had last been employed was the applicable legislation (para. 11). It was also in that state where the 'competent institution' pursuant to article 18(1) Regulation 1408/71 was located, i. e. in the case at hand Italy. It was for that institution exclusively, rather than for the British authorities, to aggregate periods of insurance for the purpose of acquiring rights to sickness benefits (para. 12).

In *Brusse, 1984* the Netherlands and the United Kingdom had come to the agreement that Dutch legislation be applied to a specific person for a period of time in the past, because that person had been wrongly affiliated to a Dutch insurance scheme during that time. The Court ruled that such an agreement was lawful under article 17 Regulation 1408/71 even for time periods in the past and even if the wrong affiliation had been the worker's fault. The agreement was subject only to the condition that it was done in the interest of the worker (paras 18, 21, and 25). Such an agreement fully replaced articles 13 to 16 Regulation 1408/71 in their function to determine the applicable legislation. Hence, when the worker applied for family allowances for the period concerned the applicable legislation had to be determined in accordance with the agreement. Consequently, article 73 Regulation 1408/71 had to be applied fully. It was not defeated by a residence clause contained in national law (paras 30-1).

The Court came back to the judgment in *Coppola, 1983* in *Ten Holder, 1986*. It declared that the *Coppola, 1983*-ruling, according to which a worker who had ceased work continued to be subject to the legislation of the member state in which he had last been employed, applied regardless of how much time had elapsed since he had last worked, provided that he did not begin to work anew elsewhere (para. 14). There was also another aspect to *Ten Holder, 1986*. Ms Ten Holder returned to the Netherlands where she had worked at an earlier point in time. After her right to continued sickness benefits based on Regulation 1408/71 in Germany had been exhausted, she claimed sickness benefits in the Netherlands. However, the Court reiterated that only one legislation was applicable at a time. The Court referred to *Kuijpers, 1982* and *Koks, 1982* to rule that the title II of Regulation 1408/71 constituted a complete system of conflict rules which had the effect that the member states were not able any longer to determine the scope and the criteria for the application of their legislation as far as persons and territory were concerned (para. 21). The Court also limited the *Petroni, 1975*-ruling – according to which rights acquired on the basis of national law alone were not to be lost – to national rules against overlapping. It was not applicable when it came to determining the applicable legislation. A person could therefore not be insured under the systems of two states at the same time (para. 22). This second aspect of *Ten Holder, 1986* was confirmed in *Luijten, 1986* for the right of a self-employed person to family allowances. The Court, finally, in *Agegate, 1989* referred back to *Luijten, 1986* to hold that it was in accordance with article 13 Regulation 1408/71, when a ship flew the flag of a member state and consequently that state's law was applicable on board that ship, to require a worker on board that ship to pay contributions to the social security system of that member state, as long as the exception in article 14b Regulation 1408/71 was respected (paras 27-9).

Non-discrimination and residence

The Court relied on non-discrimination and the waiver of residence clauses in article 10 Regulation 1408/71 in a number of cases in the 1980s. In *Überschär, 1980* the Court addressed the obligation to buy-in retrogressively lacunae in a pension insurance career. Annex V of Regulation 1408/71 in conjunction with German law established a distinction. On the one hand, there were persons who were German nationals or nationals of other member states who resided in Germany. They could buy into the German insurance scheme for periods during which they had paid contributions to a compulsory insurance scheme in another member state. However, they were obliged to do so retrogressively, i. e. the latest period had to be bought into first. On the other hand, there were persons who had been affiliated to the German system in the past, but who were not German nationals or did not at the moment reside in Germany. They could *not* in Germany buy into periods of compulsory insurance completed abroad. However, they could in turn buy-in periods during which they had not at all been affiliated to an insurance scheme and they could do so freely, i. e. without having to buy-in retrogressively (para. 13-4). The Court held that the financial consequences of the distinction varied with the objective facts of the situation of each person who was concerned (para. 17). The distinction therefore did not breach non-discrimination.

In *Camera, 1982* the Court was faced with a case to be assessed under Regulation 3. Belgium required residence for the acquisition of a right to invalidity benefits. The Court first briefly dealt with the submission of a claim to the wrong authority and the fact that national law considered certain cases of residence as irregular. Then the Court extended the reasoning in *Smieja, 1973*, which had concerned the effects of a residence transfer on rights already acquired, to the case at hand which was about the effect of such a transfer on rights to be acquired. Consequently, Belgium's residence requirement was precluded by article 10(1) Regulation 3. The Court built on this ruling when it decided in *Van Roosmalen, 1986* that a residence period required for the acquisition of an invalidity benefit in the Netherlands had to be interpreted in the light of article 10(1) Regulation 1408/71. A person could therefore not be prevented from acquiring a Dutch invalidity benefit on the sole ground that that person did not reside in the Netherlands (para. 39). The Court relied on *Camera, 1982* in the same vein in *Giletti, 1987*. A pensioner who was paid a pension in France while residing in Italy could not be prevented from acquiring or maintaining the right to a French supplement to that pension on the sole ground that he did not reside in France (paras 15-6).

The Dutch transition

Spruyt, 1986 concerned the arrangement made in the Netherlands to manage the transition from the old to the new old-age insurance system. The new system was based on residence as the main criterion to determine entitlement. As before, a wife's pension was accessory to the pension of her husband which in turn was increased proportionately. In essence, the transitional arrangement was as follows. A person who resided in the Netherlands when he retired had a right to have periods completed before 1957, when the new system came into force, taken into account for a pension awarded under the new system. That transitional arrangement was adapted in the annex to Regulation 1408/71 to the situation of migrant workers. Generally speaking, workers who did not reside in the Netherlands when they retired were entitled to claim a pension under the new system based on time periods completed before 1957, if and to the extent they had had a sufficient link to the Netherlands during that time. Such a link could consist in residence or employment in the Netherlands during a time period before 1957. According to the Court, that transitional arrangement and its adaptation by the annex to Regulation 1408/71 complied with non-discrimination. Without the adaption in the annex, non-discrimination and article 10(1) Regulation 1408/71 would modify the Dutch transitional system to the effect that every worker in the Community would have a valid claim for benefits with regard to periods before 1957 under the Dutch transitional arrangement (para. 21). However, the Court found the following aspect of the adaptation to be discriminatory. A husband was entitled to claim benefits for the time before 1957 under the transitional arrangement as adapted by the annex. Yet, his pension was not increased based on a specific period of residence of his wife in the Netherlands. That period was a period of residence of the woman before she married the man. In essence, the reason for that period being left out of account was legislative oversight, i. e. the case of spouses moving abroad at a certain point in time had not been envisaged when the adaptation of the transitional arrangement had been drafted (see paras. 24-7). In contrast, the same could not be said in *De Jong, 1986*. A woman had not yet been married during the time she had lived in Italy. Later on she married and settled with her husband in the Netherlands. With her not having been married at the time she lived in Italy, that period of residence was lawfully left out of account when the husband's pension was calculated in the Netherlands under the transitional arrangement as adapted by the annex (para. 17). After all, she had not had any connection whatsoever to the Netherlands when she had resided in Italy (Advocate General Mancini, p. 675). In *Rijke, 1987* the Court added that the way the transitional arrangement had been interpreted in *Spruyt, 1986* and *De Jong, 1986* did not invalidate the requirement in Dutch law for a married woman to submit an application within one year after she had left the Netherlands to reside abroad, if she wanted to benefit from continued voluntary insurance in the Netherlands. Such a requirement was covered by the power of the member states to determine the conditions of insurance affiliation (para. 17-8).

Further non-discrimination

In *Roviello, 1988* the Court struck down a provision in the annex to Regulation 1408/71, because it was discriminatory. Germany's system of awarding invalidity pensions was based on a categorization of work into four classes, namely highly skilled, skilled, semi-skilled, and unskilled work. The idea was that an invalidity pension was only awarded, if an incapacitated worker was unable to work in the class right below the class his previous work had been in. For migrant workers point 15 of section C of annex VI to Regulation 1408/71 determined, according to the Court, that only activities were to be taken into account for the purpose of this categorization that were subject to compulsory insurance under German legislation (para. 15). That approach violated equal treatment, because migrant workers were refused pensions that would have had to be granted if previous work of higher qualification in other member states had been factored in (paras 15-18). Point 15 section C annex VI Regulation 1408/71 was therefore invalid in so far as it had to be interpreted in that sense.

Finally, the Court held non-discrimination to be violated in three more judgments with a social security dimension. *Stanton, 1988* was a case that concerned the time before Regulation 1408/71 had been amended to include self-employed activities. Since the Regulation was therefore not applicable, the Court decided the case on the basis of the Treaty instead. Mr Stanton had been employed in the United Kingdom where he was subject to social security insurance. At the same time, he pursued a self-employed activity in Belgium. The exemption from contributions to the Belgian social security system for self-employed activities was not applied to Mr Stanton, because it was only applicable by law when the principal work in employment was subject to Belgian social security. The Court found that the free movement of persons was concerned, because a person worked in one member state and at the same time pursued a self-employed activity in another member state. The ruling in *Klopp, 1984* which validated more than one place of work also covered simultaneous employment and self-employment (para. 12). Belgium's approach disadvantaged persons who pursued occupational activities outside Belgium and thereby violated articles 48 and 52 Treaty (para. 14). Article 7 Treaty was not violated though, since there was no indirect discrimination (para. 9). The disadvantage could not be justified, because the contributions Mr Stanton was required to pay in Belgium did not afford him any social security protection additional to the protection he enjoyed by reason of the contributions he paid in the United Kingdom (para. 15). *Wolf, 1988* was handed down on the same day as *Stanton, 1988*. The decision was identical, though the employed activity was pursued in Germany. In *Allué I, 1989* the Court decided that the exclusion of foreign language assistants from social security coverage normally available to other workers violated non-discrimination in article 3 Regulation 1408/71 given that the majority of those assistants were nationals of other member states (paras 20-1).

Technicalities

The Court also addressed a series of technical details of the social security rules of the Community in the 1980s. In *Damiani, 1980* the Court dealt with the provisional pension to be awarded immediately pending verification of the details of the definitive pension. More specifically, court proceedings to claim such a provisional pension were not excluded by article 45 Regulation 574/72 and in such proceedings interest to be paid on the provisional pension could be ordered, if national authorities had failed to award it (paras 7-8). In the case *Giuseppe Romano, 1981* the problem of gains and losses through currency fluctuations was solved on the basis of the idea that a migrant worker's rights based on national law alone were not to be lost. The Court in this case also granted national courts the liberty to disregard decisions by the administrative commission established by the social security rules of the Community (para. 20). In short, the situation was as follows. A migrant worker was awarded a pension based on Community law retroactively in Italy. Consequently, the Belgian authorities retroactively reduced the pension that had been granted provisionally before, based on Belgian law alone. The Belgian authorities then informed the migrant worker of the amount they intended to claim back from him owing to overpayment. The amount they received from the Italian authorities as arrears, though, was lower than the amount they claimed back from the migrant worker, because the currency conversion rates had fluctuated between the date on the basis of which the amount to be claimed back was calculated and the date when the arrears were actually paid. However, the Court ruled that the amount claimed back from the migrant worker could not, in such circumstances, exceed the amount of the payment the Belgian authorities had received from the Italian institution (para. 25). *Fanara, 1981* concerned a similar constellation. In this case, however, the arrears paid by the Italian institution exceeded the amount to be claimed back from the migrant worker due partly to currency fluctuations between the two dates at which the respective amounts were calculated. The Belgian authorities refused to hand on the exceeding amount to the migrant worker based on a provision of national law, arguing that the Belgian pension had been based on national law alone and hence *all* Belgian rules could be applied. The Court rejected that argument (para. 12). Even though the Belgian pension had been awarded on the basis of national law alone, the provisions of Community law dealing with provisional payments and recovery of sums paid in excess had to be applied. Articles 45(1) and 111 Regulation 574/72 did not leave any room for the Belgian rules (para. 14).

Knoeller, 1982 concerned the forms to be used to communicate information between the member states according to Regulations 3 and 4 with regard to insurance periods completed by migrant workers. To achieve the aim of simplifying the 'complex administrative operations of aggregation and apportionment' (para. 10) authorities also had to take account of supplementary information communicated in documents other than the 'official' forms furnished by the administrative commission. In *Scaletta, 1985* the Court decided that the obligation to notify the authorities when moving abroad pursuant to article 59 Regulation 574/72 could be met in any form, be it in writing or orally, and at any time. Disregard for the obligation was not, moreover, to result in loss of rights. The authorities could examine, though, whether the conditions for receiving benefits were met up to the time when they were notified of a change of residence (paras 10 and 15-6).

In *Deghillage, 1986* the Court decided that a member state's national authority who was awarding benefits had the duty pursuant to article 57 Regulation 1408/71 to recognize the diagnosis of a migrant worker's occupational disease first made by an authority in another member state in accordance with that state's legislation (para. 17). *Rindone, 1987* followed-up on *Deghillage, 1986*. The Court held essentially that under article 18 Regulation 574/72 the findings as to the incapacity to work made by the medical officer of the institution situated where the migrant worker resided had to be accepted by the competent institution of another member state. The alternative option of having the migrant worker examined by a doctor of the choice of the institution having the power to grant benefits pursuant to article 18(5) Regulation 574/72 only meant that a medical doctor could be sent to see the migrant worker or the latter could be requested to go see a doctor in the member state where he resided. It did not mean that the migrant worker had to travel to the doctor of the institution's choice in the member state where the institution was situated (para. 21).

In *Viva, 1988* the Court dealt with the transition from Regulation 3 to Regulation 1408/71 and the resulting effect on the re-calculation of pensions. The Court decided that, since Regulation 1408/71 had entered into force pensions could not any more be awarded on the basis of Regulation 3 (para. 9). Yet, according to the Court, pursuant to *Saieva, 1976* the authorities were not allowed to re-calculate a pension awarded under Regulation 3 *ex officio*, but only upon request of the beneficiary and when the calculation under Regulation 1408/71 was more favourable for the beneficiary. Article 51 and 100 Regulation 1408/71 established an exception though, namely when a change in personal circumstances as explained in *Sinatra, 1982* supervened, the pension had to be re-calculated pursuant to Regulation 1408/71, even if originally it had been awarded pursuant to Regulation 3 and even in the absence of a request to that effect by the beneficiary (para. 11). *Delbar, 1989* in a sense also concerned a transitional problem, more specifically a problem of payment of family benefits to a self-employed person. The problem arose, because article 73 Regulation 1408/71 had not been amended regarding self-employed persons together with the general broadening of the scope of Regulation 1408/71 to encompass self-employed persons, but only at a later stage. Before that later stage, however, the Court held that self-employed persons could not claim family benefits directly based on article 51 Treaty given that article 73 Regulation 1408/71 had not yet been amended and article 51 Treaty only concerned workers (paras 8-11). With *Tiel-Utrecht, 1984*, finally, another subrogation case was tabled before the ECJ. Yet the Court did not enter the subrogation issue, because the basis of the insurance concluded in the case at issue had been purely contractual. The insurance relationship was therefore not covered by Regulation 1408/71 (para. 16).

4 Services

Broadcasting

Debauve, 1980 dealt with a prohibition in Belgium for cable television providers to broadcast advertisements. As held in *Sacchi, 1974*, the freedom of services applied to television broadcasting, provided that the situation was not purely internal to a member state (paras 8-9). Given the widely varying levels to which TV advertising was allowed in the member states, the Court did not find any issue with the freedom of services. The prohibition was applicable to all cable television providers without distinction based on the origin of the service or the nationality of the provider. Moreover, the Belgian broadcasting organizations were all subject to the same ad ban (paras 12-5). Finally, the possibilities for each consumer him- or herself to tap into television signals from abroad which naturally contained advertisements did not change the assessment. Discrimination could only arise from human activities, but not natural phenomena such as features of the landscape (paras 19-21). *Coditel, 1980* again concerned cable TV providers in Belgium. The dispute arose because of the transmission via cable of a German channel that broadcast a movie over which a company in Belgium held exclusive copyrights. According to the Court, the freedom of services did not prevent the copyright holder from opposing the Belgian cable TV companies' relaying of the German channel (para. 17). The freedom of services did not limit national intellectual property rights except when an arbitrary discrimination or a disguised restriction of trade was involved (para. 15). Exclusive assignment of copyrights along national borders was thus possible (para. 16). The case came back to the Court, though, in *Coditel II, 1982*. This time the Court was asked to rule on the compatibility with competition law of an agreement granting an exclusive right to show a movie within one member state. In this context, the Court held that the distinction inherent in the derogation clause of the free movement of goods in article 36 Treaty between the existence of an industrial and commercial property right which was not to be affected by the Treaty and its exercise which was capable of constituting a disguised restriction of trade applied in the context of the free movement of services, too (para. 13). (The Court then went on to hold that it was possible, depending on the circumstances, that an exclusive agreement for a specific area fell short of competition law when it restricted trade. However, that was not the case in general for an exclusive licence to show movies.)

Posted workers

In *Webb, 1981* a company established in the United Kingdom lawfully provided manpower to companies in the United Kingdom and extended that service to the Netherlands, though without the prerequisite Dutch licence. The Court held that the freedom of services applied even within the domain of social policy or when the free movement of persons was involved (paras 9-10). The licence requirement constituted an obstacle to the supplying of manpower as a service. The legislation of the host state could not necessarily be applied in its entirety to a service provider established in another member state. Rather, service provision could only be restricted in the interest of the general good, if the restriction was applied to all persons concerned equally, and if the same interest was not already safeguarded by 'home' state legislation (para. 17). Due to the sensitive social policy issues involved in manpower services and the diverse criteria the member states applied, a member state was entitled to require a licence, even from service providers established abroad that complied with home state legislation (paras

16-9). In turn, the member state concerned had to abstain from discrimination and give due credit to the conditions fulfilled by the service provider in the home state (para. 20).

In *Seco, 1982* the Court dealt with a similar constellation, namely French companies seconding workers to Luxembourg to carry out construction work in fulfilment of a contract. In this case, Luxembourg required the French company to pay social security contributions on behalf of the employees sent to work in Luxembourg. The workers were third country nationals who remained compulsorily affiliated to France's social security system. The Court judged that, because covert discrimination equally fell foul of the free movement of services, Luxembourg could not lawfully require the French company to pay social security contributions on behalf of the workers. The workers sent to work in Luxembourg were already insured under the French social security system. They contributions paid in Luxembourg for the same period did not yield any additional protection. The need to control immigration did not justify a discriminatory burden on service providers from other member state, either. Moreover, to impose such social security contributions in Luxembourg was unsuitable to make French companies comply with minimum wages in Luxembourg, which as such could be imposed though (paras 8-14).

Variety

In the following years, a number of cases raised issues free movement of services. In *Transporoute, 1982*, the Court applied Directives 71/304 and 71/305 on contracts of public works, found that under Directive 71/305 Luxembourg could not require a tenderer established in another member state to provide an establishment permit issued in Luxembourg, and held that result to be in accordance with the freedom of services (para. 14). In *Mialocq, 1983* the Court clarified the ruling in *Sacchi, 1974*. French law had established a monopoly of regional centres of artificial animal insemination. While article 37 Treaty did not apply to service monopolies pursuant to *Sacchi, 1974*, the Court decided that such monopolies were capable of affecting the free movement of goods indirectly when they treated imported goods less favourably than domestic goods.

Luisi and Carbone, 1984 concerned Italy's restrictions of foreign currency exports. The Court decided that not just service provision, but also service reception abroad, in particular for medical purposes and the purposes of tourism, education, or business, was covered by the free movement of services. Consideration for such services, even in cash, was the necessary corollary of the freedom of services, as such protected by it, and not to be made subject to more rigorous controls than the services themselves (paras 10-16). As a consequence, the free movement of services applied to such payments, while the free movement of capital was applicable in cases of investment of funds (paras 22-3). Whereas the member states had the right to apply certain controls to the non-liberalized flows of capital, such controls were not to impede the normal pattern of service provision. Any discretion of the authorities in this regard was, in particular, ruled out (paras 33-5).

Infringement in the insurance sector

In 1986, the Court was seized with a series of infringement procedures relating to the insurance sector. *Commission v. Germany (insurance), 1986* concerned insurance policies taken out voluntarily by consumers and co-insurance. (See the limitation of the ruling in para. 24.) Germany had required foreign insurance providers to have a German authorization and an establishment in Germany. With regard to consumer contracts the Court decided that the restriction posed by the authorization requirement was justified by the need to protect consumers, in particular since no harmonisation had taken place yet. It was necessary though that the conditions already fulfilled in the 'home' state were duly factored in to minimize the dual burden (paras 28-33 and 47). Yet to have a permanent establishment in Germany was precluded. That condition negated the very substance of the freedom of services (paras 54-6). In contrast, consumer protection was no ground to justify an authorisation requirement in the business of co-insurance, as in that business contracts were not a mass phenomenon, but rather negotiated individually (para. 64). The free movement of services and Directive 78/473 on co-insurance were therefore violated in that regard (para. 67). This violation of the freedom of services was confirmed in *Commission v. France (co-insurance), 1986*, *Commission v. Denmark (co-insurance), 1986*, and *Commission v. Ireland (co-insurance), 1986*, all of which were handed down on the same day as *Commission v. Germany (insurance), 1986*.

Public works

CEI and Bellini, 1987 added to *Transporoute, 1982* (above) in establishing in clearer terms the function of the freedom of services and establishment in the context of the directive on contracts of public works (Directive 71/305). Belgium had set a maximum value for works which a contractor was allowed to carry out at a time as a condition for the award of a contract. The Court held that the member states were free within the framework established by the Directive to set up further procedural and substantive rules, provided they complied with the freedom of services and establishment. Belgium's condition did not violate those freedoms (paras 14-6). *Beentjes, 1988* then reiterated the ruling in *CEI and Bellini, 1987* as to the function of the freedom of services and establishment (para. 20). The question whether the condition in a call for tender for contractors to be capable of employing long-term unemployed persons had a discriminatory effect and hence violated the freedom of services was then left for the national court to answer (paras 29-30).

Lawyers

Commission v. Germany (lawyers), 1988 addressed Germany's implementation of Directive 77/249 on lawyers' services, notably the requirement to work in conjunction with a lawyer of the host state. The Court held that Germany went beyond what was required to implement the Directive and the freedom of services in requiring foreign lawyers to work in conjunction with a German lawyer when representation by a lawyer was not mandatory for clients in proceedings (paras 14-5). The Court, in addition, struck down the requirements spelling out in detail what 'work in conjunction' meant (paras 26-32). Moreover, the restriction of the right to plead resulting from the principle of territorial exclusivity – lawyers were only allowed to represent clients where they were admitted to the bar – even though equally applicable to Germans, could not be applied to foreign lawyers, since not all host state rules governing established lawyers were automatically to be applied to foreign lawyers providing services (paras 41-3).

Broadcasting again

Bond, 1988 again dealt with the broadcasting of programmes via cable television. The Netherland's law contained a prohibition for Dutch cable operators that relayed programmes broadcast abroad to transmit advertisement directed at the public in the Netherlands or with subtitles in Dutch. The national television channels in the Netherlands, in contrast, were allowed to broadcast a certain amount of advertisement, although the ads were to be channelled through a foundation which made the necessary arrangements. Advertisers who had aired ads in Dutch or with subtitles on foreign channels which were then relayed by Dutch cable operators to the Dutch public complained about a violation of the freedom of services. The Court held that two sets of transfrontier services against remuneration were involved, namely Dutch advertisers contracting with foreign broadcasters and those broadcasters contracting with Dutch cable operators. It was immaterial that the remuneration was paid indirectly, i. e. that in the context of the latter set of services the Dutch consumer paid fees to the Dutch cable operator, rather than the broadcaster paying the cable operator for the service of relaying (para. 14-6). Both sets of services were restricted by the ad ban. The Dutch advertisers were precluded from contracting with broadcasters, the latter with cable operators (para. 22). The prohibition of subtitles reinforced the restriction by the ad ban. The restrictions were moreover discriminatory, as the national television stations generally could broadcast advertisement, albeit via a foundation, in contrast to foreign broadcasters transmitting via cable to Dutch viewers (paras 24-6). Such discrimination was in need of justification which only one of the grounds of derogation expressly mentioned in article 56 Treaty in conjunction with article 66 Treaty could provide (para. 32). Economic aims were excluded as grounds of justification (para. 34). Public policy grounds, such as the need to maintain the non-commercial pluralistic nature of broadcasting, were valid as such. Yet they did not prevail in this case, for more proportionate, less restrictive measures than an outright ad ban would have been available. A restriction of air time for ads, for instance would have been an alternative (para. 37). Moreover, a non-discriminatory ban on all advertisement, including advertisement by the Dutch national television stations, would comply with the freedom of services (para. 38).

Remuneration

Humbel, 1988, a judgment which mainly concerned the *Gravier, 1985*-line of authority, also clarified the term 'services' pursuant to article 59 Treaty. The characteristic of remuneration, according to the Court, was that it constituted consideration for a service normally agreed upon between the parties involved. That was not the case with national public education which was normally funded by public means, even though sometimes contributions were required. In public education, the state did not pursue a gainful activity, but rather fulfilled its basic function of providing the population with education (paras 17-9).

Transport services

In *Corsica Ferries, 1989* the Court refused to apply the freedom of services for the years 1981 and 1982, although higher charges were essentially imposed in case of ferry transports between ports in Corsica and member states (or Africa) than in case of transports between ports in Corsica and France. The reason for the Court's ruling was that transport services were subject to liberalization through the transport policy. That liberalization was implemented only by Regulation 4055/86 (paras 10-4). However, the Court emphasized that the freedom of services – like the freedoms of goods, persons, and capital – precluded restrictions even if they were only minor. Moreover, a trader's freedom to provide services could be affected by tax measures (paras 8-9).

Tourists

Finally, *Cowan, 1989* confirmed that a tourist was a service receiver who enjoyed the freedom of services. Tourists therefore had to be protected from physical harm in equal measure as a state's own citizens (para. 17). More specifically, when a tourist from the United Kingdom became the victim of a crime in France and claimed compensation under French law France could not refuse such compensation on the sole ground that the victim did not have a French residence permit – in particular when no similar requirement was imposed on French citizens – else French law ran afoul of the prohibition of discrimination on the basis of nationality. The same was valid as to the condition that the state of which the victim was a national had concluded an agreement of reciprocity with France (paras 10-3).

IV The 1990s

The case-law grew exponentially in the 1990s. During this decade, the Court handed down more decisions in our domain than in the 25 years before: more than 350 decisions. Social security and workers contributed the bulk with almost

140 and more than 80 decisions, respectively. The freedom of services and establishment also came up strong though, with almost 60 decisions and more than 70 decisions, respectively.

1 Workers and citizens

Worker

The Court continued the case-law of the previous decades on the term 'worker' in the 1990s with the judgment in *Antonissen, 1991*. According to the Court, a job seeker who came to the United Kingdom to find employment continued to be a 'worker' under article 48(3) Treaty even after a period of job seeking of six months had expired. The job seeker only had to provide evidence that he continued to seek employment and that he had genuine chances of finding employment (para. 21). *Antonissen, 1991* was confirmed in *Commission v. Belgium (residence permits), 1997*. The Court struck down an order to leave Belgium which, in accordance with national law, had been issued automatically after three months of unsuccessful job seeking. In *Merci, 1991* the Court held that the concept of a 'worker' covered persons who were employed by an undertaking and who were linked at the same time to the other persons employed by that undertaking through a relationship of association (para. 13). *Merci, 1991* was later confirmed in *Becu, 1999* (para. 28). In *Raulin, 1992* the Court clarified that a person who had concluded an on-call contract which gave rise to irregular working hours, payment only corresponding these hours, and no obligation to heed calls to work could be considered a 'worker'. Yet the national court had to assess the 'purely marginal and ancillary' nature of the activities. In that assessment it was not required to factor in activities pursued by the person concerned in other member states (paras 18 and 19). On the same day as *Raulin, 1992*, *Bernini, 1992* repeated *Lawrie-Blum, 1986* and *Bettray, 1989* to find that a national court could consider a paid trainee a 'worker'.

In *Boukhalfa, 1996* the Court reiterated in accordance with *Prodest, 1984* and *Lopes da Veiga, 1989* that Community law was capable of applying outside the territory of the member states. It held that a local employee of a member state's embassy situated outside the territory of the Community was entitled to rely on non-discrimination, provided that the employment contract established a sufficiently close link to a member state in terms of applicable law, jurisdiction, social security contributions, and taxes (paras 15-6). Thus, a local employee who was a national of a member state could rely on non-discrimination.

In *Asscher, 1996* the Court found that a person who was employed as a director in a company of which he was the sole owner could not be considered a worker for lack of a relationship of subordination (para. 26). Instead, the freedom of establishment was applicable. This was confirmed in *Meeusen, 1999*. However, the ruling in *Asscher, 1996* did not necessarily apply to the spouse of such a company director who (the spouse) was employed in the same company (*Meeusen, 1999*, para. 15-16).

The definition of the term 'worker' finally spilled over into social policy in *Nolte, 1995* and *Megner, 1995*. These cases concerned gender discrimination. However, the Court applied the definition of a worker developed in the free movement of workers in *Hoekstra, 1964*; *Levin, 1982*; and *Kempf, 1986* to find that the fact that a person worked during very few hours did not have the effect of excluding a person from the scope of Directive 79/7/EEC on equal treatment between men and women in matters of social security.

Advantages

The Court elaborated on article 7 Regulation 1612/68 in a sequence of cases in the 1990s, beginning with *Le Manoir, 1991*. In this judgment it emerged that indirect effects on the worker could be caught by article 7 Regulation 1612/68. The Court held that the situation where an employer had to pay higher social security contributions for a trainee he employed who pursued vocational training in another member state than for those pursuing 'national' training amounted to covert discrimination. Next, the Court qualified childbirth and maternity allowances as 'social advantages' under article 7(2) Regulation 1612/68 in *Commission v. Luxembourg (childbirth benefit), 1993*. A residence requirement was therefore ruled out. The Court then in *Schmid, 1993* declared unlawful a nationality condition for a disability allowance by applying *Lebon, 1987* with regard to a disabled adult descendant dependent on a migrant worker.

In *De Vos, 1996* the obligation of the employer to continue to pay contributions to a pension fund while the employee was attending military service was held to constitute neither an employment condition under article 7(1) Regulation 1612/68 nor a social advantage article 7(2), because the state reimbursed the contributions to employers. Rather, the payment of the contributions served as partial compensation by the state for the military service performed, and was thus not a benefit granted on the basis of the work or residence of a worker. *O'Flynn, 1996* established that it amounted to indirect discrimination in terms of social advantages under article 7(2) Regulation 1612/68 to cover the cost of a decent burial of a family member and the transport cost related thereto only when the burial took place in the United Kingdom. Essentially, the cost of the burial itself were the same abroad, and the transport cost covered were limited under national law in any case to those arising from local transports (para. 28). In *Commission v. Belgium (unemployment), 1996* the Court found the Belgian tideover allowance which had already been at issue in *Deak, 1985* and which was essentially granted only to graduates of educational establishments situated in Belgium to be indirectly discriminatory in the light of article 7(2) Regulation 1612/68, namely in cases of dependent descendants of migrant workers. In the same judgment, however, the Court considered a special unemployment programme under which the Belgian state assumed the costs of employers who employed young workers in their first job to be outside the scope of Regulation

1612/68, in so far as it regarded young nationals of other member states who had received their education abroad, sought access to the employment market in Belgium, and were not members of the families of migrant workers employed in Belgium (paras 36-40). Then in *Meints, 1997* the Court struck down a residence requirement for a compensatory benefit granted to those farm workers who had become unemployed as a result of farm land having been set aside by their former employer. The benefit constituted a social advantage pursuant to article 7(2) Regulation 1612/68 and the residence condition was indirectly discriminatory (para. 41 and 46, respectively). Frontier workers could also claim the benefit.

Commission v. France (pension points), 1998 dealt with the situation where frontier workers employed in France did not receive supplementary retirement pension points upon dismissal while ordinary workers did. The Court held that the pension point scheme which was mandatory for certain employees and based on a collective agreement rendered compulsory in France came within article 7 Regulation 1612/68. The Court found that the residence requirement violated the prohibition of indirect discrimination. In *Commission v. Greece (large families), 1998* the Court declared unlawful Greece's nationality requirement for certain benefits for large families and certain family allowances coming within the scope of article 7(2) Regulation 1612/68.

The Court relied on article 7(2) Regulation 1612/68 as well when it ruled in *Di Leo, 1990* that educational grants given to enable studies abroad had to be awarded not only to migrant workers according to *Matteucci, 1988*, but also under article 12 Regulation 1612/68 to the children of resident migrant workers, even if they pursued studies in the state of which they were nationals. *Di Leo, 1990* was confirmed in *Bernini, 1992*. The Court in this case also made it clear that a descendant dependent on a migrant worker could rely on article 7(2) Regulation 1612/68 directly. More specifically, if national law granted educational benefits to students themselves, a descendant of a migrant worker was also entitled to claim the benefits directly, although his rights were technically acquired through the migrant worker and he was only an 'indirect beneficiary' (para. 26). In *Gaal, 1995* the Court added to *Di Leo, 1990* that article 12 Regulation 1612/68 also applied to the children of migrant workers who were already 21 years of age or older and who were not any longer dependant on the migrant worker (para. 25). In *Meeusen, 1999*, on the other hand, the Court again relied on article 7(2) Regulation 1612/68 to find that if the domestic law of a member state did not impose a residence requirement on the children of a national of that member state in the award of study finance, the member state was precluded from imposing such a residence requirement on the children of migrant workers or self-employed persons (para. 23).

The rights of family members were also at stake in *Dzodzi, 1990*. However, the question the Belgian court asked related to the rights of a third country national who was the spouse of a Belgian worker. Although the only member state concerned was Belgium, the Court gave an answer, thus putting the approach that had removed purely internal situations from the Court's jurisdiction into perspective. Yet the answer the Court gave consisted mainly in a reiteration of the Community provisions that would have been applicable had the worker been a national of another member state than Belgium. The Court then left it to the national court to apply these provisions so as to avoid any possible reverse discrimination against Belgian nationals in Belgium. In *Taghavi, 1992* the rights of a third country national who was the spouse of a national of a member state were also at issue. Yet she was not entitled to rely on article 7(2) Regulation 1612/68 to claim a benefit in Belgium in the light of her handicap, because third country national spouses of Belgian nationals did not have a claim to such a benefit, either. A 'social advantage' for Belgians did therefore not exist (para. 11).

Education

Educational training was also discussed with regard to other norms than article 7 Regulation 1612/68. In the judgment *Kraus, 1993* the Court dealt with an authorization procedure which one had to undergo pursuant to national law to be allowed to bear an academic title acquired in another member state. Even though everyone was indiscriminately subject to this authorization procedure in the case at hand, the exercise of the freedom of movement was hampered or made less attractive (para. 32). The authorization procedure therefore had to be free, easily accessible, subject to an appeal, and based on a transparent statement of the reasons why the decision adopted. Non-compliance was to entail proportionate sanctions (paras 38-41). The Court essentially adopted these requirements from the diploma recognition case-law (see below).

Next, the Court again dealt with the *Gravier, 1985* line of authority in two cases. In *Raulin, 1992* the Court held that *Gravier, 1985* also applied when financial assistance for students was not only designed to reduce the fees for access to education but in addition to help with the cost of maintenance. In such a case, the part of the assistance relating to access to education had to be earmarked and made available on a non-discriminatory basis (para. 28). Moreover, equal access to education pursuant to *Gravier, 1985* necessarily implied a right of residence (para. 34). In *Commission v. Belgium (minerval), 1994* the Court then held that Belgium's legislation still failed to comply with Community law. It was not sufficient to make applicable the exemption from minerval to students who had already been enrolled in the state of which they were nationals and where they paid fees (para. 12). Moreover, the findings regarding discrimination made in *Commission v. Belgium (students), 1988* also applied to universities.

In *Commission v. Greece (teachers), 1995* the Court invalidated certain requirements for teachers in private schools that were stricter for nationals of other member states than for Greek nationals, namely the requirements that an authorization and certain documents were necessary and that an exemption from the need to be qualified as a public school teacher was only made for Greek nationals. (Greece had acknowledged the infringement.) Finally, the Court, saw to foreign language assistants again. It confirmed the judgment *Allué I, 1989* in *Allué II, 1993*, in particular for renewable one-year fixed-term contracts. *Spotti,*

1993 confirmed the discrimination of foreign language assistants in a situation where objective reasons were necessary in each case to justify limiting the contracts of teaching staff in time, while such reasons were presumed to exist in general for foreign language assistants. In *Petrie, 1997*, however, the Court found that foreign language assistants were not discriminated against when they were not admitted to fill certain posts that were only temporarily vacant and open to 'lecturers and established researchers'. The reason was that that category only encompassed persons who had passed a selection procedure, while foreign language assistants were not required to pass such a procedure. Foreign language assistants and established researchers were thus not in comparable situations (para. 52).

Taxes

In the 1990s, the Court initiated the tax case-law in the free movement of persons. The Court had already relied on the free movement of workers in a value added tax case, namely *Ledoux, 1988* (paras 11, 12, and 18). But the first case that was based fully on the free movement of workers was *Biehl, 1990*. The Court found that the way Luxembourg handled the refund of income tax levied at source violated the right to the same tax advantages in article 7(2) Regulation 1612/68, because it was covertly discriminatory. Luxembourg had excluded the refund of income tax levied in excess of the actual tax liability, i. e. in the case of 'overdeduction', when the taxpayer moved to another member state in the course of the year or had moved to Luxembourg in the course of the year. The ruling was later on applied again in *Commission v. Luxembourg (excess tax), 1995* for a similar rule in Luxembourg which required nine months of employment in Luxembourg for a tax adjustment.

The next step in the tax case-law was taken with a pair of judgments of 28 January 1992, *Bachmann, 1992* and *Commission v. Belgium (insurance taxation), 1992*. In these two judgments, the Court considered the refusal by Belgium to deduct from taxable income premiums paid under pension and life insurance contracts taken out with foreign insurers, while those paid under contracts taken out with domestic insurers were fully deductible, as a justified tax discrimination. The reason was that the advantage for persons having a contract with a domestic insurer, viz. the deductibility of premiums, was later offset by the taxation of the income by way of pension awarded on the basis of the insurance contract, while the income received in application of contracts with foreign insurers was not subject to direct taxation in Belgium. In other words the connection between the deductibility of premiums and the taxation of income – 'the cohesion of the tax system' in the words of the Court in *Bachmann, 1992* (para. 21) – justified the distinction between premiums paid under domestic and under foreign contracts.

In *Schumacker, 1995* the Court dealt with the taking into account of the family circumstances of migrant workers, notably frontier workers. The Court ruled that the situations of resident and non-resident taxpayers were, as a rule, not comparable for the purposes of direct taxation (para. 31). The member state where the worker was employed could therefore draw a distinction based on the place of residence of the taxpayer and refuse to take into account his personal and family circumstances. The reason was that the member state where a worker was resident was normally placed best to take into account the personal and family circumstances of a worker, because the worker's interests were concentrated there (para. 32). However, if a migrant worker gained almost all of his income and the major part of the family income in a member state where he was not resident, the risk arose that the personal and family circumstances of the migrant worker were not taken into account for tax purposes anywhere at all. Then the situations of resident and non-resident taxpayers became comparable and the member state where the income was earned had to factor in the personal and family circumstances. Consequently, in *Gschwind, 1999*, Germany's amended rules that provided that tax splitting for spouses applied to non-resident taxpayers only if they in total gained more than 90 per cent of their income in Germany or their total income gained abroad was less than 24'000 German marks were sanctioned by the Court.

Wielockx, 1995 was an establishment case in which the aspects of *Bachmann, 1992* and *Schumacker, 1995* came together. The Court ruled that it was contrary to *Schumacker, 1995* if the Dutch authorities rejected the tax deductibility of contributions made to a Dutch pension reserve to a person who was established in the Netherlands while having residence in Belgium and who gained his entire earnings through self-employment in the Netherlands. However, the *Bachmann, 1992*-justification based on the cohesion of the tax system did not prevail, according to the Court, because the Netherlands had waived taxation of the income generated by the contributions for non-residents in the double taxation convention with Belgium irrespective of the deductibility of contributions. Thus, the Court moved the notion of fiscal cohesion from the level of the individual to the inter-state level (para. 24). The need to preserve the cohesion of the tax system could therefore not justify the refusal to allow deduction of the contributions. In *Asscher, 1996* a similar constellation was at issue, namely a person who was self-employed in both Belgium and the Netherlands. However, although the *Schumacker, 1995*-requirements were not met in the Netherlands, because less than 90 per cent of the income was generated in the Netherlands, the Dutch authorities were not justified in applying a higher tax rate to non-residents than to residents on the ground that in the Netherlands social security contributions were generally not deductible any longer (para. 54). 'Fiscal cohesion' did not apply, either, because a direct link between the advantage and the disadvantage did not exist, i. e. no benefits were gained by reason of the additional tax paid (para. 60). Moreover the allocation of the competence to levy social security contributions pursuant to Regulation 1408/71 was mandatory and could not be changed indirectly through tax measures (para. 61).

Gilly, 1998 was another tax case regarding frontier workers. In this case the Court found that the connecting factors applied in the double taxation convention between France and Germany to determine the state competent to tax income were not contrary to article 48 Treaty, although they were partly based on the nationality of workers. These connecting factors were established by the member states to allocate powers of taxation and on the basis of an OECD model convention which was not 'unreasonable' (para. 31). They could lead to different levels of taxation (paras 34 and 47). Moreover, the requirements of *Schumacker, 1995* were respected (paras 49 and 50).

Derogations

In the 1990s, the Court addressed the derogations from the free movement of workers, too. In *Bleis, 1991* the Court held that employment as a secondary school teacher was not 'public service' within the meaning of article 39(4) Treaty. The Court thus implicitly rejected a nationality condition for competitions for posts as secondary school teachers. In *Commission v. Greece (public service), 1996* and *Commission v. Luxembourg (public service), 1996* the Court sanctioned the infringement procedure brought by the Commission, as part of a strategy to open national public services in general for nationals of other member states, against Greece's and Luxembourg's withholding of a vast array of posts to their own nationals. The Court held that generally posts 'in the areas of research, health, inland transport, posts and telecommunications and in the water, gas and electricity supply services' were not part of 'public service' (para. 31, *Commission v. Luxembourg (public service), 1996*). Moreover, primary school teachers were not within the scope of 'public service', either (para. 34, *Commission v. Luxembourg (public service), 1996*). On the same day as these two judgments were delivered, the Court in *Commission v. Belgium (public service), 1996* recalled that the public service derogation did not serve to exclude entire sectors from the scope of the freedom of workers. A violation of the public service derogation was only conceivable, if the state had a controlling authority over an entity. This was not the case for some of the semi-public and private entities affected by the infringement procedure (para. 22).

In *Pereira Roque, 1998* the Court, next, addressed the public security derogation in the special context of the Channel Islands. The Court held that the protocol relating to the islands, which had been annexed to the Act of Accession of the United Kingdom and which refrained from extending the free movement of persons to the islands, essentially precluded only deportations based on arbitrary distinctions (para. 49). Finally, the Court dealt with some derogations in *Commission v. Spain (private security guards), 1998*, a case that concerned both the free movement of persons and services. The Court rejected both nationality and residence requirements for private security guards. The companies providing security services were private, so that the public service exception was not applicable; the connection to any official authority was indirect and unspecific (para. 35); the exclusion by reason of the nationality of a guard was too general to be covered by the public security exception (para. 41); a residence requirement was not necessary for the public security aims to be met.

Non-discrimination

In the 1990s, the Court also dealt with a number of cases on the basis of non-discrimination. *Ramrath, 1993* was such a case. It concerned the freedom of workers, establishment, and services at the same time. The Court did not distinguish clearly between the freedoms. The Court made it clear that, although the rules of the Community generally left the matter at issue to the member states, a state was not to require an auditor from another member state to be permanently established in its territory when the auditor occasionally came to this member state to audit companies in the service of an auditor authorized in the member state concerned (para. 36). In *Scholz, 1994* the Court ruled that it was unjustifiably discriminatory not to take into account periods of employment in the public service of another member state when a job advertisement had announced that previous job experience acquired in the public service of the member state concerned would be taken into account in the selection of a candidate. In a similar vein, the Court ruled in *Schöning, 1998* that periods of employment in a specific profession had to be factored in equally in the categorization of an employee into a salary group, regardless of whether they were completed abroad or not. Different organizational rules of member states' public services could not affect that conclusion. Similarly, in *Commission v. Greece (foreign public service), 1998* the Court invalidated a Greek rule that excluded periods of employment in foreign public service from consideration for salary and age benefit purposes.

In the judgment *Bosman, 1995* the Court built on previous sports case-law, namely *Walrave, 1974* and *Donà, 1976*, and reiterated that sport did not fall outside the scope of the Treaty freedoms in so far as it was an economic activity. The Court then struck down the elaborate mechanism of the European football associations and their umbrella federation to impose a transfer fee to be paid by the club who acquired the services of a player to the former club of the player, essentially because it hindered the access of the player to the market. Moreover, the Court invalidated the rule which limited the number of players from other member states that clubs could field, as it was discriminatory.

One aspect of the judgment in *Commission v. France (ship registration), 1996* concerned the registration of a ship for leisure purposes. (For the main part of the judgment concerning the freedom of establishment, see below.) The Court ruled that the 'access to leisure activities' was a 'corollary' of the freedom of movement (para. 21). Thus, the registration of a ship, even though it would be used for non-economic purposes, was not to be subject to a nationality condition. *Dafeki, 1997* was a judgment that concerned the probative value of birth certificates. The Court held a German rule to be discriminatory that provided that birth certificates issued in other member states had less probative value than German certificates. Pursuant to that rule in a case in which more than one foreign birth certificate existed because of a rectification, was presumed as valid the certificate which had been issued at the point in time closest to the date of birth, while a German certificate that had been officially rectified was considered valid.

According to the Court, the rule was too abstract to address situations of abuse in which the date of birth had allegedly been moved forward with the intention to benefit from earlier retirement. Instead, such abuse had to be established in each specific case.

In *Clean Car, 1998* the Court struck down a residence requirement for managers of companies, as it was indirectly discriminatory and thus precluded by article 48 Treaty. It also held that a company itself, as an employer, could rely on the free movement of workers of its managers to attack the residence rule that was addressed to the company (paras 19-24). In the judgment in *Terhoeve, 1999* residence as a connecting factor was also an issue. *Terhoeve, 1999* concerned a ceiling that applied to the amount of social security contributions to be paid by residents. The Court found that it amounted to an unjustified obstacle to the free movement of workers to refuse to apply this ceiling to a person who had worked in another member state as a posted worker for a part of the year, it being understood that an additional entitlement to benefits was not created by reason of the amount paid in excess of the ceiling. Conversely, in *Becu, 1999* discrimination was not found in the requirement to have recourse for port service to officially recognised dock workers. The conditions to be recognised as a dock worker were not based on nationality (para. 33). It was left to the national court though to determine whether an obstacle existed nonetheless, in particular with regard to the freedom of services.

Union citizenship

In the late 1990s the Court was faced with European Union citizenship for the first time. *Uecker and Jacquet, 1997* was a case involving a purely internal situation. The question being asked whether Union citizenship moved a purely internal situation to within the scope of Community law and whether it precluded reverse discrimination, the Court answered that Union citizenship was not intended to expand the scope *ratione materiae* of Community law (para. 23). Hence, what had been a purely internal situation before the advent of citizenship remained so even after. That *Martínez Sala, 1998* actually had a citizenship dimension was not very obvious. The problem was that it was unclear whether Ms Martínez Sala was a worker within the meaning of Regulation 1612/68 and an employed person within the sense of Regulation 1408/71. Confronted with this uncertainty, the Court ruled that she came within the scope of Community law by reason of her Union citizenship and for that reason benefitted from non-discrimination with regard to a benefit within the ambit of Community law (para. 61-3). *Wijsenbeek, 1999* was not a full-blown Union citizenship case, yet his Union citizenship was one of the arguments Mr Wijsenbeek relied upon when he refused to produce a document to prove his identity upon arrival in the Netherlands after a flight from France. The Court, however, ruled that the member states could still require from nationals of the member states that they identify themselves, because the full abolishment of internal border controls required harmonization. Yet the Court also hinted at the fact that the right of Union citizens to move was unconditional (para. 43).

Ankara

In the 1990s the Court tackled a first, massive wave of judgments concerning the Ankara Agreement, after it had handed down a first judgment with *Demirel, 1987*. The Court in *Sevince, 1990* recognized the direct effect of articles 2(1)(b) and 7 Decision 2/76 and articles 6(1) and 13 Decision 1/80 of the association council. However, a temporary employment permit granted for the duration of proceedings with suspensory effect, while necessarily implying the granting of a concomitant residence permit (para. 29), did not amount to legal employment within the meaning of articles 2(1)(b) Decision 2/76 and 6(1) Decision 1/80, because such a permit did not mean that the person concerned was in a 'stable and secure situation as a member of the labour force' (para. 30). This ruling was confirmed in *Kus, 1992* for the third indent of article 6(1) Decision 1/80 (para. 16). Yet the Court made it clear that an outcome of the pending proceedings in favour of the Turkish worker concerned would mean that the periods completed during the proceedings would have to be counted retroactively as legal employment (para. 17). The reasons why a Turkish worker had been admitted to the labour market of a member state, such as marriage or other reasons, were moreover irrelevant for the purpose of determining whether the time periods laid down by article 6(1) Decision 1/80 had been completed (para. 22). Such reasons were equally irrelevant under article 7 Decision 1/80, as the Court ruled in *Eroglu, 1994* (para. 22). *Eroglu, 1994* also extended the ruling that a work permit necessarily implied a residence permit to article 7 Decision 1/80 (para. 20); held article 7(2) Decision 1/80 to be directly effective (para. 20); and established that the first indent of article 6(1) Decision 1/80 only permitted continued work for the first employer after one year of legal employment (para. 13). A person was not allowed to switch back from the second to the first employer under this provision (para. 14). In *Bozkurt, 1995*, the Court ruled that the criteria applied in *Lopes da Veiga, 1989* to establish a link to a member state that was sufficiently close to warrant application of Community law also had to be fulfilled under the Ankara Agreement, given that the Community principles of the free movement of workers were to be 'transpose[d], so far as is possible' to Decision 1/80 (para. 20). A Turkish lorry driver was therefore subject to the Ankara Agreement in certain circumstances, subject to the assessment of the national court. *Bozkurt, 1995* established two more points, namely, that the administrative documents issued to Turkish workers only had declaratory force and hence did not influence the rights under the Ankara Agreement (para. 30); and that a right to remain in a member state could not be derived from the Ankara Agreement as such for persons who had definitely left the labour force, such as retired persons and persons totally and permanently incapacitated (para. 39).

In the year 1997 alone, the Court decided six cases based on the Ankara Agreement. *Tetik, 1997* revealed that Turkish workers who came within the third indent of article 6(1) Decision 1/80 could not be considered to have left the duly registered labour force when they themselves had terminated their employment contract. Moreover, a reasonable period of time had to be accorded for them to search for new employment in the host member state (para. 30). An argument to the contrary could not be derived from article 6(2) Decision 1/80 (para. 39). *Kadiman, 1997* established that a member state was in principle entitled to require spouses to live together during the period required in the first indent of article 7(1) Decision 1/80 (para. 40), given that the aim of the article was to favour employment of the worker by the possibility to maintain family links (para. 34). However, neither short periods of absence for reasons of sickness or holiday nor circumstances beyond the power of one of the spouses were capable of influencing the completion of the period. In *Eker, 1997* the Court held that the first indent of article 6(1) Decision 1/80 required stable and continuous employment with one and the same employer for an entire year (para. 22). Changing employment repeatedly and then at the end of the first year continuing to work for the last employer did not therefore suffice to meet the requirement of the first indent of article 6(1). If the authorities allowed a person to change employment during the first year, a one-year period would thus re-commence anew (para. 25). *Kol, 1997* established that a 'stable and secure situation as a member of the labour force' for the purpose of the first indent of article 6(1) Decision 1/80 required that the person concerned had not committed fraud to obtain a residence permit (para. 25). The Court in *Ertanir, 1997* essentially ruled that article 6(3) Decision 1/80 did not allow the member states to impose conditions or limitations additional to those already contained in article 6(1) Decision 1/80, such as a maximum period of work or residence (para. 31). Moreover, the categorization of a specific activity in national law was irrelevant under article 6(1) provided that the economic activity was genuine and effective (para. 43). 'Legal employment' was a Community term which needed to be defined objectively and uniformly (para. 59). In addition, brief spells during which a person did not hold a valid residence or work permit were immaterial under article 6(1) (para. 68). *Günaydin, 1997* was a judgment of the same day as *Ertanir, 1997* and essentially ruled in the same way as the latter regarding additional conditions imposed on employees. *Günaydin, 1997* in addition clarified that work merely intending to prepare a person for work in the Turkish subsidiary of a company established in a member state could also be considered as normal employment for the purpose of article 6(1) Decision 1/80 (para. 33). Moreover, a statement made in the application for a residence permit was not to lead to a loss of the rights pursuant to article 6(1), save when the statement had been made with the sole intention of obtaining a residence permit based on a false premise (para. 60). Yet the Court limited this ruling to the specifics of the case.

The Court then ruled in *Akman, 1998* that it was not necessary in order to claim a right of access to the employment market pursuant to article 7(2) Decision 1/80 that a parent was still in employment or even present at the time his child sought access to the employment market, provided that the requirements in article 7(2) were met. Thus, the conditions of article 6(1) Decision 1/80 were not to be imposed on a child in such a situation (para. 48). In *Birden, 1998*, the Court elaborated on the two criteria Turkish nationals had to meet to benefit from article 6(1) Decision 1/80. The temporary or social nature of work did not imply either that an employee was not belonging to the duly registered labour force (para. 39) or that his employment was not legal (para. 64). Moreover, the notion of 'work' used in article 6(1) Decision 1/80 was congruent with the term in the free movement of workers as the Court had interpreted it. Thus, it encompassed employment regardless of where the funds used to finance the employment came from (para. 28). Lastly, the Court refused to transpose the case-law developed in the context of the Ankara Agreement to the Rabat Agreement between the Community and Morocco in *El-Yassini, 1999* (para. 61), given the differences in the object, purpose, and wording of the two agreements. A member state could therefore lawfully refuse to extend the residence permit of a Moroccan national, even though it could not decline to extend it for a Turkish national in the same situation. However, after a member state had granted a Moroccan national a work permit valid for a certain duration, a residence permit was not to be refused for the same duration (paras 64-6).

Technicalities

The Court addressed a number of technical details of the free movement of workers in the 1990s as well. In *Roux, 1991*, the Court ruled that the issue of a residence permit was not to be made dependent on (i) prior registration with a social security scheme, (ii) classification of an activity as 'employed' or 'self-employed', provided that it was an *economic* activity, or (iii) compliance with social security legislation. *Giagounidis, 1991* determined that an identity card was valid under Community law for the purposes of identification even when the card had been issued before the accession of the state that had issued the card or when that card in the latter state was not sufficient to leave the territory. Moreover, a migrant worker did not always have to produce the identification document he had used when he immigrated. Migrant workers were allowed to produce either a valid identity card or a valid passport. *Commission v. Netherlands (questions at border), 1991* clarified that, apart from situations involving public policy, security, and health issues, questions as to the financial means available and the purpose of a journey were not to be asked when a person entered a member state. That the requirements for residence were met needed to be proved only when a residence permit was applied for. In *ASTI, 1991* the Court judged that the exclusion of migrant workers from the elections to occupational guilds in which membership was compulsory in Luxembourg violated the rights attached to the membership in trade unions pursuant to article 8(1) Regulation 1612/68. This judgment was confirmed in *Commission v. Luxemburg (ASTI II), 1994*.

The Court annulled the directive on the right of residence of students in the case *Parliament v. Council (student Directive), 1992*, because in the light of

Raulin, 1992 the directive was wrongly based on article 235 Treaty, rather than article 7(2) Treaty. In *Gallagher, 1995*, the Court laid down further details of the role and composition of the 'competent authority' within the meaning of article 9 Directive 64/221. The independent authority need not have been a court, but it was not to be controlled by the authority ordering an expulsion. Technically, it was not precluded that the latter authority appointed the independent authority (para. 24). The notification to the person concerned need not have contained the names and titles of the members of the independent authority (para. 25). Moreover, the opinion pursuant to article 9(1) Directive 64/221 had to be given before the expulsion decision was taken, rather than after the person concerned had objected to an order (para. 20). In *Commission v. Belgium (residence permits), 1997* the Court ruled that the total of the charges Belgium levied for the issue of a residence permit was excessive and the procedure to obtain a residence permit too burdensome. Moreover, Belgium could not lawfully demand that persons who came to Belgium in order to work for less than three months obtained a residence permit. *Shingara, 1997* concerned legal remedies. It established that in an admission procedure of a national of a member state or in a procedure involving a measure to safeguard public order or security, legal remedies did not necessarily have to be identical to those in procedures dealing with a member state's own nationals' right of entry. Two more points were clarified by *Shingara, 1997*. First, the conditions for an independent authority to intervene in article 9(1) Directive 64/221 also applied in cases coming within article 9(2). Second, a national of a member state who had been refused entry to another member state had the right to a fresh decision subject to all procedural safeguards after a reasonable period had passed after the first decision, regardless of whether he had exhausted the procedural safeguards available against the initial decision refusing entry. The Court held in *Commission v. Germany (ID checks), 1998* that Germany had imposed excessive fines on nationals of other member states when they had failed to produce their residence permits in an identity control in contrast to the fines imposed for similar failures by German nationals. *Awoyemi, 1998*, finally, dealt with the obligation to exchange a driving licence in the host state pursuant to Directive 80/1263. The Court found that third country nationals could not rely on the case-law it had established in *Skanavi, 1996* (see below). More specifically, a fine for having failed to exchange a driving licence obtained abroad was not attackable by third country nationals on the ground that it was so disproportionate that it amounted to an obstacle to free movement, because third country nationals did not enjoy rights of free movement (paras 27-30). The provisions of the new Directive 91/439 which had turned the duty to exchange a foreign driving licence into a mere right, moreover, were capable of having direct effect, save when a licence issued in a third state had previously been recognized in a member state (paras 42-4).

Purely internal situations

Purely internal situations gave rise to eleven judgments in the free movement of workers. In *Steen, 1992* a German national claimed that he was discriminated on the basis of nationality, because he was asked to declare that he would become a civil servant after two years of training with the German postal service, while such a declaration was not asked from nationals of other member states. The Court held the case to concern a purely internal situation without any link to a situation governed by Community law. Community law did therefore not apply. The case, however, came back to the Court in *Steen II, 1994*. The Court answered to the national court that it was free to consider the case in the light of German constitutional law. *Morais, 1992* also concerned a purely internal situation. There was no connection to the free movement of persons when a Portuguese driving instructor working for a driving school in Portugal was fined for offering driving services beyond the boundary of the municipality where the school was established. In *Koua Poirrez, 1992* Community law did not apply to the situation where a third country national who had been adopted by a French national who had never made use of his Treaty freedoms was refused a disability benefit on the ground of his nationality. Community law did thus not preclude the refusal. The Court did not enter into the matter, although the national court had stated that the situation possibly involved reverse discrimination of French nationals (para. 8). *USSL No. 47 Di Biella, 1997* was about two Italian entities that allegedly made a fictitious arrangement for the procurement of labour. As all aspects were confined to Italy, the Court ruled that the case concerned a purely internal situation (para. 22). *Uecker and Jacquet, 1997* was also rejected for being purely internal to a member state. Two third country nationals who were married to German nationals had sought to rely on the case-law regarding foreign language assistants in Germany. However, since the German nationals had never exercised their freedom of movement, the case did not have any connection to a situation governed by Community law. In *Kremzow, 1997* an Austrian national claimed that his fundamental rights of due process had been violated by the criminal proceedings conducted against him for murder in Austria and by the ensuing imprisonment. He claimed damages on that ground and claimed that the Court had jurisdiction, since he had been unable to exercise his right of free movement as a citizen of the European Union because of the imprisonment. The Court found that no aspect of the situation was connected to any of the situations contemplated by the Treaty. As he had been sentenced pursuant to national provisions which did not seek to ensure compliance with Community law, the situation was not within the scope of Community law. It was therefore not for the Court to guarantee that fundamental rights had not been violated (paras 15-9). In *Kapasakalis, 1998* the Court rejected the situation of several Greek nationals as purely internal. They had obtained diplomas in Greece, but never exercised their freedom of movement, and then sought damages from the Greek state for failure of having transposed Directive 89/48, after the Court had ruled to that effect in *Commission v. Greece, 1995*. The Court ruled that their situation was connected neither to the Treaty freedoms nor to scope of the Directive.

In contrast, the Court refused arguments based on the logic of purely internal situations in *Kraus, 1993*. The fact that Mr Kraus had obtained a university qualification in a member state was sufficient to establish a link to a situation governed by Community law when he applied in his home state for the authorization to bear the title he acquired by the degree (paras 15-22). In *Scholz, 1994* the Court refuted the logic of a situation being purely internal by holding that Community law applied, although the person concerned had acquired the nationality of the member state in which she lived and from which she requested a benefit. The reason was that before the nationalization the person had held the nationality of another member and made use of her right to free movement to come to the member state concerned. In short, *any* national of a member state who had made use of the freedom of workers to move and had been employed in another member state came within the scope of Community law (para. 9). This approach was corroborated in *Terhoeve, 1999* where a worker who had been posted to another member state challenged the social security contributions levied upon his return by the member state of which he was a national (para. 27). With *Wijsenbeek, 1999* the Court admitted the case of a national who returned to his own country by flight from a member state, because he had made use of his freedom to move. He could avail himself of this freedom even against the state of which he was a national (para. 22).

The Court refused to address a question relating to the freedom of workers that a national court had asked in *Grado, 1997* on a ground that seems different, though related to a matter being purely internal to a member state. In criminal proceedings involving a migrant worker, the public prosecutor had not used the regular German way of addressing a male person, namely 'Herr', for the migrant worker when he gave the written order, whereas seemingly the prosecutor did so when addressing German nationals. The Court ruled that the national court had failed to provide evidence that the court was required to apply provisions implementing Community law in criminal proceedings regarding a fine in the context of a traffic accident (paras 14-5). The case was, according to the Court, outside the Treaty's area of application (paras 13 and 15).

Transition and remainders

In the free movement of workers, the Court was also faced with a few cases that arose because of transition. *Pereira Roque, 1998* was already mentioned. It concerned the accession of the United Kingdom to the Community and the special situation of the Channel Islands in the light of accession. But even before *Pereira Roque, 1998*, the judgment in *Barr and Montrose, 1991* had dealt with a similar situation as that of the Channel Islands, namely the situation of the Isle of Man. The Court ruled that the equal treatment clause in the protocol annexed to the Act of Accession, did not preclude the general requirement of a work permit for all types of employment in the Isle of Man, even though some derogations from that requirement for specific professions had the effect that only nationals of the United Kingdom and Ireland had access to these professions (paras 15-9). *Commission v. United Kingdom (fishing licences), 1992* dealt with nationality and residence requirements that the United Kingdom applied to Spanish and Portuguese fishermen during the transitional phase following the accession of Spain and Portugal to the Community. The Court found that the nationality condition deteriorated the situation of Spanish and Portuguese fishermen in contrast to their situation before accession in so far as fishing outside British fishery limits was concerned. In that regard, the condition was therefore precluded by the standstill clause in the Act of Accession (para. 30). More generally, the freedom of establishment precluded the condition for self-employed fishermen (para. 23). The residence requirement was dealt with in the same way as in *Factortame II, 1991* (see below). In *Tsiotras, 1993* the Court ruled that a person needed to have exercised the freedom to work in another member state in order to benefit from the right to remain in the host state (para. 11). This was not the case with a Greek national who had worked in a member state before the accession of Greece, but had always remained unemployed since the accession.

Finally, for the sake of completeness *Commission v. Germany (directives), 1997* must be mentioned. In this case, the Court confirmed that Germany had infringed two directives on the right of residence, viz. Directives 90/364 and 90/365, because implementing legislation had not been adopted.

2 Establishment

Kaefer, 1990 concerned the French overseas territory in the South Pacific, French Polynesia. Two nationals of member states in vain sought permission to reside there. The Court decided that, in the absence of agreements concluded to address the free movement of workers with French Polynesia pursuant to article 135 Treaty, a freedom to work in French Polynesia could not be recognized (para. 13). As regarded the freedom of establishment and services, article 176 of Council Decision 86/283 had direct effect also in French Polynesia and was to be understood to the effect that French Polynesia's obligations were limited. French Polynesia was merely obliged not to discriminate between French citizens from metropolitan France and nationals of other member states, save for lack of reciprocity. Within that framework, French Polynesia – like any other overseas territory of the member states – had to guarantee the right effectively to pursue self-employed activities and to provide services, including the right of entry and residence (paras 16-9).

Ships and aircrafts

In *Factortame II, 1991* and later on in *Commission v. United Kingdom (ship registration), 1991* the Court dealt with the new British fishing vessel register. In essence, only British nationals or companies that were either established in the

United Kingdom or dominated by British owners were allowed to register a ship flying the flag of the United Kingdom. The Court judged that compliance with Community law was necessary, although the member states could determine the conditions for the award of flags. The analogy between granting citizenship and awarding flag was rejected (para. 27 of *Factortame II, 1991*). Since establishment meant the 'actual pursuit of an economic activity through a fixed establishment in another member state for an indefinite period' (para. 20 of *Factortame II, 1991*), the British registration requirement could affect the freedom of establishment of nationals of other member states when the vessel was a part of their economic activity of establishment (para. 30 of *Factortame II, 1991* and paras 21-4 and 31 of *Commission v. United Kingdom (ship registration), 1991*). In contrast, the mere requirement that a ship be directed from within the member state of which the ship was about to fly the flag was compatible with establishment, provided that that requirement was considered to be met by a secondary establishment receiving instructions from abroad (paras 34-5 of *Factortame II, 1991*). The restriction arising from the nationality requirement could not be justified by the Community's national quota system for fishing, as the ship registration legislation was not designed to implement that system (para. 41 of *Factortame II, 1991*). In a similar vein, the Court in *Commission v. Ireland (fishing vessels), 1991* struck down the Irish requirement for a fishing vessel owner wanting to obtain a general fishing licence to be either an Irish national or a company established in Ireland. That requirement was discriminating against nationals of other member states who owned and operated a fishing vessel registered in Ireland, because it forced them to found an Irish company to obtain a fishing licence, in contrast to Irish nationals in the same situation (paras 8-11). The freedom of establishment precluded the requirement, for the discrimination could not be justified for the same reason as in *Factortame II, 1991*. In *Commission v. France (ship registration), 1996* the Court reiterated the *Factortame II, 1991*-line of authority, since France did not contest the infringement, and added under the freedom of establishment and workers (for the latter, see above) that even when no economic activity was pursued by means of the ship to be registered, but the ship was only used for private leisure purposes establishment precluded the nationality requirements. Such leisure activities were a corollary of the freedom of establishment (paras 21-2). *Commission v. France (ship registration), 1996*, in turn, was confirmed in *Commission v. Ireland (ship registration), 1997* with regard to the corresponding requirements in Irish law. *Commission v. Greece (ship registration), 1997* again confirmed it for the corresponding Greek law. The Court added that Greece's power to requisition ships when they were needed for military purposes could lawfully be exercised with regard to any ship flying the Greek flag, irrespective of the owner's nationality. Hence, that power did not justify a requirement for ship registration related to nationality (para. 26). The *Factortame II, 1991*-line of authority was finally applied by analogy in *Commission v. Belgium (aircraft registration), 1999*. Belgium required nationals of other member states to have had residence for one year in Belgium and legal persons established in other member states to have had an establishment in Belgium for one year in order to be allowed to register an aircraft in Belgium. The Court found that the registration of an aircraft could not be dissociated from the freedom of establishment when the aircraft constituted a means to exercise an economic activity which involved an establishment in another member state. Belgium's special regime applicable to nationals of other member states and companies established there was discriminatory and impeded the freedom of establishment. Consequently, it was precluded (paras. 12-3).

Doctors

In *Commission v. Luxembourg (single practice), 1992* requirements by Luxembourg similar to those at issue in *Commission v. France (doctors), 1986* were scrutinized. In a similar way as in the latter judgment, the Court found that Luxembourg's requirement for doctors, dentists, and veterinary surgeons to have only one single practice went against the grain of the freedom of establishment and workers. Employed and self-employed practitioners were entitled to have more than one place of work in one member state. While respect for the professional rules of conduct could lawfully be required so far as necessary for protection of health, Luxembourg law was not to restrict exceptional authorizations to operate more than one practice to Luxembourg nationals (para. 15). Again, the rule proved too absolute and general in nature, as presence for continued care was not always necessary and other elements, such as replacements, would have to be factored in (paras 22-3). In *Micheletti, 1992* a dentist wanted to establish himself in Spain. Mr Micheletti held both Italian and Argentinean nationalities. Spain refused the prerequisite resident permit arguing that he had effective links only with Argentina, because he had lived there before arriving in Spain. The Court rejected that argument. While a member state was free to determine the conditions for granting nationality, it was not allowed to limit the effects of the nationality granted by another member state when a person exercised a freedom of the Treaty. More specifically, Spain was not allowed to subject the recognition of the Italian nationality of Mr Micheletti to the condition that he entertained effective links with Italy. A person's citizenship of a member state could not be challenged on the ground that that person also held the nationality of a non-member state (paras 10-4).

Purely internal situations

In *Lopez Brea, 1992* two Spanish nationals who were resident in Spain questioned certain conditions in Spanish law for the exercise of the profession of real estate agent. The Court held that the freedom of establishment did not apply, for the relevant situation was purely internal to Spain and no factor connected it to the situations governed by Community law (paras 8-9). Directive 67/43 on certain activities in self-employment, moreover, did not harmonize those conditions, but only prohibited direct and indirect discrimination. A similar constellation was at issue in *Ferrer Laderer, 1992*. The Court again did not apply the freedom of establishment, though this time because it was not applicable to a Swiss national acting as an estate agent in Spain. In *Aubertin, 1995* French nationals who had not obtained any qualification in other member states claimed that a practice of the French authorities was to be applied to them. According to that practice nationals of other member states who had worked as hairdressers in the Community were allowed to work in France, although they did not hold the prerequisite French diploma. The Court did not address the argument put forward on the basis of reverse discrimination. It did not deal with the merits, because the case was confined in all aspects to France (paras 10-1). Moreover, the profession of hairdresser was not harmonised in the Community. In a similar vein, the Court refused to address the case in *Van Buynder, 1995*. In that case, a Belgian national who had not acquired qualification abroad was subject to prosecution in Belgium for having performed some dental operations on horses without having the qualification needed in Belgium. The Court refused to hear the argument that the neighbouring countries of Belgium did not subject that activity to any qualification. The situation was in all aspects confined to Belgium (paras 11-2). In *Esso, 1995*, a Spanish company challenged the obligation contained in the local law of the Canary Islands to supply petroleum to at least four islands of the Canaries Archipelago as a condition to supply petroleum to the Islands at all. The Court declined to enter into arguments based on the freedom of establishment, for the situation was purely internal to Spain and the obligation applied indistinctly (paras 14-6).

In some contrast to this case-law on purely internal situations, the Court did apply the freedom of establishment in *Singh, 1992*. The case concerned a British national who had gone to work in Germany. She was accompanied by her husband who was a third country national. When they returned to the United Kingdom to establish themselves her husband was refused leave to enter and reside. According to the Court, a national of a member state had the right to rely on the freedom of establishment against the state of which she was national after having exercised a freedom of the Treaty. In such a case the same conditions had to apply as in the analogous situations under Regulation 1612/68, Directive 68/360, or Directive 73/148, else the national of a member state could be deterred from using her Treaty freedoms to leave her 'own' state. Abuse of rights could lawfully be counteracted though (paras 19-20). *Werner, 1993*, in contrast, was a tax case in which the Court ultimately held that the situation was purely internal to Germany. Mr Werner was a German national who was established as a dentist in Germany where he had also received his medical training. He was resident with his wife in the Netherlands. Because of his residence abroad the German authorities refused to apply the more favourable income tax regime normally available for spouses. Emphasising that the case at hand was about Germany's tax treatment of a German national, the Court did not find any issue with article 52 Treaty. The situation was confined to Germany in all aspects bar residence. The case was different from *Biehl, 1990*, *Knoors, 1979*, and *Commission v. France (tax credit), 1986* (paras 13-7).

Taxation

Wielockx, 1995 was the next tax case concerning natural persons. In this case, the Court essentially applied in the freedom of establishment the ruling in *Schumacker, 1995* which had been handed down about six months before. Mr Wielockx was established as a physiotherapist in the Netherlands while he was resident in Belgium. The Dutch authorities refused the regular deduction of sums he had used to constitute a pension reserve from his taxable income, because Mr Wielockx resided in Belgium. In line with *Schumacker, 1995*, since all of his income was earned in the state where he was working, the Court held that he had to be treated like a resident and notably benefit from the same deductions as those resident there (paras 18-22). Significantly, the *Bachmann, 1992*-justification, i. e. the need to ensure the cohesion of the tax system, did not apply. The cohesion of the Dutch tax system was guaranteed by the double taxation convention with Belgium. In that convention each of the state parties had waived the right to levy income tax on pensions paid to persons resident in the other state party. The direct link required by the *Bachmann, 1992*-ground was, therefore, not given with regard to one and the same person. The idea of tax cohesion was thus shifted from the level of the individual to the inter-state level (paras 24-5). Next, in *Asscher, 1996* a distinction established by the Netherlands' tax law was at issue. The Netherlands taxed non-residents at the rate of 25 per cent, if they generated less than 90 per cent of their income in the Netherlands, while residents, even if *less* than 90 percent of their income was generated in the Netherlands, were taxed at the rate of 13 per cent. Mr Asscher was a Dutch national resident in Belgium who pursued self-employed activities in both the Netherlands and Belgium. He earned less than 90 per cent of his world wide income in the Netherlands. The amount of income generated by his activity in the Netherlands was taxed there, the amount generated in Belgium was taxed in Belgium. In application of Regulation 1408/71 he was affiliated to the social security regime of Belgium and paid contributions there. His income in the Netherlands was taxed at the rate of 25 per cent, because he did not reside in the Netherlands. Even though Mr Asscher challenged the taxation by the state of which he was a national the Court accepted the case, because he had made use of his freedom of establishment (paras 32-3). After having reiterated the *Schumacker, 1995*-ruling, the Court held the situations of residents and non-residents to be comparable. The higher tax rate could not be based on the need for progressive taxation, since the double taxation convention between Belgium and the Netherlands provided that the entire income generated by activities within the state parties could be factored in to determine the tax rate. The situations of residents and non-residents were therefore comparable (paras 47-9). The indirect discrimination could not be justified. Where he was affiliated to the social security system was immaterial to determine the tax rate (para. 54). The *Bachmann, 1992*-ground, i. e. cohesion of the tax system, did not apply, either, since a link did not exist between the higher tax rate, viz. the disadvantage, and the fact that social security contributions were not levied on the income generated in the Netherlands, viz. the advantage (paras 59-60). The higher tax rate did not afford any additional social security protection. The allocation of powers in social security by Regulation 1408/71, moreover, was not to be counteracted by means of taxation (paras 61-2).

Official authority

Commission v. Greece (transport), 1991 concerned the alleged non-transposition of Directive 82/470, which essentially dealt with some aspects of transport and travel agencies as well as storage and warehousing. The Court decided in this case that an opinion of a traffic accident expert delivered in a court did not come within the purview of the exercise of official authority pursuant to article 55 Treaty, as in that particular case the opinion did not bind the courts (paras 6-7). In *Thijssen, 1993*, article 55 Treaty did not apply, either. The activities of an approved commissioner who supervised insurance companies was not directly and specifically connected to the exercise of official authority. Although such a commissioner held a suspensory veto over certain decisions of insurance companies, ultimately, the responsibility of supervision lay with the public authority in charge. Nationality could therefore not be a requirement for an appointment as an approved commissioner.

Names

In *Konstantinidis, 1993* a Greek national was established in Germany. Based on an international norm the German authorities translated his name from his birth certificate in Greek into Roman characters. Mr Konstantinidis claimed that the translation distorted his name. The Court ceded to that argument. While Greek names could be transcribed in principle into Roman characters, the freedom of establishment was violated when a transcription caused an established person such a degree of inconvenience that he was disadvantaged, because the pronunciation of his name was distorted and confusion as to his person was caused (paras 14-6).

Gebhard

In 1995, the Court decided the case *Gebhard, 1995*. Mr Gebhard, a German national admitted to the bar in Germany, practised law in Milano. He founded his own chambers there and mainly advised German-speaking clients in Italy and Italian clients in Germany. He was prosecuted for having practised law in Italy under the title of an Italian lawyer, without being admitted to the Italian bar. The Court first distinguished establishment from services. Establishment meant participation on a stable and continuous basis in the economic life of the host state (para. 25). In contrast, services were always temporary. Whether they were temporary was to be determined in the concrete case in the light of their duration, regularity, periodicity, and continuity. Sometimes services also involved having infrastructure in the host state (paras 26-7). Since Mr Gebhard had practised continuously for some years, the freedom of establishment applied. The fact that a professional activity was subject to admission to a professional organization in the host state did not mean that the freedom of establishment was only exercised once the person concerned had been admitted. In other words, membership in such an organization was never constitutive for the freedom of establishment (para. 31). The professional rules of the host state had to be complied with, in particular where a specific qualification or admission to an organization was required. Yet, in case national measures were liable to hinder or make less attractive the exercise of the freedom of establishment, as in the case at issue, a four-pronged test had to be applied to find out whether the obstacle was compatible with the freedom of establishment. The relevant measure had to apply indistinctly and be suitable and necessary to ensure that an imperative requirement in the general interest was attained (para. 37). Moreover, when a person was lacking the qualification of the host state, the latter had to make the comparison of qualifications required by *Vlassopoulou, 1991* (see below).

Driving licences

In *Skanavi, 1996* a Greek national had failed to exchange her Greek driving licence within one year after having taken residence in Germany, as Directive 80/1263 would have required. She and her husband were established in Germany. Shortly thereafter, the new Directive 91/439 would have removed the obligation to exchange the licence. However, although driving affected the pursuit of establishment, the obligation to exchange the driving licence before entry into force of the new directive did not contravene the freedom of establishment, since the Council had the power to harmonize driving licences progressively (para. 27). The driving licence of the host state was not constitutive of the right to drive. In analogy to the case-law as to residence permits, sanctions for having violated the obligation to exchange the licence had to be proportionate to the gravity of the infringement. The person concerned therefore was not be treated as if she did not have a valid licence at all and be subject to criminal penalties or heavy fines (para. 34-8). Apart from that, the Court saw no need to address the freedom of Union citizens to move and reside within the Union which had been newly introduced by the Maastricht Treaty in article 8a, since it found specific expression in the freedom of establishment (para. 2).

Sunday trading

Semeraro Casa Uno, 1996 then concerned the prohibition to open shops on Sundays, which was primarily addressed under the free movement of goods in keeping with the Sunday trading case-law of the Court. However, the allegations that the freedom of establishment was violated by the prohibition to trade on Sundays was rejected by the Court. The measure applied indistinctly to all traders on the national territory. Its purpose was not to regulate establishment. Any restrictive effect it might have was 'too uncertain and indirect' for the measure to hinder the exercise of the freedom (para. 32).

Non-profit

Sodemare, 1997 dealt with a requirement for the reimbursement of expenses in Italy's social security law. Only private non-profit organizations received the authorization to provide certain health care-related services, such as offering services in nursery homes. Accordingly, only their expenses were eligible for reimbursement. According to the Court, rules of the kind at issue were not affected by the exclusion of not-for-profit companies from the part of the Treaty on establishment (para. 25). A member state was free to organize its social security system and to decide that only private non-profiteers guaranteed that the social aims were attained. Italy's welfare system was based on solidarity (paras 29-2). Non-profiteers from Italy and the member states were treated alike under the Italian system (para. 33). A Luxembourg company which had established a number of for-profit companies in Italy could therefore not successfully challenge the Italian system under the freedom of establishment.

Austria

Konle, 1999 and *Beck, 1999* both concerned similar transitional issues which arose because of the accession of Austria. Since the Court found in *Konle, 1999* that the free movement of capital was violated, it was not necessary any longer for the Court to deal with the freedom of establishment (para. 55) – thus rendering the reasoning under capital applicable under establishment, at least potentially. The reasoning in *Konle, 1999* was the following. The new authorization procedure for the acquisition of secondary homes in Austria was at stake. Essentially, the procedure had been streamlined after accession to remove a second track which had applied only to nationals of other member states. The Act of Accession concerning Austria contained a clause which for five years froze the restrictions on the acquisition of secondary homes in Austria which (the restrictions) existed at the time of accession. The Court ruled that the new authorization procedure was a discriminatory restriction of the free movement of capital (para 39). Austrians notably benefitted from an accelerated procedure and the examination of the requirements to be met to be allowed to acquire a secondary home was more thorough for non-Austrians. Moreover, the authorities had considerable discretion (para. 41). Even under the assumption that the needs of town planning and of maintaining a certain amount of activities unrelated to tourism were capable of justifying such discrimination, a prior authorization scheme was unnecessary. A prior declaration scheme coupled with sanctions, such as penalties, nullity of the contract, etc., in case the requirements were not met was an alternative (para. 46-7). Since the new authorization procedure had introduced a different approach and a new procedure in comparison to the legislation existing at the time of accession, the freezing clause in the Act of Accession did not cover it (para. 53). The free movement of capital was thus violated. In contrast, in *Beck, 1999* the Court decided that certain Austrian provisions concerning fictitious or fraudulent real estate transactions constituted existing legislation covered by the freezing clause, since the various amendments of the legislative act concerned had not changed the substance of the provisions at stake (para. 36). More generally, amendments that rendered provisions less restrictive of the rights provided by Community law did not remove the amended legislation from the scope of the freezing clause (para. 34 of *Beck, 1999*; para 54 of *Konle, 1999*).

Non-discrimination

In *Saldanha, 1997* the Court essentially transposed the case-law developed under the free movement of goods for the judicial enforcement of claims related to cross-border trade in goods and transport, viz. *Data Delecta, 1996*, *Pastoors, 1997* and *Hayes, 1997*, to the freedom of establishment. When a claim that was within the scope of the Treaty, because it was related to the freedom of establishment – such as the claim of a shareholder who was a national of one member state against the company established in another member state of which he held shares – was enforced in the courts of a member state, the procedural rules applicable were not allowed to discriminate on the basis of nationality pursuant to article 6 Treaty (para. 23-4). Austrian law could notably not lawfully require claimants resident abroad who were nationals of another member state to lodge security to cover the costs of the proceedings, while Austrian nationals, irrespective of where they resided and whether they held assets in Austria, were not required to do so (paras 26 and 29). In *Commission v. Belgium (associations), 1999* article 6 Treaty was also applied in a context related to establishment. Belgian laws required for an association to be recognized as having legal personality that a minimum number of the persons involved were of Belgian nationality. In the administration of certain associations at least one person had to be Belgian and a minimum number of the members of certain associations had to be Belgian as well. The provisions concerned 'regulate[d] the right to form, in Belgium, associations with legal personality' (para. 12). Hence, the provisions concerned 'one of the fundamental freedoms guaranteed by the Treaty' (para. 12) and came within its ambit. As they discriminated on the basis of nationality, they contravened article 6 Treaty (para. 13). Advocate General Cosmas had argued that at least some of the associations concerned provided services against remuneration and thereby participated in economic life. Therefore, the freedom of establishment was concerned and the exception for non-profit companies (article 58(2) Treaty) did not apply (paras 11-4 of the opinion).

Legal persons

In *Centros, 1999* the establishment of a company by natural persons was at issue. Two Danish nationals had established a company in the United Kingdom which was to do business exclusively via a branch in Denmark. The minimum capital requirements for the establishment of a company were considerably more permissive in the United Kingdom than in Denmark. It was undisputed that the two Danish nationals wanted to profit from that advantage. The Court decided that the Danish authorities had unlawfully refused the registration of the branch.

The refusal was an obstacle to the freedom of establishment. While abuse of Community rights to circumvent national law could be prevented on a case-by-case basis, an abuse of the freedom of establishment was not to be inferred from the fact that the two Danish nationals eschewed the application of the Danish minimum requirements for the formation of a company (para. 24). The four requirements of the *Gebhard, 1995*-test were, moreover, not met. Neither the protection of creditors and the public nor the combat against fraud required the refusal to register the branch (paras 35-8).

Even before *Centros, 1999* the Court had addressed the freedom of establishment of companies in a series of decisions in the 1990s. They were as follows. In *Commerzbank, 1993* the Court found a violation of the freedom of establishment in that the United Kingdom paid interest on tax levied in excess only when the company concerned had fiscal residence in the United Kingdom. More specifically, a German company's branch that had received interest payments from loan agreements with companies in the United States and paid tax on those interests in the United Kingdom was entitled to the same supplement on the reimbursement of tax overpaid as companies having tax residence in the United Kingdom, else the German company would unlawfully be discriminated. It was irrelevant that the concrete refund of the tax overpaid was only available to non-resident companies. With *Halliburton, 1994* taxation of intra-group transfers of real estate came under scrutiny in the light of freedom of establishment. The Court decided, in essence, that the Netherlands could not lawfully limit the exemption from a tax on real estate transfers within a group to transfers between 'daughter' companies constituted as limited companies under Dutch law; rather, tax relief had to be granted equally when one of the 'daughter' companies involved in the real estate transfer was constituted as a limited company pursuant to the law of another member state and operated via a permanent establishment in the Netherlands, although the effect on the foreign company as transferor was indirect, since technically the Dutch company as transferee was liable for the tax (paras 17-20). In *Commission v. Italy (securities dealing), 1996* the Court invalidated Italy's requirement of companies to be established in Italy in order to be authorized to deal in securities. Operation via a branch or an agency had to be allowed, though it could be subjected to certain requirements, such as financial guarantees, checks, etc. (paras 20-4). The requirement was thus contrary to the freedom of establishment and services. *Futura, 1997* sanctioned Luxembourg's approach to profit taxation which limited the carrying forward to those losses by branches in Luxembourg which had an economic link to the profits generated and subject to profit taxation in Luxembourg. It was in keeping with fiscal territoriality and did not give rise to discrimination (para. 22). The effectiveness of fiscal supervision did not justify the requirement to keep separate book accounts in Luxembourg, though. Other means had to be admitted to prove losses.

In *ICI, 1998* legislation of the United Kingdom was found to violate the freedom of establishment, because the setting-off of losses incurred by a subsidiary held by a holding which was in turn held by a consortium was allowed for a partner in the consortium who was subject to taxation in the United Kingdom only when the majority of subsidiaries controlled by the holding was established in the United Kingdom. With *Royal Bank of Scotland, 1999* the Court ruled, relying on *Asscher, 1996*, that a tax rate that was sometimes higher for the profits of the Greek branches of companies established in other member states than for the profits of companies established in Greece was contrary to the freedom of establishment. In *Pfeiffer, 1999* the Court decided that the lawful protection of a trade name in Austria justified a restriction of the freedom of establishment. The German company that was lawfully using the term 'Plus' in Germany had to accept that it could not lawfully use that term in Austria due to a risk of confusion with a trade name lawfully protected in Austria and had to put up with the resulting hindrances, such as changes in its corporate identity for the Austrian market. In *Baxter, 1999* it was only the cost of research conducted in France that was factored out of the calculation of a special levy payable by companies producing medicinal products. According to the Court, the cost of research done in another member state by a company established there which had a secondary place of business in France had to be treated in the same way as research conducted in France, else indirect discrimination contrary to the freedom of establishment arose (paras 12-3).

In *Saint-Gobain, 1999* the Court declared incompatible with the freedom of establishment that Germany granted certain tax concessions – which were designed to avoid that dividends received from companies established abroad which had been taxed abroad were taxed again in Germany (para. 24) – to companies established in Germany, while it denied them to the permanent establishments in Germany of companies established in other member states. In *X and Y, 1999* the Court decided that a distinction in Swedish tax law for the purpose of tax relief violated the freedom of establishment. Swedish tax law distinguished between certain intra-group transfers depending on whether the seats of the subsidiaries concerned by the transfer were in a single member state other than Sweden or in several other member states other than Sweden. According to the Court, such a distinction entailed a difference in treatment according to the subsidiaries' seats which was not justified.

Technicalities

In the interest of completeness, a number of further cases which mostly concerned rather technical details of secondary legislation must be mentioned. *Commission v. Greece (vehicles), 1993* was about car imports and the compatibility of the Greek system with certain directives, namely Directives 83/182, 83/183, and 73/148. The Court found that the Greek practice of stamping the passport with the number of the vehicle imported so that it could be tracked how long the vehicle was in Greece complied with the free movement of persons as implemented by article 2(1) and 3(1) Directive 73/148 (paras. 34-8). In *Commission v. United Kingdom (TV broadcasting), 1996*, the Court essentially applied the concept of establishment under the 'television without frontiers' directive, i. e. Directive 89/552 (para. 42). The Court rejected an argument based on the freedom of establishment made by the United Kingdom in the context of that directive (paras 57-8). *RTI, 1996* and *Denuit, 1997* applied the provisions of Directive 89/552 without any further elaboration on the freedom of establishment. In *VT4, 1997* the Court confirmed *Commission v. United Kingdom (TV broadcasting), 1996* and implicitly rejected the argument that the establishment in one member state with the aim of broadcasting exclusively towards another member state under Directive 89/552 necessarily constituted an abuse of a Treaty freedom. In *Kontogeorgas, 1996* and *Bellone, 1998* the Court applied the directive on self-employed commercial agents, Directive 86/653. In *France v. Commission (pension funds), 1997* the Court found that the Commission could not lawfully issue a Communication containing new rights and duties just because the negotiations in the Council in the topic concerned, namely pension funds, had been deadlocked. The freedom of establishment, services, and capital did not necessarily contain the obligations to be laid down in secondary legislation (paras 20-4).

Secondary law as to companies and further technicalities

A series of judgments concerned the secondary law of the Community adopted to implement the freedom of establishment of companies. *Marleasing, 1990* dealt with the First Council Directive 68/151. (The judgment also established some limited horizontal direct effect of Directives.) So did *Daihatsu, 1997* and *Rabobank, 1997*. *Karella, 1991*, *Sindesmos Melon, 1992*, *Kerafina, 1992*, *Siemens, 1996*, and *Kefalas, 1998* all concerned the Second Council Directive 77/91. In *Pafitis, 1996*, the Court *inter alia* rejected again in the context of Directive 77/91 an argument by analogy based on the *Bachmann, 1992*-justification of the cohesion of the tax system which (the argument) had been made to defend the appointment of a temporary administrator for a failing bank in order to save the cohesion of Greece's banking system (paras 47-52). *Tomberger, 1996* and *DE + ES Bauunternehmung, 1999* interpreted the Fourth Council Directive 78/660. *Les Assurances du crédit, 1991* rejected a claim for damages based on the exclusion of certain public export credit insurances from the scope of the direct insurance directive, i. e. Directive 73/239 as amended by Directive 87/343. In *Skandia, 1999* the Court again interpreted the third non-life insurance directive, i. e. Directive 73/239 as amended, and moreover the third life assurance directive, i. e. Directive 79/267 as amended. *Commission v. France (mutual societies), 1999* confirmed that France had not fully implemented those two directives. In *Germany v. Parliament and Council (deposit guarantee), 1997* the Court in essence held that Directive 94/19 on deposit-guarantee schemes had been lawfully adopted on the basis of article 57(2) Treaty and that the Directive did not violate that article or the principle of proportionality (paras 41-4). In *EITO, 1997* Regulation 2137/85 on the European Economic Interest Grouping was interpreted.

Diploma

The establishment case-law concerning diploma recognition in the 1990s began with *Bouchoucha, 1990* and *Nino, 1990*. In *Bouchoucha, 1990*, the Court addressed the situation of a French national who had obtained the qualification necessary to practice osteopathy in the United Kingdom. He was prosecuted in France later on though for having practised as an osteopath, a practice which France reserved to qualified medical doctors. According to the Court, a definition of a medical act did not exist on the Community level. The member states were therefore free to define that term, subject to non-discrimination (para. 12). The British diploma held by Mr Bouchoucha was, moreover, not the subject of mutual recognition under Community legislation. France could legitimately prevent evasion of its provisions on professional training when the practice in question was reserved to doctors whose qualification in turn enjoyed mutual recognition (para. 15). In *Nino, 1990* the Court rejected a situation as purely internal, given that the Italian nationals concerned had obtained a diploma in Italy and then practised bio- and pranotherapy there, although Italian legislation allowed only qualified medical doctors to practice that kind of therapy (para. 10).

In *Vlassopoulou, 1991* the Court then established based on *Heylens, 1987* the approach to be applied when a type of qualification was not harmonized and hence not the object of express mutual recognition. In *Vlassopoulou, 1991* a Greek lawyer sought admission to the German bar. In that situation a member state had the power to lay down the conditions a person had to meet to be allowed to exercise the profession concerned. However, a member state was required to compare objectively the abilities and the knowledge acquired by the person concerned in another member state as it was evidenced by diplomas with the knowledge and abilities its own legislation required (paras. 15-6). Only if the knowledge and qualification evidenced by diploma and practice were not equivalent was the member state concerned allowed to require additional proof of abilities and knowledge, i. e. impose an exam or a practice period. If they were equivalent, the freedom of establishment required the member state to recognize the qualifications (paras 17 and 19). Differences in legal systems could be factored into the objective comparison required (para. 18). Finally, judicial proceedings had to be made available to challenge the decision adopted concerning recognition. The approach of *Vlassopoulou, 1991* was fully confirmed in *Borrell, 1992* in the context of Directive 67/43 concerning real estate agents. The Court added merely that a failure to seek verification of a diploma could entail criminal sanctions (para. 19).

In *Commission v. Italy (health care auxiliaries), 1991* the Court confirmed that Italy had failed to fulfil its obligations under the freedoms of establishment, workers, and services in that it restricted the recognition of professional qualifications obtained in other member states in the domain of health-care auxiliaries to Italian nationals or subjected it to a condition of reciprocity. Italy in essence did not dispute the infringement (paras 8-11). In *Egle, 1992* the Court interpreted Directive 85/384 on diplomas in architecture to the effect that it covered a diploma obtained from an institute of technology, namely a 'Fachhochschule' in Germany, after four years of studies including integrated practical semesters (paras 9-14). According to *Bauer, 1992* the same interpretation applied for transitional cases, i. e. when the studies had been begun before the directive became applicable (para. 12). In *Dreessen, 1994* the Court held, in contrast, that the transitional arrangement under Directive 85/384 did not cover an engineer's diploma in general construction (paras 9-13).

In *Tawil-Albertini, 1994*, the Court decided in the context of Directives 78/686 and 78/687 on diploma and activities in dentistry that a diploma in dentistry awarded in a non-member state need not have been recognized by a member state even when another member state had previously recognized it as equivalent. The reason was that the minimum training requirements established by Directive 78/687 did not apply in relation to third states. On the same day, the Court in *Haim, 1994* gave essentially the same answer in the case of an Italian national who had obtained a diploma in dentistry in Turkey which had subsequently been recognized as equivalent in Belgium and who then sought recognition in Germany (paras 16-7 and 21). The Court, in addition, confirmed the approach developed in *Vlassopoulou, 1991* (para. 28). In *Commission v. Italy (dentists), 1995* the Court invalidated Italy's implementation of the two Directives that were already at stake in *Tawil-Albertini, 1994*. In violation of the Directives Italy had created a special category of dentists for a transitional period; the dentists within that category were allowed pursuant to Italian law to practice in Italy, but not in other member states (paras 23-4). In *Commission v. Spain (doctors), 1994* the Court held that Spain had to provide adequate remuneration under Directives 75/362 and 75/363 on recognition of diplomas in medicine and activities of doctors, respectively, for the periods of training necessary to obtain a qualification in a medical specialty. In the case at issue the specialty was 'stomatology'.

After having formally confirmed that Greece had failed fully to transpose Directive 89/48 on a general system of recognition for the award of higher-education diplomas in *Commission v. Greece, 1995*, the Court in *Aranitis, 1996* defined the term 'regulated profession' and thus the scope of that Directive. According to the Court, whenever the host state 'create[d] a system under which that professional activity [wa]s expressly reserved to those who fulfil[led] certain conditions and access to it [wa]s prohibited to those who d[id] not fulfil them' (para. 19), then a profession was regulated. Whether that was the case depended on the legal situation rather than on the conditions prevailing on the employment market (para. 23). The profession of 'Diplom-Geologe' (graduate geologist) in Germany which was at stake in *Aranitis, 1996* was not regulated in the sense explained, neither directly nor indirectly. Hence, instead of the Directive only the general approach based on *Vlassopoulou, 1991* was applicable (paras 31-2). In the year 1996, the Court also confirmed that Italy had violated Directive 85/432 on activities in pharmacy in *Commission v. Italy (pharmacy studies), 1996* by unilaterally extending the time period for transposition and allowing those pharmacy students who had commenced their university studies during that extended period to read for a diploma in pharmacy which would not benefit from mutual recognition under Directive 85/433 on recognition of diplomas in pharmacy (paras 12-4).

In *Garofalo, 1997* the Court interpreted the transitional provision of Directive 93/16 which had incorporated the transitional provision of Directive 86/457 on doctors' diplomas to the effect that it guaranteed acquired rights of doctors established in general medical practice under Directive 75/362 even if they had not entered into a service relationship at the end of the transitional period (paras. 30-3); beyond that minimum requirement, though, the member states had discretion to recognize acquired rights in other situations (para. 34). In *Fédération Belge, 1998* the Court accepted that under Directive 93/16, which had codified Directives 75/362 and 75/363 on doctors' diplomas and activities, respectively as well as incorporated Directive 86/457 on training in general medical practice, a person need not have a basic diploma in medicine before commencing training in general medical practice. Indeed, the member states had discretion to allow that training to begin before the award of a basic diploma (paras 28 and 36-7).

In *De Castro, 1998* the Court again after *Van de Bijl, 1989* dealt with certificates issued under Dir. 64/427 concerning some activities of self-employed persons in manufacturing and processing industries. A certificate issued by a member state which confirmed that a person had pursued several activities simultaneously was not, according to the Court, to be interpreted by another member state in the sense that the person concerned had pursued only one activity, else the binding nature of such certificates and, as a consequence, the freedom of establishment as well as services would be disregarded (paras 23-4 and 31-4).

Carbonari, 1999 dealt with the adequate remuneration for trainees in specialties in medicine under Directives 75/362 and 75/363 which had already been at issue in *Commission v. Spain (doctors), 1994*. As the provisions concerning remuneration were not unconditional, notably as to the body liable to pay the remuneration, they could not be applied directly after Italy had failed to transpose them properly (paras 38-47). If *interpretation conforme* of national legislation was not possible, Italy would be liable for damages, subject to the regular conditions of liability (paras 48-53). *De Bobadilla, 1999* once more concerned the interpretation of the term 'regulated profession' in Directive 89/48 and Directive 92/51. The Court decided that a nationwide practice, followed on the basis of collective agreements concluded by the social partners, possibly implied that a profession was 'regulated' (paras 20 and 22). Nonetheless, a single agreement concluded by one employer with its employees would not amount to 'regulation' (para. 23). In any event, if the Directive did not apply for want of a regulated profession, the *Vlassopoulou, 1991*-approach had to be applied, if necessary by the public body acting as a potential employer itself when a national procedure for validation did not exist (paras 34-5). The Court also reiterated that this approach had to be applied by a state to its own nationals who had obtained a diploma in another member state (para. 30). Finally, for the sake of completeness *Commission v. Italy, 1991* and *Commission v. France, 1999* must be mentioned. In *Commission v. Italy, 1991* the Court confirmed that Italy had failed to transpose Directive 85/384 concerning architects. In *Commission v. France, 1999* the Court confirmed that France had failed to transpose the articles amending Directives 78/1026 and 78/1027 concerning veterinary surgeons. Neither Italy nor France had disputed the substance of the Commission's allegations.

3 Social Security

Scope and definitions

A large number of judgments in the 1990s clarified the scope of the social security rules of the Community. *Buhari Haji, 1990* dealt with a British national who had been subject to Belgian social security for his work in the Belgian Congo and who had later on acquired the nationality of Nigeria. Such a person was not within the scope *ratione personae*, because the United Kingdom had not joined the European Community yet when he had worked in the Belgian Congo. At that point in time he did not hold a nationality of a member state. When the United Kingdom joined the Community he was not any longer subject to Belgian social security, because he was not working in the Belgian Congo any more and he did not hold the nationality of the United Kingdom (para. 19). Hence, the necessary link between the person concerned and the free movement of workers was missing (para. 22). Moreover, the Act of Accession did not contain any provision that declared Regulation 1408/71 applicable in such a case (para. 23). Conditions that required reciprocal rights in a convention and nationality of or residence in a member state of the Community were therefore not precluded.

Social security v. assistance

In *Newton, 1991*, the Court again applied the distinction established between social security and social assistance to a British mobility allowance. That allowance was a flat-rate, not means tested cash benefit granted on a weekly basis which was subject to a residence requirement. Given that the benefit fulfilled a dual function, namely of supplementing the income of handicapped persons subject to social security and of ensuring that those who were entirely outside the social security system had an income (paras 14-5), the Court drew a distinction. The mobility allowance only constituted a social security benefit within the meaning of Regulation 1408/71, an invalidity benefit to be more specific, when it was granted to persons who had not been subject exclusively to the legislation of another member state, else the stability of the social security system of the United Kingdom could be seriously affected (paras 16-8). As a consequence in those cases only, a residence condition was precluded by article 10(1) Regulation 1408/71. In *Hughes, 1992* the Court categorized the United Kingdom's family credit as a family benefit within the ambit *ratione materiae* of the Regulation 1408/71. Although need was a criterion for the award of the benefit, the authorities did not have any discretion in their decision to take into account the applicant's personal circumstances other than asset, income, and number and age of the children. Moreover, at least one of the functions of the benefit was to help a worker meet family expenses (paras 17-20). In *Commission v. Luxembourg (childbirth benefit), 1993*, the Court held that Luxembourg's non-contributory maternity allowance was to be categorised as a maternity benefit under article 4(1)(a) Regulation 1408/71 even before Regulation 1408/71 had been amended, because it was based on a legally defined right and the authorities did not make any individual and discretionary assessment of the personal needs (paras 30-2).

Conventions with third states

Grana-Novoa, 1993 concerned the scope of the term 'legislation' pursuant to article 1(j) Regulation 1408/71. The Court decided that social security conventions concluded with third states could not be considered as 'legislation'. Since Regulation 1408/71 regulated expressly conventions between the member states in articles 6-8, it would not be logical to assume that the Regulation covered conventions concluded by one member state with third states although it did not address such conventions expressly. Hence, the principles governing conventions between the member states could not be applied to a convention between a single member state and a third state. Equal treatment did not apply to it, either. The incorporation of such a convention into domestic law by statute was irrelevant in that regard (paras 22-7). Ms Grana-Novoa thus could not successfully challenge certain conditions contained in a convention between Germany and Switzerland, *inter alia* a nationality condition, to have insurance periods completed in Switzerland taken into account in Germany.

Further scope

In *Zinnecker, 1993* the situation of a person who was self-employed in the Netherlands and at the same time in Germany where he also resided came to the Court. The person concerned was not affiliated with any social security system. In Germany, old age insurance was voluntary for self-employed persons and he did not join the scheme. in the Netherlands, it was subject to a residence requirement. The Court held that it was sufficient in such a situation to bring a self-employed person within the scope of Regulation 1408/71, if the person was merely subject to one of the two relevant legal systems (para. 10). As the definition of self-employed persons for the Netherlands contained in annex I.I did not mention residence as a requirement to have the status of a self-employed person, a person like Mr Zinnecker came within the scope *ratione personae* of the Regulation (paras 12-3). In *Van Poucke, 1994* the Court held that a person employed by the army as a professional doctor who was subject to the general compulsory sickness and invalidity insurance scheme in Belgium was covered by Regulation 1408/71. Civil servants were included *ratione personae* according to article 2(3) Regulation 1408/71. The scheme was not 'special' (article 4(4) Regulation 1408/71). It was sufficient to be affiliated only to one branch of a social security system constituting 'legislation' within the scope of Regulation 1408/71 (paras. 7-10). In *Rheinhold & Mahla, 1995* the Court excluded a particular part of a legislative act from the scope of Regulation 1408/71. Dutch law had introduced one single, harmonized social security contribution for all risks. The law also included the liability of a contractor established in another state for the social security contributions its sub-contractor in the Netherlands had failed to pay. While Regulation 1408/71 encompassed social security schemes in their entirety, i. e. including coordinating and overarching provisions, according to the Court, the specific provision had to be examined to find out whether it was within the scope of Regulation 1408/71. The provision at stake addressed only a question of liability of a third party established in another member state for contributions that had not been paid by a domestic party. For lack of a direct and sufficiently relevant link between the provision concerned and the risks regulated by Regulation 1408/71 such legislation did not come within the scope of the Regulation, save where fraud by the contractor was involved (paras 26-31).

In *Otte, 1996* the Court found that an adaptation allowance for miners which was designed to bridge unemployment periods until retirement age was reached combined elements of unemployment benefits and old-age benefits. However, a sufficient link between the benefit and either unemployment or old age was not given so that it did not fall within the ambit *ratione materiae* of Regulation 1408/71. The benefit was in essence a measure of employment policy (para. 31). To include it in Regulation 1408/71 would have the consequence that the benefit would be reduced in most cases, because the pro rata calculation would become applicable (para. 34).

Scope and applicable legislation

In *Kits van Heijningen, 1990* and *Daalmeijer, 1991* questions of both scope and applicable legislation were raised. In *Kits van Heijningen, 1990*, first, persons who worked only part-time were held to be 'employed persons' within the scope of the Regulation 1408/71. Since no provision of the Regulation 1408/71 relied on the period of working time, a person who worked only for two hours on each of two days of the week was also an 'employed person' (para. 10). As Mr Kits van Heijningen resided in another member state than where he was employed in part-time, article 13(2)(a) determined the legislation of the member state of employment as applicable. That legislation, although it lawfully established the conditions of insurance affiliation, was not to include two points, namely first that a person who was part-time employed was only subject to that legislation during the days he actually worked, but not during the days he did not work (para. 14); second, that a person was only subject to an insurance scheme, if he had residence in the state concerned, else the legislation would have the effect of excluding persons from its scope to which it in fact had to apply pursuant to article 13(2)(a) Regulation 1408/71. That article had the effect of replacing a residence requirement in national law with the requirement to be employed in the member state concerned (paras 20-1).

Ceasing occupation

Daalmeijer, 1991 stood in some contrast to *Kits van Heijningen, 1990*. It concerned the situation of a civil servant who moved residence to another member state only after he had definitely ceased his occupational activities. The Court ruled that, while such a person was within the scope *ratione personae* of the Regulation 1408/71 as a former civil servant, the title on the applicable legislation did not contain any provision that applied to a person who had definitively ceased any occupational activity (paras 12-3). A residence requirement for the affiliation with the social security scheme of the state where the person had worked and resided before was therefore not excluded (para. 14). *Noij, 1991* repeated the interpretation that title II of Regulation 1408/71 did not declare any legislation applicable to persons who had definitely ceased employment. (For the consideration of title III in *Noij, 1991*, see below.) So did *Commission v. Netherlands (early retirement), 1991*. In this latter case the Court ruled that a residence clause for family benefits was not precluded when these benefits were claimed by persons in early retirement, because title II and articles 73 et seq. Regulation 1408/71 did not apply to persons who had definitively ceased any occupational activity. That was the case even if such persons were still insured pursuant to national law, because such continued insurance was not the consequence of the application of article 13(2)(a) Regulation 1408/71 (paras 10-3). (The Court did not take into account a second argument based on indirect discrimination, because the Commission had advanced it too late in the infringement proceedings.)

In *Twomey, 1992* a similar problem as in *Ten Holder, 1986* was raised: was a person who quit employment in the United Kingdom and moved residence to Ireland still a worker capable of claiming sickness benefits under article 19 Regulation 1408/71, if she fell ill before beginning to work in Ireland? Based on *Ten Holder, 1986*, and *Noij, 1991* the Court ruled that such a person continued to be subject to the legislation of the member state of employment for the purpose of sickness benefits until she definitively ceased employment. Given that she would still have been able to claim sickness benefits in the United Kingdom had she only maintained residence there, she had a claim to sickness benefits in kind pursuant to article 19 Regulation 1408/71 in Ireland after having moved residence. That approach was not at odds with the system of limited exportability of unemployment benefits and concomitant sickness benefits under Regulation 1408/71 (para. 15). In *Commission v. France (pension deductions), 1992* a similar issue as in *Commission v. Belgium (pension deductions I), 1985* was brought up, viz. the deduction of sickness insurance contributions from pensions, but this time it concerned supplementary, rather than statutory pensions. The Court judged that the principle that only one legislation was to be applied at a time to one person pursuant to article 13(1) Regulation 1408/71 was not applicable, again because pensioners had definitively ceased any occupational activity and accordingly were not covered by any of the situations regulated by articles 13(2) to 17 Regulation 1408/71 (paras 13-4). Article 33 Regulation 1408/71 which regulated deductions from pensions for sickness insurance purposes, in turn, did not apply, because the supplementary pensions were based mainly on collective agreements which did not constitute legislation within the meaning of article 1(j) Regulation 1408/71 (paras 19-20). This decision was followed-up by *Commission v. Belgium (pension deductions II), 1992* in which the Court ruled in identical terms for the corresponding situation in Belgium. The ruling that collective agreements were not 'legislation' even if they had been rendered compulsory was later on confirmed by *Commission v. France (pension points), 1998* (paras 34-5).

In *Kuusijärvi, 1998* the Court addressed the gap that *Ten Holder, 1986* had uncovered and which was supposedly filled by an amendment of Regulation 1408/71 in article 13(2)(f). According to this article a person who had ceased any activity became subject to the legislation of the state of residence. *Kuusijärvi, 1998* raised the question whether a woman who became unemployed in Sweden, gave birth to a child, and then moved residence to Finland could be prevented from claiming a parental benefit in Sweden by a residence clause. After having held that Regulation 1408/71 applied to a person who was receiving unemployment benefits when the Agreement on the European Economic Area entered into force (para. 22), the Court decided that a distinction was not inherent in article 13(2)(f) as to whether a person ceased all employment definitively or only temporarily. If the person ceased employment, then the legislation of the state of residence simply applied, in this case Finnish legislation (paras 39-41). A residence clause in the law of the state where the person had been employed previously was therefore not precluded by article 13(2)(f), in contrast to article 13(2)(a) as established in *Kits van Heijningen, 1990* (paras 32-33). Article 13(2)(f) was the fallback provision, if no other provision determined the legislation applicable (para. 34). A residence clause in Swedish law was not precluded by articles 73 or 74 Regulation 1408/71, either. True, those articles covered the parental benefit at issue, as it was a family benefit according to *Hoever and Zachow, 1996* (see below) allowing the parents to devote themselves to raising the child and substituting for a loss of income. However, those articles did not apply in the case at hand, because the person concerned had never been subject to the legislation of a state other than the state where she had resided as a consequence of the application of article 13(2)(f) (para. 71). Hence, the Swedish residence requirement was not precluded.

Derived rights

The Court also developed the approach that family members could only claim rights derived from migrant workers in a series of judgments in the 1990s. In *Taghavi, 1992* the Court re-applied established case-law. As a Belgian benefit for a handicapped person was based on a personal right of the worker and as third country nationals who were spouses of Belgian nationals could not claim such a benefit in Belgium, a third country national who was the spouse of migrant worker could not claim such a benefit, either, under articles 2 and 3 Regulation 1408/71 (paras 8-9). This approach was confirmed in *Schmid, 1993* for a migrant worker's descendant who had never worked, was disabled and dependent on the migrant worker, and claimed a disability allowance in Belgium. The descendant of the migrant worker was precluded from relying on articles 2 and 3 Regulation 1408/71 to claim the allowance, because she only enjoyed derived rights (paras 10-2). In contrast, in *Hughes, 1992* a non-working spouse of a migrant worker could claim the family credit the Court had categorised as a family benefit within the scope of Regulation 1408/71 in the same judgment (see above). The Court decided that the spouse of a worker had a derived right to a family benefit under article 73 Regulation 1408/71 when the worker fulfilled the conditions in that article and the benefit was provided for family members under national law (paras 25-7).

With *Cabanis-Issarte, 1996* the Court put the derived rights-approach into a new perspective. Ms Cabanis-Issarte sought to rely on non-discrimination to be allowed to pay-in voluntarily past old-age insurance periods at the same rate as Dutch nationals. She was not a migrant worker herself, but had always accompanied her husband who had been a migrant worker before he had died. The Court expressly limited the derived rights-approach to unemployment benefits as they had been at issue in *Kermaschek, 1976* (paras 24 and 34) in spite of the case-law that had extended it to other benefits. The Court discussed a whole series of arguments, but the essential points were (i) that the free movement of workers would have been hindered, if the derived rights-approach had applied in the circumstances of the case at issue (para. 30); (ii) that the member states would have been in a position to undermine the uniformity of Community law by designating certain benefits as personal and thereby exclude them from Regulation 1408/71 (para. 31) and (iii) that the derived rights-approach would have led to a split within one and the same person regarding the scheme of one and the same member state, because certain of her periods of insurance would have been treated as giving rise to personal acquired rights while others would not have for being only derived rights (para. 32). Moreover, in the specific case of Ms Cabanis-Issarte, she wanted to supplement periods of compulsory insurance she had acquired while accompanying her husband (paras 41-2). Hence, according to the Court, equal treatment pursuant to article 3 Regulation 1408/71 applied with the consequence that the same rate had to be applied to the voluntary insurance contributions. In *Hoever and Zachow, 1996* the Court next affirmed that the derived rights-approach applied only to unemployment benefits as held in *Kermaschek, 1976*, but not to family benefits such as the child-raising allowance in the case at hand (para. 33). That allowance was a family benefit as it was designed to meet family expenses (para. 23). It would have deterred migrant workers, if the benefit could have been made subject to a residence requirement for family members (paras 34-6). In addition, it was not tenable to examine single family members in isolation of the family circumstances to determine entitlement to such a family benefit (para. 37). Spouses who were not employed persons could therefore lawfully claim the allowance under article 73 Regulation 1408/71.

Special non-contributory benefits, social assistance

In *Snares, 1997* the Court dealt for the first time with the amended articles 4(2a) and 10a Regulation 1408/71. These amendments were introduced to regulate special non-contributory benefits which had the characteristics of both social security and social assistance and had been categorized by the Court's case-law as social security benefits. Article 10a, in particular, exempted that kind of benefit from exportability, i. e. from the waiver of residence clauses. In *Snares, 1997*, the Court classed the British disability living allowance which had a mobility and a care component as such a special non-contributory benefit, for it was listed in Annex IIa. The sanctioning of residence clauses by article 10a Regulation 1408/71 did not go against the grain of article 51 Treaty. The special non-contributory benefits covered by article 10a Regulation 1408/71 were closely linked to the particular social and economic context where they were granted (para. 43). Hence, article 10a was not invalid. *Partridge, 1998* essentially confirmed *Snares, 1997*. It only added that persons who had been awarded the precursor of the British disability living allowance before entry into force of the amendment of Regulation 1408/71 by articles 4(2a) and 10a were still entitled to benefit from exportability (para. 39).

Farming

In *Meints, 1997* the Court decided that a Dutch benefit was not within the scope *ratione materiae* of Regulation 1408/71. The benefit was provided when farm workers were dismissed, because a farming business set aside arable land. Such a benefit did not address the risk of unemployment covered by Regulation 1408/71. The benefit did not replace the remuneration the worker lost and contribute to his maintenance. It was not recurrent, but a lump sum payment. It had to be repaid in case of re-employment. It did not vary depending on the duration of unemployment. And it cushioned the structural reorganization necessary because of Community legislation (paras. 29-33).

(Not) purely internal situations

In *Petit, 1992*, the Court applied the notion of a situation being purely internal to a member state in circumstances concerning Regulation 1408/71. Mr Petit alleged discrimination in violation of articles 48 and 51 Treaty as well as Regulation 1408/71 in an action against the Belgian pension office, because he was not entitled to submit his claim in French. Since Mr Petit was a Belgian national and all circumstances were confined to Belgium the said articles did not, however, apply to the case at hand (paras 8-9). In *Kulzer, 1998*, the Court applied

Regulation 1408/71 to a retired German civil servant who had never himself made use of his freedom. He had spent his entire working life in Bavaria. However, the fact that he claimed children allowance with regard to his daughter who lived in France was enough to render Regulation 1408/71 applicable (paras 27-30). Apart from that, the Regulation applied to civil servants as well as pensioners, and consequently to retired civil servants (paras 24-6).

Monopoly, periods of insurance

The scope of the social security rules was, in a certain sense, also at issue in *José García, 1996*. According to that judgment, the national statutory social security schemes, including those governed by Regulation 1408/71, did not come within the scope of the third non-life insurance Directive 92/49, because to apply that Directive would have meant to break up the monopoly of the state with regard to those schemes and to jeopardize the solidarity and the compulsory contributions on which the social security schemes were based (para. 14). Lastly, *Vella, 1990* should be mentioned. It was only summarily published. In this case the Court apparently reiterated *Murru, 1972* in that, subject to articles 48 to 51 Treaty, the national legislation under which a period had been completed exclusively determined the criteria to be fulfilled for that period to be treated as a period of insurance under Regulation 3 and Regulation 1408/71.

Applicable legislation

In a number of further judgments the Court dealt with the legislation applicable to certain facts. *De Paep, 1991* concerned the situation where a person residing in Belgium was employed by a Belgian undertaking. The person worked aboard a ship flying the flag of the United Kingdom. According to article 14(2)(c) Regulation 1408/71 the applicable legislation was the legislation of the state of employment, i. e. Belgian legislation in the case at issue. In such a situation, Belgian law was not to require for a survivor's benefit that the ship concerned flew the Belgian flag, because in keeping with *Kits van Heijningen, 1990* the requirements of an insurance system were not to be such that they excluded persons to whom the system should apply pursuant to the determination of the applicable legislation under Regulation 1408/71 (para. 19). The same applied to national provisions concerning the nullity of a contract of employment in so far as they had the effect of preventing the conflict rules from applying (para. 20). In *Maitland Toosey, 1994* the Court ruled that when it came to invalidity benefits the state was competent whose legislation was applicable when the invalidity occurred. According to the regular rule in article 13(2)(a) Regulation 1408/71 that was the legislation of the member state of employment. A subsequent change of residence did not change anything in that regard, even if the person went back to the member state where she had originally come from. In particular, it did not render article 71(i)(b)(ii) Regulation 1408/71 applicable (paras 13-6). The authorities of the state where the person has moved to merely needed to forward the application to the state whence she had come from (paras 22-4).

In *Van Poucke, 1994* the Court clarified which legislation was applicable to a person who was employed in Belgium and at the same time pursued a self-employed activity in the Netherlands. The Court decided that the legislation of the member state where the person was employed was also applicable pursuant to article 14c(1)(a) Regulation 1408/71 to the self-employed activity pursued abroad, as if that activity had been pursued in the member state of employment. That the applicable rules were limited by Regulation 1408/71 to certain branches of social security with regard to the activity as an employed person, did not have an impact on the application of the rules regarding the self-employed activity (para. 25).

In *Aldewereld, 1994* the Court had to determine the legislation applicable in a case Regulation 1408/71 did not address. Mr Aldewereld was resident in the Netherlands and was employed by a German company which posted him to a third state. Given that there was a sufficiently close link between the employment and the Community as required by *Prodest, 1984* in that a national of one member state was employed by a company in another member state, the application of Regulation 1408/71 was not per se excluded (para. 14). Having discarded the option for the worker to chose the legislation applicable, the Court fell back on the idea underlying title II of Regulation 1408/71 that the law of the member state of residence only applied, if some professional activity was also pursued there. Hence, the Court opted for the law of the member state where the company was established which employed Mr Aldewereld (paras 22-5).

In *Calle, 1995* a worker was employed by a company in Germany, while the worker was resident in Denmark. The worker also performed in Denmark regular activities on a minor scale on behalf of his German employer. As those activities in Denmark extended beyond twelve months, he was not a posted worker pursuant to article 14(1)(a) Regulation 1408/71. Instead, the legislation of the member state where he was resident fell to be applied. Article 14(2)(b)(i) Regulation 1408/71 also covered the case when an employee pursued an activity in several states on behalf of one and the same employer (paras 13 and 18). With *De Jaeck, 1997* one of the few situations in which two legislations were applicable at the same time to one and the same person came before the Court. Article 14c(1)(b) Regulation 1408/71 in conjunction with Annex VII point 1 provided that a person who was employed in a member state other than Luxembourg and who pursued at the same time a self-employed activity in Belgium was to be subject to two legislations, one for each activity. The Court decided that the terms 'employed person' and 'self-employed person' had to be defined by the applicable national social security law, as indicated by articles 1(a) and 2(1) Regulation 1408/71. To be consistent, the terms used in articles 14a and 14c Regulation 1408/71, i. e. 'persons who are employed' and 'persons who are self-employed', equally needed to be determined by national social security law (paras 22 and 30). That interpretation was not at variance with the definition of a worker by Community law under article 48 Treaty (para. 28). It was, moreover, confirmed on the same day as *De Jaeck, 1997* had been handed down in the judgment

Hervein I, 1997. In *De Jaeck, 1997*, the Court, in addition, went on to hold that Article 14c(1)(b) Regulation 1408/71 did not prevent a member state from insuring a person merely against some of the risks governed by the Regulation. Yet, each member state could only levy contributions on the part of the income generated in its territory when two legislations applied.

Aggregation

During the 1990s the Court elaborated its case-law as to aggregation in more than 40 judgments. In two cases, *Pian, 1990* and *Bianchin, 1990*, the Court merely reiterated the calculation principles pursuant to article 46 Regulation 1408/71 and the case-law relating thereto. The main issue had already been decided in *Di Felice, 1989*, namely that an early retirement pension was of the same kind as an invalidity pension for the purpose of article 12(2) Regulation 1408/71. In *Spits, 1990* the Court also mainly reapplied the calculation rules in article 46 Regulation 1408/71. National rules against the overlapping of benefits were not to be applied in the calculation of the independent amount pursuant to article 46(1) Regulation 1408/71. That was why the Belgian authorities calculating a retirement pension were not entitled not to apply a certain administrative practice. That practice consisted in factoring in years of work before the 20th birthday when a person's insurance record in Belgium was not complete in the sole light of the years of work after the 20th birthday. The Belgian authorities had to apply that practice even when that person's insurance record in the Netherlands was complete.

With *Di Prinzio, 1992* the Court again was seized with the adding of notional years to a miner's insurance record. The case concerned an invalidity pension turned into a retirement pension and then a survivor's pension and the national rule against the overlapping of benefits according to which such notional years were reduced when they corresponded to actual years which gave rise to a pension under another scheme, in particular a foreign scheme. In the case of Ms Di Prinzio her Belgian survivor's pension based on the invalidity turned retirement pension of her late husband was reduced, because one notional year was not granted in the light of her husband's invalidity pension being paid in Italy. Various points raised by this case had already been settled in previous case-law. The Court, however, took this case as an occasion to walk through all the steps to be taken to calculate a pension under article 46 Regulation 1408/71. In addition, the Court clarified four points. (i) The first point arose because the retirement ages differed in Italy and Belgium. Was it possible for the Belgian authorities to calculate the theoretical amount under article 46(2)(a) Regulation 1408/71 when the retirement age had not yet been reached in Italy? The problem was that the Belgian institution normally had to know how long the insurance period completed in Italy was, because only then could it add up all the periods completed in all member states and treat them as if they had all been completed in Belgium which was necessary to arrive at the theoretical amount. In other words, under ordinary circumstances one was not able to know how long an old-age insurance period was until it was completed by reaching the retirement age. The Court answered that, in the circumstances of the case at hand, it was possible to calculate the theoretical amount, because the worker had the right to a full pension already pursuant to Belgian legislation. Accordingly, it was not necessary to feed into the calculation of the theoretical amount the insurance periods completed in Italy (paras 25-6). (ii) The second point was that the pro rata amount pursuant to article 46(2)(b) Regulation 1408/71 always had to be calculated, even if the person had a right to a full pension under the legislation of the state where the award of a pension was sought (para. 51). (iii) The third point related to the taking into account of notional periods in the calculation of the pro rata benefit under article 46(2)(b) Regulation 1408/71. In clarification of *Menzies, 1980*, those periods were to be taken into account in that calculation when they came to pass before the materialization of the risk (para. 54). (iv) The fourth point had actually already been rather clear. The pension pursuant to *Petroni, 1975*, i. e. the pension on the basis of a calculation based on the entirety of national law, had to be compared with the 'Community pension', i. e. the pension based on the calculation pursuant to article 46 Regulation 1408/71, after the latter had been adjusted in application of article 46(3) Regulation 1408/71 to avoid passing the 'ceiling' of the highest theoretical amount (paras 64-5). The entire explanation given in *Di Prinzio, 1992* was repeated in *Di Crescenzo, 1992* for the basically identical case of a miner who had also worked in Italy and Belgium. The Court emphasized the separate calculation based on the law of a single member state in its entirety, viz. the *Petroni, 1975*-calculation, the result of which was then to be compared to the outcome of the calculation pursuant to article 46 Regulation 1408/71, because the national Court had doubted that *Petroni, 1975* still applied (para. 11; see the opinion of Advocate General Jacobs, paras 16-7).

With *Marius Larsy, 1993* the Court came back to the interpretation given to article 46(3) Regulation 1408/71 in *Collini, 1987*. The situation in *Marius Larsy, 1993* was new. Mr Larsy had been pursuing a self-employed activity both in Belgium and in France at the same time and had paid contributions for each activity under the respective social security system. The Belgian authorities reduced the Belgian pension awarded in the light of the French pension. The Court replied on the basis that the calculation pursuant to article 46 Regulation 1408/71 was at issue. The situation was different from *Collini, 1987*, because Mr Larsy had been obliged to pay contributions under two systems during one and the same time period, while *Collini, 1987* had concerned notional periods (para. 21). Article 46(3) Regulation 1408/71 was not to be applied to reduce a benefit in those circumstances (para. 19). In *Lepore, 1993* the question was raised whether, in the calculation of an old-age pension under article 46 Regulation 1408/71, Belgian law could lawfully treat as periods of employment only those periods of invalidity that had followed upon employment in Belgium. The Court rejected that approach for both the calculation pursuant to article 46(1) and (2) Regulation 1408/71. In spite of the freedom of the member states to define insurance periods pursuant to article 1(r) Regulation 1408/71 Belgium had to treat invalidity periods after work in another member state equally as insurance periods in the calculation pursuant to article 46 Regulation 1408/71 (para. 23). The reason was, according to the Court, that the risk of losing the right to have such periods of invalidity taken into account as periods of insurance would deter migrant workers in certain circumstances from making use of their freedom of movement (para. 22).

In *Fabrizii, 1993* the Court added an element to the calculation of the theoretical amount in accordance with article 46(2)(a) Regulation 1408/71. To determine whether a period completed was a period of insurance and thus had to be factored into the calculation of the theoretical amount, it was not the law of the state that was about to award a pension that had to be examined. Instead, the legislation under which a period was completed determined whether such a period constituted a period of insurance. Thus, if Italian law treated a period of military service in the Italian army as an insurance period, then Belgium had to treat it so as well in the calculation of the theoretical amount. The Belgian authorities were not allowed to object that periods of military service did not constitute periods of insurance according to Belgian law (paras 22 and 25). Furthermore, the Court reiterated how notional periods and provisions against overlapping had to be treated under article 46 Regulation 1408/71. In addition, the Court added that the way the Belgian authorities handled a Belgian provision limiting the total amount of years of insurance to the maximum of years permitted in Belgium implied that the provision came down to a rule against overlapping which was not to be applied in the calculation pursuant to article 46 Regulation 1408/71. Rather, it was to be applied in the calculation under national law alone pursuant to *Petroni, 1975* (see the opinion of Advocate General Darmon, para. 52; and *Fabrizii, 1993*, paras. 39 et seq.). When it was applied in that latter calculation the national rule did not violate articles 48 to 51 Treaty (see the opinion of Adovate General Darmon, paras 78-80).

In *McLachlan, 1994* the Court essentially sanctioned France's approach to awarding a retirement pension when a person who was 60 years of age or older was made redundant, i. e. 5 years before the retirement age in France. As indicated by article 49 Regulation 1408/71, in case the respective retirement age had not been reached in all the member states concerned, the member state where it had been reached calculated the pension due under its legislation pursuant to article 46 Regulation 1408/71. According to the regular rules, that state factored in periods of insurance completed in another member state for the purpose of the acquisition of a right to a pension. That state was also entitled to take them into account in the determination of the rate applicable to the pension. However, that state had to leave them out of account in the calculation of the amount of the pension due in that state, i. e. when applying article 46 Regulation 1408/71 (para. 31), which was due to the fact that the migrant worker had separate pension rights under each of the social security systems concerned for each insurance period completed (para. 37). In brief, article 49 Regulation 1408/71 did not modify the regular approach of article 46 Regulation 1408/71. Non-discrimination was, moreover, not violated by France's approach. Yet because of the way the national court asked the question and due to the substance of the national proceedings, the Court did not address a further aspect of the case (see paras 25 and 35). The taking into account of the 30 quarterly insurance periods completed by Mr McLachlan in the United Kingdom made it possible for the French authorities to award him an early retirement pension rather than unemployment benefits, because he consequently had completed the minimum number of insurance periods required for awarding such a pension, namely 150 quarterly periods with him having completed 120 periods in France and 30 in the United Kingdom. However, since the *rate* of the pension was also determined by taking into account the insurance periods completed in the United Kingdom, merely a partial pension resulted, presumably four fifth of a full pension, corresponding to 120 out of 150 quarterly periods. The amount of that partial pension was lower than the unemployment benefits he would have received had he not been eligible for an early retirement pension at all, viz. had the periods completed in the United Kingdom been totally left out account (see para. 23).

In *Reichling, 1994*, the Court adopted a similar approach for aggregation with invalidity benefits as it had for unemployment benefits in *Fellinger, 1980*. When a type A invalidity benefit came together with a type B benefit the relevant salary on the basis of which the theoretical amount pursuant to article 46(2)(a) Regulation 1408/71 had to be calculated to determine the benefit due under the type A regime was, according to the Court, the salary the person concerned had last received in employment regardless of where in the Community the person had been employed (para. 28). When the worker had been employed in Luxembourg before becoming invalid the remuneration paid in Luxembourg was relevant for the Belgian type A invalidity benefit, even before the amendment of Regulation 1408/71 (paras 26 and 29). To rely on the minimum salary in Belgium in the absence of paid employment there had the effect of depriving a migrant worker of rights because of him having exercised his freedom to move (para. 25).

Previous conventions

In *Rönfeldt, 1991* the Court had been faced with a tricky challenge, namely the question whether the rights contained in a convention between two member states were replaced by Regulation 1408/71, although those rights went further. The question arose, because a convention between Denmark and Germany had provided that 15 years of insurance completed in Denmark were to be taken into account in the calculation of the benefit in Germany. In other words, 15 years were added to the insurance period completed in Germany, resulting in a significantly higher benefit in Germany than under the pro rata approach pursuant to article 46 Regulation 1408/71. The Court ruled that the need to safeguard rights which were granted by the national law of a single member state to the migrant worker and which were more favourable than those provided by Community law was not just pertinent in the case of national law as such pursuant to

Petroni, 1975, but also in the case of conventions between member states (para. 27). Hence, the pension had to be awarded based on the more favourable calculation under such conventions, although Regulation 1408/71 had replaced them (para. 14). *Rönfeldt, 1991* was, however, limited in *Thévenon, 1995*. In this case also, a social security convention that had existed already at the time Regulation 1408/71 entered into force was more favourable for a migrant worker. Mr Thévenon could notably have claimed higher invalidity benefits in Germany based on the convention between Germany and France than on the basis of the pro rata calculation in article 46(2) Regulation 1408/71. However, according to the Court, he did not have a valid claim, since he had exercised his freedom to move to Germany in order to work only *after* Regulation 1408/71 had entered into force and replaced the convention between Germany and France (para. 26). He could, therefore, only rely on Regulation 1408/71, even if the convention would have been more favourable. The approach developed in *Rönfeldt, 1991* and *Thévenon, 1995* was confirmed in both *Naranjo Arjona, 1997* and *Grajera Rodríguez, 1998*. Spanish workers who had moved in order to work abroad before Regulation 1408/71 had entered into force for Spain were entitled to rely on a social security convention that already existed at that time when it was more favourable than the Community rules (para. 27 and para. 29, respectively).

Changing circumstances

The Court in a number of cases dealt with the problem that the circumstances in which a pension had been awarded initially changed later on. In particular, the economic circumstances in Italy that changed rapidly at the time gave rise to a series of judgments. In *Cabras, 1990* a constellation was at issue in which a type A invalidity benefit was awarded based on Belgian law alone and a type B invalidity benefit in Italy based on the rules of the Community. In such a constellation the full Belgian type A invalidity benefit constituted the highest theoretical amount and thus the ceiling in article 46(3) Regulation 1408/71 (para. 20). That was, according to the Court, in accordance with articles 48 to 51 Treaty, since the Community calculation applied only when the application of national law in its entirety including national rules against overlapping was not more favourable than the application of Community law. As the highest theoretical amount, i. e. the ceiling, in such a constellation did not vary, the substantial adjustments made over time to the pension under the Italian type B legislation due to changing economic circumstances could essentially be cancelled out when the type A benefit was recalculated based on article 51 Regulation 1408/71. These effects were, according to the Court, the quid pro quo for the advantages the migrant worker drew from the Community rules (para. 27). The migrant worker concerned had to accept them like the disadvantages arising from the receipt of two different benefits, viz. the 'splitting' of benefits and the uncertainty associated with it (para. 30). Furthermore, the amount of benefit that was overpaid since a re-calculation was triggered by a revision of national law could be reclaimed from the beneficiary (paras 41-2).

A similar situation as in *Cabras, 1990* was addressed in *Ravida, 1990* which was also handed down on 21 March 1990. The difference was that in *Ravida, 1990* in both Belgium and Italy a retirement pension had been awarded together with a survivor's pension. According to Belgian law a survivor's pension could only be aggregated with retirement pensions and other benefits in Belgium and abroad up to a certain ceiling. In the light of the Italian benefits the Belgian survivor's pension had accordingly been scaled down to the ceiling. When the Italian retirement pension was increased to reflect the changing economic circumstances – in other words when it was revalorized – the Belgian survivor's pension was reconsidered and further reduced to comply with the Belgian ceiling. The Court decided that in such circumstances article 12(2) first sentence Regulation 1408/71 could not simply be applied repeatedly, although the survivor's pension which was adapted was of a different kind than the retirement pension awarded in Italy. The reason was that article 12(2) only applied *in* the calculation (para. 17). However, one first had to determine whether a re-calculation was in order at all. Article 51 Regulation 1408/71 addressed that question exhaustively. Pursuant to that article, however, the mere fact that one of the benefits that had been adjusted to the changing economic circumstances was not of the same kind as the retirement pension did not as such justify a recalculation (para. 23). *Cassamali, 1991* was based on facts that were essentially the same as in *Ravida, 1990*. Accordingly, the Court answered in the same terms. It merely added two points: (i) Article 51 had to be applied in all situations, notably also when a pension had been calculated solely pursuant to national law; and (ii) Article 51 was mandatory in the sense that the national authorities were only allowed to recalculate benefits in the cases mentioned in article 51(2) and in no other cases (paras 20-2). The first point (i) was confirmed in *Bogana, 1993 mutatis mutandis* for two invalidity benefits. Article 51 Regulation 1408/71 governed the recalculation of benefits, even if the benefit on the basis of article 46 Regulation 1408/71 was the same or less favourable than the benefit calculated on the basis of national law alone including the national rules against overlapping (para. 19). Thus, national rules addressing the recalculation of benefits were excluded even if they were designed to ensure continuous compliance with a ceiling applicable to a benefit (para. 21). In *Levatino, 1993* the Court nevertheless created an inroad for recalculation due to changing economic circumstances, albeit in a particular case, namely when the income a retired migrant worker received by reason of his pensions in Belgium and Italy had been increased by a Belgian non-contributory old-age pension supplement to reach the minimum means of subsistence. The Court fitted the continuous adjustment of that Belgian supplement, especially in the light of significant increases in the Italian pension, into the changing of personal instead of economic circumstances, i. e. into article 51(2) rather than (1). Essentially, the reason was that the supplement was special, because a dimension of personal circumstances was inherent in it in that it had been designed to guarantee a minimum means of subsistence (paras 33-4 and 42-3). The supplement thus had to be recalculated every year under article 51(2).

That such recalculation was possible for the supplement meant that article 51 did not have the effect of disrupting the system set up by Belgian legislation within the meaning of paragraph 21 of *Frilli, 1972* (para. 45 of *Levatino, 1993*). Apart from that ruling, the Court reaffirmed that the fact that migrant workers could be better off than workers who had spent their entire working life in one member state was irrelevant, for the two situations were not comparable (para. 49). The Court refused to apply the same reasoning developed in *Levatino, 1993* as to article 51(2) Regulation 1408/71 in the judgment in *Cirotti, 1997*. In this case the former spouse of a migrant worker received an old-age pension in Belgium on the basis of the insurance of her former husband and an invalidity pension in Italy which was increased significantly based on the economic circumstances. The pension in Belgium did not pursue the same aim as the supplement to the pension that was granted in *Levatino, 1993* (para. 28). The *Levatino, 1993*-line of reasoning was therefore not pertinent. Article 51(1) instead of (2) Regulation 1408/71 had to be applied. Besides, equal treatment in article 3 Regulation 1408/71 did not concern equality of treatment between spouses (para. 30).

In *Bettaccini, 1994* the Court clarified that the recalculation pursuant to article 51 Regulation 1408/71 applied only when benefits covered by chapter 3 of title III of Regulation 1408/71 were changed (para. 16). Hence, a change in a family benefit did not give rise to a recalculation of an invalidity benefit. More specifically, a Belgian invalidity pension could not lawfully be re-calculated when the general Italian family allowance which the person concerned was receiving together with an Italian invalidity pension was changed (para. 19). With *Van Munster, 1994* the Court was faced with exactly the same constellation as in *Bakker, 1988* (see above). In *Bakker, 1988*, however, the question was exclusively answered with regard to article 12(2) Regulation 1408/71. In *Van Munster, 1994* the full implications of the situation had to be dealt with, namely what were the consequences of a change in legislation in the Netherlands for the Belgian legislation? The Netherlands had brought their legislation in line with the Directive on gender equality in social security, Directive 79/7, by essentially abolishing old age pensions based on a household rate. Instead two separate pensions were awarded when both spouses reached the retirement age. Belgium's legislation also complied with that Directive owing to an opt-out therein enabling the continued application of a household rate. Could the Belgian authorities switch the basis of the worker's pension in Belgium from the household rate to the single rate – thereby reducing it – because the other spouse, a non-migrant worker who had never worked herself, received upon reaching retirement age her own income in the Netherlands, i. e. her own independent pension? The Court answered that they could not lawfully do so. The aims that articles 48 to 51 Treaty pursued would else be frustrated. The total amount awarded in the Netherlands had not been increased when the non-working spouse reached retirement age. The Belgian authorities were not allowed to apply national legislation literally in the same way to migrant workers as well as non-migrant workers without regard to the legislation applicable in other member states, else the co-operation in good faith required by article 5 Treaty would not be achieved (paras. 30-4).

Benefits of the same kind, overlapping

With the judgment in *Del Grosso, 1995* the Court clarified two points as to aggregation. First, an apportioned benefit according to article 46(2) Regulation 1408/71 did not become an independent benefit pursuant to article 46(1) merely because its amount was the same owing to a supplement as that of the independent benefit (para. 16). Second, the Court interpreted the second sentence of article 12(2) Regulation 1408/71, which excluded the application of national rules against the overlapping of benefits. For that sentence to be applicable three requirements had to be met, namely two benefits a person received had to be of the same kind; each of these two benefits had to be equivalent to benefits 'in respect of invalidity, old age, death (pension) or occupational disease'; and the benefits had to be awarded pursuant to articles 46, 50, and 51 or article 60(1)(b) Regulation 1408/71 (para. 22). The Court then classified the Belgian benefit at issue as a sickness benefit and the Italian benefit as an invalidity benefit. They were therefore not of the same kind. Moreover, the Belgian benefit failed to meet the second and third requirement. In *Schmidt, 1995* the Court again had to decide whether two benefits were of the same kind for the purpose of article 12(2) Regulation 1408/71. That was not the case for a Belgian old-age pension a divorced woman received on the basis of insurance periods completed by her former husband and a German old-age pension she received on the basis of the insurance periods she had completed herself. The two benefits did not have the same purpose and had not been completed by the same person (paras 25-6 and 28-9). This interpretation was confirmed in *Cordelle, 1998*. A survivor's pension awarded in Belgium which was based on the insurance periods completed by the late husband was not of the same kind as a French old-age pension based on the insurance periods completed by the survivor herself (para. 21). In *Cordelle, 1998*, the amendment of article 12(2) Regulation 1408/71 did not apply, as the pension had been awarded before the amendment's entry into force and the person concerned had not submitted a request for application of the amended rules (paras 13-7). However, in *Conti, 1998* the amended articles 12(2) and 46b Regulation 1408/71 did apply. The Court ruled that the case-law relating to article 12(2) continued to apply, since the amendment did not modify the substance of the rules, but rather smoothed them out (para. 19). Belgium's provisions governing miners' benefits had been changed since *Romano, 1985*, namely they did not any longer reduce notional years in the light of a pension awarded abroad, but supplemented a miner's pension when a foreign benefit did not have the effect of bringing that pension up to the full amount available in Belgium. Yet, the Belgian provisions were still at variance with the ruling sent in *Romano, 1985*, although they were seemingly part of the calculation of the benefit. They constituted rules against the overlapping of benefits that had to be left out of account in the calculation pursuant to article 46 Regulation 1408/71 (paras 24-9).

In *Van Coile, 1999* and *Platbrood, 1999* the Court refused to classify a Belgian rule as a rule against the overlapping of benefits. If a person had been employed at a specific point in time in Belgium during World War II and had paid a minimum amount of contributions there, the Belgian war years presumption treated the rest of the period of World War II from that specific point in time onwards as a period during which contributions had been paid in Belgium. A Belgian pension that was awarded on the basis of that presumption was reduced, however, when another pension was awarded – notably abroad – for the same period. The presumption was then deemed to be rebutted. According to the Court, the mere fact that national law considered the war years presumption as a rule of evidence was irrelevant to determine whether it was a rule against the overlapping of benefits. However, the presumption could not be classed as such a rule against overlapping, since it merely intended to alleviate the damaging consequences of the War on Belgian pension rights (paras 27-8 and 32).

Aggregation in Spain

With *Lafuente Nieto, 1996* the first aggregation case concerning Spain came to the Court. It concerned the particular approach used in Spain to calculate a type A invalidity pension when a type B pension was awarded in another state. Spain relied on the average amount of the bases of social security contributions over a reference period of time, namely 84 months, before invalidity set on. If for a part of that reference period contributions had not been payable, Spain simply took the general minimum basis of contributions to calculate the average amount. As that had the effect that periods of work abroad were always factored in on the basis of that minimum, migrant workers were disadvantaged. Article 47(1)(e) Regulation 1408/71, which was applicable, did not authorize that way of calculating. According to the Court, Spain did not have to take into account social security contributions actually paid abroad, though. But the bases of contributions applicable for the time period during which contributions had been paid in Spain had to be 'extended', revalorized, and updated, or in other words taken into account again as if the person had continued to contribute under the Spanish system for the rest of the reference period. Put simply, for the purpose of calculating the average amount a worker had to be treated as if he had continued to work in Spain (paras 35-40). That solution was underpinned by an amendment of the annex provisions concerning Spain, which had not been applicable yet at the time of *Lafuente Nieto, 1996*. Finally, the Court held that article 46(2)(c) Regulation 1408/71 regarding the maximum period was not applicable to type A schemes. The interpretation in *Lafuente Nieto, 1996* was confirmed in *Naranjo Arjona, 1997*. The amended annex was not applicable in *Naranjo Arjona, 1997* in the absence of a request to that effect by the person concerned. In *Grajera Rodríguez, 1998*, the Court confirmed that the interpretation given in *Lafuente Nieto, 1996* was compatible with articles 48 to 51 Treaty. Moreover, the differences concerning the average amount between the approach applicable according to *Lafuente Nieto, 1996* and the approach pursuant to annex VI(D)(4), including its amendment, were negligible, since pursuant to *Lafuente Nieto, 1996* the existing bases of contribution were updated, while the annex revalorized the amount of the pension as such and left out of account the last year before the risk materialized (paras 21 and 25).

Aggregation and special non-contributory benefits

In *Stinco, 1998* the Court decided that the exclusion of certain special, non-contributory benefits from exportability pursuant to article 10a Regulation 1408/71 did not have an impact on the calculation of the theoretical amount pursuant to article 46(2) Regulation 1408/71 (paras 17-8). A non-contributory supplement to an old-age pension paid in Italy which was intended to bring the pension up to the statutory minimum had to be taken into account in the calculation of the theoretical amount of an Italian old-age pension. That applied even in the calculation of a pension to be awarded to a person residing in another member state than Italy, although the supplement was ultimately not paid to such a person because of article 10a.

Differing retirement ages

In *Lustig, 1998*, the Court was again faced with a problem that arose because retirement ages differed among the member states. Article 49 Regulation 1408/71 had been amended since *McLachlan, 1994*. As a consequence, article 49(1)(b)(ii) allowed a state to ignore for the calculation of an old-age pension pursuant to article 46 Regulation 1408/71 insurance periods completed in another member state until the retirement age was also reached in that other state. However, the Court ruled that periods completed abroad had to be taken into account nevertheless in the specific circumstances of the case in contrast to *McLachlan, 1994*. Ms Lustig only sought to have them taken into account for the purpose of rendering a higher pension rate applicable, i. e. for the purpose of coming into the category of persons eligible for the Belgian guaranteed minimum pension (para. 40, see the opinion of Advocate General Fennelly, para. 20). If the periods were not taken account of in those circumstances, article 48 to 51 Treaty would be violated.

Aggregation and civil servants

In a few cases in the 1990s the Court dealt with the aggregation of periods completed under special insurance schemes for civil servants. Such schemes were excluded from the scope of Regulation 1408/71 by reason of article 4(4). *Olivieri-Coenen, 1995* concerned Annex VI point 4(a) of section I regarding the Netherlands according to which all periods of paid employment completed before 1967 when the new social security legislation came into force in the Netherlands had to be considered as periods of insurance under the new legislation. The Court held that even periods of paid employment during which a person had been affiliated to a special scheme for civil servants before 1967 were covered by Annex VI. As there was no hierarchy between the regular body of Regulation 1408/71 and its annexes and given the aim of freedom of movement, the annex provision had to prevail. Such a period of affiliation to a special scheme for civil servants therefore had to be aggregated pursuant to article 46 Regulation 1408/71 (para. 15). (In a similar vein, though not with regard to special schemes for civil servants, the Court later on in *Grahame, 1997* ruled that periods of service in the military of the Netherlands before 1967 constituted paid employment for the purpose of annex VI. Such periods therefore had to be aggregated for an invalidity benefit.)

In *Vougioukas, 1995* the Court again addressed a special scheme for civil servants, albeit not with regard to the Netherlands. According to the Court the restrictive notion of public service in article 48(4) Treaty could not be applied under article 4(4) Regulation 1408/71. Moreover, a scheme need not have been 'special' for article 4(4) to apply. It was enough if it was 'different' from the general social security system (para. 27). Next, the Court found that the Council had failed to discharge its duty pursuant to article 51 Treaty to adopt the measures needed to regulate such special insurance schemes for civil servants (para. 34). Therefore, when the Greek authorities, in the case of Mr Vougioukas, refused on the basis of article 4(4) Regulation 1408/71 to take into account periods of affiliation to an insurance scheme for civil servants in Germany, the Court decided that aggregation had to be granted directly based on article 51 Treaty else the migrant worker would be discriminated. However, the Court implied that its ruling applied only in cases where aggregation was possible despite the lack of implementing provisions (para. 36). When *Nijhuis, 1999* came to the Court, the amendment of Regulation 1408/71 had taken place. The exemption of special schemes for civil servants had been removed and new articles governing such schemes had been introduced. However, in *Nijhuis, 1999* the Court decided that the new rules were not applicable to a period before entry into force of the amendment. Moreover, the rules on aggregation in force before the amendment could not be applied by analogy in the case at issue, either, because in contrast to *Vougioukas, 1995* positive coordinating measures were needed for aggregation (paras 30-2).

Broader aggregation

The Court also dealt with aggregation of periods in a less technical sense than that addressed by article 46 Regulation 1408/71. In *Paraschi, 1991* German law extended the reference period of insurance relevant for invalidity benefits by certain periods. However, the reference period was only extended when the event or circumstance that gave rise to such a particular period, like sickness or unemployment, was confined to Germany. The Court rejected that approach for being discriminatory. For migrant workers such events and circumstances typically occurred abroad, for they in particular tended to return to their home state in case of sickness or unemployment (para. 24). Germany thus equally had to take into account such periods occurring in other member states when it came to prolonging the reference period. Apart from that the Court also reconfirmed in *Paraschi, 1991* that the member states were free to establish the conditions to become a member of their social security schemes. Accordingly, the member states could also amend those conditions so as to make them stricter, provided that they respected non-discrimination (para. 16). In *Moscato, 1995* the Court was faced with a problem arising from a requirement for the award of an invalidity benefit in the Netherlands. Dutch law awarded a benefit for invalidity materializing within six months after insurance cover had begun only if it had not been foreseeable at the beginning of insurance cover that the person would become incapable of work. Based on article 51 Treaty and article 38 Regulation 1408/71, which concerned aggregation of insurance periods for the purpose of acquisition of invalidity benefits, the Court ruled that previous insurance cover in another member state had to be taken into account to determine whether the incapacity of work had been foreseeable at the time the insurance cover had begun. When a migrant worker had worked in another member state previously the relevant date could therefore not be set to the beginning of the insurance cover in the Netherlands (paras 29-30). On the same day the Court delivered *Moscato, 1995* the judgment in *Klaus, 1995* was handed down. Based on the aggregation rule for sickness benefits in article 18(1) Regulation 1408/71, the Court in *Klaus, 1995* applied the same reasoning as in *Moscato, 1995* for sickness benefits in Dutch law. Cash sickness benefits were subject to the condition of being fit for work at the beginning of sickness insurance cover. While the condition was not excluded by article 35(3) Regulation 1408/71, the beginning of the insurance cover in another member state had to be taken as the relevant date (para. 24). Moreover, a lapse of a few days between the end of the previous insurance cover and the beginning of the new insurance cover had to be disregarded when setting the relevant date (para. 28).

In *Martínez Losada, 1997*, the Court dealt with an issue of aggregation with regard to a particular benefit granted in Spain to those beyond the age of 52 years. The requirements for the award of the benefits were that a person had contributed to unemployment insurance for at least six years and had a right to a retirement pension based on 15 years of contribution. Ms Martínez Losada had returned to Spain, after having worked abroad, though never in Spain. The Spanish state paid contributions to sickness insurance and family benefits schemes on her behalf while she was receiving unemployment benefits in Spain which were granted as usual to a returning migrant worker. However, she was refused the benefit. That benefit was an unemployment benefit, as Spain had declared it so under article 5 Regulation 1408/71. Article 48 Regulation 1408/71 concerning periods shorter than one year did not apply for lack of a reference in the section relating to unemployment benefits. The key issue, however, namely whether the contributions paid on her behalf by the Spanish state implied that a period of insurance had been last completed in Spain pursuant to article 67(3) Regulation 1408/71 thus triggering aggregation of unemployment insurance periods completed abroad, and ultimately the right to the Spanish benefit, was left to the national court to decide. It was up to national law to determine 'periods of insurance' pursuant to article 1(r) Regulation 1408/71 and, particularly, whether a period during which the Spanish state paid contributions on behalf of a person who had never been employed in Spain constituted such a period (para. 37). A further issue relating to this Spanish scheme was clarified in *Ferreiro Alvite, 1999*. Another condition of national law for the award of that particular Spanish benefit was that the person had to have contributed to the Spanish social security system during a qualifying period of 15 years. In *Martínez Losada, 1997* the Spanish government had recognized that periods completed in other member states would be taken into account for the purpose of that qualifying period (para. 41). In *Ferreiro Alvite, 1999* the Court reaffirmed that Spain was required to do so (para. 25)

Iurlaro, 1997 concerned questions that were somewhat similar to those raised in *Martínez Losada, 1997*. Germany extended the reference period for its type B invalidity pensions as regarded the minimum contribution required by periods during which unemployment benefits were drawn and for such periods factored in notional contributions in order to determine the amount of the benefit. Italy counted such periods of unemployment as proper invalidity insurance periods both for the acquisition and the calculation of its own type B invalidity benefits, if contributions had been paid. How were the Italian authorities to deal with periods during which a migrant worker drew unemployment benefits in Germany when they were asked to award an invalidity pension? Italy was not required to extend the Italian reference period by the period of unemployment in Germany, because it did not do so for periods of unemployment in Italy, either. A member state was entitled to lay down in a non-discriminatory fashion the conditions governing the right to become a member of a social security scheme (paras 23-5). However, given that the law under which a period was completed determined whether such a period constituted a 'period of insurance' pursuant to article 1(r) Regulation 1408/71, Italy had to factor in periods of invalidity insurance completed and recognized as such in Germany when determining whether a right to an Italian invalidity benefit was acquired. Italian law could not lawfully require periods to have been completed on the national territory to count towards the minimum period required (para. 29). Yet limiting the recognition of unemployment periods as insurance periods to six months in general was lawful (paras 31-2).

Family benefits

In the 1990s, the Court also dealt with family benefits. *Bronzino, 1990* rejected a requirement for the children of migrant workers to be registered with the employment office of the host state for migrant workers to be eligible for a particular benefit awarded when children were unemployed. The benefit was a family benefit, as it intended to help parents meet the cost incurred because their children were unemployed. As such it fell within the scope of article 73 Regulation

1408/71. The obligation for the children to hold themselves available to the employment office of the host state could also be fulfilled with the employment office at the place where they resided. Moreover, it was the parents rather than the children who received the benefit (para. 11-4). It seems that the Court gave the same answer in *Gatto, 1990*. (The case was only summarily published.) In *Kracht, 1990*, the Court re-affirmed the case-law that had begun with *Ragazzoni, 1978*, namely that all requirements of substance and form had to be met for a family benefit to be 'payable' within the meaning of article 76 Regulation 1408/71. Only then did the rule against overlapping benefits become applicable. That the migrant worker, or her spouse, was in a position, as a consequence of the case-law, to chose where to receive benefits by ceasing to apply for them in the state of residence, as in the case at hand, did not invalidate that case-law. The amendment of article 76 which targeted specifically an outright refusal to apply for family benefits was moreover not applicable before it entered into force.

After Pinna

Yáñez-Campoy, 1990 was an aftermath of *Pinna, 1986*. Before *Pinna, 1986* was handed down, the Act of Accession of Spain had relied on the stipulation in article 99 Regulation 1408/71 to find a uniform solution to the situation which article 73(2) Regulation 1408/71 had addressed by means of a derogation for France. In the meanwhile the Act of Accession had established a transitional regime that would have applied until the uniform solution would have been found. According to that regime, article 73(2) Regulation 1408/71 and certain social security conventions applied to Spanish workers. When *Pinna, 1986* supervened and invalidated the special treatment of France in article 73(2) Regulation 1408/71, the consequences for the transitional regime in the Act of Accession were uncertain. The Court replied that the uniform solution stipulated in article 99 Regulation 1408/71 and taken into account by the Act of Accession had been achieved by *Pinna, 1986*. The transitional regime therefore need not have been applied any longer. Spanish workers therefore were allowed to rely on article 73(1) Regulation 1408/71 (paras 20-1). *Alonso-Pérez, 1995* confirmed this approach. However, *Alonso-Pérez, 1995* also made it clear that national procedural law governed the limitation of retroactive applications for family benefits. Thus, even though *Pinna, 1986* had been handed down and the amendment to Regulation 1408/71 had later on repealed the special treatment of France in article 73(2) Regulation 1408/71 retroactively as per the date of the judgment in *Pinna, 1986*, German law could still impose a six month limitation on retroactive claims for family benefits. More specifically, Germany could limit a migrant worker's retroactive application for family benefits with regard to his non-resident family members to six months counting backward from the time of application, even though the time period between the date of the judgment in *Pinna, 1986* and the entry into force of the amendment of article 73 Regulation

1408/71 was concerned, provided that such a limitation also applied to purely domestic claims (para. 31).

More family benefits

Middleburgh, 1991 concerned the right of a self-employed person to child benefits. Mr Middleburgh was first employed and then pursued a self-employed activity in the United Kingdom. However, as article 73 Regulation 1408/71 only applied to *employed* persons for the time relevant in the case – article 73 had been excluded from the extension of Regulation 1408/71 to self-employed persons by Regulation 1319/81 – he could not lawfully rely on that article to attack a residence clause in British law for child benefits as regarded the time during which he had exercised a self-employed activity. The fact that he had a claim to unemployment benefits during that time owing to his prior employment did not make him an employed person entitled to rely on article 73 (para. 8-9). Before the amendment of article 73 as to self-employed persons had entered into force, a residence requirement concerning child benefits for self-employed persons was, moreover, not precluded by article 52 Treaty (para. 15). In *Durighello, 1991* the Italian authorities refused a migrant worker a supplementary benefit for his dependent spouse based on Italian law on the ground that his pension was not due on the basis of Italian law alone, but rather on the basis of Regulation 1408/71. Moreover, that Regulation made no provision for benefits for dependent spouses, but only for dependent children. The Court ruled that those grounds in themselves were not sufficient to refuse a benefit for a dependent spouse which was due under national law, given that under Regulation 1408/71 the national social security systems co-existed and that benefits due under such systems were not to be lost merely because a worker made use of his freedom of movement on the basis of Community law (paras 14-7).

Imbernon Martínez, 1995 again concerned article 73 Regulation 1408/71 in so far as it precluded a residence requirement for family members, or in other words in so far as it required a member state to treat them as if they had residence – so-called 'notional residence' (para. 23). The Court ruled that the article applied regardless of whether a family benefit was refused/reduced on the basis of the act governing the benefit, viz. the social legislation, or as a consequence of a distinction made in the tax law of the member state concerned (para. 23). That also applied where the residence of the spouse of the migrant worker or any family member had an influence on the entitlement to the family benefit or its extent (para. 27). Thus, the entitlement to the family allowance concerned and the amount thereof had to be determined as if the family members, including the spouse, resided in the member state concerned.

Moreno, 1996 dealt with article 74 Regulation 1408/71. In the case of Mr Moreno unemployment benefits in cash were in a first phase suspended, because he received a compensation from his former employer due to the termination of his contract. In a second phase they were temporarily excluded, because Mr Moreno's employment contract had been terminated by reason of a fault of his.

For both phases, the Court considered that he was 'dra[wing] unemployment benefits' within the meaning of article 74, since the compensation in the first phase was a substitute for unemployment benefits (paras 17-9) and when the payment of unemployment benefits was excluded in the second phase, he was still insured against sickness and accident (para. 23). Article 74 therefore required the state concerned to grant family benefits, as if Mr Moreno's family members were residing in that state.

In *Stöber and Pereira, 1997* the Court came back to the factual constellation in *Middleburgh, 1991* in a changed legal setting. Article 73 Regulation 1408/71 now also applied to self-employed persons by reason of the amendment by Regulation 3427/89. In this case the problem was, however, that the annex relating to Germany now stated that only self-employed persons who were *compulsorily* insured in Germany were 'self-employed persons' entitled to German family benefits under chapter 7, title III of Regulation 1408/71. The persons concerned in *Stöber and Pereira, 1997*, however, were only *voluntarily* insured. Article 73 Regulation 1408/71 therefore did not be apply to them (para. 34). Yet, the Court ruled in some contrast to *Middleburgh, 1991* that the requirement that the family members resided in Germany for the migrant self-employed person to have been eligible for the German children's allowance was excluded by article 52 Treaty, because it was discriminatory. The difference to *Middleburgh, 1991* was that for the period at stake in *Stöber and Pereira, 1997* the Community provisions implementing family benefits for self-employed persons had been adopted by Regulation 3427/89. The rules applicable to self-employed persons within the scope of Regulation 1408/71 therefore had to be applied by analogy to the self-employed persons in the case at hand, thus excluding the residence requirement (para. 40). In *Merino García, 1997* the Court ruled in a very similar vein for 'employed persons' with regard to family benefits in article 73 Regulation 1408/71. That article similarly was applicable only to employed persons in Germany, if they were subject to compulsory unemployment insurance pursuant to article 1(a) Regulation 1408/71 in combination with the annex concerned. Mr Merino García had not paid unemployment insurance contributions, but had been subject to sickness insurance during a period of unpaid leave from his employment in Germany. For that period, he was refused family benefits for his children living in Spain. The Court, in keeping with *Stöber and Pereira, 1997* for article 52 Treaty, found the approach of Regulation 1408/71 based on compulsory unemployment insurance to be in compliance with article 48 Treaty (paras 30-1). The requirement of German legislation, though, that the family members be resident in Germany (para. 9) for a migrant worker, who was on leave and did not pay unemployment insurance contributions but was subject to sickness insurance, to be eligible for family benefits was discriminatory as well as in *Stöber and Pereira, 1997* and therefore excluded by article 48 Treaty. The Court confirmed the approach to the definition of who was an 'employed person' for the purpose of article 73 Regulation 1408/71 as it had been modified by the annex for Germany in *Kulzer, 1998*. As a retired civil servant did not fulfil the requirements in the annex, he could not lawfully rely on article 73 Regulation 1408/71 to claim Germany's child allowance. However, since Mr Kulzer had stayed his entire life in Germany and only his daughter had moved to France, article 48 Treaty did not preclude the residence requirement, in contrast to the rulings in *Stöber and Pereira, 1997* and *Merino García, 1997*. The question whether Union citizenship had such a preclusive effect was raised by Advocate General Fennelly (para. 62), but the Court did not discuss it.

In *Romero, 1997* the Court dealt with non-discrimination concerning orphans. When an orphan interrupted educational training to serve in the military of any member state, German law suspended an orphan's entitlement to benefits. It then prolongated the entitlement to the orphan's benefit beyond the usual statutory age limit of 25 years for a time period commensurate with the duration of the military service completed. Yet the prolongation was only granted in the case of service in Germany's armed forces. According to the Court, to refuse that prolongation to an orphan who served in Spain's instead Germany's army was discriminatory, in particular as the prolongation of entitlement constituted deferred payment of the orphan's benefit rather than compensation for the disadvantages of military service (paras 33 and 35).

In *Gómez Rivero, 1999*, the Court dealt with the special situation of a consulate worker who had opted out of the social security legislation of the host state pursuant to article 16(2) Regulation 1408/71. The Court ruled that such an opt out did not impact on the rights of the worker's family members in the host state which were guaranteed by that state irrespective of the insurance cover of the worker (para. 25). If that approach came down to a cumulation of family benefits, the rules against the overlapping of benefits would have to be applied (para. 28).

Post Rossi

The supplement to family benefits to be paid in accordance with the *Rossi, 1979*-line of authority also came up in the 1990s. In *Athanasopoulos, 1991* the Court mainly clarified two points. (i) The supplement also had to be paid under articles 77 and 78 Regulation 1408/71, if the entitlement to the benefit only arose after the migrant worker had moved residence, because the worker was awarded a pension or the children were born after the change of residence (paras 32-7). (ii) An indiscriminate reduction of the family benefit by the state paying the benefit or the supplement in proportion to the current net annual income of the worker was lawful. To that effect the authorities of both states had to cooperate to establish the income of the migrant worker in the state where she or he resided (paras 43, 46, and 49). *Doriguzzi, 1992* also concerned a *Rossi, 1979*-supplement to an orphan's benefit. In this case it was doubtful in as how far the benefits granted in the state of residence had to be factored in when calculating the supplement due from the state where the child was not residing. More specifically, Italian law provided for an orphan's benefit together with a family supplement. The role of the latter family supplement in the calculation of the *Rossi,*

1979-supplement due in Germany was at issue. The Court decided that all the benefits due in the state of residence for the maintenance of orphans, regardless of their character or designation, had to be taken into account in the comparison of benefits necessary to determine whether a *Rossi, 1979*-supplement had to be paid (para. 15-7). Essentially, a *Rossi, 1979*-supplement was therefore reduced by the Italian family supplement. *Doriguzzi, 1992* was confirmed in *Gobbis, 1993*. The Court only added that the increase the surviving spouse received when her total income did not reach Italy's minimum income could lawfully be disregarded in the calculation of the orphan's *Rossi, 1979*-supplement under article 78 Regulation 1408/71, since it did not serve the purpose of maintaining the orphan (para. 19). In contrast, a supplementary family allowance had to be factored in since it helped maintaining the family (para. 20).

In *McMenamin, 1992* the Court clarified a point as to the suspension of family benefits governed by article 73 Regulation 1408/71. *Robards, 1983* had extended that suspension to the case of a divorced spouse. Consequently, the Council amended the relevant provision of Regulation 574/72 accordingly, i. e. article 10(1)(b)(i) as to the overlapping of family benefits. In *McMenamin, 1992* the Court then clarified that the rules of priority established by Regulation 574/72 applied generally and regardless of who was technically entitled to family benefits. In case one of the persons having the care of the children was entitled to family benefits in the state where the family resided, the benefits due in the other member state, i. e. the state where the frontier worker was employed, were to be suspended as far as the benefits overlapped pursuant to *Rossi, 1979* (paras 25-7).

The Court in *Bastos Moriana, 1997* then drew a clear limit to the *Rossi, 1979*-supplement case-law. In *Bastos Moriana, 1997* the question was whether the *Laterza, 1980*- and *Gravina, 1980*-judgments as to the supplements for pensioners and orphans also applied when the pension or the orphan's benefit was not granted on the basis of insurance periods completed in Germany alone, but rather based on the Community rules regarding aggregation. The Court made clear that the case-law was based on *Petroni, 1975*, viz. the right to benefits acquired on the basis of national law alone was not to be lost because of the exercise of the right to free movement. When, however, the pension or the orphan's benefit had not been based solely on national law but on aggregation pursuant to Community law the application of articles 77 and 78 Regulation 1408/71 did not deprive the migrant worker of such a right. The state providing the pension or the orphan's benefit, in this case Germany, was then not required under articles 77(2)(b)(i) or 78(2)(b)(i) Regulation 1408/71 to grant a *Rossi, 1979*-supplement to guarantee the higher amount of benefit to beneficiaries residing abroad (para. 19). The limitation of the supplement-case-law in *Bastos Moriana, 1997* was confirmed in *Gómez Rodríguez, 1998*. German law was more favourable than Spanish law, because it granted orphan's benefits beyond the age limit of 18 years which applied in Spain. However, an orphan residing in Spain could not lawfully claim the more favourable German benefit as a *Gravina, 1980*-supplement after having reached the age of 18 years when the orphan had not acquired a German benefit by reason of insurance periods completed under German law alone (para. 25). Neither had the orphan a claim to the application of article 78(2)(b)(ii) Regulation 1408/71 after having exhausted the rights with the competent state pursuant to article 78(2)(b)(i) (para. 26). Moreover, the orphan was not allowed to fall back on the social security convention between Spain and Germany, either. While the *Rönfeldt, 1991/Thévenon, 1995*-requirements were met, viz. the convention rather than Regulation 1408/71 had been in force when the worker had completed the insurance periods in Germany, the situation at issue was different. The comparison of the benefits due under the convention with those due under Regulation 1408/71 had already been made upon the award of the orphan's benefit pursuant to article 118(1) Regulation 574/78. It was not to be re-assessed when the benefit under the other instrument, i. e. the instrument based on which the benefit was not awarded, became more favourable later on, as it was the case when the orphan reached the Spanish age limit, else the benefits would have to be re-compared continuously which would cause considerable administrative difficulties (paras 46-7).

Unemployment

In the 1990s, the Court also dealt with unemployment benefits in a series of cases. *Di Conti, 1990* concerned the case of a late returner under the regime established by article 69 Regulation 1408/71. Article 69(2) Regulation 1408/71 established that a worker who returned late after having searched for employment abroad for three months forfeited his rights to unemployment benefits in the competent state. Article 69(4) which required three months of work to re-qualify for benefits after having returned late within the sense of article 69(2) to Belgium from abroad, was a special concession to Belgium for its maintaining entitlement to unemployment benefits for an extra long time. According to the Court, Belgium could therefore not lawfully impose further conditions such as a qualifying period (paras 11-3 and 16). The Court in *Spataro, 1996*, however, clarified that article 69(4) only applied to a returning job seeker asking for re-qualification for unemployment benefits. Conversely, it did not apply when a returning job seeker sought acquisition of a new entitlement to unemployment benefits based on Belgian law (para. 16).

Van Noorden, 1991 confirmed that the state where the worker had lastly completed periods of employment/insurance was competent for unemployment benefits pursuant to article 67(3) Regulation 1408/71. Beyond the regime established by article 69 Regulation 1408/71 for job seeking abroad Community law did not require another state to pay unemployment benefits to a person who had never worked in that other state (paras 10-1). Article 69 Regulation 1408/71 apart, a state could lawfully refuse those benefits to such a person even if national law by itself granted a claim to benefits. In *Gray, 1992* the Court confirmed that the scheme established by articles 67(3) and 69(1) Regulation 1408/71 complied with article 51 Treaty. The Council was notably allowed to attach conditions to the right to claim unemployment benefits in the state where a person had been employed and to the right to export those benefits (para. 12).

Acciardi, 1993 concerned a Dutch benefit that followed upon the regular unemployment benefit. Despite its non-contributory nature, the Court classed it as an unemployment benefit, mainly because it was not subject to a discretionary assessment, addressed the risk of unemployment, was only available to unemployed persons, and was granted exclusively to persons seeking employment (paras 15-8). As the benefit varied when the unemployed person had spouse and children, its amount was linked to the number of family members within the meaning of article 68(2) Regulation 1408/71 (para 24-6). Therefore, in accordance with that article the Netherlands were not to leave the unemployed worker's spouse out of account merely because she resided in another member state.

Reibold, 1990 was only published summarily. It seemed to have reiterated *Di Paolo, 1977* and *Bergemann, 1988*, adding only that 'residence' in article 71(1)(b)(ii) Regulation 1408/71 had to be determined by taking into account that academic work was performed under a university exchange scheme which allowed the worker to return to his accommodation in another member state for prolonged periods every three months (see the summary). In *Knoch, 1992* article 71 Regulation 1408/71 was also at stake. The Court elaborated a number of details. In application of the criteria developed in *Di Paolo, 1977* residence in Germany was not lost for the purpose of article 71(1)(b)(ii) when a person had remained registered in Germany while she was working as a university assistant in the United Kingdom for two years and receiving an allowance to support her from Germany (para. 25). Such a person still had the possibility under article 71 to claim unemployment benefits in Germany, even if she had initially opted to claim such benefits and sought work in the United Kingdom (paras 28, 33-4). The provision against the overlapping of benefits in article 12(1) Regulation 1408/71 had to be applied to unemployment benefits, when two benefits were of the same kind. That was the case when they both were granted after employment had been lost, as a substitute for the salary for maintenance purposes, and when the conditions and the bases of calculation of the benefits differed only because of structural differences in the social security systems concerned (paras 43-4). Pursuant to article 12(1) periods of insurance completed and actual benefits paid in one state had to be factored in when the other state determined acquisition of entitlement to benefits and the actual amount of benefits (para. 49). Finally, the Court ruled, after having reiterated that the national authorities were entirely free to appreciate a statement made pursuant to article 84(2) Regulation 574/72, that entitlement under article 71(1)(b)(ii) could only be suspended when all the conditions of article 69 Regulation 1408/71 had in fact been fulfilled (para. 59). Moreover, the duration of entitlement under article 71(1)(b)(ii) was reduced by the number of days during which article 69 applied (para. 62). In *Grisvard, 1992* the Court clarified a point that had not been addressed in *Fellinger, 1980*. While according to *Fellinger, 1980* the state where a wholly unemployed frontier worker was resident had to calculate the unemployment benefits due on the basis of the salary last received in the state of employment, the ceiling which limited unemployment benefits in the member state of employment could not lawfully be applied by the state of residence. According to article 71(a)(ii) Regulation 1408/71, that state had to apply its own legislation as if the frontier worker had been subject to it during his last employment. Moreover, the salary had to be converted based on the official exchange rate applicable on the day of payment (paras 22-3).

Van Gestel, 1995 concerned a particular application of article 71 Regulation 1408/71. The authorities of Belgium and the Netherlands had agreed on the basis of article 17 Regulation 1408/71 that Mr van Gestel would continue to be subject to Dutch legislation for a certain time, despite the fact that he worked for a company in Belgium and resided there. After he had become unemployed, the question arose which state was competent for unemployment benefits. The Court replied that article 71(1)(b)(ii) Regulation 1408/71 was applicable, although Mr van Gestel worked in the same state as he resided, namely Belgium. It was sufficient for the article to apply that pursuant to the agreement between the Belgian and Dutch authorities the competent state, viz. the Netherlands, was not the state where the worker resided, viz. Belgium (paras 17 and 25). Moreover, the Court confirmed *Brusse, 1984* in that an agreement under article 17 was also capable of covering periods in the past.

In *Naruschawicus, 1996* the Court dealt with an employee of the Belgian army who had been stationed in Germany and in fact resided there, while maintaining her legal residence in Belgium. According to article 13(2)(d) Regulation 1408/71, Belgian law applied, because she was a Belgian civil servant, irrespective of the fact that Belgian law categorized her retroactively as an ordinary employed person. Moreover, article 71(1)(b)(i) Regulation 1408/71 was applicable to a civil servant as to any other employed person. Such a person made herself available to an employment service in the sense of that article by registering with that service. It did not have any impact that she in fact still resided a long distance away in Germany (para. 27).

Huijbrechts, 1997 largely confirmed *Cochet, 1985*. When a wholly unemployed frontier worker was receiving unemployment benefits where he resided and then moved to the state where he had been employed, the special rule of article 71(1)(a)(ii) Regulation 1408/71 ceased to be applicable and the general rule that the state of employment was competent became applicable. When providing unemployment benefits pursuant to national law the then competent state would have to take into account the benefits previously granted by the formerly competent state as if it had granted them itself (para. 28).

Perrotta, 1995, finally, was at the nexus of unemployment and sickness benefits. It concerned cash sickness benefits for which an unemployed worker applied who had gone to seek employment abroad under the regime of article 69 Regulation 1408/71. Article 25 Regulation 1408/71 provided that in such cases the state of last employment, i. e. the state whence the unemployed person came to seek work, was competent for cash sickness benefits during the period of three months authorized by article 69(1) Regulation 1408/71. Beyond that period, that state remained liable only in cases of *force majeure* pursuant to article 25(4). The Court held that a sickness having befallen an unemployed person during the three months and extending beyond it could not stretch out the entitlement to cash sickness benefits beyond the three months period (para. 17). A formal application to apply article 25(4) was not required (para. 19-2). Moreover, sickness did not automatically equal *force majeure* under article 25(4) (para. 32). Instead, *force majeure* in this context designated 'abnormal and unforeseeable circumstances, outside the control of the unemployed person, the consequences of which, in spite of the exercise of all due care, could not be avoided except at the cost of excessive sacrifice' (para. 27). Thus, a case-by-case assessment was necessary to establish whether the unemployed person was able to travel back to the competent state (para. 29).

Sickness and invalidity

Sickness and invalidity benefits also came up before the Court during the 1990s. In *Noij, 1991* the Court decided that a state could not lawfully charge a retired migrant worker, who received a pension from another member state, sickness insurance contributions simply because he was a resident when the state which paid the pension was competent for sickness benefits. Article 33 Regulation 1408/71 which was based on the general idea that a state only levied contributions from resident pensioners if it granted them benefits, precluded the levying of such contributions. That applied even if the pensioner had previously worked in that state (paras 14 and 17). (The amended article 33 did state so explicitly, but was not applicable at that time yet.)

Vidal, 1991 concerned the award of invalidity benefits to a person living abroad. The Court held that article 51(1) Regulation 574/72 was inconclusive as to whether the person could be summoned to the member state concerned and that *Rindone, 1987* which had concerned sickness benefits could not be applied by analogy. The fitness to travel had to be assessed on a case-by-case basis. As a broad range of examinations involving various experts was necessary to determine invalidity and as the conditions varied between states, a person who was, subject to the verification by the competent state, fit to travel could lawfully be required under article 51(1) to travel to the member state concerned, at the expense of the latter (paras 13-6). In *Voeten, 1998*, the Court again applied article 51 Regulation 574/72. The rule laid down in that article applied to frontier workers in the same way as to other workers. A re-assessment of the invalidity of a person because of a change in legislation still came within the purview of article 51 (paras 33-4). The person concerned was, moreover, able to waive his right to be examined first in the state of residence, if he had been properly informed (para. 38). In contrast, under article 40 Regulation 574/72 relating to the first determination of invalidity a prior examination in the member state of residence was not required. Nevertheless, the competent institution had to take into account documents and reports drawn up previously in the member state of residence or in any other member state (paras 47-9).

Paletta, 1992 categorized the obligation of the employer to continue to pay a sick worker's salary for six weeks as a sickness benefit subject to Regulation 1408/71, since the method of financing the benefit was irrelevant. The employer was the competent institution which was bound by the diagnosis of sickness in another member state. As such it was allowed to have the diagnosis verified by a doctor of its choice. *Paletta II, 1996* clarified that the continued wage payment was a cash sickness benefit pursuant to article 22(1)(a) Regulation 1408/71, although it was only paid with the usual delay for salaries. Moreover, a national approach designed to avoid abuse or fraudulent conduct which required workers in general to bring additional proof that they were sick, i. e. proof beyond the determination required by the Community rules, was not to be applied as such under Regulation 1408/71. However, since abuse could lawfully be counteracted on a case-by-case basis, the employer was allowed to bring evidence before the national court that the worker was not in actual fact sick.

Delavant, 1995 was about a worker who did not reside in the state where she worked and about the sickness benefits for her family members. Under article 19 Regulation 1408/71, according to the Court, the legislation of the state of employment was applicable to determine entitlement to sickness benefits. It was then up to the state of residence, subject to a refund, to provide benefits in kind according to its own legislation and within its limits, as if the worker was insured there. According to article 19(2) that also applied by analogy to the family members of the worker, if they were not entitled to benefits under the legislation of the state where they resided. Thus, if French law provided certain sickness benefits for children, the German sickness fund had to grant them to the children of a worker insured in France and residing in Germany, regardless of what German law dictated (para. 18).

In *Molenaar, 1998* the Court dealt with a new type of social care insurance with certain special characteristics which was introduced by Germany (see para 5-7). Essentially, the benefits provided under care insurance included reimbursement of certain expenses as well as compensation for home care provided to sick persons by third parties. Those benefits were sickness benefits (paras 23-4). Given their characteristics, part of them were to be classified as benefits in kind, while another part, notably the care allowance, was a cash sickness benefit (paras 32-5). Consequently, France provided the benefits in kind in accordance with its own legislation to persons who were resident in France and working in Germany subject to a refund, while Germany had to grant the care allowance, i.e. the cash benefit, to persons insured in Germany, even if they were resident in France. That applied to employed and unemployed persons as well as pensioners all of whom resided in another state than the competent state. Such persons were not to be exempted from paying the contributions required under care insurance, even if they possibly never claimed benefits thereunder. Conversely, if such persons contributed to care insurance, they were basically also entitled to claim the benefits provided by that insurance when the other conditions, i. e. the conditions complying with Community law, were met (paras 41-3).

Non-discrimination and residence

The Court also dealt with non-discrimination and residence clauses in the 1990s. In *Winter-Lutzins, 1990*, the Court came back to the arrangement the Netherlands had established for the transition to the new old-age insurance system in the year 1957. The Court mainly confirmed *Spruyt, 1986* and *De Jong, 1986*. The legal situation in brief was as follows. Dutch law equalled periods completed before 1957 with insurance periods under the new system, if a person was resident in the Netherlands after her 65th birthday. Such 'continuing-residence' (para. 4) in the Netherlands thus had transformative power. Depending on whether the requirement was met, the years before 1957 were 'gold or dross' according to the opinion of Advocate General Darmon (para. 14). Given that, the annex to Regulation 1408/71 watered down that requirement for persons who had resided for six years in a member state after their 59th birthday. To be more specific, those who were not resident in the Netherlands at the moment of their 65th birthday were still entitled to equal periods before 1957 if during those periods there had been a sufficient connection to the Netherlands. This was the 'second chance' according to Advocate General Darmon (para. 12). That was the case for periods during which they either resided in the Netherlands or worked in the Netherlands for an employer established in the Netherlands while residing in another member state (see *Spruyt, 1986* above). According to the Court, that Dutch transitional regime as attenuated by the annex to Regulation 1408/71 was in compliance with the waiving of residence clauses in article 10(1) Regulation 1408/71. In particular, a person who came to the Netherlands after 1957, but then went back to Germany and was resident there on her 65th birthday could not rely on article 10(1) to force the Dutch authorities to feed time periods before 1957 into her Dutch pension (para. 19). In *De Wit, 1993* the Court added a further element to the transitional arrangement. If Dutch law deemed periods of employment for a legal person governed by Dutch public law as giving rise to rights under the transitional arrangement, even though the employee was resident outside the Netherlands – i. e. in case of 'notional residence' – that same interpretation had to be applied under the annex of Regulation 1408/71 that adapted the transitional arrangement to the free movement of workers. Periods of employment in the Dutch foreign service before 1957 during which the person concerned had been resident outside the Netherlands therefore had to be taken into account, provided that the other conditions were met, since during those periods a sufficient link to the Netherlands had been established (para. 20-1).

In *Commission v. France (supplementary allowance), 1990* the Commission brought infringement proceedings, because France continued to apply the residence requirement to the supplementary allowance which (the residence requirement) the Court had struck down in *Biason, 1974* and *Giletti, 1987*, and because the negotiations in the Council to solve the issue were stalling. Not having an ear for the specific economic and social environment in France or practical difficulties, the Court confirmed the infringement. In a similar vein, the Court in *Commission v. France (allowance), 1991* struck down a residence and a reciprocity requirement for a French supplementary old-age allowance. Similarly, the Court confirmed an infringement in *Commission v. Belgium (minimex), 1992*, since residence in Belgium for a certain period of time was required for the award of certain benefits such as minimex. Neither France nor Belgium had disputed the infringement in these two cases.

In *Masgio, 1991* the Court found discriminatory a specific method of calculation used in Germany when an accident pension and an old-age pension were granted at the same time. When both pensions were granted in Germany, German law required the suspension of an overlapping amount of the old-age pension. The overlapping amount was calculated in two ways, namely by reference to the annual earnings based on which the accident pension was calculated and to the basis of calculation of the old-age pension. The lower amount of the two was then suspended. If, however, the accident pension had been awarded abroad, the amount to be suspended was only calculated by reference to the basis of calculation of the old-age pension. As a consequence, the amount suspended in such cases was regularly higher than in cases when the accident pension had also been awarded in Germany. That was contrary to articles 7 and 48 to 51 Treaty and article 3(1) Regulation 1408/71 (paras 20-2).

In *Baglieri, 1993* the Court mainly confirmed the established case-law as to voluntary or optional continued insurance under article 9(2) Regulation 1408/71. It was up to national law to determine the conditions for the acquisition of rights, provided that periods of insurance completed in other member states were taken into account when periods of a certain length of time were required for admission to voluntary or optional continued insurance pursuant to article 9(2) Regulation 1408/71. Yet a returning migrant worker could not on the ground of having been affiliated to an insurance scheme in another member state lawfully claim admission to a scheme of voluntary continued insurance in Italy for the admission to which prior compulsory insurance affiliation in Italy was required. The Court then rejected a challenge of this approach on the basis of non-discrimination. Italian nationals returning from third states were allowed to be affiliated to social security insurance, while Italian nationals returning from a member state did not have a possibility to join insurance. However, Community law did not preclude Italy from treating its own nationals more favourable when they returned from working in a third state than when they came back from working in a member state (para. 18).

In *Leguaye-Neelsen, 1993* the Court also rejected a challenge based on non-discrimination. Normally, persons entering the public administration in Germany were reimbursed the compulsory social security contributions they had previously paid under the German social security system, if their contributions did not suffice in themselves to acquire a right to a pension. Ms Leguaye-Neelsen's contributions were not reimbursed though when she entered the

French public service on the ground that she was entitled to voluntary continued insurance in Germany. The Court decided that Regulation 1408/71 applied (para. 12). However, non-discrimination was not violated, since normally contributions were not reimbursed if they were insufficient to acquire a pension; rather, continued insurance was offered. Contributions were only reimbursed when a person joined the German public administration to make up for the fact that continued insurance was not offered. That approach aimed at avoiding the duplication of insurance periods. Germany, however, was not required to prevent such duplication with regard to foreign insurance schemes (paras 13-6).

Hoorn, 1994 again rejected a claim of discrimination. Based on a convention concluded between the Netherlands and Germany, periods of forced labour of Dutch nationals in Germany during World War II gave rise to pension rights in the Netherlands. The argument that such an approach was discriminatory since pension rights in Germany granted to German forced labourers would have been more favourable was rejected by the Court. The convention, which continued to apply for it was mentioned in the annex to Regulation 1408/71, only determined the legislation applicable. That a German pension would have been more favourable was only the consequence of Germany granting higher pensions to forced labourers than the Netherlands (paras 12-3). There was no discrimination, either, in that those who had continued to work in Germany became subject to the Regulation instead of the convention (para. 16). Furthermore, article 8 Regulation 1408/71, which required the member states to conclude conventions in the spirit of the Regulation, only applied to conventions concluded after the entry into force of Regulation 1408/71 (para. 19).

In *Drake, 1994*, again, the Court did not find any violation of article 48 Treaty. In this case, the Netherlands refused Mr Drake an invalidity pension, because he had not had any income in the year before the onset of invalidity since he had quit working after a certain time after having gone to Germany. The problem was the following. Before the amendment of Regulation 1408/71, which had brought self-employed persons within the scope of the Regulation, a first Dutch act had been applicable with regard to invalidity pursuant to article 45(3) Regulation 1408/71 when a worker had become eligible for benefits in another member state because he had become incapable of work. Article 45(3) declared the materialization of invalidity anywhere in the Community as sufficient for systems, such as the Dutch, which relied on materialization of risk rather than the progressive constitution of rights. *After* the amendment of Regulation 1408/71, however, pursuant to the annex relating to the Netherlands that first Dutch act applied to employed persons, while another, a second Dutch act, applied to persons who were not employed. It was, therefore, after the amendment not sufficient any longer to be eligible for benefits in another member state to render the first Dutch act applicable; rather, one had to be employed at the time invalidity materialized. Moreover, application of the second act required a person to have some income at the time invalidity overcame (para. 16). The Court found that the new approach in the annex to Regulation 1408/71 relating to the

Netherlands was not invalid in the light of article 48 Treaty. Mainly, rights based on national law were not lost by reason of the movement of the person concerned to another member state. Rather, it was the ceasing of work which had had the consequence that Mr Drake did not receive any benefits under Dutch legislation (para. 24). Moreover, as to the income that was needed pursuant to the annex for the second act, the member states had the power to determine the conditions of the right to become a member of a social security scheme; they could render them stricter, too. Since the condition of having income before becoming incapable of work was not discriminatory, article 48 Treaty was not violated (para. 27-8).

Kemmler, 1996 dealt with the social security contributions of a self-employed person before the relevant amendment of Regulation 1408/71 applied. The Court ruled that Belgium was not allowed to require a self-employed lawyer who practised in Belgium as well as in Germany where he was also habitually resident and was subject to social security to pay social security contributions as a self-employed person in Belgium, even if he partly also resided in Belgium. The otherwise resulting restriction of the freedom of establishment in article 52 Treaty was not justified as the contributions did not afford any additional protection (paras 12-3). In *Commission v. Greece (large families), 1998* the Court ruled that the nationality condition applied by the Greek authorities when awarding certain sickness and family benefits for large families violated the principle of non-discrimination in article 3(1) Regulation 1408/71 (para. 28). *Swaddling, 1999*, finally, concerned the residence requirement contained in article 10a Regulation 1408/71. The Court held that the notion of 'residence' in that article was a Community term for the application of which all circumstances in a concrete case needed to be taken into account (para. 29). In particular, the United Kingdom could not lawfully consider a British national who returned as a migrant worker from another member state to have 'residence' for the purpose of article 10a only after an appreciable period of time. As the intention to remain in the United Kingdom was clear from the circumstances, such a time limit could not lawfully be applied (para. 30).

Third states

The Court addressed social security in agreements with third countries in a few judgments in the 1990s. *Kziber, 1991* dealt with the Rabat Cooperation Agreement with Morocco. The Court held based on *Demirel, 1987* that article 41(1) of that Agreement relating to non-discrimination in social security had direct effect, although implementing measures had not been adopted (para. 19). In analogy to Regulation 1408/71 unemployment benefits were covered. A Moroccan worker who had retired was to be considered a worker under article 41(1). Owing to non-discrimination, his daughter could not be refused an unemployment benefit in Belgium where they both lived because of her Moroccan nationality, if she met all other requirements of national law (para. 28). In a similar vein, the Court rejected a nationality requirement in *Yousfi, 1994* for a Belgian disability allowance. Mr Yousfi had fulfilled all the requirements of Belgian law for the award of the allowance after having become disabled because of an accident at work, except that he was a Moroccan national. The Court categorized him as a worker and the Belgian allowance in keeping with the case-law under Regulation 1408/71, namely *Newton, 1991*, as an invalidity benefit despite the dual function of the benefit. Hence, the nationality requirement was precluded by article 41(1) (paras 23-9).

In *Krid, 1995* the Court essentially extended the approach developed for the Rabat Agreement to the Algiers Cooperation Agreement with Algeria. The Algerian wife of an Algerian worker who (the worker) was deceased had applied for a French supplementary allowance to her survivor's pension. She had never worked herself. Her application was refused on the ground of her nationality. The Court held the non-discrimination clause in article 39(1) Algiers Agreement to be directly effective. As the wife of a former worker, she was covered by the Algiers Agreement. In analogy to *Giletti, 1987*, and *Commission v. France (supplementary allowance), 1990* and in the light of the amendment of Regulation 1408/71 which had expressly included special non-contributory benefits in its scope, the supplementary allowance was a social security benefit for the purpose of the Algiers Agreement (para. 33-6). The derived rights-approach developed under Regulation 1408/71, however, was not applicable under the Algiers Agreement, since the scope *ratione personae* of the latter was different (para. 39). The nationality requirement was therefore precluded by the non-discrimination clause in article 39(1). That approach was confirmed later on in *Babahenini, 1998* for a Belgian disability allowance under the Algiers Agreement. In particular the rejection of the derived rights-approach, which the Court had restricted some time before *Babahenini, 1998* in *Cabanis-Issarte, 1996*, for the Algiers Agreement was upheld.

Hallouzi-Choho, 1996 concerned the transitional arrangement established by the Netherlands for the transition from the old to the new old-age pension legislation in 1957 which had been at issue in the line of case-law that began with *Spruyt, 1986*. In *Hallouzi-Choho, 1996* that arrangement was at stake in the light of the Rabat Agreement. The Hallouzi-Chohos were Moroccan nationals residing in the Netherlands. The husband had worked, but then retired. The wife had not worked and claimed application of the transitional arrangement. That claim was rejected on the ground of their nationality. The Rabat Agreement did not include an adaptation of the transitional arrangement for migrant workers like the annex to Regulation 1408/71. According to the Court, that was irrelevant, since except for nationality Ms Hallouzi-Choho fulfilled all the requirements of Dutch law for the application of the transitional arrangement, in particular the requirement to have residence in the Netherlands (paras 32-36). Hence, since she was within the scope of the Agreement (para. 30), the non-discrimination clause in article 41(1) of the Agreement precluded the Dutch authorities from relying on her Moroccan nationality to refuse her the benefit of the transitional arrangement (para. 28). Moreover, residence or employment requirements had to be imposed in the same way as for Dutch nationals (para. 37).

In *Mesbah, 1999* the Court refused to transpose the reasoning in *Micheletti, 1992*, an establishment case in which the effects of dual nationality were in question (see above), to the case at hand which concerned a retired worker who held both Moroccan and Belgian nationality and was resident in Belgium. According to the Court, Belgian law was not precluded from considering such a worker as a Belgian national only. Accordingly it could lawfully refuse to allow him and his family members to rely on the Rabat Agreement (para. 39). Apart from that, the Court also ruled that the term family members in article 41(1) Rabat Agreement included not just the spouse and the children, but also the parents of a worker as well as close relatives related by marriage, such as the parents-in-law if they lived together with the worker (paras 44-6).

Ankara

In *Taflan-Met, 1996* the Court was faced with Decision 3/80, i. e. the analogon of Regulation 1408/71 which had been adopted by the association council under the Ankara Agreement with Turkey. According to the Court, Decision 3/80 was binding as per its adoption by the association council. Implementing measures by the parties to the Ankara Agreement were not needed for its entry into force (paras 18-21). However, although Decision 3/80 had virtually the same content as Regulation 1408/71 and included some implementing provisions, it did not have direct effect in the absence of an implementing measure governing the details regulated by the 'voluminous' Regulation 574/72 for the Community (para. 28). Without such a measure, which had been pending before the Council at the time, Decision 3/80 could not be applied properly (paras 30-7). In *Sürül, 1999* the Court put *Taflan-Met, 1996* in a different perspective. Ms Sürül was the wife of a Turkish student in Germany. He had a limited work permit and he worked, but was only ensured against accidents. She only had a limited residence permit and was insured against old-age for a certain time when she gave birth to their child. She then applied for family allowances, which were refused on the ground of her having only a limited residence permit. The Court ruled that the limitation in *Taflan-Met, 1996* was not applicable in this case. In contrast to the aggregation at stake in *Taflan-Met, 1996*, implementing provisions were not required for the case at issue. Hence, the prohibition of discrimination in article 3(1) Decision 3/80 had direct effect and applied directly (paras 57-8 and 63). The limitation of the term 'employed person' for the purpose of family benefits awarded in Germany that was contained in the annex to Regulation 1408/71 which was applicable to Decision 3/80 based on a reference, was not to be applied in this constellation, since the chapter on family benefits was not at issue. Only Germany was concerned, while the restrictive definition in the annex was designed to limit the availability of German family benefits pursuant to the chapter on family benefits in situations where two member states were concerned (para. 90). As Mr and Ms Sürül were each ensured against one risk covered by Decision 3/80, which was sufficient by analogy to the case-law under Regulation 1408/71 (para. 86), Decision 3/80 applied, namely either to her being a family member of a person covered by the Decision himself or to her being insured herself on the basis of old-age insurance due to childbirth (paras 93-4). As a consequence, non-discrimination in article 3 Decision 3/80 precluded Germany from refusing the family allowance on the sole ground that the person concerned only held a limited residence permit (paras 101-3).

Technicalities

A number of technical details of the Community social security rules were also clarified by the Court during the 1990s. In *Iacobelli, 1993* the Court ruled that it was entirely up to national law to determine whether a person could validly waive an invalidity benefit in favour of an old-age pension, since the member states laid down the conditions for the award of benefits. Articles 44(2) Regulation 1408/71 and 36(4) Regulation 574/72 were purely procedural provisions. In *Picard, 1996* the Court decided based on article 86 Regulation 1408/71 that benefits had to be awarded in all member states concurrently as per the date of the first claim submitted in any one member state (para. 20). Article 36(1) Regulation 574/72, which required a person to submit the claim to the institution at the place of residence, only simplified the administrative procedure. A failure to comply with it was not to amount to an obstacle to the award of benefits. In *Baldone, 1997* the Court confirmed that an invalidity pension awarded pursuant to Regulation 1408/71 could only lawfully be re-calculated in the light of the amendment to Regulation 1408/71 by Regulation 1248/92 to the detriment of the person concerned upon that person's explicit request pursuant to article 95a(4) to (6) Regulation 1408/71 which had been introduced by the amending Regulation. Moreover, a benefit had to be considered to have been awarded under Regulation 1408/71 before the amendment when the authorities rectified after the entry into force of the amended Regulation the erroneous calculation made before its entry into force (paras 13 and 15-7). Article 95a(4) to (6) therefore applied fully.

Subrogation

Two judgments in the 1990s concerned subrogation. *DAK, 1994* was about the subrogation of a German insurance company into the rights of an insured person against the person having caused an accident in Denmark. The Court decided that the nature and the extent of the claim subrogated as well as the question whether a subrogation occurred in the first place was to be determined by the law of the state where the insurance company was established pursuant to article 93(1) Regulation 1408/71, i. e. German law in the case at issue (para. 18). If that law provided for subrogation, all member states had to recognize it and could not rely on their national law to exclude it (para. 22). That was the counterpart for insurers being liable to cover accidents throughout the Community suffered by persons insured with them. The subrogation included the costs that arose in another member state by reason of transport and hospital treatment. However, the substance of the claim against the person having caused the accident or against the corresponding insurer – in particular, with regard to whether the person was liable for the injury caused – was governed by the legislation applicable pursuant to the rules of private international law of the member state concerned, viz. typically the legislation of the state where the accident had taken place, i. e. in this case Denmark (para. 21). In *Kordel, 1999* the Court confirmed this interpretation. It merely clarified two points. First, that restrictions of the subrogation in the law of the member state where the institution subrogated was established needed to be taken into account by all member states; and second, that the subrogation was not capable of creating additional rights going beyond those the victim had against the person having caused the accident (para. 23).

Social security more broadly

Finally, three more judgments which were handed down in the 1990s were related to social security. (i) *Faux, 1991* regarded frontier workers under Regulation 36/63. The Court ruled that a worker retained the status of a frontier within the meaning of Regulation 36/63, although he had become wholly unemployed. Moreover, according to that Regulation and Regulation 1408/71, the member state where a frontier worker had last been employed was competent for both incapacity of work and invalidity benefits. When that state made the acquisition of a right to incapacity of work benefits dependent on the completion of insurance periods and counted periods during which unemployment benefits were paid towards such insurance periods, periods during which unemployment benefits were drawn abroad had to be counted in equally, even though such periods were not regarded as insurance periods in the state of residence (para. 24). The reason was that it was Regulation 36/63 that determined that unemployment benefits had to be granted in the member state of residence (para. 23). If such periods during which unemployment benefits were granted abroad did not count towards periods of insurance for invalidity purposes in the state of employment as article 1(r) Regulation 1408/71 indicated, an unemployed frontier worker would as a consequence never acquire invalidity benefits (para. 26). (ii) A question of social security law was also raised in *Zabala Erasun, 1995*. However, the Court did not address the merits of the case, because it was inadmissible for lack of jurisdiction. (iii) In *Poucet and Pistre, 1993* the Court rejected a challenge against certain national social security systems on the basis of competition law. Essentially, the Court ruled that the entities involved in the social security systems were not undertakings in the sense of articles 85 and 86 Treaty, for they implemented the law on the basis of solidarity and non-profit. As such, they were not engaged in an economic activity.

4 Services

Posted workers

The first judgment in the free movement of services in the 1990s, *Rush Portuguesa, 1990*, concerned services in the context of the Act of Accession of Portugal. Rush Portuguesa was a Portuguese undertaking in the construction business that provided services in France under a contract. For that purpose, Rush brought its own employees to France. The question arose whether the transitional limitations of the free movement of workers in the Act of Accession also applied to the provision of services, which had been liberalized as per accession, through construction workers. According to the Court, the freedom of services itself covered such service provision. Hence, work permits or engagement *in situ* could not lawfully to be required (para. 12). The purpose of the limitations in the Act of Accession was, so the Court, to avoid disruption of the employment market (para. 14). The provision of services at issue did not risk such disruption, since the workers came to France only temporarily, did not seek employment, and later on would return to Portugal, all while they were employed and insured against risks by Rush Portuguesa (para. 15). Hence, the limitations in the Act of Accession did not apply. However, the Court adjusted its answer to the services in question, viz. performance of a contract via workers in the construction business (para. 16). France was, moreover, entitled to apply its own labour laws and prevent abuse (paras 17-8).

In *Vander Elst, 1994* the Court came back to posted workers. A company established in Belgium lawfully employed Moroccan workers. The workers had work and residence permits, received regular pay, and were covered by the Belgian social security system. When they were posted to France to execute a project, they had short-stay visas, but France required a work permit for them and the payment of a fee. The Court first re-cited services case-law, emphasizing the right to enter a member state to provide and receive services (para. 13), and then implied that the French rules applied indiscriminately, as French firms also had to comply with them when their employees sought access to France's employment market. Yet the posted workers did not seek access to that market (para. 21). That was why in those circumstances the French requirement to have a work permit and to pay a fee went beyond what was required, as a prerequisite for service provision, to enforce French employment rules, in particular given that the supervision by the Belgian authorities prevented exploitation of the workers. In addition, those workers benefitted from non-discrimination under the Rabat Agreement with Morocco (paras 18-25).

Guiot, 1996 also dealt with posted workers. The posting of workers by a company established in Luxembourg to Belgium for construction work prompted a charge under Belgium's collective labour agreements payable by the Luxembourg company. The charge was levied to secure construction workers an income, when they were laid off due to bad weather, and an end-of-year premium.

However, the company concerned was already subject to a similar charge in Luxembourg for the workers it employed. According to the Court, although the Belgian charge was indistinctly applicable, the service provider was required to pay two charges with respect to the same workers for the same period. The higher financial burden to be shouldered by the service provider was liable to restrict its freedom (paras 14-5). While the host state was certainly entitled to impose its own legislation on social protection of workers, it could not do so in so far as the workers' interests were already protected as a consequence of the charge in the state where the provider was established. In that regard it was sufficient if the corresponding charge covered the same risks and pursued a similar purpose, whereas the way the charge was levied was immaterial (paras 16-21).

Arblade, 1999 again clarified a number of points with regard to workers posted temporarily to another member state. Belgium required companies, such as Arblade, posting workers to Belgium to fulfil certain requirements. The Court reiterated that the host state could impose minimum wages applicable in the host state, even when the 'home' state legislation was complied with, provided however that the rules on minimum wages were sufficiently precise, accessible, and clearly communicated (paras 41-3). However, the Belgian loyalty and bad weather stamps were not necessarily part of a minimum remuneration (paras 46-7). Whether contributions to finance those stamps and the requirement to furnish the corresponding documentation could lawfully be imposed depended on whether the posted workers concerned already enjoyed similar protection against the relevant risk in the state where the service provider was established. Even if that was not the case, the freedom of services required that contributions resulted in real additional social protection for those workers (paras 50-5). The keeping of separate social and labour documents on site was a restriction of the freedom of services when the state where the service provider was established already required book-keeping (paras 58-9). However, having documents available was necessary to enable controls at least where Directive 96/71 on posting of workers did not bring the member states' documentation requirements in line. Whether those documents would necessarily have to be drafted in accordance with *host* state legislation as well hinged on the national authorities' and court's assessment of the likeness of the documentations required by the two national legal orders, as assessed in the light of the relevant Community social policy directives (paras 61-70). It could only be required lawfully within certain narrow limits that documents be retained with an agent in Belgium after the posting had come to an end. Documents needed could be forwarded on demand by the authorities. Moreover, Directive 96/71 would make that requirement redundant after its entry into force (paras 76-9).

Tourist guides

In a series of infringement procedures, the Court next dealt with restrictions imposed on services in the context of tour operators working with tourist guides. In *Commission v. Italy (tourist guides), 1991* the Court explained that two kinds of services were involved. Either a service providing tour operator from one state employed a tourist guide and brought her or him along to another member state, or such an operator availed itself of an independent guide. In either case, the freedom of services was involved (paras 5-6), as it always was when a service provider established in one state provided services in another state, irrespective of where the recipient of the service was established (para. 9). Italy's requirement for tourist guides to have an Italian licence, although applicable irrespective of nationality, constituted a restriction of services (paras 15-6). Justification was conceivable as far as the grounds argued were not already covered by 'home' state legislation. A licence requirement, however, went beyond what protecting the consumer and the cultural heritage, though as such legitimate grounds, called for (paras 17-20). Consumers and cultural heritage were sufficiently protected by the competition among and the reputation concerns of tour operators. Moreover, tourists benefited if they were familiar with tourist guides and if they had language options. Those two aspects suffered when the number of tourist guides was low because of a licence requirement (paras 22-4). In *Commission v. France (tourist guides), 1991* and *Commission v. Greece (tourist guides), 1991* the Court ruled in the same way as in *Commission v. Italy (tourist guides), 1991. Commission v. Spain (tourist guides), 1994* later on established that Spain had committed the same infringement of the freedom of services as the other member states in the corresponding cases (paras 21-2). Spain, moreover, failed to open the examination required to qualify as a tourist guide for nationals of other member states, thus violating the free movement of workers and establishment (paras 8-9), and to provide a procedure to examine the equivalence of tourist guide qualifications obtained in other member states (paras 14-7). In *SETTG, 1997* a different measure in the context of tourist guides was at stake. Based on a settlement of a collective labour dispute, Greece required that tourist guides who held a Greek licence and provided services to a tourist agency, regardless of where that agency was established, in essence had to be given an employment contract subject to social security contributions. That arrangement, according to the Court, concerned the free movement of services, because the provision of services by self-employed tourist guides established in other member states and holding a Greek licence, which they did not need, but could obtain, was affected (paras 12-3). It established an indiscriminately applicable barrier by excluding such service provision (para. 17). Maintaining industrial peace and preventing adverse effects on tourism were economic aims which were not capable of justifying a restriction. In any case, industrial peace did not require that tourist guides established abroad could not provide services in Greece (paras 23-4).

Lawyers

In *Commission v. France (lawyers), 1991* the Court mainly reiterated for France what had already been decided for Germany with regard to the implementation of Directive 77/249 on lawyers in *Commission v. Germany (lawyers), 1988*. To require a person to retain a lawyer established on site when representation was compulsory was only allowed within the confines of 'work in conjunction' as elaborated in *Commission v. Germany (lawyers), 1988*, while it was precluded for administrative proceedings and when representation was not compulsory (paras 15-9 and 28-36). France, moreover, had to recognize French nationals authorized to practise abroad as lawyers in France like nationals of other member states (paras 10-1).

Säger

Säger, 1991 was about reminders sent to patent holders indicating that their patents were up for renewal. Such reminders were dispatched by service providers in the United Kingdom who coupled them with the advancement of the patent fees to be paid. In the United Kingdom such a service could be provided freely, while in Germany it was reserved to patent agents who were licensed. The Court decided that the free movement of services was about abolishing all restrictions on cross-border services, regardless of whether those restrictions applied indiscriminately, in particular when a restriction impeded the services provided by a provider established in another member state where that provider offered those services lawfully and when it was not necessary to visit the host state to provide a service (paras 12-3). The German licence requirement was such a restriction which, as all restrictions of services, had to be justified by imperative reasons in the public interest not yet protected by 'home' state legislation and had to apply indiscriminately, while being necessary to meet those imperative reasons (paras 14-5). The protection of the service recipient from unqualified legal advice, while being a valid ground as such, could not justify Germany's licence requirement, as it was unnecessary. No particular legal knowledge was required to send out a patent reminder; and the risk was limited, as the patent office in any case dispatched a reminder later on, charging a higher fee at that point in time though (paras 16-20).

Broadcasting

ERT AE, 1991 concerned the television monopoly in Greece. ERT had the exclusive right to produce radio and television programmes in Greece. This included retransmitting in Greece programmes produced abroad. While a broadcasting monopoly was not *per se* incompatible with the free movement of services, the Court held that, in the case of Greece, production and transmission powers were all aggregated in one hand. Consequently, the risk arose that programmes produced abroad would be discriminated against and the programmes ERT AE produced itself were favoured in broadcasting. If the national court found that that was the case, the limitation in numbers of channels available would not justify such discrimination as long as channels were left unused (paras 20-5). Moreover, the freedom of expression as guaranteed by article 10 European Convention of Human Rights would have to be taken into account when assessing justification. According to the Court, a derogation from free movement could only apply, if it was compatible with fundamental rights (para. 43).

In *Gouda, 1991* the Court next addressed the Netherlands' regulation of broadcasting which had been amended after the ruling in *Bond, 1988*. Dutch law in *Gouda, 1991* established certain requirements which applied to foreign companies broadcasting television advertisements in the Netherlands as well as Dutch companies, while advertisements in the Netherlands were still channelled through a Dutch foundation. In a preliminary remark, the Court emphasized that discriminatory requirements were only susceptible to justification by the grounds explicitly mentioned in article 56 Treaty, while indiscriminately applicable requirements could be justified by the broader 'overriding reasons relating to the public interest' (para. 13; paras 10-5). The restriction was twofold in that Dutch cable operators were hindered in broadcasting programmes produced by foreign broadcasters, while foreign broadcasters were hindered in their opportunities. The conditions concerned the structure of broadcasting companies and the advertisements to be broadcast and amounted to restrictions (paras 17-9). The conditions as to the structure of companies could not lawfully be imposed on foreign bodies; to do so was not justified by the needs of cultural policy – which otherwise was a valid ground in particular in the light of the freedom of expression (para. 23) – as there was not any essential connection between the two (paras 24-5). The conditions as to the ads, i. e. as to types of ads, timing, etc., still had the effect of protecting the revenues of the Dutch foundation and could for that reason not be justified, whereas in principle they were capable of being justified by the need to protect the consumer and by cultural policy (paras 27-9). *Commission v. Netherlands (broadcasting), 1991*, handed down on the same day as *Gouda, 1991*, added that the Netherlands were not allowed to require those producers that were allocated broadcasting time in the Netherlands to use the technical facilities of a specific Dutch public company for production. Such a restriction had a protective effect, for it disadvantaged similar companies in other states, and could not be justified by the needs of cultural policy to which it was not connected (paras 22-5 and 31-2).

Commission v. Belgium (broadcasting), 1992 dealt with the Belgian rules on broadcasting. The Flemish community, in particular, precluded cable operators in the Flemish territory from transmitting programmes of broadcasters established in other member states in languages other than the official language of the member state where the broadcaster was established. In other words, a Dutch broadcaster's programme in Flemish could lawfully be re-transmitted in Belgium by a cable operator, while a German broadcaster's programme in Flemish, e. g. a 'Flemish window', could not. The Court held that regime to be discriminatory. The same restriction did not apply to Belgian national companies and it prevented distribution of foreign programmes in the Flemish territory (paras 5-6). The restriction could not be justified by cultural policy or the needs to maintain media pluralism and the revenue of national broadcasting companies, as those grounds were not explicitly mentioned in article 56 Treaty. Therefore, they could not justify discriminatory restrictions. Moreover, to safeguard the revenue of a national company was incompatible with the freedom of services (paras 9-11).

That the programmes concerned were principally directed at Belgian territory also failed to provide any justification, as trans-border service provision as such could not be prohibited, else the freedom of services would be abolished (para. 12). Belgium, moreover, did not dispute that the authorization requirement applied by the Flemish community as well as the definition it applied of 'own cultural productions' violated the freedom of services; nor did it dispute that to reserve the majority of the share capital in the Flemish broadcasting company to certain shareholders was contrary to the freedom of establishment (paras 14-5).

Veronica, 1993 then addressed a situation under the Netherlands' broadcasting system again. Veronica was a Dutch broadcasting association of viewers which was indirectly funded by viewer's fees and advertisement revenues, could produce programmes, and was allocated programme time, but was not allowed to make profit. Veronica helped found a company in Luxembourg which was to broadcast its programmes in particular towards the Netherlands, by providing *inter alia* advice and a bank guarantee. However, the Dutch authorities prohibited that specific activity of Veronica. The Court confirmed that the Dutch system, as a pluralistic, non-commercial system justified by the freedom of expression which was characterized by viewer's associations such as Veronica, was in accordance with the free movement of services and capital. The idea of prohibiting the support provided to the Luxembourg company was to avoid diverting funds to purely commercial ends (paras 9-11). Moreover, the freedom of services would be misused in order to evade professional rules applicable in the Netherlands by directing a service from Luxembourg towards the Netherlands (paras 12-3). *TV10, 1994* further elaborated that aspect of prevention of abuse under the Dutch broadcasting system. The Dutch authorities had treated a broadcaster established in Luxembourg which aired principally towards the Netherlands as a domestic undertaking. The Court explained that the case-law established did not remove such services from the scope of the freedom of services. Rather, the Netherlands were entitled, in the circumstances of its broadcasting system designed to implement media pluralism and a certain cultural policy, to take measures to prevent that kind of evasion of Dutch rules (para. 15). To treat a broadcaster as domestic was such a measure (paras 21-6).

Leclerc-Siplec, 1995, apart from applying *Keck and Mithouard, 1993* under the free movement of goods, then dealt with a French television ad ban for the distribution sector, which affected a company importing goods, under Directive 89/552 on television broadcasting services. The Court ruled that the Directive left the member states free to adopt stricter rules than those in the Directive. The ad ban thus did not go against the grain of the Directive (paras 37-47). The implementation of Directive 89/552 was also at issue in *Commission v. Belgium (TV broadcasting), 1996*. The idea underlying the Directive was that the state in the territory of which broadcasts originated was to ensure that these broadcasts complied with that state's law and the Directive (see paras 34-9 and 86). In contrast, Belgium – more specifically, the language communities in Belgium – maintained certain requirements for 'incoming' broadcasts, such as requirements of prior authorization. In essence, the Court ruled that the Directive covered broadcasts via cable (paras 19-25); that cable retransmission was concerned by the Belgian measures (paras 27-8); that a measure's compliance with the freedom of expression as laid down in the European Convention of Human Rights did not guarantee compliance with Community law (para. 45); that neither of the newly adopted provisions of the Maastricht Treaty concerning cultural policy and subsidiarity justified Belgium's measure (paras 46-53); that Belgium had failed to demonstrate the measure's necessity and proportionality in the light of cultural policy and copyright protections (paras 55, 57, 90, and 92); that the measures were too general to combat abuse of law in the sense of the case-law (para. 65); and that the member states had to have mutual trust with regard to the supervision of broadcasters (para. 88).

RTI, 1996 equally concerned Directive 89/552. The Court decided that 'telepromotions', which were common practice in Italy, could, but need not necessarily benefit from the option provided by article 18(1) to increase total ad time (paras 34-6); and that nothing in the Directive required sponsors only to be named at the beginning or the end of a programme (paras 43-7). *De Agostini, 1997* again dealt with broadcasting of advertisements. Certain transmissions from the United Kingdom were prohibited in Sweden because the ads they contained violated certain Swedish rules as to content; in particular, they addressed minors. The Court decided that Directive 89/552 did not preclude the application of rules that protected consumers and ensured fairness by the host state (paras 32-5). Under the freedom of services, too, the restriction the Swedish rules established (paras 50-1) were amenable to justification by consumer protection, subject to the national court's assessment (para. 52). However, as the Directive contained a set of rules to ensure that the broadcasting state guaranteed the control of programmes with regard to protection of minors, the host state no longer could control content in this regard (paras 59-61). (The judgment also had a dimension of free movement of goods.) Finally, *ARD, 1999* also raised issues under Directive 89/552. Germany applied the net rather than the gross principle to television ads. The ad time allowed per movie was calculated on the basis of the net length of a movie, rather than the overall time required to screen a movie together with advertisements. The Court held that the Directive had to be read so as to embody the gross principle, because that reading chimed more with the freedom of services (paras 29-32). However, as the Directive did not prevent a member state from applying stricter standards to broadcasters under its jurisdiction, Germany could lawfully require application of the net principle (paras 37-42) and still be in compliance with the freedom of services, for the restriction posed by the net principle was justified by the need to protect consumers (paras 49-52).

No connection to services, purely internal

In *Grogan, 1991* students in Ireland distributed information material about possibilities to have a legal abortion in clinics in the United Kingdom. Those student officers were not in any way affiliated with the British clinics. Irish law prohibited abortion and the distribution of materials about it. The Court decided, after having confirmed that the freedom of services applied to medical services in general and to legal abortions more specifically (paras 18-20), that the link between the persons handing out the information and the service provided by the British clinics was too tenuous for the prohibition to distribute information material on abortions to constitute a restriction of the freedom of services (para. 24). The distribution of information was a way to make use of the freedom of expression, but it was independent of the economic activity (para. 26). Hence, in those circumstances the freedom of services was not restricted by Ireland's prohibition. Consequently, the Court did not have jurisdiction to examine any violation of fundamental rights, either (para. 31). In *Hoefner and Elser, 1991*, a competition law case, the Court, also ruled that the free movement of services was not concerned. German consultancy companies provided advice with recruitment of German nationals for German companies. There was no link to any situation governed by Community law (paras 38-9). In *Boscher, 1991* the Court decided that the free movement of services was not applicable when a trader occasionally sold goods belonging to him by public auction in another member state and challenged the rules governing that sale. The freedom of services only applied when no other market freedom was applicable. In that case the free movement of goods was indeed applicable (paras 8-9).

In *Gervais, 1995* the Court characterized a situation as purely internal to France, because a French national had practised artificial insemination of animals without proper qualifications and in violation of the monopoly established in France. The free movement of services and establishment were not in any way concerned by the situation (paras 24-6). The Court merely reiterated *Mialocq, 1983*, viz. that a monopoly in services could indirectly affect the free movement of goods which would render article 37 Treaty applicable (paras 35-7).

The Court in *RI.SAN., 1999* declined to assess whether equal treatment and transparency obligations flowing from the freedom of movement were violated, for the situation concerned was purely internal to Italy. An Italian company which had previously provided waste disposal services to a municipality in Italy had objected to those services being entrusted offhandedly to a newly formed Italian company partly owned by that municipality (paras 21-3). In *Jägerskiöld, 1999* the Court again refused to apply the freedom of services, because the dispute was confined in all aspects to a member state. Two Finnish nationals resident in Finland had been in dispute over fishing rights in Finland (paras 43-4). Yet the Court clarified that granting a right to catch fish meant to provide a service. That the right was transferable and certified in a document did not render the free movement of goods applicable (para. 36).

Public works

In *Commission v. Italy (public works), 1992* the Court dealt with certain conditions which Italy required tenderers to meet to be awarded a contract, in the light of the freedom of services and Directive 71/305 on public works contracts. More specifically, Italy insisted that tenderers entrusted a minimum amount of services to sub-contractors established in the region. Moreover, in an invitation to tender preference was to be given to groups that pursued their main activities in the region concerned. The Court found that approach to be discriminatory. It was true that Italian undertakings were also treated unfavourably. However, the decisive point was that it were essentially Italian undertakings that were favoured (paras 8-9 and 12). The idea to counter disadvantages experienced by local and regional undertakings because of the award of a single, large contract was unsuitable as a ground to justify that discrimination (paras 13-4). (Directive 71/305 was violated, too, by the preference to be given to local groups, para. 21.)

Various services

In *Fedicine, 1993* Spain linked the licence to dub movies from third countries into the Spanish national languages to the filming and distribution of Spanish movies. According to the Court, foreign film distributors, who provided services within the meaning of article 59 Treaty (paras 10-1), were thereby disadvantaged, because Spanish distributors and producers gained an advantage (paras 14-5). As the measure was not indiscriminately applicable, only express derogation grounds could be argued. None of them applied. Apart from that, cultural policy could not provide justification, as Spanish producers were favoured independently of the quality and content of films. Moreover, the measure pursued an economic aim in that it sought to safeguard revenues of national producers (paras 16-21). In *Hubbard, 1993* the Court was faced with a German measure which required a British executor to lodge a deposit in proceedings in Germany in order to obtain possession of real property in Germany belonging to the testator's estate. (The relevant conventions either contained a reservation or were only applicable to those resident in the host state.) As the service was provided in a member state other than that where both service recipient and provider were established, the freedom of services applied (paras 11-3). The measure was discriminatory, as it applied only to nationals of other member states, and as such precluded (para. 14). That Germany's law on succession was involved was irrelevant, since procedural law had to comply with the freedom of services (para. 19). In *Wirth, 1993* the Court confirmed *Humbel, 1988* in that the freedom of services did not apply to public education. In particular, it was not applicable to courses at institutes of higher education which were in essence financed out of public funds. In contrast, it did apply to private for-profit institutions where students paid for training (paras 15-7). Furthermore, in the answer to the second question the Court confirmed *Lair, 1988* in that maintenance grants were held to be outside the scope of the Treaty.

Games of chance

Schindler, 1994 was the first case that concerned games of chance. Agents of a German public large-scale lottery had sent ads and application forms to persons in the United Kingdom where such lotteries were prohibited, in contrast to small-scale lottery-like activities. The agents were prosecuted in the United Kingdom. The Court first decided that the freedom of services applied rather than the free movement of goods, because the materials sent to the persons in the United Kingdom embodied a larger service, i. e. a service that combined the sale of a hope to win with the collection of the bets, the determination of the winner, and the payment of prizes for the price of a ticket. The service was not prohibited in all the member states. Even the United Kingdom allowed it, though on a smaller scale. Thus, the import of the tickets was not to be likened to an import of illegal products. The activity was moreover economic, despite the elements of chance and recreation and the use of the profits in the public interest (paras 22-35). According to the Court, the British prohibition was applicable without distinction as small-scale lottery-like activities were not comparable to large-scale lotteries. But it raised an obstacle to the provision of a service across the border which (the service) was lawfully provided within Germany (paras 43-4 and 47-52). As such it was amenable to justification by overriding considerations in the public interest. The need to protect the service recipient and to maintain order justified the restriction, given the general tendency of the member states to restrict lotteries and the need to prevent crime, fraud, and excessive spending. That the revenues were used for public interest purposes was not a ground of justification in itself, but fed into the protection of the recipient. Hence, the member states had a certain latitude which allowed them to prohibit large-scale lotteries (paras 57-63). *Commission v. Italy (lottery machinery), 1994* also concerned lotteries, but in a different perspective. Italy had required the undertaking that delivered the automated system used for running lotteries to be publicly owned for the main part. The Court countered that the official authority derogation in article 55 Treaty did not apply, for the responsibility to organize lotteries was not transferred. The computerization system merely registered, checked, and transmitted data; the draws were still made by a state committee; the public administration approved and paid the prizes; the concession merely defined the terms of operation; and players' payments did not constitute fiscal charge (paras 6-12). Thus, the freedom of services and establishment was violated. Besides, the Court thereby validated the president of the Court's interim measures in *Commission v. Italy (lottery machinery interim I), 1992*, as confirmed in *Commission v. Italy (lottery machinery interim II), 1992*. (Directive 77/62 on public supply contracts was also violated.)

Läärä, 1999 dealt with the monopoly to operate slot machines in Finland. A British company which lawfully operated slot machines in the United Kingdom had challenged the exclusive right of the public licence holder to run slot machines in Finland. That licence holder forwarded the proceeds to the Finnish state. The Court transposed the *Schindler, 1994*-case-law to other forms of gambling such as slot machines. The repetitive nature of slot machines put into perspective the relatively modest stakes and prizes contrasting it with the crosswords at issue in *Familiapress, 1997*, a free movement of goods case (paras 15-8). In contrast to *Schindler, 1994*, a monopoly rather than a full prohibition was at issue (para. 21). The impediment to the freedom of services resulting from that monopoly, which was according to the Court a non-discriminatory restriction (paras 28-9), could be justified by the grounds admitted in *Schindler, 1994*. A member state had discretion on how to pursue those aims on its territory. A tax on gambling or the control of operators could prove less effective. The proceeds were paid over to the state. In addition, a monopoly had the advantage of keeping gambling within controllable channels (paras 27-42). In *Zenatti, 1999* the Court extended the *Läärä, 1999*-ruling to bets on sporting events. An intermediary had channelled such bets from the United Kingdom where they were lawfully offered as a service to Italy where they were subject to authorization. Certain operators in Italy held the prerequisite Italian licence. The service intermediary in Italy who cooperated with the British provider, in contrast, was barred. The Court validated the Italian approach in keeping with *Läärä, 1999*, but emphasized that it was not sufficient that the proceeds gained contributed to the financing of social activities. Rather, a genuine concern to limit gambling opportunities was required (para. 36).

Maritime transport

In *Corsica Ferries, 1994*, the Court applied Regulation 4055/86 on maritime transports in the light of the freedom of services. In the port of Genoa different tariffs for piloting were applied based on whether the ship piloted flew the flag of Italy or another member state. The Court decided that Regulation 4055/86 implemented the freedom of services in maritime transport and assessed the tariffs under non-discrimination. The freedom of services applied, because some of the ferries operated between Genoa and ports in other member states (paras 30-1). The tariffs affected the operators in their freedom of services when they received piloting services as well as when they provided transport services (para. 21). The undertakings operating ships flying the Italian flag were essentially Italian. That was why the tariffs were indirectly discriminatory (paras 32-4). Even if navigational safety, environmental protection or the national transport policy were capable of providing justification, those objectives did not necessitate the distinction in tariffs (para. 36). In conclusion, article 1(1) Regulation 4055/86 ruled out the distinction in tariffs. In *Peralta, 1994* the Court also applied free movement of services case-law under Regulation 4055/86, though to little avail. The captain of a ship which flew the Italian flag and was held by an Italian owner, after having flushed containers at sea in breach of Italian law, was tried on less favourable terms than he would have been had he been a national of another member state. According to the Court, the case did not give rise to discrimination. The same technical legislation was applicable across the board when Italy had jurisdiction. The fact that other member states applied less stringent rules, did not amount to discrimination. Moreover, any restrictive effect was simply due to a regular application of Italian legislation (paras 41-52). Besides, the free movement of workers did not apply in a purely internal situation when a member state treated one of its own nationals less favourably than nationals of other member states (paras 27-8). The freedom of establishment was, finally, not concerned when a member state imposed technical rules on undertakings subject to its jurisdiction. That situation was comparable to when national laws on labour, social security, or tax systems diverged (paras 30-5).

In *Commission v. France (maritime transport), 1994*, the Court revisited charges on intra-Community passenger transports. Those charges were, ultimately, lower for domestic transports than for transports between France and other member states, but all operators were subject to the same charges. The Court, after having confirmed that the services case-law applied under Regulation 4055/86 else the freedom of services would become nugatory (paras 13 and 20), struck down the differential charge, for it made service provision across borders more difficult than within a member state and secured a special advantage for domestic transport (paras 17-8 and 21).

Corsica Ferries France, 1998 again dealt with services in the context of maritime transport, more specifically, with the mooring regime in certain Italian ports. In the light of the security aspects of mooring services certain mooring groups were given a *de facto* monopoly. It was mandatory to use their services and the prices of the services were fixed at a level beyond the usual for such services in order to take account of security-related aspects. Having not found any indirect discrimination of service receivers, the Court ruled that the mooring service provision constituted a service of general economic interest within the meaning of article 90(2). Given that, any potential restrictive effect of the mooring regime on the service provision was justified (paras 57-9 and paras 45-6). As far as maritime transport services, in contrast to mooring services, were affected, if at all, the potential restriction caused by the requirements to use the services of specific mooring groups and to pay the fixed price were justified by the need to safeguard public security (para. 60). (Any restrictive impact on the free movement of goods was, according to the Court, too uncertain and indirect to be of relevance; paras 30-1.)

Again various services

The Court in 1994 ruled that Spain infringed the free movement of services by requiring non-resident nationals of other member states who were older than 21 years to pay entrance fees for museums, while admission was free for everybody else (*Commission v. Spain (museum admission), 1994*). *Van Schaik, 1994* dealt with the Netherlands' roadworthiness test for registered vehicles. Dutch law allowed only garages established in the Netherlands which had to fulfil certain requirements and were supervised by the Dutch authorities to offer that roadworthiness test. A side-effect of that approach was that Dutch vehicle owners usually, for the sake of convenience, had their cars maintained in garages in the Netherlands, too, although maintenance work in garages abroad was generally less expensive. The Court acknowledged the restrictive effect of the Dutch approach on the freedom of services, while the freedom of goods was only incidentally affected (para. 14), but found it justified by the need to maintain road safety. To allow foreign garages to offer the Dutch test would, moreover, come down to delegating state authority to foreign agents (paras 16-20). A test taken pursuant to the law of another member state for a vehicle registered in that state would, furthermore, have to be recognized in accordance with Directive 77/143 on roadworthiness tests (para. 22).

In *Alpine Investments, 1995* the Netherlands' prohibition of cold calling for dealers in commodities futures was at issue. The Dutch authorities prohibited a Dutch trader from calling potential customers in the United Kingdom unless those customers had given their written consent to being contacted, while British law did not in general forbid it. The free movement of services was applicable, because the service recipient was resident in another member state. It was irrelevant that the service was merely offered or that it was offered via telephone (paras 18-21). The prohibition was restrictive in that the trader was, by the state where he was established, stripped of an effective method of marketing his services and of contacting clients. That British law allowed cold calling, in turn, was immaterial. The Court also refused to transpose the *Keck and Mithouard, 1993*-ruling. The Dutch prohibition was not analogous to certain selling arrangements. It impeded access to the market of customers in another member state (paras 27-38). The needs to protect consumers and the integrity of the Dutch capital market, however, were valid justifications. While the British customers were best protected by British, rather than Dutch regulation, it was the 'home' state, viz. the Netherlands in the case at issue, that was best positioned to regulate cold calling. Proportionality was ensured, because it was possible to obtain written consent, only a specific sector was concerned, and less intrusive measures did not exist (paras 42-54).

In *Svensson, 1995*, Mr Svensson, a resident of Luxembourg, was denied an interest rate subsidy available essentially to those who had dependent children and took out a loan to construct a house in Luxembourg. The reason was that he had taken out the loan with a credit institution in Belgium rather than Luxembourg. The Court found that the freedom of services and free movement of capital were applicable to a loan agreement with a bank in another member state. The measure was discriminatory, because it relied on the place where banks were established (para. 12). Hence, Luxembourg's social policy argument that the profit tax on financial establishments in Luxembourg funded its social policy went unheard for not coming within the scope of an express derogation ground. Moreover, the *Bachmann, 1992*-ground, i. e. the need to ensure the cohesion of the tax system, did not apply for lack of a direct link (paras 13-8). In conclusion, the measure was precluded.

In *Perfili, 1996* a British insurance company was denied leave to intervene in proceedings in Italy concerning an Italian national who had taken out an insurance policy with the company. The reason essentially was that the company had granted legal authority to its representative under English law, which failed to live up to the requirements of Italian procedural law (see para. 6). The Italian procedural requirements, according to the Court, affected the ability of foreign service providers to defend their interests in Italy. However, the freedom of services and establishment was not concerned with disparities in treatment resulting from differences existing between the laws of the member states, if they applied based on objective criteria rather than nationality. Yet it was impossible for the Court by means of the information given to assess whether the national legislation which applied indiscriminately constituted an unjustifiable obstacle to the freedom of services (paras 16-8). Moreover, the Court did not have jurisdiction to apply fundamental rights outside the scope of Community law (para. 20).

In *Reisebüro Broede, 1996* the Court sanctioned Germany's reservation for lawyers to recover debt in court. A company established in France had argued that that reservation violated the freedom of services and establishment. The Court conceded that the freedom was restricted. That restriction did not occur on a discriminatory basis, though (paras 26-7 and 30). Applying the *Gebhard, 1995*-test under the freedom of services (para. 28), the Court found the restriction justified by the need to protect service recipients. Germany was entitled to ensure that those who recovered debts in court on behalf of legal persons were properly qualified and that justice was correctly administrated (para. 31). Germany was allowed to assess what was necessary to protect service recipients (paras 36-42).

Parodi, 1997 focused on the requirement to have a banking licence in the host state at a time when only the first banking Directive 77/780 was applicable. France required banks established in other member states to have a banking licence and to be established in France. In the case at hand, a company established in France had taken out a mortgage loan with a bank in the Netherlands. Ruling that the freedom of services applied, because capital movements had been liberalized in that regard already (paras 8-16), the Court found the French requirement to restrict the freedom of services, because banks established abroad already had to hold a licence in the state where they were established (para. 19). However, at that point in time, banking authorizations had only been subject to mutual recognition to some extent in the Community. That was why consumer protection, which was particularly sensitive in banking, still justified the restriction, subject to the national court's assessment which needed to distinguish between savers and borrowers (paras 20-9). The prerequisite of being established in the host state was only justifiable if it was indispensable (para. 31).

Medical services

Kohll, 1998 then essentially rendered the freedom of services applicable in situations that basically came within the scope of article 22 Regulation 1408/71, viz.

when medical treatment was sought in another member state and the 'home' state's social security system subjected reimbursement of the cost incurred to prior authorization. *Kohll, 1998* only concerned treatment *extra muros*, i. e. outside hospital. In Luxembourg Mr Kohll sought reimbursement of the cost incurred by reason of his daughter's medical treatment in Germany – treatment for which the authorization required by Luxembourg law had not previously been given. Yet Mr Kohll only requested reimbursement to the extent the Luxembourg social security system would have covered the cost had treatment been provided in Luxembourg. The Court first decided that the freedom of services applied in the domain of social security (paras 19-21). Article 22 Regulation 1408/71 only governed prior authorization in case of medical treatment in accordance with the law of the host state. In contrast, the freedom of services, as part of primary law from which secondary legislation could not derogate, could apply when reimbursement pursuant to 'home' state law, i. e. the law of the state to the social security system of which the person concerned was affiliated, was requested (paras 25-7). Medical services *extra muros* were covered by the freedom of services (para. 29). Luxembourg's prior authorization requirement, as a condition for the reimbursement of cost for medical treatment provided abroad, amounted to a restriction of the freedom of services (paras 34-5). While the need to maintain the financial balance of the social security system of a member state basically was a ground for justification, the ground was not plausible in the case at hand, because Mr Kohll had not requested more than what he would have received, had the treatment been provided in Luxembourg (paras 41-2). Public health considerations did not justify the restriction, either. The public health sector could not lawfully be excluded as a whole from the freedom of services. The Community rules on the mutual recognition of medical professional qualifications ensured the quality of the services. Moreover, the maintenance of a balanced medical and hospital service accessible to all did not require a prior authorization scheme (paras 46-52). As a result, Luxembourg could not lawfully subject the reimbursement of cost arising out of *extra muros* treatment provided abroad to authorization. Besides, the day *Kohll, 1998* was handed down the Court also ruled in *Decker, 1998*, on the same grounds as in *Kohll, 1998*, that the free movement of goods ruled out a scheme under which the cost of corrective eyeglasses were only reimbursed if the glasses had been purchased within the member state concerned or if the authorization to buy them abroad had been given beforehand.

Taxation

Safir, 1998 dealt with the Swedish approach to taxation of life assurances. Under Swedish law, capital life assurance policies were taxed in the hand of the insurer. The insured neither deducted the premiums paid from tax nor paid any tax on the proceeds. To level the playing field for domestic and foreign insurers, policies taken out with foreign insurers were taxed in the hand of the insured established in Sweden, i. e. the premiums paid were subject to tax. The insured was entitled to prove to the Swedish authorities that a similar tax had already been levied on the assurance policy by another member state and thereby have the Swedish tax reduced in steps, viz. by 50 per cent, if the foreign tax amounted to at least a quarter of the Swedish tax normally due, or by 100 per cent if it amounted to at least half of the Swedish tax. The Court found the Swedish approach to have a dissuasive effect on the freedom of services for several reasons (para. 30). The insured had to register, declare the premiums, and apply for a reduction of Swedish tax (para. 26). It was more costly to surrender a foreign policy after a short period of time (para. 27). It was burdensome for the insured to prove the tax levied by another member state (para. 28). Sweden's diverging decisions as to the tax paid by foreign insurers established in one and the same country resulted in a state of uncertainty for the insured (para. 29). Finally, the reduction of the Swedish tax in steps had a threshold effect resulting in higher taxes (para. 31). That it was not possible to apply the Swedish standard tax regime or that a fiscal vacuum ensued if the foreign policies were not taxed in the hand of the insured did not justify the restriction. It would be possible to tax all life assurances equally by taxing the yield on life assurance capital across the board. The freedom of services would then be less restricted and the system more transparent (paras 32-4).

Lease Plan, 1998 was a value added tax-case which also had a dimension of freedom of services. The Court decided that Belgium violated the freedom of services in that companies established abroad which regularly conducted business in Belgium, in contrast to companies established in Belgium, had to give notice to receive interest and, even if they did, received less interest on the amounts of tax they had advanced than companies established in Belgium (paras 32-3). According to the Court, the proper comparison for the purpose of assessing discrimination was between companies established in Belgium and those established abroad providing services on a regular basis in Belgium, rather than between the latter and those who did not at all, or only irregularly, pursue an economic activity in Belgium and sought reimbursement of the tax (paras 36-9).

Eurowings, 1999 concerned the effects of Germany's tax regime in cases of cross-border leasing contracts. In essence, a lessee established in Germany and subject to German trade tax had to add back to the taxable total a certain amount, if the lessor was not subject to tax in Germany; had the lessor been subject to tax in Germany, add-backs did not apply in general for the lessee. The idea of that approach was to avoid taxing a taxable amount twice, i. e. once in the hands of each taxable person. As a result of the add-backs the tax burden of the lessee was increased. That was the case for the German company Eurowings when it rented a plane from an Irish company. Applying the freedom to receive services, the Court found a difference in treatment in that German companies such as Eurowings in the majority of cases had to pay higher taxes when they leased planes from companies established abroad than when they leased them from companies established in Germany (paras 35-40). The cohesion of the German tax regime within the meaning of *Bachmann, 1992*, did not justify that difference in treatment for lack of a direct link (para. 42). Neither did the fact provide justification that the Irish company was generally subject to a lower tax burden. According to the Court, compensatory tax regimes jeopardized the foundations of the single market (paras 43-5).

A tax regime was also challenged in *Vestergaard, 1999*. Denmark applied a presumption that a stay abroad in a tourist resort, even if in the context of an educational course, had a touristic purpose. As a consequence, the corresponding expenditures were only tax deductible, if a taxable person rebutted the presumption by proving that a stay abroad had served for professional training. In the case at issue, Mr Vestergaard was established in Denmark and had followed a course in Crete offered by a Danish provider. The presumption of non-deductibility was applied. It would not have been applicable, had the course been given in a tourist resort in Denmark. The Court confirmed that the freedom of services applied when the service was provided in another member state than the state where both the provider and the receiver were established (paras 18-20). The Danish tax regime applied a distinction based on where the service was provided (paras 21-2). The restrictive effect of that distinction was not justified by the need to safeguard the cohesion of the Danish tax system, since a direct link between taxation and deductibility was missing. Neither did the effectiveness of fiscal supervision provide justification, given Directive 77/799 on mutual assistance (paras 23-8).

Public procurement

In *Gemeente Arnhem, 1998* the Court was faced with issues under Directive 92/50 on public services contracts which were raised when two municipalities in the Netherlands entrusted the collection of refuse to an entity they had founded and owned. The Court resorted to the freedom of services on two occasions in the detailed reasoning on the provisions of the Directive. On the one hand, after having decided that the fact that other private companies also offered waste disposal services did not have an impact on the qualification of the entity founded by the municipalities under Directive 92/50, the Court defined the objective of that Directive to be the elimination of barriers to the freedom to provide services and the protection of operators offering services to contracting authorities in other member states (para. 41). On the other hand, the Court ruled that the nature of the provisions setting up the entity in question were not relevant in determining whether it was a 'contracting authority' within the meaning of the Directive, because that term needed to be interpreted functionally in order to give the freedom of services full effect (para. 62).

Mannesmann, 1998 was a public works contract case in which, in general, the qualification of an Austrian entity that fulfilled certain public and commercial tasks, such as printing identification cards and newspapers, as a contracting authority under Directive 93/37 on public works contracts was at stake. In this context, the Court *inter alia* ruled that the transfer of a public works contract pursuant to article 1(a) from a contracting authority pursuant to article 1(b) to an entity it controlled but which did not itself qualify as a contracting authority did not have an impact on the classification of the contract as a public works contract, else the aim of the Directive, which was to realize the free movement of services and establishment in public works contracts, would be frustrated (para. 43).

Further services cases

In *Bickel, 1998* a German tourist and an Austrian truck driver challenged the legislation in the German-speaking part of Italy which offered the option to have criminal proceedings conducted in German exclusively to Italian nationals who resided in that part of Italy and spoke German. The Court accepted the applicants' argument. The situation was within the scope of the Treaty, as they were potential service recipients and as union citizens had the right to move freely and reside in other member states. Hence, the principle of non-discrimination in article 6 Treaty had to be applied, even though the rules governing criminal proceedings were at issue (paras 15-7). German-speaking nationals of other member states were disadvantaged, while Italian residents of the region who spoke German were put in a favourable position by the rule (paras 23-6). The protection of a national minority, as such a legitimate ground, did not justify the residence and nationality requirements, as that aim would not have been undermined, if the rule had been extended to cover German-speakers from other member states. Moreover, additional costs would not arise in that case (paras 28-30).

In *Ambry, 1998* the Court applied the freedom of services under Directive 90/314 on package travels and the banking Directives 89/646 and 92/49. French law required the guarantee, which travel agencies had to provide under Directive 90/314 to secure the risk of certain costs, *inter alia* for the repatriation of customers in case of insolvency of an agency, essentially to be issued by a financial institution established in France. In case of a guarantee from a bank established in another member state an additional agreement between that foreign bank and a French bank was required (para. 27). An interpretation in the light of the freedom of services revealed that the use of foreign banks by travel agents was discouraged due to the cost the additional agreement with a French bank generated (paras 28-30). The justification of that restriction failed, as Italian legal procedures were sufficiently expedient even if immediate funds were needed, e. g. in case of repatriation. Moreover, travel agents did not have the possibility to prove that the guarantee provided by a foreign bank was sufficient in terms of rapid availability of funds (paras 33-8).

In *Calfa, 1999* the Court dealt with the lifelong expulsion of a tourist from Greece as a consequence of the possession of drugs. According to the Court, expulsion for life of a national of another member state for possession of drugs for the possessor's own use constituted an obstacle to the freedom of that national, as a tourist, to receive services in the host state, as it would have constituted an obstacle to the free movement of persons had the person concerned been (self-)employed (para. 18). Drawing on established case-law, notably *Bouchere-*

au, 1977, the Court went on to find that, while the use of drugs endangered public policy within the meaning of article 56 Treaty as interpreted in the light of Directive 64/221 on public policy, security or health measures (para. 22), an expulsion order was only justified if the conduct of the person concerned amounted to a sufficiently serious threat to society (para. 25). The Greek legislation at issue did not live up to that requirement, for under Greek law foreigners guilty of drug possession for their own use were to be expelled automatically, without due account being taken of their personal conduct (paras 27-8).

Ciola, 1999 concerned mooring places on Lake Constance. Austria had restricted the number of places capable of being rented out to persons residing abroad. Mr Ciola, an Austrian owner of mooring places, was prosecuted for disregarding an administrative decision ordering him not to lease out any further places to persons not resident in Austria. The Court reiterated that an Austrian service provider such as Mr Ciola could rely on the freedom of services against Austria, as long as the service recipient was resident abroad (paras 11-2). To require residence in Austria for a person to be eligible to receive a service amounted to indirect discrimination, since the majority of those residing abroad were nationals of other member states (paras 13-4). In the absence of an exception in the Act of Accession such discrimination was only amenable to justification by the regular express derogation grounds. None of those applied in this case. Economic grounds in particular, such as the pressure on prices for mooring places, were excluded (paras 15-9). (The rest of the judgment concerned the primacy of Community law over a measure taken to enforce an individual administrative decision adopted before accession.)

For the sake of completeness, a number of further cases related to services must be mentioned. In *Commission v. Denmark (Storebælt), 1993* Denmark had accepted that a Danish content clause requiring the use of Danish materials and services to the greatest possible extent in an invitation for tenders to build a bridge violated *inter alia* the freedom of services. In *Ballast Nedam, 1994* the Court applied Directives 71/304 and 71/305 on public works contracts in the context of holdings and their subsidiaries. The *Opinion on GATS and TRIPS, 1994* dealt with the power of the Community to conclude the Marrakesh agreements, one part of which was the General Agreement concerning Trade in Services (GATS). Finding overall that the Community shared the competence to conclude those agreements with the member states, the Court found specifically that cross-frontier supplies, the so-called mode 1 under the GATS, were covered by the common commercial policy of the Community, in contrast to the other modes of service provision under the GATS, i. e. consumption abroad, commercial presence, and the presence of natural persons (paras 41-7). Moreover, the free movement of services and establishment the nationals of the member states enjoyed within the internal market did not imply the power of the Community to enter into agreements with third countries to liberalize services and first establishment for third county nationals; neither was an exclusive power to be derived from certain acts addressing third country nationals or from the harmonization of certain service sectors as it remained partial (paras 81, 86, and 95-7). In *Job Centre, 1997* the Court exclusively applied competition law, which was violated by a refusal to grant permission to open a job recruitment agency in Italy on the ground that this activity was reserved to public agencies. Given that violation, the Court did not continue to assess the case under the freedom of services (para. 39). In *Romanelli, 1999* the Court interpreted the term 'other repayable funds' in article 3 Directive 89/646 on banking. In *Commission v. Luxembourg, 1999* the Court confirmed that Luxembourg had failed to transpose in time Directive 93/22 on investment services in the securities field.

V The 2000s

The first decade of the millennium was by far the most fruitful of the history of the Court. The Court handed down about 500 judgments in the free movement of persons and services. The free movement of workers and citizens contributed more than 150 judgments. The coordination of social security remained rather stable with a little more than 80 judgments. The exponential growth of the case-law was most visible in the free movement of services and establishment which together accounted for some 240 judgments.

1 Workers and citizens

Worker

In the first decade of the millennium, the Court added little to the term 'worker'. *Fahmi and Amado, 2001* clarified that a migrant worker who had definitely ceased work and then returned to her home state could not lawfully rely on article 48 Treaty and article 7 Regulation 1612/68 to claim a benefit for her children in the state where she had worked (paras 41-51). In *Ninni-Orasche, 2003* the Court mainly elaborated that objective criteria and the circumstances were decisive in determining whether a person was a 'worker' (para. 27). Thus, were irrelevant the conduct of the person before and after having begun to seek work (para. 28) or the short duration of the work in relation to the entire residence period (para. 30). The Court also generally disqualified the argument that a person had possibly obtained the position of a 'worker' abusively as a means to benefit from the advantages linked to that status (para. 31). In *Collins, 2004* the Court ruled that a person was not to be regarded as a 'worker' by reason of him having last worked in a member state 17 years before (para. 28). The Court also reiterated the distinction between persons who had worked in a member state and then sought employment there, i. e. 'workers', and those who just came to a member state to search for employment, i. e. job seekers (paras 30-32).

Advantages

The Court consolidated its case-law on article 7(2) Regulation 1612/68 during the first decade of the 2000s. (As to the case-law relating to tax advantages, see below.) The *Kaba, 2000*-judgment in essence rubberstamped the approach of the United Kingdom which distinguished between persons who were 'present and settled' in the United Kingdom and those who were not. Essentially, as nationals of other member states were capable of becoming 'present and settled' as well, a problem under article 7(2) Regulation 1612/68 did not arise. The problem was again referred to the Court in *Kaba II, 2003*, apparently for lack of clarity in the first decision, but the Court simply stuck to its ruling in *Kaba, 2000*.

In *Ferlini, 2000* the Court held that a social advantage within the meaning of article 7(2) Regulation 1612/68 was not involved when the fees for maternity care payable by a person not affiliated to the sickness insurance scheme of a member state exceeded by more than 70 per cent those payable by a person affiliated to that scheme. Such a person who was not affiliated to the scheme did not seek a 'social advantage' with the reimbursement of the maternity expenses, but the application of the same scale of fees as that applicable to persons affiliated to the scheme (para. 44). Given that the scale of higher fees had been imposed unilaterally by hospitals in *Ferlini, 2000* (para. 49), the distinction was caught and precluded as indirect discrimination by the general principle of non-discrimination in article 6 Treaty rather than article 48 Treaty.

Leclere, 2001 reiterated that a worker was allowed to claim certain rights even after the employment relationship had ended. However, a worker who ceased work because of invalidity and then received an invalidity pension was not simply to be likened to a worker entitled to benefits under article 7(2) Regulation 1612/68. Such a person only had a claim to such benefits under that article as were linked to her or his former employment. New benefits, such as a benefit on account of a child born after the employment had ended, could, in contrast, not be claimed lawfully (paras 59-60). In *Commission v. Luxembourg (minimum income), 2002* Luxembourg conceded the violation of article 7(2) Regulation 1612/68 that resulted from the requirement to have completed a residence period of five years in Luxembourg during the last 20 years to be eligible for the minimum income guaranteed in Luxembourg.

Hartmann, 2007 concerned a residence requirement for a child-raising allowance in Germany. The Court ruled that such a benefit constituted a 'social advantage' for a migrant worker when his spouse claimed the benefit, because it allowed a member of the family of a migrant worker to devote him- or herself to raising the child. This benefitted the migrant worker's family as a whole, regardless of who actually claimed the benefit (para. 26). The Court then struck down the residence requirement largely on the specifics of the case, because the link to the society of Germany – as such a justified requirement for a child-raising benefit – was not only given when a person was resident in Germany, but also when a person contributed significantly to Germany's labour market (paras 34-7). The 'significant contribution to the national labour market' was thrown into sharp relief on the very same day *Hartmann, 2007* had been handed down in *Geven, 2007*. The Court essentially held in *Geven, 2007* that work of 4 to 13 hours per week could lawfully be regarded as minor employment, i. e. an insignificant contribution to the national labour market. As a consequence, a person who was in minor employment could, although still having the status of migrant worker, lawfully be refused the child-raising allowance for lack of a link to the society of Germany.

In *Hendrix, 2007* the Court dealt with a benefit made available in the Netherlands to young disabled adults who were unable to gain as much through their work as workers who were not disabled. Article 10a Regulation 1408/71 validly exempted that benefit from exportability (see below). However, the Court continued to examine article 7(2) Regulation 1612/68. The restriction of free movement resulting from the residence requirement, however, was justified by the close link of the benefit to the socio-economic environment (para. 55). Moreover, a hardship clause in Dutch law allowed for the necessary flexibility in cases where it would be disproportionate to refuse the benefit. That was the case of Mr Hendrix who had moved abroad, but maintained close ties to the Netherlands' employment market (para. 57).

In *Commission v. Germany (savings-pension bonus), 2009*, the Court, finally, categorized the bonus Germany awarded in case of contributions to a complementary savings-pension scheme as a social advantage, although the bonus had the form of an additional tax deduction (paras 41-3 and 49). Limiting this bonus to persons liable to full taxation in Germany affected mostly persons who pursued work across the borders and was thus, in the absence of proper justification, precluded. Those workers were sufficiently closely linked to the German society to take advantage of the benefit, since only those could subscribe to a savings-pension scheme who were affiliated to the mandatory statutory pension scheme in Germany (para. 60). Moreover, to require reimbursement of the bonus when full tax liability in Germany ended was equally precluded for having a deterrent effect on those workers wishing to leave Germany. The ruling handed down was also valid under Union citizenship for economically non-active citizens (para. 115).

Family members

The Court dealt with the family of migrant workers in a number of judgments. *MRAX, 2002* concerned the position of spouses of nationals of the member states who were third country nationals. The Court elaborated that the member states could lawfully require such persons to produce an identity card or a passport as well as proof of their marriage to a national of a member state upon entering their territory. Basically, an entry visa could be required, too. However, only proportionate sanctions were to be taken when a person had entered a country or had remained there without having observed the formalities required. In particular, it was disproportionate to send back a third country national spouse who was able to provide the necessary evidence (para. 62). The Court followed up on *MRAX, 2002* in *Commission v. Spain (visa prior to entry), 2005* to hold unlawful Spain's requirement that third country nationals who were members of a migrant worker's family first obtained a visa at the consulate of Spain where they last were resident (para. 38).

Baumbast, 2002 also dealt with some aspects concerning family members. According to the Court, the children of a migrant worker who had resided with the worker while he had worked in the host state could invoke a right of residence and access to education pursuant to article 12 Regulation 1612/68 even after the migrant worker had ceased work in the host state (para. 55). *All* the children of the family of the migrant could benefit from these rights, including the descendants of just one of the spouses (para. 57). The nationality of the children was irrelevant (para. 56) and so was the fact that the migrant worker and the spouse had divorced in the meantime (para. 60-61). Moreover, the right of the children under article 12 Regulation 1612/68 also conferred a right of residence to their parent as the primary carer (para. 71).

In *Givane, 2003* the Court decided that the two year-period of continuous residence pursuant to article 3(2) Regulation 1251/70 had to precede immediately the death of the migrant worker to give rise to the right of the late worker's family to remain in the host state (para. 50). *Akrich, 2003* established that a third country national who was the spouse of a national of a member state could only lawfully rely on the rights of spouses pursuant to Regulation 1612/68, in particular the right to family reunification with the migrant worker, if the third country national spouse had already had lawful residence in a member state (para. 50). In other words, a third country national who was married to a national of a member state did not have a claim under Community law allowing her or him to come to the territory of the Community from a third state. The member states alone had the power to regulate such direct family reunification. The Court, moreover, held that a marriage of convenience could possibly amount to abuse of rights (para. 57).

In *Mattern and Cikotic, 2006* the Court evoked *Gül, 1986* to reason that the rights of third country nationals under article 11 Regulation 1612/68 were linked to the migrant worker. According to *Mattern and Cikotic, 2006* a member of the family of a migrant worker was therefore only allowed to rely on article 11 Regulation 1612/68 in the member state where the migrant worker was employed. When a Luxembourg national worked and resided in Belgium, her third country national spouse could therefore not rely on Community law in order to work in Luxembourg (para. 27).

Family members and Union citizenship

The advent of Union citizenship gave the case-law regarding family members a new turn. The Court in *Baumbast, 2002*, after having answered the first questions on the basis of the freedom of workers, established the direct effect of the right of residence of Union citizens pursuant to article 18 Treaty (para. 84). The only conditions were that a Union citizen was insured against sickness and had sufficient resources so as to not to become an unreasonable burden on the public finances of the host state (para. 90). Those criteria were subject to a proportionality assessment (para. 91). In *Zhu and Chen, 2004* the Court added that the interpretation given in *Baumbast, 2002* was also valid for minors (para. 20). It did not matter where their resources came from (para. 33). Moreover, in extension of *Baumbast, 2002* (para. 71) the right of residence of minor children as Union citizens also conferred a right on their parents to reside with them, despite article 1(2)(b) Directive 90/364 which covered only *dependent* relatives in the ascending line (para. 45).

Jia, 2007 was not necessarily a citizenship case. Rather, it was handed down on the basis of the freedom of establishment of self-employed persons. However, its main aspect concerned the judgment in *Akrich, 2003*. The Court emphasised the element of abuse that characterized *Akrich, 2003* to find that Community law did not require a member state to insist on prior lawful residence of third country nationals in another member state, but rather left each member state the option to insist on such residence. Furthermore, the Court held that 'dependence', i. e. the need for material support, of a member of the family of a migrant worker or a self-employed person had to be assessed in the light of the situation of that family member in his or her home state or the state where he or she had come from (para. 37). In *Eind, 2007*, in turn, the impact of Union citizenship was apparent. The Court held that when a national had returned to his home state after having exercised his freedom of movement her or his dependent descendant could still reside with her or him, even though the returning national was not economically active in any way.

In *Metock, 2008*, the Court then expressly broke with *Akrich, 2003* (para. 38 of *Metock, 2008*). It reduced *Akrich, 2003* to the specifics of the facts, namely the element of abuse that was prominent in that case, and held based on a number of considerations – union citizenship and the citizenship Directive 2004/38 among them – that third country nationals who were the spouses of Union citizens could immigrate directly into the territory of the Community from a third country based on Community law. They were no longer required to have lawful residence in a member state before being able to benefit from family reunification based on Community law. Neither did it matter when the family ties were founded. The new approach of *Metock, 2008* was promptly confirmed in *Sahin, 2008*.

Union citizenship, minimex, and students

In *Grzelczyk, 2001* the Court began to revise its case-law on students in the light of Union citizenship. The Court ruled that Belgium's minimum subsistence allowance (minimex), a non-contributory social benefit, could no longer be withheld from students on the grounds that they were not migrant workers. Given that Union citizenship was 'destined to be the fundamental status of nationals of the Member States' (para. 31), a student who had studied for three years in Belgium while sustaining himself by means of work and then encountered temporary financial difficulties in his final year of studies (para. 44), was allowed to benefit from the Belgian benefit on an equal footing with Belgian nationals, despite the wording to the contrary in Directive 93/96. The Court expanded on *Grzelczyk, 2001* in *Trojani, 2004*, though not with regard to students. The Court held that it was possible for a member state to consider that a Union citizen who had applied for minimex did not have sufficient resources to avoid becoming a burden on the host state (para. 36). However, if a member state granted him a residence permit in spite of his lack of resources, the state would also have had to apply the principle of equal treatment (para. 40). In these circumstances, the member state had to grant the minimex.

In *Bidar, 2005* the Court reconsidered students' maintenance grants in the light of Union citizenship. The students case-law previously had been based exclusively on article 12 Treaty. However, the Court in *Bidar, 2005* held that the exclusion from Community law of maintenance grants for students who had exercised their freedom to move was no longer warranted. *Brown, 1988* and *Lair, 1988* were thus not good law any longer (with regard to article 12 Treaty; see *Bidar, 2005*, para. 42). While the principle of non-discrimination thus had to be applied to maintenance grants, member states could lawfully require that students demonstrated a 'certain degree of integration' and thus a 'genuine link with the society' of the host state (paras 57 and 62, respectively) so as not to become an unreasonable burden on the finances of the host state. That link need not necessarily have been evidenced by employment in the host state (para. 58). A period of residence of certain duration, such as three years, would suffice (paras 59 and 61). A person having received a substantial part of secondary education in the host state could also possibly have established a 'genuine link' to the host state's society (para. 62). In a similar vein, the Court struck down the German conditions to be fulfilled to obtain an education and training grant to study abroad in *Morgan, 2007*. Germany had required resident students to have pursued studies for at least a year in Germany and to continue the same studies in another member state to be eligible for a grant. However, the Court found that the genuine link required by *Bidar, 2005* was already established when a student had been raised and had completed schooling in Germany (para. 45). The conditions Germany imposed did therefore not cover all the situations in which the genuine link to the German society existed (para. 46). They were thus not necessary to ensure that a student did not become an unreasonable burden for Germany. The Court also rejected a number of other grounds – such as ensuring that students pursued studies in as brief time as possible, that they had chosen the right studies for them, or that grants were not duplicated. Those grounds were inappropriate or unnecessary to justify the obstacle Germany had created to the free movement of Union citizens. In *Förster, 2008*, in some contrast, the Court upheld the requirement of five years of residence in the Netherlands for students to be eligible for maintenance grants. That condition satisfied, according to the Court, the 'genuine link'-requirement of *Bidar, 2005* (*Förster,*

2008, paras 52-5). The citizenship Directive 2004/38, which had not been applicable at the time of *Förster, 2008*, in essence relied on the very same condition (para. 55).

Education without Union citizenship

Judgments were also handed down in the 2000s that merely developed the case-law on education without that Union citizenship had much impact. Before *Bidar, 2005*, *Ninni-Orasche, 2003* had clarified the requirement that unemployment had to be involuntary for a worker seeking re-training after having lost employment in order to justify application of article 48 Treaty and article 7(2) Regulation 1612/68 to lay claim to student maintenance assistance. (See *Lair, 1988* for the requirement of continuity.) The Court explained that even when temporary employment ended the worker could be involuntarily unemployed depending on the circumstances (para. 42). Such circumstances could exist in a practice that was usual for this type of employment, in the chances of finding long-term employment, and in the possibility to renew a contract (para. 44). The Court also held in *Commission v. Belgium (CESS), 2004* that Belgium could not lawfully require prospective students who did not have a Belgian *certificat d'enseignement supérieur*, but had passed secondary education in another member state, to pass an aptitude test to gain access to higher education in Belgium. In *Commission v. Austria (university), 2005* an even less restrictive requirement in Austria was invalidated by the Court, too. Austria had required prospective students to show that they had access in the state where they had obtained their secondary education to the studies they wished to pursue in Austria. Austria had failed to show that, without the requirement, the existence of the Austrian university system as such or its homogeneity would have been jeopardised (para. 66). Non-discriminatory entry examinations or minimum grades for access to certain studies would have been in accordance with article 12 Treaty though (para. 61).

Tideover allowance and Union citizenship

The impact of Union citizenship on the tideover allowance Belgium granted to jobseekers who looked for the first job after their studies was at issue in *D'Hoop, 2002*. The Court ruled that in view of Union citizenship the allowance could no longer be reserved to students who had passed secondary education in Belgium. A real link of the applicant to the geographic employment market could lawfully be required, but the criterion applied by Belgium was too 'general and exclusive' (paras 38-9). The Court also held that Union citizens were entitled to invoke Union citizenship against the member state of which they were nationals, after having made use of the freedom of movement (para. 30). In *Ioannidis, 2005* the Court further developed the tideover allowance. The allowance was not to be refused to a Union citizen, either, on the sole ground that the parents of the citizen were not migrant workers in the host state. While the parents' work in the host state was possibly indicative of the 'real link' to the geographic employment market, it could not be excluded, according to the Court, that a Union citizen had established such a real link on other grounds (para. 33).

Job seekers and Union citizenship

Building on *D'Hoop, 2002*, the Court in *Collins, 2004* further elaborated on the benefits of job seekers in the light of Union citizenship. The Court held that, in view of Union citizenship, the job seeker's allowance provided by the law of the United Kingdom could no longer be excluded from the scope of article 48(2) Treaty (para. 63). A genuine link of the job seeker to the employment market could, however, be required lawfully. The allowance could be subject to the job seeker having effectively and genuinely searched for employment for a certain time (para. 70). Residence as a criterion was apt to ensure that the genuine link to the job market existed, provided that the period of residence required was not excessively long (para. 72). This interpretation of the freedom of workers in the light of Union citizenship was confirmed in *Vatsouras, 2009*. Given that the legal basis of the claim of job seekers to benefits was still free movement of *workers*, the Court also held in *Vatsouras, 2009* that article 24(2) of the citizenship Directive 2004/38 was valid, for it was susceptible to a reading in accordance with article 39(2) Treaty (paras 44-5).

Genuine link again

The requirement of a genuine link to the society of the host state was also applied under Union citizenship by the Court in *Gottwald, 2009*. Austria had required disabled persons, for whom a reduced price for the toll disc necessary to use highways in Austria was available, to be resident in Austria to benefit from the reduced price. The Court ruled that the residence requirement ensured that disabled Union citizens had a connection to the society providing the benefit (para. 36). Decisive elements in that consideration were (i) that the disadvantage, i. e. the higher price for the toll disc, merely affected those who passed through Austria only occasionally, (ii) that a minimum period of residence was not required (para. 37) and (iii) that 'residence' was interpreted by the Austrian authorities so as to include situations where there was a connection of a similar degree as in the case of ordinary residence (paras 38-9).

War victims and Union citizenship

With *Tas-Hagen, 2006* benefits granted to civilian war victims came under the scrutiny of Union citizenship. Yet before *Tas-Hagen, 2006*, the Court in *Baldinger, 2004* rejected the claim of a former Austrian national, who had become a Swedish national before the accession of Austria to the Community, for a benefit provided by Austria for prisoners of war in World War I or II who were Austrian nationals at the time they applied for the benefit. In keeping with *Even, 1979* the Court held the benefit to be outside the scope of free movement of workers and, in particular, Regulation 1408/71. The Court did not enter into the argument to the contrary that Advocate General Ruiz-Jarabo Colomer had made on the basis of Union citizenship (paras 24-47 of the opinion in *Baldinger, 2004*). In *Tas-Hagen, 2006*, however, the Court applied Union citizenship and decided that the Netherlands were not to refuse a civilian war victims benefit merely because one of its own citizens had made use of the freedom as a citizen to move and therefore lived in Spain at the time of the application for the benefit. To require residence at the time of the application had a dissuasive effect on the freedom of Union citizens to move and was too selective as a criterion to establish the link to the Dutch society which the Netherlands legitimately required for such a benefit (para. 39). In the same vein, the Court rejected a requirement of continued residence imposed by Poland for the award of a war victim benefits in *Nerkowska, 2008*. It would have been less restrictive to require regular visits rather than residence in order to verify that the conditions of the benefit continued to be met (para. 45). For a similar war victim benefit the Court in *Zablocka-Weyhermüller, 2008* rebuffed Germany's way of reducing the benefit when the beneficiary resided abroad. The aspect that made the reduction disproportionate was that it only applied in the case of residence in certain countries, namely those that had belonged to the Soviet Union or to Yugoslavia but not some member states where the cost of living was equally low (para. 43). Moreover, the monitoring of the beneficiary's situation was necessary to the same extent, no matter which member state was involved (para. 44).

Union citizenship and expulsion

In *Jipa, 2008* the Court examined an order adopted by Romania against one of its own citizens ordering the citizen not to leave Romania for three years, because he had been expelled from France. A national was entitled, the Court stated, to rely on the freedom of movement of Union citizens to leave his country of origin (para. 18). The Court in essence applied under Union citizenship the expulsion case-law developed in the domain of workers (paras 23-4). The order by another member state to leave the country by itself was, according to the Court, not sufficient as justification for a member state to restrict the freedom of movement of one of its own nationals to its own territory. The domestic authorities had to conduct a full examination within the meaning of the expulsion case-law into which the public security considerations of the other member state could be fed (paras 25-6).

Names and Union citizenship

In *Garcia Avello, 2003* the Court relied on Union citizenship to decide that it was contrary to the right to equal treatment of Union citizens for Belgium to refuse to register the dual last name of a national of Spain and Belgium as it was current in Spain. The fact that two countries, namely Spain and Belgium, registered two different names for the same person could bring about a 'serious inconvenience' for that person (para. 36). This inconvenience was not justifiable by the need to avoid the general risk of creating confusion (para. 42). The Court decided in *Grunkin, 2008* on similar grounds that the refusal to register in Germany the double-barrelled surname lawfully conferred to a German national in Denmark violated the free movement of citizens.

Union citizenship and institutional issues

The Court also addressed institutional issues in the light of Union citizenship. In *Kaur, 2001* the Court ruled that the declaration made by the United Kingdom upon accession to the Community, which was later on amended, was relevant to determine who was a Union citizen. Those persons who did not fulfil the conditions in the declaration were not entitled to claim that they lost rights under Community law because of the declaration, as the declaration prevented rights from arising in the first place (para. 25). Issues related to the constituency of the United Kingdom also came up in *Spain v. United Kingdom (Gibraltar), 2006.* The Court ruled that the member states had the power to determine the franchise and eligibility in elections for the European Parliament, as long as Union citizens from other member states were allowed to participate. In other words, the United Kingdom could lawfully determine who were 'its' citizens that were allowed to participate in the elections to the European Parliament in the United Kingdom. Thus, the United Kingdom validly extended the right to vote in European parliamentary elections in Gibraltar to third country nationals who had close links to the United Kingdom based on historical constitutional traditions. Similarly, the Court decided, on the same day as *Spain v. United Kingdom (Gibraltar), 2006* was delivered, in *Eman and Sevinger, 2006* that it was up to the Netherlands to determine its constituency for the European Parliament elections. However, the Dutch citizens in Aruba and the Netherlands Antilles, which were Dutch overseas territories, were not to be excluded from such elections, if Dutch citizens in non-member states were generally allowed to participate in them (paras 58 and 60).

Union citizenship and other policies

In *Wolzenburg, 2009*, the Court made it plain that provisions implementing framework decisions of the Union had to respect Community law, in particular the rights *qua* Union citizenship (para. 45). The Netherlands complied with the limits imposed by Union citizenship and non-discrimination when it restricted the cases in which it refused to execute a European arrest warrant seeking the execution of a judgment (which was an option offered by the relevant framework decision) to those warrants targeting either Dutch nationals or Union citizens who had resided in the Netherlands for five years. The main reason was that only persons in those two categories had a connection to the Dutch society that was sufficient to outlast the prison sentence. Only for them it was therefore reasonable to serve the sentence in the Netherlands instead of being extradited (see paras 67-73). However, the Netherlands were not to require a permit of indefinite duration as evidence of the permanent residence, because the right to permanent residence in article 16(1) citizenship Directive 2004/38 did not depend on administrative documents (paras 49-52).

As to the Schengen system, the Court held in *Commission v. Spain (Schengen alert), 2006* that Schengen law had to respect the rights individuals derived from Community law. When an alert concerning a third country national married to a Union citizen was entered into the Schengen information system the reasons why the Schengen alert had been entered had to be available rapidly to the authorities which were in a position to refuse entry into a state belonging to the Schengen area, because such third country nationals benefitted from the enhanced protection against public policy and security measures in Community law (para. 58).

In a similar vein, the Court examined Germany's register of foreigners in the light of the data protection Directive 95/46 and Union citizenship in *Huber, 2008*. The Court found that a separate register for Union citizens residing in Germany which contained the data Union citizens had to provide under the relevant Community legislation was, under certain conditions, in accordance with the rights of Union citizens to free movement, given the need to control residence (paras 58-62). However, registering the crimes committed by Union citizens separately, i. e. besides and in addition to the general register of crimes, was not justified to fight crimes, for with regard to the fight against crimes the situation of Union citizens was not different from that of German nationals (paras 77-9).

Taxation

Taxes occupied the Court repeatedly during the first decade of the millennium under the free movement of workers as well as Union citizenship. *Zurstrassen, 2000* expanded the *Schumacker, 1995*-case law. The Court ruled that a member state could not lawfully refuse the joint tax assessment of spouses, merely because one spouse was resident abroad, if the couple gained almost all of their income in that member state. The reason was, as in *Schumacker, 1995*, that that member state was the only state that could possibly take into account the personal and family circumstances of the taxpayer (para. 23). In *De Groot, 2002* the Netherlands refused to take into account all the personal and family circumstances of a resident taxpayer. The problem was that Mr de Groot had also earned income in several other member states. The Netherlands refused to factor in fully the maintenance payments Mr de Groot made by reason of his divorce, but – unlike for residents who earned all their income in the Netherlands – took into account only the amount proportionate to the income in the Netherlands. Consequently, a part of the payments was not taken into account for income tax purposes anywhere. The Court ruled that a situation in which personal and family circumstances were taken into account for income tax purposes in no member state at all was contrary to free movement of workers (paras 101-2). The Netherlands thus had to either adjust their tax system unilaterally or amend their double taxation conventions with other member states accordingly (para. 99).

In *Wallentin, 2004* the Court again applied *Schumacker, 1995* to find that the refusal to apply the allowance that was tax free, i. e. the amount of income not subject to income tax, to a migrant worker, because he had stayed less than six months in the host state, violated the free movement of workers when the worker had not gained any taxable income in other member states. The allowance constituted a 'personal circumstance' within the meaning of *Schumacker, 1995*, as its aim was to alleviate the tax burden of persons with low income. *Turpeinen, 2006* was again a tax case decided on the basis of *Schumacker, 1995*. However, in this case the Court *per analogiam* applied *Schumacker, 1995* to Union citizenship. The case concerned a similar constellation as *Pusa, 2004*, namely a Finnish national who had moved to Spain after retirement (see *Pusa, 2004* below). Finland, however, applied a flat rate withholding tax to pensions paid in Finland in case of non-resident retired taxpayers, whereas a progressive tax rate applied to resident pensioners. In the case of Ms Turpeinen this led to a higher tax burden than if she had maintained her residence in Finland. With Finland being the only state where she received a pension, the Court found that *Schumacker, 1995* applied by analogy (para. 29). The higher tax burden therefore violated the free movement of citizens and equal treatment (paras 31 and 33).

Based on the free movement of workers the Court also invalidated an approach Belgium used to tax persons who were simultaneously self-employed in Belgium and employed in Germany in *Mertens, 2002*. The Court in this case relied heavily on *AMID, 2000*, an establishment case that concerned company taxation, to order that Belgium for tax purposes was not to set off losses incurred because of a self-employed activity in Belgium against income gained by reason of work in Germany when determining the losses to be carried over to the following tax year. The crux was that when a person who was self-employed in Belgium was simultaneously employed in Belgium rather than Germany the losses were deductible from the taxable income gained from employment in Belgium (para. 28), whereas with simultaneous employment in Germany the losses made in Belgium were not deductible from income. As a result, the losses incurred in Belgium were not deductible *anywhere* (para. 23), which hindered free movement of workers (para. 33). The Court decided so based on the facts that (i) the two cases, i. e. employment and self-employment both in Belgium v. employment in Belgium and self-employment in Germany, were not comparable and Belgium was therefore precluded from applying the same approach in both cases (para. 31); (ii) Belgium's approach was unilateral (para. 36); (iii) the losses incurred in Belgium as a result of the self-employed activity were, in keeping with the double taxation convention, not taken into account in Germany in the taxation of the income earned by reason of the employment in Germany (para. 31).

Taxes and houses

The Court addressed losses for tax purposes in the light of free movement of workers in *Ritter-Coulais, 2006* as well. In this case, Germany had applied a difference in treatment depending on whether a loss of income by reason of an owner living in his own house arose from either the house being situated in Germany – in which case the loss of income was taken into account to determine the applicable income tax rate – or the house being situated in another member state

– in which case the loss of income was left out of account, save to offset positive income from the same source. However, the positive income from real estate was always factored in irrespective of where the real estate was situated. The Court found that difference in treatment to be an unjustified restriction of the freedom of workers (para. 37-8). The Court then came back to *Ritter-Coulais, 2006* under slightly different circumstances in *Lakebrink, 2007*. Luxembourg legislation never took into account the yields of real estate situated abroad for the purpose of determining the tax rate; in other words, it was not just negative income that was disregarded as in *Ritter-Coulais, 2006*, but also positive income from real estate. Moreover, whether the owner used the real property concerned to live there himself was irrelevant. In short, Luxembourg treated residents differently than non-residents in that, for residents, positive and negative income from real estate was factored in to determine the applicable tax rate, while for non-residents neither positive nor negative income was factored in (para. 18). The Court ruled that the advantages such legislation created for migrant workers when they declared positive income from real estate abroad, did not offset the disadvantages in cases where negative income having arisen from such real estate was left out of account (paras 22-24). Moreover, the Court ruled, falling back on *Schumacker, 1995*, that when a non-resident taxpayer gained almost all of his income in Luxembourg the personal and family circumstances had to be taken into account for tax purposes. That included all the factors affecting the taxpayer's ability to pay tax (para. 34), including negative income originating in real estate situated abroad. Thus, the Luxembourg legislation constituted discrimination contrary to article 39 Treaty (para. 35). In *Renneberg, 2008* the Court again came back to *Ritter-Coulais, 2006* and *Lakebrink, 2007* read in the light of *Schumacker, 1995*. In *Renneberg, 2008*, the Netherlands refused to take into account negative rental income originating in an owner-occupied dwelling situated in Belgium for the purpose of determining the income tax base. The person concerned earned all of his work-related income in the Netherlands. According to the Court, the Netherlands had to apply *Schumacker, 1995* (paras 64 and 71), even though the relevant double taxation convention allocated to Belgium the power to tax income from real estate situated in Belgium. If the Netherlands took negative income from real property situated in Belgium into account for residents, they had to do so for non-residents as well (paras 56-8).

Cohesion of the tax system

In *Commission v. Denmark (insurance taxation), 2007* the Court addressed a similar constellation as in *Bachmann, 1992* and *Commission v. Belgium (insurance taxation), 1992*. Denmark required pension or life insurance contributions to have been made under a pension scheme taken out with an insurer established in Denmark to be income tax deductible. The Court found a restriction of the freedom of workers and establishment, in particular of those persons coming to Denmark and having previously taken out insurance abroad which they intended to maintain, but also of services because of either the requirement of being established in Denmark or the deterrence for receiving services abroad (paras 39-44). Those restrictions were not justified. Effective supervision was made possible by Directive 77/799 on mutual assistance and by evidence to be provided by the taxpayer (paras 52-6). A general presumption of tax avoidance was not to be applied (para. 57). The cohesion of the Danish tax system was only in peril when a person moved abroad *after* having deducted the contributions from income but *before* receiving the benefit that would be taxable as income in Denmark. The Court held that that possibility alone was not sufficient to establish a direct link which could justify a general requirement of establishment in Denmark for insurers (paras 72-4).

Taxation of employees of the Communities

The Court dealt with the special tax situation of workers employed by the European Communities in *Schilling, 2003*. In that specific context, the Court held that it was contrary to the freedom of workers for the 'home' state, which was competent to tax all income other than the salary of persons employed by the Community, to refuse the deduction from income originating in real estate for the cost incurred by reason of employment of a household help – cost that were normally deductible from income – on the sole ground that the social security contributions for the help were not paid to the home state's social security scheme, but to another member state's social security scheme.

Taxes and Union citizenship

In *Pusa, 2004* taxes were examined in the light of Union citizenship. A pensioner had moved from Finland to Spain where he paid income tax on his retirement pension received in Finland. However, the Finnish authorities calculated the attachable part of the pension without taking into account the income tax payable in Spain, while they would have deducted the income tax prepayment normally due in Finland. The Court found that approach acceptable under Union citizenship given that it allowed the debtor to shield part of his income from the creditor's right of recovery, provided, however, that the tax had not yet been due at the time the creditor claimed a part of the pension (paras 26-7). Moreover, a provisional tax assessment was available in the debt enforcement procedure in Finland for income tax not yet payable (paras 40-2). However, in this assessment any discretion of the authorities had to be excluded for it to be in accordance with Union citizenship (para. 45).

In *Schempp, 2005* the Court applied Union citizenship and non-discrimination. It did not find a violation in that Germany rejected the deductibility of maintenance payments made to a former wife resident in Austria, although such payments would have been deductible from income had the recipient lived in Germany. Germany could lawfully reject the deductibility when payments were made to a recipient in another member state which did not subject these payments to income tax in the hands of the recipient (paras 30-5). The Court also relied on the *Lindfors, 2004*-ruling (see below) on the absence of a guarantee of tax neutrality when Union citizens exercised their freedom to move (para. 45-6). In *Rüffler, 2009* the Court, in turn, based on Union citizenship invalidated the way Poland taxed the income of a retired pensioner resident in Poland. The pension was paid in Germany and compulsory sickness insurance contributions were deducted at source in accordance with Regulation 1408/71. However, Poland had calculated the income tax due on the basis of the gross pension, i. e. before the deduction of the contributions in Germany, although the contributions had not been taken into account for income tax purposes in Germany in any way, while Poland would have computed on a net basis had the pension been paid in Poland. The Court found a difference in treatment (paras 67-8) which was not justified given that Germany compensated Poland for the benefits in kind provided in actual fact to pensioners residing in Poland in keeping with Regulation 1408/71.

Taxes on cars

Taxes other than income tax were also scrutinized by the Court in the light of the free movement of workers and citizenship. In *Weigel, 2004* the Court did not find a violation in the tax due in Austria when a used car was registered. Mr Weigel had claimed that his freedom to move as a worker had been violated, because he had been forced to re-register his car and pay the tax due in Austria, after he had moved there to work. However, the Court found that the Treaty did not contain a guarantee of tax neutrality of movements of migrant workers. The migrant worker was not placed at a disadvantage compared to those who had already been subject to the legislation of the host state (para. 55). In *Lindfors, 2004* the very same reasoning as in *Weigel, 2004* was applied under Union citizenship to a car tax levied by Finland (paras 34-5). In *Alevizos, 2007*, *Weigel, 2004* and *Lindfors, 2004* were confirmed. However, the Court further elaborated in *Alevizos, 2007* on the aspect that the taxation of the vehicle imported had to avoid any disadvantages for Union citizens. The level of the tax on the vehicle imported had to take into account the vehicle's depreciation (para. 78).

Taxes and real estate

In *Commission v. Portugal (capital gains deduction), 2006* the Court applied the freedom of workers, establishment, and citizens to strike down an exemption from the tax on capital gains realised upon selling real estate which had served as a home to the owner or her family. The law of Portugal had limited that exemption to the situation where the proceeds of the sale were used to acquire another home *in Portugal*. The Court held that restriction to be unjustified. This judgment was confirmed in *Commission v. Sweden (tax deferral), 2007* for the deferral of the taxation of capital gains on real estate situated in Sweden. In a similar vein, the Court in *Commission v. Germany (housing subsidy), 2008* invalidated the German housing subsidy in the light of the free movement of persons and Union citizenship in so far as it was only granted when persons subject to unlimited income taxation in Germany had acquired real estate for their own occupation that (the real estate) was situated in Germany. The Court found that the aim the subsidy pursued, namely allowing taxpayers to acquire their own dwelling, was equally attained when the real property acquired was situated abroad (para. 28). This was confirmed in *Commission v. Germany (savings-pension bonus), 2009* for the use of certain subsidized capital to acquire a dwelling in Germany (para. 82).

Interim assistance and taxation

In *Merida, 2004*, finally, the way income tax was dealt with had an influence on another benefit. The German interim assistance for unemployed persons had been calculated on a basis of assessment as if the income gained by a worker in Germany had been subject to income tax in Germany, i. e. in the calculation of the benefit the German tax was notionally deducted from the wage the dismissed worker had gained. In the case at hand, this resulted in a lower benefit than if the income tax paid in actual fact in France, which was lower than the income tax in Germany, had been taken as a basis. According to the Court, this approach violated the free movement of workers, more specifically, article 7(4) Regulation 1612/68), for having an unfavourable effect on the migrant worker concerned (para. 28).

Derogations

In the first decade of the millennium, the Court also dealt with the derogations from the free movement of workers. In the year 2000, the Court mainly re-applied established case-law regarding the public service exception pursuant to article 48(4) Treaty in *Österreichischer Gewerkschaftsbund, 2000*. The Court ruled that once access to public employment had been granted, non-discrimination applied. Austria, however, failed to live up to that standard when it applied stricter conditions to take into account periods of employment in another member state than those applicable to periods of comparable employment completed in Austria. In the absence of transitional provisions, that also applied to periods of employment completed before accession of a member state to the Community (para. 55). In the twin judgments of 30 September 2003, *Marina Mercante, 2003* and *Anker, 2003*, the Court addressed the reservation of the captaincy and first office on ships flying the flag of a member state to the nationals of that state. The Court ruled that the mere employment by a private person was not sufficient to render the public service exception inapplicable in the case of ship masters and chief mates (*Marina Mercante, 2003*, para. 43). The exception in principle applied when a person exercised official authority by means of certain notarial and police powers (*Marina Mercante, 2003*, para. 42). However, the exception only applied when those powers were exercised on a regular basis and were not a very minor part of the activities concerned (*Marina Mercante, 2003*, para. 44). The Court had to repeat the ruling in four more infringement proceedings almost five years after *Marina Mercante, 2003* and *Anker, 2003* before the message had finally sunk in (*Commission v. France (ship officers), 2008; Commis-*

sion v. Greece (ship officers), 2009; Commission v. Italy (ship officers), 2008; Commission v. Spain (ship officers), 2008). In *Alevizos, 2007* the Court, in addition, made it clear that even with an army officer whose employment squarely came within the public service exception taxation which had no link to him being an officer, such as taxation at the occasion of a transfer of residence to another member state, could be challenged under the free movement of workers (para. 71).

In a series of infringement cases – *Commission v. Finland (military equipment), 2009*; *Commission v. Germany (military equipment), 2009*; *Commission v. Sweden (military equipment), 2009*; *Commission v. Italy (military equipment), 2009*; *Commission v. Italy (dual use equipment), 2009*; *Commission v. Greece (military equipment), 2009*; *Commission v. Denmark (military equipment), 2009* – that concerned the member states' duty to contribute to the Community's own resources, and more specifically the duty to communicate imports of military equipment to the Commission giving rise (the imports) to a duty to contribute, the Court elaborated the public safety derogation under all the market freedoms, including the freedom of workers. The Court in all those judgments held that the public safety derogations to the market freedoms were not to be interpreted to the effect that a general exception was inherent in Community law which allowed to remove whole domains related to public security from the scope of Community law (see e. g. *Commission v. Finland (military equipment), 2009*, paras 45-6).

The Court applied the public policy derogation as well, namely in *Olazabal, 2002*. *Rutili, 1975* was put into perspective as the Court held that the freedom of movement of a Spanish national could lawfully be restricted to parts of the territory of France when the migrant worker concerned could as well have been expelled from France on grounds of public order (para. 41). In *Orfanopoulos, 2004*, the Court held that the public policy derogation had to be applied particularly restrictively in the light of Union citizenship (para. 65). Any automatism and presumption were excluded when it came to the expulsion of a migrant worker on public policy grounds (paras 70 and 93). The threat to public policy had to be reviewed, moreover, whenever a lengthy period had passed after the expulsion decision was adopted (para. 81). The Court also elaborated the proportionality analysis the national court had to undertake into which the human rights of the person concerned had to be fed (paras 97-9). Moreover, the Court clarified the procedural safeguards applicable in case of expulsion. *Orfanopoulos, 2004* was by and large confirmed in *Commission v. Netherlands (automatic expulsion), 2007*. In addition, the Court made it plain that all Union citizens, even those who did not reside lawfully in a member state, benefitted from the safeguards of Community law in case of expulsion (para. 35). The case *Commission v. Germany (expulsion), 2006* also concerned derogations from free movement. The Commission had challenged Germany's implementation of the Community rules on expulsion. However, the Court mainly found that the Commission had failed to meet the standard of evidence required to establish an 'administrative practice' contrary to Community law. The Commission had merely put forward a number of cases spanning almost a decade in which the expulsion standards had allegedly been violated.

Sufficient resources

In a similar vein as in the expulsion case-law the Court dealt with the issue of a Union citizen not having sufficient resources to avoid becoming a burden to the host state. In *Commission v. Belgium (own resources), 2006* the Court held that a member state could not lawfully require a Union citizen to have a legal right to the financial resources she used to maintain herself (para. 46-7). Thus, an agreement as to assistance concluded before a notary could not be required where a partner supported the Union citizen concerned. Nor could automatic expulsion ensue from a lack of evidence as to the existence of sufficient resources (para. 68). Both measures were found to be disproportionate to ensure protection of the financial interests of a member state. Similarly, the Court rejected in *Commission v. Netherlands (own means), 2008* the requirement of the Netherlands to have sufficient resources for an entire year to be eligible for a residence permit (para. 29).

Non-discrimination

The Court also ruled on the basis of non-discrimination of migrant workers in a series of other cases during the first decade of the millennium. In *Graf, 2000* the Court judged that a rule according to which an employee forfeited the right to a compensation worth two months of salary when he himself rather than the employer had terminated the employment contract did not violate the migrant worker's access to the internal labour market. The entitlement to compensation was conditioned on a 'future and hypothetical event' (para. 24). The possibility that the employer would have eventually terminated the contract, had not the employee done so, was 'too uncertain and indirect a possibility' for the legislation to constitute an obstacle to market access (para. 25). The rule therefore respected the principle of non-discrimination.

In *Lehtonen, 2000* the Court came back to sports, this time basketball. The Court validated the transfer window rule which was recommended by the European basketball federation to the national federations. This rule established that all transfers of players within Europe had to be concluded before the end of February of each year. The rule was justified to ensure the 'regularity of sporting competitions' (para. 53), i. e. that transfers were not made after the regular season was over and the play-offs and relegation games had begun (paras 54-5). However, while it seemed unnecessary to the Court that the transfer window remained open a month longer for transfers of players from outside Europe, the Court left it to the national court to find objective reasons to justify that discrepancy.

In *Angonese, 2000*, the Court found that the requirement to have a specific language certificate which could only be obtained in a specific region violated the free movement of workers. While a language requirement as such did not pose any problem as such, migrant workers had to be allowed to prove language proficiency by other means (paras 44-5). Moreover, the Court held based on the line of authority that had begun with *Walrave, 1974* that the principle of non-discrimination applied as well to regulations adopted by private persons, such as banks in this case (para. 36). The latter ruling was confirmed in *Raccanelli, 2008* for private associations, such as the German *Max Planck Gesellschaft* as an employer.

Commission v. Italy (language assistants), 2001 dealt with Italian language assistants again. This time the Court invalidated the conversion of fixed-term contracts of language assistants into contracts of indeterminate duration, because in doing so the rights acquired previously as language assistants were, in contrast to regular workers, left out of account. This was confirmed in *Delay, 2008*, provided, however, that there was continuity between the duties under the first and the second contract.

Burbaud, 2003 concerned France's recruitment system for civil servants in hospitals which combined an initial selection with ensuing training and provisional civil servanthood. The Court ruled that migrant workers who had passed similar training in another member state, if it had to be recognized under the Community rules (see below), had to be offered a simplified option to access employment as civil servants in hospitals – to be more specific, an option that exempted them from undertaking again the training they had already passed in another member state, but still ensured the legitimate selection of the candidates most suitable for employment (para. 109).

In *Köbler, 2003* the Court held that a special salary supplement awarded after 15 years of employment could not lawfully be reserved to those professors who had performed their duties exclusively at Austrian universities. The reward for the loyalty of an employee embodied by the supplement did not justify the obstacle created to free movement of workers, since it applied to the duties performed at *any* Austrian university, while universities in Austria in effect competed amongst themselves for the most able professors in a similar way as with foreign universities (para. 84).

With *Commission v. Italy (teaching experience), 2005* the Court held in the light of *Scholz, 1994* that Italy could not lawfully attribute a different value to a teacher's experience acquired abroad than to that acquired in Italy (para. 21). This was again confirmed for the impact of work experience in public service abroad on the salary paid in *Commission v. Spain (work experience), 2006*. *Commission v. Italy (work experience), 2006* reiterated this ruling regarding professional experience and seniority acquired in public service abroad and added that it was immaterial in this regard whether a member state recruited civil servants based on a public competition or not (para. 18) and whether a civil servant worked under a contract or not (para. 19).

Car registration

In *Van Lent, 2003* it was prohibited in Belgium to use a car registered in another member state which an employer established there had leased for his employee residing in Belgium. In fact, such a vehicle could not be registered in Belgium, neither by the employer nor by the employee. The Court held that the obstacle to the free movement of workers which arose by reason of the fact that a migrant worker residing in Belgium was prevented from benefitting from a leased car provided by his employer established abroad (paras 19-20) was not justified by the need to ensure road safety. This applied even if it had been possible to register such a car in Belgium (para. 25). Car registration was also at issue in *Commission v. Denmark (car registration), 2005*. Denmark required resident persons who worked for an employer established abroad providing them with a car to obtain an authorization in Denmark to use the car and to pay a tax. The Court, similarly as in *Van Lent, 2003* held that the access of workers and employers to the labour market was hindered. That restriction of the free movement of workers would only have been justified, if the car had been used in Denmark on a permanent basis rather than just occasionally (paras 76-8). This applied regardless of whether that use was for business purposes only or also for private purposes. This judgment was confirmed in *Commission v. Finland (car registration), 2006*.

Further non-discrimination

In *Kranemann, 2005* the Court rejected Germany's limiting the reimbursement of trainee lawyers' travel expenses for training purposes to journeys within Germany. The financial obstacle for trainee lawyers to seek training in another member state was not justifiable by budgetary considerations (paras 29 and 34). *Öberg, 2006* was handed down on the same day as *Rockler, 2006*. Both judgments essentially concerned the same constellation. The Court ruled that Sweden violated the free movement of workers pursuant to article 39 Treaty when it refused to take into account insurance periods a worker had completed with the insurance scheme of the Community for the purpose of determining whether the 240-days period of insurance needed for the award of a parental benefit in Sweden was fulfilled.

Lyyski, 2007 concerned the efforts in Sweden to train a sufficient number of teachers to address an acute lack of teaching personnel. Mr Lyyski had claimed that he intended to fulfil the practical part of an educational course for teachers given in Sweden in a Swedish-speaking school in Finland. Given the urgency of the lack of teachers in Sweden and the temporary nature of the measures, the Court in principle accepted the restriction of the freedom of workers inherent in the Swedish requirement that the practical part be passed at a school in Sweden. But the Court ultimately left the proportionality assessment to the national court, requiring the latter, however, to factor in the need to monitor candidates in their practical training and a potential lack of candidates qualifying for the course (paras 43-4 and 46).

In *ITC, 2007*, the Court rejected in light of the free movement of workers Germany's approach to finding employment for unemployed workers. The approach essentially consisted in paying a fixed amount of money for each unemployed person a private recruitment agency managed to place, provided though that the job concerned was subject to contributions to the German social security system. With reference to *Clean Car, 1998* the Court found that a private recruitment agency was entitled to rely on the freedom of workers of the person placed, although it acted only as an intermediary between the employer and the employee (paras 24-6). The restriction to employment subject to the German social security system was not justified, though. Germany had failed to bring sufficient evidence that the restriction in the new social policy instrument was necessary to encourage recruitment. Equally it seemed unnecessary to protect the national social security system – in particular the financial balance of the social security system was not at risk of being upset, given that the fee paid was counterbalanced by the unemployment benefits that need not have been paid any longer – or to prevent the loss of qualified labour, if the latter was a ground suitable for justification at all (paras 39-44). In a similar vein, the freedom of recruitment agencies to provide services and of recipients to receive them was unlawfully restricted. The freedom of services was, in particular, restricted when a recruitment agency established in Germany, after having found employment for a worker in another member state, then had to rely on the worker, rather than the state, to pay the fee (paras 57-9). As the freedom of workers and services gave specific expression to Union citizenship, the Court did not deal with the latter (paras 64-5).

In *Wood, 2008*, the Court turned down France's approach to compensate persons for damage suffered by reason of criminal offences. Union citizens were only entitled to receive compensation, if the relevant act had been committed in France, in contrast to French nationals who were always eligible. The approach was considered directly discriminatory in the case of a Union citizen who had made use of his freedom to come to work and reside in France (para. 15).

Ankara

In the first decade of the millennium the Court addressed the rights of workers under the Ankara Agreement with Turkey in more than twenty judgments. In *Nazli, 2000*, the Court held that a worker who came under the third indent of article 6(1) Decision 1/80 belonged to the duly registered labour force despite short absences from the labour market. In Mr Nazli's case the absence lasted 13 months due to detention pending trial. However, the Court added the proviso that the person concerned found employment again after a reasonable period (paras 40 and 42). This applied also when enforcement of the prison sentence had been suspended, because such a measure usually aimed at a person's integration in the host state's society (para. 48). Moreover, the expulsion case-law developed for the internal market equally applied under the Ankara Agreement (para. 56). In *Kocak, 2000*, however, the Court refused to apply *Dafeki, 1997* to the facts at issue. The reason was that Germany had amended its practice as to changes of dates of birth since *Dafeki, 1997*. Of late, the first declaration of the date of birth was consistently relevant, except where a document that had existed before the first declaration had been made proved an earlier date of birth. With all documents regardless of whether they originated in Germany or Turkey having the same probative value (para. 41), Germany was not required to take into account any special circumstances in Turkey (paras 50-1).

In *Ergat, 2000* the Court held that the member states were not entitled any longer to impose conditions after the periods pursuant to article 7(1) Decision 1/80 had passed (paras 38-9). In that case, that article also implied a concomitant right of residence (para. 40). The rights were only lost if a ground for expulsion was given or if the person concerned left the host state for a prolonged period of time without any legitimate reason (paras 46 and 48). Thus, the failure to have a residence permit extended and the resulting temporary unlawful residence of a Turkish worker in a member state was not to entail disproportionate sanctions. A Turkish worker namely was not to be deprived of his rights under article 7(1) Decision 1/80, or to be imprisoned or deported (paras 57-8). In *Eyüp, 2000* the Court relied on the *de facto* continued family life of a Turkish couple (para. 34), even after their divorce and second marriage, to calculate a continuous period under article 7 Decision 1/80. The Court in *Kurz, 2002* transposed the case-law as to the term 'worker' from the internal market to the Ankara Agreement (para. 31) in order to qualify an apprentice as a 'worker' within the meaning of article 6(1) Decision 1/80. Mr Kurz as an apprentice also met the other requirements of that article despite the temporary nature of his employment, i. e. the due integration into the labour force and a legal, stable, and secure situation (paras 45 and 53).

Wählergruppe Gemeinsam, 2003 established the direct effect of article 10(1) Decision 1/80 and transposed *ASTI, 1991* and *Commission v. Luxemburg (ASTI II), 1994* to the context of the Ankara Agreement. Consequently, it was not lawful to consider Turkish migrant workers as ineligible in elections to workers' representation bodies on the sole basis of their nationality (para. 78), although the regime established by the Ankara Agreement did not include an analogon to article 8 Regulation 1612/68 (para. 81). The Court then in *Ayaz, 2004* relied on *Wählergruppe Gemeinsam, 2003* to justify the transposition to the Ankara context of the part of the judgment in *Baumbast, 2002* concerning a migrant worker's children. Thus, as held in *Baumbast, 2002*, the stepchildren of a Turkish worker belonged to his family for the purpose of article 7 Decision 1/80.

In *Cetinkaya, 2004* the Court decided that the son of a Turkish migrant worker who had been born in the host state and had always lawfully lived there had to be considered as having been authorized to join the Turkish migrant worker within the meaning of article 7 Decision 1/80 (para. 23). The rights acquired on the basis of that article, in addition, were not lost when the migrant worker ceased to belong to the duly registered labour force (paras 29 and 32). Moreover, applying *Orfanopoulos, 2004*, the Court held that the danger to public policy exuding from an individual had to be re-assessed, if circumstances that arose after a deportation order had been handed down suggested that the danger was no longer present (para. 47). The Court in *Dörr, 2005* added to that and the ruling in *Nazli, 2000* that, since the expulsion case-law of the internal market was applicable under the Ankara Agreement, the procedural guarantees provided by Community law in expulsion cases, i. e. articles 8 and 9 Directive 64/221, applied to Turkish migrant workers as well (para. 65).

In *Aydinli, 2005*, the Court replied to the referring Court that a member of the family of a Turkish migrant worker, once he had fulfilled the requirements of article 7 Decision 1/80, need not have continued to fulfil them (para. 26). Such a person was not subject to the conditions of article 6 Decision 1/80, either (paras 30-1). Thus, the person need not have been integrated into the duly registered labour force. Residence in the host state on its own was sufficient. Moreover, a member of the family of a Turkish worker who came within the first paragraph of article 7 Decision 1/80 equally could lose his rights only if he represented a danger to public policy or left the host state (para. 27). This latter ruling was confirmed for the second paragraph of article 7 Decision 1/80 in *Torun, 2006* (para. 25). Moreover, according to *Torun, 2006*, the second paragraph of article 7 also applied to descendants who were not minors any longer (para. 27).

In *Gürol, 2005*, the Court held that article 9 Decision 1/80 regarding access to education had direct effect and did not presuppose that the children lived together with the Turkish migrant worker under the same roof (para. 29). Moreover, given that all forms of education were covered, educational grants had to be granted on the basis of equal terms to Turkish as well as German nationals under article 9 Decision 1/80 (paras 36-8). An educational grant to study abroad – even in Turkey – was therefore not to be subject, in the case of Turkish nationals, to the stay abroad being a mandatory requirement of the curriculum of the studies pursued, whereas in the case of German nationals the stay abroad only had to be beneficial to the studies pursued and recognizable as a normal part (para. 35).

In *Dogan, 2005*, the Court explained that workers who fulfilled the requirements of the third indent of article 6(1) Decision 1/80 were no longer subject to article 6(2) Decision 1/80 (para. 16). Moreover, the interpretation given in *Nazli, 2000* did not just apply to short periods of absence from the labour market, but also to any period short of a definitive absence from the labour market, regardless of the cause for the absence. The only proviso was that the worker was able to find employment again within a reasonable period of time (para. 23). Even a long term spent in prison did not harm the rights (para. 22). A Turkish worker therefore also had a right to seek employment under the third indent of article 6(1) Decision 1/80 and meanwhile have residence in the host state (para. 19). In *Sedef, 2006* the Court somewhat tempered the otherwise strict formal criteria in article 6 Decision 1/80 for the case of a Turkish seaman who had worked for many years, in accordance with the usual practice in the métier, under consecutive short-term employment contracts. Because of the short-term nature of these contracts, formally, he only met the requirements of the first indent of article

6(1). According to the Court the periods in between each contract during which Mr Sedef had not worked came within the scope of the second sentence of article 6(2), although he had never reported to the unemployment office (para. 56). Mr Sedef was therefore entitled to rely on the third indent of article 6(1). Yet the ruling was specifically tuned to the facts of the case (see paras 61, 66-7). More generally, the Court also decided that the stages of article 6(1) Decision 1/80 had to be fulfilled in turn, i. e. the third indent *after* the second indent (paras 37 and 43).

In *Güzeli, 2006* the Court essentially bounced the case back to the national court for the assessment of whether Mr Güzeli had been duly registered as belonging to the labour force of the host state, given that he had changed employers although his work permit did not allow him to do so. Yet the Court also stated that Article 10 Decision 1/80, like article 6(1) Decision 1/80, only applied if a person was duly registered as belonging to the labour force of the host state (para. 48). However, the Court also ruled that the second sentence of article 6(2) Decision 1/80 regarding interruptions of employment only applied when rights had already been acquired under the three indents of article 6(1) (paras 43-4).

Ankara more favourable than the internal market

In *Derin, 2007*, the Court stuck to its interpretation that the rights in article 7 Decision 1/80 were only lost in two situations, namely prolonged absence and threat to public order. Any other aspect was irrelevant (para. 57). The Court would not hear that this implied to treat the descendants of Turkish migrant workers more favourably than those of Community migrant workers pursuant to article 10 Regulation 1612/68. According to the Court, the legal situation of the former was not comparable to that of the latter (para. 68). Article 59 of the Additional Protocol to the Ankara Agreement was therefore not violated (para. 69). This interpretation was confirmed by *Polat, 2007*. Additionally, the Court ruled in *Polat, 2007* that, in keeping with the expulsion case-law, several criminal convictions as such did not necessarily constitute a ground for expulsion (para. 36). *Derin, 2007* was further confirmed by *Er, 2008*. Even if a descendant who fulfilled the conditions of article 7 Decision 1/80 had never found employment, even with government help and after several years, the rights flowing from article 7 remained intact (paras 33-4).

Altun, 2008 concerned the son of a Turkish migrant worker. The migrant worker had initially come to Germany as a refugee, but had made some false representations in this regard. The Court held that during the periods required by article 7 Decision 1/80, the Turkish migrant worker had to belong to the duly registered labour force as required by article 6(1) Decision 1/80 (paras 27 and 33), else rights could not come into existence for the descendant under article 7. *After* the periods of article 7 had been completed, however, the criteria of article 6(1) became irrelevant for the purpose of article 7 (para. 36). Even if the Turkish worker's residence permit was withdrawn at a certain point in time, because it then turned out that the criteria of article 6(1) had not been met in the first place because of false representations made by the worker, the autonomous rights the descendant had acquired at that point in time by reason of the completion of the periods in article 7 were not to be questioned owing to the need for legal certainty (paras 58-60). In addition, the reason why a migrant worker had originally been granted access to a member state, namely that he had been a political refugee under the Geneva conventions, did not have an impact on the rights acquired by his family members pursuant to article 7 (para. 49).

Payir, 2008 revealed that students who worked part-time and au pairs were capable of qualifying as 'workers' within the meaning of article 6 Decision 1/80 (para. 35). The criteria for 'work' as established in the internal market case-law had to be met (para. 28), students and au pairs had to be duly registered (para. 29), and their situation had to be stable and secure (para. 30). Besides these three conditions other considerations were not relevant, bar in cases of downright fraud (paras 44 and 6). Moreover, Directive 2004/114 was not to be applied in the context of the Ankara Agreement, not even for interpretive purposes (para. 48). In *Kahveci, 2008* the Court found that non-discrimination in the context of the Ankara Agreement precluded any limit on the number of Turkish football players a club in a member state could field. In deciding so, the Court effectively transposed *Deutscher Handballbund, 2003* and *Simutenkov, 2005*, which are both explained below, to the Ankara Agreement.

Sahin, 2009, finally, concerned the administrative charges payable upon the extension of a residence permit. The Court decided that the standstill clause in article 13 Decision 1/80 did not prevent the introduction of new charges payable by Turkish nationals and Union citizens alike (paras 67 and 69). However, in the light of article 59 Additional Protocol the charges levied from Turkish nationals were not to be higher or lower than those levied from Union citizens (para. 71).

Agreements with other third states

The Court also dealt with the free movement of workers in the context of a number of other agreements than the Ankara Agreement with Turkey. In *Fahmi and Amado, 2001*, the Court held that the children of a Moroccan migrant worker had to reside in the Community, else neither them nor the migrant worker were entitled to rely on the principle of non-discrimination contained in article 41(a) and (3) of the Rabat Cooperation Agreement with Morocco to claim a family allowance (para. 57).

In *Gottardo, 2002* the Court indirectly dealt with a bilateral convention between Italy and Switzerland which essentially provided that Italy aggregated old age insurance periods an Italian national had completed in Switzerland. According to the Court, non-discrimination of workers required Italy to extend that benefit to migrant workers who were nationals of a member state and had completed insurance periods in Italy and Switzerland (paras 33-4), in essence because that extension did not affect the balance and reciprocity of obligations between Italy and Switzerland (paras 36-7).

Pokrzeptowicz, 2002 concluded that the principle of non-discrimination in the Europe Agreement with Poland had direct effect. In light of the text, purpose, and context of non-discrimination in the Europe Agreement there was no reason not to interpret it in the same way as in the case-law regarding language assistants developed in the internal market, notably *Spotti, 1993*. Given that the very same national provision was at issue in *Pokrzeptowicz, 2002* as in *Spotti, 1993*, the ruling as to article 48(2) Treaty was transposable to the Europe Agreement (para. 39). As the rules of non-discrimination in the Europe Agreements with Slovakia and Poland were identical, the Court in *Deutscher Handballbund, 2003*, next transposed to the Agreement with Slovakia the ruling in *Bosman, 1995* that had increased the number of Union citizens a club in a member state could field. However, this applied only to Slovakian players who had already gained access to the labour market.

The Court then transposed the ruling in *Deutscher Handballbund, 2003* to the Partnership Agreement with Russia in *Simutenkov, 2005*, which (the Agreement) also included a directly applicable provision of non-discrimination in terms of conditions of work. With *Commission v. Austria (trade unions), 2004* the Court then transposed the decision in *ASTI, 1991* and *Commission v. Luxemburg (ASTI II), 1994* regarding participation in workers' representation bodies to the Agreement on the European Economic Area, all Europe Agreements, and 'other agreements' (para. 47) establishing non-discrimination of workers regarding working conditions, much like the Court had done for the Ankara Agreement in *Wählergruppe Gemeinsam, 2003*. In *Gattoussi, 2006* the Court finally transposed the ruling in *El-Yassini, 1999* as to the Rabat Agreement with Morocco to the Association Agreement with Tunisia, in so far as it precluded a member state from refusing a residence permit after a work permit of a certain duration had been issued (para. 40).

Two more agreements were dealt with by the Court. In *Grimme, 2009* the Court dealt for the first time with the Agreement on free movement of persons with Switzerland in the light of free movement of workers. After having held that internal market case-law was not to be transposed automatically to the Agreement, the Court decided first that the Agreement encompassed only natural persons. The freedom of establishment of legal persons was not within the scope of the Agreement. The freedom of services was limited to 90 days per year. Second, as regarded the freedom of workers, a German employee of the German branch of a Swiss company was not entitled to rely on the principle of non-discrimination in the Agreement to claim applicability of an exemption provided by German law from the compulsory affiliation to a pension scheme for members of the managing board of German companies merely because he was at the same time a member of the managing board of the Swiss parent company (para. 49). The Court also addressed the Agreement on the European Economic Area, namely in *Commission v. Portugal (capital gains deduction), 2006* and *Commission v. Sweden (tax deferral), 2007*. The Court in these two decisions extended the rulings it delivered re the internal market to the Agreement on the European Economic Area (paras 40-2 and 32-3, respectively).

Technicalities

During the first decade of the millennium, the Court also interpreted several technical provisions of the directives implementing the free movement of workers. *Commission v. Italy (resources), 2000* concerned the sufficient resources migrant workers, the members of their family, as well as students had to have in order not to become a burden to the host state and the proofs relating thereto. The Court on the one hand rejected the Commission's allegation that Italy had exceeded the latitude it enjoyed under these directives; on the other hand, it refuted Italy's restriction of evidence to prove sufficient resources.

In *Yiadom, 2000* the Court decided that a Union citizen who had been temporarily admitted to the territory of a member state pending a decision concerning entry, but then had to wait 'for a period which [was] manifestly longer than [was] required' (para. 41) for such a decision, benefitted from the procedural safeguards in article 9, rather than just those in article 8 Directive 64/221. In *Dörr, 2005* the Court found, subject to the national court's assessment, that the requirements of a review of expediency under articles 8 and 9 Directive 64/221 were not respected (para. 47). Moreover, the suspensory effect of procedures had to be automatic (paras 51-2).

Driving licences

In *Commission v. Netherlands (driving licence), 2003*, the Court struck down the requirement to have a driving licence registered in the host state after having transferred residence, because the formality was contrary to article 1(2) of Directive 91/439 on mutual recognition of driving licences (para. 63) and unjustifiably hindered the free movement of persons (paras 66-70). That ruling was confirmed in *Krüger, 2004* in which the Court also made it plain that as a consequence a state's requirement for its own nationals to renew driving licences every 10 years amounted to reverse discrimination with which to deal was up to national law (paras 35-6). *Kapper, 2004* also concerned the recognition of driving licences. According to the Court, Directive 91/439 did not leave any room not to recognize a driving licence issued in another member state, even if the host member state had concrete indications that the residence requirement had been disregarded by the state issuing the driving licence (para. 47). That point had already been established in *Commission v. Netherlands (driving licence), 2003* and confirmed in an order by the Court, *Da Silva Carvalho, 2003*. Certain measures to restrict, suspend, withdraw, or cancel a driving licence could be taken, though. However, that possibility was not to be used to refuse indefinitely the recognition of the validity of a licence issued in another member state, in particular in case of a licence which was issued in one state after a temporary ban imposed by an another state had expired (para. 76). In *Commission v. Spain (driver licence), 2004*, the Court confirmed *Commission v. Netherlands (driving licence), 2003* and added the following points. The registration of a licence could be offered on a voluntary basis (para. 61). It was sufficient to register the details of an offender at the occasion of the offence (para. 63). Roadside checks did not violate the free movement of persons or non-discrimination, even if they were selective (para. 64). Even when licences issued before the entry into force of the Directive were renewed the minimum medical standards of the Directive had to be observed (paras 77-80). *Kapper, 2004* was in turn confirmed in *Halbritter, 2006*. Accordingly, Germany could not lawfully require the holder of a driving licence issued in Austria to comply with conditions established by German law for the re-issuing of a German licence after Germany had previously withdrawn his German licence, in particular when the person concerned had been resident in Austria when the Austrian licence had been issued (paras 29-30 and 37-8). The two cases were again confirmed in *Kremer, 2006*. The Court added that when a temporary ban on driving had not been ordered by Germany, recognition of a licence issued in Belgium later on could *a fortiori* not be refused (para. 34). In *Wiedemann, 2008* the Court further clarified that case-law and qualified it to some extent. When a member state had withdrawn a driving licence and the period during which it was prohibited to apply for a new licence had passed, recognition of a driving licence issued in another member state could be refused or suspended when it was evident from the driving licence document itself or other information provided by the issuing member state that it had been issued in violation of the residence requirement pursuant to Community law (paras 69-72 and 84). *Zerche, 2008* was handed down on the same day as *Wiedemann, 2008* and confirmed it. *Möginger, 2008* confirmed that a licence issued in a member state, while a ban on re-application had been ordered after a withdrawal in another member state, need not have been recognized by the latter state. The possibility to refuse recognition was not limited in time (paras 41-2). *Weber, 2008* again clarified a detail. When a person's right to drive was temporarily suspended in one state, because the person had driven under the influence of a substance, and then later on was definitely revoked in the light of the same incident, a driving licence issued in another member state during the time of suspension need not have been recognized (paras 31-40). *Schwarz, 2009* further refined that case-law. The question in *Schwarz, 2009* was whether a driving licence issued by Austria before accession to the Community had to be recognized, after a subsequently issued German licence had been withdrawn due to driving under the influence of a substance and the period set by Germany during which no new licence could be applied for had expired. In the light of the case-law, the Court denied the obligation to recognize the Austrian licence, although the licence was in principle equivalent. The reason was that road safety could be compromised, because the person concerned had simply fallen back on the old Austrian licence without having undergone any kind of test of the fitness to drive (paras 89-97). *Wierer, 2009* refined *Wiedemann, 2008* with regard to a licence issued in violation of the residence requirement in Directive 91/439 and the evidence needed in this regard for the host state to justify a refusal to recognize a licence issued in another member state. The evidence admitted did not include statements made by the licence holder in the administrative procedure in the state issuing the licence, or even that state's statement not to have verified the residence requirement; it included information furnished by the host state's local authorities in charge of residence registration, but not by employers or landlords (paras 53-61).

Purely internal situations

In the 2000s the Court also developed its approach to purely internal situations and clarified it with regard to Union citizenship. In *Garcia Avello, 2003* the Court decided that article 12 Treaty applied as soon as a national of one member state resided in another member state, even if he also held the nationality of the host state (paras 27-8). In *Zhu and Chen, 2004*, the Court found that the situation of a national of a member state who was born in another member state which he had never left was not a purely internal situation (para. 19). In *Schempp, 2005* the Court decided that it was enough to bring a situation within the scope of articles 12 and 18 Treaty that a German national residing in Germany, who had never made use of his Treaty freedoms, had a tax issue with the German authorities with regard to maintenance payments made to his former wife who was resident in Austria. The reason was that the possibility for him to deduct maintenance payment from income for tax purposes in Germany was influenced by her exercising her freedom of movement (para. 24).

In *Tas-Hagen, 2006* the refusal of a benefit by a member state to one of his own nationals on the ground that he resided in another member state was found not to be a purely internal situation for the purposes of Union citizenship (paras 26-8). This was confirmed in *Nerkowska, 2008* (paras 28-9). In *Eman and Sevinger, 2006* the Court ruled that article 19(2) Treaty did not apply to a Union citizen residing in an overseas territory who wished to vote in European Parliamentary election in the state of which he was a national (para. 53). The Court went on to examine equal treatment nonetheless only to find that a member state was precluded from drawing a distinction for voting purposes between his own nationals living in a third state and those living in an overseas territory (paras 58 and 60).

In *French Community, 2008* the Court dealt with a care insurance scheme established by the Flemish region in Belgium which was only available to persons residing in the Flemish region or nationals of other member states who worked in the Flemish region, but resided in another member state. The Court replied to the questions asked by the national court for two reasons, namely (i) to give the national court the possibility to exclude reverse discrimination of Belgian nationals which could be prohibited by national law; and (ii) to exclude discrimination of nationals of the member states who resided in the French region of Belgium or in Brussels and worked in the Flemish region (paras 40-1). The Court then found that the exclusion from the scheme of nationals of member states other than Belgium who resided in Brussels or the French region violated non-discrimination pursuant to articles 39 and 43 Treaty. Essentially, the residence condition was liable to prevent certain Union citizens from moving to parts of Belgium (para. 48).

However, the Court also refused to examine certain situations, because they were purely internal to a member state. This was the case in *Mayeur, 2008*, because the spouse of a third country national had never made use of his freedoms as a Union citizen. The third country national could therefore not rely on the diploma recognition rules of the Community to have a diploma recognized in the member state concerned which (the diploma) she had obtained in a third state, although previously the diploma had already been recognized by another member state (para. 20). In *Mariano, 2009* the Court refused to deal with a situation in Italy in which a survivor received lower benefits because she had not been married to the person having died in an accident. Given that all circumstances were confined to Italy, no connection whatsoever to Community law was given (paras 22-3). The Charter of Fundamental Rights did not change that assessment (para. 29). In a similar vein, the Court refused to enter into the case in *Pignataro, 2009*. An Italian national who had never made use of her right of free movement was not entitled to rely on her rights as a Union citizen to challenge her exclusion from the elections to the regional assembly in Sicily on the ground that she was not resident there, but elsewhere in Italy. According to the Court she was not hindered in exercising her right of free movement. The purely hypothetical perspective of her exercising her rights at a later point in time was not sufficient to establish a connection to Community law (paras 15-6).

2 Establishment

Dentists

In *Haim II, 2000* the Court considered a language requirement for dental practitioners in the light of the freedom of establishment. While such a requirement could be justified by the need for the communication skills required to exercise the profession, in particular with patients, the Court found that the requirement was not to go beyond what such communication required. In particular, the needs of patients speaking a foreign language in the host state to communicate with dentists in their native language had to be taken into account (paras 57-60). In *Commission v. Italy (dentists), 2001* the Court rejected two requirements for dentists practicing in Italy. Both requirements resulted from an unclear interpretation of certain Italian provisions. That only Italian nationals could maintain their registration in Italy as dentists when they moved to reside abroad was discriminatory (paras 31-2). The requirement for nationals of other member states to reside in Italy in the district concerned in order to be admitted to practice as dentists constituted a restriction, for it prevented dentists established in other member states from establishing a second practice or working as employees in Italy (para. 20). Both requirements, therefore, violated the freedom of establishment and workers. Italy had to bring to an end the state of uncertainty created by the interpretation of the norms concerned.

Hartlauer, 2009 developed the medical services case-law which had been formed mainly under the freedom of services. Hartlauer, a German company, was refused the authorization to establish outpatient dental clinics in Vienna and Wels in Austria. Such authorizations depended on the need for such a clinic in a region which in turn depended on different factors in each region, such as the waiting time for patients or the number of doctors per capita in the region concerned. The Court ruled that the refusal to grant the authorization for lack of need constituted a restriction of Hartlauer's access to the Austrian market and thus of the freedom of establishment (paras 37-9). That restriction concerning *extra-muros* treatment in kind was, in principle, susceptible of justification by the need to maintain a balanced high quality medical service open to all and to prevent serious harm to the financial balance of the social security system (paras 51-3). However, Austria had pursued those aims in a manner unsuitable for inconsistent and unsystematic. Group practises run by several dental practitioners which essentially covered the same market as outpatient dental clinics were not subject to an assessment of need (paras 54-63). Moreover, the criteria subject to which the authorization was normally granted were not sufficiently fixed and well known in advance, in part because they differed for each region (paras 64-70).

Opticians

In *Mac Quen, 2001* the Belgian authorities opened criminal proceedings, because a company established in the United Kingdom offered certain new examinations of eyesight via a daughter company in Belgium. Such services were reserved in Belgium to qualified ophthalmologists, while in the United Kingdom they could lawfully be provided by ordinary opticians. The profession of ophthalmologist was not harmonized in the Community. The Court found that the four-pronged test established in *Gebhard, 1995* was satisfied, namely the requirement was indiscriminate, public health concerns applied, and it was suitable and basically necessary to protect public health. That other member states were satisfied with a lower level of public health protection did not necessarily render one member state's high level of protection disproportionate (paras 26-34). However, in assessing the necessity of the restriction the national court had to factor in two points, viz. that Belgium's restriction was based on an early interpretation by Belgium's highest court and the assessment of public health concerns could possibly differ at the time given the scientific progress; the German Federal Constitutional Court had, moreover, ruled shortly before that the services the British company offered were provided safely by opticians in Germany (paras 35-6).

In *Commission v. Greece (opticians), 2005* the Court rejected Greece's requirements for the operation of an optician's shop, namely (i) an authorized optician as a natural person was allowed to run only one shop; (ii) such an optician had to hold at least 50 per cent of the share capital of a company running an optician's shop and participate at least to that extent in the profits and losses of the company which had to be established in the form of a collective or limited partnership; (iii) an optician running a shop was allowed to participate at most in one other company owning an optician's shop. According to the Court, the first requirement (i) restricted the freedom of establishment of natural persons, while the other requirements restricted the freedom of establishment of legal persons (paras 28-9). The protection of public health did not justify those restrictions, since less restrictive measures were available, namely qualified opticians could simply be required to be present at the shop and civil liability and professional indemnity insurance rules could address the risks involved (para. 35). In *Commission v. Greece (opticians II), 2009* the Court confirmed that Greece had failed to comply with the judgment for about four years and ordered Greece to pay a lump sum.

Psychotherapists

In *Commission v. Germany (psychotherapists), 2007*, Germany had introduced a new quota system based on regions for practices of psychotherapists. The Commission challenged the way Germany safeguarded established rights. In essence, Germany only allowed those practitioners to practice outside the quota system who had practised previously for three years under German statutory sickness insurance schemes and who wanted to continue to do so in the very same region. Even for psychotherapists who were established in Germany, comparable professional activities in other member states were not taken account of to determine whether the requirement of having practised for three years was met (para. 52). The Court held that that exclusion amounted to indirect discrimination (paras 53-9). While safeguarding established rights was a ground that could potentially justify a restriction, the measure was not necessary. According to the Court, the aim of the new system of quotas which was to limit the number of psychotherapists would not have been jeopardized, if practice in other member states would have been taken into account in all the cases of psychotherapists who were already established in Germany (paras 63-73).

Pharmacies

In *Apothekerkammer, 2009* Germany's prohibition for non-pharmacists, such as the Dutch company DocMorris, to own and operate a pharmacy was at issue. In a similar vein as in *Hartlauer, 2009*, the restriction of the freedom of establishment inherent in Germany's prohibition was in general justifiable by public health grounds. The independence of pharmacists, a 'moderating factor' (para. 39) which a member state was entitled to consider as necessary to run a pharmacy in a way that avoided overemphasizing profits and that did not jeopardize the financial balance of the medical system could be factored into that assessment (paras 27-40). In contrast to *Hartlauer, 2009*, the German measure was appropriate, because it was consistent and systematic. The existence of internal hospital pharmacies as well as the possibility for non-pharmacists within narrow confines to run an inherited pharmacy both complied with those criteria; so did the fact that pharmacists under certain conditions could run three branches of a pharmacy, while remaining responsible for the overall operation (paras 42-50). Finally, given the member states' large discretion less restrictive, but equally effective measures were not available (paras 52-8). With almost identical reasoning, though also extending to the free movement of capital, the Court then approved Italy's requirements to run pharmacies in *Commission v. Italy (pharmacies), 2009*. Italy also limited the right to operate pharmacies to pharmacists and to companies composed exclusively of pharmacists. In addition, companies distributing pharmaceutical products were not allowed to acquire stakes in public municipal pharmacies.

Lawyers

In *Luxembourg v. Parliament (lawyer directive), 2000* the Court rejected Luxembourg's challenge of a new lawyer directive governing practice under the title acquired in the 'home' state, viz. Directive 98/5. Equal treatment was not violated by the possibility for lawyers admitted to the bar in a member state to practise fully in the host state under the 'home' state title, as the situations of a 'domestic' lawyer and a lawyer coming to practice in the host state under her 'home' state title were not comparable (paras 24-8). The protection of the consumer was sufficiently guaranteed by the directive (para. 43). Article 57(1) Treaty was, moreover, the right legal basis for the directive, as it was about the recognition of professional titles rather than the rules governing the professions pursuant to article 57(2) Treaty (paras 56-7).

Wouters, 2002 also concerned lawyers. In the Netherlands, the bar association prohibited multidisciplinary partnerships. Lawyers were therefore not allowed to offer their services together with accountants. Most of the judgment dealt with competition law. However, the freedom of establishment and services was also concerned, since the bar as a private association regulated establishment and services collectively. The Court found that any possible restriction of the freedoms inherent in the prohibition were justified – like the restriction of competition – by the rules of professional conduct established in the Netherlands, namely the need for lawyers to be independent and maintain professional secrecy and the prevention of conflicts of interests (para. 122, referring to paras 97-108).

In *Commission v. Italy (lawyers), 2002* the Court held that Italy could not lawfully require a lawyer to reside in the judicial district where she or he was admitted to practise, because owing to the freedom of establishment it had to be possible for lawyers to have more than one place of work (paras 27-8). Moreover, the aptitude test Italy required foreign lawyers to pass did not live up to the requirements of Directive 89/48 on a general system of recognition, because the subjects to be tested and the yardsticks applied were not known in advance. That resulted in a situation of fluidity and uncertainty (paras 51-4). Apart from that, the Court struck down the requirement Italy imposed on foreign lawyers practising in Italy not to have an establishment in Italy, for it was irreconcilable with the freedom of services; the freedom allowed for some infrastructure in the host state (paras 22-3).

In *Mauri, 2005*, admission to practice as a lawyer came under scrutiny. It was not the exam to be taken by candidates as such that was at issue, but rather the composition of the committee examining a candidate's ability. The Court, however, did not find any restriction of the freedom of establishment in that the committee concerned in Italy included, apart from two judges and one professor, two lawyers who acted as president and vice-president of the committee. In any event, a possible restriction would have been justified by the need to ensure the proper qualification of candidates. After all, lawyers themselves were particularly well placed to assess the abilities of candidates (paras 43-5). Moreover, the state retained important supervisory powers (paras 32-5). An additional dimension of the case was that the Court entered the merits, although all the facts of the case exclusively concerned Italy. The Court accepted the argument that the national court required an answer to its question in order to exclude reverse discrimination, thus disregarding that the situation was purely internal to Italy (para. 21).

With *Wilson, 2006* the Court came back to Directive 98/5. Luxembourg had made the admission to practice as a lawyer under the 'home' state title subject to a language test. The Court found that the Directive had completely harmonised the conditions. The aims pursued by such a test were sufficiently safeguarded by the Directive. There was therefore no room left for such an exam (paras 66-76). The Court, in addition, elaborated on the composition of the instance hearing appeals against refusals to be admitted to practice in the light of the fundamental right to effective judicial protection. On the same day *Wilson, 2006* was handed down the Court in *Commission v. Luxembourg (lawyers), 2006* dealt with other aspects of Luxembourg's implementation of Directive 98/5. Apart from fully confirming the ruling sent in *Wilson, 2006* regarding the language test, the Court held that lawyers practising under the 'home' state title in Luxembourg were not to be barred from providing certain services on behalf of companies, if such services could be provided by domestic lawyers, because full access to the profession of a lawyer had to be granted, bar the exceptions contained expressly in the Directive (paras 57-60). Finally, the Directive equally precluded the requirement for lawyers to submit proof of continued registration in the 'home' state on a yearly basis (paras 67-70).

Eschig, 2009 concerned the legal expenses insurance Directive 87/334. The Court decided that the Directive included a general right of the insured person to chose the lawyer representing her or his interests, even in the absence of a conflict of interest. The insurer could, therefore, not lawfully retain the right to appoint a lawyer for mass tort claims proceedings.

Pay slips for workers

In *Payroll, 2002* Italy had reserved the service of issuing the pay slips of workers of companies with less than 250 employees to companies staffed exclusively with certain qualified employment consultants. The Court found that this measure constituted an obstacle to the freedom of establishment (para. 27). The national court had to assess whether it was suitable for the protection of the workers receiving the pay slips, or whether the service consisted merely in implementing instructions and was thus of administrative nature (paras 34-5). In any event, the rule went beyond what was necessary to protect workers, as for no apparent reason it applied only to small companies with less than 250 employees (para. 37).

Games of chance

Gambelli, 2003 concerned a similar gambling constellation as *Zenatti, 1999*. In the latter case the Court had owing to the question referred by the national court exclusively applied the freedom of services. In *Gambelli, 2003* the Court in addition applied the freedom of establishment. A British company which was authorized to offer gambling services in the United Kingdom collected bets in Italy via agencies without having obtained the licence required in Italy. That the freedom of establishment and services was restricted was undisputed, in particular because the conditions under which an authorization would have been obtainable worked to the effect that one Italian licence holder enjoyed a monopoly in gambling services (paras 47-9). However, in applying the four-pronged *Gebhard, 1995*-test the Court held that national legislation had to pursue the aims of gambling legislation in a consistent and systematic manner to be suitable for justification (para. 67). Italy notably could not lawfully insist on a licence requirement, while denying such a licence to companies established abroad where they were duly authorized for gambling purposes, in the name of reducing gambling, whereas at the same time actively encouraging gambling with the only Italian service provider pursuing the aim of collecting more taxes (paras 68-9). Furthermore, the national court had to ensure that the licence requirement was applied indistinctly and penalties for violating it were proportionate (paras 71 et seq.).

Commission v. Greece (gaming), 2006 also concerned the entertainment and gaming industry. Greece had prohibited the public operation of all electric, electromechanical and electronic games, including all computer games, on public and private premises outside casinos. The Court looked at the prohibition through the lenses of the free movement of goods first, finding an unjustified restriction, and then the freedom of establishment and services. The Court ruled that the prohibition prevented persons lawfully offering those services in other member states from establishing themselves in Greece. Similarly, the prohibition prevented the operation of gaming machines, which was a service (paras 52-4). Those restrictions were, moreover, not justified by the grounds argued in *Schindler, 1994* and *Läärä, 1999*, namely the protection of consumers and public order, since the activities prohibited were not comparable to games of chance. In particular, they were not played with a view to winning money (para. 36). According to the Court, even if the justification based on public order as such was not precluded, less restrictive measures than an outright prohibition would have been available, like technical and organisational measures (paras 39-40). In *Commission v. Greece (gaming II), 2009* the Court then ordered Greece to pay a penalty and a lump sum, because Greece had not brought an end to the violations.

In *Placanica, 2007*, the Court followed up on *Zenatti, 1999* and *Gambelli, 2003* and again dealt with games of chance offered in Italy. In essence, Italy had tendered a thousand licences for each sports and horse race betting activities. Listed companies were not allowed to participate in the tender procedure though, for Italian law necessarily required that the owners of the licensed companies were clearly identifiable at all times. That requirement worked to exclude the major service providers established in member states other than Italy, since they were all public companies. Consequently, the Italian agents of a company listed and licensed in the United Kingdom were subject to prosecution in Italy for having offered betting services without the prerequisite licence. According to the Court, the objective of reducing gaming opportunities did not justify the restrictions inherent in the licence and the tender requirements, because Italy pursued a policy of expanding betting and gambling to raise revenues. However, the aim of channelling betting and gambling away from illegal to controllable operators could provide such justification (para. 55). Yet, the blanket exclusion of listed companies from the tender procedure was unnecessary to achieve that aim. Information on owners and representatives of listed companies could be gathered as an alternative to a downright exclusion of the companies concerned (para. 62). *Placanica, 2007* was backed up on the very same day it was handed down by four decisions dealing with identical constellations, namely *D'Antonio, 2007*, *Damonte, 2007*, *Di Maggio, 2007*, and *Gallo, 2007*.

Taxation

Baars, 2000 concerned an exemption from Dutch wealth tax which was only granted when substantial long-term shareholdings were held in companies established in the Netherlands. Mr Baars, a Dutch national resident in the Netherlands, was denied the exemption for his holdings in a company established in Ireland. According to the Court, the freedom of establishment was violated. A Dutch national was entitled to invoke that freedom against the member state of which he was a national (paras 28-9). When the shareholder exercised definite influence on the company concerned, the difference in treatment based on the seat of the company hindered the freedom of the shareholder to establish himself abroad (paras 30-1). (Where definite influence was not exercised over the company, free movement of capital was hindered; paras 20-2.) The hindrance was not justified, since the wealth tax did not correspond in any way to the taxation of a company's profits (paras 39-40).

De Lasteyrie du Saillant, 2004 also concerned taxation. In specific cases, France levied a tax on latent increases in the value of securities in companies subject to taxation in France when the holder of the securities transferred residence to another member state. In case the taxpayer stayed in France, the tax only became due when the increase in value was actually realized. The exit tax could be suspended when a sufficient guarantee was lodged, a declaration was submitted, and a representative in France was designated. In that case, the duty to pay the tax lapsed after five years, if the increase in value was not in fact realized. A tax levied by another member state on the same increase in value was credited in any case against the French tax. The Court held that the freedom of establishment was restricted, because persons were dissuaded from leaving a member state. That applied even if a national of a member state wanted to leave that member state and if the restriction was minor. The conditions to be fulfilled for the suspension of the tax, in particular the guarantee, constituted a restriction, too (paras 42-8). The restrictions were not justified by the prevention of tax avoidance, for the French approach was not designed exclusively to counteract short-term transfers of residence undertaken to escape taxation. The taxation of latent increases in value could be limited to cases of relatively brief stays abroad (paras 51-7). The coherence of the French tax system did not provide justification, either. The direct link in the sense of *Bachmann, 1992* between the postponement of the taxation of increases in value and the collection at the moment when the taxpayer transferred residence was not given. The aim of the French exit tax was to prevent tax evasion, rather than to tax increases in value generally (paras 63-7). In *N, 2006* a similar exit tax on latent increases in the value of shares as in *De Lasteyrie du Saillant, 2004* was at issue. The freedom of establishment was concerned, because the shares conferred substantial influence on the company concerned (para. 28). However, the Court found that the restriction of the freedom of establishment inherent in the Dutch tax at issue was, in the absence of harmonizing measures, justified by the proper allocation of the power to tax increases in the value of shares among the member states, i. e. by the principle of territoriality (paras 46-7). Yet to avoid going beyond what was necessary in the light of that aim, the lodging of a security to guarantee payment of the tax debt in case that payment was deferred, could not be required. Moreover, decreases in the share value which occurred after residence had been transferred had to reduce the actual tax debt when the payment of the tax had been deferred (paras 51-4 and 57).

In *Conijn, 2006* deductions for the purpose of direct taxation were at stake. Mr Conijn resided in the Netherlands, while he was established in Germany. He gained less than 90 per cent of his total income in Germany and sought to deduct the cost of the advice he had needed to file the tax declaration in Germany from his taxable income. However, German law allowed such a deduction only for persons fully taxable in Germany, i. e. mostly residents. The Court found that residents and non-residents were in comparable situations with regard to the deduction of the cost of tax advice, since both of them were in need of similar advice given the complexity of national tax law. The cost of the advice was, moreover, linked directly to the income taxed in Germany in both cases.

The freedom of establishment thus precluded the indirect discrimination inherent in Germany's refusal to grant non-residents the deduction (paras 22-4). *Meindl, 2007* also concerned direct taxation in a *Schumacker, 1995*-like situation. When one spouse was resident in Austria and received a tax-free children allowance there, while the other spouse resided in Germany and generated the entire taxable family income through self-employment there, according to the Court, the freedom of establishment required Germany to disregard the Austrian children allowance and to treat the couple, tax-wise, as if they both resided in Germany. Consequently, Germany had to apply the regular joint assessment.

As discussed under the freedom of workers, the Court in *Commission v. Denmark (insurance taxation), 2007* dealt with the requirement that a pension and life insurance institution had to be established in Denmark for tax relief to be available to insured persons subject to direct taxation in Denmark. The Court found that such an approach did not only restrict the freedom of service provision by foreign insurers as well as the freedom of recipients in Denmark to receive services abroad, but also the freedom of self-employed persons and workers to move to Denmark (para. 44). Those restrictions were not justified, since the cohesion of the Danish tax system was not sufficiently threatened within the sense of *Bachmann, 1992*. A risk arose exclusively when an insured person left Denmark's fiscal jurisdiction right before the pension became payable, while tax relief was refused in other situations, too (paras 72-4). The restrictive measure was not required by the need to supervise taxation effectively or to prevent tax avoidance, either (paras 52-8).

In *Talotta, 2007*, the Court addressed a distinction drawn by Belgian tax law. When a person resident in Luxembourg who was established in Belgium had failed to submit a tax declaration based on which his income taxable in Belgium could be assessed, a tax based on a minimum tax basis became due, because the person was a non-resident taxpayer. If he had been a resident taxpayer a different method to estimate the tax due would have been applied, namely either the income taxable in Belgium would have been estimated on the basis of the income of three taxpayers in comparable situations or a flat-rate method of taxation would have been applied on the basis of signs and indications that the person concerned was indeed better off than indicated by the income accounted for (paras 21-2). The Court decided that the situations of resident and non-resident taxpayers pursuing a self-employed activity in Belgium were comparable. A distinction could therefore not be drawn on the basis of residence, else non-resident taxpayers would be subject to indirect discrimination (paras 24-6 and 31). The practical difficulties to assess the tax due from a person who pursued an activity in Belgium and was resident in Luxembourg were the same as when the person resided in Belgium and pursued a self-employed activity in Luxembourg. Those practical difficulties could be overcome by exchanging information based on Directive 77/799 (paras 28-9).

In *Filipiak, 2009* the Court invalidated the way Poland's tax law dealt with social security contributions paid by a Polish national who was resident in

Poland and pursued a single professional activity in self-employment in the Netherlands. This self-employed activity was compulsorily subject to social security contributions in the Netherlands pursuant to Regulation 1408/71, while those contributions were not factored into the income taxation in the Netherlands (para. 51). The Court held that the situations of a person who contributed to the social security system in Poland and a person who contributed to the system of another member state were comparable, since both were subject to unlimited tax liability in Poland (paras 66-70). Therefore, Poland had to treat social security contributions made in the Netherlands in the same way in terms of taxation as those made in Poland, i. e. Poland had to allow deductibility (para. 63), else the freedom of establishment and services were breached. That the Polish constitutional court had not rendered invalid the relevant Polish act right away was irrelevant, as any Polish court was directly obliged not to apply the act, since it was contrary to the Treaty (paras 82-4).

Car registration

Nadin and Durré, 2005 again after *Commission v. Denmark (car registration), 2005* concerned the registration of company vehicles and the tax imposed on that occasion. In *Nadin and Durré, 2005*, Belgium required the registration of a vehicle along with the payment of a tax, when a person resident in Belgium was established as a self-employed person in another member state and was provided, based on that establishment, with a 'company' car. After having directed the national court to assess whether the persons concerned were indeed self-employed, the Court re-applied the ruling delivered in *Commission v. Denmark (car registration), 2005* to self-employed persons (paras 36-7 and 41-2). Essentially, the vehicle's registration in the member state where the person concerned was resident could lawfully be required, if the vehicle was used there on a permanent basis. In addition, the Court rejected the justification of the restriction on the grounds of road safety and environmental protection (paras 49 and 52). *Nadin and Durré, 2005* was confirmed in all aspects in *Schmitz, 2006*. In *Vandermeier, 2008* the Court again confirmed the approach and held that it also applied in the case of a self-employed journalist who pursued his professional activity in another member state, had leased the car himself and was not the director of a company, but a regular natural person (paras 34-5).

Diploma

Neri, 2003 was at the nexus between diploma recognition and establishment. A company established in the United Kingdom offered courses in Italy via branches to prepare students for the bachelor degree to be awarded by a university in the United Kingdom. The company had an agreement to that effect with the British university concerned. The students were enrolled with the British university. Italy refused to recognize the bachelor diplomas awarded in the United Kingdom as a result of the preparatory courses in Italy. According to the Court, the freedom of establishment was restricted, because non-recognition of the diplomas had the effect that students were deterred from seeking those educational services provided by branches in Italy (paras 43-4). While maintaining a high standard of university education was a reason apt to justify a restriction of the freedom of establishment, non-recognition of the diploma awarded was not a suitable measure, since it was only applied when Italian nationals had obtained such a diploma. Moreover, Italian universities were allowed to offer similar courses under comparable arrangements within Italy (para. 47). Finally, Italy's categorical non-recognition also went beyond what was required in that it precluded any assessment of the concrete situation (paras 49-50).

Private security

Commission v. Portugal (private security), 2004 concerned the freedom of services as much as the freedom of establishment. To be allowed to provide private security services certain conditions had to be fulfilled in Portugal. The provider had to be constituted as a legal person with a minimum share capital. An establishment in Portugal and an authorization by the Portuguese state were also necessary; and employees had to be in possession of a Portuguese professional certificate. Relying on *Schnitzer, 2003*, a freedom of services case, the Court reiterated that an abstract rule did not exist to determine the duration and frequency of services necessary to distinguish them clearly from establishment. The freedom of services was possibly concerned though, even when the services were provided over a long time span like more than one year (paras 26-8). The Court then went on to reject each of Portugal's requirements. The minimum share capital went against the grain of both the freedom of establishment and services and was not justified by the protection of creditors (paras 53-4), as did the requirement to be constituted as a legal person for excluding natural persons and secondary establishments (paras 42-3). The authorization requirement was also rejected, because it created a double burden and was not necessary to ensure supervision (para. 60); so was the requirement to be established (paras 33-4). Finally, the condition of having a Portuguese certificate violated the freedom of workers and services for it created a double burden for service providers (para. 66).

Bovine semen

In *Commission v. France (insemination), 2008*, the Court dealt with certain requirements in French law for services related to insemination with bovine semen. Semen had to be stored at specific centres which enjoyed territorial exclusivity. Each service provider had to have a licence which was subject to an agreement with a service centre. The conclusion of such an agreement was subject to the discretion of the centre concerned. The Court found that the territorial exclusivity and the need for an agreement violated the freedom of establishment, while the exclusivity and the licence requirement including the need for an agreement contravened the freedom of services (paras 53-55 and 64-66). The restrictions were not justified, as the protection of pure-bred bovine stock had been harmonized in the Community and they were not necessary for the collection of data on insemination (paras 73-81). The protection of public health did not require exclusive rights and a licence subject to a discretionary agreement, either (paras 91-5). The necessities of food safety, traceability of semen, and of town planning were, moreover, not proven to a sufficient degree.

Family members

Jia, 2007 was already discussed under free movement of workers above, because it was mainly related to *Akrich, 2003* and *Metock, 2008*. Technically though, it concerned the freedom of establishment and Directive 73/148. The Court in *Jia, 2007* left the member states an option, namely each member state could – but did not have to – require a third country national who was the parent of the third country national spouse of a migrant worker to have had legal residence in another member state before that parent was entitled to rely on the right to family reunification pursuant to Community law (para. 33). Moreover, the Court clarified the concept of 'dependence'. The situation of dependence of the relative must have existed in the state of origin or the state where the person concerned had been resident (para. 37).

Cars

In *Commission v. Italy (motor insurance), 2009* Italy had laid down an obligation to contract for companies that offered insurance policies for third-party motor vehicle liability. The Court found that access of foreign insurance companies to the Italian market was impeded, since the obligation to contract constituted a substantial interference with the liberty to contract which companies normally enjoyed and in particular required insurance companies to adapt their policies (paras 66-71). However, that restriction of the freedom of establishment and services was justified by the need to protect victims of road traffic accidents (paras 74-82). The restriction was proportionate given that Italy had shown that young drivers in southern Italy would have difficulties taking out insurance policies without the obligation to contract and that the rates were still subject to variation based on statistical evidence (paras 87-91). Moreover, problems of equal treatment under Italian law would have arisen, if the obligation to contract was limited to southern Italy (para. 92). Finally, two complaints by the Commission relating to Directive 92/49 were rejected.

In *Commission v. Portugal (vehicle inspection), 2009* Portugal had required companies that tested vehicles on roadworthiness to have an authorization which was only granted, if it was in the public interest to grant it, the company had a share capital of 100'000 Euro, the objectives of the company were limited to providing that service, and certain incompatibility rules for shareholders, managers, and directors of the company were respected. The Court found that those conditions restricted the freedom of establishment, in particular since the public interest criterion was subject to potentially arbitrary discretion. Justification by the public authority derogation, though not inconceivable for non-discriminatory measures as such (para. 33), was not plausible. If at all, only the second stage of the test, i. e. the attachment of the certifying badge to the vehicle after the actual test, could possibly come within the scope of the derogation. However, in this stage the companies concerned were supervised by the public authorities and did have neither the independence in decision-taking nor the power of coercion characteristic of public authority (paras 38-44).

Ankara

In *Savas, 2000* two Turkish nationals had stayed in the United Kingdom after their tourist visas had expired and had opened a business there. The Court ruled that article 13 of the Ankara Agreement with Turkey did not have direct effect in the absence of the implementing provisions mentioned therein, in contrast to the standstill clause in article 41(1) of the Additional Protocol to the Ankara Agreement. However, that standstill clause was not capable by itself of conferring a right to establishment in the case at hand, since in analogy to the case-law developed for workers under the Ankara Agreement the situation of a person who remained in the host state after a tourist visa had expired was not to be considered stable and secure. Such a person was therefore not entitled to claim a residence permit. Each member state on its own regulated the first admission of Turkish nationals to its market (paras 63-7). In *Tum, 2007*, the Court again ruled on the basis the freedom of establishment under the Ankara Agreement. According to the Court, the standstill clause in article 41(1) of the Additional Protocol to the Ankara Agreement, which had been at stake already in *Savas, 2000*, prevented the introduction of any new procedural and substantive requirements for the establishment in a member state. The standstill clause notably also covered the conditions of first admission to a member state, while not in itself conferring a right of first admission (paras 52, 55, 58, and 63).

Europe Agreements

In *Kondova, 2001* a similar situation as in *Savas, 2000* came up under the Association Agreement with Bulgaria. A Bulgarian national had made false representations when entering the United Kingdom, and later on began to work as a self-employed cleaner there, after having married a third country national having indefinite leave to remain in the United Kingdom. The Court ruled that the freedom of establishment in article 45(1) of the Europe Agreement with Bulgaria had direct effect. However, despite the same wording of the freedom of establishment in the Europe Agreement as in the Treaty the case-law developed for the internal market was not to be applied mechanically under the Europe Agreement, since the aims of the internal market and the Agreement differed (paras 50-5). Hence, the freedom of establishment under the Europe Agreement did not automatically entail the same right of entry and residence as in the internal market. While the economic needs of the British market, nationality, and residence were all banned by the Europe Agreement as criteria under the freedom of establishment, a system of prior control of the requirements in the Europe Agreement was compatible with it. More specifically, to prevent illegal immigration the person concerned could lawfully be required not to make false statements upon entering the United Kingdom, and, if she did nonetheless do so, be forced to file a new application from Bulgaria or another state outside the United Kingdom. Such a person had placed herself wilfully outside the protection of the Europe Agreement and was not entitled to invoke it (paras 77-80 and 87). The family life had to be respected, though (para. 88). Shortly after *Kondova, 2001* the Court applied an identical approach under the Europe Agreements with Poland and the Czech Republic in *Gloszczuk, 2001* and *Barkoci, 2001*, respectively. However, in *Barkoci, 2001* an abuse had not been committed by the Czech nationals concerned. Yet those Czech nationals had to meet the substantive requirements which were tolerated by the Europe Agreement and in case of failure to do so could lawfully be required to file new applications from the Czech Republic, even if they had been admitted temporarily to the United Kingdom on grounds of human dignity and solidarity (para. 78).

Jany, 2001 again concerned an activity under two Europe Agreements, namely that with Poland and that with the Czech Republic. Polish and Czech prostitutes claimed to be established to conduct business in the Netherlands. The Court applied the same principles as it had in *Kondova, 2001*. Moreover, according to the Court, internal market case-law could be applied to determine whether an activity was covered by the freedom of establishment (paras 37-8). Prostitution was an economic activity in the sense of the Europe Agreement (para. 48). Whether a restriction of prostitution was covered by a derogation, notably the public order derogation, was essentially for the national institutions to assess. Certainly though, similar restrictions had to be enforced against Dutch nationals as for nationals from the associated states. That was not the case in *Jany, 2001* (para. 62). Finally, a member state was not to apply a general presumption that prostitutes were employed. Rather, a case-by-case assessment was necessary (paras 67-70). (The distinction between employment and self-employment was relevant, because the admission requirements were not the same for the two categories under the Europe Agreements.)

In *Panayotova, 2004* the Court again ruled on the basis of the Europe Agreements. The Court reiterated that the relevant Europe Agreements did not confer a right for persons to submit an application in the host state to become established there, in that case the Netherlands, when they were present there illegally or based on a tourist visa. Rather, national law could lawfully require an application in the 'home' state via the consular representation (para. 24). The Court added that procedural guarantees and fundamental rights had to be respected (paras 26-7). Moreover, even when the host state authorities did not have any discretion pursuant to domestic law and the substantive requirements of the Europe Agreement concerned were manifestly met they were entitled automatically to reject an application made on the basis of illegal or tolerated presence, else the conditions of the Europe Agreements ran the risk of being circumvented (paras 29-38).

In *Commission v. Austria (self-employment), 2008* the Court dealt with a measure Austria had adopted to prevent circumvention of the transitional limitation of access to the labour market for workers from the new central and eastern European member states which (the limitation) was contained in the Act of Accession. Austria had claimed that workers from the new member states established themselves in Austria as self-employed persons in partnerships and limited liability companies and thereby bypassed the limitations applying to employed persons. However, the Court found that the prior authorization requirement for such entities which had been introduced by Austria and was applicable in the case of nationals from the new member states established a difference in treatment which was contrary to the freedom of establishment. The authorization was essentially granted only if the person concerned proved that she or he was not working as an employed person. Moreover, during the authorization proceedings 'work' was not to begin yet (paras 29-30). Being discriminatory, the measure was amenable to justification solely by the express grounds provided by the Treaty, but the public policy ground did not hold, since it would have been sufficient to provide the authorities with the information they needed. The persons concerned could then have immediately begun with their activities and the authorities would have undertaken controls later on (paras 31-40).

Switzerland

Stamm, 2008 was the first judgment that applied the Luxembourg Agreement on Free Movement of Persons with Switzerland. (*Grimme, 2009* was handed down later on, see above.) Mr Stamm was a farmer established in Switzerland who had leased farmland across the border in Germany. Could such a farmer, as a self-employed frontier worker, rely on the equal treatment clause contained in the Luxembourg Agreement? The Court, reasoning mainly in analogy to employed frontier workers (paras 41-3), answered in the affirmative.

Purely internal situations

In *Kurt, 2008*, the Court refused to address the question asked by the Austrian court on the ground that the situation was purely internal to Austria. Mr Kurt had complained that he was only allowed to work as a teacher for driving instructors in Austria, but not to run his own school, while German nationals with an educational background comparable to his were allowed to run their own school in Austria based on the freedom of establishment. Moreover, he himself was entitled to run such a school in Germany. According to the Court, all aspects of the situation were confined to Austria. It was up to national law to address reverse discrimination (paras 21-3).

Secondary law

In the 2000s, the Court also in a number of judgments applied further, rather technical secondary legislation which implemented the freedom of establishment, though without elaborating on that freedom itself. In *Centrosteel, 2000* the

Court applied Directive 86/653 on self-employed commercial agents by confirming the judgment in *Bellone, 1998*. In *Ingmar, 2000*, *Caprini, 2003*, *Mavrona, 2004*, *Poseidon, 2006*, *Honyvem, 2006*, *Chevassus-Marche, 2008*, and *Semen, 2009* the Court again interpreted that Directive. In *Vogel, 2003* the Court applied Directive 78/687 concerning dental practitioners.

Open skies

The opens skies judgments, eight of which had been handed down on 5 November 2002 (*Commission v. Austria (open skies), 2002; Commission v. Belgium (open skies), 2002; Commission v. Denmark (open skies), 2002; Commission v. Finland (open skies), 2002; Commission v. Germany (open skies), 2002; Commission v. Luxembourg (open skies), 2002; Commission v. Sweden (open skies), 2002; Commission v. United Kingdom (open skies), 2002*) with one trailing in 2007 (*Commission v. Netherlands (open skies), 2007*), mainly dealt with the powers of the Community and the member states to conclude agreements with third states, namely in these cases agreements allowing free air transport with the United States of America (see the main part of *Commission v. Denmark (open skies), 2002*). One aspect of the cases, however, concerned the freedom of establishment. The open skies agreements with the United States contained a clause of ownership and control of airlines. That clause allowed the United States to withdraw the licence of an airline which had been designated by the other party of the treaty, if no substantial part of ownership and effective control over the company was vested in the state party or nationals of the parties to the specific treaty, for instance in the United Kingdom or British and/or American nationals (para. 47 of *Commission v. United Kingdom (open skies), 2002*). The Court found that the freedom of establishment applied in the air transport sector, in contrast to the freedom of services (paras 39-40), even if the company established in a member state provided air transport exclusively towards a third country (para. 43). Owing to equal treatment, a member state was under the obligation to grant nationals of other member states the benefits provided by treaties with third states, as held in *Saint-Gobain, 1999* and *Gottardo, 2002* (para. 46). The clause treated nationals of other member states and companies established there less favourably, as the United States were obliged to grant a licence when an airline operator of a state party (or one connected thereto) was concerned and could just exceptionally withdraw it, while they were always free to exclude airline operators connected to the other member states (paras 48-50). The public policy and safety derogations did not exempt the distinction, since it was too general to address a threat to the fundamental interests of society, for it was not limited to airlines that actually posed a threat and there was no direct link between the threat and the discrimination (paras 58-9).

Legal persons and taxation

The freedom of establishment of companies more generally occupied the Court in a large number of cases. *Germany v. Commission (Länder), 2000* was one such case, though it mainly concerned state aid. Yet the Court found that Germany's limitation of a tax concession, namely the carrying forward of investments in the new German Länder, to companies established in Germany, thus in effect excluding foreign companies operating via an establishment in eastern Germany, violated the freedom of establishment (para. 86). *AMID, 2000* was a case of company establishment in which the Court declared unlawful Belgium's requirement to offset for company tax purposes a Belgian company's losses made in Belgium against profits made by its permanent establishment in Luxembourg, essentially because that resulted in a situation where the losses made in Belgium could not be deducted anywhere from taxable profit, whereas such losses would have been deductible had the permanent establishment not been in Luxembourg, but in Belgium (para. 23).

Dividends

Metallgesellschaft, 2001 developed the case-law on dividends. The law of the United Kingdom made available a regime called group income election only to groups the parent company of which had its seat in the United Kingdom. Group income election essentially had the effect that a tax on intra-group dividends which operated as an advance payment of corporation tax did not become due. The result was a cash-flow disadvantage for foreign groups with subsidiaries in the United Kingdom. According to the Court that constituted a restriction of the freedom of establishment (paras 43-4 and 53-4) which was not justified, notably by the need to maintain the cohesion of the tax system. A direct link did not exist between the cash-flow disadvantage due to the tax on dividends, i.e. the refusal to grant group income election, and the exemption of foreign parent companies from profit taxation as regarded dividends received from subsidiaries in the United Kingdom, since such dividends were not subject to profit taxation in any case regardless of whether the parent company had its seat in the United Kingdom or in another member state (paras 69-73).

Lankhorst, 2002 added to the case-law on taxation of dividends. Germany treated interest paid on the basis of an intra-group loan as a covert distribution of profits, viz. as dividends, to the extent that the loan was not at arm's length and taxed it accordingly. Such an approach was applied almost exclusively to foreign parent companies – such as Lankhorst which was a German subsidiary of a foreign parent company – technically because they did not have any tax credit in Germany. According to the Court, the freedom of establishment was restricted (paras 27-32). The approach was too general to be justifiable by the need to prevent tax evasion. The tax advantage necessary for justification by the cohesion of the tax system was also absent (paras 37-42).

Incorporation

In *Ueberseering, 2002*, a German court had refused, in application of the principle of the company seat, a Netherlands corporation, in which all the shares had been acquired by two German nationals resident in Germany, the right to stand before court. The Court found that the freedom of establishment which applied in such a situation despite the appearance created in *Daily Mail, 1988* was violated, for what Germany's approach essentially required was the winding-up of the Dutch company and the consequent re-incorporation in Germany. That approach thus unjustifiably negated the freedom of establishment (paras 81 and 93).

In *Inspire Art, 2003* the Court mainly based on *Centros, 1999* struck down some of the Dutch requirements for the registration of a branch. Inspire Art was a company formed under the law of England and Wales with a sole director who resided in the Netherlands. It was founded solely for the purpose of doing business in the Netherlands via a branch. In such a case, however, the Netherlands imposed requirements for the registration of a branch some of which, according to the Court, were contrary to provisions of the Eleventh Council Directive 89/666 (paras 55-72). In addition, the branch registration requirements for the foreign company concerned to have a higher minimum share capital and for the directors of the company to be subject to stricter liability than in the case of a Dutch company constituted obstacles to the freedom of establishment (para. 101). Those obstacles were not justified by the prevention of abuse, for the Dutch measure was too general, or the protection of creditors, for Inspire Art clearly displayed that it was a foreign company (paras 135-40).

Taxation of capital gains and profits

X and Y, 2002 rejected Sweden's approach to the taxation of capital gains. In short, Sweden deferred taxation when shares were transferred at undervalue to a company established in Sweden, but not when the transferee was a company established abroad or when it was a Swedish corporation in which a foreign company had a holding (see paras 30-1). The consequent deterrent effect *qua* cash flow disadvantage amounted to a restriction of the freedom of establishment and the freedom of capital (paras 36 and 38) which was not justified, in particular by the cohesion of the Swedish tax system which was guaranteed by the relevant double taxation convention and in any event could be safeguarded by less restrictive means (paras 53-9). *X and Y, 2002* was confirmed in *De Baeck, 2004*. Belgium's tax on increase in value when shares were sold to foreign companies was equally contrary – in fact, *a fortiori* contrary since the alternative was not the deferral of taxation (para. 24) – to the freedom of establishment and the freedom of capital.

In *Bosal, 2003* Dutch law required that the cost incurred by Dutch parent companies through foreign subsidiaries were indirectly instrumental for creating a profit taxable in the Netherlands to be deductible from taxable profits. While not precluded by the relevant directive, namely Directive 90/435, the Court found that approach to be contrary to the freedom of establishment for having a dissuasive effect (para. 27). The restriction was not justified by the logic of *Bachmann, 1992* of the cohesion of the tax system for lack of a direct link or by the principle of territoriality (paras 31-40).

Sight account with banks

With *Caixa-Bank, 2004*, the Court was confronted with a prohibition in French law for banks to offer remuneration on sight accounts. Like all banks operating on the French market, a French bank which was the subsidiary of company established in Spain was prohibited to offer interest on sight accounts. The Court found that prohibition to violate the freedom of establishment, since it prevented banks established in other member states from penetrating the French market. It blotted out the price of services as a parameter of competition and hindered banks in raising capital (paras 12-4). The prohibition, moreover, went beyond what was necessary to encourage long-term saving and to protect the consumer from excessive charges. As to the latter, banks could offer the consumer the choice between remuneration coupled with a service charge and a free account without service charge (para. 22).

Ship registration

In *Commission v. Netherlands (ships), 2004* the requirements for ship registration came under scrutiny again. This time the case was about the requirements established by the Netherlands which mostly concerned the structure of the ship-owning companies wanting to register a ship in the Netherlands. One the one hand, the Dutch ship registration scheme required shareholders and directors of a company to be nationals of a member state of the Community or of the European Economic Area, if the company wanted to register one of its ships in the Netherlands. On the other hand, the ship management scheme required directors to be such nationals and to have residence within the territory of the Community or the European Economic Area. The Court rejected both schemes for violating the freedom of establishment of companies. The restructuring of the companies concerned and the redefining of their recruitment policy, both necessitated by the Dutch requirements, as obstacles to the freedom of establishment were not justified by the need to control ships effectively and to exercise jurisdiction (para. 19). The nationality of the shareholders and directors and their residence was irrelevant for control purposes and the real link to the actual owner of a ship needed for such purposes could also be established through a place of business in the Netherlands which was managed on a day-to-day basis by a person with powers of representation (paras 21, 25-6, 32-7).

Ship registration was also at issue in *Viking, 2007*. The Finnish company that operated a ferry service between Helsinki and Tallinn intended to reflag its ship, the 'Rosella', to Estonia in order to escape the application of the collective agreements of Finland and employ Estonian seamen at lower wages. The Finnish union invoked union solidarity and obstructed the re-flagging of 'Rosella' through the international union umbrella association. That association resisted flags of convenience as a matter of policy. The Court decided that collective action measures taken by unions were not *per se* removed from the scope of the freedom of establishment (paras 35-7 and 47). In holding so, the Court in turn recognized a fundamental right to collective action (paras 43-4). In the case at hand, the unions' measures taken to ward off 'Rosella's' reflagging were subject to the freedom of establishment, although the unions were, technically speaking, private organizations (paras 57-66). The unions' measures amounted to a restriction of Viking's freedom of establishment which was exercised through the registration of a ship (paras 72-3). As far as the Finnish union's actions were concerned, they were in principle justified to protect Finnish workers if the national court found so and if a commitment offered by Viking not to make Finnish workers redundant did not prove effective in protecting their work and employment conditions (para. 82-7). However, the international union association's general policy to combat flags of convenience was not justified by the protection of workers, since the policy prevented re-flagging of ships even when the labour force was not at risk (paras 88-9).

Taxation of groups

In *Marks & Spencer, 2005* the Court again dealt with the taxation of groups. The United Kingdom refused group relief to parent companies established in the United Kingdom for losses incurred by subsidiaries in other member states, while it was granted for losses by domestic subsidiaries. Losses made abroad could therefore not be set-off against profits generated in the United Kingdom. While restricting the freedom of establishment by denying a cash advantage (para. 33), the British scheme was, according to the Court, justified by a combination of three grounds, namely the three needs to maintain a balanced allocation of the powers to impose taxes between the member states, to avoid that losses were taken into account twice, and to forestall tax avoidance. If it was not justified, parent companies could have avoided paying taxes by transferring losses within the group to the state that applied the highest tax rate to profits (paras 45-50). However, group relief had to be granted in one specific constellation, viz. when the possibilities to offset a loss in the state where the subsidiary was established were exhausted and it was impossible to offset the loss in the future, for instance because the subsidiary was sold (para. 55-6).

Cross-border merger

In *Sevic Systems, 2005* the German authorities refused to register a cross-border merger between a German and a French company. According to the Court, such mergers were a particular method of exercising the freedom of establishment (paras 17-20). Not to register cross-border mergers, while purely national mergers were registered, constituted a difference in treatment which deterred from exercising the freedom of establishment (paras 21-3). While harmonisation could not be a precondition for establishment, a difference in treatment such as that was in principle susceptible of justification based on various grounds, such as the protection of minority shareholders, creditors, and employees, the effectiveness of fiscal supervision, or the fairness of commercial transactions. However, an downright refusal to register the merger went beyond what was necessary to safeguard those needs (paras 26-30).

Further companies, taxation (2006)

In the year 2006, the Court dealt with a number of cases concerning establishment of companies. *CLT-UFA, 2006* invalidated a distinction in Germany's tax law between branches and subsidiaries of foreign companies. The situations of a German branch and a German subsidiary of a company established in Luxembourg were comparable, given that the profits of branches and subsidiaries were treated equally under the double taxation convention (paras 23-30). Germany could therefore not lawfully apply a higher tax rate to the profits of branches than to those of subsidiaries in Germany, else the free choice under the freedom of establishment between branches and subsidiaries would be impaired and disadvantageous treatment would result (paras 15-7). In *Keller Holding, 2006* the Court was seized with a dispute about dividends again. The Court again invalidated a difference in treatment established by German tax law in comparable situations. The cost associated with dividends paid was deductible for a German parent company in the case of domestic indirect subsidiaries, but not so in the case of indirect subsidiaries in Austria, although in both cases dividends paid were in reality not subject to tax in Germany (paras 31-4 and 37). That difference in treatment violated the freedom of establishment under the Treaty and the European Economic Area, for neither the need to maintain the coherence of the tax system nor the territoriality principle justified it (paras 43-4).

Cadbury Schweppes, 2006 addressed the tax scheme of the United Kingdom which aimed to counteract low tax rates in other states. In essence, the United Kingdom levied a tax on the profits of a foreign subsidiary in the hands of the domestic parent company, if the tax rate applied abroad to those profits was below a certain level, that was three quarters of the rate applicable in the United Kingdom in a similar situation. According to the Court, the difference in treatment based on whether a subsidiary was established abroad or not (paras 43-6) could only be justified by the need to combat abusive practices, viz. tax avoidance, if the exemptions from the British tax were properly interpreted so that only wholly artificial arrangements which did not reflect any genuine economic activity were targeted (para. 55). For that purpose, an objective element, namely no real economic activity in the 'host' state, and a subjective element, namely the intention to obtain a tax advantage, had to be proven to reflect tax avoidance (paras 61-70). In *ACT Group, 2006* the Court again dealt with the United Kingdom's tax regime. The Court mainly determined that the situations of non-resident and resident shareholders were not comparable as regarded the tax treatment, by the member state where the distributing company was resident, of dividends distributed by that company (para. 57), else a member state would be required to forgo its right to tax profit generated in its territory. (Conversely, the situations were comparable when a resident shareholder received dividends from a resident and from a non-resident company, as regarded the tax legislation of the state where the recipient was resident. That was established in *Lenz, 2004* and *Manninen, 2004*, two cases concerning the free movement of capital.) That ruling applied as long as the taxation of the profits of the resident company was at stake, but not when it came to the taxation of the income of shareholders. As regarded the latter, the situations of resident and non-resident shareholders were comparable again (para. 68). That latter point was confirmed shortly after *ACT Group, 2006* in *Denkavit, 2006* in which the Court consequently struck down a French withholding tax on dividends which applied almost exclusively when the dividends were distributed to foreign parent companies (paras 36-9). The reduction of that tax by the relevant double taxation convention between France and the Netherlands and the authorization in it to offset the French withholding tax could not overcome the restriction, as foreign-sourced dividends were exempt from taxation in the Netherlands. Thus, credit was not given in the Netherlands for tax withheld in France (paras 46-9).

FII Group, 2006 was handed down on the same day as *ACT Group, 2006* and also dealt with British taxes in the context of dividends. *FII Group, 2006* dealt with many aspects of the British system. *Inter alia*, the United Kingdom applied for foreign-sourced dividends a system of partial imputation regarding the corporation tax paid by a foreign company distributing dividends. For nationally-sourced dividends a system of exemption applied which had the effect that dividends were not taxed in the hands of the recipient due to tax credit. The Court basically did not find any issue with the freedom of establishment (paras 33-57 and 51-3), while it found some issues under the freedom of capital (see paras 61-71). However, the differences in the operation of the British advance corporation tax fell afoul of the freedom of establishment, essentially because companies receiving foreign-sourced dividends did not receive any credit for the British advance corporation tax (paras 79-98). The way surplus advance corporation tax was dealt with raised an issue only in a specific constellation, namely the surrender of surplus advance corporation tax (paras 113-134). However, the new foreign income dividend regime did not comply with the freedom of establishment or the freedom of capital (paras 140-173). Finally, in the year 2006, the Court in *Innoventif, 2006* held that the freedom of establishment did not preclude national law from requiring all companies wanting to register branches to advance the administrative costs of the publication of the relevant articles of association, a publication which was in accordance with Eleventh Council Directive 89/666 (paras 37-42).

More dividends case-law

The dividend case-law then continued with *Thin Cap, 2007*. In this case the Court addressed the scheme established and repeatedly amended by the United Kingdom to counteract a practice known as thin capitalization. Within groups share capital was kept 'thin' and replaced by intra-group loans with the aim of paying interest rather than distributing dividends, thus steering clear of taxes due on dividends. The United Kingdom essentially responded to this practice by taxing such interest like dividends in so far as the loan went beyond what would have been agreed at arm's length. The Court found a restriction of the freedom of establishment in so far as the British practice treated interest as dividends even though the relevant loan had been granted at arm's length, notably when a loan had been granted intra-group by a company not established in the United Kingdom (paras 38-45 and 59-63). The resulting disadvantageous tax position was not justified by the balanced allocation of powers of taxation or the cohesion of the tax system, since the increased tax on interest in the United Kingdom was not mirrored by a decrease in tax liability in other member states based on double taxation conventions. Essentially, the British approach was based on a unilateral decision taken by the United Kingdom (paras 49-69). While the British approach to counter thin capitalization was designed to prevent tax avoidance as an abusive practice, the approach went beyond what was necessary in so far as it taxed, in cases of international intra-group loans, interest paid under market conditions. Moreover, even when a loan was agreed at more favourable terms than those available on the market, a group had to have the possibility to put forward, in a specific case, a commercial justification for the favourable terms of the loan (paras 76-91).

Companies and third countries

In *Lasertec, 2007* a covert distribution of profits in Germany was at stake in a similar constellation as in *Thin Cap, 2007*. However, the Court held that the freedom of establishment could not be relied upon, because it was a company established in Switzerland, a third country, that had a definite influence through shareholdings in a German company (para. 27). In a similar vein, the Court in *A and B, 2007* held that the freedom of establishment could not be relied upon when a branch or a subsidiary in a non-member state was held by a company established in a member state. Thus, in a situation where a Swedish group had an establishment in Russia, the freedom of establishment could not be relied on to determine whether the salaries paid to employees of the Russian establishment had to be taken into account when assessing a Swedish legal threshold which depended on the total amount of salaries of employees. In both cases, *Lasertec, 2007* and *A and B, 2007*, the Court made it clear that it was the freedom of establishment, rather than the freedom of capital that was at issue. According to the Court, it was unnecessary to examine the freedom of capital, as any restriction of that freedom was the inevitable consequence of a restriction of the freedom of establishment (paras 25-7 of *Lasertec, 2007* and paras 27-9 of *A and B, 2007*). The Court reiterated in *Holböck, 2007* that the freedom of establishment could not be invoked in situations involving third countries. Accordingly, the full taxation of dividends distributed by a Swiss company to a shareholder resident in Austria as income, while dividends distributed by an Austrian company would have been taxed at only half the rate, was not precluded by the freedom of establishment (para. 29). Even assuming that the free movement of capital applied, the Austrian distinction would not have been precluded, for it was a restriction of a movement of capital that in substance had existed already at the time when the Treaty had entered into force (paras 31-44). In *Ergste, 2007* the Court confirmed that line of authority by holding that the freedom of establishment could not be relied on to challenge Germany's refusal to allow profits to be offset by losses incurred by branches in the United States of America.

Further group cases

Rewe, 2007 also dealt with groups. The parent company of an international group established in Germany challenged the conditions to allow partial write-downs on subsidiaries established in other member states as losses. According to the Court, the possibility to write-down holdings in domestic subsidiaries immediately, while foreign subsidiaries could be written down only under certain conditions constituted a difference in treatment notably due to the cash-flow disadvantage (paras 28-35). That difference in treatment was not justified. None of the grounds put forward held water, neither a combination of the balanced allocation of the power to tax, the danger of losses being taken into account twice, and tax avoidance as in *Marks & Spencer, 2005* (paras 41-53) nor the effectiveness of fiscal supervision (paras 55-8), the coherence of the tax system (paras 60-67), or territoriality (paras 68-9). In contrast, the *Marks & Spencer, 2005*-ground(s) stood firm in *Oy AA, 2007*. In case of intra-group transfers from a subsidiary 'upwards' Finland allowed the deduction of the financial transfers from the income of the subsidiary, though only if the receiving parent company was established in Finland. The Court found that the difference in treatment based on the place of establishment of the parent company (paras 31-43) was justified by the combination of the three grounds admitted in *Marks & Spencer, 2005*, namely the balanced allocation of the power to tax, the danger of losses being taken into account twice, and tax avoidance, while the first and the third ground were in the focus in *Oy AA, 2007* (paras 53-65). The Court, in particular, held that a less restrictive alternative to the Finnish measure did not exist, although it was rather general and not particularly designed to counteract wholly artificial arrangements (para. 63). The Court further clarified that case-law in *Lidl, 2008*. Germany had refused to allow the deduction of losses incurred by a permanent establishment in Luxembourg from income generated by the 'parent' limited partnership established in Germany. The Court found that the restriction of the freedom of establishment which consisted in discouraging the permanent establishment in other member states (paras 20-2 and 23-6) was justified by each of the two reasons of preserving a balanced allocation of powers of taxation and of forestalling that losses were taken into account twice (paras 31-7). The Court, in addition, made it clear that it was not required that each of the three reasons on which the justification in *Marks & Spencer, 2005* was based – more specifically the balanced allocation of powers to tax, the risk of losses being taken into account twice, and tax avoidance – was given. Instead, as already implied in *Oy AA, 2007* a combination of two grounds was sufficient (paras 36-42). In contrast to *Marks & Spencer, 2005*, moreover, the two conditions required by necessity, viz. the exhaustion of possibilities to offset and the impossibility to take into account a loss in the future, did not pose a problem in *Lidl, 2008* (paras 49-51).

Inheritance tax

In *Geurts, 2007*, an exemption from inheritance tax was applicable in the Flemish region of Belgium, if the family company which was part of the estate employed a minimum number of workers in the Flemish region for a certain time. The Court ruled that the difference in treatment based on where the workers were employed constituted indirect discrimination (paras 18-23). Even if ensuring the survival of local companies and the maintenance of employment possibly constituted grounds of justification, it was not necessary to limit the exemption to companies that employed workers in the Flemish region. The effectiveness of fiscal supervision as a ground for justification was not plausible, either, although Directive 77/799 did not apply to inheritance tax (paras 26-8).

Taxation of limited partnerships

In *Columbus, 2007* the partners of a limited partnership established in Belgium were resident in Germany. Since Belgium applied a tax rate to the profits of the partnership which was less than 30 per cent, Germany did not apply the double taxation convention which exempted profits made in Belgium from taxation in Germany, but instead the regular offset-method. Germany thus took into account the taxes paid in Belgium, but taxed the profits again as income up to the overall level to which such profits were normally taxed in Germany. Because of that method the tax burden of the partners increased by 53 per cent. The Court did not find a restriction of the freedom of establishment. Germany treated all partnerships alike, regardless of whether they were established in Germany or abroad, by applying the same tax rate. The Court did not have jurisdiction for possible violations of the double taxation convention. The choices made available by the freedom of establishment were not impeded, either (paras 39-54).

More dividends

In *Lammers, 2008* the Court followed-up on the *Thin Cap, 2007*-case-law. Belgium's approach to re-classify as dividends payments made by a Belgian subsidiary on claims by a parent company established in another member state which was a director of the subsidiary, as soon as the total of loans exceeded the paid-up capital plus taxed reserves at the beginning of the taxable period, was qualified as a restriction of the freedom of establishment, since such re-classification was not applied when the parent was established in Belgium. The restriction was not justified, as it could not be excluded that interest paid pursuant to agreements entered into on an arm's length basis would be re-classified as dividends as well (paras 31-3).

Currency loss

Deutsche Shell, 2008 dealt with a currency loss on start-up capital injected in a permanent establishment in Italy. When the capital invested was reimbursed later on to the German company Deutsche Shell, the German tax authorities refused to take into account the loss that had occurred due to the depreciation of the Lira in Deutsche Shell's corporation tax assessment. According to the Court, an obstacle with a deterrent effect on the establishment in other member states was inherent in the German tax approach which ignored the financial loss suffered (paras 29-32). That restriction was not justified by the coherence of the tax system, because no direct relationship existed between Deutsche Shell's currency losses and gains (para. 40). Moreover, by nature only Germany could take into account the currency losses incurred, because the capital was denominated in Lira. That was why the need for a balanced allocation of the powers to tax did not justify the restriction, either (para. 44).

Expenses for research and development

In *Commission v. Spain (R&D), 2008* companies' expenses for research and development were deductible to a larger extent when the investment had been made in Spain. The Court held that the freedom of establishment – and the freedom of services as far as subcontractors and centres of research were concerned – was restricted, because investments abroad by Spanish companies and investments in Spain by companies abroad, both by means of establishments, were deterred (paras 22-4). Justification was not available, as fiscal incentives with a view to investments in the member state concerned were not a ground for justification and as tax evasion was to be excluded by requiring proof from taxpayers and by means of cooperation under Directive 77/799 (paras 33-42).

Further group taxation

In *Burda, 2008* a corrective tax mechanism applied by Germany was at issue. As a tax audit revealed, Burda, a German subsidiary of a Dutch and a German company, had distributed more funds than it had had taxable income. The German authorities then applied a corrective mechanism that in essence charged Burda's capital. However, only the German parent company received a corresponding tax credit in Germany, while the Dutch parent company did not. That treatment, according to the Court, did not constitute a restriction of the freedom of establishment, while Directive 90/435 did not preclude it, essentially because the subsidiary was charged irrespective of the seat of the parent company. Its tax burden was not altered according to whether it distributed its profits to a resident or a non-resident parent company (para. 83). It was up to the member state where the parent company had its seat to ensure that a tax credit for corporation tax paid in the member state where the subsidiary was established was granted and thus economic double taxation was excluded (para. 89-94).

In *Bauer Verlag, 2008* a company established in Germany which was wholly owned by a German parent company held an unlisted holding in a limited partnership established in Spain. The German tax authorities assessed those holdings in a different way than holdings held in a partnership established in Germany for the purpose of the wealth tax liability of the parent company. The former were taken into account on the basis of their net asset value to which prospective earnings were added, while for the latter the net asset value was relevant. According to the Court, the resulting tax disadvantage for the parent company had a dissuasive effect (paras 31-3) and was not justified by the cohesion of the tax system for lack of a direct link (para. 38). Furthermore, evidence supplied by taxpayers sufficed for fiscal supervision, even though Directive 77/779 was possibly not applicable in the case at issue (para. 41).

The judgment in *Lidl, 2008* was further elaborated in *Wannsee, 2008*. In this case, in some contrast to *Lidl, 2008*, Germany had permitted a company established in Germany to take into account for the German tax assessment losses incurred by a permanent establishment in Austria in the years before 1994. As a result profits generated in and subject to taxation in Germany were essentially reduced. However, the German tax authorities reintegrated those losses when the establishment in Austria generated profits in the year 1994, by taxing those profit made in Austria, although they were subject to taxation in Austria, too – and lawfully so pursuant to the relevant double taxation convention. Austria did not set of the losses incurred in Austria against the profits made in Austria, because the losses had already been taken into account in Germany in the assessment of the 'parent' company. As Austria was a member of the European Economic Area in 1994, the freedom of establishment as interpreted by the Court for the internal market applied uniformly (paras 23-6). According to the Court, a restriction of the freedom of establishment occurred because a tax disadvantage resulted when Germany withdrew the previous taking into account of the losses by factoring in the profits generated by the permanent establishment in Austria (paras 32-8). However, the need to maintain the coherence of the German tax system justified the restriction, because Germany's assessment of profits made in Austria mirrored the previous factoring in of losses made in Austria, in other words, there was a direct personal and material link between the treatment of the losses and the profits, the 'reintegration being the logical complement of the deduction previously granted' (para. 42). Due to this symmetry the restriction was justified (paras 42-5). That the German company was by law unable to have the losses incurred in Austria taken into account by the Austrian tax authorities to set them off against the profits generated in Austria was irrelevant, for Germany was not required to adapt its tax system to the particularities of the Austrian tax system (paras 47-52).

France offered an integration regime for consolidated taxation of groups which was at stake in *Papillon, 2008*. Its application was refused to a parent company established in France as far as its sub-subsidiary in France was concerned by reason of a subsidiary being interposed which was established in the Netherlands (see para. 17). At issue thus was the refusal to apply the tax integration regime to the French parent company given that an interposed subsidiary was established abroad. As losses could not lawfully be taken into account immediately, the refusal to apply the integration regime when a foreign subsidiary was interposed constituted a restriction of the freedom of establishment (paras

18-22). Since the aim of the regime was consolidation and that aim was not necessarily jeopardized when the integration regime was extended to cover situations where an interposed subsidiary was established abroad, groups that did not have an interposed subsidiary were comparable to groups that had one (paras 25-30). France's refusal to apply tax integration was, however, covered by the need to maintain the coherence of the tax system, though not by the balanced allocation of powers of taxation, as taxation in only one member state was at issue (paras 36-40). The mechanism of neutralisation of transactions applicable in the integration regime did not apply in the case of an interposed foreign subsidiary. A risk arose that losses would be taken into account twice, in France and in the Netherlands, in the case of Papillon. In such a case, a parent company would benefit from the advantage, namely tax integration, while it eschewed the disadvantage, viz. neutralisation of intra-group transactions, which would upset the coherence of the system (paras 45-51). Yet the outright refusal to apply tax integration went beyond what was necessary. Quite apart from information provided under Directive 77/799, a parent company also had to be given the possibility to prove that the risk of profits being taken into account twice was inexistent in a specific case (paras 55-61).

Truck Center, 2008 concerned a withholding tax Belgium charged on interest payable by a resident company to a non-resident company based on a loan agreement. Such withholding tax was not due when a loan had been agreed between two resident companies. While the procedures for the charging of tax differed according to whether a company was resident in Belgium or not (para. 34), the situations of resident and non-resident recipient companies were, however, not comparable, according to the Court. The Belgian state was involved in two different capacities, namely as the state where two companies were resident and as the state in which interest originated. In the case of a non-resident recipient company withholding tax applied. In the case of a resident recipient company withholding tax did not apply; instead, the recipient company was subject to corporation tax in Belgium, a tax to which the interest paid was subject as any other income. The non-resident recipient company was not necessarily worse off, either, as withholding tax was usually lower than corporation tax. Belgium and Luxembourg – the other state involved in the case – had, in addition, agreed in the double taxation convention that each state was at liberty to charge a withholding tax. Finally, the situations for the recovery of the sums due differed (paras 41-9).

With *Commission v. Greece (dividends), 2009* the Commission challenged two elements of Greece's tax system. The Court confirmed that it violated the freedom of establishment and the freedom of capital to subject foreign-sourced dividends to a heavier tax burden than nationally-sourced dividends. In Greece, the latter were exempt from income tax at the level of the shareholder in the light of the Greek corporation tax paid, while the former were not (paras 24-8). Moreover, the higher tax rate Greece applied to foreign partnerships as compared to domestic partnerships unlawfully dissuaded partnerships established in other member states from operating an establishment in Greece (paras 38-42).

In *Aberdeen Alpha, 2009* the Court dealt with Finland's charging of withholding tax on dividends paid by a Finnish subsidiary company to a parent shareholder established in Luxembourg, while if the parent shareholder had been established in Finland withholding tax would not have been due. In the case at hand, Directive 90/435 did not apply, because the recipient company, which was to hold all the shares in the Finnish company concerned, was established in a special form in Luxembourg, namely an open-ended investment company called SICAV, and was only subject in Luxembourg to a tax on capital at a rate of 0.01 per cent. The Court reiterated that the positions of foreign and domestic shareholders became comparable by reason of Finland's exercising its income tax jurisdiction over dividends by means of a withholding tax (para. 43). Even if the Luxembourg company were exempt from income tax in Luxembourg, the series of charges to which Finnish dividends paid to shareholders abroad were subject entailed a restriction (paras 39-55) which was not justified by the grounds argued – namely neither by the prevention of tax avoidance, because the Finnish measure did not exclusively target wholly artificial arrangements (para. 65), nor the need for a balanced allocation of powers of taxation, essentially since Finland itself decided not to tax resident shareholders on such income (paras 67-70), nor the coherence of the tax system, as the exemption from withholding tax was not subject to the taxation of the dividend in the hands of the resident shareholder (para. 73).

In *KBC Bank, 2009* the Court decided that Belgium's tax law could lawfully distinguish between subsidiaries and permanent establishments by limiting the possibility to deduct profits distributed by a subsidiary to the extent of the profits of the parent company during the taxable period concerned, provided that there was not any discrimination between subsidiaries in Belgium and those abroad or between permanent establishments in Belgium and those abroad (para. 81). (The Court also ruled on questions relating to the freedom of capital and Directive 90/435 on the taxation of groups in this judgment.) In *Gaz de France, 2009* the Court *inter alia* ruled that the Community legislature had not restricted the freedom of establishment or the freedom of capital by not including the French *société par actions simplifié* within the scope of Directive 90/435 (para. 61).

Moving the seat

Cartesio, 2008 dealt with a Hungarian company which wanted to move its seat to Italy while remaining subject to Hungarian law. The Hungarian authorities refused registration on the ground that in Hungary the real seat approach was applicable. Accordingly, the company concerned would have been forced to wind down and re-establish itself in Italy. The Court did not find a restriction of the freedom of establishment in Hungary's refusal. Companies were creatures of national law pursuant to *Daily Mail, 1988* and the national law of each member state chose between the various connecting factors possible, i. e. the registered office, the central administration, or principal place of business, to determine whether a company came into existence according to its own law. Only after that choice had been made and applied in a specific case and a company had come into being, could that company then rely on the freedom of establishment. Thus, the freedom of establishment, or secondary legislation, did not govern the transfer of the real seat or the registered office from one member state to another, while the company maintained the personality under the first state. Rather, future Community legislation would have to address the question. In contrast, the freedom of establishment applied when a company wished to become subject to the law of another member state (paras 100-14).

Secondary law re companies

In the 2000s, the Court also interpreted the secondary law concerning the freedom of establishment of companies in a series of judgments. *Diamantis, 2000* and *Commission v. Spain, 2008* took on the Second Council Directive 77/91, as did *Audiolux, 2009*. *BIAO, 2003* dealt with the Fourth Council Directive 78/660. *Springer, 2004* concerned Directive 90/605, which had amended Directives 78/660 and 83/349, and its validity in the light of the fundamental right to exercise a trade or profession and the freedom of the press. *Markopoulos, 2004* was about the Eighth Council Directive 84/253 and, in part, about the *Vlassopoulou, 1991*-line of authority in the context of that Directive. *Berlusconi, 2005* dealt with the First, Fourth, and Seventh Council Directive, i. e. Directives 68/151, 78/660, and 83/349, respectively, and the *lex mitior* principle as a fundamental right in the context of the implementation of a Directive. In *Berlusconi, 2005* the questions asked later on in *Mulliez, 2006* had already been answered. Moreover, *Epikouriko Kefalaio, 2004* dealt with Directives 73/239 and 79/267 on direct insurance. *Ntionik, 2007* concerned Directive 2000/34 on stock exchange listings.

Diploma recognition in 2000-2002

Hocsman, 2000 initiated the diploma recognition case-law of the 2000s. The Court decided that the *Vlassopoulou, 1991*-line of authority also applied when a Directive, while regulating the specific profession at issue, was not applicable. According to the Court, the scope of *Vlassopoulou, 1991* was not to be reduced by a Directive (para. 31). In the case at issue, a general diploma in medicine had been awarded in a third state, namely Argentina. It was later on recognized as equivalent in Spain. That allowed the person concerned to obtain the specialization in urology in Spain. While France was not obliged to recognize the specialization based on Directive 93/16 on doctors, since the general diploma had been awarded in Argentina, France was required, according to the Court, to apply the *Vlassopoulou, 1991*-comparison (paras 32-6).

Erpelding, 2000 further elaborated on Directive 93/16. The Court decided that the use of the title 'specialist doctor' in the language and according to the nomenclature of the host state was the necessary corollary of the automatic and compulsory mutual recognition under Directive 93/16, if it applied (paras 23-7). On a more technical note the Court also interpreted the right to use the 'home' state title and the possibility for the host state to authorize the use of the title in a language other than that of the 'home' state under article 10(1) of the Directive (paras 31-2).

In *Dreessen II, 2002* the Court confirmed the approach taken in *Hocsman, 2000* and clarified that the *Vlassopoulou, 1991*-line of authority applied regardless of the reason why a directive in a specific field was not applicable, be it that a diploma had been obtained in a third country as in *Hocsman, 2000* or that a diploma in a specific profession was not covered as in *Dreessen, 1994* with an engineer diploma under Directive 85/384 on architects (para. 28). *Commission v. Spain (doctors), 2002* again confirmed that approach. Spain was not allowed systematically to require doctors who had followed specialist training in other member states but did not benefit from automatic recognition under Directive 93/16 to sit the same state examination as Spanish doctors in order to begin specialist training, else the *Vlassopoulou, 1991*-case-law would be disregarded (paras 37-40). A second complaint by the Commission under Directive 93/16 challenging registration as a condition for reimbursement by the Spanish health system was, moreover, rejected (paras 46-56.)

In *Gozza, 2000* the Court reiterated the ruling given in *Carbonari, 1999* and extended it to the adequate remuneration in case of part-time training in specialised medicine (paras 41-4). In *Commission v. Spain (architects), 2000* the Court held that Spain had failed to implement Directive 85/384 on architects by limiting the occupation of migrant architects benefitting from mutual recognition under that Directive to the activities they were allowed to pursue under 'home' state legislation. According to the Court, if mutual recognition applied pursuant to the Directive, the architects benefitting from it had to be allowed to pursue the same activities as architects holding the host state title (paras 35-40). Moreover, the Court held that recourse to the derogation clause in article 56 Treaty was no longer possible once directives had achieved harmonisation (para. 42; the Court had previously ruled so for derogations from the free movement of goods). In a similar vein, *Commission v. Italy (architects), 2002* confirmed that Italy's implementation of Directive 85/384 was improper in several regards. Italy had (i) failed to include some German diploma in the list of diplomas benefitting from automatic recognition (paras 21-4) and to clearly state which diplomas benefitted from automatic recognition (paras 30-1). Italy had (ii) violated the freedom of establishment and services by consistently requiring submission of the original diploma or a certified copy for recognition (paras 37-40) and of a certificate of nationality as well as certified translations of all documents (paras 45-6). Italy had (iii) set the wrong reference date to apply the transitional arrangement (paras 51-3). Italy had (iv) violated the freedom of services by prohibiting architects who merely provided services and were thus not permanently established in Italy from having some infrastructure in Italy (paras 56-7) and by requiring those architects to follow an overly cumbersome registration procedure before the end of which services could not lawfully be provided (paras 62-5). Similarly, Greece had failed to implement Directive 85/384 properly, according to the Court in *Commission v. Greece (architects), 2004*. The Greek authorities unlawfully required migrant architects to submit a certificate attesting that their diploma benefitted from recognition (paras 19-21). They also took too long to deal with migrant architects' requests to be registered (paras 29-35), a failure that could not be justified, as Greece had argued, by the frequency of earthquakes in Greece (para. 33).

In *Commission v. France (psychologists), 2001* France admitted not having properly transposed Directive 89/48 on general diploma recognition with regard to psychologists, a regulated profession in France. *Commission v. Italy (doctors), 2001* concerned the Italian scheme for dentists. The Court held that Italy had failed to implement Directive 78/687 on the coordination of dentists' activities, as Italy had established a second training track for dentists which combined general medicine with a specialisation in dentistry, in stark contrast to the unadulterated five years of dental training in accordance with the Directive (paras 37-40). However, according to the Court, Italy's transitional regime was in keeping with the Directive in that it enabled dentists subject to that regime – and exclusively those dentists – to be registered at the same time as ordinary doctors as well as dentists (paras 48-55).

In *Commission v. Italy (ski-monitors), 2002* the Court confirmed that Italy had failed to live up to Directive 92/51 on a second system for recognition by applying a reciprocity requirement to diplomas of ski-monitors. *Paracelsus, 2002* concerned lay medical practitioners (*Heilpraktiker*). Paracelsus was a school established in Germany offering training courses to become a lay medical practitioner. Parts of those courses were offered in Austria where the courses were also advertised. However, in Austria the activities of lay medical practitioners were reserved for doctors. Applying the case-law delivered under Directive 89/48, i. e. *Aranitis, 1996* and *De Bobadilla, 1999*, the Court found that the profession of lay medical practitioner was not 'regulated' within the meaning of Directive 92/51 merely due to the fact that Austria reserved the corresponding activities to doctors (paras 31-6). The Austrian reservation – essentially a prohibition of the profession of lay medical practitioner – amounted to a restriction of the freedom of establishment and services. Yet, that restriction passed the *Gebhard, 1995*-test, in particular since member states were entitled to decide on the level of public health protection required (paras 39-50). Similarly, Austria could lawfully prohibit that parts of the training took place in Austria given the need to ensure the efficacy of the prohibition of the profession (para. 61), but only in as far as 'confusion in the minds of the public' (para. 65) was created. Conversely, Austria had to permit advertising of the school's services in Germany, provided that it clearly stated that the profession could not be exercised in Austria (para. 68).

Klett, 2002 dealt with diploma recognition in the context of the Act of Accession of Austria. The Court ordered that an amendment to Directive 78/686 on dentists which had been introduced when Austria acceded to the Community did not violate the Treaty, since it was based on the Act of Accession which itself belonged to primary law. Austria, consequently, was not obliged to open a post-doctoral course for the training of doctors to become dentists to doctors holding doctoral degrees from universities in other member states, since the course was to be abolished progressively under the regime of Directive 78/686 and was only maintained temporarily to allow participants to finish their studies (paras 30-41).

Diploma recognition in 2003-2004

In *Tennah-Durez, 2003* the Court dealt with the automatic recognition of diplomas under Directive 93/16 on doctors. After having explained that that Directive was different from Directives 89/48 and 92/51 in that it harmonized the educational system for doctors (paras 29-34), the Court decided that, as long as a doctor diploma – a 'doctor's passport' (para. 57) – had been awarded in a member state, Directive 93/16 made recognition mandatory, even if parts of the training had been followed in a third country and the member state awarding the diploma had then recognized that training as equivalent. In other words, Directive 93/16 did not contain a requirement as to a minimum duration of training in a member state, in contrast to Directives 89/48 and 92/51. As a consequence, France had to recognize a diploma awarded by a Belgian university after seven years of medical training, six of which had been followed in Algeria (paras 49-69). France was, moreover, bound by a certificate issued by Belgium attesting that training pursuant to Directive 93/16 had been completed (paras 75-80).

In *Vogel, 2003* the Court ordered Germany not to permit doctors in general to practise dentistry, else an additional category of dental practitioners in violation of Directives 78/686 and 78/687 would be created. The title under which such doctors were allowed to practise dentistry in Germany was, according to the Court, irrelevant (paras 25-31). *Rinke, 2003* must also be mentioned in this context, although the case was not strictly about diploma recognition. In this case, a doctor challenged under the fundamental right to equal treatment of sexes the requirement for doctors to have worked for at least six months full-time to qualify for residence, which arose from a combination of a Directive 93/16 on doctors and German law. The Court agreed that there was unequal treatment between women and men for statistical data proved it (para. 35). However, full-time work for six months was an appropriate and reasonable requirement to ensure that doctors acquired the necessary experience and followed the evolution of certain pathological conditions. Neither Directive 93/16 nor the implementing legislation, in consequence, violated the fundamental right.

Morgenbesser, 2003 dealt with the registration of trainees which was required in Italy to be admitted for the bar exam. The Italian authorities refused to register Ms Morgenbesser as a *practicante* (trainee) on the ground that she held a diploma from a French rather than an Italian university. Directive 98/5 on lawyers did not apply, as she had not yet been admitted to a bar in a member state, neither did Directive 89/48, as the traineeship required to be admitted to the Italian bar could not be considered a regulated profession separate from the lawyer's profession (paras 44-55). As a consequence, the *Vlassopoulou, 1991*-line of authority only forced the Italian authorities to make the comparison of qualifications (paras 57-71).

Burbaud, 2003, a case that also concerned the free movement of workers (see above), dealt with the French way of recruiting hospital administrators. That way combined recruitment with training in a school and based on that, ultimately, provided access to civil service. Ms Burbaud had acquired the qualification needed to become hospital administrator in Portugal, but her application to be recruited in France was rejected. The Court held that public service as such was not removed from the scope of Directive 89/48 on a general system of recognition, save when article 48(4) Treaty or a particular directive applied (para. 39). Applying standard case-law on the 'regulated profession', a Community term (para. 43), the Court decided that passing the French system was equal to obtaining a diploma within the meaning of Directive 89/48, although a formal document was usually not issued (paras 44-53). It was up to the national court to decide whether the qualification Ms Burbaud obtained in Portugal was a diploma as well, and if so, to assess equivalence under the Directive (paras 54-7).

Beuttenmüller, 2004 was about acquired rights under Directive 89/48 on general recognition. According to the Court, Ms Beuttenmüller was entitled to rely directly on that Directive in order to set aside the practice of a German Land that required teachers to have passed three years of training under any circumstances or that training to have had a particular content (paras 51-2). Her teacher diploma, awarded after two years of training in Austria only, had been certified by Austria as equivalent to the current regular educational track taking three years to complete. She thus benefitted from an established right under the Directive (paras 40-4). In addition, the Court ruled that the four years of training required in the exception in article 3 Directive 92/51 on a second system of recognition – an article that applied only in the event that article 3 Directive 89/48 was not applicable (para. 60) – was not to be understood so as to include probationary practice of teachers following after training (para. 64).

Fascicolo, 2004 was also about acquired rights, though those of doctors under Directive 93/16. The Court, in essence, sanctioned the Italian system of awarding posts as general medical practitioners. According to the Court, that system in distinguishing to some extent between doctors having obtained the right to practice general medicine before 31 December 1994 and those having obtained that right after that point in time, i. e. under the regime set up in accordance with Directive 93/16, was covered by the discretion afforded to the member states, since the Directive only required safeguarding the rights of doctors who had made use of the freedom of establishment before 1 January 1995 (para. 30). For completeness, the Court in *Mosconi, 2004* declined to deal with the exclusion of an Italian civil engineer holding an Italian diploma from certain works on classified heritage buildings under Directive 85/384 on architects, because the situation was purely internal to Italy.

Diploma recognition in 2005-2006

Peros, 2005 confirmed *Beuttenmüller, 2004* in that article 3(a) Directive 89/48 on a general system for recognition was directly applicable, since Greece had failed to transpose the Directive in time. It was so even though Greece had not designated the competent authorities pursuant to article 9(1) of that Directive. *Aslanidou, 2005* was delivered on the same day as *Peros, 2005* and ruled in the very same terms for article 3(a) Directive 92/51 on a second general system for recognition. (*Peros, 2005* had concerned a mechanical engineer, *Aslanidou, 2005* an occupational therapist.)

Commission v. Austria (dentists), 2005 again dealt with Directives 78/686 and 78/687 on dental practitioners. According to the Court, Austria breached those Directives by allowing dentists (*Dentisten*) to pursue the profession of dental practitioner under the title *Zahnarzt* (dental practitioner), although they had not followed any university training and thus failed to fulfil the requirements of the Directives (paras 25-7). Moreover, Austria was wrong to apply article 19b Directive 78/686 to those dentists (paras 29-30). In contrast, Austria was right to authorize the remaining medical specialists in dental surgery, a profession Austria had abolished to implement the Directives, to choose between the titles of 'medical specialist in dental surgery' (*Facharzt für Zahn-, Mund- und Kieferheilkunde*) and 'dental practitioner' (*Zahnarzt*). The Directives did not impose on those medical specialists the obligation to bear the title 'dental practitioner'. Austria had not created an additional category of dental practitioners but implemented article 19b Directive 78/686 properly (paras 35-42).

Colegio, 2006 concerned the problem of partial recognition of a professional qualification. Is it possible to recognize a qualification only partially when a qualification allowed the pursuit in the 'home' state of an activity which in the host state was part of a wider profession? Was it possible to take up a regulated profession partially? These questions were raised with Mr Imo who held an Italian diploma of civil engineering with a specialization in hydraulics and required recognition in Spain where only a more general category of engineering existed. The Court decided that Directive 89/48 on a general system for recognition did not as such preclude partial recognition in the sense that the activities allowed in the host state could be limited to those permitted in the 'home' state; indeed partial recognition was possibly more in keeping with the freedom of movement, in particular when the compensatory measures to be imposed in the light of the difference between two professions were such that they, in fact, prevented the person from making use of the freedom (paras 17-25). Yet a distinction was to be drawn, because not to allow the partial taking-up of a profession amounted to a hindrance of free movement (paras 31 and 33), namely between (i) situations in which compensatory measures needed to be applied, for two professions were so similar that they both came within 'the profession in question' pursuant to article 3(a) Directive 89/48 (para. 34) and (ii) situations not covered by the Directive, because the differences were so significant that full and fresh educational training would have been required to establish equivalence (para. 35). In the latter case, if the activity in question could objectively be separated, partial recognition needed to be granted in combination with the obligation to bear the original 'home' state title together with a translation. That measure sufficed not to confuse consumers (paras 36-8).

In *Commission v. France (diploma), 2006*, *Commission v. Austria (diploma), 2006*, and *Commission v. Germany (diploma), 2006* the Court formally confirmed that the member states concerned had failed to transpose Directive 2001/19 amending several diploma directives in time – a fact which they essentially did not dispute. In *Sam Mc Cauley, 2006* the Court decided that the recognition of diplomas in pharmacy was only partially harmonised by article 2 Directive 85/433, making automatic recognition mandatory only with regard to pharmacies that had been open for more than three years, i. e. not with regard to 'new' pharmacies, while leaving the member states the option to go further. As far as 'old' pharmacies were concerned, though, the member states did not have any discretion. Whether to proceed in steps in such a way, by means of partial harmonisation, was up to the Community legislature to decide (paras 25-32).

In *Price, 2006* the Court first delimited the scopes of Directives 89/48 and 92/51 and then decided that the profession of director of voluntary sales of chattels by public auction in France, seemingly in contrast to the situation in the United Kingdom, was a regulated profession for the exercise of which precise knowledge of national law was necessary, since French law required the person concerned to have passed substantive legal educational training. If the national court found that such directors in addition regularly provided advice or assistance in matters of national law – which was possible, for such advice was not just given in the traditional legal profession – possibly in a specialised area (paras 58-9), the choice of compensatory measures, viz. an adaptation period or an aptitude test, could be taken by the state rather than the individual concerned pursuant to article 4(1) third subparagraph Directive 89/48.

Diploma recognition in 2007-2009

In *Commission v. Czech Republic (diploma I), 2007* and *Commission v. Czech Republic (diploma II), 2007* the Court formally confirmed that the Czech Republic had failed to transpose in time Directive 93/16 on doctors and parts of Directive 78/686 on dental practitioners, respectively. *Commission v. Portugal (architects), 2007* confirmed that the recognition of professional qualifications of architects was automatic under Directive 85/384. Hence, Portugal could not lawfully require migrant architects who were not registered with the order of architects in the 'home' state to take the regular exam to be passed for admission to the Portuguese order of architects (para. 28).

Commission v. Spain (hospital pharmacists), 2008 established that Directive 89/48 on a general system for recognition was applicable in Spain to the regulated profession of hospital pharmacist which was a specialisation of the profession of pharmacist in general. Neither the existence of Directives 85/432 and 85/433 on pharmacists, which applied only to the profession of pharmacist and not to specialisations of pharmacists, nor article 47(3) Treaty as such precluded Directive 89/48 from applying. As a consequence, Spain had to provide the option for nationals of other member states with equivalent qualifications to take up the profession of hospital pharmacist within the limits of Directive 89/48 (paras 36-43). In *Commission v. Portugal (pharmacists), 2008* this approach was confirmed for the profession of pharmacist specialized in medical biology which was regulated in Portugal.

In *Commission v. Greece (doctors), 2008* the Court held that Greece had failed to transpose Directive 93/16 on doctors, because Greece had recognized certain doctors with acquired rights protected by article 36 Directive 93/16 as holding the specialisation of general medical practitioner, although they had not followed the training required by articles 30 and 31 Directive 93/16 (paras 11-4). In *Commission v. Spain (air traffic controller), 2008* the Court affirmed that the profession of air traffic controller was regulated in Spain within the meaning of Directives 89/48 and 92/51 on general recognition. Neither the fact that a set of qualifications was needed to be allowed to exercise the profession (paras 34-47) nor the fact that Directive 2006/23 on an air traffic controller licence had been adopted (paras 48-51) had any impact on that assessment for the time before Directive 2006/23 became applicable. Since recognition was not automatic under Directives 89/48 and 92/51, any particularities of the Spanish qualification could be factored into by way of compensatory measures (paras 52-6).

In *Commission v. Greece (diploma), 2008* the educational regime that worked on the basis of so-called homologation agreements was mainly at stake. Under that regime training provided in one member state by private institutions led to the award of a diploma under the educational system of another member state based on a homologation agreement. Greece refused to recognize such diplomas on the basis of Directive 89/48 on a general system of recognition, claiming that higher educational training was reserved in Greece to public institutions, notably Greek universities. The Court rejected that line of argument, holding that nothing in Directive 89/48 indicated that a member state could treat diplomas awarded in another member state differently on the basis of where in the Community the training had been provided (paras 28-35). Diplomas were not recognized owing to their intrinsic value, but because they granted access to a specific profession (para. 29). The Directive had established a system of mutual trust based on a presumption of equivalence of qualifications in which it was the task of the authorities issuing diplomas to examine whether the conditions for their award were met (para. 30). Greece thus had to recognize such diplomas issued in other member states, even if the training provided on Greek territory was not recognized as higher education in Greece (para. 35). Furthermore, the Court acceded to a number of claims made by the Commission, namely that Greece had not respected that the choice of compensatory measures under Directive 89/48 had to be with the holder of a diploma, rather than the state (para. 44); that a certain Greek body was not entitled to verify facts established by diplomas to be recognized (para. 48); and that the law had to be unambiguous as to the re-classification of holders of equivalent diplomas in the Greek public service who had been wrongly classified (paras 50-9). Finally, the Court rejected a further challenge by the Commission, as it incorrectly categorized the Greek technical chamber (paras 71-5). In the judgment *Commission v. Spain (diploma), 2008* of the same day the Court ruled in the same way as in *Commission v. Greece (diploma), 2008*. Spain had essentially refused to recognize diplomas in engineering awarded in Italy by an Italian university. The training had been pursued entirely at a university in Spain which had awarded a diploma that did not give access to the profession of engineer in Spain. Based on an agreement with the Italian university, the persons concerned took an exam in Italy and were awarded the Italian diploma of engineer (paras 43-4). The Court decided in the same way as in *Commission v. Greece (diploma), 2008* that Spain had to recognize such diplomas subject to potential compensatory measures, irrespective of the fact that all training had been provided in Spain. The Court, in addition, rejected the arguments advanced by Spain that the situation was purely internal to Spain (para. 67) and that Spanish law was fraudulently circumvented (paras 72-3). Finally, the Court emphasized that, once such diplomas were recognized, the holders had to have the same promotion possibilities as those having the equivalent national qualification, irrespective of the shorter duration of training (para. 80). *Kastrinaki, 2008* in (paras 50-2) confirmed the two judgments in *Commission v. Greece (diploma), 2008* and *Commission v. Spain (diploma), 2008*. *Khatzithanasis, 2008* and *Commission v. Greece (diploma II), 2008*, both of the same day, transposed this line of authority to Directive 92/51 on a second general system for recognition (para. 33 and para. 28, respectively). *Commission v. Greece (diploma II), 2008*, moreover, established that recognition of a diploma under Directive 92/51 could not lawfully depend on the 'home' state's answering of certain questions posed by the host state (paras 35-7). *Cavallera, 2009* then established the limits of that case-law. In that case, Mr Cavallera, although having obtained a junior engineer diploma from a university in Italy, did not gain access to the profession of engineer in Italy for lack of having passed the Italian state examination. The certificate of homologation he obtained in Spain, which was granted solely on the basis of the Italian diploma and without any further education or examination, and the registration on the relevant register in Spain entitled Mr Cavallera to pursue the profession of engineer in Spain. However, according to the Court, he was not allowed to rely on Directive 89/48 to obtain registration as an engineer in Italy on the basis of the Spanish certificate of homologation, else he would be able to take up the profession of engineer in Italy without having passed the prerequisite Italian state examination. This was so in particular because the Spanish certificate was awarded without further ado and thus did not provide evidence of any further qualification (paras 56-7).

In *Pesla, 2009* the Court then followed-up on the *Vlassopoulou, 1991* line of authority for lawyers. The Court held that, in the comparative examination required by articles 39 and 43 Treaty (para. 38) and when determining the corresponding measures to be imposed to ensure that qualifications were equivalent, a member state was entitled to require knowledge of the law of its own legal system rather than of the law in general. Evidence of a comparable level of training in law was not sufficient. Thus, a person who had not taken the first state examination in Germany, but held degrees based on educational training in Polish and German law, need not have been admitted for a traineeship in Germany – a traineeship which was required to be admitted to the second state examination in Germany – without providing further evidence of qualification (paras 44-8). While partial recognition within the sense of the *Vlassopoulou, 1991*-line of authority was sufficient to guarantee the freedom of movement, it had to be a real, not merely a notional option. However, a member state was not required under articles 39 and 43 Treaty to lower the level of knowledge required for nationals of other member states, while it was free to do so (paras 50-64). *Rubino, 2009*, finally, applied Directive 2005/36 on the recognition of professional qualifications which replaced Directives 89/48 and 92/51 on general recognition. According to the Court, the fact that a temporary list of candidates successful in a selection procedure was established in Italy from which, later on, university lecturers were recruited did not imply that the profession of university lecturer became a regulated profession within the meaning of Directive 2005/36 under which the case-law established under Directives 89/48 and 92/51 concerning the term 'regulated profession' continued to apply (paras 23, 27 and 29-32). Selection and recruitment procedures to fill posts were not concerned by those Directives (para. 27). Consequently, Mr Rubino who had acquired a qualification as a lecturer in Germany – the 'facultas' and 'venia legendi', i. e. something called a *Habilitation* in Germany – need not have been exempted from the selection procedure in Italy. However, the qualification had to be taken into account duly in this procedure (para. 34).

3 Social security

Scope and definitions

In the 2000s, the Court clarified the scope of Regulation 1408/71 in several cases. In *Movrin, 2000*, the Court categorized a subsidy to sickness insurance contributions which Germany paid to recipients of old-age pensions as an old-age cash benefit according to article 1(t) Regulation 1408/71. The supplement aimed at alleviating the cost of sickness insurance for pensioners and was paid directly to the sickness insurance institution. As its amount indirectly depended on the amount of the pension and was paid exclusively to pensioners by the pension insurance institution, it was an old age rather than a sickness benefit (para. 40). As such it was not be made subject to a residence requirement pursuant to article 10(1) Regulation 1408/71. Even if sickness insurance contributions had been generally lower in the Netherlands, Germany would have had to grant the subsidy (para. 51). In *Offermanns, 2001* the Court addressed Austria's stepping in when a parent failed to make maintenance payments owed to a child of whom the other parent had custody. Austria was subrogated into the claim, when it advanced the payments due. The Court classed that support as a family benefit under articles 1(u) and 4(1)(h) Regulation 1408/71, because it helped a family to meet expenses incurred due to the maintenance of the family. It was a public contribution to a family's budget to alleviate the financial burdens involved in the maintenance of children (para. 41). From the perspective of the recipient the benefit was not provisional (para. 44). The Court moreover confirmed that the derived-rights approach did not apply anymore to family benefits. The children of a self-employed worker were therefore covered by Regulation 1408/71 as far as family benefits were concerned (para. 34-5). Hence, the benefit had to be provided to nationals of member states other than Austria on an equal footing. *Laurin Effing, 2005* confirmed that the maintenance payments advanced by Austria constituted a family benefit. That the person concerned served a prison sentence and that the payments were advanced for that reason did not have an impact on the assessment (para. 27). Moreover, a prisoner who was insured against the risk of unemployment was within the scope *ratione personae* of Regulation 1408/71 as he was insured against a risk it covered.

Special non-contributory benefits

With *Jauch, 2001*, the Court continued its case-law on special non-contributory benefits. Article 4(2a) Regulation 1408/71 had definitely brought such cash benefits within the ambit of the Regulation, because they addressed risks it typically covered, although only in a substitute, supplementary or ancillary way. Article 10a Regulation 1408/71, in turn, exempted such benefits from exportability, since they had some atypical properties which brought them close to social or medical assistance. The Court in *Jauch, 2001* examined an Austrian care allowance. Although the care allowance was listed in annex IIa among the special non-contributory benefits, the Court proceeded to verify whether it was special and non-contributory (paras 19-22). It found that the allowance was not special – a point which had already been decided for the similar German care insurance benefits in *Molenaar, 1998*. It was granted objectively on the basis of a legally defined position and could not be likened to social assistance (paras 26-8 of *Jauch, 2001*). It was contributory, too, albeit only indirectly, since sickness insurance contributions had been raised in Austria to create the budgetary room to introduce the allowance (para. 33). As a regular sickness benefit it therefore had to be granted to persons resident abroad.

Leclere, 2001 concerned several benefits provided by Luxembourg law in case of child birth to those who resided in Luxembourg. The applicants claimed that the provisions of Regulation 1408/71 which had the effect of sanctioning those residence requirements were contrary to articles 48 to 51 Treaty. The exclusion from the scope of Regulation 1408/71 of certain childbirth and adoption allowances, including the Luxembourg childbirth and antenatal allowances, in article 1(u)(i) was, so the Court, in accordance with the Treaty, since a restriction of the scope of the Regulation itself did not add further disparities to those resulting from the lack of harmonization (para. 29). In contrast, while article 10a Regulation 1408/71 validly sanctioned residence requirements for special non-contributory benefits, the Luxembourg maternity allowance could not lawfully be made subject to a residence requirement. It came within the scope of Regulation 1408/71, but was not 'special' within the meaning of article 4(2a). It was part of the general legislation addressing one of the risks covered by Regulation 1408/71 and was available to every woman giving birth to a child. Thus, annex IIa, in so far as it listed the benefit, was incompatible with articles 48 to 51 Treaty (paras 34-7). Finally, the Luxembourg child-raising allowance was not a family *allowance* within the meaning of article 77 Regulation 1408/71. Its purpose was to replace income that was lost when a child was raised. Its amount did therefore not depend on the number of children as required by article 1(u)(ii) Regulation 1408/71 (para. 43). More generally, the Court ruled that articles 1(u)(i) and 10a Regulation 1408/71 did not establish a principle of non-exportability. Quite the contrary, those articles were just exceptions from the general rule that benefits could not lawfully be made subject to residence requirements (para. 26). Apart from those issues of scope, the Court also ruled in *Leclere, 2001* that a pensioner was not entitled to rely on article 73 Regulation 1408/71, which applied to active workers, or any other article of the Regulation instead of article 77 Regulation 1408/71 which applied to pensioners claiming family allowances.

Skalka, 2004 was a judgment which again exclusively dealt with the question whether a benefit was 'special and non-contributory'. Austria granted a supplement to pensions to allow the pensioners concerned to maintain their standard of living, subject to certain ceilings. Since it was conditional on residence, Mr Skalka who lived in Tenerife was not entitled to claim the benefit under national law. According to the Court, the benefit was 'special', as it pursued an aim of social assistance in guaranteeing a minimum subsistence income. As such, it was linked to the socio-economic situation and the amount was determined by reference to the standard of living in Austria (paras 24-26). Moreover, it was 'non-contributory', since it was not in any way financed by contributions by the beneficiary (para. 29). Owing to the listing in annex IIa the benefit could therefore lawfully be made subject to residence pursuant to article 10a Regulation 1408/71.

In *Hosse, 2006* the Court again dealt with a care allowance that was similar to those that had been at issue in *Molenaar, 1998* and *Jauch, 2001*. The Court made it plain that 'social security benefits' and 'special non-contributory benefits' were two concepts that were mutually exclusive (para. 36). The Austrian municipal care allowance was not 'special', since it did not pursue aims of social assistance, but intended to improve the state of health and the life of persons reliant on care. As such it supplemented sickness benefits and was to be considered as a sickness benefit pursuant to article 4(1)(a) Regulation 1408/71. It compensated additional expenditure arising from the need for care; its amount depended on the degree of reliance on care; and other income gained had no effect on the amount of the allowance (paras 38-42). The derived rights-approach, moreover, did not apply to sickness benefits under article 19 Regulation 1408/71 (para. 53). Therefore, a residence requirement was contrary to 19(2) Regulation 1408/71.

Kersbergen, 2006 also concerned the categorization of a benefit as 'special and non-contributory', in this case the Netherlands' allowance for young disabled persons. It was 'special', because it provided a socially disadvantaged group with minimum means of subsistence. As such it constituted social assistance provided on the basis of socio-economic grounds. Moreover, the majority of the beneficiaries did not have any means without the benefit; and it was closely linked to the Netherlands environment for based 'on the minimum wage and the standard of living' in the Netherlands (paras 31-33). Since it was also 'non-contributory' for not linked in any way to contributions, a residence requirement was in order. Finally, the persons concerned in this case had made use of the freedom to move only after the residence requirement had been introduced in the relevant Dutch act. Therefore, acquired rights were not violated (paras 41-3). The interpretation delivered in *Kersbergen, 2006* was fully confirmed in *Hendrix, 2007* (paras 35-8).

In *Perez Naranjo, 2007* the Court came back to the French supplementary allowance which *Giletti, 1987* and *Commission v. France (supplementary allowance), 1990* had held to be exportable. The Court assessed the allowance in the light of the case-law on the new article 10a Regulation 1408/71. While the allowance was 'special' for it pursued aims of social assistance (para. 34), the 'non-contributory' nature was more challenging. The supplementary allowance was financed by a general social contribution. However, the Court found that the link between that general contribution and the allowance was not sufficiently direct. The general contribution also served to finance other schemes; the institution concerned also had funds available from other sources; and the contributions did not necessarily come from the recipients of the allowance (paras 46-52). The French supplementary allowance which was listed in annex IIa was therefore within the ambit of article 10a and, hence, need not have been exportable. As a result, the *Giletti, 1987*-case-law was overruled on the basis of article 10a Regulation 1408/71.

Commission v. Parliament (special benefits), 2007 dealt with the amendment of article 4(2a) and annex IIa Regulation 1408/71 by Regulation 647/2005, which the Community legislature had enacted to fit the Regulation to the case-law of the Court on special non-contributory benefits, notably the judgment in *Jauch, 2001*. The Commission did not challenge the adaptation of article 4(2a) as such. However, several benefits concerning disabled persons had been listed in annex IIa and thereby exempted from exportability. The Commission did not agree with this. The Court reviewed whether the five benefits challenged were 'special' in the sense of the case-law and the new article 4(2a). It first ruled that concepts of 'family benefit' and 'special benefit' were mutually exclusive. It then held all six benefits at issue, i. e. the Finnish and Swedish care allowances, the Swedish disability allowance, and the British disability living allowance, attendance allowance, and carer's allowance, not to be 'special'. While the benefits did 'promote the independence of the persons who receive[d] them and [did] protect the disabled in their national social context', that was not their sole purpose, since they also ensured the care and supervision of the disabled in their social context (all in para. 54; see the new article 4(2a)(a)(*ii*) Regulation 1408/71). However, the benefits did not fit under article 4(2a)(a)(*i*) Regulation 1408/71, either. Under that paragraph, a benefit had to 'either replace or supplement a social security benefit, while being distinguishable from it, and be by its nature social assistance justified on economic and social grounds and fixed by legislation setting objective criteria' to be 'special' (para. 55). Despite their specific characteristics (paras 58, 60, 63, and 66), all allowances were sickness benefits and as such not 'special'. Only the British disability living allowance included an element of social assistance, namely the mobility component, which the British legislature technically could split off. It would then be 'special' and could be made subject to a residence requirement (para. 69). That the British disability living allowance and the attendance allowance had been held to comply with article 10a Regulation 1408/71 in *Snares, 1997* and *Partridge, 1998* was not at odds with the new decision of the Court, since *Jauch, 2001* had in the meanwhile introduced the examination of the 'special non contributory' nature of a benefit, in spite of its listing in annex IIa (para. 71). Hence, annex IIa was annulled in so far as it listed the five benefits at issue.

Annex issues

In *Habelt, 2007*, the Court transposed the *Jauch, 2001*-case-law to another annex issue. If the person concerned resided in Germany, Germany took into account periods of old-age insurance contribution completed during World War II in territories that had belonged to the German *Reich* at that time, but were not any longer part of modern day Germany. Annex VI(c)(1) to Regulation 1408/71 sanctioned that residence requirement. The Court first held that the scheme was within the scope of Regulation 1408/71, as the periods were not taken into account in recognition of efforts during the war within the meaning of article 4(4) Regulation 1408/71, and because contributions had been paid during that time (para. 66). That the institution which had administrated the scheme originally did not exist any longer was immaterial (paras 70-1). In analogy to the *Jauch, 2001*-line of authority it was not sufficient for a benefit to be listed in an annex to Regulation 1408/71 in order to validate a residence requirement and comply with article 42 Treaty, formerly article 51 Treaty. In addition – as with 'special non-contributory' benefits – the benefit had to be closely linked to the social environment. That was not the case for the German benefit of recognition of wartime periods of contribution. Hence, the residence requirement and the annex, in that regard, were contrary to article 42 Treaty (paras 81-4). Moreover, the Court confirmed the continued applicability of a convention that had been in force when the person concerned had moved to work in a member state before Regulation 1408/71 became applicable, in keeping with *Rönfeldt, 1991* and *Thévenon, 1995*. That even applied when a person had moved to a member state from outside the Community (para. 121), provided that a link to the Community was given within the sense of the *Prodest, 1984*-line of authority (para. 121-3).

Further scope and definitions

In *Noteboom, 2005* the Court categorized a Belgian benefit as an old-age benefit pursuant to article 4(1)(c) Regulation 1408/71. 'Holiday pay' was granted to pensioners to supplement their pensions so that they could go on holiday. It was linked to the pension and financed by the same resources. Regardless of the facts that it was not funded by contributions and consisted in a flat-rate amount, it was an old-age benefit (paras 22-9). In *De Cuyper, 2006*, the Court again dealt with a Belgian benefit, namely an allowance which was granted as a means of subsistence to persons aged over 50 years who had lost employment. The Court discarded the argument that the benefit constituted social assistance, as it was granted without a discretionary assessment of the personal circumstances and based on an objective, legally defined position (para. 23). The allowance addressed the characteristic risk of loss of employment, was a substitute for the salary lost, and calculated on that basis. The amount of the allowance was determined in the same way as regular unemployment benefits. The allowance was subject to a minimum qualifying period of employment having given rise to social security contributions during a reference period. The exemptions from the obligations to register as a person seeking employment and to be available for work were immaterial. The allowance was thus an unemployment benefit (paras 27-31). Consequently, a residence requirement was not precluded by Regulation 1408/71. That outcome was compatible with the freedom of Union citizens to move pursuant to article 18 Treaty, as surprise monitoring was an appropriate method of ensuring that the conditions for the grant of the benefits continued to be fulfilled, in particular with regard to the family and employment situation of the person concerned. Less intrusive means than a residence requirement were not available (paras 41-6).

Finally, in *Petersen, 2008* the Court dealt with a particular Austrian benefit. Persons resident in Austria were granted a benefit which served to bridge the period of uncertainty while a person was awaiting a decision regarding an invalidity benefit. Since that benefit was obviously only granted, if the person concerned did not work during that time, it was unclear whether the benefit was an invalidity or an unemployment benefit under article 4(1)(b) or (g) Regulation 1408/71. The benefit was considered retroactively as an unemployment benefit by national law, in case the decision on invalidity did not turn out in the affirmative. It was financed by the unemployment scheme, subject to refunding in case of invalidity.

The purpose of the benefit was to replace income lost during the period of uncertainty. Moreover, the benefit was subject to the same conditions as unemployment benefits and calculated in the same way. Given those characteristics, the Court concluded that it was an unemployment benefit. That the person concerned was dispensed from being available for, capable of, and willing to work was irrelevant (paras 23-34). Consequently, a residence requirement would have complied with Regulation 1408/71, subject to article 69 and 71 Regulation 1408/71 – if the Court had not invalidated it on other grounds, namely the indirectly discriminatory effects on the free movement of workers which could not be justified. The Court mitigated the ruling, though. The benefit was on average only available for three to four months. Moreover, the ensuing invalidity benefits in the event of an affirmative decision were exportable in any event pursuant to article 10(1) Regulation 1408/71, while the ensuing unemployment benefits in case of a non-affirmative decision were subject to articles 69 and 71 Regulation 1408/71. Moreover, the return of the person concerned for checks could lawfully be required (paras 55-62).

Applicable legislation: posted workers

In the 2000s, the Court also decided several cases which mostly centred on the applicable legislation. With *Fitzwilliam, 2000* the Court came back to *Manpower, 1970*, which had concerned posted workers under Regulation 3. The Court essentially confirmed the criteria developed in that decision for posted workers under article 14(1)(a) Regulation 1408/71. Two of the conditions to be met for article 14(1)(a) to apply, and hence for the 'home' state legislation to continue to be applicable, were that (i) the posted workers had a necessary link to the undertaking posting them in the sense that the undertaking had authority over them (paras 22 and 24) and (ii) that the undertaking posting workers normally conducted its business in the state where it was established (paras 23 and 30). Only that interpretation was in accordance with the exceptional nature of article 14(1)(a) (para. 41). The second point (ii) had to be deduced from all the circumstances, namely including the law applicable to the employment contracts of the posted workers, the places where those contracts had been concluded and where the workers had been recruited, the turnover, administration, seat, and staff of the undertaking, but not the nature of the work performed (paras 42-4). Apart from that, the E 101 certificate that posted workers took along to prove that they remained subject to 'home' state legislation pursuant to article 11(1)(a) Regulation 574/72 established a presumption that bound the host state authorities. Those authorities were, however, entitled to ask the 'home' state authorities to verify the certificate (paras 53-6). *Banks, 2000* confirmed that latter point and added, on the one hand, that the person in the host state that (the person) called on the services to be performed under certificate E 101 was also bound by it, and, on the other hand, that such certificates could also be issued with retroactive effect (paras 47 and 52-3). Moreover, *Banks, 2000* clarified that 'work' within the meaning of article 14a(1)(a) Regulation 1408/71, which concerned self-employed persons who went to 'work' in another member state, included activities in an employed as well as a self-employed capacity (para. 23). Artists who were self-employed in the United Kingdom and went to 'work' in an employed capacity for a theatre in Belgium for several months therefore remained subject to the legislation of the United Kingdom. In analogy to posted workers pursuant to *Fitzwilliam, 2000*, however, a significant part of the persons' activities had to be performed for a certain amount of time where they were established. The circumstances – offices, value added tax number, registration, etc. – were equally decisive here. The 'work' performed in the host state by such self-employed persons, in addition, had to be genuine and clearly delimited in advance (paras 25-7). Such circumstances given, Belgium could not lawfully collect social security contributions from the Belgian employers for the 'work' of such self-employed persons. In *Plum, 2000*, the criteria developed in *Fitzwilliam, 2000* were put to the test. The owner of construction companies in Germany had established a company in the Netherlands in order to benefit from the lower labour costs there by posting workers to Germany. The Court found that the purely managerial activities of the company in the Netherlands were not sufficient for it to conduct its business normally in the state of establishment within the sense of *Fitzwilliam, 2000* (para. 21 of *Plum, 2000*) and hence to benefit from the scheme established by article 14(1)(a) Regulation 1408/71. In *Herbosch Kiere, 2006*, the Court confirmed the ruling delivered in the previous judgments as to the binding nature of certificate E 101. The Court added that the host state authorities could not have the certificate declared invalid by the courts in the host state, either. Such courts did not have the power to scrutinize the validity of the certificate as to the existence of a direct link between posting undertaking and posted workers. As long as the certificate had not been withdrawn by the state having issued it, the certificate remained valid (paras 30-2).

One legislation

Commission v. France (social debt repayment), 2000 concerned a charge France imposed on all income gained in France. The aim of the charge, 'the social debt repayment contribution', was to raise the funds necessary to redress a budgetary imbalance in the French social security system. The Court assessed that the charge was not a tax, but rather a social security contribution, since its purpose was to finance a deficit in the French general social security system. That sufficed to establish a direct and sufficiently relevant link between the charge and the social security system, notwithstanding that the charge was levied together with taxes and did not yield any concrete benefit for the person charged (paras 36-41). As a social security contribution, it could not be imposed without violating the principle that only *one* legislation was to be applied pursuant to article 13 Regulation 1408/71 and equal treatment in articles 48 and 52 Treaty on persons who, while residing in France, received income abroad and paid contributions to the social security systems of other member states pursuant to Regulation 1408/71 (paras 45-8). In *Commission v. France (general social contribu-*

tion), 2000, handed down on the same day as *Commission v. France (social debt repayment), 2000*, the Court applied identical reasoning to the French general social contribution which fed the social security branches concerning old-age, survivor's, sickness, and family benefit and was designed to alleviate the burden on low- and mid-level incomes (paras 35-6). In contrast, in *Commission v. Germany (artists' contribution), 2001* the Court validated a similar social contribution Germany charged on Belgian artists' remunerations paid in Germany. The crux was that according to German law the undertakings that marketed the artists' work and were liable to pay the charge were prohibited from passing on the burden of the charge to the artists. That prohibition had the effect that artists who were established in France and only occasionally performed work in Germany and who were therefore subject to French social security were not concerned – not even indirectly – by the German charge (paras 26-37). Thus, neither article 13 Regulation 1408/71 nor articles 51, 52, and 59 Treaty were infringed.

In *Vogler, 2000* the Court declined, in an order, a challenge to the approach chosen by the Community legislature to address the situation of persons who simultaneously pursued self-employed activities in two member states. According to the Court, to rely on the residence of the self-employed person to determine the legislation applicable pursuant to article 14a(2) Regulation 1408/71 was not unreasonable. In laying down that rule, the Council did not commit a manifest error or misuse his powers (paras 24-7). Germany could therefore not lawfully impose social security contributions regarding farming activities in Germany of a person who at the same time was a hotelier in Austria where he resided. In a similar vein, the Court rejected a challenge in *Allard, 2005*. The Belgian 'moderation contribution' was within the scope of Regulation 1408/71, because it served to finance a Belgian social security scheme (paras 17-8). Pursuant to article 14d(1) Regulation 1408/71 Belgium was not just allowed, but indeed required to levy social security contributions not only on the proceeds of the self-employed activities in Belgium of a person resident there but also on the proceeds of that person's self-employed activities in France (para. 23). That requirement, moreover, did not violate the freedom of establishment (paras 32-3). The ruling in *Allard, 2005* was, however, put in a different perspective in *Derouin, 2008*. This case concerned the two contributions which had been at issue in *Commission v. France (social debt repayment), 2000* and *Commission v. France (general social contribution), 2000*. It was therefore obvious that those two contributions were subject to Regulation 1408/71. According to the ruling in *Allard, 2005* France was entitled to levy those contributions on the entire income generated by a person resident in France through self-employed activities in France and the United Kingdom. However, France could forgo that right unilaterally or in a double taxation convention with the United Kingdom. According to the Court, *Allard, 2005* could not be interpreted in the sense that France *had to* levy the charge equally on the income stemming from the self-employed activity in the United Kingdom (paras 27-30 of *Derouin, 2008*).

Ceasing occupation

Elsen, 2000 raised the question whether article 13(2)(f) Regulation 1408/71 according to which the legislation of the member state of residence was applicable to persons who ceased work applied to the situation of Ms Elsen. She had worked in Germany, then moved to reside in France while continuing to work in Germany as a frontier worker. She had then given birth to a child whom she had raised while not continuing to work and not working later on, either. She claimed that the child-rearing periods were to be taken into account for her German old-age pension. The Court denied that article 13(2)(f) was applicable in that specific situation, because a close link existed between the employment in Germany, which had given rise to social security insurance there, and the following period of maternity (para. 26-8). German law was therefore applicable. The Court then went on to examine the German requirement that the child-rearing, essentially, had to take place in Germany, for the corresponding period to be credited towards the old-age pension. The Court explained that the freedom of movement of Union citizens had to be complied with even when the member states organized their social security systems. Regulation 1408/71 helped to guarantee not only the freedom of workers but also that of citizens. Hence, the German requirement was contrary to freedom of movement of workers and citizens (paras 29-36).

The Court also addressed article 13(2)(f) Regulation 1408/71 in *Commission v. Belgium (contributions), 2001* and equally held that article not applicable, though for another reason. Belgium imposed social security contributions on occupational disease pensions paid in Belgium to persons resident abroad. The Court held that article 13(2)(f) was not to be applied generally, since it was uncertain whether any other legislation was applicable to the persons concerned and, in particular, whether the legislation to which each of the persons concerned had been subject previously in actual fact had ceased to apply (paras 29-32 and 38). Hence, the law of the member state of residence could not generally be held to be applicable when a person received a pension by reason of an occupational disease. Belgium was, therefore, not precluded on that general level from levying the contributions. In *Laurin Effing, 2005*, in contrast, the Court steered clear of article 13(2)(f). The person concerned in that case served a prison sentence in Germany, after having been transferred from a prison in Austria where his family lived and he had been employed previously. As he worked during the prison term in Germany, it did not matter whether article 13(2)(a) or (f) applied. In either case, German legislation was applicable to the person concerned (para. 45). Consequently, he did not have a claim to benefits on the basis of Austrian law and the residence requirement in Austrian law was not precluded either by Regulation 1408/71 or by article 12 Treaty.

Van Pommeren, 2005 concerned article 13(2)(f), too. A person residing in Belgium had been compulsorily insured owing to employment in the Netherlands and then become incapacitated and received invalidity benefits in the Netherlands. By reason of those benefits, the person continued to be subject pursuant to Dutch law to some branches of insurance on a compulsory basis, while for others continued insurance became optional. In those circumstances, the Court considered, article 13(2)(f) was not applicable, since the person concerned had not ceased to be subject to Dutch legislation (para. 36). However, the Court found discrimination in that the conditions of continued insurance for non-residents were less favourable than those under compulsory insurance which applied to residents. Notably, the levels of contributions were not the same. In the light of the low rate of affiliation to continued insurance in the Netherlands – which was indicative of difficulties encountered by non-residents – the Court concluded that article 39 Treaty was violated, because non-residents were put in a less favourable position than residents (paras 40-3).

Two legislations

Piatkowski, 2006 again dealt with an exception to the rule that only one legislation was applicable, namely article 14c(b) Regulation 1408/71 according to which two legislations applied in case of simultaneous employment in one state and self-employment in another. Mr Piatkowsi had been pursuing a self-employed activity in Belgium, while he was employed in the Netherlands as a director of a Dutch company. The Netherlands authorities treated the interest paid on a debt which a Dutch company owed him as income and subjected it to Dutch social security contributions. The Court did not find any issue with that. Despite the revision of article 14c which had deleted the passage 'as regards the activity pursued in its territory', still each member state was entitled to levy contributions on the part of the income generated in its territory (paras 28-9). That Regulation 1408/71 did not regulate the way interest on debts had to be attributed between two member states was irrelevant, since Belgium did not subject the interest paid to contributions (paras 30-1). Moreover, the Dutch levy applied without distinction, contributions were not left without return, and income was not subject to contributions twice for the same period of time. That the contributions levied on the debt did not afford any concrete additional protection was immaterial given that in a system of solidarity the protection afforded was independent of the amount of contributions paid (paras 30-38).

Aggregation

As to aggregation, the Court decided about a dozen of cases during the 2000s. In *Engelbrecht, 2000*, the Court dealt with essentially the same situation as in *Van Munster, 1994*, though the national provision at stake was different. Yet the provision still had the effect of reducing a married couple's pension in Belgium by switching from the household to the single rate due to the 'splitting' of a worker's pension in the Netherlands when the non-working spouse reached retirement age – a 'splitting' which did not increase the couple's overall pension in the Netherlands. That the non-working spouse's part of the split Dutch pension was partly based on periods of compulsory insurance in the Netherlands did not change anything in the assessment made in *Van Munster, 1994*. The national authorities still were not entitled mechanically to apply a national provision which had been plainly designed to deal with overall increases in a couple's income through retirement benefits, in a situation in which an overall increase had not taken place, else they violated the free movement of workers (paras 32-3, 41, and 43).

Insalaca, 2002 was a typical aggregation case in application of article 46 Regulation 1408/71. It arose because a Belgian provision was unclear (see the opinion of Advocate General Léger, paras 21 and 32). The effect of that provision was that the ceiling applicable to a Belgian survivor's pension which had been granted concomitantly with a Belgian old-age pension was lowered in the light of a simultaneously awarded survivor's pension in Italy. The Court, in application of standard case-law, classed that provision as a rule against overlapping which could not lawfully be applied in the calculation under the Community rules, viz. the calculation of the independent and *pro rata* amounts, in contrast to the calculation of the benefits pursuant to national law alone.

Barreira Pérez, 2002 dealt with particular years added in the calculation pursuant to article 46 Regulation 1408/71. Spain added certain years in the calculation of old-age pensions when those years concerned periods during which rights had been arising under the old Spanish retirement scheme. The Court decided that such notional years constituted periods of insurance pursuant to 1(r) Regulation 1408/71), even though they were not added in the qualifying period, but only in the calculation of the benefit (paras 25-6). As such they had to be fed into the calculation both of the theoretical amount as well as the *pro rata* amount under article 46(2), although those years did not relate to a specifically identifiable time period and potentially could overlap with periods of insurance completed in other member states (paras 34-41).

In *Koschitzki, 2005* the Court was asked whether the Italian supplement to bring an old-age benefit up to the minimum pension was to be taken into account generally in the calculation of the theoretical amount under article 46(2) Regulation 1408/71 or merely when the person concerned was actually entitled to it. The Court clarified *Stinco, 1998* which had not addressed the point and ruled that the supplement was to be included only when the person concerned was actually entitled to it (para. 29). When the income threshold was crossed and the person concerned was therefore not entitled to the supplement, the theoretical amount had to be calculated without it.

In *Chuck, 2008* the Court was faced with the question whether article 48(2) Regulation 1408/71 concerning periods of insurance of a duration of less than one year also applied to a national of a member state who had worked in several member states, but resided in a non-member state, in this case the United States, when applying for an old-age benefit. On the basis of the scope *ratione personae* of Regulation 1408/71, which was based exclusively on the national of a member state having been subject to the social security system of a member state, the Court decided that residence in a third country was not an obstacle to the application of article 48(2) (para. 34). However, it was a matter of national law whether the benefit awarded based on that article was exportable to a third state (para. 38).

Leyman, 2009 concerned an intricate case in which Belgium's type A invalidity scheme was confronted with Luxembourg's type B invalidity scheme. In such a constellation, article 46 Regulation 1408/71 undoubtedly applied to invalidity pensions awarded. However, the Belgian system was based on a sequence of sickness benefits and invalidity benefits. During the first year, thus, a person received a primary incapacity allowance which was then followed by invalidity benefits, if need be. Because of that approach article 40(3)(b) Regulation 1408/71 specifically provided that invalidity benefits were only acquired as per the date when the sickness benefits expired. However, in *Leyman, 2009* that led to a peculiar situation. Ms Leyman had become invalid in Luxembourg and was awarded a pro rata invalidity pension there right from the first year on. However, based on article 40(3)(b) Belgium refused to award her a pension for the first year after having become incapable of work. Only for the period after that first year invalidity benefits were granted. In doing so, Belgium relied on Luxembourg's binding determination of invalidity which in Belgium could only trigger the benefit due after the first year of incapacity. According to the Court, Belgium's refusal disadvantaged migrant workers, since they lost a year worth of benefits in Belgium. In addition, contributions that had been paid there went without return. Therefore, based on the free movement of workers, good cooperation pursuant to article 10 Treaty, and despite article 40(3)(b) Belgium had to grant an invalidity benefit also for the first year of incapacity of work (paras 42-6).

Aggregation and child-rearing in Austria

Kauer, 2002 concerned periods of child-rearing which Austrian law generally took into account as substitute periods for old-age insurance purposes. Ms Kauer had worked in Austria. She had then stopped working. Without having received any benefits, she had given birth to three children whom she had mainly raised in Belgium after having moved there. She had never worked in Belgium and then came back to Austria to work in 1975. Austria refused to recognize those child-rearing periods as substitute periods, as (i) they had been completed before entry into force of the Agreement on the European Economic Area and (ii) because Ms Kauer had not received Austrian benefits during the periods. According to the Court, Regulation 1408/71 applied, because risks having materialized before entry into force of Regulation 1408/71 were relevant and the effects of situations having come about before that entry into force were on-going in accordance with articles 94(2) and (3) Regulation 1408/71. Austrian law applied to determine whether the periods were insurance periods within the sense of article 1(r) Regulation 1408/71, based on either *Ten Holder, 1986* or article 13(2)(f) Regulation 1408/71 as interpreted in *Elsen, 2000* due to the sufficiently close link to Austria (paras 29-33). The Court discarded the first condition (i) in the light of article 94(2) Regulation 1408/71 (paras 35-6). The second condition (ii) was also rejected. The condition violated article 94(2) in conjunction with articles 8a, 48, and 52 Treaty (paras 44-9). Thus the periods of child-rearing had to be considered as periods of insurance under Austrian law as interpreted in the light of the Treaty. Via article 94(2) Regulation 1408/71 they had to be taken into account for the purpose of old-age insurance in Austria. *Klöppel, 2008* also concerned the taking into account of periods of child-rearing in Austria, tough in different circumstances. Ms Klöppel had raised her child in Germany. Her partner helped her and received child care allowance in Germany for that purpose. When they moved to Austria, she received child care allowance in Austria. However, in the determination of the period for which the allowance was granted, it was not taken into account that her partner had received child-care allowance in Germany. As a consequence, the benefit was only granted for 30 months, rather than 36 months. The Court found that reduction to constitute indirect discrimination contrary to article 3 Regulation 1408/71 (paras 17-9).

Aggregation and employment with the Community

In *My, 2004* the Court dealt with insurance periods completed during work for the institutions of the Community. Mr My, an Italian national, had moved to Belgium as a child and later worked in Belgium and then for the Community. Belgium refused to take the insurance periods into account for the purpose of entitlement under Belgian old-age insurance. The Court refused to examine Union citizenship (paras 32-3) and reiterated that Regulation 1408/71 did not apply to officials of the Community. Regulation 1612/68 did not apply either, because Mr My's entire working life had been confined to Belgium. The situation was purely internal to Belgium. Employment with the Community was not the same as employment in the civil service of another member state (paras 39-42). Instead, the staff regulations of the Community applied. Based on those and the principle of cooperation, Belgium had to take into account those periods (para. 44 et seq.).

Further aggregation

In *Salgado, 2005* the Court dealt with a Spanish unemployment benefit granted to persons aged over 52 years. Those persons received a particular benefit and Spain, in addition, paid old-age insurance contributions on their behalf. However, the periods during which that benefit was granted did not count towards the qualifying period of 15 years for Spanish old-age insurance, i. e. they were only taken into account in the calculation of an old-age benefit. The Court did not find an issue with that approach, since it was up to national law to determine which periods constituted periods of insurance pursuant to article 1(r) Regulation 1408/71. As the approach was not discriminatory and insurance periods completed abroad were factored in, the Spanish approach was compatible with the free movement of workers. In *García Blanco, 2005*, the Court declared inadmissible another question asked by a Spanish court as to the same Spanish scheme, since the claims of the applicant had already been met.

In *Noteboom, 2005*, the Court ruled that a frontier worker who drew unemployment benefits in Belgium based on article 71(1)(a)(ii) Regulation 1408/71, although he had been affiliated to the unemployment insurance scheme of the Netherlands, had to be considered to have been insured in Belgium for the purpose of entitlement to 'holiday pay' in the first year of retirement. That much followed from the 'as if'-clause for aggregation pursuant to article 45(6) Regulation 1408/71 (para. 34).

Nemec, 2006 concerned an occupational disease benefit awarded in France to those who were exposed to asbestos during their work. The benefit essentially allowed those persons to retire early. To determine the benefit in the case of Mr Nemec, the French authorities relied on Mr Nemec's last salary in France, although he had made use of his freedom and had gone to Belgium to work where he had earned a higher salary. According to the Court ruling on the basis of article 58(1) Regulation 1408/71, the French authorities did not have to take into account the actual salary gained in Belgium. However, they were not allowed to rely simply on the last salary paid in France, either, else migrant workers would be disadvantaged. Instead, they had to calculate on the basis of what Mr Nemec would have earned had he continued to work in France rather than Belgium. In other words, the salary paid had to be updated and revalorized (para. 42).

Sickness benefits, medical services

The Court ruled on the basis of the provisions concerning sickness benefits in a number of cases in the 2000s. *Vanbraekel, 2001* concerned the situation where the authorization to seek medical treatment abroad was granted retroactively after it had been refused previously. The question came up whether the costs the patient had faced due to the treatment abroad were to be reimbursed to him in accordance with host state or 'home' state legislation. In the case of the Vanbraekels' relative the cost of the treatment provided in France was lower than it would have been had the treatment been provided in Belgium, the 'home' state. The Court decided that article 22(1)(c) Regulation 1408/71 did not regulate the question. While article 22 did require the 'home' state institution to reimburse the person concerned directly in such circumstances, article 22(1)(c) left the 'home' state free to reimburse the lower cost actually incurred in the host state or the higher cost under its own system (paras 36-7). However, the freedom of services, i. e. the freedom of the recipient of medical services, required that the higher amount pursuant to the 'home' state legislation be reimbursed, else service recipients would be deterred from seeking medical services abroad (para. 45). In *Inizan, 2003* the Court confirmed that the authorization scheme established by article 22(1)(c) Regulation 1408/71 complied with the freedom of services. The crux was that article 22 allowed persons to receive medical treatment abroad in accordance with the host state's legislation. That option would not be available without article 22. Accordingly, the Community legislature was entitled to attach conditions to that option (paras 22-4). Apart from that, when an authorization to seek *intra muros* medical treatment abroad was sought, the conditions for the refusal of the authorization applicable under article 22 had to be interpreted in the same way as those the case-law under the freedom of services had developed for cases of medical treatment abroad. For clarity, the latter applied when medical treatment abroad was to be reimbursed in accordance with the legislation applied by the competent institution itself (see paras 19 and 52). Notably, it was required that the same or equally effective treatment was not available within due delay in the member state of residence (paras 45 and 59) and procedural safeguards applied (paras 48 and 57). France was, in particular, entitled to refuse the authorization only if equal medical treatment was available without undue delay in France. (See the case-law under the free movement of medical services below.)

In *Bosch, 2004* the practice of a German sickness insurance fund to reimburse in full and without any formality expenses up to 200 German mark incurred by insured persons abroad was at issue. The German authorities opposed that practice. According to the Court, akin to *Vanbraekel, 2001*, article 34 Regulation 574/72, which governed situations where an insured person was unable to complete the formalities required by Regulation 574/72 when receiving benefits abroad, was not to be interpreted so as to exclude the practice of the German fund, since it ensured that the person received the same, or even a higher reimbursement than if article 34 had been applied (paras 22-4).

In the case *Keller, 2005* Ms Keller had received the authorization from the competent Spanish institution to be treated in Germany under article 22(1)(c) Regulation 1408/71. German doctors then decided that the particular operation she needed could only be performed in Switzerland. The Court held that the authorization granted in due form covered that situation, because sickness insurance according to German law would cover the cost of such an operation in Switzerland. Pursuant to article 22 Regulation 1408/71 the host state institutions applied the law of the host state and the authorized person had to be treated as if she were insured under host state law (para. 48). The Spanish authorities were therefore 'in the hands of the doctors authorised' (para. 50) and bound by their assessment even if it led to treatment in a non-member state. They could neither require the return of the person concerned nor reserve further approval. The authorization also covered vital treatment needed urgently which could not have been anticipated at the time the authorization had been granted (paras 53-60). The Spanish authorities had to reimburse the German institution, or the insured person directly, to the same extent as her operation was covered by German law (paras 67-9).

Watts, 2006 again concerned the authorization to receive *intra muros* treatment abroad. The Court confirmed expressly what had already been evident in *Inizan, 2003*, namely that the criterion 'within the time normally necessary for obtaining the treatment' in article 22 Regulation 1408/71 had to be interpreted in the same way as the term 'undue delay' used under article 49 Treaty (paras

57-61). The Court also clarified the details of the medical assessment to be made in that regard. This was particularly important for the United Kingdom with its universal health system which was at stake in *Watts, 2006* and which sometimes resulted in considerable waiting periods for patients. An 'exodus of patients' (para. 77) was therefore possible depending on the interpretation of Community law. The Court, in particular, held that all the circumstances of each case had to be assessed individually – for instance the medical condition and history of the patient and the degree of pain – if necessary flexibly and dynamically. Within that assessment, however, waiting periods, and waiting lists in particular, were not per se excluded, as already held in relation to the freedom of services, provided that the waiting period did not exceed what was acceptable in the light of the medical needs of the person concerned (para. 63). Potentially higher cost abroad were not to be fed into the assessment, though. The framework the Court described was necessary to prevent overcapacities, wastage, and imbalances in the medical system of a member state. (For the dimension of the freedom of medical services, see below.)

Acereda Herrera, 2006 next dealt with the extent of the cost covered when the authorization to receive treatment abroad had been granted. It was, in particular, uncertain whether certain ancillary costs were covered, such as the cost of travelling to the hospital, certain meals and accommodation outside the hospital, or the cost of relatives who accompanied the person for the treatment. With the benefits listed in article 22(1)(c) Regulation 1408/71 being exhaustive, the Court decided that only the cost directly connected to the medical treatment and cost linked thereto, like accommodation and meals in the hospital, were benefits in kind covered by article 22 Regulation 1408/71. In turn, cash benefits under article 22(1)(c)(ii) Regulation 1408/71, which was also a Community term, related to loss of income and was not to be interpreted to mean ancillary cash cost incurred in hospital treatment (paras 33-5). Consequently, certain ancillary cost was not covered by the authorization pursuant to article 22. That ruling, however, did not affect the assessment under non-discrimination, if the freedom of services was applicable.

In *Von Chamier-Glisczinski, 2009* a person who was subject to German sickness insurance was receiving German home care benefits. When her medical condition deteriorated she moved to Austria to receive full care in a home of her choice. The German care benefits were then discontinued. The powers were clearly allocated in such a case, irrespective of whether article 19 or article 22(1)(b) and (3) applied, namely Germany provided cash benefits and Austria benefits in kind in accordance with Austrian legislation on behalf of the German insurance. The care benefits were benefits in kind, since they served to finance full in-patient care (paras 48-9). However, as Austrian law did not know such care benefits, the Austrian institutions were not obliged to provide them and the German institutions rightfully ceased providing them (para. 53), while Regulation 1408/71 did not force Germany to stop providing them (paras 55-6). Since it was unclear whether Mr von Chamier had sought work in Austria, the above result was not at variance with article 39 Treaty. Union citizenship in turn did not preclude the result, either, since it was the natural consequence of a lack of harmonisation in social security. It did not amount to discriminatory or disadvantageous treatment of a Union citizen that full in-patient care provided in a home in Germany would have been covered by German insurance, while care in a home in Austria was not covered. A guarantee that moving residence in such a constellation would be neutral did not exist in Union law (paras 85-7).

Pensioners and sickness benefits

In *Rundgren, 2001* Finland's authorities levied sickness insurance contributions on pensions paid in Finland. In the case of Mr Rundgren, who was receiving a pension in Sweden and then moved to reside in Finland, Finnish law treated him as if he received a pension in Finland, because in theory he had a right to a state pension in Finland. That treatment had the effect, in fact, that contributions were levied on his Swedish pension. As Mr Rundgren's situation was within the scope of Regulation 1408/71, the Court interpreted article 28a Regulation 1408/71 to mean that only the state that in fact paid a pension, i. e. Sweden, was entitled to deduct contributions. There was a connection between the actual provision of pensions and the obligation to bear the cost of benefits in kind (para. 47). Furthermore, by levying contributions, Finland required a pensioner to pay contributions for benefits which were actually payable by Sweden. Since Mr Rundgren did not receive any additional protection, either, Finland's approach was precluded by article 33 Regulation 1408/71 (para. 55). The waiver of reimbursement of the cost arising from the provision of benefits in kind in the convention between Finland and Sweden did not have an impact on that assessment (para. 62). The judgment in *Nikula, 2006* dealt with the sickness insurance of a pensioner in Finland, too. However, the circumstances were slightly different. Ms Nikula received two pensions, one in Sweden and one in Finland, while she was resident in Finland. In such circumstances, the Court concluded that Finland could take into account the pensions paid in Finland *and* Sweden to determine the income on the basis of which the sickness insurance contributions due in Finland were calculated. The only caveats the Court applied was that the contributions levied as a consequence in Finland were not to be higher than the pension paid in Finland pursuant to article 33(1) Regulation 1408/71 and that, if the Swedish pension had already been the subject of sickness insurance contributions earlier on, Finland was not to factor it, or the part of it concerned, into the Finnish calculation (paras 32-6).

IKA, 2003 also concerned a pensioner, though with regard to medical treatment abroad. Greek law established an ex post facto authorization for treatment abroad that was given, if the illness had manifested itself abroad and treatment had become necessary immediately. The Court interpreted article 31 Regulation 1408/71, which required that *intra muros* treatment had become necessary abroad, i. e. treatment abroad had not been planned. That article need not have been interpreted in harmony with article 22(1)(a) Regulation 1408/71, which dealt with the same question for (self-)employed persons but required immediate necessity of treatment, since the Community legislature wanted to create a special regime designed for the specific needs of pensioners (para. 38). In that light, Greek law could not lawfully require an authorization as such or, indeed, that treatment had become immediately necessary during a stay abroad and that the illness had come to light abroad (paras 41-3). Consequently, the direct reimbursement of the cost advanced by the patient could not lawfully be subjected to those conditions, either (para. 62). In contrast to *IKA, 2003* the judgment in *Van der Duin, 2003* dealt with planned medical treatment of pensioners abroad. In that case Mr Van der Duin, a pensioner, was resident in France and registered there in accordance with article 28 Regulation 1408/71. He went to seek hospital treatment in the Netherlands, the state in which he received his invalidity pension. It was doubtful whether the authorization scheme in article 22(1)(c)(i) Regulation 1408/71 was applicable in such a case. The Court replied in the affirmative, because the regime Regulation 1408/71 set up for pensioners residing abroad was based on the idea that those pensioners received benefits in kind in the host state as if they received pensions from the host state. It was different from the regime applicable to persons in active employment. The cost incurred by reason of a pensioner's medical treatment in the host state were reimbursed by the state paying the pension by lump sum based on the average cost caused by a pensioner. If the authorization scheme did not apply and a right to receive benefits in the state paying the pension existed for pensioners registered abroad pursuant to article 28 Regulation 1408/71, a risk would arise that the state paying the pension would face the cost caused by a single pensioner twice (paras 40-6).

Unemployment benefits

Thelen, 2000 continued the Court's case-law on unemployment benefits in the 2000s. In *Thelen, 2000* the Court transposed its case-law as to rights acquired under conventions that applied when the Regulation entered into force to unemployment benefits (para. 19). In the case of Mr Thelen, it was a convention between Germany and Austria which allowed him as a German national to return to Germany and claim unemployment benefits there, while his work in Austria was taken into account for the German qualifying period. Under the regime of Regulation 1408/71 which entered into force for Austria when it joined the European Economic Area he could only claim benefits in Austria. The exportability of benefits was subject to article 69 Regulation 1408/71. For the Court there was no reason not to apply the *Rönfeldt, 1991*-line of authority. Mr Thelen had moved to Austria at a time when Regulation 1408/71 had not yet been in force and so he could legitimately expect the convention to apply (para. 22). The short interruptions in his employment in Austria, one of which happened to fall on the date of entry into force of the Agreement on the European Economic Area, did not deprive him of his rights under the convention (para. 21). In *Kaske, 2002* the Court further clarified that case-law, again with regard to the convention between Germany and Austria. The Court made it clear that movements between member states which the worker concerned made after the entry into force of Regulation 1408/71 did not have an impact on the worker's established rights under a convention that had been in force when the worker first moved to a member state and neither did subsequent interruptions of employment. The situation of such a worker as regarded unemployment benefits had to be assessed entirely in the light of the more favourable convention (para. 32). Regulation 1408/71 only applied once the rights under the relevant convention had been exhausted, in other words typically when the basis of the worker's rights was laid entirely after entry into force of Regulation 1408/71, for instance when all the periods giving rise to a right to benefits were completed after entry into force of Regulation 1408/71 (paras 33-4). Quite apart from that, Austria could not lawfully provide that a worker was entitled to claim unemployment benefits in Austria, instead of the competent state pursuant to Regulation 1408/71, if that person had previously stayed in Austria for at least 15 years, for that option would result in discrimination (para. 38).

In *Stallone, 2001* Belgium's increase of unemployment benefits for heads of household was at stake. Belgian law increased unemployment benefits by five per cent when the unemployed person, the spouse and the children who were dependent on the unemployed person lived together. The Court found that the condition implicitly amounted to a residence clause which was prohibited under article 68(2) Regulation 1408/71, for it amounted to indirect discrimination. It was therefore not to be applied, not even for reasons of monitoring, when the family of the unemployed worker lived in another member state (paras 16-22). *Ruhr, 2001* confirmed that *Kermaschek, 1976* was still good law for unemployment benefits (para. 21). A spouse who was a third country national and had worked in Luxembourg, while residing with her German husband in Germany, could not rely on article 71 Regulation 1408/71 to claim unemployment benefits, since she only enjoyed rights derived from her husband. Whether the husband had himself made use of his freedom under article 39 Treaty was immaterial.

In *Verwayen, 2002* the Court ordered that the aggregation of periods pursuant to article 67(1) and (2) Regulation 1408/71 only applied when insurance or employment periods had been last completed in the member state from which benefits were claimed. Since that was not the case of Ms Verwayen, article 67 Regulation 1408/71 did not apply (para. 25). *Kristiansen, 2003* mostly concerned the Commission's conditions of employment and the unemployment benefits that could be claimed by reason thereof. However, the Court also rejected the claim of Ms Kristiansen of being discriminated as a post-graduate fellow. Belgium was not required to take periods completed as such a fellow into account under the national unemployment scheme, as long as similar periods were not taken into account for Belgian nationals, either. The fact that some member states considered such periods as relevant under their unemployment schemes was irrelevant (paras 36-9).

Exporting unemployment benefits

Rydergård, 2002 concerned the 'export' regime for unemployment benefits set up in article 69 Regulation 1408/71. Swedish law offered a special benefit to a parent who had to take care of a sick child. That benefit interrupted Swedish unemployment benefits. The question in *Rydergård, 2002* arose whether the period of four weeks under article 69 during which one had to have received unemployment benefits in order to rely on the possibility to 'export' the benefit had to be continuous. The Court reiterated that the regime set up by article 69 went beyond mere coordination and established proper, exhaustive criteria to be fulfilled. However, national law still determined unemployment benefits, and in particular the condition when a person could be considered to have been available to the unemployment services of a member state (paras 25-6). It was not required, though, that the person concerned had been receiving those benefits continuously, provided that the total period amounted to at least four weeks (para. 31).

Unemployed frontier workers

In *De Laat, 2001* the Court dealt with partly unemployed frontier workers. 'Wholly' and 'partially unemployed frontier workers' were Community terms in need of uniform interpretation under article 71(1)(a) Regulation 1408/71 (paras 16-8). A partly unemployed frontier worker was supposed to receive unemployment benefits in the conditions most favourable to finding new employment, like all other unemployed workers, and only one social security legislation was to apply to him. For partly unemployed frontier workers the institutions of the place of residence would not be well placed to help the worker find new employment. A worker who used to work full-time and then was forced to reduce to part-time work maintained the links with the state of employment. He could therefore only lawfully claim benefits in the member state where he was still employed. Only when those links were totally severed would he become a wholly unemployed frontier worker who was entitled to claim benefits in the state where he resided (paras 31-6). *Commission v. Netherlands (frontier worker), 2003* made it plain that the 'export' regime of article 69 Regulation 1408/71 applied also in the context of wholly unemployed frontier workers which were covered by article 71(1)(a)(ii) Regulation 1408/71. Since such workers were only entitled to unemployment benefits from the member state where they resided, that state also had to make available the three months 'export' option to them, when they wanted to seek work in a third member state, i. e. a state other than the member states of former employment or of residence.

In *Adanez-Vega, 2004* a Spanish national who was born in Germany had lived most of his life in Germany, except for a training spell in Spain. He went to serve in Spain's military. Thereafter his claim for unemployment benefits in Germany was rejected for he failed to meet the qualifying period within the reference period, because the period of military service was left out of account. Subject to the national court's assessment of the facts, in particular of whether Mr

Adanez-Vega had maintained residence in Germany during military service, the Court found that German law was applicable by reason either of article 13(2)(f) Regulation 1408/71 with residence being the relevant factor, after the Spanish legislation pursuant to article 13(2)(e) had ceased to apply (paras 23-6), or of article 71(1)(b)(ii) with a worker who was employed in another state than where he resided making himself available to the unemployment services of the state of residence (paras 32-40). However, it was essentially up to Spanish law to determine whether the period of military service constituted a period of employment. If that was the case, Germany would have to aggregate the period pursuant to article 67(3) Regulation 1408/71, if a period had lastly been completed in Germany, except when article 71(1)(b)(ii) applied (para. 49). In that regard, it was irrelevant how much time had lapsed between the period last completed and the point in time when the application for benefits was made, if no other period had been completed in the interim (para. 52).

Family benefits

Family benefits were addressed by the Court in a number of decisions in the 2000s. In *Humer, 2002* the Court came back to the advanced maintenance payments by the Austrian state which had been at issue in *Offermanns, 2001* (and later on in *Laurin Effing, 2005*, see above). In *Humer, 2002* the Court added that a minor child whose parents were employed was able to rely on articles 73 and 74 Regulation 1408/71. Its claim to family benefits following a divorce of the parents was, moreover, not excluded by Regulation 1408/71 (para. 42). When the child moved residence with one of its parents who went to reside in another member state, Austria was not to rely on a residence requirement vis-à-vis the child. For articles 73 and 74 to apply it need not necessarily have been the worker who moved residence, it could be the members of his family, too (paras 48-9). Moreover, not just the worker and the spouse were entitled to apply for family benefits under articles 73 and 74, but also other family members, such as the child, since an individual was not to be considered in isolation under those articles (paras 50-1).

In *Maaheimo, 2002*, a Finnish benefit was at stake. Finland offered a place in a nursery for each child. However, parents could also instead opt for a home care child allowance, if they preferred to care for their child themselves. When Mr Maaheimo was posted to another member state for a year under his employment contract in Finland and his wife accompanied him, the allowance was discontinued because of a residence requirement. According to the Court, the allowance was a family benefit, because it was designed to meet family expenses and alleviate the financial burden on the family (para. 26). Since Finnish law continued to apply to a posted worker pursuant to article 14(1)(a) Regulation 1408/71), article 73 Regulation 1408/71 applied in such a case, because the place of residence differed from the place of employment. Moreover, the benefit was not listed in annex IIa as not exportable. Hence, in particular in the light of the option to choose the home care allowance instead of care in a nursery, the residence requirement was precluded (paras 30-5).

Dodl and Oberhollenzer, 2005 brought the Court back to Austria. In each of the two cases at hand, a wife had worked in Austria, while residing in Germany with her husband who worked in Germany. When she stopped working in Austria due to maternity it was unclear which of the two states had to supply a child raising allowance. Germany relied on the husband and refused an allowance, because he worked. Austria in turn refused an allowance, because the wife did not work, since her employment was suspended according to Austrian law and she did not reside in Austria. Provided that the national court found that the wife was insured in Austria within the sense of Regulation 1408/71 (paras 31-3), according to the Court, in principle the state of employment, i. e. Austria, as the competent state pursuant to articles 13(2)(a) and 73 Regulation 1408/71, was obliged to grant the allowance. However, in the cases at issue a risk of overlapping of benefits arose. In Germany benefits could be due owing to one of the parent's residence, while in Austria they could be due at the same time owing to the wife's employment (para. 50). In such a situation, article 10 Regulation 574/72 as interpreted in *McMenamin, 1992* applied, since employment in the state of residence was given when the couple was considered as a whole. Thus, the reversal of priorities in article 10(1)(b)(i) Regulation 574/72 applied, suspending the competence of the state of employment of the wife in favour of the state of residence, although the husband was not himself entitled to an allowance because of his work in Germany. A proviso was, however, that the wife was entitled to the allowance in Germany, which was the case due to residence (paras 57-62). In the second case, however, the allowance in Germany was excluded, because the income threshold was crossed. The reversal of priorities was then not justified and Austria had to grant the allowance (paras 62-3). This ruling was confirmed later by the Court in *Weide, 2005* for a constellation concerning Luxembourg and Germany. The Court merely clarified what had already been implicit in *Dodl and Oberhollenzer, 2005*, namely that a top-up payment, i. e. a supplement to guarantee the higher benefit pursuant to national law, in that case Luxembourg law, was required (para. 33). In *Bosmann, 2008*, however, the constellation was slightly different. Ms Bosmann alone was working in the Netherlands, while she resided with her family in Germany. A reversal of priorities was not triggered in those circumstances. Article 10(1)(b)(i) Regulation 574/72, i. e. the *Dodl and Oberhollenzer, 2005*-precedent, did not apply, since work was not performed in the state of residence, Germany; neither did article 10(1)(a) Regulation 574/72 apply, because a benefit was not due in the Netherlands, since the children had already passed the age of 18 years (paras 22-5). Therefore, the Netherlands were the regular competent state to provide family benefits. That those benefits had expired in the Netherlands, in contrast to the family benefits under German law, did not imply that Germany was consecutively required by Regulation 1408/71 to grant benefits (para. 27). However, Regulation 1408/71 was not to be relied upon to exclude a benefit that was indeed due under German law alone. More specifically, the German authorities could not lawfully discontinue the payment of the family benefit when Ms Bosmann took up work in the Netherlands after having previously worked in Germany, solely on account of Regulation 1408/71, while German law on its own would require granting the benefit by reason of residence as the sole criterion (paras 27-32).

In *Slanina, 2009* family benefits in Austria had been discontinued, because the mother had moved to reside in Greece with the child. She did not work in Greece, while her former husband, the father of the child, worked in Austria. Subject to the national court's assessment that the child was a member of the family pursuant to article 1(f)(i) Regulation 1408/71, the Court decided that Austria had to continue to pay family benefits in application of article 73. As held in *Humer, 2002*, the fact that the parents were divorced was irrelevant. Moreover, a family member was not to be considered in isolation. The Austrian benefits could only lawfully be discontinued pursuant to article 76 Regulation 1408/71, if the mother took up employment in Greece and if – and in so far as – she thus became entitled to family benefits in Greece.

Family benefits and pensioners

Martínez Domínguez, 2002 concerned the claims of pensioners to family benefits pursuant to articles 78 and 79 Regulation 1408/71. Several persons who were receiving pensions in both Germany and Spain were granted family benefits in Spain, because they were resident there. When the children who were the beneficiaries of the family benefits turned 18 years of age the Spanish benefits ceased. In other cases, the conditions for the award of family benefits in Spain were not met in the first place due to an income ceiling or an option exercised. In those circumstances, the Court judged, those children could not pursuant to articles 77(2)(b)(i) or 78(2)(b)(i) fall back on Germany's family benefits, although German family benefits expired only when the children were older or the benefits would have been available in the first place. As already held in *Bastos Moriana, 1997* and *Gómez Rodríguez, 1998*, the crux was that the German pensions had been awarded in application of Community law. Only when the pensions had been awarded on the basis of national law alone, could the German right to family benefits be activated after the Spanish benefits had come to an end or had not arisen in the first place (para. 25). The same applied if the pension had been awarded on the basis of a convention which had been preserved owing to the *Rönfeldt, 1991*-line of authority, as clarified by *Kaske, 2002*. That case had to be treated as if the relevant pension had been awarded in application of national law alone (para. 31).

Non-discrimination

In a number of social security cases in the 2000s the Court dealt with non-discrimination. Some of those cases have already been discussed, like *Commission v. France (social debt repayment), 2000*. In that case the Court found that the French levy on salaries gained abroad and subject to social security there violated the principle that only one legislation was applicable (see above). For the same reason the Court found that non-discrimination was violated. The principle that only one legislation was to be applied to one and the same worker at a time implemented the principle of equal treatment inherent in articles 48 and 52 Treaty. France had thus created an obstacle which could, furthermore, not be justified by the facts that the contribution levied was minor or that only a limited number of workers was concerned (paras 45-9). The Court ruled identically in *Commission v. France (general social contribution), 2000* (paras 42-6).

Sehrer, 2000 was about a rather particular situation. Mr Sehrer, who was resident in Germany, received an old-age pension in Germany and a supplementary pension in France. Germany subjected the German pension to sickness insurance contributions and added the gross amount of the French supplementary pension, although a French solidarity contribution which fed France's sickness insurance funds but yielded no benefit to Mr Sehrer had already been levied on the latter pension. (The validity of the latter contributions was not challenged in the national proceedings.) As the French pension was paid pursuant to an undeclared industrial agreement, Regulation 1408/71 did not cover it pursuant to article 1(j) Regulation 1408/71. Mr Sehrer, therefore, had to be treated as if he received only one pension, namely in Germany. In those circumstances, Regulation 1408/71 did not apply (para. 27). Instead, article 48 to 51 applied, since his pension was intrinsically linked to his former status as a worker. The German approach, however, disadvantaged those who had made use of their freedom, while it did not so for those who had remained in Germany. Only for the former a risk existed that sickness insurance contributions would be levied twice on the gross amount of their pension (para. 34). Germany could therefore not subject the gross amount of the French pension to contributions again.

In *Borawitz, 2000* Germany distinguished between retroactive pension payments made within Germany and payments directed toward another member state. Such payments in general were only to be made if they exceeded a certain minimum amount. That amount, however, was lower for payments made within Germany than for those directed to another member state. The Court found that this approach clashed with non-discrimination pursuant to article 3 Regulation 1408/71. It essentially had the same effect as a residence requirement, since it affected those residing in Germany less than those living abroad (para. 28). The latter, however, were typically nationals of other member states. There were proportionately more nationals of other member states among those receiving a German pension while residing abroad than among those receiving such a pension while residing in Germany. In other words, the ratio, within the group of persons living *abroad* and receiving a German pension, between Germans and nationals of other member states had to be compared to the same ratio within the group of person living *in* Germany and receiving a pension. Since the first ratio was greater in the case at hand, there was indirect discrimination (paras 29-31). While additional expenses could in theory justify the approach, Germany used a clearing system which had the effect that the cost of payments to recipients established abroad were not different than those of domestic payments. Moreover, the payments could technically just be added to the next tranche of the pension paid in Germany (paras 33-4). Thus, the indirect discrimination was not properly justified.

With *Hervein II, 2002* the compatibility of Regulation 1408/71 with articles 48 to 52 Treaty was questioned in so far as it provided in article 14c(1)(b) in conjunction with annex VII that the legislations of two member states applied at the same time when a person was simultaneously employed in one member state and self-employed in another member state. The Court held that the validity of article 14c(1)(b) could only be judged on its own. The differences resulting in terms of contributions and benefits as such were due to a lack of harmonization and the fact that separate national systems remained in existence (para. 54). The Court admitted that the regime applicable pursuant to article 14c(1)(b) was liable to complicate matters in some cases, as the application of merely one legislation was easier. However, even if only one legislation applied in a given situation similar problems were liable to arise, since typically there were different compulsory schemes within the legislation of one and the same member state which applied to employment and self-employment (paras 55-7). Furthermore, migrant 'workers' could not expect 'neutrality as regard[ed] the complexity [...] of the administration of their social security cover' (para. 58). The Council thus validly undertook to coordinate the social security dimension of such cases and made special provision for them. Finally, even under article 14c(1)(b) it was required that social security contributions basically did not go without return in terms of additional social security protection for the migrant worker (para. 64) and the *Rönfeldt, 1991*-caveat concerning social security conventions had to be respected.

Gaumain-Cerri, 2004 concerned Germany's care allowance scheme, which incidentally also covered the old-age insurance contributions of the third person providing home care to the person insured under the German care scheme. However, those contributions of third persons were only provided, if that third person or, as the case may be, the person reliant on care was resident in Germany. The care allowance was in keeping with *Molenaar, 1998* part of a sickness insurance scheme and the part covering the old-age insurance contributions of the third person a cash sickness benefit for the person reliant on care despite the fact that, sometimes, a private insurer offered the insurance (paras 20-1 and 27). Thus, German legislation applied to the benefit (paras 28-30). There was no need, though, to determine whether a third person providing the care was a worker, because his or her Union citizenship precluded Germany from relying on residence in Germany as a requirement. The requirement established a difference in treatment in comparable situations. Thereby, it discriminated against Union citizens who had made use of their freedom to reside in another member state, while providing care in Germany. Hence, Germany could not lawfully refuse to cover the third persons' old-age insurance contributions under the care allowance scheme (paras 32-5).

In *Chateignier, 2006* the Court dealt with Belgium's unemployment insurance. In accordance with article 67 Regulation 1408/71, Belgium required that migrant workers had worked for at least one day in Belgium, before periods of work in other member states were aggregated for the purpose of Belgian unemployment benefits. However, for Belgian nationals that condition did not apply. They were directly entitled to claim unemployment benefits. According to the Court, that approach was contrary to equal treatment as laid down in article 39 Treaty and article 3 Regulation 1408/71 and, as such, was precluded.

In the judgment in *Celozzi, 2007*, a specific German practice was at stake. Mr Celozzi, an Italian national resident in Germany, had received daily sick pay under German sickness insurance commensurate with the categorization of his income for tax purposes. As a migrant worker, he had been categorized automatically for tax purposes as being separated from his wife, although in reality he was not separated from her; she had just kept residence in Italy. Upon his application he was subsequently re-categorized as married for tax purposes, which had the effect of entitling him to higher sick pay. However, that effect was limited to future sick pay. He applied for the higher sick pay with retroactive effect, i. e. right from when he was first sick, but that application was rejected, for retroactive effect was usually not granted. The Court judged that German practice to be contrary to non-discrimination in article 3 Regulation 1408/71. Sick pay clearly was a cash sickness benefit. Hence, Regulation 1408/71 applied. The German practice of automatically categorizing migrant workers and of refusing retroactive effect when the categorization had been rectified subsequently, for the purpose of sick pay, worked to their disadvantage and was indirectly discriminatory. In particular, the fact that a migrant worker was not informed of a possible change in categorization and that documentation involving the home state was required for re-categorization put him in a less favourable position (paras 31-2). Administrative difficulties – if they were capable of providing justification at all – did not justify the German approach, in particular since retroactive rectification was possible in at least one other case under German law (para. 39).

Agreements with third countries, Ankara

Social security Agreements with third countries were also addressed by the Court in a few decisions. *Alami, 2003* was an application of *Kziber, 1991*. The Belgian seniority supplement to unemployment benefits for workers beyond 50 years of age was an unemployment benefit within the scope of Regulation 1408/71 and, thus, of the Rabat Agreement with Morocco, although it was not mentioned in its article 41(2) (para. 25). As non-discrimination applied pursuant to article 41(1) Rabat Agreement, Belgium could not lawfully require in the case of Moroccan nationals that an international agreement provided for the aggregation of employment periods completed in France in order to meet the Belgian qualifying period, while it did not so require for Belgian nationals (paras 33-4). *Öztürk, 2004* regarded a similar constellation under the Ankara Agreement. Mr Öztürk had worked in Germany and Austria and was receiving in Germany, where he was resident, an early retirement benefit because of old-age unemployment. The corresponding benefit in Austria was refused, as periods completed in Germany were not aggregated for Austria's qualifying period. The Court decided first that Decision 3/80 did not just apply in the member state where the Turkish worker was resident, but in all member states (paras 51-2). Then the Court ruled that the case was not about a question of technical aggregation, which could not be solved in the absence of provisions implementing Decision 3/80, like Regulation 574/72 for Regulation 1408/71. Rather, it was a simple question of taking into account periods completed abroad for a minimum qualifying period (paras 63-5). Non-discrimination pursuant to article 3(1) Decision 3/80 – which also caught the measure at hand since it was liable to affect Turkish workers more than Austrian workers – precluded Austria's refusal to take into account the German periods. That refusal could, moreover, not be justified by the employment policy goal of the early retirement benefit, as it was an old-age rather than an unemployment benefit (para. 67).

In *Echouikh, 2006* France refused to award an invalidity pension based on service in the French army in Indo-China during the 1950s on the ground that Mr Echouikh was not French. Mr Echouikh, a Moroccan national, had claimed that pension based on the Brussels Association Agreement with Morocco which had replaced the Rabat Cooperation Agreement. The Court transposed the relevant Rabat Agreement case-law to the Brussels Agreement, *inter alia* regarding the direct effect of non-discrimination pursuant to article 41(1) Rabat Agreement and article 65(1) Brussels Agreement. A pensioner had to be considered a worker for the purpose of a pension. Service in the army constituted 'work' and a link to France was given, although he had worked abroad, since he had served in the French army (paras 46-7 and 54). Non-discrimination, therefore, precluded France from relying on the Moroccan nationality to refuse a pension (paras 58-60) and it was not necessary to enter into any fundamental rights issue (paras 64-5).

El Youssfi, 2007 concerned a Moroccan national resident in Belgium who in vain claimed the minimum income guaranteed for elderly persons in Belgium. As held in *Nemec, 2006*, Regulation 883/2004, the successor to Regulation 1408/71, did not yet apply for lack of implementing legislation. Regulation 1408/71 had been amended to extend its scope to third country nationals. However, that applied only as far as the situation of such third country nationals concerned at least two member states. Since Ms El Youssfi's situation was confined to Belgium, she was not within the scope of the amended Regulation 1408/71 (paras 41-3). Hence, it was only the Brussels Association Agreement that applied. The benefit was a social security benefit within the meaning of Regulation 1408/71 and the Brussels Agreement (para. 60). The derived rights-approach did not apply under the Agreement in any case (paras 61-2). Ms El Youssfi could lawfully claim the benefit either herself if she had worked, through her husband if he was a worker, or through her son if he was a worker (paras 63-70). Consequently, the guaranteed minimum income could not lawfully be refused on the basis of Ms El Youssfi's Moroccan nationality (paras 54-5). Fundamental rights needed to be applied by the national court (para. 75). Furthermore, for completeness, the order in *Haddad, 2004* has to be mentioned. The Court referred to it twice in *Echouikh, 2006*. It apparently concerned the application of the Rabat Cooperation Agreement to an unemployed student. However, apart from the notice in the Official Journal, which is inconclusive, no other information whatsoever has been published on the case.

Technicalities

Four more judgments dealt with more technical provisions implementing the coordination of social security. *Camarotto, 2001* clarified based on *Baldone, 1997* that article 95a Regulation 1408/71 applied not only to decisions that were final on 1 June 1992, but also to decisions that were taken in proceedings that had been brought before that date, but were still pending at that date. (The rest of the judgment concerned procedural issues of implementation.) In *Gervais Larsy, 2001* the Court held that article 95a(4), (5), and (6) Regulation 1408/71 only applied when an application made for review of a pension was based on the more favourable new provisions inserted by amending Regulation 1248/92. It did not apply when an application concerned the provisions of Regulation 1408/71 as they had been in force before the amendment (para. 31). In applying article 95a(4), (5), and (6) Regulation 1408/71 to the case of Mr Gervais Larsy, the national court had, moreover, committed a serious breach of Community law giving rise to responsibility for damage caused (para. 34 et seq.).

Duchon, 2002 concerned the application of Regulation 1408/71 in Austria to the consequences of an accident that had taken place in Germany in 1968, i. e. before the accession of Austria to the Community. According to Austrian legislation (i) the qualifying period under Austrian disability insurance was waived only when the accident at work had been suffered by a person covered by the Austrian pension insurance scheme. The relevant reference period was, moreover, (ii) prolongated only for periods during which a benefit was received under the Austrian accident insurance scheme. The Court held that Regulation 1408/71 applied in such a situation pursuant to article 94(3) Regulation 1408/71, as the contingency had taken place before entry into force of Regulation 1408/71 but had 'future' effects. In other words, a pension was not claimed as from the accident in 1968, but as from 1 January 1998; it were only those effects, viz. benefits as from 1 January 1998 onwards which were at stake in the case at hand (para. 43). As the waiver of the qualifying period (i) worked to the detriment of migrant workers, it was precluded (para. 29). In the same vein, the prolongation of the reference period exclusively when Austrian benefits were received disadvantaged migrant workers in the sense of article 48 Treaty. In addition, in so far as article 9a Regulation 1408/71 expressly provided that possibility for national law, i. e. to exclude prolongation of the reference period when foreign benefits were paid, it was invalid in the light of article 48 Treaty (paras 38-40).

In *Pasquini, 2003* an application by analogy of the two-year limit in article 94 Regulation 1408/71 was rejected. The Italian authorities had overpaid an Italian pension due to a migrant worker, because they had not been aware that a pension was paid concurrently in Luxembourg. Consequently, the Italian authorities claimed back the amounts overpaid for more than thirteen years. The amount was more than 29'000 Euro. The Court decided that the two-year limit in articles 94 to 95b Regulation 1408/71 could not be applied to the claim for repayment, because it only concerned situations of transition (para. 54). However, for domestic pensions Italian law required a yearly review of income to avoid overpayment for more than a year. Based on the procedural Community principles of equivalence and effectiveness, that review had to apply to the pension at stake as well. As a result, an action for repayment was limited to overpayment for one year (paras 66-9).

Further social security cases

Finally, two more social security judgments were handed down in the 2000s. In *Khalil, 2001* the Court was seized by stateless persons and refugees who wanted to rely on Regulation 1408/71. It was not in dispute that Regulation 1408/71 in general applied to such persons. Incidentally, however, the power of the Community legislature to regulate the social security issues pertaining to stateless persons and refugees, who as such did not enjoy the right of free movement, on the basis of article 51 Treaty was challenged. The Court rejected that challenge by means of a historical reading. Before Regulation 1408/71 had entered into force, the member states had already contracted obligations to treat stateless persons and refugees on an equal basis with their own nationals as regarded social security, notably in the Geneva refugee convention and the New York convention on stateless persons (para. 49). That was repeated in the European convention of 1957 which had served as a model for Regulation 3, which in turn served as the basis of Regulation 1408/71. Not to have included stateless persons and refugees would have meant to establish an entirely separate coordinating regime for those persons only (para. 57). The Community was thus justified in regulating the matter together with the coordination of social security of migrant workers. In the concrete case, however, the stateless persons and refugees could not lawfully rely on Regulation 1408/71, since their cases were all confined to one member state and no factor linked them to any situation governed by Community law (para. 69). They had all come to Germany directly from a third state. Their cases were therefore purely internal to Germany and as such not within the scope of Regulation 1408/71 (paras 69-71). In *Commission v. Greece, 2004*, finally, the Court confirmed without further ado Greece's failure to transpose in time Directive 98/49 on safeguarding the supplementary pension rights of employed and self-employed persons moving within the Community.

4 Services

Posted workers

In the 2000s, the Court decided a long series of posted worker cases. *Mazzoleni, 2001* was the first. The posted workers directive 96/71 was not yet applicable (para. 17). Instead, the Court applied the freedom of services and clarified that the national authorities under proportionality had to take into account a number of points when the host state imposed a minimum wage requirement on the employees of a private security company located in the frontier zone, namely a rotation of the security guards could lawfully be required to carry out a contract with a company in the host state; the application of an additional legislation increased the administrative burden on the company providing the service; to apply the host state's minimum wage could result in wage inequalities within the work force of that company and thus create tension; and it was necessary to compare the overall situation of the workers, i. e. the salaries including social security and taxation (paras 30-40).

In *Finalarte, 2001*, in which the posted workers directive was not yet applicable, either, the Court confirmed the existing services case-law on posted workers, but gave the national court some indications on how to assess justification. Germany required businesses established abroad, like German businesses, to contribute to paid leave funds for the benefit of workers, be they posted or regular workers. The funds financed the salaries of construction workers during holidays which was necessary, because those workers usually worked for an employer only for a brief time. The Court emphasized that the additional burden for foreign businesses seemed to amount to a restriction (paras 35-6). A protectionist intent of the legislature when enacting a measure was not conclusive, but indicative, and called for a more careful, objective assessment by the national court (paras 38-42). That assessment needed to extend to the question whether the workers posted obtained a real, additional advantage owing to the contributions paid (paras 43-51). The Court then examined three distinctions Germany drew between foreign and German businesses with regard to the paid leave fund. (i) That, in contrast to regular German workers, posted workers themselves rather than their employer had a direct claim against the fund did not amount to discrimination, since that approach was more efficient and objective differences existed between foreign and German businesses (paras 62-4). (ii) That foreign businesses had to provide additional information could be justified, provided that controls could not be made on the basis of documents drawn up under 'home' state legislation (paras 69-74). (iii) Discrimination resulted from the fact that posted workers were always treated as a business and consequently became subject to German collective agreements in the construction industry, while German organisational entities in some circumstances were not treated as businesses (paras 81-2).

Construction business

Commission v. Germany (contract labour), 2001 also dealt with the protection of workers in the construction industry, though not in the context of posted workers. German law prohibited the contracting out of labour to fulfil a contract, unless all parties involved within a consortium or, in general, parties belonging to the construction industry in essence were subject to the relevant collective agreements. This was the case for foreign companies only if they had an establishment in Germany (paras 14-7). Moreover, a German branch of a foreign company was only considered to belong to the construction industry and thus to be subject to the relevant collective agreements, if 50 per cent of the staff's working time was spent on construction sites. That requirement had the effect that foreign companies could not lawfully establish a branch in Germany for instance just to launch a project and later contract out labour. The Court, in briefest terms, found a restriction of the freedom of services because of the need for an establishment in Germany, a restriction which the protection of workers did not justify for it was not indispensable (paras 18-23). The working time requirement, in addition, violated the freedom of establishment, as it limited the possibilities for foreign companies to establish purely administrative branches, thus impeding their access to the German market (paras 31-6).

More posted workers

Portugaia, 2002 came back to posted workers, again in the construction business with Germany as host state, while Directive 96/71 on posted workers still did not apply. Germany imposed a minimum salary on the basis of collective agreements to be paid to all workers, including posted workers. In keeping with case-law the Court accepted that approach, subject to the national court's assessment of necessity and proportionality as in *Finalarte, 2001*. Yet Portugaia, a Portuguese company posting workers to Germany, had to have the same possibility as German undertakings to negotiate special collective agreements which lowered the minimum wage, else discrimination resulted (para. 34).

Wolff & Müller, 2004 for the first time applied Directive 96/71 on the posting of workers. German law provided that those German companies who contracted with companies in other member states to post workers to Germany had to guarantee the minimum rates of pay for the workers posted. Accordingly, a posted worker could basically claim her or his salary from two persons, namely her or his employer and the German company. The Court found that approach to be in compliance with Directive 96/71, which left the member states a large margin of discretion in implementation. As it had already been held that a minimum wage could be imposed as a justified restriction of the freedom of services, so could measures to implement a minimum wage (paras 36-7). Yet the national court had to determine whether a restriction arose at all and, under proportionality, examine the legislation at issue objectively and closely, given the protectionist aims pursued by the German legislature. Any practical difficulties in enforcing the minimum salary against the German guarantor and the prevention of unfair competition also had to be taken into account (paras 33 and 38-42).

In *Commission v. Luxembourg (posted workers), 2004* the Court assessed certain conditions Luxembourg law imposed when a company established in another member state posted third country nationals who were lawfully resident in that state to Luxembourg. Was required either an individual work permit issued by Luxembourg subject to the situation in the employment market; or a collective work permit, which Luxembourg exceptionally granted to the entire work force posted, if the workers concerned held employment contracts of indefinite duration with the posting company which had entered into effect at least six months previous to the posting. Moreover, a minimum bank guarantee was to be provided to secure the cost in case the workers needed to be repatriated. The Court found that the free movement of services was impeded, because an additional administrative and financial burden was imposed on the service provider (para. 23). The posting of third country nationals had not yet been harmonised (para. 25). According to the Court, the work permit mechanism was not appropriate to ensure the social protection of workers. A duty to report before the posting of workers would have been just as effective. The mechanism made the deployment of workers considerably more complicated. Short-term service provision became difficult. The social measures adopted by the 'home' state of the service provider or in an agreement concluded by the Community with a third state were not factored in, either (paras 30-6). The discretion the authorities had to grant the permit – they took the situation in the labour market into account – was not warranted by the need to avoid disturbances of the labour market, since the posted workers did not seek access to that market (paras 38-43). An obligation imposed on the service provider to furnish information was, in addition, just as well suited to protect the labour market as the conditions relating to the employment contracts (paras 44-6). The bank guarantee was excessive, too. An order to pay the cost when third country nationals had to be repatriated was just as effective (para. 47). The free movement of services, thus, precluded Luxembourg's measure.

Commission v. Germany (minimum wage), 2005 concerned the elements to be taken into account under Directive 96/71 to determine the minimum wage to be paid under the law of the host state. The Commission had claimed that certain bonuses an employer paid to workers posted to Germany had to be taken account of when it was calculated whether those workers' remuneration was equivalent to the minimum wage payable by law in Germany. Germany had accepted most of the Commission's claims with regard to additional payments. As that acceptance was belated, the Court ruled that the Directive and the freedom of services had been violated (paras 29-33 and 41-2). For the rest, the Court ruled that the Commission's claims were either unclear or unfounded, because quality bonuses and bonuses for dirty, dangerous, or heavy work were not to be considered constituent elements of the minimum wage (paras 39-40).

Commission v. Germany (posted workers), 2006 ruled in a similar vein as *Commission v. Luxembourg (posted workers), 2004*. The visa Germany required for third country nationals posted from another member state to Germany, which (the visa) was handed out within seven days without being subject to the authorities' discretion or any substantive condition, and the requirement that a worker posted to Germany had been employed for at least a year by the company posting her or him, both contradicted the free movement of services. A prior declaration, instead of an advance control measure resulting in a visa, sufficed to prevent abuse of the freedom of services and to guarantee the protection of the workers (paras 33-50). In particular, ensuring that a posting of workers was lawful was certainly in the interest of both the service provider and the host state, but the responsibility for unlawful conduct could not be imposed on those who did comply (para. 50). Furthermore, a simple prior declaration, rather than the condition of having been employed for at least a year, also ensured equally effectively that the worker was in lawful and habitual employment within the meaning of *Vander Elst, 1994* with the company posting him or her to Germany (paras 55-62). Similarly, in the light of the option of a prior declaration, the Court struck down Austria's legal provisions applicable in cases of postings of third country nationals in *Commission v. Austria (posted workers), 2006*. Austrian law required the company posting workers *de facto* to seek prior authorization and to have employed the workers for at least a year or under non-temporary contracts (paras 41-57). Moreover, it was impossible by law to regularise on site the situation of workers lawfully employed but posted without visa (paras 61-7).

In *Commission v. Germany (posted workers), 2007* the Commission again challenged some rules Germany imposed on undertakings posting workers to Germany. The Court decided that the Commission had failed to establish an infringement by the requirement that undertakings paid contributions to a German paid-leave fund on behalf of the workers they posted to Germany, unless a similar obligation existed in the 'home' state. It was not proven that the workers did not receive additional social security protection based on the contributions or that the requirement was disproportionate, as posited in *Finalarte, 2001* (paras 50-54). The free movement of services was not infringed by Germany's requirement that the posting undertaking held available on site four documents in German for each worker, namely the contract, pay-slips, time-sheets, and proof of payment of wages. The restriction resulting from the additional expenses caused by that requirement was justified by the social protection of the workers and the need to monitor that protection. Monitoring would be extremely difficult if those four documents, which need not have been held available after the posting or the project had ended, were only accessible in a foreign language. The documents were often simple, for national law standardized them. A multilingual Community instrument did not exist. Information exchange between authorities was not an alternative, since the authorities in the 'home' state did not have those documents available (paras 66-79). In contrast, the notification of the authorities required when the posted workers began to work or changed the place where they worked violated the freedom of services. It was discriminatory, since German undertakings were not subject to such an obligation. As such it was only susceptible of justification by grounds expressly mentioned in the Treaty. None of those grounds was pertinent in this case, though (paras 84-7).

Laval, 2007 was handed down on the same day as *Viking, 2007*. Both cases raised similar issues, though in different circumstances, and the Court addressed them in the same way. In *Laval, 2007* a Latvian company posted workers to Sweden to fulfil a construction contract through its subsidiary. The workers posted were subject to collective agreements in Latvia. Laval refused to conclude a collective agreement in Sweden, because an agreement necessarily left open in accordance with Swedish law for later negotiation the salaries to be paid to the workers. Swedish law, including the collective agreements, did not establish a mandatory minimum wage to be paid to workers. Because of Laval's refusal to conclude an agreement collective action was commenced. Ultimately, that collective action forced Laval to bail, its subsidiary in Sweden filing for bankruptcy. Since Directive 96/71 on the posting of workers was applicable *ratione temporis*, the Court found that the freedom of services was to be applied in the light of the Directive. The Directive allowed a member state to lay down a mandatory minimum wage. Conversely, a member state, such as Sweden, could opt not to implement that option, but consequently it could not lawfully force a minimum wage upon an undertaking posting workers to its territory or an obligation to negotiate such a wage on a case-by-case basis. In a similar vein, Sweden could not require an undertaking posting workers to Sweden to comply with provisions going beyond the mandatory rules for minimum protection as laid down in the Directive (paras 63-84). As ruled in *Viking, 2007* for freedom of establishment, the Court held for freedom of services that collective action, including the right to strike as a fundamental right, was not outside the purview of the market freedom. The collective action taken to force Laval into complying with terms not made mandatory for all operators in the Swedish construction business constituted a restriction of the freedom of services. Balancing the market freedom against the social policy, including the protection of workers, mentioned in the Treaty, the Court found that the collective action as an obstacle to the freedom of services was not justified in a context in which national law did not establish a clear mandatory minimum wage (paras 86-110). Finally, a particular aspect of Swedish law amounted to discrimination. Swedish law in essence prevented Swedish unions from taking collective action to force amendment of a Swedish collective agreement. In case of a collective agreement concluded in the 'home' state by an undertaking posting workers, such as with the collective agreement concluded by Laval in Latvia, that obligation did not apply, resulting in the possibility for Swedish unions to take collective action and the impossibility for Laval to oppose that action. That distinction constituted discrimination which violated the freedom of services and for which the grounds expressly mentioned by the Treaty did not provide justification (paras 112-9).

Rüffert, 2008 again concerned the posting of workers in the framework of Directive 96/71 and the freedom of services. A German company had concluded a contract with a German land to do construction work in a prison. In that contract, the German company had agreed as required by the law of the German land to abide by a collective agreement which contained a minimum wage to be paid to construction workers. The German company sub-contracted part of the work to a Polish company which then posted workers to the construction site in Germany. The Polish company paid those workers less than the minimum wage required by the collective agreement the German company had agreed to abide by. The Court refused to qualify that collective agreement as universal within the meaning of the Directive. The law of the Land seeking to make binding the collective agreement by means of a contract concluded with the contractor did not amount to a declaration of universal applicability, in particular because the German act implementing Directive 96/71 did not contain any provision having that effect and because the collective agreement covered only a part of the construction sector. Hence, the Polish company could not be held to the standard of the collective agreement (paras 24-31). The freedom to provide services confirmed that reading. The minimum wage imposed by means of the collective agreement was an obstacle to the free provision of services by the Polish company. That obstacle was not justified by the needs to protect workers, the independence in the organization of working life by trade unions, or the balance of the host state's social security system, in essence because the collective agreement was not universally applicable in the host state (paras 37-42).

In *Commission v. Luxembourg (posted workers), 2008* the Commission took issue with Luxembourg's subsuming a whole series of measures implementing Directive 96/71 under the public policy exception in this Directive. The Court stated that article 3(1) Directive contained an exhaustive list of matters in which each member state could prioritise its own rules and apply them to workers posted to its territory. The public policy exception in article 3(10), in turn, only concerned provisions that were so essential for the protection of the political, social, or economic order of the host state that they had to be applied to all persons in that state's territory and that there could be no derogation from them. The exception had to be strictly construed. Moreover, those provisions had to comply with the freedom of services (paras 24-33). That was not the case for several of Luxembourg's rules. The condition for posted workers to comply with all of Luxembourg's rules concerning written contracts of employment was not covered by the public policy exception, since a Community directive, viz. Directive 91/533, had imposed on each state certain requirements in this regards. The 'home' state thus already ensured compliance with those requirements and the worker was sufficiently protected. Luxembourg's rule failed to take that into account and deterred foreign undertakings from posting workers (paras 35-43). For the same reason, Luxembourg could not lawfully impose compliance with its rules on part-time and fixed-time work under the cover of public policy (paras 57-60). It could not lawfully be required that all rates of remuneration be automatically adjusted to the cost of living in Luxembourg based on the public policy exception, either. The list in article 3(1) already governed the aspect of the minimum wage. Luxembourg had failed to establish the prerequisite serious threat to one of the fundamental interests of society (paras 45-54). Collective agreements were only to be imposed as far as they were universally applicable (paras 64-67). Luxembourg's monitoring regime also lacked clarity in that it was uncertain whether it required prior notification (paras 78-80). The role of the ad-hoc agent to be designated in Luxembourg who held the documents required, finally, could be fulfilled by a worker posted to Luxembourg. In any case, in the absence of further justification it could only lawfully be required for the duration of the project for which the workers had been posted (paras 85-95).

In *Commission v. Belgium (posted workers), 2009* the Commission initially challenged Belgium, because Belgium's regulation required a set of document to be provided when third country nationals were posted to Belgium. However, it turned out that Belgium's requirements were satisfied by the production of a form E 101, a posting certificate issued by the social security authority of the state of origin, or any other possible evidence. That, the Court held, accorded with the possibility established in case-law to require prior notice in case of posting of third country nationals (paras 12-9).

Medical services

With *Smits, 2001* the Court began to develop the medical services case-law initiated in *Kohll, 1998*. In contrast to *Kohll, 1998*, *Smits, 2001* concerned hospital services, i. e. *intra* rather than *extra muros*. The Dutch system was based on contractual arrangements between sickness insurance funds and hospitals. Benefits in kind were provided and a contractual hospital was then reimbursed by the fund concerned. Any treatment sought in non-contractual hospitals, including hospitals established abroad, was subject to prior authorization by the sickness insurance fund concerned. According to Dutch law that authorization had to be given when the treatment sought was in accordance with medical standards and medically necessary in the light of Dutch standards. The Court refused to limit the scope of the freedom of services to services provided *extra muros*. The freedom of services applied, although benefits were provided in kind. In case of hospital care abroad the patient usually had to advance payment and then claim the sum back from the fund. Flat rate payment under contractual arrangements in any event constituted consideration for services (paras 53-8). The authorization requirement on which reimbursement of cost incurred abroad depended amounted to a restriction, for most non-contractual hospitals were situated abroad (paras 62-9). While the grounds put forward in *Kohll, 1998* to justify the restriction of services, viz. maintaining the financial balance of the system, a balanced service open to all, treatment capacity, medical competence, and satisfying planning requirements, did ultimately not prevail in that case, in *Smits, 2001* those grounds won out for the authorization of *intra muros* treatment. With hospitals, cost and wastage had to be controlled and increasing demands for services had to be met with limited financial means; a high quality of services had to be assured (paras 72-81). However, the authorization criteria applied had to be based on international standards of science, with reimbursement of a specific treatment under the insurance systems of other member states being indicative of such standards; under no circumstance could the place where a hospital was established be a criterion. Yet a member state could lawfully limit reimbursement to specific treatments, e. g. by means of a list; and it was not necessary to extend reimbursement solely because other member states were more liberal. Medical necessity of the treatment abroad, that is whether the same treatment was available without undue delay in a contractual hospital, i. e. in the Netherlands, as a criterion was in order, though it was not to be used to prefer Dutch hospitals over hospitals in other member states. Finally, the standard case-law regarding authorizations requiring objective standards made public in advance and procedural guarantees and precluding any discretion of authorities had to be complied with (paras 83-106).

Müller-Fauré, 2003 again concerned the Dutch sickness benefit scheme, prompting the Court to reiterate in a first step what had been ruled for *intra muros* treatment in *Smits, 2001*. The Court spelled out, though, that the question whether treatment was available in the 'home' state 'within undue delay' was to be decided in the light of a specific patient's condition and situation (para. 90). The existence of waiting lists as such did not automatically mean that there was no 'undue delay' and, therefore, did not in itself justify a refusal to grant the authorization to seek treatment abroad (para. 92). In a second step, the Court in *Müller-Fauré, 2003* held for *extra muros* treatment – which, as the Court admitted, was sometimes distinguishable from *intra muros* treatment only with difficulty (para. 75) – that a prior authorization requirement was contrary to the freedom of services. The grounds that prevailed in *Smits, 2001* for *intra muros* treatment and justified the restriction of free movement of services failed to win out for *extra muros* treatment. There was no evidence that the financial balance of the system concerned was undermined, if the prior authorization requirement was abandoned (para. 93). Patients would not travel abroad in masses to seek medical treatment *extra muros*, either (para. 95). Mainly frontier regions were concerned and in practice doctors established abroad already had concluded agreements allowing the costs to be reimbursed (para. 96). The impact on social security systems based on benefits in kind would be limited, since *inter alia* article 22 Regulation 1408/71 already required such systems to be adjusted so that they allowed for reimbursement of the cost for treatment received abroad (paras 105 and 102). The member states still had the power to lay down the limits of the cost to be covered and the conditions to be met, such as the prior consultation of a general medical practitioner, provided they did so without discriminating or creating obstacles to the freedom of services (paras 106-7). The legislation of the state to the social security system of which the person concerned was affiliated continued to apply and determined the benefits and the cover available, in contrast to when article 22 Regulation 1408/71 was applied (para. 98).

Leichtle, 2004 added to that case-law. Mr Leichtle was a civil servant in Germany who received health cure in a spa in Italy. He had not waited for the outcome of court proceedings that arose over the authorization needed for such cure to be covered by the German social security scheme he was affiliated with. Instead he had gone on to have the treatment and had sought reimbursement afterwards. The German scheme covered the cost only if a medical report confirmed that the treatment abroad was absolutely necessary owing to the greatly increased chances of success of the cure abroad. The relevant spa had to be included in a list of spas recorded by the scheme. The dispute was about the 'ancillary' cost of the treatment only, namely the cost of travel, lodging, board, visitor's tax, and the cost of a medical report at the end of the cure. The Court ruled that the ancillary cost was closely connected or inextricably linked to the treatment which qualified as medical services. Whether the cost was covered or not influenced the decision where to seek services. The issue was, therefore, within the scope of the freedom of services (paras 31-6). The additional report required on the necessity of the treatment abroad was an obstacle to service provision, in contrast to the general criteria of eligibility. It applied only to services provided abroad and thus discouraged such services (paras 37-42). A state was, indeed, free in general to set objective, transparent, and non-discriminatory limits to the treatments covered. Yet an additional report was not necessary to ensure the financial equilibrium of the social security scheme or to guarantee treatment capacity or medical competence (paras 46-7). It was for the national court to determine whether the need for a spa to be registered in Germany to qualify for reimbursement had a deterrent effect (paras 49-50). In keeping with *Vanbraekel, 2001*, if the person concerned had not awaited a court decision, but rather advanced the expenditures and the final outcome of court proceedings was that they were covered, the person had to be reimbursed (paras 53-8).

In *Watts, 2006* the Court then examined the authorization required by the British national health system, which was funded by public finances and essentially provided health treatment free of charge, to seek treatment abroad in the light of the freedom of services. For the *intra muros*-treatment at issue in the case, the Court first confirmed that article 22 Regulation 1408/71 had to be interpreted congruently with the corresponding medical services case-law under the free movement of services, in particular as to the question of undue delay (para. 60; see above). Both article 22 and the freedom of services could apply concurrently (paras 46-8). Apart from that, the authorization to seek treatment abroad constituted a restriction of the freedom of services which applied even to a free of charge-system such as the British, because it was not required for treatment in hospitals affiliated with the British national health system (paras 97-8). While a prior authorization required for hospital treatment abroad was as such compatible with the freedom of services, each of the conditions under which the authorization was granted had to be tested against that freedom. As established by the case-law on authorizations, discretion by the authorities was ruled out; criteria had to be made public in advance; a decision had to be subject to procedural review and where necessary be based on expert opinions; and it had to include the reasons based on which it had been adopted (paras 114-7). Certain other factors, however, were not to be factored in, like a potential distortion of the regular order of priorities due to urgency as expressed in waiting lists or the facts that funds needed to change to cover the cost of the treatment abroad or that medical services had to be compared for the purpose of reimbursement. The member states could be required to adapt their systems to realize the internal market freedoms. Hence a mechanism for reimbursement had to be established (paras 118-22). As to the amount to be reimbursed, the Court found that an obstacle to the free reception of services could arise where the legislation of the host state did not provide for full cover of a specific treatment, while the treatment in the 'home' state was free of charge. In such a case, the 'home' state, in this case the United Kingdom, had to top up. It also had to reimburse the difference between the actual amount charged and the amount covered in accordance with host state legislation, though only up to the objective value of the treatment in the 'home' state. To establish that value the United Kingdom could orient itself by means of the amounts the British national health system charged foreigners for specific treatments they received in the United Kingdom (paras 131-3). As to the ancillary cost of travel and accommodation incurred because of the treatment received abroad, the Court found that such cost was only to be covered in so far as it was paid for in case of treatment within the United Kingdom. It was also possible to impose objective and transparent limits (paras 139-42). Beyond the limitations the case-law established for the authorization to seek treatment abroad further budgetary considerations could not be taken account of (paras 145-7).

In *Stamatelaki, 2007* the Court further refined the medical services case-law. Greek law excluded the reimbursement of cost that arose from treatment in private hospitals abroad, save for children under the age of 14. The national court asked the question exclusively with regard to the freedom of services. That is why the Court refrained from addressing article 22 Regulation 1408/71. The Greek sickness insurance scheme established a restriction of the freedom of services which applied to private and public hospitals alike (para. 22), as treatment in Greek private hospitals under contract or in emergency cases was covered, while treatment in private hospitals abroad was not (paras 26-8). The grounds of justification acknowledged in the medical services case-law applied in this case equally, but the Greek measure was disproportionate. Instead of a downright exclusion of reimbursement it would have been possible to grant reimbursement only for treatment that had been authorized previously or within certain limits, for instance in accordance with a scale of reimbursable cost. Moreover, the controls to which foreign hospitals were subject in other member states as well as the professional qualifications of doctors working in foreign hospitals guaranteed the quality of the services provided in those hospitals (paras 35-7).

Games of chance

Anomar, 2003 confirmed the Court's gambling case-law established in the 1990s. Portugal subjected the operation of gaming and gambling machines to a licence requirement and restricted it to certain designated places, such as casinos. Several Portuguese companies challenged that regulation. The Court, after having admitted the case since the national court could be in need of an answer to exclude reverse discrimination in an otherwise purely internal situation (paras 39-42), found that all games of chance and gambling constituted economic activities (para. 47). The free movement of services was affected, because Portugal's rules addressed the operation of gambling machines as a service rather than their import – in the latter case the free movement of goods and the provisions on monopolies would have been applicable (paras 55-6 and 59-60). The indiscriminate restriction imposed by Portugal (paras 65-6) could be justified by the grounds developed in the case-law, i. e. the need to protect the consumer combined with the need to maintain order (73-4), while the proportionality of the restriction was to be assessed by the national authorities, which were entitled to disregard lower standards of protection set by other member states (paras 78-80 and 87).

Lindman, 2003 again concerned lotteries. Finland taxed the winnings from a lottery in Sweden in the hands of the winner, while winnings in Finnish lotteries remained tax-free. The Court reiterated that the freedom of services applied to lotteries. Finland drew a distinction based on where the lottery was organised and this distinction induced players to participate in domestic lotteries in which the winnings were not taxed. The taxes paid by the Finnish organizer of lotteries in Finland could not be likened to the taxes levied on the foreign lottery winnings of the winner (paras 21-2). The distinction was not justified, as no evidence proved that participation in foreign lotteries, in contrast to domestic lotteries, increased the risks inherent in gambling (para. 26).

In *Liga Portuguesa and Bwin, 2009* the Court further refined that gambling case-law. Portugal reserved all games of chance, i. e. lotteries, betting, etc., including those provided via internet, to a single national public provider. Bwin was established in Gibraltar where it lawfully offered online games of chance, including sports betting based on football matches of the Portuguese football league. Bwin also sponsored that league as well as some football clubs. The Portuguese authorities fined Bwin. The Court examined only the freedom of services, since any capital movement was entirely secondary to the provision of gambling services (para. 47). The restriction in the prohibition to offer games of chance via internet was justified by the need to fight crime. Portugal was free to determine the level of protection required. The proportionality of Portugal's measure was to be assessed with regard to Portugal only. That Bwin lawfully offered services in one state did not necessarily imply that another state had to tolerate the provision of the same service. The aim to fight crime was pursued in a consistent and systematic way. Given that harmonisation had not taken place, it was appropriate to reserve the online offer of games of chance to a single national provider which was under strict control of the state. In the domain of online gambling the risk of fraud was high, because the consumer did not enter into personal direct contact with the service provider. Moreover, the combination of sponsoring with the provision of gambling services in one and the same company created the risk of the outcome of sporting events being influenced. Hence, the restriction was justified (paras 60-71).

Taxes

In the 2000s, the Court was practically inundated with services cases having a tax dimension. In the following, the cases are described in roughly chronological order. *Commission v. Portugal (flight tax), 2001* established that the freedom of services-case-law applied to taxes on air services. Consequently, the applicable Regulation 2408/92 on access to air routes had to be read in the light of that case-law (paras 21-2). Portugal had levied higher security and passenger services taxes on international than on domestic and regional flights. The obstacle to cross-border services thus created was not justified. Portugal had failed to demonstrate any difference in the services offered to passengers depending on whether their flight was domestic or international. While a special treatment for flights to the Portuguese Azores and Madeira would have been in order, the taxes in question were not designed to address that situation. Finally, to treat all flights equally in terms of taxation did not imply that the fees had to be raised for domestic flights (paras 27-36). In the same vein, the Commission in *Commission v. Italy (departure tax), 2001* challenged the higher departure tax Italy levied on international flights. Italy did not dispute the violation of the freedom of services and the Court adjudicated accordingly.

De Coster, 2001 also dealt with taxes. A municipality in Belgium had introduced a tax on satellite dishes. That it was a local authority that had introduced the tax, according the Court, was irrelevant (para. 27). According to the Court's case-law, the free movement of services covered broadcasting of television signals. The tax only affected signals received via satellite, but not those received via cable. As many foreign television programmes could only be received via satellite dish, the tax dissuaded viewers in the municipality concerned from receiving services from abroad. It also hindered the activities of operators in the field of satellite transmission and gave broadcasters in Belgium an advantage (paras 31-5). The control of the proliferation of satellite dishes and thus the preservation of the quality of the environment – if acceptable at all as a ground for justification – did not compensate the restriction, since other less restrictive means would have been available, such as requirements as to the size and position of dishes (paras 37-8).

In *Danner, 2002* Mr Danner, a German-Finnish dual national, voluntarily continued to pay contributions under a pension insurance scheme established in Germany when he moved to Finland. However, Finland refused to allow him to deduct the contributions he continued to pay from his taxable income in Finland to the same extent contributions paid to a voluntary pension insurance scheme established in Finland would have been deductible. According to the Court, the freedom of insurers to offer the service of voluntary pension insurance (paras 25-7) was restricted, since residents of Finland were deterred from taking out policies with insurers established abroad and the latter from offering them in Finland. Tax relief was an important consideration in the decision to take out a voluntary pension insurance policy (paras 30-1). The cohesion of the Finnish tax system, viz. the *Bachmann, 1992*-ground, failed to justify the restriction, as under Finnish law the income eventually resulting from voluntary pension insurance would be taxable in Finland if the person concerned was resident there, regardless of whether contributions had been deducted previously or not. The double taxation convention with Germany did not alter that assessment (paras 35-41). The need for effective fiscal supervision did not justify the restriction, either, given Directive 77/799 on mutual assistance and the possibility to ask the taxpayer for documentation (paras 48-52). Finally, the aim of preventing the reduction of tax revenue was not a suitable ground to justify a restriction (paras 54-6).

Taxation in the framework of pension insurance was also at issue in *Skandia and Ramstedt, 2003*. In this case, a Swedish company had taken out a pension insurance policy for the benefit of an employee with a company established in another member state. The Swedish tax authorities refused to deduct immediately the contributions the employer paid under that policy, because Swedish law allowed immediate deduction only if the insurer was established in Sweden. If it was established abroad, premiums paid could essentially be deducted only once the pension was paid out. According to the Court, Swedish tax law unlawfully restricted the freedom of insurers established in other member states to provide services in Sweden. That freedom applied, because the premiums the employer paid constituted the consideration for the service the employee received (paras 22-4). It was restricted, because foreign insurers were dissuaded from offering pension policies in Sweden, as were Swedish employers from taking out policies with foreign insurers (paras 27-8). The cohesion of the Swedish tax system was not in peril, because an employer which had taken out a policy with an insurer established abroad did not benefit from any compensatory measure that set off the disadvantage suffered, namely the delayed deductibility. The pension paid out was subject to income tax in the hands of the employee at the same time and in the same way irrespective of where the insurer was established (paras 34-7). Again as in *Danner, 2002*, Directive 77/799 on mutual assistance and proof furnished by the taxpayer guaranteed the effectiveness of fiscal supervision (paras 41-5). Further, the need to preserve the tax base could not justify the Swedish compensatory tax approach (paras 51-3). A final ground Sweden argued was rejected by the Court, in essence because the argument was hardly understandable at all (paras 57-8.)

Gerritse, 2003 dealt with the direct taxation of income in the light of the freedom of services. Mr Gerritse was resident in the Netherlands where he earned around 55'000 German mark. He went to Germany to perform as a drummer.

For this performance he gained a little more than 6'000 mark, while he incurred expenses of about 1'000 mark. The German authorities taxed this income at the source at a rate of 25 per cent and refused to allow deduction of the expenses. Had he been resident in Germany, roughly the first 12'000 mark of income would not have been taxable at all, but his income would have been subject to progressive taxation at the source and expenses would have been fully deductible. Mr Gerritse could not request taxation as a resident for two reasons, namely he earned more than 12'000 mark abroad and he did not earn more than 90 per cent of his income in Germany. The Court examined the situation from the angle of the free movement of services, because Mr Gerritse was not established in Germany. First, the free movement of services ruled out the non-deductibility of business expenses, because they were connected to the generation of the earnings. Residents and non-residents were, therefore, in a comparable situation and the consequent discrimination was precluded (paras 27-29). Second, with regard to the taxation at the source at a flat rate of 25 per cent, the Court enquired into whether the difference in the situations of residents and non-residents was such to make it possible to disregard the discrimination (para. 47). The 12'000 mark tax-free allowance granted solely to residents could, according to the Court, lawfully be reserved to residents, in particular since it was possible for those who earned more than 90 per cent of their income in Germany to be treated like residents. Moreover, the Netherlands granted a similar tax-free advantage on income taxable in the Netherlands (paras 48-52). As to progressivity, the Court explained that the Netherlands also applied a progressive tax rate after having integrated the income gained abroad. Thus, the situation of residents and non-residents in Germany was comparable in that regard and, consequently, a higher tax burden for non-residents would be precluded. To determine whether the tax burden was indeed higher the national court had to add the net income – 6'000 mark minus expenses – to the tax-free allowance – 12'000 mark – and then see whether the application of the progressive table for residents resulted in a lower tax rate than the 25 per cent-rate generally applicable to non-residents (paras 53-4).

In *Stylianakis, 2003* the Court invalidated Greece's distinction in the passenger tax on flights. Twice the amount of tax was levied in case of flights covering a distance of more than 750 kilometres than in case of those covering a shorter distance. All flights covering the shorter distance, bar one, were domestic. This fact, according to the Court, made the free movement of services more difficult. That freedom applied because it expressed specifically the prohibition of discrimination of Union citizens (paras 18-20). It was applicable in the transport sector where it was implemented by Regulation 2408/92 on access to air routes (para. 24). Even if the tax constituted consideration for services, passengers of international flights did not require twice as many services as passengers flying domestically (paras 25-8).

In *Commission v. France (fixed levy), 2004* natural persons who took out certain contracts, such as debt instruments or deposits, with persons established in

France could opt for a fixed levy at the source on the proceeds from those contracts rather than the taxation of the proceeds as regular income. That option was not available for contracts concluded with persons established abroad. The Court found that the services offered by foreign companies became less attractive, because they could not offer the fixed levy option. Service recipients were, consequently, discouraged from concluding contracts with foreign service providers. That the advantage the fixed levy offered was in some circumstances minor was irrelevant. Service recipients usually only opted for it when it was advantageous (paras 22-5). The effectiveness of fiscal supervision and the prevention of tax avoidance did not justify a presumption of such a general nature as that applied by France. Proportionality was crucial when a national rule excluded trans-border transactions from its scope altogether. The simplicity of the French approach and the administrative difficulties involved in applying the fixed levy to foreign service providers were not valid grounds of justification. Directive 77/799 on mutual assistance was sufficient to guarantee cooperation, any banking secrecy notwithstanding. As an alternative, moreover, France could require foreign service providers to file a voluntary annual declaration (paras 27-33).

In *Viacom, 2005* the Court validated a tax an Italian municipality levied on advertisements displayed in the public space of the municipality. The tax, the level of which was modest, was levied from the agent providing the service of displaying the ads for a third person. The Court did not find a restriction. The tax applied equally to all agents providing the service, no matter where the service receiver was established or where the product or service advertised originated from. The level was modest. Moreover, it only applied to ads placed outdoors (paras 37-8).

Fournier, 2005 dealt with a tax credit for research expenses in France. According to French law, expenses made to conduct research gave rise to a tax credit as long as the research was conducted in France. In the judgment of the Court this approach violated the free movement of services. The cost of research services provided by a company established in another member state was not tax creditable for the service receiver established in France, while in case the service provider was established in France they were. That differentiation based on the places of service provision and, indirectly, establishment was contrary to the freedom of services, despite the principle of fiscal territoriality (paras 15-8). It was not justified by the cohesion of the tax system for lack of a direct link between the corporation tax and the tax credit for research expenses. While the promotion of research basically was a ground to justify a restriction, the French measure ran directly counter to the Community's policy aim of encouraging research within the area of the internal market. The effectiveness of fiscal supervision did not prevail, either. A taxpayer had to have the possibility to prove that research conducted abroad had given rise to relevant expenses (paras 21-5).

In *Mobistar, 2005* two municipalities in Belgium levied taxes on mobile telephony antennae and other communication infrastructure. According to the

Court, while those taxes added additional cost to the provision of services, they affected in the same way all service provision, no matter whether across the border or within Belgium. Such measures were outside the scope of services. Moreover, the taxes applied indistinctly and affected the tariffs of all service providers equally. There was no cumulation of local taxes that had the effect of compromising the freedom of services (paras 31-4).

In *Commission v. Finland (VAT), 2006* the Court in the light of the relevant value added tax directive invalidated Finland's requirement for those not established in Finland to appoint an agent there when value added tax became payable in Finland. Given that the value added tax directive regulated the matter exhaustively, there was, according to the Court, no need to apply the freedom of services (para. 55).

Scorpio, 2006 concerned certain German tax rules which obliged certain service receivers established in Germany to retain at the source the income tax a service provider established in the Netherlands owed in Germany as a consequence of the service provision, in this case artistic and cultural performances subject to income tax in Germany. Failure to retain the tax resulted in the liability of the service receiver vis-à-vis the German state. Business expenditures the service provider had incurred could not be deducted right away from the amount retained, but only in a subsequent procedure. The benefits due under the double taxation convention between the Netherlands and Germany could only be claimed, if a German office had certified that the conditions to be fulfilled were met. The duty to retain taxes did not apply in case the service provider was established in Germany. The case at issue concerned specifically a Dutch-German cooperation in the organization of concerts, as a result of which the German company involved incurred liability for having failed to retain the tax due at source. The Court ruled that the duty to retain the tax due and the liability in case of failure to do so constituted restrictions of the free movement of services, because service receivers were deterred from calling on providers established abroad. However, the Court found the restrictions legitimate, appropriate, and proportionate, and thus justified by the need to collect income tax effectively (paras 33-8). The Court pointed out, though, that the facts had taken place before the Maastricht Treaty had entered into force. Moreover, no legal instrument governed mutual administrative assistance for debt recovery between the Netherlands and Germany (para. 36). In contrast, expanding on *Gerritse, 2003*, that expenditures directly connected to the service provision were only refunded in an ex post facto procedure amounted to an unjustifiable restriction. The service provider had to have the possibility to report expenses directly related to the service, but only those expenses – though a member state was free to allow that other expenses were taken account of (para. 51) – to the service receiver who would then have to take them into account (paras 42-8). As to the certificate attesting that tax needed not to be retained owing to the double taxation convention, the Court held the restriction of the freedom of services inherent in the requirement to obtain such a certificate to be justified. The service receiver could only be released from the obligation to retain the tax at source once it was definitely certain that no tax was due, else the proper functioning of the procedure for taxation at source was compromised (paras 56-60). Finally, when the service provider was a third country national the freedom of services was not applicable, irrespective of whether the service provider was established in a member state or not and whether the service was provided within the Community (paras 66-8).

In *Commission v. Belgium (contractors), 2006* an approach was at stake that was quite different from that in *Scorpio, 2006*. Belgium required all those in the construction industry who contracted with service providers who were not registered in Belgium to withhold a certain amount of the payment due under the contract to secure possible tax debts of the non-registered contractor. Moreover, both contractors became jointly liable for tax debts owed by the non-registered contractor in Belgium as a result not just of the contract they had concluded, but more generally of any activity in Belgium. According to the Court, the issue of the registration of the contractor could be separated from the withholding/liability obligations (paras 13-4). Each of those obligations constituted a restriction of the freedom of services for they deterred service provision. It was irrelevant that the joint liability applied indistinctly to all providers who were not registered in Belgium, for it was sufficient, so the Court, that it impeded access to the Belgian market (paras 30-2). The obligations were not justified by the prevention of tax fraud. The duty to withhold a part of the payment due under a contract was too general to combat fraud and failed to take into account the specific circumstances of each case. In essence, not everyone who had not been registered in Belgium committed tax fraud. Nor was everyone liable to pay tax in Belgium in the first place. Less restrictive measures, such as a system to exchange information with the tax authorities on such contracts, would have been available. The joint liability could also be replaced by less restrictive means, such as the possibility to prove tax compliance. Moreover, the withholding obligation and the joint liability applied cumulatively (paras 34-41).

Centro Equestre, 2007 concerned taxation of income generated through services provided in Germany. Centro Equestre was a company established in Portugal which provided certain artistic services in Germany. Those services gave rise to income which was subject to restricted taxation in Germany pursuant to the applicable double taxation convention. The tax was deducted at the source. Centro Equestre then claimed repayment of the tax corresponding to the amount of the operating expenditures incurred in providing the services in Germany. According to German law, only those expenditures could be taken into account that were made to provide the services subject to taxation in Germany. Moreover, expenditures were only taken account of, if they amounted to more than 50 per cent of the income taxed. For persons subject to unrestricted taxation in Germany, such a limitation did not apply. According to the Court, in a situation where residents were taxed on their net income, it followed from *Gerritse, 2003*, *Scorpio, 2006*, and from territoriality as established in *Futura, 1997* that it was consistent with the services freedom to allow non-residents to deduct solely those expenditures that were directly connected with the provision of the services. Such expenditures were those that were inextricably linked to the provision of the service concerned, such as travel and accommodation cost, irrespective of where and when they had been incurred (para. 25). However, to require that the amount of expenses added up to half of the income, raised an obstacle to the freedom of services which was not justified by the need to avoid that costs were deducted twice. The German mechanism of information exchange as well as Directive 77/799 on mutual assistance prevented double deduction. Moreover, Portugal set off taxes paid in Germany against taxes due in Portugal. It was therefore possible for Portugal to examine which costs had been deducted in Germany (paras 29-37).

In *Commission v. Denmark (insurance taxation), 2007* the Court held that Denmark's requirement that insurers be established in Denmark for income tax relief to be applicable violated the freedom of services (see above). In *Commission v. Belgium (tax matters), 2007* the Commission challenged several of Belgium's tax rules before the Court. The Court found that the following rules amounted to obstacles to the free movement of services for the internal market as well as the European Economic Area. (i) Supplementary contributions employers made to pension and life assurances could only be deducted for tax purposes, if the fund or undertaking with which the assurance had been taken out was established in Belgium. (ii) Tax reductions for long-term savings were only granted, if the contributions were paid to funds or undertakings established in Belgium. (iii) A tax was levied, when capital or surrender values which had been built up through contributions by an employer were transferred to a fund or insurance undertaking established outside Belgium. (iv) Insurers established abroad had to have a personally liable representative in Belgium to ensure payment of taxes due as a result of insurance contracts (paras 39-46). Belgium only argued justification for the last rule (iv) on the ground that it was necessary to ensure collection of taxes. The Court rejected that argument, because Belgian law itself knew less restrictive measures (paras 52-7). In addition, the limitations of tax deductions and reductions for long-term savings (i and ii) as well as the tax levied in case of transfers (iii) violated the free movement of persons and, in case of rule (iii), the free movement of Union citizens, as did a further rule according to which a tax was triggered when certain savings were forwarded to an insurance institution established outside Belgium (paras 61-76).

In *Gootjes-Schwarz, 2007* Germany refused tax relief to a married couple for school fees charged by a private school their children attended in Scotland. Had the school been approved in Germany, which was the case only for schools established in Germany, tax relief would have been granted. The Court held that the free movement of services was breached. The freedom covered education provided by private schools when such schools were mostly financed by private funds. Those funds need not necessarily have stemmed from parents or pupils. It was irrelevant whether schools in Germany provided services in the sense of the freedom of services. What mattered was that the school in Scotland provided a service (paras 34-45). The Court found an obstacle to the freedom of services in the refusal to grant tax relief on the ground that the school was established in another member state. Service receivers were deterred from seeking services abroad, service providers were hindered in providing them (paras 64-7). The justification of the discrimination failed. The German measure did not constitute a subsidy for schools, but tax relief for taxpayers (paras 70-1). Even if it were arguable based on *Bidar, 2005* that it needed to be avoided that tax relief for school fees became an unreasonable burden for the state concerned so that the overall level of aid that state could grant would be reduced and even if the fact that the reduction of tax receipts were a ground capable of justifying a restriction, Germany could have applied a less restrictive measure. Instead of automatically excluding tax relief for foreign school fees, Germany could have limited the amount of private school fees for which tax relief was granted for all private schools, irrespective of where they were established, based on objective criteria (paras 72-3 and 76-81). In as far as the freedom of services did not apply, so the Court, Union citizenship had to be examined (paras 34-5). Children who were Union citizens and went to another member state to attend a private school exercised the right to move freely flowing from Union citizenship. There was a difference in treatment between taxpayers depending on where their children attended school, resulting in a disadvantage for the children. In the same vein as with the freedom of services Germany's measure was disproportionate under citizenship. Thus, even where a school was not covered by the freedom of services, Germany's refusal was precluded (paras 90-8). In *Commission v. Germany (private schools), 2007*, handed down on the same day as *Gootjes-Schwarz, 2007*, the Court addressed the same German legislation. The substance of the judgment was largely identical to *Gootjes-Schwarz, 2007*, save that the Court added that the German legislation also violated the free movement of workers and the freedom of establishment of self-employed persons when those freedoms were applicable in certain particular constellations. The freedom of establishment of private schools was not violated though (paras 114-22).

In *Jundt, 2007* a university teacher who was subject to taxation in Germany taught a university course in France. He received an expense allowance. Germany, however, refused to factor out that allowance from taxable income, although it would have been had the expense been paid by a German university. The Court ruled that the situation was within the scope of services. Although a public university had granted the expense allowance and courses taught within publicly financed educational institutions as such were not services, the freedom of services applied in that case, because the university had called for and paid remuneration for the services of a natural person on a secondary basis. That the service was quasi-honorary and the remuneration hence did not include a profit was irrelevant. It was sufficient when the service was provided for some reward at all (paras 31-5). Teaching at university was not connected to the exercise of official authority (paras 36-8). The refusal to grant a tax concession in case of teaching abroad amounted to a restriction of the freedom of services (paras

53-4). It was not justified by the promotion of teaching and research and development, even if that were a ground suitable for justification, for the measure essentially discouraged teaching abroad, while the Community encouraged cooperation in education. The free movement of Union citizens in educational matters was particularly important, as established in *Morgan, 2007*, and the German measure infringed the freedoms of teachers without necessity, given that the aims of Germany's educational policy could be attained without excluding the tax exemption (paras 57-64). The direct link required for the cohesion of the tax system to justify a restriction was missing. The link between the tax exemption and the contribution to public teaching was too general and indirect (paras 66-70). Finally, in spite of the member states' powers to organize their education systems they were required to comply with the freedoms, in particular with the tax exemption being a fiscal, rather than a measure organizing the educational system (paras 81-8).

In *Jobra, 2008* the Court addressed a tax premium Austria's tax law afforded to those who invested in goods that were possibly then leased out, provided that those goods were primarily used on Austrian territory. Jobra was a company established in Austria that invested in lorries and leased them to a company in Germany which was part of the same group. Jobra's claim for the tax premium was rejected, because the lorries were mostly used in Germany. That the tax premium was only granted, when leased goods were used in Austria, the Court held, discouraged the leasing out of goods to persons in other member states. The restriction thereby established violated the freedom of services (paras 22-6). It was not justified by the balanced allocation of powers of taxation, irrespective of whether all conditions tied to that ground were met, because the income from such leasing agreements was taxable in Austria (paras 32-3). As a direct link did not exist between the premium granted to the lessor and the subsequent taxation of the income of the lessee, the cohesion of the tax system did not justify the restriction, either (para. 34). The prevention of abuse through the establishment of wholly artificial arrangements also did not justify the restriction, for the premium did not target such arrangements. The rule relied on a general presumption of abuse, and in particular proof could not be brought showing that a specific transaction was not abusive (paras 36-38).

In *X and Passenheim, 2009* the regime the Netherlands applied in case of undeclared taxable assets or income came before the Court. In case a taxpayer had failed to declare assets situated in the Netherlands, such as a bank account, under Dutch law taxes that would have been due were recovered for the five years preceding the assessment. In case of assets situated in other member states the recovery period was twelve years. The fine imposed in case of concealment corresponded to that recovery period. Consequently, it was higher when the assets were situated abroad. The Court judged that the distinction drawn on the basis of where the assets were situated had the effect of restricting the freedom of services and the freedom of capital, notwithstanding the taxpayer's possibility to declare assets. Receivers of financial services were dissuaded from seeking services abroad (paras 34-9). The effectiveness of fiscal supervision and the prevention of tax evasion could justify the restriction (paras 45-6). The measure contributed to the achievement of those aims and hence was suitable (paras 49-52). While the period did not reflect the time needed for the authorities to find and tax the tax items concerned, a member state was not required to adapt its law to the law of other member states, in particular those with banking secrecy (paras 57-61). However, a distinction had to be drawn. (i) In the case of taxable items of which the authorities did not have any knowledge, because the taxpayer concealed them, a longer recovery period of twelve years in case of assets situated abroad was justified. The period in that case reflected the fact that the longer the period was the higher the chances were of discovering concealed assets. The instruments on exchange of information, namely Directive 77/799, could not apply in that case, because the authorities did not know about the items (paras 63-73). (ii) In the case of tax items the authorities knew about, the period of recovery merely reflected the time needed to obtain the necessary information. Thus, the recovery period had to be adapted to the circumstances. Directive 77/799, a double taxation convention, automatic information exchange, banking secrecy in another member state – all those were factors that could influence the time needed to obtain the information necessary to assess the taxes payable. The recovery period therefore needed to be set in function of those factors, else the restriction was disproportionate (paras 74-5). Apart from that, the difference in the amount of the fine imposed depending on whether assets were situated abroad merely reflected the length of the recovery period and as such it was justified (paras 82-5).

In *Commission v. Spain (lotteries), 2009* Spain's tax law drew a distinction. On the one hand, there were certain organizers of games of chance established in Spain. The gains made in games of chance organized by them were exempted from income tax, since they presumably pursued certain social purposes. On the other hand, other organizers of games of chance established in Spain as well as all organizers established abroad – irrespective of the purpose they pursued – did not benefit from such a presumption. The winnings made in games of chance organised by them were not exempted from income tax in Spain. The Court decided that the organizers established abroad that pursued social purposes – and only them – and those Spanish organizers that could distribute tax-exempt gains were in comparable situations. Hence, Spanish law was discriminatory in that it refused to treat the two organizers in the same way, notably by refusing the foreign organizers the benefit of exempting gains made in their games from income tax in Spain (paras 33-5). The restriction, as it was discriminatory, was not justifiable by the grounds recognized by the case-law which were not expressly mentioned in the Treaty (paras 36-7). More specifically, the grounds Spain argued did not prevail. Even assuming that the prevention of money laundering came within the public policy derogation, a general presumption that games of chance organized abroad were connected to money laundering could not lawfully be applied. As the measure encouraged participation in games of chance it did not pursue the aim of public health protection in a coherent and systematic way, even assuming that preventing gambling addiction, the spread of which was not proven, came within the public health derogation. Since the exemption was applicable to winnings made in all games organised by the privileged organizers, it could not be argued that the measure served to channel betting towards less addictive forms of games of chance. The financing of activities with a social purpose was not a ground in itself. The protection of consumers as well as the social order were not mentioned expressly by the Treaty and the measure did not have any direct link to administrative measures to protect consumers, much like it encouraged participation in games of chance (paras 39-46).

Presidente, 2009 concerned a tax that was levied at the occasion of stopovers of pleasure boats and airplanes in Sardinia. The tax was only payable by persons who did not have tax domicile in the region. Since the tax was not technically levied on transports of persons such as tourists, the Court first established that the tax had an indirect impact on the provision of cross-border services, for instance when the operator of a boat rented it out to tourists who then harboured in Sardinia and on that occasion received services (paras 24-8). The tax supplied those having tax domicile in the region with an advantage (paras 29-32). The Court confirmed that residents and non-residents were usually not in a comparable situation with regard to direct taxation. However, in assessing comparability the specific characteristics of the tax levied had to be examined. In the case at issue, the taxable event was a stopover by boat or plane in Sardinia. There was no objective difference in the situations of persons liable or not to pay the tax. The impact on the environment was the same, irrespective of whether the taxpayer had domicile in Sardinia or not. That persons domiciled in Sardinia contributed to the protection of the environment through the regular taxes they paid, like income tax, while others 'behave[d] like environmental 'free-riders'' (para. 33), was irrelevant for the comparison to be made, since the regular taxes were not of the same nature and did not pursue the same purpose as the stopover tax (paras 34-8). The same considerations led the Court to reject justification. The pollution was the same regardless of whether it originated from persons domiciled in Sardinia or elsewhere. The need to maintain the cohesion of the tax system did not provide any justification, either, for lack of a direct link between the advantage, i. e. the exemption from the stopover tax, and the disadvantage, i. e. payment of income tax (paras 44-8). In conclusion, while a tax on stopovers as such was legally possible, the way it was implemented contravened the freedom of services (para. 43).

Private security firms

Commission v. Belgium (security firms), 2000 began the case-law on private security firms in the 2000s. The Commission challenged certain prerequisites for foreign private security firms to operate in Belgium. After having found that the official authority exception did not apply for lack of a direct connection (paras 24-6), the Court rejected each of the Belgian conditions. A place of business in Belgium could not lawfully be required, since private security firms as such were not a genuine threat to one of the fundamental interests of society within the sense of the public security exception, which, in any event, could only be relied upon to refuse entry or residence to individuals, not to exclude an entire business sector from a treaty freedom (paras 27-30). To require a prior authorization in Belgium went beyond what was necessary to supervise such firms and failed to give due regard to 'home' state regulation (paras 35-8). Security guards could moreover not lawfully be required to have a specific identification card, given that service providers in general had to have an identity card when entering another member state (paras 39-40). Apart from those violations of the freedom of services, the Court also found that a residence requirement for managers and staff violated the free movement of persons, as less intrusive measures existed to obtain the information needed about the person concerned (paras 31-4). The Court followed up in *Commission v. Italy (private security guards), 2001* confirming that a general nationality condition was not to be applied to bodies and individuals providing private security services. The Court also ruled that the official authority exception was not pertinent, since the powers of private security guards to arrest people did not go beyond the powers of ordinary citizens (paras 18-21). Besides, a nationality condition also restricted the free movement of workers. The public service exception did not make up for that restriction, given that the security entities concerned were private (para. 25.)

Commission v. Netherlands (private security), 2004 largely confirmed the private security firms case-law. The Netherlands failed to take into account 'home' state legislation, with which a company already complied, with the Dutch requirement for firms and managers to have an authorization (paras 17-20). A certificate issued by the Dutch authorities could not lawfully be required, either, since an identification card was needed to enter the Netherlands anyway. Possible exemptions from the authorization requirement did not change that assessment, as long as they were subject to the authorities' discretion (paras 27-31). In *Commission v. Spain (private security), 2006* the Court confirmed what had been established in *Commission v. Portugal (private security), 2004* (see the freedom of establishment, above). Previously, the Court had already invalidated certain conditions contained in Spanish law in *Commission v. Spain (private security guards), 1998*. The Court added several points, though. A minimum share capital for private security firms could not be justified by the prevention of terrorist threats for lack of a direct connection (paras 36-7). Spanish legislation requiring the lodging of a security deposit with a Spanish bank was disproportionate in that it failed to take into account similar guarantees already provided in the 'home' state (paras 41-4). The minimum number of employees of private security firms Spanish law required went beyond what was needed to guarantee a certain level of security, except in the case of transports of explosives (paras 48-51). To require a fresh authorization for each staff member in the host state, without taking into account compliance with 'home' state regulation, went against the grain of the freedom of services and establishment (paras 55-7). Finally, private detectives were a regulated profession under Directive 92/51 for which Spain had failed to establish a system of mutual recognition (paras 64-65).

The Court in *Commission v. Italy (private security), 2007* rejected as incompatible with the freedom of services, and partially with the freedom of establishment, a series of conditions Italian law required private security undertakings to meet. (i) The obligation to swear on oath of allegiance to the Italian Republic hindered access to the Italian market and was more easy to fulfil for Italian nationals. Private security undertakings did not exercise official authority, as established previously. Neither did they constitute a threat to the public order which had to be countered by an oath of allegiance (paras 36-51). (ii) An authorization of limited territorial validity – thus an authorization that had to be requested in each of the 103 provinces in Italy – failed to take into account the requirements undertakings already complied with in the 'home' state and therefore violated the freedom of services (paras 58-64). (iii) The limited territorial validity and the account taken of, for the purpose of assessing whether a licence was to be granted or not, the number and size of private security undertakings already operating in a specific region, violated the freedom of services and establishment. The needs to supervise undertakings effectively and to prevent infiltration by local criminal organizations did not prevail, for less restrictive measures were available, such as administrative controls coupled with a general authorization and sanctions if necessary. Moreover, foreign private security undertaking did not generally intend to usurp the role of the public authorities (paras 74-8). (iv) The freedom of services also ruled out a condition to have an establishment in each region. Effective supervision did not depend on a place of business (paras 84-7). (v) Staff members could not lawfully be required to obtain individual fresh authorizations, either (paras 93-4). (vi) The approval of the authorities needed for any change in the number of staff violated access to the market in a way contrary to the freedom of services and establishment. It was not necessary to guarantee effective supervision (paras 100-4). (vii) The lodging of a guarantee with an Italian depositor, required for each province, failed to factor in 'home' state regulation, and was thus unnecessary for effective supervision (paras 109-14). (viii) The prices for the services which were fixed by the Italian authorities, despite the margin for variation applied, finally, deprived foreign competitors of possibilities to compete effectively and to factor in cost which Italian undertakings did not incur, resulting in a violation of the freedom of services (paras 124-7).

Leased cars

The Court dealt with leased cars in a number of judgments during the 2000s. *Cura Anlagen, 2002* dealt with certain requirements Austria imposed in relation to such cars. A company established in Germany concluded long-term leasing contracts with customers in Austria. The Court assessed Austria's requirements in the light of the free movement of services, for the lease of a car constituted a service (paras 18-20). Austria could lawfully require cars leased from companies established abroad to be registered in Austria, if the cars were primarily used in Austria, for Austria retained that power for lack of harmonisation in the Community. The registration, moreover, was the natural corollary of the power to tax vehicles (paras 37-43). However, to require registering a car in Austria within three days after arrival was excessive. The period was too short to comply with the freedom of services (paras 46-7). The lessor could likewise not be expected to have an establishment in Austria in case the lessee was not authorized to register the vehicle in his or her own name. It would equally satisfy the need to identify the responsible person in case of an accident, if the lessor simply had to communicate the details of the lessee upon registering a car in its own name in Austria (paras 48-51). Austria was only allowed to insist on insurance in Austria within the confines of Directives 2000/26 on civil liability insurance for vehicles and third non-life insurance Directive 92/49 (paras 53-6). Similarly, a roadworthiness test could be required only in accordance with the corresponding Directive 96/96, since such a test constituted an obstacle in need of justification in terms of road safety. In particular, tests to be taken in Austria could not again examine requirements that had been tested previously abroad, though if the vehicle had been used in the meanwhile, a check for deterioration was in order (58-63). A tax based on the fuel consumption of the car concerned, in turn, was justified in the light of environmental protection, provided that the tax varied according to the duration of the leasing (paras 68-9).

In *Leroy, 2006* the Court confirmed for the freedom of services what had been established in *Nadin and Durré, 2005* for the freedom of establishment, namely that registration of a vehicle leased in one member state was lawfully required by another member state where the lessee was resident when the vehicle was used on a permanent basis in the latter state (para. 14). In keeping with that case-law the Court added in *Van de Coevering, 2006* that a vehicle tax levied on vehicles leased abroad was, as a restriction of the freedom of services (para. 21), subject to the same condition. However, the Court reiterated, a member state could still levy a tax on vehicles which had been leased abroad – even if they were not used permanently in its territory – if further justification existed and, in particular, the amount levied was proportionate to the time during which the car was used in its territory (paras 28 and 30-2). In *Ilhan, 2008* the Court re-applied that case-law on cars leased and registered abroad. A tax imposed at the occasion of registration was only lawful when the leased car was intended to be used, or in fact used, in the host state. Further, the tax had to be proportionate to the use made of the car in the host state, notably the duration of the leasing contract and the nature of the use made of the car (paras 21-4).

Maritime transport

Maritime transport occupied the Court in a few decisions during the 2000s. *Analir, 2001* concerned maritime cabotage to, from and between islands. Spain required of maritime transport service providers to obtain an authorization which was subject to the service provider being in good financial standing, i. e.

having no outstanding tax or social security debts. Spain also imposed certain public service obligations on providers of maritime transport from, to and between Spanish islands. Concurrently, Spain concluded some public service contracts with transporters as to the same routes. The Court confirmed that Regulation 3577/92 on maritime transport implemented the freedom to provide maritime cabotage services and went on to apply the freedom of services in that context (paras 17-20). An authorization requirement was not mentioned by the Regulation. It constituted a restriction of the freedom of services (paras 22-4) which could basically be justified by the need to ensure an adequate level of transport to and between islands. However, a real public service need had to be demonstrated in the sense that no adequate level of transport would be provided under market conditions and a declaration ex post facto had to be shown to be insufficient. Relying partly on free movement of capital case-law, namely *Bordessa, 1995* and *Sanz de Lera, 1995*, the Court also ruled that an authorization requirement would have to meet certain other conditions. The criteria applied had to be objective and specified in advance so as to circumscribe the discretion of the authorities and exclude arbitrary decisions. Legal remedies also had to be available (paras 27-39). Within those confines, the financial standing of a service provider could serve as a criterion, particularly since the Regulation relied on the capacity of a company to provide a service (paras 47-50). The Court did not object, either, to the method of concluding a public service contract concurrently with imposing public service obligations with regard to one and the same route, provided a real public service need had been established and necessity as well as non-discrimination were respected (paras 60-70).

Commission v. Italy (passenger tax), 2002 confirmed the case-law as to passenger transports. A passenger tax which was only levied on ship transports to and from ports in other member states, but not in case of transports between two ports in Italy, violated the freedom to provide services, as laid down for maritime transport in Regulation 4055/86. (Italy had not disputed the violation.) *Sea-Land, 2002* also dealt with the freedom of services in the context of Regulation 4055/86. A Dutch company and a US company challenged a charge the Netherlands imposed on those seagoing ships that exceeded a length of 41 meters. The charge was supposed to compensate for the specific services such large ships needed. However, ships that only used inland waterways were not subject to the charge. The Court found that the charge was not indirectly discriminatory, since the situations of inland water vessels and seagoing ships were objectively different and not comparable (paras 33-7). The obstacle to the provision of services which the charge nevertheless raised was justified, since the services performed in exchange for the charge contributed to public security. Moreover, the amount charged was commensurate with the cost of the services received (paras 38-43).

In *Naftiliaki, 2002* the dues imposed on passenger transports between Rhodes in Greece and Turkey were challenged under Regulation 4055/86. Those dues were higher than the dues imposed in case of purely domestic transport or transport between Greece and other member states. The Court confirmed that higher dues on journeys to and from ports in other member states than on purely domestic journeys were precluded by the freedom of services as implemented by the Regulation. That ruling applied even if a due was payable by the passenger, for it increased the cost of the journey. Since the Regulation had rendered applicable the entire freedom to provide services to maritime transport – thus precluding restrictions – and then extended it to cover traffic with third states as well, higher dues on journeys to and from Turkey than on journeys within the Community were precluded (paras 19-22). The Court also clarified that the dues imposed could only vary depending on the cost of the service a passenger received. For lack of objective justification, dues were not to be higher the further a destination was away, either (paras 26 and 28).

Commission v. Greece (cabotage), 2004 then came back to maritime cabotage under Regulation 3577/92 which had already been at issue in *Analir, 2001*. Greece required those who wanted to provide maritime cabotage services to furnish a certificate issued by the flag state that proved that the ship was authorised for cabotage services. Moreover, Greek law designated the Peloponnese as an island, thus rendering applicable the provisions of the Regulation as to transport to and from islands. The Court held that the certificate to be provided constituted a restriction of the freedom of services which was not clearly excluded by the Regulation (paras 30-1). The Court did not find any less restrictive approach to ensure that the ship concerned complied with flag state regulation and thus validated the Greek requirement (paras 34-5). The Peloponnese could not be designated as an island, though, essentially because it was only separated from the Greek mainland by a narrow man-made canal (paras 43-8). Finally, the Court held that all matters relating to the manning of cruise liners exceeding a certain size were the responsibility of the flag state, irrespective of whether such cruise liners also provided island cabotage services (paras 53-6). *Commission v. Spain (Vigo), 2006* also concerned sea cabotage. Under Spanish regional law a concession was required to operate transport in the Vigo estuary, with only one single concession on offer which was valid for 20 years and subject to experience with transport in the Vigo estuary. According to the Court, Regulation 3577/92 applied, although the Vigo estuary was situated inland, 'a river valley inundated by the sea' (para. 29), the impact on the internal market was limited, and only limited port infrastructure existed. Based on Regulation 3577/92 the free movement of services was applicable (paras 23-35). The single concession and the conditions subject to which it was granted amounted to a restriction of the freedom of services. It was unjustified, since a system of booking of available seats would equally allow the traffic to be adapted, while being less restrictive. Further grounds argued by Spain, namely in essence the protection of the environment and the lack of profitability of the service, remained unsubstantiated (paras 43-9). A public service obligation could not lawfully be imposed under Regulation 3577/92, either, as a well established road existed, too, and parts of the transport were only seasonal (paras 58-9). The application of the standstill clause referred to in article 7 Regulation was, finally, restricted to the cases mentioned in article 6 Regulation which did not cover the Vigo estuary (paras 62-6).

In *Agip Petroli, 2006* the Court next decided that the exception from the applicability of host state legislation in a case of island cabotage when it was followed by an international voyage, in which case article 3(3) Regulation 3577/92 rendered flag state legislation applicable, applied regardless of whether the vessel concerned had cargo on board or not during that international voyage (paras 13-7). However, abuse of Community law by ship owners could lawfully be prevented. That required objective evidence though that the aim of the international voyage without cargo was to circumvent application of the host state's legislation and that the ship owner actually benefitted from the application of flag state law (paras 18-24). In *Enosi, 2006* the Court confirmed that article 6(3) Regulation 3577/92 did not confer any rights on individuals in Greece before 1 January 2004 (paras 16-21; the rest of the judgment concerned Directive 98/18 on passenger ships).

In *Commission v. Greece (towage), 2007* the Commission claimed that Greece violated Regulation 3577/92 on maritime cabotage in that only ships under Greek flag could provide certain towage services in Greek waters. The Court rejected that claim finding that towage did not constitute maritime cabotage, for cabotage implied transport of persons or goods, while towage did not involve a straightforward carriage of goods or persons, but rather assistance for the vessel transporting goods or persons. Hence the Regulation did not govern towage (paras 29-33). (The Commission did not allege violation of the free movement of services.) In contrast, in *Commission v. Greece (ports), 2007* the Court held that Regulation 4055/86 on maritime transports was violated in that Greece tolerated that certain entities levied several duties that were higher in cases of transports between Greek ports and ports in other states than in cases of transports between two domestic ports (paras 24-9).

Broadcasting

The Court dealt with television and broadcasting in a broad sense in numerous decisions. In *Canal Satélite, 2002*, Spain required operators of pay television services via satellite to obtain an administrative authorization subject to technical specifications and to be registered in Spain together with the products they marketed like decoders, etc. After having decided that Directive 95/47 on standards of TV signals did not preclude an authorization procedure (para. 27), the Court examined the case from both angles of the free movement of goods and services at the same time, since in pay TV and telecommunications in general services and goods were intricately linked (paras 31-3). The Court accepted Spain's registration requirement owing to the need to protect consumers, but reminded the national authorities of the Court's case-law relating to administrative authorizations, namely the exclusion of discretionary conduct by the authorities, the need to make the criteria public beforehand, and the requirement to take account of 'home' state regulation. The ruling, in addition, emphasized two points, namely that a prior authorization could only lawfully be required when ex post facto control was not at least as effective (paras 39-40); and that the authorization procedure was not to have a deterrent effect because of the duration, the cost, the ambiguity in conditions, and delays (paras 41-2). In *RTL, 2003* the Court then interpreted the terms 'films made for television' and 'series' under Directive 89/552 on television broadcasting in the light of consumer protection in order to define the amount of advertising that could be inserted in those broadcasts, concluding that the freedom of expression was not violated.

In *Commission v. France (alcohol ads), 2004* certain French rules designed to minimize the presence of alcohol in television were at issue. Generally, advertising alcoholic beverages on television was prohibited in France, while ads in other forms, such as in the press, were permitted. French law required broadcasters established in France when broadcasting sporting events taking place abroad which were especially targeted at the French public, viz. bi-national events, to use all means, including technical, to make sure that advertisement of alcoholic beverages did not appear on screens, for instance on t-shirts of players or billboards. In particular, they had to use all means to prevent foreign organizers of such sporting events to show such advertisement. According to the Court, the freedom of services of a number of actors was restricted, namely of French broadcasters who had to refuse to retransmit certain sporting events; of the organizers of sporting events in other member states who could not sell certain retransmission rights; and of the owners of advertising hoardings who had to refuse certain advertising (para. 26). In particular, the use of technical means to prevent ads from appearing on the screen entailed additional cost (para. 28). The restrictions involved were justified, though, on grounds of public health. The French rules discouraged alcohol consumption by reducing the visibility on screen. It was not inconsistent with that aim that advertising beverages with an alcohol content of less than 1.2 per cent and advertising tobacco were not prohibited. Those exceptions were covered by the discretion a member state had in this regard. Moreover, the rules applied only to bi-national events and, generally, less restrictive measures were not available. That other member states administered a lower level of public health protection did not render the French rules disproportionate. Further, a duplication of the regulatory burden was not involved. The rules were, finally, sufficiently clear and precise (paras 30-9). *Bacardi, 2004* was handed down on the same day as *Commission v. France (alcohol ads), 2004* and was identical in content. The Court only added, first, that Directive 89/552 on television broadcasting was not applicable, because indirect advertising, such as on hoardings, did not constitute advertising within the meaning of the Directive (para. 27), and, second, that the member states' discretion allowed them not to prohibit advertising in the background of film sets without being inconsistent (para. 40).

In *Mediakabel, 2005* the Court qualified the 'filmtime' pay-per-view service provided by a Dutch company as a television broadcasting service within the scope of Directive 89/552. The customer could purchase the right to view a specific movie at a certain pre-set time on Mediakabel's channel and a key the customer obtained after the purchase allowed the customer to decode the channel during the time the movie was screened. According to the Court, that service was a broadcasting service within the meaning of Directive 89/552, rather than an information society service governed by Directive 98/34 (paras 29-32 and 37-44). In particular, the Court rejected Mediakabel's argument that Directive 89/552 could not be applied since the obligation contained in the Directive to broadcast for the main part works of European origin could not be implemented with such an on-demand service. In the view of the Court, (i) the overall broadcasting time was clear and European programmes could be allocated broadcasting time in proportion to that time, irrespective of how often movies were in fact demanded, (ii) possible adverse consequences for a trader to whom a piece of legislation was intended to apply were not to determine the scope of that legislation, and (iii) a narrow interpretation of the term television broadcasting service possibly jeopardized the aim of Directive 89/552 (paras 48-51).

ORF, 2007 again concerned Directive 89/552 on television broadcasting. The Court qualified under the Directive a prize game offered on Austrian television in which the viewer was encouraged to call a toll number in order to be selected to participate on air in a game or alternatively to participate in a weekly prize drawing. Depending on the circumstances, the prize game could constitute 'teleshopping' or 'television advertising' within the meaning of the Directive. According to the Court, the offer to the viewers possibly constituted a service, since the cost of the call were higher than for a regular call. The service consisted in the participation in a game in the hope of winning, in keeping with the *Schindler, 1994*-line of authority (paras 32-4). To be qualified as 'teleshopping' the national court in addition had to assess whether a real service was offered – notably in the light of the purpose of the broadcast, the importance of the game within the entire broadcast in terms of economic effects and benefits and time-wise, as well as the questions the candidates were asked – in contrast to mere entertainment within the broadcast (paras 35-8). As to whether the game constituted 'television advertising' the national court had to examine all aspects of the broadcast and was not to confine itself to finding that the game was intended to make the broadcast more attractive. It was significant *inter alia* that the offer intended to make the viewer participate in the content of the broadcast itself, while it did not seek to extol the interest of the broadcast (paras 41-5).

United Pan-Europe, 2007 again concerned television broadcasting, although exclusively in the light of the free movement of services. Belgium's law knew a special must-carry status for television broadcasters in the region of Brussels. Cable network distributors were under an obligation to transmit the broadcasts of broadcasters with must-carry status, resulting in better economic conditions for the latter. However, the status was de facto obtained only by broadcasters established in Belgium. The Court judged that the status resulted in a restriction. It conferred an unconditional guarantee. It was more difficult for broadcasters without must-carry status to have their programmes broadcast. It was more likely that the status was granted to broadcasters established in Belgium. It was not necessary that all domestic broadcasters enjoyed an advantage (paras 32-7). Yet the restriction could be justified by a pluralist cultural policy and the freedom of expression given the wide discretion of the member states in that matter, if certain requirements were met. The award of the must-carry status had to be based on objective criteria and pursuant to a transparent procedure; the conditions and public service obligations the status involved had to be known in advance; the authorities' discretion had to be excluded; the number of broadcasters enjoying the status had to be limited and the programmes enjoying the must-carry status had to be restricted to those that were suitable to attain the aims of the cultural policy. In contrast, it could not be taken account of where a broadcaster was established, else the requirements were discriminatory; when the requirement could more easily be met by domestic broadcasters, they had to be essential (paras 46-50).

In *Centro Europa 7, 2008* an undertaking was granted certain rights in Italy for broadcasting. However, due to a transitional arrangement implementing the switch from analogue to digital broadcasting that undertaking was not in fact allocated frequencies to broadcast. Instead, the incumbent networks merely continued to broadcast on those frequencies, thus blocking them, without having been subject to a selection procedure. The Court addressed the freedom of services, although the situation seemed purely internal to Italy, mainly to allow the national court to exclude reverse discrimination, while the Court refused to address a whole range of issues, notably under competition law, for lack of factual details (paras 64-70). According to the Court, the freedom of services and, from the time on it had become applicable, the new common regulatory framework for electronic communications services and networks consisting of a set of directives precluded the granting of rights to broadcast while the allocation of frequencies necessary to make use of those rights was refused (paras 85-9). Were equally unlawful the perpetuation of the positions of the incumbents, since they had not been selected in a procedure applying transparent, objective, non-discriminatory, and proportionate criteria. The transitional arrangement for the transit from analogue to digital broadcasting, assuming that it constituted a ground to justify a restriction of the freedom of services, did not provide justification, particularly because the incumbents' privilege to broadcast was not limited in time (paras 95-115).

In *Dermoestética, 2008* a Spanish company offered cosmetic surgery services via a subsidiary in Italy. It concluded a contract with an Italian company to organise an advertisement campaign in Italy. However, the Italian company was unable to fulfil the contract, because Italian law prohibited broadcasting of ads for cosmetic surgery in private clinics on national television. On local television such ads were, however, permitted. The Court held that the prohibition of television ads was a serious obstacle to market access in Italy (paras 33-4). While the restriction could be justified on the ground of public health protection, because it was indistinctly applicable, Italian law was inconsistent in that it allowed ad campaigns on local television while prohibiting them on national television. The Italian prohibition was thus unsuitable to achieve the aim of protection of public health (paras 36-40).

In *Kabel Deuschland, 2008* the Court had the occasion to clarify the must-carry status under the Universal Service Directive (Directive 2002/22, a specific directive in the framework established by Directive 2002/21). The Court found the obligations imposed by the regulatory authority of a German Land on an analogue cable network distributor to be in compliance with Directive 2002/22. Subject to the national court's assessment of public interests and proportionality, such a distributor could basically be obliged to transmit channels which were already receivable through other terrestrial transmission means. Moreover, such a distributor could not lawfully oppose an order of priority of channels to be transmitted which the regional authority imposed, even if that order meant that all channels on the analogue cable network were fully utilised and the economic activity of the distributor was strongly restricted (paras 20-55). The Court, finally, decided that certain telemedia services, such as teleshopping, could constitute television services within the meaning of Directive 2002/22 (paras 58-68).

Uteca, 2009 was concerned with Spain's implementing legislation of Directive 89/552 which required television companies established in Spain (i) to earmark five per cent of their operating revenue of the previous year for funding European cinematographic and television films. Of these five per cent (ii), 60 per cent had to be used for productions in one of Spain's national languages. Given that the Directive did not regulate the issue at all, Spain merely needed to comply with the market freedoms (paras 17-8). The Court did not find any restriction in the five per cent requirement (i) (paras 22-3). The other allocation requirement (ii), however, restricted the free movement of services as well as free movement of workers, establishment, and capital (para. 24). It was justified by the need to protect and defend national languages though, which need not have been laid down in more detail, given that the amount of funds concerned was relatively modest (paras 27-36).

Public procurement

In the 2000's, the Court developed public procurement case-law on the basis of the free movement of services in rather long series of cases. *Commission v. France (public tender), 2000* was a case concerning the construction of certain public schools in a French department. The judgment mainly applied the public works directives, i. e. Directives 71/305 and 93/37. However, the Court also held that certain contract notices which were published in the Official Journal of the European Communities pursuant to the public works directives, violated the freedom of services. The notices made references to French standards and were, in essence, easier to comprehend for French undertakings. The resulting dissuasive effect amounted to indirect discrimination violating the freedom of services of providers established in other member states (paras 80-3). Furthermore, it could not lawfully be required in a notice that architects be registered with the order of architects in France (para. 87).

In *University of Cambridge, 2000* the Court clarified the status of universities, such as the university of Cambridge, under the public contracts directives, viz. Directives 93/36, 93/37, and 92/50. The Court notably explained when a university was to be considered as being 'financed, for the most part' by the state or other public bodies, and hence could qualify as a 'body governed by public law' within the meaning of articles 1(b) of the Directives. In that context, the Court remarked preliminarily, much like in *Gemeente Arnhem, 1998*, that the purpose of coordinating awarding procedures was to eliminate barriers to the free provision of services and goods (para. 16). The Court again relied on that passage in *SIAC, 2001* in the context of the award of a public works contract under Directive 71/305 on public works contracts, which (the award) had been based on the opinion of an expert evaluating the most advantageous tender (para. 32).

In *HI, 2002*, the Court was faced with an issue in a public service contracts case. An Austrian authority had withdrawn an invitation to tender, after tenders had been submitted. A tenderer tried to challenge that decision in court, but Austrian law did not provide any possibility for legal review. When interpreting Directive 92/50 on public service contracts the Court fell back on the free movement of services and establishment and the judgments in *Unitron, 1999* and *Telaustria, 2000*, a public supply and a public service contract case, respectively, in which the Court had inferred an obligation of transparency from the principle of non-discrimination on grounds of nationality (paras 31 and 60-63, respectively), to find that Directive 89/665 on review procedures for public contracts was applicable to the effect that a legal review in case of a decision to withdraw a call for tenders was indispensable (paras 43-8).

In *Coname, 2005* the Court applied the freedom of services to a public service concession. In Italy, a municipality held 0.97 per cent of the shares of a company; the rest of the shares were predominantly held by other public, but also by private entities. The municipality concerned directly awarded that company a concession for the distribution of gas. Coname, the company that had previously provided those services, claimed that the municipality had failed to tender publicly the concession. The Court first assumed that the public contracts directives 92/50 and 93/38 were not applicable (paras 9-10 and 16). Instead, the freedom of services and establishment were to be applied. A lack of transparency when awarding such concessions amounted to a difference in treatment that worked to the detriment of service providers established in other member states that could be interested in such concession. Such providers then lacked the opportunity to express that interest. The concession needed not have been tendered publicly, but the appropriate information had to be made available. Further, it could not be argued that the effect on the freedom of services and establishment was too uncertain and indirect, despite the municipality's modest stake in the company licensed (paras 16-22). The need to control a concessionaire managing a public service – even assuming that that consideration could generally justify a lack of transparency – did not prevail in the case at issue, given the municipality's lack of control over the company and the fact that the company was open to private capital (paras 23-26). *Parking Brixen, 2005* confirmed that the freedom of services and establishment and non-discrimination required transparency when the public contracts directives were not applicable. Equal treatment of tenderers for a public service concession was necessary even in the absence of discrimination on the basis of nationality. The concession to be awarded had to be advertised sufficiently so that competition was possible and the impartiality of the proceedings could be reviewed. Not to call for tenders at all was in any case unlawful (paras 48-50). Drawing on public contracts case-law the Court further elaborated that that obligation to act transparently was dispensable only when the company to which a public service concession was awarded met certain conditions, namely (i) it was controlled by the awarding public entity in a similar way as the public entity's own departments and (ii) the essential part of the activities of the company was carried out with the public entity concerned (paras 57-63). The Court then further clarified the condition of control (i). In particular, control was not given in the case at issue, because the company concerned had been newly incorporated as a company limited by shares and its objectives had been broadened, private individuals were basically allowed to acquire shares, the municipality did not have control over the management of the company, and the activity of the company was not limited geographically to the municipality (paras 65-71).

In *Commission v. France (project delegation), 2005* the Court further clarified this strand of case-law. In cases in which the public service contracts directive 92/50 was not applicable, in particular because the threshold it set was not reached, France was required to admit companies established abroad on an equal level as French legal persons to serve as agents with specific tasks in relation to public service contracts under French law, else an obstacle to the freedom of services subsisted which, in addition, was not justifiable by the official authority derogation (paras 68-9). In *Contse, 2005* the Court again tested a call for tenders against the free movement of services. In a call for tender to provide certain services related to home respiratory treatments and other breathing techniques, notably oxygen delivery, only companies that had an office in town which was open during certain hours were admitted. This criterion was also relevant for the evaluation of the answers to the call, as were certain production plants situated within 1000 kilometres from the province concerned and operated by the company answering the call. The evaluation also depended on the production capacity of those plants. In the event the evaluation resulted in a tie between two tenderers, the tenderer that had provided the service previously was awarded the contract. The Court decided that the admission condition raised the costs of answering the call for tenders and, as a result, made it less attractive. The evaluation criteria also hindered the free movement of services, in particular the requirement to operate certain plants within a given perimeter. The preference in case of a tie hampered the freedom of services, because the market was homogenous and all players essentially provided similar products (paras 29-32). Subject to the national court's assessment, the condition of having an office in town did not stand the *Gebhard, 1995*-test the Court applied, since it was not essential for the service or necessary to guarantee the health of patients (paras 35-45 and 55). Having a production plant within reach, even assuming that that criterion was not discriminatory, could not be an evaluation factor, either, as the health and life of patients could be guaranteed by storing a certain amount of the gas required locally. Delivery delays could also occur when producing within the perimeter (paras 56-68). The maximum production capacity of the plant had to be left out of account, too, for it was not tailored to the contract to be awarded (paras 69-76). Discrimination, finally, resulted from the bias in favour of the previous contractor in the event of a tie (paras 77-8). In *ANAV, 2006* the Court reiterated that in case of a public service concession, i. e. when Directives 92/50 and 2004/18 on public services did not apply, the freedom of services did not require transparency to take effect when the municipality concerned had control over the undertaking receiving the concession. Conversely, if a third entity acquired stock in such an undertaking serving as a public service concessionaire, transparency applied with all the consequences established in the case-law based on free movement of services (paras 27-32).

In *Commission v. Italy (horse races), 2007* Italy had decided to increase the number of licences available for horse-race betting operations from 329 to 1000. While Italy had invited tenders publicly for 671 licences, the existing 329 licences had simply been extended. Those licences were, according to the Court, public service concessions which were not covered by Directive 92/50 on public service contracts. In keeping with the case-law, an extension of existing licences violated transparency and thus constituted a restriction of the freedom of services and establishment (para. 25). Italy had failed to show that the extension of the licences was suitable to prevent the development of clandestine betting. Consequently, the freedom of services was violated (paras 30-4).

In *Commission v. Ireland (An Post), 2007*, the Irish state had contracted out the service of payment of social welfare benefits on behalf of the Irish state to the Irish postal company An Post, without having followed any competitive tender procedure first. That contract came within the scope of Directive 92/50, namely Annex 1B which in cases of non-priority such as that at issue did not require a call for competitive tenders, but merely a certain degree of ex post publicity. Nonetheless, the Court reiterated, a member state had to comply with the freedom of services and establishment and the public service contracts case-law established based on them when the contract to be awarded had a cross-border dimension despite the listing in Annex 1B (para. 29) – a dimension which the Commission had failed to establish in the case at issue (paras 32-4).

In *Asociación Profesional, 2007* a Spanish ministry had offhandedly concluded a contract with the Spanish universal postal service provider Correos. According to that contract Correos basically provided the postal services for the Spanish state. After having found that public procurement case-law did not apply to the services lawfully reserved to a universal postal service provider in accordance with Directive 97/67 on postal services and having confirmed the violation of Directive 92/50, the Court went on to examine the freedom of services and establishment in case the contract concluded did not cross the pecuniary threshold established by Directive 92/50. The Court ruled that the case-law created on the basis of the freedom of services, in particular the duty to establish transparency, then applied. The in-house exception developed in that case-law was not pertinent in the case at issue, since the non-reserved services were equally provided to a wide range of customers, not just to the Spanish state (paras 86-7 and 58-63). The contract was only outside the scope of the case-law, if the contract was in fact a unilateral administrative measure that created only obligations for the universal postal service provider and departed from regular commercial terms, leaving no possibilities to negotiate or cancel it (paras 85 and 54-5).

In *Commission v. Italy (public works), 2008* the Court, apart from examining the public contracts directives, reiterated that the case-law on the freedom of services and establishment applied below the thresholds of those directives in cases of cross-border interest. Given that application, Italy was not required to adopt particular rules in that regard when implementing the directives (paras 67-8 and 81-2). The Court, finally, in the context of the Commission's general claim that Italy had violated equal treatment, mentioned that the freedom of services and establishment did not contain a general obligation of equal treatment, but rather a prohibition of discrimination on the basis of nationality (para. 106).

The general approach in public procurement was confirmed and refined in *Secap, 2008* in which Italian law had required public authorities that called for tenders to exclude automatically those offers submitted that were abnormally low, except when only five offers or less had been submitted. Abnormality was determined by means of a mathematical formula. The authorities notably did not have the possibility to examine those abnormally low tenders. According to the Court, where the public works Directive 93/37 did not apply due to the threshold not being exceeded and where a cross-border interest was at stake, which could be the case due the location of the work to be performed, even with contracts of very low value (para. 31), the automatic exclusion of low tenders was liable to undermine the principles established by the case-law on the freedom of services and establishment. Foreign competitors sometimes had different price structures and economies of scale and at times undercut the market with their offers in order to enter a market. With the automatism they were deprived of the possibility to prove why their tenders were low. Moreover, the automatic exclusion could give rise to collusion by local companies. Thus, access of foreign competitors to the Italian market and effective competition were impeded. Automatic exclusion could only be an option where a very large number of tenders had been submitted, while five tenders did not amount to a very large number (paras 24-33).

In *Brescia, 2008* the Court sanctioned the way an Italian municipality ended a long-term gas distribution concession, which would have been valid until the year 2029, with the aim of freeing space for a common gas market by a transitional regime. The end of the concession provided by that regime, however, was removed for two years. According to the Court, the award of a new concession would have been subject to the requirements flowing from the freedom of services and establishment, viz. transparency, etc., given the cross-border interest. Thus, the extension of the old concession under the transitional regime raised a restriction to the freedoms (paras 57-63). That restriction could be justified by the need to guarantee legal certainty, in essence since in 1984 when the concession had been awarded the Court had not yet ruled on the applicability of the market freedoms to such a concession. It was up to the national court, however, to decide whether the extension of the concession was necessary to ensure legal certainty (paras 64-72).

Thereafter, *Coditel, 2008* clarified the in-house exception to the requirement of transparency under the freedom of services and establishment, i. e. when the public contracts directives were not applicable. The Court decided, after having examined in detail the legal nature of the inter-municipal cooperative concerned in the case at issue, that the award of a concession for the management of a municipality's cable television network to that cooperative came within the in-house exception, essentially because it was wholly owned and fully controlled by municipalities the interests of which it was bound to pursue (paras 28-40). Joint control by public authorities was sufficient for that purpose, provided that the body concerned worked mainly with the authorities concerned (paras 44-53). In *Sea, 2009* the Court refined the in-house exception. The Court confirmed that it fell to be applied in the same way under the freedom of services and establishment as under the public contracts Directive 2004/18 (para. 37). Moreover, in essence prospective ownership in a public company by private owners, which would exclude the in-house exception, had to be a real possibility in short term to be taken into account (para. 50). If that possibility turned into reality, though, a competitive tender for a running contract was required (para. 53). The Court also added that the level of control exercised by public authorities over a company had to be assessed in the light of the applicable legislation, the market-orientation of the company, and the control mechanisms (para. 66). The Court then applied those criteria to the company at issue (paras 67-89).

In *Eurawasser, 2009* the Court confirmed that public service concessions did not come within the scope of Directive 2004/17, but were subject to the case-law established under the freedom of services and establishment (para. 44). The Court then went on to elaborate the distinction between a public service contract and a public service concession, notably with regard to the consideration for the service and the risk to be born by the service provider (paras 49-79).

In *Acoset, 2009* an Italian municipality intended to set up a public-private company and entrust it with the management of water services. The Court, after having found that a public service concession was at issue (paras 40-2), ruled in the light of the freedom of services and establishment that it was not necessary to organize two public calls for tenders, one for the selection of the private minority shareholder with the capacities to perform the services needed and a second to entrust the entity founded for the sole purpose of providing a service with the concession. One public invitation for tenders to find a proper private partner was sufficient, provided, however, that the corporate purpose of the entity founded remained the same for the duration of the concession (paras 58-62).

In *Serrantoni, 2009* the Court invalidated an Italian rule which automatically excluded a consortium and a member of that consortium from a tendering procedure, whenever that member submitted a tender in the same procedure at the same time as the consortium itself. The rule also threatened criminal sanctions in such a case. While recognizing a certain amount of discretion of the member states to adopt rules to ensure compliance (para. 31-2), the Court found that, in a case in which the threshold established by Directive 2004/18 was not crossed, the automatism in the rule amounted to a restriction of the freedom of services and establishment, quite apart from the fact that the measure at issue discriminated against some consortia. It was not possible for a tenderer to rebut the presumption. Moreover, the restrictive effect on tenderers established abroad was not justified by the need to forestall collusion between tenderers (paras 38-45).

Ankara

Some cases in the 2000s dealt with free movement of services in the context of the Ankara Agreement with Turkey. In *Abatay, 2003* Germany required Turkish drivers who transported goods in lorries registered in Germany from Turkey to Germany on behalf of Turkish subsidiaries of German companies to have work permits. The Court decided that those workers could not lawfully rely on articles 6 and 13 Decision 1/80, because they did not seek access to the employment market in Germany. They were employed by the Turkish subsidiary, stayed in Germany only for brief terms, and returned to Turkey immediately thereafter (paras 89-91). According to the Court, essentially for lack of a title on transport in the Ankara Agreement, the internal market case-law according to which the freedom of services did not apply in transport until implementing secondary legislation was adopted was not applicable. Instead, the freedom of services applied directly in the transport sector under the Ankara Agreement. Moreover, the standstill clause addressing services as well in article 41 Additional Protocol to the Ankara Agreement which essentially froze the level of service restrictions as per its entry into force was to be applied directly and, in addition, to be interpreted for services, workers, and establishment in the same way (paras 67, 92-103). The Turkish nationals whom the Turkish company employed and who were indispensable for the provision of its services were entitled to rely on the freedom of services and on the standstill clause, since the service was destined for a recipient in a member state, whereas the German company could not lawfully rely on the freedom of services against Germany, because it received the service in Germany (paras 106-8). Given that the internal market case-law on the free movement of services needed to be extended as far as possible to the Ankara Agreement, the requirement for the Turkish drivers to have a work permit in

Germany constituted a restriction of the freedom of services. Further, it was an unsuitable restriction, because the workers were not intent on access to the German labour market. Whether the restriction had already existed in national law at the time the Additional Protocol had entered into force and it was thus within the scope of the standstill clause was up to the national court to decide (paras 111-6).

Soysal, 2009 also concerned the free movement of services under the Ankara Agreement. Turkish lorry drivers who were employed by a Turkish company lawfully transported goods in Germany in lorries owned by a German company and registered in Germany. Initially, at the entry into force of the additional protocol to the Ankara Agreement which contained the standstill clause in article 41(1), a visa was not required for the kind of services these drivers provided in Germany. Later on, a visa was required, but it was consistently granted up to a certain point when the German authorities learnt that the lorries they drove were registered in Germany. Then the visa were no longer granted. Together with the legislation of the Union in the area of Schengen the German legislation had changed again. Pursuant to that legislation, a visa was required which was valid for the entire Schengen area. In keeping with its case-law on the standstill clause in the Additional Protocol, the Court reiterated that more restrictive measures could not be enacted than those applicable at the time the standstill clause had entered into force. Since a visa had not been required at that time for the provision of such services in Germany, a visa requirement was not to be imposed now (paras 51-3 and 57-8). It was not relevant whether the requirement was based on a measure of the Union or a member state's measure implementing legislation of the Union; or whether the Schengen visa had some advantages as compared to the regime originally in force. The visa requirement introduced an additional burden and if a visa was denied, provision of services became impossible (paras 54-5). Apart from that, an international agreement such as the Ankara Agreement took precedence over the secondary legislation of the Union which, therefore, had to be interpreted in accordance with the agreement (para. 59).

Further services cases

A whole series of other cases concerned the free movement of services, but resists a similar categorization as above. In rough chronological order they were the following. *Commission v. Italy (cleansing services), 2000* invalidated Italy's registration requirement which applied to all undertakings offering certain cleansing services such as rodent-control. Italy had failed to take due account of 'home' state registration and, as a consequence, violated the free movement of services (paras 13-4).

With *Deliège, 2000*, certain aspects of *Bosman, 1995* were applied in the freedom of services. Ms Deliège was a judoka performing on the highest level in Belgium. She was repeatedly ignored in the Belgian federation's selection of judokas for international tournaments, the results in which *inter alia* determined how many athletes could be fielded for the Olympic games. She alleged violation of her freedom to provide services. The Court first reiterated, mostly in keeping with the *Bosman, 1995*-case-law, that the Treaty applied to professional sports such as judo. Then the Court ruled that the selection made in the case at issue was not for national teams the activities of which had been considered as non-economic in *Bosman, 1995* (paras 43-8). For the question whether judokas offered services it was relevant that they were usually supported by public grants and private sponsors (paras 51-2). Moreover, the activities of high-level athletes involved a number of separate but closely related services within the sense of the freedom of services, although not all of them were paid for by those who received them. They allowed other service providers, such as event organizers or broadcasters, to offer services (paras 56-7). As for the question whether the case was purely internal to Belgium, the national court had to bear in mind that a certain degree of extraneity was involved when an athlete performed abroad (paras 58-9). Unlike in *Bosman, 1995*, however, the Court did not find a restriction of a Treaty freedom. The federations did not select candidates based on nationality, nor was access to the labour market denied. It was in the nature of such sport events that a selection had to be made. Participation in the events had to be limited in some way. A whole number of considerations unrelated to the individual athlete were factored into the decision on whom to select. It was therefore appropriate that national federations laid down a selection procedure and selected athletes (paras 61-9).

In *Corsten, 2000* Germany required persons established abroad to be registered on the German skilled trades register to be allowed to provide the corresponding services in Germany. In the case at issue, Mr Corsten, a German architect, had had a Dutch company lay floors in Germany, an activity which that company lawfully pursued in the Netherlands. In keeping with case-law on the freedom of services, compliance with which was required despite Directive 64/427 on industry and small craft industries, the Court struck down the registration requirement (paras 30-4). Acknowledging that the need to guarantee the quality of skilled trade work could justify a restriction (para. 38), the Court held that Germany had failed to draw a distinction between those established in Germany and those merely providing services, imposing the same requirement on both (para. 44). The examination which Directive 64/427 permitted could be one of form only (paras 41-2). The Court further clarified that any authorization procedure was not to delay or impede the provision of services when the conditions to exercise the activities in question had been met. Moreover, no additional expense was to arise, nor could payment of subscriptions to chambers of trade be lawfully imposed (paras 47-8). In *Commission v. Italy (register), 2000* the Court struck down Italy's requirement for persons providing services in haulage to have an Italian authorization and to be registered in Italy. The requirement was incompatible with the free movement of services and establishment. (Italy had not contested the Commission's allegation).

The primary interest of *Gourmet, 2001* was in the free movement of goods under the *Keck and Mithouard, 1993*-line of authority. However, it also had a service dimension. Sweden prohibited all advertising of alcoholic beverages bar comments in the editorials of magazines and advertising directed at traders. That prohibition restricted cross-border services of the domestic press in advertising (paras 38-9). Like the restriction of free movement of goods, it was justifiable by public health concerns, except if the national court found the measure to have been diverted from its original towards protective purposes (paras 40-1 and 26-33).

In *Commission v. Italy (transport consultants), 2001* the Court reviewed a number of requirements Italy imposed on transport consultants, namely an authorization was needed which was only granted after a security deposit had been lodged; minimum and maximum fees applied; nationals of other member states had to have residence in Italy. The latter requirement negated the freedom of services and, as regarded the freedom of establishment, was discriminatory (paras 14 and 21). The authorization coupled with the deposit constituted a restriction of the freedom of services which was not justified, because Italy failed to take into account similar 'home' state regulation with which a service provider established abroad had complied already (paras 22-4). In contrast, the Commission had failed to show how the minimum and maximum fees violated the free movement of services (paras 25-6).

In *Commission v. Italy (trade-fairs), 2002* the Court struck down a series of restrictions by local and regional entities in Italy relating to the organisation of trade-fairs. Since Italy did not dispute the infringement (para. 19), the Court in brief terms invalidated the requirements for trade-fair organizers (i) to obtain official recognition from the relevant authorities, (ii) to have a permanent establishment in Italy and a particular legal form or status, (iii) to organize exclusively trade-fairs, (iv) to operate on a not-for-profit basis, (v) to hold fairs periodically, (vi) to conform to the aims set by the region concerned, (vii) to abide by particularly strict time-limits in the procedure to obtain the necessary administrative authorization, and (viii) to have fairs included in the official calendar (paras 28-33). Yet certain subsidies were considered not to be restrictive (para. 32). Moreover, a number of requirements were contrary to the freedom of services and establishment, namely (i) the involvement of public authorities in administrative appointments, (ii) the inclusion of at least one local territorial institution among the founders or the members of the body concerned, and (iii) the involvement of bodies made up of operators already established in the region concerned in certain decisions (paras 36-40. Only the involvement of certain persons who did not compete with the trade-fair organizers was considered justified (para. 41).

In *Commission v. Italy (temporary labour), 2002* the Court invalidated a number of requirements Italy imposed on those who provided temporary labour to businesses in Italy. The requirement to have an establishment in Italy was not indispensable within the sense of *Parodi, 1997* for the protection of workers, as some workers possibly were not in need of protection in Italy, particularly when they resided abroad or usually worked in Italy under an employment contract, and the Brussels framework allowed workers to sue employers in a court at the place where they worked (paras 20-5). It could not be demanded from a foreign provider of temporary labour services to provide the same bank guarantee as Italian providers, as that requirement failed to take into account comparable guarantees provided in the 'home' state (paras 32-4). Moreover, if that guarantee was to be provided through a bank established in Italy, the freedom of banks established in other member states to provide services was unlawfully restricted, too, as was the freedom of capital of the service provider (paras 36-9).

In *Carpenter, 2002* Mr Carpenter, a British national, was resident in the United Kingdom. He had several clients in other member states to whom he sold advertising space in certain British journals. For that purpose he also travelled to other member states. His wife was a national of a third country, who had initially entered the United Kingdom with a visitor visa. She stayed beyond the validity of her visa and later on married Mr Carpenter, thenceforth taking care of his children stemming from his first marriage. This in turn allowed Mr Carpenter to devote more time to his business activities. As her stay in the United Kingdom was illegal, she was going to be deported. The Court decided that Mr Carpenter's freedom to provide services was affected since he provided a significant part of his services to receivers in other member states (paras 29-30). In contrast, Directive 73/149 did not apply vis-à-vis the state of which a person was a national (paras 34-6). Mr Carpenter's freedom of services would have been violated by his wife's deportation. The separation would have been detrimental to the Carpenters' family life and deterred him from providing services (paras 38-9). Any assessment of the justification of that interference would have to be compatible with the Carpenter's right to family life, protected by article 8 European Convention of Human Rights. To deport her would not strike a fair balance between the right to family life and public order and safety, in particular since she had not committed any offence other than staying in the United Kingdom beyond the validity of her visa. Moreover, the Carpenters' marriage was genuine (paras 40-5).

The Commission in *Commission v. Italy (local museums), 2003*, again after *Commission v. Spain (museum admission), 1994*, challenged admission fees for cultural sites. Some local and decentralised authorities in Italy had granted Italian citizens and local residents of a certain age free admission to the local museums and monuments they ran. In keeping with *Commission v. Spain (museum admission), 1994* the Court found the freedom of services to be violated. Relying on Italian citizenship was discriminatory. Residence as a criterion for distinction resulted in indirect discrimination, though not all of those disadvantaged were nationals of other member states (paras 12-5). Justification of the direct discrimination failed, for none of the grounds expressly mentioned in the Treaty applied. The residence requirement was not justified by the cohesion of the Italian tax system, not merely because the direct link required was missing, but also because not just local residents, but all residents of Italy paid tax. Finally, Italy could not validly plead its federal structure to justify the discriminations, either (paras 19-27).

In *Commission v. Italy (patent services), 2003* again a residence condition was at stake. Italy required those who provided certain services related to patents and the patent office in Italy to have residence or a place of business and to be registered in Italy. The Court assessed the situation from the angle of the freedom of services rather than the freedom of establishment, because the services concerned did not necessarily involve stable and continuous participation in the economic life in the host state (paras 23-5). The registration requirement was an obstacle. The corresponding aptitude test which all applicants had to take failed to take into account qualifications already acquired by those established abroad in their 'home' state. Hence, the registration requirement was not necessary to ensure the quality of the services provided or the protection of the service recipient (paras 27-32). Equally, the residence condition was an obstacle which was not justifiable for it went beyond what was needed to determine the court having jurisdiction in patent lawsuits or for the proper administration of justice (paras 42-5). In any event, Italy could not lawfully require reciprocity from other member states (para. 46). In a similar vein, the Court in *Commission v. Luxembourg (patent agents), 2003* overruled Luxembourg's requirement for foreign patent agents to elect domicile with an approved agent in Luxembourg in order to provide services (para. 19). (Luxembourg had not disputed the infringement.)

In *Freskot, 2003* the Court assessed an insurance scheme Greece had established. The Greek state levied a charge on the sale and purchase of domestic agricultural products. That charge served to feed a public entity which in turn covered natural risks farmers in Greece typically faced. Besides the free movement of goods, agricultural policy, and state aid, the Court also examined the freedom of services. According to the Court, a service was not provided by means of that insurance scheme. The charge levied was not consideration for a service, because it was levied by tax authorities, it applied equally to all operators, and its characteristics were determined by the legislature (paras 56-8). Hence, the freedom of services and, as a consequence, Directive 73/239 on direct insurance were not applicable in that respect. The freedom of foreign insurers to insure in Greece the kind of risk the Greek scheme covered was possibly restricted, though. However, it was unclear whether the risks covered were insurable profitably by private insurers. Yet even if they were, the restriction was susceptible of justification. The scheme pursued the social policy goal of ensuring an adequate level of protection for all farmers, regardless of the individual risk each of them faced, and the rate of the charge was the same across the board, again irrespective of the individual risk. It was up to the national court, though, to assess the proportionality of the cover. It had to factor in that the Greek scheme provided only minimal cover and farmers were free to conclude contracts to increase insurance protection (paras 63-73).

In *AMOK, 2003* an Austrian company won a court case in a German court. Consequently, it required the losing party to pay the fees of the Austrian lawyer who had conducted the lawsuit on its behalf in accordance with the scale of fees applicable in Austria. In addition, it requested reimbursement of the fees the work in conjunction with a German domestic lawyer had occasioned. According to German law it was mandatory to work in conjunction with a local lawyer for foreign lawyers. Both requests were rejected by the German court of appeal, which instead applied the German scale of fees which was less advantageous for the Austrian company and declared the fees of the local lawyer as not recoverable. Both rejections, according to the Court, constituted restrictions of the freedom of services, for they rendered services supplied by providers established in other member states less attractive (paras 27 and 36). The German scale of fees could lawfully be applied, though, because host state rules and conditions could in principle be applied to trans-frontier services, a point also emphasized by Directive 77/249 on lawyers. Moreover, application of the German scale was predictable and thus complied with legal certainty (paras 29-30). In contrast, to reject reimbursement of the additional fees resulting from the work of the local lawyer violated the freedom of services, because German law, making use of an authorization in Directive 77/429, required foreign lawyers to work in conjunction with a domestic lawyer. The fees such domestic lawyers charged were, in addition, modest, since their role was limited (paras 38-40).

Schnitzer, 2003 followed up on *Corsten, 2000*. A German company charged a Portuguese company with plastering work in Bavaria which took around three years to complete. The head of the German company was fined, because the Portuguese company was not entered into the German trade register as required by law. The Court reiterated that the distinction between the freedom of services and freedom of establishment had to be made on the specifics of each case. No abstract rule determined the point in time when services became establishment. Even regular services provided over several years did not necessarily amount to establishment within the meaning of the Treaty. If the national court found that the Portuguese company merely provided a service, given that it did not have any infrastructure in Germany and did not seek to evade German legislation (paras 30-3), the registration requirement constituted an obstacle as held in *Corsten, 2000*. That obstacle was susceptible of justification by the needs to protect those who commissioned the work and to ensure the quality of services. However, when 'home' state legislation demonstrably guaranteed the quality of services, the registration was not to complicate or delay the work, give rise to fees or contributions to trade chambers, or be a condition precedent to the provision of the service, irrespective of whether the service was provided repeatedly or just once (paras 37-9).

In *Commission v. France (bio-medical labs), 2004* France required firms running bio-medical laboratories to have an establishment in France to be allowed to provide bio-medical analysis services. Such an establishment also rendered the cost of the service provision reimbursable under the French social security system. The requirement, according to the Court, restricted the freedom of services, though not the freedom of establishment, because a French branch could operate a laboratory and foreign nationals could act as directors (paras 59-62 and 65). It was an excessive requirement, however, even to guarantee the quality of medical services in order to ensure a high level of health protection. Inspections and controls which ensured that French standards were met obviously were in order, but an authorization requirement would have served those purposes just as well. Any such requirement would have to avoid duplicating the standards already met in the 'home' state. Proof of the fact that those 'home' state standards were not less strict and were actually complied with could lawfully be required from the foreign service provider who also had to ensure that French doctors and biologists understood the laboratory reports it supplied (paras 69-76). Similarly, a foreign service provider could lawfully be required to obtain an authorization in France which then rendered the cost of the services provided reimbursable under the French social security system. Such a requirement would be less restrictive than the condition to have a branch or a subsidiary in France (paras 91-4).

In *Omega, 2004*, a British company concluded a franchise contract with a Germany company to provide a fully functioning game hall where customers could 'play at killing' with laser guns. The German authorities prohibited that activity on the ground that it violated public order. According to the Court, the freedom of services was applicable exclusively, since the goods imported were entirely secondary to the services provided (paras 25-7). The prohibition was a restriction that was justified by public policy considerations, which could in principle justify indistinctly and distinctly applicable measures (para. 29). That the game was tolerated in other member states did not render Germany's prohibition disproportionate. On the contrary, the member states had a margin of discretion to define what public policy meant. A conception of public policy common to all member states was not necessary, either, contrary to what might have been inferred from *Schindler, 1994* (paras 31 and 37-8). The objective of protecting human dignity, on the basis of which the German authorities had prohibited the game, was compatible with Community law. It was to be taken into account as a ground justifying restrictions of the market freedoms, as in fact any fundamental right (paras 34-5). The prohibition, finally, was not unnecessary, as it was limited to 'playing at killing' and the German constitution sought to guarantee a level of public policy protection that corresponded to the prohibition (para. 39).

In *Burmanjer, 2005* the Court found the free movement of goods applicable, in contrast to *Omega, 2004*. Vendors had sold to pedestrians in the public sphere of a town in Belgium subscriptions to periodicals on behalf of a German company without having obtained the authorization Belgian law required for such itinerant activities. The Court ruled that the activity of the vendors consisted in the marketing of certain goods. The services associated with that marketing were entirely secondary. Hence, solely the free movement of goods and with it the *Keck and Mithouard, 1993*-case-law was to be examined, instead of services (paras 33-6). Free movement of workers did not apply, because the vendors were not employed by the German company (paras 18-20.)

In *Oulane, 2005* a French national was deported from the Netherlands, because he had failed to prove his identity. He claimed to be in the Netherlands for the purpose of receiving services. The Court clarified a number of points. First, pursuant to Directive 73/148 on movement and residence based on establishment and services and the freedom of services nationals of other member states could be required by the host state to establish their identity when asked to do so. Yet proof of identity could be provided not only by means of an identity card, but by other means suitable to establish identity unequivocally (paras 16-25). Second, the host state could insist on nationals of other member states carrying a valid identity card or a passport only if its own nationals were required to do so, too, else discrimination arose (paras 32-4). Third, deportation and detention, as sanctions in case a national of another member state who received services in the host state had failed to present a valid identity card, were out of proportion to the need to ensure public security. The sanctions had to correspond to the penalties imposed for similar offences committed by nationals of the host state. The award of damages after a sanction had turned out to be unjustifiable did not render deportation or detention proportionate (paras 41-3). Fourth, it was up to the person concerned to prove her or his right of residence as a service receiver in accordance with Directive 73/148 by any means appropriate, failing which she or he could lawfully be deported subject to the limits imposed by Community law (paras 49-5).

In *Servizi ausiliari, 2006* Italy reserved the provision of certain services related to the declaration of taxes – advice, assistance, etc. – to particular companies constituted under Italian law. Although the situation seemed to be confined in all aspects to Italy, the Court gave an answer, because the national court possibly needed an answer to preclude reverse discrimination (para. 29). The freedom of services and establishment were restricted. The requirements were discriminatory in as far as the services were reserved to companies already established in Italy. They restricted access to the market, as far as the services were reserved to companies meeting certain requirements (paras 33-7). The grounds expressly mentioned in the Treaty did not provide justification in the case of discrimination (para. 36). Apart from that, the restrictions were not justified either (i) by the protection of service recipients, for the services were either simple and hence could not be reserved to persons having certain qualifications or, when more complex, the requirements to be met were not suitable to protect recipients, or (ii) the official authority derogation, for lack of a connection, since the services were provided only in the preparatory stage before the official authorities became involved (paras 36-48).

In *Commission v. France (performing artists), 2006* France treated artists who came to France to perform as service providers as if they were in employment and consequently applied French social legislation, unless that presumption was rebutted. An additional requirement was undisputed; France admitted that the requirement to have a licence to pursue the activity of engaging performing artists which was issued subject to need on the French market violated the freedom of services (para. 29). As to the first requirement, according to the Court, France's approach amounted to a restriction of the free movement of services, irrespective of whether the presumption was hard or easy to rebut (paras 38-42). For lack of harmonisation, the restriction was susceptible of justification. Though as such a legitimate ground, the social protection of service recipients failed to justify the obstacle, as Regulation 1408/71 already provided social security protection for them. Further, the idea of guaranteeing paid leave could not be reconciled with self-employment. The need to combat concealed employment, finally, did not justify such a general approach. Instead, ex post facto controls and deterrent penalties on a case-by-case basis sufficed (paras 43-52).

In *Meca-Medina, 2006*, an annulment appeal in which professional swimmers attacked the rules against doping enacted by the international olympic committee, the Court held in accordance with its case-law that the freedom of services – and other internal market law such as competition law – applied to swimming as a professional or semi-professional sport governed by said committee, and more specifically to the rules against doping (paras 22-33). Yet the initial complaint had been solely based on competition law, which essentially was not violated, since the rules at issue were justified by the need to keep the sport fair, provided that the sanctions ordered in case the rules had been violated were proportionate. In the light of this initial complaint the Court refused to enter into the merits of the claim alleging a violation of the freedom of services (paras 58-9).

Fidium Finanz, 2006 delineated the freedom of services from the free movement of capital. Fidium was a company established in Switzerland which offered short-term consumer credits in Germany via internet and credit intermediaries. Fidium operated lawfully in Switzerland, but was not established nor had a licence in Germany as required by German law in case of companies established in third countries. At the time the facts took place, the Association Agreement with Switzerland liberalising free movement of persons and services partially had not yet been in force. According to the Court, it was possible that both the freedom of service and the freedom of capital were applicable at the same time. With no order of priority existing between the two freedoms the Court would only examine one freedom, if the other was entirely secondary and could be considered together with the first (paras 25-34). In the case at issue, providing consumer credits constituted a service. However, a company established in a third country was not entitled to rely on the free movement of services, in contrast to the free movement of capital. The restriction in the flow of capital was merely the inevitable consequence of the limitation of the freedom of services inherent in Germany's licence and establishment requirements. The freedom of capital therefore need not have been considered (paras 38-49).

Cipolla, 2006 concerned Italian legislation which fixed on a scale the minimum and maximum fees lawyers were allowed to charge in Italy for in- and out-of-court counsel. Derogations from those fees were not possible. Replying although the situation was purely internal to Italy so to enable the national court to deal with any potential reverse discrimination (para. 30), the Court decided that the Italian measure restricted the freedom of lawyers established in other member states to provide services in Italy. Like in *Caixa-Bank, 2004*, those service providers were prevented from competing effectively on the basis of prices and the choices for service recipients were limited (paras 58-60). Whether the protection of the service recipient and the proper administration of justice justified that restriction was left for the national court to decide. In taking the decision, the national court had to take into account the typical asymmetry of information between attorneys and clients, the possible lack of a link between the quality of the service and the price, the high number of lawyers operating on the Italian market, and other means to prevent destructive competition, such as professional rules, liability, and supervision (paras 64-7).

In *Commission v. Austria (boilers), 2006* Austria required service inspectors of boilers and pressure tanks to be established in Austria. The restriction, the existence of which Austria did not dispute (para. 22), was not justified by public security and health considerations. An undertaking did not constitute a threat to public security by the sole reason of being established in another member state, in particular when a directive, like Directive 1999/36, had established minimum requirements for boiler inspectors to be met. With regard to the protection of public health less restrictive alternatives were available. An entire sector of services could, moreover, not lawfully be removed from competition on the ground that undertakings established in other member would otherwise have gained an unfair competitive advantage, else the freedom of services became dependent on harmonisation of all national rules. The protection of the domestic industry alone was not a ground justifying a restriction of the freedom of services (paras 25-31).

In *Commission v. Italy (debt enforcement), 2007* the Court scrutinized a series of requirements Italian law imposed on those who offered the service of extra-judicial debt enforcement on a commercial basis. According to the Court, while a licence requirement necessarily restricted the freedom of services, a general declaration of good conduct for which to make a form could be downloaded from the internet, to be filled out and submitted to the authorities, did not amount to a licence in the sense of an authorization. Availability on the internet guaranteed sufficient publicity. Such a declaration was less onerous than an authorization. It could not validly be argued that it failed to take into account 'home' state regulation (paras 24-30). The Court also sanctioned the discretion of the Italian authorities to impose additional requirements on a case-by-case basis for police licence holders. The Commission had failed to show a single example in which such a requirement was imposed in a manner contrary to the freedom of services or establishment. There was no legal uncertainty (paras 35-9). In contrast, the requirement to have business premises in Italy and to display there the services offered was the very negation of the freedom of services and violated the freedom of establishment. Less intrusive means would have been available to guarantee the supervision of debt enforcement activities (paras 43-6 and 65-6). A territorial limitation of the 'licence' within the sense described above and, alternatively, the option to authorize an agent in regions other than where the 'licence' had been issued violated the freedom of services and establishment, for both requirements were unnecessary. Although indistinctly applicable, they provided domestic operators with better opportunities, since those operators were in a better position to establish contacts with agents in other regions. A declaration given in a single province would have sufficed for the purposes of supervision in all of Italy (paras 57-63). Although prices fixed by a member state could, according to case-law, amount to an obstacle to service provision given that an important variable for competition was eliminated, a non-binding recommendation of the prices to be charged for services, which in fact solely meant that an undertaking had to set objective and uniform price standards, was in accordance with the freedom of services and establishment, particularly when it was not proven beyond doubt that such a recommendation existed at all (paras 70-7). The simple clarification in a circular that the 'licence' to pursue extra-judicial debt enforcement activities did not imply a licence to offer banking and credit services, for which a separate licence was required, did not fall foul of the freedom of services (paras 83-5).

In *Commission v. Austria (bio inspections), 2007* the Court dealt with controls of production in accordance with Directive 2092/91 on organic agricultural products. Austria required private bodies that conducted those controls to be established in Austria even when those bodies had already been approved abroad. According to the Court, the Directive had not harmonised the monitoring of organic agricultural production by bodies established in the member states. Accordingly, the member states had to comply with the market freedoms, in particular the freedom of services, in that regard (paras 28-30). The requirement to have an establishment in Austria, as a restriction of free movement of services, was not justifiable. The official authority derogation failed to provide justification for lack of a direct and specific connection. In spite of the tasks performed by the monitoring bodies – implementation, reporting, supervision, granting and withdrawal of the right to market products, etc. – it were the Austrian authorities that supervised those bodies and were ultimately responsible. The issue of certificates of conformity and certain powers to impose penalties could be separated from the other supervisory tasks. Hence, they did not justify a removal of the entire supervisory tasks under the Directive from the freedom of services (paras 31-49). The protection of consumers, in turn, was sufficiently guaranteed by the Directive's harmonisation of the approval of private supervisory bodies. It was less restrictive to require bodies established in other member states to submit proof of their approval. Moreover, a system of exchange of information was in place (paras 54-60).

Van Leuken, 2008 concerned a real estate agent lawfully established in the Netherlands. He specialized in services with regard to real estate situated in Belgium. The Belgian authorities ordered him to cease his activities on the ground that he did not have a Belgian authorization. He then cooperated with a real estate agent properly authorized in Belgium who was responsible for the legal aspects of the activities in Belgium. Belgium's authorities again opposed that practice. At one point he applied for authorization in Belgium, but he was told to take an aptitude test comprising nine legal subjects as a compensatory measure. The Court applied Directive 89/49, since the profession was regulated in Belgium, and the freedom of services. The person concerned, according to the Court, had to have the possibility to choose between a period of adaptation and an aptitude test, since knowledge of Belgian law was not required to exercise the profession (paras 37-8). The compensatory measure was, moreover, disproportionate to the need to protect consumers given that he did no longer exercise the profession fully, but cooperated with a local real estate agent (paras 40-1). Accordingly, a penalty could not be imposed for his failure to comply with national law (para. 42).

In *Kattner, 2009* a German company challenged the compulsory affiliation to an association which provided statutory minimum insurance against the risk of accidents at work. Kattner wanted to take out accident insurance with a company established in Denmark. Having ruled that competition law was inapplicable, the Court found that the compulsory affiliation amounted to a restriction of the freedom of services, which applied despite the power of the member state to organise their social security systems (paras 72-6). Although it was uncertain whether accident insurance could be run profitably by private insurers, the compulsory affiliation prevented service receivers from taking out some insurance with insurers established abroad (paras 80-3). Yet the need to maintain the financial equilibrium of the social security system based on solidarity justified the restriction. Companies could still take out additional insurance with private insurers. That the affiliation was mandatory was necessary because of the risk of leaving the insurance association with 'bad' risks only (paras 85-91).

Commission v. Austria (patent lawyers), 2009 addressed two requirements Austrian law imposed on patent lawyers established abroad when they provided services in Austria, namely that they had to have a civil liability insurance which need not have been taken out necessarily in Austria but had to cover a minimum insurance sum; and that they needed to appoint an agent in Austria for the communication with authorities and courts. The first requirement was, according to the Court, a restriction of the freedom of services, because foreign patent lawyers had to take out an insurance policy which was not necessarily required in their 'home' state (paras 27-9). However, the protection of service recipients justified that restriction, in particular because it was not an alternative to inform the recipient that the lawyer he consulted did not have insurance, given the risk that recipients failed to comprehend the implications of that information (paras 32-37). In contrast, the second requirement was not justified. The requirements of regular procedure could be met through the use of postal services, as expressly acknowledged by Community regulation, or electronic means (paras 47-53). In a similar vein, in *Commission v. Austria (bank account), 2009* Austrian law in combination with the regulation issued by a professional association required self-employed doctors established in the Land Vorarlberg to have a bank account with a specific regional bank in Austria. This account was meant to simplify the administration of credits and reimbursements received from sickness funds and to secure possible claims. The Court examined the free movement of services, as the services of banks came within the scope of that freedom. The Court reiterated that not just regulation by the state was covered by the freedom of services, but also collective private regulation (paras 32-37). Austria's requirement restricted doctors in Austria in accepting services from foreign banks and those banks in providing them (paras 40-1). The simplification of administrative procedures was not a ground suitable to justify a restriction of the freedom of services. As to the prevention of abuse or the need to secure claims, less restrictive alternatives existed, like the exchange of information between the entities involved and the authorization for a bank to debit an account directly (paras 46-49).

Services more broadly

In the interest of completeness, a few more services cases need to be mentioned. In *Commission v. France (insurance), 2000* the Court invalidated based on the third non-life insurance and the third life assurance Directives 92/49 and 92/96 France's requirement to notify systematically some conditions of insurance contracts offered in France. In *Commission v. Belgium (insurance), 2000* the Court again interpreted Directive 92/49, holding that it applied to insurance offered by undertakings at their own risk even when that insurance was part of a statutory social security scheme. In *ABBOI, 2000* the Court clarified the framework for insurance undertakings under the third non-life insurance Directive for the setting up of undertakings pursuing business other than insurance. In *Kvaerner, 2001* the Court clarified the power to tax insurance premiums under the Second non-life insurance Directive 88/357 when a parent company had concluded insurance contracts for the benefit of subsidiaries in other member states. In *Axa Royale, 2002* the Court held that Belgium could not, under the third life assurance Directive 92/96, require companies to include in proposals and policies a general and vague warning as to the disadvantages of cancelling, surrendering or reducing a life-assurance contract. *Testa and Lazzeri, 2002* clarified the term 'management of investment portfolios' in the context of Directive 93/22 on investment services in the securities field and the latitude the Directive left to the member states.

The case *Der Weduwe, 2002* was rejected by the Court as inadmissible. The situation related to the freedom of services and seemingly raised a puzzling question: How was a service provider whom Luxembourg law obliged, under the threat of criminal penalties, not to disclose information owing to the banking secrecy to behave when Belgian law obliged him, under the threat of criminal penalties, to disclose that very same information in criminal proceedings? According to the Court the question was hypothetical though, since it was based on an unsound interpretation of Luxembourg law. That law equally seemed to allow such persons to disclose the information in criminal procedures (para. 37).

In *Commission v. Italy (direct insurance), 2003* the Court again applied the third non-life insurance directive 92/49, this time, firstly, striking down certain measures Italy took to freeze specific insurance rates, because those measures failed to live up to the freedom to set premiums contained in the directive and, notably, failed to come within the exception of general price-control systems. Secondly, the Court validated Italy's gathering of certain data to combat insurance fraud. In contrast, both in *Commission v. Luxembourg (insurance rates), 2004* and in *Commission v. France (insurance rates), 2004* the Court found a compulsory bonus-malus system for contracts insuring third-party liability arising out of motor vehicle accidents to be compatible with the third non-life insurance directive, because the system did not fix the premiums.

In *Asempre, 2004* the Court clarified the scope of the services that could be reserved to a national universal postal service provider under Directive 97/67 on postal services, in particular with regard to self-provision and money order services. In *Paul, 2004* the Court applied the Community banking legislation, namely Directives 94/19, 77/780, 89/299, and 89/646, to the effect that a depositor did not have a right against the competent authority to have certain supervisory measures taken, if the minimum deposit amount was guaranteed. Moreover, the relevant directives or state liability did not confer a depositor rights, bar the guarantee of the minimum deposit, in case his deposit was unavailable as a consequence of defective supervision.

In *Commission v. Belgium, 2005* the Court rejected the case, because the Commission had failed to prove that Belgium's legislation governing transparency to protect the consumer in certain customer loyalty programmes, which (the legislation) in itself was not contrary to the freedom of services, was implemented by an administrative practice which on its own breached the free movement of services. In *Ostermann, 2005*, the Court explained how the setting of a reasonable period for payment chimed with article 4(6) fourth motor insurance Directive 2000/26. In *Commission v. Spain (direct insurance), 2007* the Court rejected the Commission's allegation that Spain's regime governing cancellation of insurance contracts in case of cessions of bundles of contracts had violated Directive 92/49 and 2002/83 on non-life insurance and life assurance, respectively.

In *International Mail, 2007* the Court came back to postal services under Directive 97/67 as well as Directive 2002/39, which had taken liberalization a step further, to clarify when certain cross-border postal services could lawfully be reserved to a universal postal service provider. In particular the Court elaborated that the financial balance of such a provider had to be at risk to allow reservation of those services and that mere expediency was not sufficient to justify a monopoly in cross-border mail services. In *Deutsche Post, 2008* the Court essentially ruled that the universal service provider under Directive 97/67, which opened part of the postal distribution chain to some business customers and granted them preferential tariffs, had to offer the same tariffs to all customers willing to provide similar bulk mail at the same point in the distribution chain.

Finally, the Court in *Opinion on GATS amendments, 2009* addressed the modifications to the GATS that had become necessary because new member states had joined the Community. The Court opined that the competence to modify the GATS commitments was still shared between the Community and the member states despite the amendments the Treaty of Nice had made to the common commercial policy. Article 133(6) Treaty declared the competence to be shared with regard to certain sensitive policy fields. Moreover, the act of the Community approving the amendments to the GATS had to be based both on the common commercial policy and the common transport policy.

VI The 2010s

Not quite half of the decade is over and it is already clear that the case-law of the Court continues to grow – perhaps not exponentially, but certainly steadily on a very high level. The free movement of workers and citizens has already yielded more than 60 decisions and social security some 30 decisions, while the free movement of services and establishment have contributed the bulk, with more than 120 decisions.

1 Workers and citizens

Advantages

The Court developed its case-law on advantages migrant workers enjoyed in the first years of the 2010s. *Commission v. Netherlands (portable funding), 2012* dealt with a requirement the Netherlands imposed when support for studies abroad was applied for. According to Dutch law, funding to study at a university outside the Netherlands, so-called portable funding, was only granted when a prospective student had resided in the Netherlands during three out of the six years preceding enrolment at the foreign university, pursuant to the so-called 3 out 6 years rule. The Commission took issue with the 3 out 6 years rule, but only with regard to article 7(2) Regulation 1612/68, i. e. for workers and their children. The Court sided with the Commission and found free movement of workers and article 7(2) violated. The residence requirement amounted to indirect discrimination, as the majority of those migrant workers, viz. their children, and frontier workers residing abroad were nationals of other member states (paras 39 and 55). The comparability of situations required to find unequal treatment was given between, on the one hand, workers residing in the Netherlands and, on the other, frontier workers or migrant workers falling short of three years of residence (paras 42-44). Such comparability required objective and easily identifiable criteria, not simple probabilities. (The Netherlands had argued that it was more probable that prospective students who resided in the Netherlands would study in the Netherlands; paras 40 and 42). The Court then confirmed that article 7(2) had an independent meaning for the members of the family of a migrant worker, i. e. independent from article 12 Regulation 1612/68, as far as they (the members) were supported by the migrant worker (paras 48-53). That an unreasonable burden would result, if the 3 out 6 years rule was precluded by article 7(2), was not admitted by the Court as a ground to justify the indirect discrimination. If that consideration was admitted, the scope of the market freedoms would vary in time and place in function of the state of public finances. Migrant workers, after all, *per se* had a link to the host state's society, in particular because they paid taxes there. Moreover, the case-law in *Bidar, 2005* and *Förster, 2008* required such a link for Union citizens who did not work, in contrast to workers (paras 58-69). The aim of encouraging student mobility, though, could be a ground to justify the discrimination. The measure was appropriate to achieve that aim, given that most prospective students studied where they resided and most would return there after having studied abroad (paras 75-9). However, the Netherlands had failed to provide evidence that the 3 out 6 years rule was necessary and did not go beyond what the aim required. It was not sufficient to cite two alternatives which would have been more restrictive, namely a language or a local diploma requirement. The Netherlands at least had to show why they had opted for such an exclusive rule in the first place (paras 84-7). The Court, therefore, struck down the rule, while leaving the Netherlands the option of finding less restrictive alternatives.

In *L.N., 2013* a Union citizen had applied for a study course at an educational establishment in Denmark, then went to Denmark while the application was pending and began to work in full-time employment. When he commenced the studies, he continued to work part-time and applied for a maintenance grant in Denmark. For the Court, this was a standard case of a worker seeking benefits under article 7(2) Regulation 1612/68, provided that the national Court found that the work pursued was genuine and effective. The Court also reiterated that the motives of a person to exercise the freedom to work in another member state were irrelevant, as long as the person genuinely pursued or wished to pursue an activity in employment (para. 47). (Denmark had claimed that his motives had been *ab initio* to study in Denmark, because he had submitted his application before arriving in Denmark.) Apart from that, the Court clarified that the status of a Union citizen enrolled at an educational establishment under article 7(1)(c) Directive 2004/38 did not preclude a person from relying on the right of a worker to obtain a maintenance grant (para. 36). More generally, the rights conferred by both Union citizenship and free movement of workers were available at the same time to a Union citizen (para. 30).

In *Prete, 2012* the Court further explained the real link to the host state's employment market that migrant job seekers could lawfully be required to have established, before they came in a position to claim a benefit facilitating access to that employment market. Belgium required six years of studies at a Belgian establishment of higher education before entitlement to the tideover allowance arose. Abstaining from ruling on the exact duration of studies corresponding to the real link-requirement, the Court made it plain that other factors were capable of establishing a real link in the sense of the case-law, namely registration as a job seeker, periods of residence in the host state, or marriage in the host state and other family circumstances (paras 37-51). Article 39(2) Treaty therefore excluded the Belgian criterion as too general and exclusive, hence violating the rights of job seekers.

Residence

With *Radziejewski, 2012* the Court then came back to residence requirements. Swedish law made the availability of a debt relief procedure which granted private individuals relief from debt enforcement by creditors dependent on residence in Sweden. Mr Radziejewski had had residence in Sweden, but went to reside in Belgium, while remaining in employment in Sweden. He was refused a debt relief procedure in Sweden. The residence requirement, in the view of the Court, dissuaded workers from leaving Sweden (para. 31). The need to guarantee the authority of debt relief decisions, though a legitimate ground (para. 36), did not necessitate residence in Sweden. Even with residence in Sweden, a debtor could be sued by his creditors in a court in another member state where the debt relief decision was not recognized, since it was not within the scope of the Brussels framework. Even with residence abroad, the authority of the decision could be guaranteed in debt enforcement proceedings in Sweden (paras 37-43). Moreover, monitoring was legitimate, but could be implemented even in the absence of residence in Sweden, in particular when the person concerned was employed and subject to income taxation in Sweden and could be required to furnish information. To require residence just on the day when the debt relief procedure was opened was ineffective in any case (paras 46-50).

Next, *Caves Krier, 2012* also dealt with a residence requirement, this time in connection with a subsidy Luxembourg granted to employers who engaged unemployed persons of advanced age. Caves Krier, a Luxembourg company, engaged Ms Krier, a frontier worker residing in Germany who had previously lost her employment in Luxembourg and registered with the unemployment office in Germany. Caves Krier was refused the subsidy, because Ms Krier was resident in Germany. The Court held that there was a disadvantage for workers having used their freedom to move in that the benefit was denied based on the residence clause (paras 43-7). The employer was entitled to invoke the free movement of workers to oppose the resulting deterrent effect (paras 28-9). Luxembourg had not argued any justification. In any event, the member states' broad discretion in social policy did not justify the refusal, in particular since frontier workers as a rule entertained links with the employment market of the host state by reason of their (former) employment and the taxes they paid (paras 51-4).

Taxation

Numerous cases then concerned various taxes the member states imposed. In *Commission v. Greece (transfer tax), 2011* certain distinctions Greece drew in its tax regime for real estate transfers came to the Court. Greece exempted, first, anyone with permanent residence in Greece and, second, Greek nationals resident abroad from the tax that became due whenever ownership in real estate was transferred. Those exemptions applied whenever such persons acquired a first home in Greece. According to the Court, the requirement to have permanent residence in Greece amounted to indirect discrimination (paras 47-50) and the exemption of Greek nationals resident abroad to direct discrimination (para. 69), with both going against the grain of the freedom of workers and establishment. The first restriction was not justified by the aim of avoiding speculation, even if it were admitted as a ground for justification, as it was unsuitable for that purpose. An obligation to reside at the acquired home did not apply and the property could be rented out (para. 54). Similarly, low-income families were not protected, either, as all families benefitted from the exemption (para. 55). To avoid possible tax evasion or prevent abuse by persons resident abroad and acquiring several 'first' homes in Greece, less restrictive means were available, namely a requirement to register, provide documentation or a declaration, or checks by the authorities (paras 56-7). That ruling applied not just in case of workers, but also of Union citizens who were not economically active (para. 60). For the second restriction, i. e. the exemption of Greek nationals abroad, encouraging the return of Greek nationals from abroad and preserving the links between Greek nationals abroad and their home country were not objective circumstances which were independent of nationality (paras 70-1). For both restrictions, the same assessment applied with regard to the European Economic Area (paras 62 and 75).

Schulz-Delzers, 2011 next concerned comparability of certain allowances for tax purposes. 'German' civil servants received certain allowances from the German state when they worked abroad. Those allowances were not factored in at all for the purposes of income taxation in Germany. In a similar vein, 'French' civil servants received certain allowances from the French state when they worked in Germany. The German state took the French allowances into account for the purpose of determining the tax rate applicable in Germany. This resulted in a higher tax rate and thus a higher tax due owing to progression. In the case of Ms Schulz-Delzers, a French civil servant working in Germany and married to a German national, the taking into account in Germany of the allowances she received from the French state, led to a higher tax rate applicable in the joint income assessment with her husband, to which splitting applied. The Court did not find an issue under article 39 Treaty, because the situations of a civil servant working abroad for Germany and of a civil servant working for France in Germany were not comparable. Comparability had to be assessed within one and the same tax system, in this case within the German tax system (para. 40). An allowance the German state paid to one of its civil servants abroad was designed to compensate for the higher cost of living abroad and hence did not increase the civil servant's ability to pay tax in Germany; in contrast, the French allowance by nature increased the French civil servant's ability to pay tax in Germany. The resulting higher tax due, therefore, was not the result of discrimination, but of a determination by the German state of the tax criteria applicable (paras 35-42).

Commission v. Hungary (property tax), 2011 was about the property tax that became due upon the acquisition of real estate in Hungary. If such real estate served as the principal residence for the acquirer, the tax that had been paid previously on the occasion of acquisition of real estate was offset against the tax becoming due upon the new acquisition. The aim was to avoid double taxation of assets. In brief, only the amount that was invested in addition was taxed. However, that offsetting mechanism applied only within certain time-limits and when the first piece of real estate had been situated within Hungary and it had equally served as principal residence. The Court first found that the freedom of workers and establishment were applicable, since they gave specific expression to Union citizenship pursuant to article 18 Treaty (para. 44). The Court found a restriction of those freedoms, since those having paid property tax abroad previously were excluded from the benefit of offsetting (paras 66-7). The line of authority as to the lack of comparability of residents and non-residents for the purposes of taxation, viz. the *Schumacker, 1995*-line, did not apply to taxes such as property tax (paras 50-64). It had been developed for income taxation where objective differences existed between residents and non-residents (paras 57-8). The two situations at issue – first residence abroad and in Hungary – were thus comparable. However, the distinction Hungary drew was justified by the cohesion of the tax system. A direct link existed between the advantage, i. e. the offsetting of tax, and the disadvantage, i. e. the tax previously paid. A logical symmetry was reflected in that only the hitherto untaxed part of the invested assets was taxed and that Hungary did not have the power to tax property abroad. Moreover, the same taxpayer and the same taxation were concerned. If taxes paid abroad had been factored in on an equal footing, the persons moving to Hungary from abroad would have benefitted unduly from the host state's tax system (paras 70-78). Further, the distinction was proportionate, essentially because the benefit was a tax advantage and had not become a disguised exemption for Hungarians, because a rebate was not given if the tax previously paid had been higher. Moreover, the member states enjoyed some degree of autonomy in taxation and were not obliged to adapt their systems to those of other member states (para. 83-4). A restriction of the freedom of Union citizens who were not economically active was justified on the same ground (para. 89). The same assessment applied for the European Economic Area for the freedom of workers and establishment (paras 91-2). On the same day as *Commission v. Hungary (property tax), 2011* was handed down, the Court decided a similar case with nearly identical reasoning in *Commission v. Belgium (registration duties), 2011*. The Court only applied the free movement of capital rather than persons to a Flemish registration duty that could be offset against a duty previously paid when acquiring real estate as the principal residence in the Flemish region of Belgium. The Court found that the freedom of establishment was not applicable, since any breach of that freedom was the unavoidable consequence of an interference with the free movement of capital (para.32). Union citizenship pursuant to article 18 Treaty was not relevant, either, since the freedom of capital was the particular provision the Treaty laid down for such situations. Moreover, real estate acquisition in Belgium by persons who were not economically active was covered by the freedom of capital (paras 30 and 32).

In the order in *Notermans, 2012*, the Court confirmed the existing case-law as to registration taxes on imported cars. A registration tax was compatible with the free movement of workers and establishment, in essence if a car was primarily used in the host state and the duration of the use and the depreciation of the vehicle were taken into account. The day before *Notermans, 2012* was handed down the Court decided *van Putten, 2012* which was about the same car registration tax in the Netherlands. However, the facts in *van Putten, 2012* lacked any connection to the freedom of workers or establishment. Persons resident in the Netherlands had, in fact, used cars registered abroad which were provided to them free of charge. For lack of an economic dimension, the national court asked about the implications of Union citizenship pursuant to article 18 Treaty. However, the Court found that the cross-border loan of a car free of charge constituted a movement of capital. The Court then essentially went on to apply the established case-law as to the registration tax under the free movement of capital. Hence, Union citizenship need not have been addressed (para. 55).

In *Commission v. Estonia (tax allowance), 2012* the Court further refined the *Schumacker, 1995*-line of authority. In this case a resident of Finland received pensions of nearly equal amounts in Finland and Estonia. Because the overall amount of the pensions was modest, he was not taxed in Finland at all. Estonia taxed the pension due in Estonia and refused him a tax allowance on the ground that he was not resident in Estonia and did not receive more than 75 per cent of his income in Estonia. The Court found that *Schumacker, 1995* applied, although he received only about 50 per cent of his income in Estonia. In the situation where Finland did not tax the pension due in Finland because the worldwide income was modest, the personal and family circumstances as well as the ability to pay tax were not taken account of in Finland. Estonia's refusal to take into account the circumstances of a non-resident person when taxing a pension due in Estonia and to grant a tax allowance in such a situation came down to penalising the person concerned for having made use of the freedom to move. In such circumstances, the situations of a non-resident person and a regularly resident person in Estonia were comparable (paras 55-6). As advantages were not accumulated in an unjustified way, the free movement of workers was infringed (para. 57).

In *Commission v. Spain (income tax), 2012*, Spain required those moving residence to another member state to pay immediately the income tax relating to past periods of work, while those remaining in Spain could pay them at a later point in time. According to the Court, the resulting cash-flow disadvantage for those leaving Spain had a deterrent effect and constituted a restriction of the free movement of workers and establishment (para. 59). The situations of those leaving Spain and those remaining there were not objectively different with regard to income taxation (para. 60). The restriction was not justified by the need to recover tax debts effectively, since the instruments of cooperation available in Union law were sufficient for that purpose. Even if those instruments sometimes did not work fully effectively, the member states could not lawfully restrict a fundamental freedom on the basis of a lack of cooperation for the purposes of taxation (para. 72). In contrast to *Truck Center, 2008*, the restriction did not concern a different technique of taxation applicable to non-residents, viz. taxation at source, but the obligation to pay taxes immediately upon leaving a state (para. 74). Fiscal territoriality did not provide justification, either, since Spain's right to tax income generated in its territory was not in doubt. It was only the immediate recovery of tax debts that was at issue (para. 81). The direct link required by the *Bachmann, 1992*-case-law of the cohesion of the tax system was not given, either. In the case at issue the idea of cohesion in any case overlapped with the notion of territoriality (paras 86-7). Under article 18 Treaty the same assessment applied for Union citizens that were not economically active (paras 91-3). For the European Economic Area, though, Spain's measure was justified, as an equally effective instrument of mutual assistance between tax authorities did not exist in that framework and the bilateral conventions with Spain did not contain such an instrument, either (paras 96-8).

Petersen, 2013 again concerned income tax. Germany exempted income generated in the field of development aid from taxation when the employer concerned was established in Germany. Mr Petersen was a Danish national residing in Germany. He was employed in Denmark by an employer in the context of a development project in Benin. Mr Petersen worked in Benin under that contract. Germany, however refused to exempt his income which was taxable in Germany pursuant to the double taxation convention, because the employer was not established in Germany. The Court ruled that the free movement of workers was applicable. Any restriction on the freedom of services was the unavoidable consequence of a restriction of the freedom of workers (para. 33). That freedom was applicable in principle to a measure adopted by the member state where a worker was resident who was employed in another member state (para. 37). While the work was performed in a third state, a sufficiently close link to the European Union existed when a worker resident in one member state performed work under an employment contract with an employer established in another member state, in particular when the contract was subject to Danish law and Danish social insurance applied (paras 40-3). The refusal to grant the tax exemption was liable to dissuade workers from seeking employment in other member states (para. 46). The need for effective fiscal supervision did not justify that restriction even though the mutual assistance framework did not apply with regard to the third state. The taxpayer could lawfully be asked to furnish the information required regarding the Danish employer, as in fact it was also required from workers employed in Germany. Information from the third state was not necessary (paras 51-7). Germany, in addition, had failed to explain why development policy goals required the exclusion of workers employed in another member state from the income tax exemption (para. 61).

Family members

The Court also addressed the benefits family members enjoyed in the 2010s, namely in *Teixeira, 2010*. The Court ruled that the primary carer of a child in educational training and the child herself who was born in the host state had a right of residence under article 12 Regulation 1612/68, as in principle established in *Baumbast, 2002*. (All other grounds possibly conferring a right of residence were not applicable in the case at issue.) That right was independent for based on article 12 alone, rather than on article 12 in conjunction with article 10 Regulation 1612/68. Hence, the conditions of article 10 need not have been met on a continuous basis (paras 46-9). That independence was in particular significant, because the citizenship directive 2004/38 had repealed articles 10 and 11, but not article 12 Regulation 1612/68. The Court found that amendment not to have changed the right under article 12 (paras 56-60). The primary carer, a former worker and Union citizen, could apply for social assistance without forfeiting her right of residence under article 12 (paras 64-9). The independent right of residence of the child under article 12 lasted, while she was in training, even after having reached majority. The right of the parent also endured, provided that the child was still in need of the parent's care and presence (paras 78 and 86). That the parent had not worked at the exact moment the child had begun her educational training, but only generally during that training, was immaterial for the application of article 12 (paras 72-4). *Ibrahim, 2010* confirmed the independence of the right contained in article 12 Regulation 1612/68. The judgment in addition made it clear that the ruling in *Teixeira, 2010* also applied when the parent who was the primary carer was a national of a third country (para. 29). *Czop, 2012* confirmed the ruling in *Teixeira, 2010* as to article 12 Regulation 1612/68. The Court, furthermore, refused to apply article 12 to self-employed persons, given the clear and precise wording of that provision and the fact that it had been incorporated in the new regulation 492/2001 on workers rather than the citizenship directive 2004/38 (paras 31-3). The Court also confirmed that periods of residence completed before accession to the Union of the state of which the person concerned was a national counted towards the five year-period required for the right to permanent residence pursuant to article 16(1) citizenship directive (paras 34-5; see below).

Collective agreement

Erny, 2012 was a case that concerned article 7(4) Regulation 1612/68, i. e. the nullity of discriminatory individual and collective agreements. Mr Erny was a

French national who resided in France and worked for Daimler, a German company. His salary was subject to taxation in France pursuant to the applicable double taxation convention, because he was a cross-border worker. The net income that resulted for him was higher than that of a comparable worker subject to taxation in Germany. He entered a German scheme of part-time work prior to retirement which was partly based on a collective agreement. The idea of that scheme was to guarantee elderly employees 85 per cent of their previous salaries while they worked part-time. The employer paid a top-up amount in addition to the part-time salary to guarantee 85 per cent of the salary paid before part-time work was begun. The calculation of the top-up amount for cross-border workers was made based on a notional tax position, rather than the actual income the cross-border worker received. In the case of a worker residing in Germany the tax position was more in line with the actual income. The result of this method was that a German worker received roughly 85 per cent of his previous salary, with the top-up amount not being taxed in Germany, while a cross-border worker, such as Mr Erny, received less than 85 per cent and faced taxation of the top-up amount in his state of residence. In the view of the Court, that approach violated the free movement of workers. It created a disadvantage for cross-border workers (paras 42-5) which was not justified by administrative difficulties or the additional financial burden. The grounds suitable for justification of a restriction did not differ depending on whether a collective agreement or a public measure was at issue (para. 48). The autonomy of social partners, codified in article 28 of the Charter of Fundamental Rights, did not imply that Union law could be disregarded (para. 50). Since the relevant provisions were null and void pursuant to article 7(4) Regulation 1612/68, it was up to the parties involved to find suitable solutions (para. 53).

Non-discrimination

The Court also addressed non-discrimination more directly in the 2010s. With *Olympique Lyonnais, 2010* the Court was again faced with a sports case. The professional charter of the French football association, a national collective agreement, required players who were trained by a club in France under a specific contract for young players to sign the ensuing contract with the club that had trained them, else they became liable to pay damages. The Court, in keeping with *Bosman, 1995*, found that the obligation to pay damages constituted a restriction of the freedom of movement a worker, for it was liable to discourage the worker from exercising it (paras 35-6). While the restriction was generally susceptible of justification by the need to ensure the recruitment and training of young footballers, which was distinctive for sports in general, the measure went beyond what was required to attain that aim. The payments footballers were required to make when they signed a contract with a new club were not calculated on the basis of the cost generated by training and recruitment of players in general, but on the basis of an unspecified loss the club had suffered (paras 39-48).

In *Barth, 2010* the Court next dealt with a follow-up to *Köbler, 2003*. Mr Barth had been a professor in Germany and then was employed by an Austrian university, before *Köbler, 2003* was handed down. After *Köbler, 2003* he applied for the special length-of-service increment that had been at issue in that judgment and received it. However, he received the increment only for the three years that had passed before he applied. With regard to the period before that, his application was rejected based on a three-year limitation period in Austrian law. The Court found that the Austrian rejection did not amount to indirect discrimination. The actions of all professors at Austrian universities whose salaries had been calculated wrongly were subject to a three-year limitation period. Further, a worker was not possibly discouraged with regard to periods that took place entirely in the past (paras 37-40). The principles of effectiveness and equivalence flowing from non-discrimination were not violated, either (paras 16-36.)

In *Casteels, 2011* the Court was faced with the multiple successive affiliation of an employee of British Airways with subsidiaries in Belgium, France, and Germany. As Mr Casteels, when he moved on to work for another subsidiary, each time concluded a new employment contract with each subsidiary, albeit on the basis of a coordinating contract, he suffered certain disadvantages in terms of supplementary occupational pension benefits. Notably in Germany the collective agreement applicable provided that periods completed with subsidiaries in other member states were not taken into account for the purpose of the qualifying period for supplementary pension benefits in Germany. Moreover, when Mr Casteels left to be employed by another subsidiary of British Airways he was only reimbursed the contributions he himself had paid in Germany, rather than both his and his employer's contributions. According to the Court, article 48 Treaty could not be relied upon directly for lack of direct effect (paras 14-5). However, the approach of the collective agreement was relevant under article 45 Treaty (paras 19-20). The refusal to take into account periods completed with the subsidiaries in other member states of the same group, despite the existence of a coordinating contract, amounted to a restriction of the free movement of workers. Mr Casteels was disadvantaged in contrast to a worker who had never made use of his freedom, because he suffered financial losses and an adverse effect on his pension rights (paras 23-9). The restriction was not justified, since Mr Casteels would not be enriched unjustly if his claim was met. Staff loyalty could not be argued, either, as Mr Casteels had continuously been employed by one and the same employer (paras 31-2). Moreover, the relevant collective agreement seemed to be susceptible to an interpretation in compliance with article 45 Treaty (paras 34-5).

In *Las, 2013* Flemish legislation that required all employment contracts to be drafted in Dutch, on pain of nullity to be declared by the courts on their own motion, came under the Court's scrutiny. Mr Las, a Netherlands national, had concluded an employment contract in English with a Belgian company which was part of a multinational group. After having been dismissed he claimed based on Flemish law that the contract was null and void. After having confirmed that an employer was also entitled to rely on the freedom of workers (para. 16), the Court found a restrictive effect on employers and employees fluent in languages other than Dutch (para. 22). Whereas the promotion and protection of official languages, the social protection of workers and the monitoring of that protection were all grounds suitable to justify a restriction, the Flemish requirement went beyond what was required to attain those aims. Arguably, the Charter of Fundamental Rights protected the member states' cultural and linguistic diversity and their national identity (para. 26). Yet it would have been less restrictive to allow contracts drafted in two languages, one being Flemish, the other being a language which both parties understood. The need for free and informed consent of both contracting parties required that, given that sometimes the parties to a contract did not know the official language (paras 31-2).

Driving licences

The mutual recognition of driving licences under Directive 91/439 came back to the Court with *Scheffler, 2010*. The case concerned a driver whose driving licence had been withdrawn in Germany because of him having driven under the influence of alcohol. He then obtained a new driving licence while resident in Poland. Immediately after having received the new licence in Poland a psycho-medical report was drawn up in Germany, based on a request by him, in the light of the conduct that had led to the previous withdrawal of his licence in Germany. That report attested negatively with regard to fitness to drive. In these circumstances the Court left it to the national court to assess whether this report was 'new' evidence casting such doubt on the driver's fitness to drive as to allow the German authorities to rely on the exception from the obligation to recognize driving licences issued abroad. The Court merely indicated that this did not seem to be the case (paras 72-5).

Grasser, 2011 then established that a foreign driving licence need not have been recognized if it had manifestly been issued in disregard of the residence requirement. That was the case when a licence issued in the Czech Republic stated itself that the driver was resident in Germany (para. 24). It was irrelevant in this regard whether the licence concerned was the first licence ever issued to the driver or whether another licence had previously been withdrawn from her (paras 26-32). In *Apelt, 2011* the Court clarified that the confiscation of a driving licence equalled a withdrawal within the meaning of Directive 91/439 and the case-law (para. 33). Moreover, when a licence for category B, viz. cars, was vitiated by an error which justified a refusal of recognition, a licence for category D, i. e. buses, which was issued subsequently need not have been recognized, either (paras 38-47). According to *Köppl, 2011*, the latter ruling was also valid when a category C licence was added to a category B licence – even if the error, which was a failure to comply with the residence requirement which in turn was evident from the category B licence itself – was not evident from the category C licence (para. 48).

Akyüz, 2012 added to this case-law that a refusal to issue a first driving licence in one state was not a ground for that state to refuse to recognize a licence issued in another state later on. In other words, a refusal to grant a licence was not the same as a withdrawal, even if the ground for the refusal – in the case at issue aggressiveness of the person concerned – would have justified the withdrawal of a licence (paras 50-8). The Court in *Akyüz, 2012* also broadly transposed the case-law established under Directive 91/439 regarding the withdrawal of driving licences to the new driving licence Directive 2006/126 (paras 40 and 34). The Court added that 'indisputable evidence' concerning a driver's lack of residence in the issuing state, which justified a refusal to recognize a licence, included the information conveyed by the authorities of the issuing state to the host state, even if it was conveyed through a state's representation in the issuing state. The national court, moreover, had to assess whether residence in the issuing state had been purely fictional (paras 67-8, 71-2, and 75-6). In *Hofmann, 2012* the Court ruled that the case-law established under Directive 91/439 as to the obligation to recognize a licence issued in another member state after a temporary ban on re-application for a new licence had expired continued to apply under Directive 2006/126, despite the slightly changed wording (paras 65-89).

Ankara

In the 2010s, the Court addressed the Ankara Agreement with Turkey in a long series of decisions beginning with *Bekleyen, 2010*. Ms Bekleyen was a Turkish national and the daughter of a Turkish worker. Her father had been admitted to work in Germany, but had returned to Turkey with his entire family. After several years, Ms Bekleyen returned to Germany alone to pursue the higher education she had begun in Turkey. The question arose whether she could lawfully claim rights under article 7(2) Decision 1/80 to take residence and access the employment market, despite her and her parent's prolonged absence from Germany and despite the lack of a temporal link between her parent's work and residence in Germany and the educational training she continued in Germany. The Court answered in the affirmative. The idea of article 7(2) was to grant a worker's child an autonomous right to access the employment market, rather than to foster family unity (paras 22-31). It was immaterial that a child returned to the host country alone and that a long time had passed since the worker and his family had first left that country. The children of Turkish workers were, moreover, not treated more favourably than the children of Union citizens – a difference in treatment which article 59 of the Additional Protocol would have precluded. There were more grounds to restrict the rights of those Turkish children than in the case of Union citizens under the Citizenship Directive 2004/38. Their rights could, for instance, be lost when they left the host state for a long time without any legitimate reason (paras 35-44).

With *Genc, 2010* the Court again added to the Ankara Agreement case-law. Ms Genc, a Turkish national, initially had come to Germany to reunify with her husband who was a lawful worker of Turkish nationality in Germany. She received a residence and a work permit. After they had separated, she worked lawfully but only during 5.5 hours per week, i. e. her employment only amounted to 14 per cent of a standard full-time job, earning her only 25 per cent of the regular minimum means of subsistence. Her contract was subject to the collective agreement concerned, she enjoyed paid holidays and continued salary payment in case of sickness. During a certain time, she received social security benefits, but she later asked for them to be stopped. The Court applied the internal market definition of a worker, as elaborated in *Megner, 1995* with regard to very few hours of work, to find that she was a regular worker within the meaning of the Ankara Agreement. The national Court had to ascertain, though, that her work was real and genuine, rather than marginal and ancillary, factoring in paid holiday, sickness insurance, union protection, and the long-standing contractual relationship with her employer (paras 18-28). The reason why she had come to the host country initially was not relevant any longer, as it was not one of the conditions exhaustively enumerated in article 6(1) Decision 1/80. Hence, it was irrelevant that the family with which she had at first reunified was not lived any longer in actual fact. She was therefore entitled to claim rights under article 6(1), provided that she met the conditions established by that article (paras 36-40) and that her presence did not constitute a threat to public security or that she was not absent from the host state for a prolonged period of time (paras 41-3).

Next, in *Toprak, 2010* the standstill clause in article 13 Decision 1/80 was at issue. Two Turkish nationals had come to the Netherlands for family reunification with Turkish workers. However, before three years had elapsed, their marriages failed. The marriages had lasted more than one year after their arrival in the Netherlands, though. At the time Decision 1/80 had entered into force, Dutch law had required a period of cohabitation in the Netherlands of three years for an independent right of residence to arise for a spouse. That period was later on reduced to one year, and then again increased back to three years. The Court decided that the standstill clause applied in such a context, because the Netherlands regime, while technically applying only to spouses of foreign nationality, affected also Turkish workers (paras 40-6). Moreover, the objective of the standstill clause required that it be applied with reference to the point in time when the one-year period had become applicable. Thus, any subsequent increase of that one-year period constituted a new restriction precluded by the standstill clause. More generally, conditions were not to be made more stringent than they had been at any point in time after the entry into force of decision 1/80 (paras 49-60). The Court essentially transferred that interpretation to article 41(1) Additional Protocol in *Dereci, 2011*. The Court held with regard to the establishment of a Turkish national in Austria that the tightening of a provision which had relaxed the rules applicable at the entry into force of the Additional Protocol to the Ankara Agreement fell foul of article 41(1) of that Protocol, as it constituted a new restriction (paras 94-8). (For the citizenship dimension of the case, see below.)

In *Metin Bozkurt, 2010* a situation with regard to article 7(1) Decision 1/80 was at issue. A Turkish national had joined his wife in Germany. He unquestionably fulfilled the period of cohabitation in article 7(1). They divorced after he had been convicted of having violated his wife. The Court decided that the divorce was irrelevant, once a spouse had acquired separate rights under article 7(1). So was any kind of employment of the person concerned for the purpose of article 7(1). Beyond the two grounds acknowledged, viz. a prolonged absence and a threat to public policy, security or health, other grounds for removal could not be acknowledged (paras 30 and 35-45). Further, fraudulent conduct to secure rights under Decision 1/80, such as a sham marriage, was no at issue. In particular, the reliance on rights did not amount to such conduct (paras 49-52). Hence, the only point where the crime committed could be taken into account was in the assessment, in keeping with case-law, of the public policy or security threat posed by the person concerned (paras 54-60).

Pehlivan, 2011 again concerned article 7(1) Decision 1/80. Ms Pehlivan, a Turkish national, had lawfully joined her Turkish parents who were workers in the Netherlands and resided with them for more than three years, as required by article 7(1). During that time, she married a Turkish national. Under Dutch law that marriage broke the family link with her parents, which resulted in the loss of the right of residence under article 7(1). According to the Court, the member states were entitled to impose certain limited conditions that complied with the objective of article 7(1), which was to foster family unity, during the three years of cohabitation with the parents (paras 52-3). However, article 7(1) only required the child to live with her parents. If she had done so, it went against the grain of the objective of that article to consider her marriage during those three years as having broken the link with her parents. Having lived for three years with her parents, she was entitled to claim rights under article 7(1), irrespective of her marriage (paras 57-61 and 64). In *Unal, 2011* the Court interpreted article 6(1) Decision 1/80 in a similar way. A Turkish national had joined his wife in the Netherlands. He received a residence permit and worked lawfully. After he had worked for more than a year with the same employer, it turned out that he had failed during his first year of employment to abide by the condition contained in the residence permit to reside with his wife. The Dutch authorities withdrew his residence permit retroactively, as per the point in time when he stopped residing with his wife. The Court rejected that approach under article 6(1). While a member state had the power to regulate the conditions during the first year of work, once a Turkish national who had lawfully entered the host state had worked there for more than a year – in the absence of a provisional admission to the territory or fraudulent conduct – that Turkish national acquired the rights under article 6(1). Those rights were not to be made dependent any longer on the continuing existence of the circumstances which had given rise to them (paras 49-50). *Gülbahce, 2012* confirmed this decision.

Ziebell, 2011 raised the question of the impact of Union citizenship under the Ankara Agreement. The case involved a second generation Turkish immigrant, the son of a Turkish worker who (the son) was born in Germany and had spent all his life there. After several criminal convictions, his expulsion from Germany was ordered. The Court refused to apply by analogy the enhanced protection regime established by the citizenship directive 2004/38 for union citizens having permanent residence in the host state to Turkish nationals having long-term residence in the host state. That regime required that imperative grounds of public security were given to justify an expulsion (paras 57 and 60). The purpose of the Ankara Agreement was purely economic (para. 64). It applied to workers, whereas Union citizenship relied only on nationality and went further than economic integration. The effects of Union citizenship were reserved to the nationals of the member states (paras 69-73). The right frame of reference for the expulsion of a Turkish national therefore was, since Directive 64/221 had been repealed by the citizenship directive, the framework established by the Union for third country nationals having long-term residence in the Union, i. e. article 12 Directive 2003/103. Within that framework, additional guarantees for long-term residents were provided and the traditional established expulsion case-law of the Court applied. That case-law, in essence, required a weighing of the circumstances, but in principle allowed expulsion in case a threat to public *policy* was given, rather than a threat to public *security* under the citizenship directive in case of Union citizens having long-term residence (paras 79-85).

Kahveci, 2012 then came back to article 7 Decision 1/80. The Court ruled that a family member that had fulfilled the conditions required by article 7 was still entitled to claim the corresponding rights and enjoyed the protection of article 14 Decision 1/80, even if the Turkish worker concerned had been naturalized in the host state while retaining his Turkish nationality. The Court reached this conclusion based on the objective of article 7 which was to promote family reunification. Moreover, a member state was not entitled to add conditions to article 7 or alter rights acquired under that article. That would have been the case, if the article had not been applied any longer after the Turkish worker concerned had gained the nationality of the host state while keeping the Turkish nationality (paras 35-8). *Dülger, 2012* added that the members of the family of Turkish workers who were nationals of third states, viz. third states other than Turkey, also enjoyed the protection of article 7 Decision 1/80. In addition to the objective of that article, the Court relied on a number of other grounds, namely the need for uniform interpretation of the term 'family members' (para. 36); that the parties to the Ankara Agreement had gone 'well beyond considerations of a purely economic nature' (para. 45) with article 7 Decision 1/80; the right to private and family life as enshrined in article 7 Charter of Fundamental Rights which was to be observed as a part of Union law having the same value as the Treaties (para. 53); the corresponding rules applicable to the members of the family of Union citizens (paras 48-51); Regulation 1408/71 and Decision 3/80 which both covered family members who were third country nationals (paras 54-7); and the power the member states retained to authorize family reunification in the first place, subject to the respect of fundamental rights (paras 61-2).

Bulgaria

Two cases in the 2010s concerned Bulgaria before and immediately after its accession to the Union. *Pavlov, 2011* concerned non-discrimination in the context of the Association Agreement with Bulgaria before its accession to the Union. Mr Pavlov was refused inclusion in the list of trainee lawyers in Austria by reason solely of his Bulgarian nationality. The Court decided that the inclusion in the list concerned access to a regulated profession, rather than a condition of work. Such access was not, in contrast to the conditions of work, subject to non-discrimination pursuant to article 38(1) of the Association Agreement. Hence, the refusal to include him in the list was in accordance with that article (paras 23-8). In *Sommer, 2012*, an employer in Austria wanted to employ a Bulgarian student lawfully present in Austria, but the work permit was refused on the ground that the relevant quota had been exceeded. The Court in essence found that Bulgarian nationals had to benefit from the same access to the labour market as under Directive 2004/114 on *inter alia* third country national students access to the labour market, although they had become Union citizens and were not any longer third country nationals. Though accession took place before this Directive had to be transposed, the Accession Protocol required that Bulgarian nationals benefitted from the treatment provided in the Directive and that they were given preference over third country nationals (paras 33-5). (The Court then interpreted the Directive on the facts of the case and found that it only exceptionally permitted a restriction based on the situation of the labour market; paras 41-4.)

Union citizenship

Union citizenship also occupied the Court in many cases during the early years of the 2010s. *Rottmann, 2010* was the first pure citizenship case of the 2010s. Mr Rottmann was an Austrian national who became the subject of a criminal investigation in Austria. He then emigrated to Germany where he was later on naturalized. He did not mention the criminal investigation vis-à-vis the German authorities. As a result of the naturalization in Germany, he lost his Austrian nationality. When the German authorities learnt of the criminal investigation and the Austrian arrest warrant, they revoked the decision granting Mr Rottmann German nationality, with the result that Mr Rottmann ran the risk of not retaining any nationality at all. The Court first found that the situation was by nature and in the light of the potential consequences within the scope of Union law. Mr Rottmann's Union citizenship was affected by the decision to withdraw the nationality (para. 42). While the member states had the power and discretion to grant and withdraw nationality, they had to respect Union law in their decisions, as established in *Micheletti, 1992*. That implied that the decision to withdraw nationality in particular was subject to judicial review in the light of Union law (para. 48). When a person had acquired nationality by means of deceptive behaviour, a member state had the power to withdraw it, a power which was in accordance with international law and served to protect 'the special relationship of solidarity and good faith' as well as 'the reciprocity of rights and duties' between a state and its nationals (para. 51). However, owing to Union law and the effect of a withdrawal on Union citizenship, a member state had to respect proportionality in the light of Union law, i. e. to take into account the consequences for the person concerned and his family as well as the circumstances such as the gravity of the deception, the length of the time period since the acquisition of the nationality, and the possibility to re-acquire the former nationality. The latter point on its own was not imperative, although the national court possibly had to offer the person concerned a reasonable period of time to regain his previous nationality (paras 55-8). The member state of which the Union citizen previously was a national equally had to respect proportionality in its decision whether to reinstate him in his nationality (para. 62).

Union citizenship and students

Next, in *Bressol, 2010* the French-speaking region of Belgium had introduced a restriction for certain undergraduate medical and paramedical study programmes at its universities, because a great number of students had come from other member states to study at those universities, while returning home immediately after the end of their studies, leaving the French community without a sufficient number of qualified medical graduates. In essence, the number of non-resident students in each of the programmes concerned was limited to 30 per cent of all students in the programme. The places for non-resident students enrolling for the first time were allocated by lot. In the judgment of the Court, the member states were free to opt for a system of free or restricted access to university education, provided they respected Union law (paras 28-9). The situation of the students concerned was within the scope of Union citizenship pursuant to article 18 Treaty and the citizenship directive 2004/38. Relying on residence to determine who was admitted amounted to indirect discrimination (paras 43-7). Justification on the basis of financial considerations was excluded (paras 49-51). The justificatory power of the need to ensure the homogeneity of the higher education system was left open (paras 52-4). However, the requirements of public health applied, in particular if the high number of students enrolled put in danger the quality of the medical education and, despite that high number, not enough qualified graduates were available in the French Community (paras 67-8). Ultimately, it was for the national court, though, to determine whether the restriction was necessary. Protective measures were possible, despite uncertain causal links between education and the situation on the market (paras 69-70). In a thorough objective assessment with figures and solid consistent data the authorities had to show for each study branch the maximum sustainable number of students and the minimum number of graduates needed for the market, along with a number of other factors (paras 71-3). It was also to be assessed whether the restriction was in fact capable of leading to an increase in the number of practitioners in the French Community (para. 76). Further, less restrictive alternatives had to be examined which could incentivize practitioners to settle in Belgium permanently or which could take into account the aptitudes and knowledge of candidates better than chance on which the drawing of lots relied (paras 78 and 80). Finally, the Court did not see a contradiction between the right of access to higher education in article 13(2)(c) of the United Nations Covenant of Civil and Political Rights and the requirements of Union citizenship (paras 85-7). The temporal effects of the judgment were not subject to any limitation (paras 89 et seq.).

Commission v. Austria (transport fare), 2012 also concerned students and Union citizenship. The law of some Austrian Länder reduced the fares for public transport for students, but only those students whose parents were receiving family allowances in Austria. According to the Court, such a benefit was within the scope of articles 20 and 21 Treaty, in so far as it indirectly helped students to cover maintenance cost (para. 43). Even if the benefit was covered by Regulation 1408/71 pursuant to article 1(u) of that Regulation, that did not imply that unequal treatment was allowed (paras 44-8). The restriction consisted in the fact that the condition of receiving family allowances in Austria was more easily fulfilled by students who were Austrian nationals, since their parents frequently received family allowances in Austria (para. 50). Article 24(2) Directive 2004/38 was not applicable, because it explicitly only applied to student grants and student loans (paras 54-6). The need for a genuine link with the society of the host state, in principle, could justify a restriction. But the criteria applied to establish such a link were not to be too general or overly favouring an element that did not represent a real and effective degree of connection with the host state. Whether that was the case had to be established in light of the nature and the purpose(s) of the benefit concerned. As an example, it could be taken into account whether the student was enrolled with a private or a public establishment which was financed or accredited by the host state in accordance with its laws. Austria had failed to establish that the benefit at issue was based on such considerations (paras 61-5).

Permanent residence

In *Lassal, 2010* the right to permanent residence of Union citizens was invoked. Ms Lassal, a French national, had resided in the United Kingdom lawfully based on Union law for more than five years. She then went back to France to live with her mother for ten months. After that she came back to the United Kingdom. All these facts had taken place before the citizenship directive 2004/38 had to be transposed. She claimed a right to permanent residence under that directive, a right that depended on a period of five years of residence in the host state. The Court reiterated that the Directive did not grant any less rights than Union citizens had before its entry into force (para. 30). Even before the adoption of the Directive, Union law had allowed migrant workers to remain in the host state after having ceased to work (para. 35). Moreover, the purpose of the Directive was to promote integration in the host state. Such integration was taking place already before the Directive became applicable (para. 37). The Directive had to be applied to present facts (paras 38-9). Hence periods of lawful residence completed before the Directive was to be transposed had to be counted towards the five year-period. Ms Lassal's absence from the United Kingdom, moreover, was not relevant, since she had already been resident in the United Kingdom for more than five years when she departed for France (para. 45). The effectiveness of the Directive which prevailed in case of conflicting interpretations and its objectives dictated that much (paras 49 and 51-3). However, they also dictated that article 16(4) Directive be applied in case she was absent from the host state for more than two years (paras 54-6). *Dias, 2011* was a similar case as *Lassal, 2010.* A Portuguese national had resided lawfully for five years in the United Kingdom. She then stopped working and failed to have sufficient resources to support herself, but continued to hold the residence permit, i. e. the document, issued to her under Directive 360/68. All this took place before the date of transposition of Directive 2004/38. In keeping with *Lassal, 2010* the period of five years of residence gave rise to a right to permanent residence under article 16(1) Directive, though obviously not before the end of the transposition date. A residence permit did not give rise to rights. It was merely declaratory. Hence, she did not have a right to reside in the United Kingdom after having completed the five year-period solely because she had a document entitled 'residence permit'. Her lack of resources meant that she did not have a right to reside in the United Kingdom (paras 47-55). In such a situation, article 16(4) Directive had to be applied by analogy. Like two years of absence from the territory of the host state extinguished the right of permanent residence, periods of residence of more than two years completed without having a right of residence – although formally the person concerned held a 'residence permit' – terminated the right to permanent residence. The integration link to the host state was not just put into question by absence from the territory, but also by qualitative elements like the lack of a right to reside (paras 57-65).

Ziolkowski, 2011 again concerned the right of Union citizens to permanent residence in the host state pursuant to article 16 Directive 2004/38. The Court held that 'having resided legally' in the host state was an autonomous concept of Community law for lack of reference to national law in article 16 (para. 33). Based on the context and purpose of the right to permanent residence the Court concluded that the conditions in article 7(1) Directive, viz. to have sufficient resources and sickness insurance, had to be met during the five years of residence in the host state which gave rise to the right to permanent residence (para. 34-47). Hence, although a period of residence might have been in compliance with the host state's law, it only counted toward the five year-period of residence, if the Union citizen had had during that period enough resources not to become a burden on the host state's finances. Secondly, for lack of a transitional provision in an Act of Accession, the Directive had to be applied *in toto* right from accession. This implied that periods of lawful residence completed before accession counted towards the five year-period, since the law was applied non-retroactively to the present facts that had their origin in the past. The person concerned had to show, though, that 'sufficient resources' were available during that period (paras 56-62).

Union citizenship and expulsion

Tsakouridis, 2010 dealt with the enhanced protection of Union citizens against expulsion after ten years of residence in the host state. The case concerned a Greek national who had been born and had always lived in Germany, but had spent two summers working in Greece. He was convicted of drug dealing and sentenced to prison for more than six years. The German authorities ordered his expulsion. For Union citizens having resided for the previous ten years in the host state, imperative grounds of public security were necessary for expulsion, rather than just serious grounds of public security in case of permanent residence or public security or policy grounds in case of regular residence pursuant to article 28(2) and (3) Directive 2004/38. The Court directed the referring court to make an overall assessment of the situation of the person concerned with regard to the ten year-period of residence. All factors had to be taken into account, in particular the duration and frequency of the absences, the reasons for them, and the centre of interest of the person concerned, in order to determine whether the link with the host state had been broken during any absence (paras 32-5). It was also for the national court to assess whether imperative grounds of public security were given. The case-law as to expulsion basically applied, but the requirements were stricter. Very good grounds and a high degree of seriousness of the threat to public security were needed. Drug dealing as part of an organized group was possibly covered; certainly it was within the ambit of 'public policy' in article 28(2) Directive. A balance had to be struck between the imperative grounds of public security and the social rehabilitation and fundamental rights of the person concerned (paras 45-52). The Court added in *P. I., 2012* that the sexual assault, sexual coercion and rape of a minor over many years could lawfully be considered by the referring court to amount to an imperative ground of public security. Sexual crimes against minors were a particularly harmful sort of crime. The national court therefore had the option to find in the case at issue that a fundamental interest of society was concerned (paras 25-8). Expulsion was not to be an automatic consequence, though. The personal circumstances of the Union citizen concerned had to be taken into account and they had to be reviewed, if the expulsion order was implemented more than two years after it had been issued (paras 29-32).

Union citizenship and names

In *Sayn-Wittgenstein, 2010* Austria's constitutional abolishment of noble titles in surnames came under scrutiny. The Austrian constitutional court had ruled that a noble surname conferred by adoption in Germany to an Austrian national violated this constitutional rule and the prohibition of distinctions between genders in surnames. This judgment by the Austrian court affected an Austrian national who had not been involved in the proceedings before the Austrian constitutional court that had led to the ruling. That Austrian national bore the surname *Fürstin von Sayn-Wittgenstein* which meant 'Princess of Sayn-Wittgenstein'. She had conducted business under that name in luxury real estate for 15 years in Germany where she also resided. Her name stemmed from the adoption as an adult in Germany by a German national called *Fürst von Sayn-Wittgenstein.* Following the judgment of the Austrian constitutional court, her surname was changed in the Austrian registers – the only registers she was listed in – to 'Sayn-Wittgenstein'. For the Court, the name change affected the interests of her business which she had pursued under a regular name in Germany for 15 years and caused her as a Union citizen serious inconveniences within the meaning of the *Garcia Avello, 2003* and *Grunkin, 2008*-line of authority (paras 60-70). The Court did not enter into the freedom of services, because the referring court had only asked about citizenship. The restriction could, however, be justified by public policy grounds, namely the constitutional rank of the norm that abolished nobility in Austria and national identity. It was covered by the margin of discretion the member states enjoyed in terms of public policy. The Charter of Fundamental Rights recognized the right to equal treatment before the law in article 20 which was underpinning Austria's approach to surnames. Moreover, the measure, on the facts of the case, did not go beyond what was necessary to achieve the aim (paras 83-94).

Runevič-Vardyn, 2011 again brought a problem regarding names to the Court. A Lithuanian national belonging to the Polish minority had married a gentleman of Polish nationality. Both were resident in Belgium. In their marriage certificate which had been issued by the Lithuanian authorities her maiden last name in the double-barrelled surname she was going to use was spelled in Lithuanian language, despite her Polish heritage, in accordance with her passport and birth certificate, essentially spelling 'č' instead of 'cz'. Her first name was also written in Lithuanian in keeping with her passport and birth certificate. *His* last name in her double-barrelled surname was spelled in Lithuanian, using 'v' instead of 'w', while it was spelled in Polish with 'w' for him in the same marriage certificate. His first name was spelled without using the diacritical marks, spelling 'L' instead of 'Ł'. After having found that the situation was within the scope of Union citizenship, as it applied immediately to the present effects of facts originating in the past and as the two Union citizens had made use of the freedom to move, the Court first did not find a restriction with regard to her maiden name in the double-barrelled surname, since it was spelled in a uniform way in her birth certificate, passport, and marriage certificate. A deterrent effect did not arise for her, either, despite her Polish origin (paras 69-70). Neither was there a restriction in the spelling of his first name in the marriage certificate. The omission of diacritical marks was frequent, in particular when computers were used (paras 79-81). However, the national court had to examine whether the divergence in the spelling of his surname – first in his name in Polish with 'W', then in her double-barrelled name with 'V' in one and the same marriage certificate – amounted to an inconvenience within the meaning of the case-law, and if that was the case, whether it was serious enough to constitute a restriction (paras 72-8). In that event, the national court also had to assess whether a fair balance was struck between the protection of the Lithuanian language as part of the national identity, the safeguarding of which the Charter of Fundamental Rights mandated and which *Groener, 1989* had recognized as a ground for justification, and the rights of the persons concerned as Union citizens and beneficiaries of the fundamental right to identity and private life. That his surname was spelled in Polish on the same certificate and that Roman letters could otherwise be used in surnames in Lithuania despite them not being part of the official language was indicative (paras 88-93).

(Not) purely internal situations, family reunification of Union citizens

In *Ruiz Zambrano, 2011* a Columbian national was refused unemployment benefits in Belgium. He and his wife had been present in Belgium while several procedures to determine their status were pending. Mr Zambrano worked without having the prerequisite work permit in Belgium. When he was ordered to desist he applied for unemployment benefits. During their stay in Belgium, Ms Zambrano gave birth to two children who both acquired Belgian nationality based on Belgian law, because they risked remaining stateless. The reason why they did not acquire Colombian nationality was that the parents did not undertake the necessary steps. Mr Zambrano then argued that he had a right to residence and work as of the birth of his first child *qua* him being the relative in ascending line of a Union citizen who depended on him. Since he had a right to work in Belgium, his argument went, the periods of his work were lawful and had to be counted toward the period of work required for unemployment benefits. The children had basically never left Belgium, the state of which they were nationals. The Court, first, rejected the application of Directive 2004/38, because it only applied to Union citizens who had made use of their right of movement. Article 20 Treaty, in contrast, applied, for the children unquestionably were Union citizens, given their Belgian nationality. Any measure that had the effect of depriving a Union citizen of the genuine enjoyment of the substance of the rights owing to that status was precluded (para. 42). The refusal to grant Mr Ruiz Zambrano a residence and work permit was such a measure. It forced the children as Union citizens to leave the territory of the Union, for they depended on their parent (paras 43-4). In *McCarthy, 2011*, the Court refined that approach. Ms McCarthy invoked Union citizenship pursuant to article 21 Treaty and the citizenship Directive 2004/38 against the United Kingdom to claim a right of residence for her husband who was a national of a third country. She was a national of the United Kingdom and of Ireland. She had been born in the United Kingdom and had never moved away. In keeping with *Ruiz Zambrano, 2011*, she was not to be considered a beneficiary of the citizenship Directive, since she had never exercised her freedom of movement. The wording, purpose and context of the Directive only guaranteed the movement. A person who was a national of a member state and who had never moved away from that state had not exercised her freedom to move. That she also held the nationality of another member state, namely Ireland, did not imply that she had exercised that freedom. Her husband could not lawfully benefit from the citizenship directive, either, since he did not have any rights which were autonomous from hers (paras 31-43). As to article 21 Treaty, the situation was not to be considered purely internal to the United Kingdom solely by reason of her never having made use of her right to move. However, she did not suffer any serious inconvenience or was deprived of the substance of her right to move within the meaning of the *Garcia Avello, 2003/Ruiz Zambrano, 2011*-line of authority. She had an unconditional right to remain in the United Kingdom by reason of her British nationality. Hence, her situation was confined in all respects to the United Kingdom and article 21 Treaty was not applicable (paras 46-55).

That strand of case-law was further expounded in *Dereci, 2011*. Several third country nationals claimed a right to reside with family members who were Austrian nationals, and thus Union citizens, in Austria. Again the citizenship Directive was inapplicable, for lack of movement by the Union citizens. As to the rights based on the Treaty, a Union citizen did not suffer a serious inconvenience in a situation where it was desirable for her to live with a family member who was a third country national and that desire was not respected. Rather, the Union citizen had to be forced by the circumstances to leave not just the state of which he was a national, but the entire territory of the Union (paras 66-8). Apart from that, it was left to the national court to apply the right to family life either in article 7 Charter of Fundamental Rights or in article 8(1) ECHR, which were two articles with the same meaning, depending on whether the national court found that Union law was implemented or not (paras 70-3). *Iida, 2012* further elaborated that line of authority. Mr Iida was a Japanese national who had married a German national in the United States of America. They had a daughter who was of German nationality. They first moved to Germany where Mr Iida worked in employment. His wife then moved to Austria together with their daughter to work there, while he remained in Germany. Thenceforth, they lived separately, but the marriage as well as the joint parental responsibility were maintained. Mr Iida then applied for a residence permit in Germany as a family member of a Union citizen. That application was rejected. According to the Court, Mr Iida would have had rights as a long-term resident third country national pursuant to Directive 2003/109, had he only filed an application to this effect. However, in the absence of such an application, such rights did not arise (paras 40-8). Under Directive 2004/38 only rights derived from Union citizens were granted to third country nationals. According to case-law, namely *Zhu and Chen, 2004*, dependence of the Union citizen daughter on the third country national parent was not sufficient to found a right of residence of the latter under Directive 2004/38 (paras 54-5). According to *Diatta, 1985*, a marriage was to be considered intact as long as it had not be dissolved officially (paras 57-9). However, a third country national spouse was only a beneficiary of the Directive, if he had accompanied the spouse to or joined her in the host state. Hence, the Directive did not grant Mr Iida any rights in his situation (paras 61-4). Article 20 and 21 Treaty, in turn, provided derived rights for third country nationals in cases of intrinsic connection with the free movement of Union citizens in the member state where the Union citizens resided. The requirement was that those citizens would be deprived of the substance of the rights conferred by citizenship, if the third country national was not granted a right of residence (paras 66-72). That was not the case for Ms and Mr Iida. He sought a right to reside in the state of which his wife and daughter were nationals, rather than where they were resident. He would have a right under Directive 2003/109. His wife and daughter had not been discouraged from moving to Austria. Purely hypothetical obstacles were irrelevant, like the purely hypothetical prospects of exercising a right to move according to *Kremzow, 1997* (paras 73-77). Again the referring court had to apply the fundamental rights of the Charter only when Union law was implemented. Whether that was the case had to be decided in the light of the purpose and character of the implementing legislation and of any possible impact of that legislation on Union law. Had he applied for a permit under Directive 2003/109, for instance, it would have been a matter of Union law and the Charter would have applied (paras 78-81).

In *O and S, 2012* the Court was seized with a further implication of the *Ruiz Zambrano, 2011*-case-law. Both cases at issue were essentially identical. A third country national had married a Finnish national. She then gave birth to a child who became a Finnish national. She had a right of permanent residence in the host state. The marriage was divorced and the mother retained sole custody. She married again, but this time a third country national. From this second reunion another child was born, but this child held the nationality of the third state. The mother then applied for family reunification with her second husband on the basis of the citizenship of the first child. Given that the Union citizen, the child, had never made use of his right of free movement, Directive 2004/38 was not applicable. The Court directed the national court to judge whether the Union citizen was deprived of the genuine enjoyment of his rights. Certain factors were relevant, namely that the third country national mother had a right to reside in the host state; that a refusal to grant family reunification could deprive the first child of the contact to his biological father and the second child of the contact to his biological father; that the consideration in *Ruiz Zambrano, 2011* were not limited to blood-relatives; that a situation of financial, legal, or emotional dependency possibly did not exist between the Union citizen and the second husband of his mother; and that fundamental rights had to be guaranteed (paras 49-59). In contrast to the situation at issue in *Chakroun, 2010* (see below), Directive 2003/86 on family reunification of third country nationals could apply, because the mother concerned had permanent residence in the host state and hence could be a 'sponsor'. In such a situation, the mere fact that one of her children was a Union citizen could not have the effect that Directive 2003/86 was not applicable when family reunification was sought with the spouse who was not the biological father of the Union citizen (para. 69).

Union citizens and prohibition to leave

In *Aladzhov, 2011* Bulgaria had imposed on a Bulgarian national a prohibition to leave Bulgaria, until the tax debt which he owed in connection with his work as one of three directors of a company established in Bulgaria had been paid or secured. For the Court, the measure was within the scope of Directive 2004/38, as a Union citizen could invoke it against the state of which he was a national when that state prohibited him from leaving its territory (paras 24-7). Article 27(1) of that directive had direct effect (para. 32). It could not be excluded that the aim of recovering tax debts came within the public policy exception, as the European Court of Human Rights had stated. However, in keeping with the Court's own case-law a serious threat to one of the fundamental interests of society was required, for instance due to the sums at stake or a possible tax fraud being involved (para. 37). The aim of recovering taxes due was not to be considered as serving exclusively economic ends, an aim which article 27(1) excluded for justification (para. 38). In the absence of sufficient facts, justification was for the national court to assess, as were the taking into account of the specific case of the individual concerned, any automatisms involved, and the availability of less restrictive means, such as mutual assistance under Directive 2008/55 (paras 43-8). *Gaydarov, 2011* was handed down on the same day as *Aladzhov, 2011* and concerned a similar situation. A Bulgarian citizen was convicted of drug crimes in Serbia. After having served a prison sentence there, he returned to Bulgaria. That state then ordered him not to leave the country on public security grounds. The Court decided in the same way for the public security ground as for the public policy ground in *Aladzhov, 2011*. In accordance with the Court's case-law the national court in particular had to assess the threat to the society's fundamental interests solely on the basis of the facts of the case, rather than on grounds of general prevention. In *Byankov, 2012*, in a similar vein, a Bulgarian national was prohibited from leaving Bulgaria on the sole ground that he had failed to serve a private debt. The Court found that it could not be excluded that such a prohibition exclusively served economic ends pursuant to article 27 Directive 2004/38. Moreover, a threat to the society within the meaning of the case-law did not exist. The personal situation was not taken into account sufficiently. Moreover, the prohibition – 'the antithesis of the freedom conferred by Union citizenship' (para. 79) – was too absolute. Exceptions, a temporal limitation, or a review of the facts were excluded. Judgments could in addition be enforced in the Union under Regulation 44/2001, with the result that the rights of creditors were not less well protected than under the right to property in the ECHR (paras 39-47). The possibility to have such a measure reviewed after three years pursuant to article 32(1) Directive applied exclusively to measures which had been adopted in accordance with Union law. However, the procedural principles of equivalence and effectiveness *a fortiori* required that a possibility for review existed when a measure was illegal under Union law, for example when a judgment by the Court implied that the measure was illegal (paras 67-81). Apart from that, the legal remedy against a restriction which (the remedy) was required by article 31 Directive applied only at the time the restriction was enacted. If the person concerned had failed to challenge a measure within the procedural time limits of national law, that article was not applicable (paras 53-5).

Union citizenship and the broader family

In *Rahman, 2012* the Court was asked to elaborate on the rights of dependent family members of Union citizens under article 3(2) Directive 2004/38, i. e. of members other than those covered by the 'close' family of a Union citizen pursuant to article 2(2) of the Directive. The obligation to facilitate entry and residence of those family members of a Union citizen did not include a right to entry and residence. Instead, it only required a member state to grant those persons a certain advantage in contrast to all other third country nationals. A member state had to deliver a reasoned decision, based on an extensive examination of the personal circumstances. But otherwise a member state had wide discretion in selecting the factors to be applied for reunification, provided only that the normal meaning of the word 'facilitate' and the effectiveness of the provision were respected. Article 2(2) did not have direct effect, but required a decision to be subject to judicial review (paras 21-5). It was not required, though, that the situation of dependence existed in the member state whence the Union citizen concerned had moved. It was sufficient that dependence existed while the third country national was resident abroad. The relevant point in time in that regard was when the third country national filed the application (paras 28-34). Finally, it was up to the member states (i) to lay down the criteria determining when dependence was genuine and stable, within the confines of the normal meaning of the word and the effectiveness of the provision (paras 37-9), and (ii) to decide whether the situation of dependence needed to endure after reunification (paras 42-5).

The Union citizenship of a president

Hungary v. Slovakia, 2012 dealt with Slovakia's refusal to grant Hungary's president access to Slovakia. He had been invited by a private association in Slovakia on a particular day, namely the day after the day that commemorated the birth of the Hungarian state and the day on which, some 40 years ago, members of the Warsaw pact had invaded Czech territory to quash the spring of Prague. The Court emphasized that the Hungarian president was a citizen of the Union. Yet the rules on citizenship had to be read in the light of international law. That law granted a special status to heads of states, including immunities and privileges, regardless of the capacity in which a foreign state was visited. That status distinguished a head of state from all other Union citizens. A visit by a head of state was thus governed by international law. In accordance with international law specific conditions could be imposed for such visits, conditions which could not be imposed on ordinary Union citizens moving to a member state. Hence, Slovakia was not obliged under Union law to grant Hungary's head of state access to its territory (paras 44-52). Slovakia's appeal to its right to block a Union citizen's free movement did not amount to abuse of rights, either (paras 56-60).

Issues left open re Union citizenship

In *Kamberaj, 2012* the Court was asked a series of questions relating to Union citizenship. The referring court notably raised the question whether the award of a housing benefit could lawfully be made dependent on a minimum of five years of residence in the province of South Tyrol and a declaration from a Union citizen with which the citizen elected to join one of the three linguistic groups of the province. The Court declared these questions inadmissible for lack of a link to the actual facts of the case. Instead, the Court ended up answering the questions asked solely in the light of Directive 2003/109 on long-term residence of third country nationals. Yet it was mostly left to the national court to determine whether the difference in treatment between Union citizens, including Italian nationals, and third country nationals resulting from the uneven funds allocated to finance the housing benefits of the two groups was compatible with the Directive, and more specifically with its concept of core social benefits, as interpreted in the light of article 34 of the Charter of Fundamental Rights. In a similar vein, the Court declined to address a comparison made with the charges levied from Union citizens under Directive 2004/38 in *Commission v. Netherlands (certain charges), 2012* (para. 78). The charges the Netherlands levied from third country nationals when they applied for residence permits were unlawful under Directive 2003/109 in itself, because the amounts charged were so high that they undermined the aims of that directive.

Further cases

For completeness, a number of further cases must be mentioned. *Chakroun, 2010* was about the rights of third country nationals who were lawfully present in the Union to family reunification with other third country nationals under Directive 2003/86. The Court in this case fell back on *Eind, 2007* and *Metock, 2008* to interpret the concepts of social assistance and family reunification used in Directive 2003/86. *Commission v. Portugal (military equipment), 2010* was a late judgment in the series of *Commission v. Finland (military equipment), 2009*. Its content was identical to that latter judgment. In *Commission v. Portugal (tax representative), 2011* the Court declined to enter into Union citizenship, given that it had found incompatible with the free movement of capital Portugal's requirement to appoint a tax representative in Portugal when a person liable for certain taxes on investments in Portugal was resident abroad.

2 Establishment

Taxes

Gielen, 2010 brought a specific aspect of the Netherlands' tax system to the Court. Dutch law determined the tax deductions allowed by means of a test which was based on the number of hours the person concerned had worked in self-employment. This test was partly based on the residence of the person concerned. Those resident in the Netherlands could factor in hours worked in the Netherlands and abroad, while those resident abroad could only factor in hours worked in the Netherlands. However, the latter could opt into the Dutch system and, consequently, be treated as residents. The Court decided that the situations of residents and non-residents were comparable for the purpose of determining tax deductions for self-employed persons. In that regard, a difference in treatment based on residence amounted to discrimination to the detriment of non-residents who were most often nationals of other member states (paras 40-8). The opt-in did not remedy the discrimination, else a discriminatory system was validated (paras 49-54).

Pharmacies

Pérez and Gómez, 2010 came back to pharmacies. The Spanish region of Asturia implemented Spanish law by structuring the distribution of medicinal products. It required pharmacists to have a licence to operate a pharmacy. Each year, a competition was organized for the award of new licences. A series of criteria was applied. Subject to certain exceptions, a minimum distance of 250 meters was to be maintained between new and existing pharmacies. There was not to be more than one pharmacy per 2'800 inhabitants in pre-determined areas. With each new slice of 2'000 persons added to the total population of an area a new licence could be offered. To select between the pharmacists who applied for a new licence, a system of points was applied. For those who had practised as pharmacists in Asturia before, 20 per cent of points were added. In case of a tie, preference was first given to those who previously operated a pharmacy in areas with low population density and then to those who had previously pursued their profession in Asturia. The Court answered the questions asked to give the national court the possibility to avoid reverse discrimination and because it was conceivable that nationals of other member state were interested in operating a pharmacy in Asturia (paras 39-40). According to the Court, Directive 2005/36 made room for a competitive examination as part of a system of geographical division, but freedom of establishment nonetheless had to be complied with (paras 45-50). The Court first (i) addressed the population and minimum distance requirements. The prior authorization requirement was indistinctly applicable, but constituted a restriction. The applicable criteria prevented pharmacists established in other member states from establishing themselves in Asturia (paras 55-9). However, the protection of public health by means of a sound and reliable distribution of medicinal products, as acknowledged by article 35 Charter of Fundamental Rights (para. 65), justified the restriction. The aim was pursued in an appropriate way, because the requirements were consistent with that aim. The rules other member states enacted were irrelevant in that regard. Planning avoided duplication of structures in densely populated areas and shortfall of supplies in disadvantaged regions. The measures channelled pharmacists towards less attractive regions. The minimum distance requirement avoided concentration of pharmacies, while guaranteeing accessibility (paras 68-83). The preference given to pharmacists who had previously operated a business in areas with less than 2'800 inhabitants supported the aim (paras 86-87). Established pharmacies were not unduly favoured by the structural approach (paras 88-92). Subject to the verification by the national court, consistency was, moreover, guaranteed by some flexibility in the parameters. In particular, if the threshold of 2'800 inhabitants proved too high for certain sparsely populated areas exceptions could be made. If the minimum distance of 250 meters was revealed as being too much for highly concentrated areas, again, exceptions were possible (paras 95-102). To set a simple minimum number of pharmacies allowed to operate in a specific area would not have been equally effective, as concentrations would have occurred and the planning through Spain's regions could have been made impossible (paras 104-12). (ii) In contrast, the preference given in the system of points to pharmacists previously established in Asturia unduly disadvantaged pharmacists established in other member states, given that Directive 2005/36 regulated the activities that holders of formal qualifications in pharmacy were entitled to pursue (paras 120-4). The judgment in *Pérez and Gómez, 2010* was confirmed in *Sáez Sánchez, 2010*, a case which concerned the same legislation of the state of Spain, and in *Polisseni, 2010* and *Grisoli, 2011*, cases stemming from Italy where very similar legislation had been enacted.

In *Susisalo, 2012* the licensing system for pharmacies in Finland was not disputed as such. Rather, a distinction within that system was at issue which allowed the university of Helsinki to operate 16 branches of its pharmacy, while private pharmacies could only run three branches, which were moreover subject to the area concerned being so sparsely populated that an independent pharmacy could not be operated. The university of Helsinki, in turn, was obliged to provide practical training for students in the pharmacies and was required to produce some rare pharmaceuticals. The Court entered the case to allow the national court to exclude reverse discrimination (para. 20). The preference the university of Helsinki enjoyed worked to the disadvantage of private pharmacies (paras 33-4). The resulting restriction could be justified by public health considerations, but only in so far as the additional branches the university was allowed to run actually contributed to the training of students and the production of the rare pharmaceuticals (paras 39-43).

Laboratories

In *Commission v. France (bio labs), 2010* the Court transposed *Apothekerkammer, 2009*, which had been about pharmacies, to biomedical analysis laboratories. In the same way as in that case the Court sanctioned France's requirement that non-biologists could not hold more than 25 per cent of the capital of certain companies operating biomedical laboratories. The criterion, while hindering access of foreign companies to the French market (paras 46-8), guaranteed the independence of biologists in running a laboratory, much like pharmacists in charge of pharmacies, but unlike opticians. That in turn ensured the protection of public health (paras 56-68). The French measure was notably consistent and systematic, as the presence of biologists in some form in the daily operation of the laboratory had to be guaranteed. Exceptions from the 25 per cent-rule were, moreover, made *inter alia* to allow companies established in other member states and lawfully running laboratories there to participate in a French company (paras 70-78). The measure was necessary, too. The independence of biologists could not be guaranteed solely by rules of professional conduct. Severing the voting rights from the financial rights of shareholders would not have been equally effective. Further, 75 per cent of voting rights were needed under French law to take decisions the law considered important (paras 82-8). The Court, however, struck down the prohibition in French law that biologists were not entitled to own shares in more than two companies formed to operate jointly one or more biomedical analysis laboratories (paras 99-102). France had not disputed this aspect of the Commission's claim.

Games of chance

In *Engelmann, 2010* games of chance came back to the Court. In Austria, all concessions to operate games of chance were held by a single Austrian company, which had obtained them for a duration of 15 years, partly because it was constituted as a public limited company in Austria. A public tender had not taken place. Mr Engelmann, a German national, was prosecuted for having illegally operated two establishments in Austria that publicly offered games of chance. The Court assessed the situation in the light of the freedom of establishment and services. In as far as a company had to be a public limited company to be allowed to operate games of chance, the freedom of establishment was restricted. In the absence of sufficient facts, the national court had to assess any possible justification (paras 28-31). In so far as a seat in Austria was required, that amounted to discrimination. Austria in any event had failed to pursue the aim of combating crime consistently and systematically. Less restrictive measures than an outright prohibition of secondary establishments would have been available, namely the requirement to keep separate accounts, the gathering of information on managers and shareholders, or the supervision on premises (paras 34-9). While it was possible to limit the number of licences so that gambling opportunities were restricted and to limit their duration to allow investors to recoup investments made (paras 45-48), a total lack of transparency in the award of licences went against the grain of the case-law developed under the freedom of services for public service concessions. This case-law was applicable to licences to operate gaming establishments, as the Court had already indicated for the freedom of services in *Sporting Exchange, 2010* (see below). Accordingly, the discretion of the authorities had to be circumscribed, competition and impartiality had to be ensured, and judicial remedies had to be available (paras 46-56).

Costa and Cifone, 2012 the followed up on *Placanica, 2007*. Italy organised a new tendering procedure for the award of gambling licences to remedy the defects found in *Placanica, 2007*. However, the Court again took issue under the freedom of establishment and services with the way the tendering procedure for the new additional licences to be granted had been set up. First, the new tender guaranteed and entrenched the market positions of licence holders who had been awarded licences in the previous procedure which *Placanica, 2007* had declared unlawful, because it required new licences holders to keep a minimum distance from established licence holders (paras 53 and 58). That disadvantage for 'new' competitors like Stanley, the company established in the United Kingdom which worked via data transmission centres in Italy and which had been at the heart of the challenge in *Placanica, 2007*, was not justified by the needs to reduce gambling opportunities and channel gambling toward controlled agencies, given the expansive gambling politics of Italy. Moreover, the national court had to examine whether the aim of the minimum distance was the protection of established competitors rather than the guaranteed nationwide provision of gambling services (paras 62-5). Second, the new criteria applied for the award and subsequent withdrawal of licences were partly contrary to the freedom of establishment and services. The withdrawal of a licence and the refusal to issue one and the corresponding forfeiture of a large sum bank guarantee could be justified only by the lawful and final criminal convictions of a licence holder for serious crimes. The mere breaking of the trust of the authorities was not such a ground (paras 76-81). Equally, the transparency of tendering procedures, legal certainty, and equal treatment required that a tenderer like Stanley knew in advance whether its business model, namely services offered via data transmission centres, could lawfully be implemented with the new licence (paras 87-90). In any case, Stanley could not be refused a licence on the basis that its managers had been prosecuted before *Placanica, 2007* had been handed down when that judgment had later on declared the prosecutions unlawful (paras 82-4). In seven orders the Court then gave the same answer as in *Costa and Cifone, 2012* in identical circumstances, namely in *Arrichiello, 2012*; *Ferazzoli, 2012*; *Minesi, 2012*; *Pulignani, 2012*; *Rizzo, 2012*; *Veneruso, 2012*; and *Sacchi, 2012*. Only in *Pulignani, 2012* an Austrian company rather than a British company was involved, while the answer remained the same. (For the gambling judgments that were decided primarily on the basis of the freedom of services, see below.)

Car insurance

In *Bejan, 2010* the Court looked at Romanian legislation which required insurers that concluded non-mandatory car insurance contracts to exclude from those contracts coverage for damages that arose because a person had driven the insured car under the influence of alcohol. After having pointed out that the Community system for mandatory insurance, viz. Directives 72/166, 84/5, 90/232, 2000/26, and 2005/14, did not apply to non-mandatory insurance contracts, the Court found a restriction of the freedom of establishment and services. Foreign insurers were hindered from offering, directly or via an establishment in Romania, non-mandatory insurance contracts that covered damages to a car which arose because a driver was under the influence of alcohol. For lack of information, the justification of that restriction was for the national court to assess (paras 39-45).

Lawyers, notaries, and courts

In *Jakubowska, 2010* the Court again dealt with the lawyer Directive 98/5. The Court accepted the case to give the referring court the possibility to exclude reverse discrimination (paras 31-2). It reiterated that the Directive harmonized completely the recognition of admission to the profession in the host state. Nonetheless the member states remained free to lay down the rules of professional conduct, provided that they applied to all lawyers alike. In accordance with article 8 Directive which generally aimed at forestalling conflicts of interests, Italian law could validly prohibit lawyers from exercising their profession in self-employment representing clients in proceedings, while at the same time working part-time as public officials (paras 56-63).

Commission v. Austria (notaries), 2011 was one in a series of cases in which the Commission attacked the nationality conditions the member states imposed on notaries. In Austria, notaries belonged to the liberal professions, but admission to practice as a notary was subject to Austrian nationality. The Court was only asked to assess this sole condition and only under the aspect of the freedom of establishment, rather than the freedom of services and workers. The direct discrimination was not, according to the Court, justified by the exercise of official authority by notaries. The direct and specific connection required was absent. The probative value and enforceability of authenticated documents was not sufficient to establish that connection, for the parties by consensus agreed to the obligations represented by those documents. The proof inherent in such documents could be refuted and was subject to the judge's unfettered assessment (paras 88-103). The tasks notaries performed notably in the law of succession were either ancillary or performed under the supervision of courts which took the most important decisions themselves (paras 105-110). The official status of notaries was irrelevant. Moreover, notaries were in competition with one another (paras 111-3). That certain acts of the Union excluded notaries from their scope was irrelevant (paras 114-6). *Marina Mercante, 2003* which concerned ship captains did not provide any ground in favour of the nationality condition for notaries (para. 117). Despite the infringement of the freedom of establishment, Austria had not failed to implement Directives 89/48 and 2005/36, given the uncertain legal situation (paras 138-46). Although the case concerned only the nationality condition, the Court indicated that other conditions restricting the access to the profession of notaries, such as the selection procedure for appointment, the limitation in number or territorial jurisdiction, or the regulation of remuneration, could be justified if they were proportionate (para. 96). The Court ruled in the same vein in five more judgments handed down on the same day as *Commission v. Austria (notaries), 2011*, namely *Commission v. Belgium (notaries), 2011*; *Commission v. France (notaries), 2011*; *Commission v. Luxembourg (notaries), 2011*; *Commission v. Germany (notaries), 2011*; *Commission v. Greece (notaries), 2011*, while in each of those decisions addressing the specificities of the liberal profession of notaries in the respective member state. The Court ruled in *Commission v. Portugal (notaries), 2011*, in addition, that Portugal had not failed to transpose Directive 2005/36 on recognition of qualifications properly. In *Commission v. Netherlands (notaries), 2011* the Court later on ruled in the same vein as in *Commission v. Austria (notaries), 2011* and the other corresponding judgments.

In *Peñarroja Fa, 2011* the Court again refused to apply the public authority exception in the context of courts. The services provided to courts by expert translators who were registered with the courts were not connected to the exercise of public authority. Such translators merely provided accurate translations, while not expressing any opinion on the substance of cases. The discretion of courts was left intact (paras 43-44). Moreover, the Court decided that the practice of courts to keep registers of expert translators from which the judges chose a translator when they needed one, did not make the expert court translator a regulated profession within the meaning of Directive 2005/36 on recognition of qualifications (para. 30). (For the services dimension of the case, see below.)

In *Commission v. Italy (fees for lawyers), 2011* the Commission challenged the maximum fees that Italy's legislation required lawyers to abide by for both in- and out-of-court work. In the view the Court, the Italian measure was binding, since it applied by default when parties had not agreed otherwise (paras 41-4). The access of foreign lawyers to the Italian market was not hindered, though. They enjoyed access under conditions of normal and effective competition. The mere facts that other member states applied less strict or more favourable rules and that foreign lawyers needed to get accustomed to the Italian rules did not amount to obstacles. Further, Italy's maximum fee approach was flexible, allowing for increased fees if the circumstances so required (paras 49-53).

Stark, 2011 again concerned Directive 87/344 on legal expenses insurance. The Court held that the Directive left a member state free to allow the parties of a legal expenses insurance contract to agree to limit the cost of a lawyer covered to those charged by a local lawyer at the place of the court having jurisdiction. That agreement did not render meaningless the free choice of a lawyer contained in the Directive, provided that *de facto* a choice was not excluded (paras 33).

Non-discrimination

A number of cases in the freedom of establishment during the 2010s concerned more or less directly non-discrimination. *Yellow Cab, 2010* was about the authorization required in Austria to operate bus services in Vienna. That authorization *inter alia* depended on two conditions, namely an establishment was required in Austria and the service to be offered was not to jeopardize the transport services already offered on the same route. Yellow Cab was established in Germany and was refused the authorization to operate a transport service in Vienna which would have been primarily addressed at tourists. According to the Court, the freedom of services did not apply since it had to be implemented by the transport policy. The transport policy measures adopted, however, did not govern the services in question. However, the freedom of establishment applied, but it was not restricted in any way by the requirement to have an establishment in the host state. Yet the detailed rules surrounding the requirement to have an establishment possibly amounted to a restriction of the freedom of establishment (paras 34-5). That was the case when an establishment in the host state was required *before* the necessary authorization was granted, given the dissuasive effect. To require an establishment after the authorization had been granted, in contrast, did not violate the freedom of establishment (paras 37-40). The freedom of establishment was restricted, though, by the authorization requirement. Potentially, the restriction could be justified by the promotion of tourism or environmental concerns. However, the need to prevent the established services of a competitor from being jeopardized was, at least with regard to transport services for tourists, a purely economic argument which did not justify the restriction. Moreover, to rely exclusively on information from such a competitor put into question the objectivity and impartiality an authorization procedure needed to have in order to live up to the freedom of establishment (paras 44-54).

In *Commission v. Spain (shopping centres), 2011* the Court was called upon to decide on a number of conditions the Spanish region of Catalonia imposed in case of the establishment of large shopping centres. Since the Commission had failed to establish that those criteria had an indirectly discriminatory effect – a difference in treatment to the advantage of certain types of retail stores which essentially benefitted Spanish traders would have been necessary (paras 59-61) – the Court examined whether any hindrance to access the Spanish market existed. A prior authorization requirement was such a hindrance, as it depended on the location, size, etc. of the retail store concerned (paras 65-70). The Court then analysed the specific conditions to which the authorization was subject under justification. While restrictions on the size and location of shopping centres were conceivable to protect the environment and the consumer – more specifically, to avoid polluting car journeys, to counter urban decay, to preserve an environmentally integrated urban model, to avoid new road building, and to ensure access by public transport – some specific restrictions Catalonia imposed were too rigorous, as essentially in some cases shopping centres could not be established at all. The necessity was not proven for those restrictions (paras 80-85). Whereas a prior authorization was necessary in an environmental perspective, that authorization was not to depend on the expected market share and the impact on existing traders. Those were inadmissible economic criteria (paras 92-8). An opinion by a committee could be required, but the committee was not to consist of potential competitors. Rather, the interests of consumers and the environment had to be represented (paras 110-1). The Court also sanctioned some soft criteria, like the safety of the project, the mobility it generated, and the need for a broad and varied supply, because harder criteria would have been even more restrictive (paras 117-8). The procedural rule that the authorities' silence implied rejection of an application for a licence after a certain time was lawful, as it was a rule that was easily managed and supervised (paras 122-5). Finally, the determination of the fees payable by reference to the size of the store to be built reflected the overall cost and deviated little from the actual cost that arose (paras 127-9).

Ankara and other Agreements with third states

A number of decisions during the 2010s concerned Agreements with third states. In *Oguz, 2011* the Court came back to the standstill clause in article 41(1) of the Additional Protocol to the Ankara Agreement. The Court clarified that the benefit of the standstill clause was not to be denied to a Turkish national in the United Kingdom on the ground that he had committed abuse of rights. The standstill clause only determined which law was applicable. That law then specified the consequences of an abuse of rights (paras 29-32). More specifically, the ruling in *Kondova, 2001* was not transposable to the case at issue. Apart from the factual differences – the Turkish national had been lawfully present in the United Kingdom, in contrast to Ms Kondova – the standstill clause did not grant a substantive right, while the Europe Agreement provided for a right to establishment and equal treatment (paras 40-5).

Graf, 2011 concerned the Agreement on free movement of persons with Switzerland. Mr Graf, a Swiss farmer established in Switzerland concluded an agreement with a German farmer to lease a plot of agricultural land in Germany. However, the German authorities refused the authorization required, because competition was distorted when Mr Graf was able to sell the products grown in Germany at a better price in Switzerland. Moreover, the distribution of agricultural land was going to be unsound. The Court found that a farmer as a self-employed frontier worker was entitled to rely on the Agreement to challenge the German rule on which the German authorities had based their decision. Substantively more Swiss nationals than German nationals were established in Switzerland while working in a self-employed capacity in Germany. Hence, the German rule primarily worked to the detriment of Swiss farmers (paras 27-8). The resulting indirect discrimination was not justified. The distortion of competition was not a ground for justification. The public order derogation in the Agreement had to be interpreted in the light of the internal market case-law and the objectives of the Agreement. The requirements of public order could vary from state to state, but they had to be interpreted strictly as derogations from fundamental rules. Hence, public order did not encompass the needs of agricultural land planning (paras 30-4). In addition, the German measure was a new restriction which the standstill clause in the Agreement prohibited (para. 35). In *Ettwein, 2013* the Court then made it plain – again after it had decided so in the context of social security family benefits in *Bergström, 2011* (see below) – that the Agreement on free movement of persons with Switzerland was not just about discrimination on the basis of nationality. Self-employed German frontier workers who resided in Switzerland while they pursued their self-employed activity in Germany were entitled to rely on the Agreement against Germany even though they were German nationals. The wording and the objectives of the Agreement required so (paras 33-40). Moreover, those frontier workers rightfully claimed application of the *Schumacker, 1995*-line of authority which required the German tax authorities to grant those frontier workers the tax advantage of split tax assessment for spouses who earned all their income in Germany. That was the meaning of Article 21(2) of the Agreement (paras 41-52).

Technicalities

In a few cases the Court also addressed the technical intricacies of secondary law. In *Volvo, 2010* the Court applied Directive 86/653 on self-employed commercial agents to allow the national court to exclude reverse discrimination. The Court ruled that a contract that the principal terminated in the ordinary way could not lawfully be terminated again with immediate effect based on a newly discovered default by the agent in order to deprive the agent of the indemnity due (paras 39-44). In *Iaia, 2011* the Court explained the framework Union law set to the statute of limitations for doctors' claims under Directive 82/76 for adequate remuneration during the specialization training and, in particular, the impact of Italy's late transposition of that Directive.

Legal persons and taxation

A long series of cases again raised issues under the establishment of legal persons, namely issues of taxation. In *SGI, 2010*, the Court scrutinized Belgium's particular tax treatment of loans granted to companies established in other member states in the light of the freedom of establishment. Belgian tax law added a certain amount to the profit of a resident company when it granted an unusual loan to another company with which it had a relationship of interdependence, namely loans at a rate beyond market conditions or at a gratuitous rate without being under a legal obligation to do so. However, the amount was only added to the profit when the other company, typically a subsidiary, was established outside Belgium. The Court applied the freedom of establishment, because in the case at issue the Belgian company had definite influence over the foreign company (para. 35). The restriction consisted in the fact that the amount was added only when the loan was granted to a non-resident recipient company, but not when a resident company received such a loan (paras 42-54). However, the restriction was justified by a combination of two grounds, namely the needs for a balanced allocation of powers of taxation and for the prevention of tax evasion. Without the restriction Belgium would have had to give up its right to tax profits generated in its territory and companies could have elected where those profits were taxed (para. 63). Tax avoidance would become possible (para. 67). Moreover, a company had the possibilities to explain the commercial rationale of a loan and thus escape the disadvantage and to have reviewed a decision taken by the tax authorities. The amount was added to the profit only in so far as to bring the loan on an equal level with loans granted at arm's length (paras 73-5).

In *X Holding, 2010* the Netherlands offered parent companies the possibility of consolidated taxation for the whole group. However, such group taxation was only available with regard to subsidiaries subject to taxation in the Netherlands. The Court found the refusal of the advantage of group taxation for foreign subsidiaries to constitute a restriction of the freedom of establishment (paras 18-9). For the purposes of consolidated group taxation, the situations of domestic and foreign subsidiaries were objectively comparable (para. 24). The restriction was justified, though, by the need for a balanced allocation of powers of taxation, else the parent company could have chosen where the profit and loss of a subsidiary was taxed (paras 30-3). Apart from that, permanent establishments and subsidiaries in other member states were not in objectively comparable situations for the purposes of taxation of the parent company in the Netherlands. Hence, it was not necessary to extend the possibility to offset profits of foreign permanent establishments to foreign subsidiaries (paras 39-42).

In *Ciba, 2010*, Hungary charged a particular levy on companies established in Hungary. That levy was calculated on the basis of the wages the company paid to its work-force. The levy served to finance a special ring-fenced fund to develop the employment market in Hungary. Ciba, a company established in Hungary, was required to pay the levy. It was calculated on the basis of all wages Ciba paid in Hungary as well as those that were paid by a branch of Ciba in the Czech Republic. That branch was subject to contributions with a similar purpose in the Czech Republic. According to the Court, the levy was a tax. That the proceeds from the levy were ring-fenced was immaterial. Moreover, the company subject to the levy did not gain any direct benefit in consideration for paying it (paras 23-4). That levies were charged for similar purposes in Hungary and in the Czech Republic did not constitute a restriction of the freedom of establishment. It was the consequence of the absence of measures to avoid double taxation and of the fiscal sovereignty of the member states (paras 25-9 and 38). Rejecting any analogy to *Arblade, 1999*, the Court went on to find a restriction, though, in that wages paid by the branch in the Czech Republic were taken into account for the Hungarian levy while any possibility to reduce the liability to pay the levy with reference to the Czech branch was excluded. In contrast a Hungarian company could reduce its liability, for instance, by organizing training for its workforce (paras 42-4). That restriction was not justified by the cohesion of the tax system (paras 47-8).

In *National Grid, 2011* a company established in the Netherlands held a claim against a company established in the United Kingdom which was denominated in pound sterling. Since the pound rose in value against the Dutch guilder an unrealised exchange rate gain was generated on that claim. That gain had not yet been taxed in the Netherlands. National Grid then transferred the place of its effective management from the Netherlands to the United Kingdom. Under the double taxation convention between those two states this had the effect that the company's gains and profits henceforth became subject to taxation in the United Kingdom, while the company remained a corporation under Dutch law. The Dutch tax authority subjected the unrealised capital gain to corporation tax as per the transfer of the place management to settle tax debts finally and immediately claimed the tax due. As the debt was denominated in sterling, the unrealised exchange rate gains disappeared at the moment the place of management was moved. According to the Court, National Grid could rely on the freedom of establishment. While it was for the member states to answer the preliminary issue of when a company came into existence and when it ended, the case at issue was about the tax consequences of a change in place of management while the company remained in existence under Dutch law (paras 28-32). The restriction consisted in a cash-flow disadvantage which National Grid suffered in contrast to a company that moved its place of management within the Netherlands (para. 37). The two situations were comparable, even though the exchange rate gain disappeared when the place of management was moved (paras 38-9). In the view of the Court, the restriction was justified by the balanced allocation of powers of taxation, viz. fiscal territoriality with a temporal element, to *determine* the tax due at the moment the change in place of management took place, else a member state risked forfeiting its right to tax capital gains that arose within the ambit of its powers of taxation. The case at issue was different from *N, 2006*, as it was up to the host state to take into account decreases in the value of the claim from the moment the place of management was moved onwards. The disappearance of the exchange rate gain was irrelevant (paras 48-64). However, the immediate *recovery* of the tax at the moment the place of management was changed was less straightforward. The company had to be given the option to choose either (i) to accept the immediate recovery of the tax and suffer the resulting cash-flow disadvantage or (ii) to pay the tax when the gain was actually realised and suffer the disadvantages of providing documentation which allowed the Dutch tax authorities to trace the tax debt and of possibly providing a bank guarantee (paras 65-78). The cohesion of the Dutch tax system did not provide further justification. It coincided mainly with the balanced allocation of powers of taxation (paras 80-2). Further, a general presumption of tax evasion was not to be applied when a company changed its place of effective management (para. 84).

The same ruling as in *National Grid, 2011* applied in two more constellations according to *Commission v. Portugal (exit tax), 2012*, namely when a company transferred its registered office and effective place of management from one member state to another and the first member state immediately taxed unrealised capital gains (paras 27-9); and when a foreign company transferred the assets of a permanent establishment in one member state to another and the unrealised capital gains on those assets were taxed immediately (para. 34). However, a restriction did not arise when capital gains were taxed when an economic activity was definitely ceased, because the treatment of foreign and domestic companies was the same (para. 30). In *Commission v. Netherlands (unrealised gains), 2013* the Netherlands did no longer contest, after *National Grid, 2011* had been handed down, that the legislation concerned violated the freedom of establishment (para. 15).

In *Philips, 2012* the tax treatment of resident companies and permanent establishments belonging to the same foreign group was dealt with. The tax legislation of the United Kingdom allowed losses sustained by a foreign group's permanent establishment in the United Kingdom to be transferred to a company established in the United Kingdom belonging to the same foreign group only under the condition that those losses could not be used for purposes of taxation abroad. A similar condition did not apply in purely internal situations. For the Court, that additional condition made it less attractive for foreign groups to establish permanent establishments in the United Kingdom, thus limiting the free choice of the appropriate legal form of establishment (paras 15-6). The situations of resident companies and permanent establishments in the United Kingdom, both belonging to the same foreign group, were objectively comparable for the purpose of the tax treatment of transfers of losses (para. 19). The resulting restriction could not be justified by the need to ensure a balanced allocation of powers of taxation. The powers of the United Kingdom to tax profits generated in its territory was not affected by a transfer of losses from a local permanent establishment to a resident company, in contrast to the hypothetical situation where losses sustained *abroad* would be transferred to a company established in the United Kingdom (paras 25-6). The prevention of a double use of losses, if a ground for justification at all, was not pertinent, either, as the possible use abroad of losses incurred by a permanent establishment in the United Kingdom was not of concern to the United Kingdom (paras 28-31).

DIVI, 2012 then concerned a tax benefit Luxembourg granted to resident companies. Capital tax was reduced, if the company concerned maintained a reserve on the balance sheet for the five years following the year the reduction was granted. DIVI was a company established in Luxembourg. When it moved its seat to Italy, the capital tax reduction was withdrawn and the tax was claimed immediately. The situation was, according to the Court, within the scope of the freedom of establishment, because, as in *National Grid, 2011*, the tax consequences of a change of seat were at stake (para. 29). The restriction consisted in the withdrawal of the tax benefit. Had DIVI maintained its seat in Luxembourg, it would have continued to enjoy the benefit. Hence, transfers of seat, i. e. the establishment in other member states, were hindered (paras 34-6). The situations of resident companies and those transferring their seat were objectively comparable with regard to the capital tax generated before a change of seat (paras 37-9). The need for a balanced allocation of powers of taxation could not by nature justify the restriction, since the tax would not have been due, had the company remained in Luxembourg (paras 44-5). The cohesion of Luxembourg's tax system did not justify the restriction, either, for lack of a direct link. The disadvantage of being subject to corporate income tax and trade tax in Luxembourg during the years the reserve was maintained on the balance sheet was too remote and uncertain (paras 48-9).

In *Commission v. Belgium (investment companies), 2012* the Court first struck down under the free movement of capital the distinction Belgium's tax law drew between (i) resident investment companies and foreign investment companies having a permanent establishment in Belgium and (ii) foreign investment companies. In both cases, a withholding tax was applied to dividends and interests distributed. However only in the first case (i) could the withholding tax be set off against corporation tax due; dividends and interests were, moreover, exempt from corporation tax. In the second case (ii) the withholding tax constituted definitive taxation. For the Court, the distinction deterred foreign investment companies from investing in Belgium (paras 38-40). In keeping with case-law the two situations of investment companies (i and ii) were not different, as they became comparable by reason of Belgium's decision to exercise its power of taxation (paras 50-1). After having rejected a series of arguments Belgium put forward – double taxation conventions did not always allow complete neutralization, unfavourable tax treatment could not be compensated by other advantages, and fund-like entities were not the right basis of comparison, for they lacked legal personality (paras 52-67) – the Court found the restriction unjustified. When a member state decided not to tax resident companies it could not lawfully rely on the need for a balanced allocation of powers of taxation to justify taxation of non-resident companies, in particular when the income earned by resident companies had already been taxed in the hands of the distributing companies as profit realised by them. The effectiveness of fiscal supervision could be safeguarded by guarantees provided by the taxable persons (paras 76-81). The Court then held that those considerations as to the unjustified restriction of the free movement of capital could be transposed *mutatis mutandis* to the freedom of establishment for cases in which an investor exerted definitive influence over a company (paras 84-6). Moreover, the same applied with regard to the European Economic Area Agreement (para. 88).

In *FII Group II, 2012*, *FII Group, 2006*, obviously, came back to the Court. The referring court asked the Court for a number of clarifications. The Court obliged and clarified (i) that the nominal tax rate that had been applied to the profits underlying foreign-sourced dividends had to be taken into account under the imputation method (see notably paras 52 and 62, clarifying para. 56 of *FII Group, 2006*); (ii) that it did not matter that the foreign company distributing dividends to a company resident in the United Kingdom did not itself pay, but rather its subsidiary did pay, corporation tax on the profits underlying the dividends (para. 74); (iii) that the freedom of establishment and capital precluded the payment of advance corporation tax on foreign-sourced dividends not just by the resident receiving company, but also by the parent company under the group income election option in which advance corporation tax was passed 'upwards' (paras 79-80). The Court, moreover, clarified the relationship of the freedom of establishment and the freedom of capital in cases in which the national legislation applied not just to shareholdings allowing the shareholder to exercise definite influence, but also to financial investments below that threshold. With regard to such legislation, the shareholder was entitled to rely on the freedom of capital with regard to companies established in third states. However, care had to be taken that such companies in third states did not, under the cover of the capital freedom, exercise the freedom of establishment which the Treaty had not extended to them. That was not the case for the legislation at issue in *FII Group, 2006* and *FII Group II, 2012*, since it only covered dividends paid by companies established in third countries to companies established in the United Kingdom (paras 99-100). Finally, surplus advance corporation tax lawfully levied according to *FII Group, 2006* in the case of foreign-sourced dividends need not have been refunded, if it could not be passed on to the non-resident subsidiary because the latter had not generated any taxable profit in the United Kingdom (para. 110).

In *A Oy, 2013* a Finnish parent company wanted to absorb a Swedish subsidiary which had sustained losses in Sweden and had gone out of business, while it remained bound by long-term leasing contracts in Sweden. Whereas the losses incurred by a subsidiary resident in Finland could be taken into account by a resident parent company to reduce its own income for the purpose of taxation in Finland after having absorbed the subsidiary, such was not the case for a Swedish subsidiary. The Court first reiterated that the freedom of establishment was applicable to cross-border mergers and that measures against tax avoidance were relevant only for justification of a restriction (paras 24-8). To refuse the tax advantage – the deduction of losses incurred by a subsidiary – in case of a merger with a non-resident subsidiary constituted an obstacle to the freedom of establishment, as its exercise became less attractive (paras 31-2). For the purpose of taxation of the income of a resident parent company, the situations of resident and non-resident subsidiaries were objectively comparable. In keeping with *Marks & Spencer, 2005* the combination of the need for a balanced allocation of powers of taxation and the prevention of the double use of losses and of the avoidance of taxation justified the restriction, though only in so far as the possibilities of having the subsidiary's losses taken into account for tax purposes in the state where the subsidiary was resident had not been exhausted. This was for the referring court to assess (paras 46-55). However, the mere liquidation of the subsidiary was not *per se* a circumstance which proved that those possibilities had been exhausted (paras 51-2). Finally, Union law did not determine the law applicable to the calculation of the losses in the circumstances of the case at issue. That calculation had to made sure that resident and non-resident subsidiaries were treated equally, though (paras 58-9).

Further company cases

In *Attanasio, 2010* Italian law required new fuel service stations to respect a certain minimum distance from existing service stations. The Court answered the question referred, because companies established in other member state were possibly interested in selling fuel in Italy (para. 24). It found that the requirement restricted the freedom of establishment, for it hindered the access of companies established in other member states, which were seeking to establish themselves in Italy, to the Italian market. The minimum distance requirement favoured existing companies, as it only applied to new companies (para. 45). The restriction was not justified by road safety or environmental and public health concerns, since those aims were not pursued in a consistent and systematic manner, given that the measure only applied to new service stations. It would have been less restrictive to examine those aims in each specific case, rather than to impose a general minimum distance requirement which applied in each and every case. The consumer, moreover, was disadvantaged, because the few existing competitors in the market were favoured (paras 52-6).

In *Idrima Tipou, 2010* a Greek law came under the Court's scrutiny that made it possible in specific circumstances to impose fines on shareholders of a company, because the company concerned had violated Greek law. When a Greek company limited by shares operated a television station and in the course of that operation violated Greek legislation or rules of good conduct for journalists, a fine could be imposed not just on the company itself, but also concurrently on share holders who held more than 2.5 per cent of the share capital of the company concerned. The Court, after having found that Directive 68/151 on co-ordination of safeguards for the protection of members of certain companies did not regulate the matter, went on to examine the freedom of establishment and capital. Those freedoms both had to be applied, since a shareholder holding 2.5 per cent of the shares of a company had or did not have, depending on the circumstances, definite influence over a company's decisions (paras 47-53). On the specifics of the case, the Greek measure deterred investors from other member states more than Greek investors. In essence, it was more difficult for foreign investors to build alliances, as Greek law expected it of shareholders controlling more than 2.5% of share capital, with other shareholders with the aim of making the company concerned comply with Greek legislation and rules of conduct (paras 57-9). The resulting restriction was not justified, because the Greek measure was not suitable to ensure that television companies complied with Greek legislation and rules of good conduct. Essentially, the Greek legislature was wrong to assume that a shareholding of 2.5 per cent or more allowed a shareholder to exercise that kind of influence over a company. Alternative measures that were less restrictive of the market freedoms were, moreover, available (paras 63-9).

Vale, 2012 concerned the transformation of a company in the sense of a cross-border conversion. Vale was an Italian company that wanted to convert into a Hungarian company. The operation was not a sham. Vale intended to pursue a genuine economic activity in Hungary. It deregistered in Italy where the authorities registered that the company had moved to Hungary and applied for registration in Hungary after having met the substantive requirements of Hungarian law, such as paid up capital, etc. Hungarian law regulated national conversions of companies. However, the Hungarian authorities refused to register Vale as a Hungarian company. The Court found the operation to be within the scope of the freedom of establishment. While it was for the member states to determine the connecting factors for companies, which in turn determined the beginning and life of a company, in this case the company would be governed solely by the rules of the host state. The obligation to allow cross-border conversions, hence, did not infringe the powers of the host state (paras 30-2). Since Hungarian law allowed domestic conversions, there was a difference in treatment in that foreign companies could not lawfully convert into Hungarian companies (para. 36). Arguably, creditors, the fairness of commercial transactions, and fiscal supervision all required protection. But Hungary prohibited cross-border conversions in a general way, regardless of whether those interests were at risk (para. 40). Since national law had to lay down the details, the freedom of establishment could not just regulate those details in the absence of secondary legislation. However, when national law allowed domestic conversions, the principles of equivalence and effectiveness were applicable. Those principles notably allowed to impose on companies the condition of strict legal and economic continuity as well as the requirement to draw up lists and inventories, etc. However, the principles precluded a refusal to register the predecessor company. Hungarian authorities could also not lawfully refuse to admit any foreign evidence relating to the deregistration abroad. However, they were entitled to apply national legislation as to the evidence required (paras 49-59).

In *Express Line, 2011* the Court dealt with Belgium's legislation which imposed on postal service providers outside the scope of universal services a mandatory out-of court complaint procedure for customers. A company established in Belgium which was part of the DHL group established in Germany was affected by that legislation. After having found that Directive 97/67 on universal postal services did not restrain the freedom of action of the member states in this regard, the Court did not find a restriction of the freedom of establishment. All service providers in Belgium were subject to such a procedure. Those providers could expect that a member state would afford legal protection to customers of postal services. Nearly all member states provided for external complaint procedures in such cases (paras 61-2).

Companies and third states

Some cases also concerned the establishment of companies with regard to third states. In *Fokus, 2010* the acquisition of real estate in Austria by legal persons established in Switzerland was at issue. In keeping with the case-law applicable, the Agreement on Free Movement of Persons with Switzerland did not apply to legal persons. Hence, when an Austrian company that was owned by a Swiss company acquired real estate in Austria, the Swiss company could not invoke the Agreement, more specifically article 25 of annex I liberalizing real estate acquisition, to challenge the authorization requirement Austrian law imposed on the Austrian company seeking to purchase real estate in Austria (paras 33-6). The Swiss company was entitled, in principle, to rely on the freedom of capital of the Treaty. But in the case at issue the Austrian authorization requirement had only been formally amended, but otherwise remained the same in substance since the freedom of capital had entered into force. It was therefore covered by the clause in the Treaty that had grandfathered restrictions of the freedom of capital as per the Treaty's entry into force (paras 43-8).

A Oy, 2012 concerned Finland's tax treatment of exchanges of shares. Exchanges of shares between companies established within the Union benefited from tax neutral treatment in Finland in implementation of Directive 2009/133. However, when one company involved in the exchange of shares was established in a state party to the European Economic Area and the other in Finland, the exchange of shares was treated as a disposal subject to taxation in Finland for the Finnish company. Directive 2009/133 was not applicable in such a constellation, because it covered only exchange of shares within the Union. However, the freedom of establishment under the European Economic Area Agreement applied. That freedom was identical to the internal market freedom (paras 15 and 21-2). Finnish law operated a difference in treatment in that purely domestic exchanges of shares did not give rise to taxation, whereas they did when a Norwegian company was involved (paras 26-9). That restriction of the freedom of establishment under the European Economic Area Agreement was not justified by the need to prevent tax evasion, since a general presumption of tax evasion could not lawfully be applied. The effectiveness of fiscal supervision was to be assessed differently for Norway, Liechtenstein, and Iceland than for Union member states, because an information exchange mechanism akin to Directive 77/799 did not exist in the European Economic Area. However, in the case at issue a bilateral mechanism compensated that lack. Hence, Finland's approach was precluded (paras 32-7).

In *Scheunemann, 2012* Germany's inheritance tax was lower on inherited shareholdings in companies established in a member state than for such holdings in companies in third states. However, the reduction applied only to shareholdings that amounted to at least a quarter of the share capital. According to the Court, solely the freedom of establishment was applicable, because the German legislation was aimed at shareholders holding at least a blocking minority that allowed them to influence a company. The idea of the legislation was to encourage heirs to exercise influence in a company of which they inherited shares, so that jobs could be saved and the survival of the company could be guaranteed. Any effect on the freedom of capital was an unavoidable consequence of the restriction of the freedom of establishment. That was why the freedom of capital need not have been examined. As the freedom of establishment, unlike the freedom of capital, was not extended to cover third countries, the German legislation did not fall within the ambit of the freedom of establishment (paras 25-34).

Diploma

A number of decisions also concerned diploma recognition during the 2010s. In *Vandorou, 2010* some persons had first obtained diplomas in a member state and then acquired the authorization to pursue a regulated profession there. Some of them (i) gained practical experience *before* obtaining the authorization; others (ii) gained practical experience *after* having received the authorization, but in another member state than the state where they received the authorization. The Greek authorities imposed supplementary requirements as a condition for the authorization to exercise the corresponding regulated professions in Greece, but refused to take into account, in the determination of those requirements, the practical experience the persons concerned had gained. According to the Court, the practical experience was not to be qualified as 'professional experience' within the meaning of Directive 89/48 on mutual recognition as it had been gained before the authorization to pursue a profession was granted (i) or in another state than the state where the authorization was granted (ii) (paras 61-4). However, the experience had to be taken into account, when determining supplementary requirements, in the assessment of knowledge and qualifications to be made due to the freedom of establishment case-law. That case-law was not inapplicable solely because of the existence of the Directive (paras 65-71).

In *Koller, 2010* diploma recognition in Austria for the purpose of practising as a lawyer was at stake. Mr Koller had obtained a master of law in Austria. He had also acquired a master of law in Spain through courses he had visited concurrently at a Spanish university. The latter master entitled him to practise as an attorney in Spain, which he did for three weeks after having been admitted in Spain. He then applied for admission to the bar in Austria. In Austria admission was contingent on five years of practice. His application to take an aptitude test in order to be admitted was rejected based on the argument that he could not be admitted to the test for lack of having practised in Austria. The Court decided that the qualification Mr Koller held constituted a 'diploma' within the meaning of the Directive 89/48. He had followed a three year-course at university and was admitted to practice in Spain where an additional part of his educational training had taken place. Hence, he benefitted from access to the profession in the host state (paras 26-35). Given that a legal profession was at issue Austria could subject him to an aptitude test for which his qualifications had to be taken into account. However, he was not to be refused access to the test, the aim of which was to establish whether he had the necessary practical experience, on the ground that he lacked practical experience in the host state (paras 38-40).

Ebert, 2011 again concerned diploma recognition of lawyers. In this case, the Court made it plain that two equivalent ways existed for a lawyer admitted in the 'home' state to practice as a lawyer in the host state under that state's title for lawyers. Either the lawyer concerned practised for three years as a lawyer in the host state and in that state's law under the 'home' state title, then the lawyer was automatically entitled to practice under the host state title pursuant to Directive 98/5; or the lawyer practised in the host state for less than three years, then he could seek admission to practise under the host state's title under Directive 89/48 and could be required to take an aptitude test (paras 30-4). In any case, a lawyer was always required to abide by the host state's regulation of the profession. A lawyer could also be required to join the bar, if that requirement was indistinctly applicable (paras 37-41).

In *Toki, 2011* the Court partly overruled *Price, 2006*. It concerned the constellation where a profession was not regulated in the member state of origin, the United Kingdom, but partly 'governed' by a professional organization with which membership was optional, while it was regulated in the host member state, Greece. The Court ruled that in that constellation the host state always had to apply point (b) of the first sub-paragraph of article 3 Directive 89/48, regardless of whether the person concerned who had obtained a diploma in the state of origin was a member or not of the professional organization in the state of origin. In other words, the host state, Greece, could insist on two years of actual pursuit of the profession concerned in the state of origin, the United Kingdom (paras 23-5). Actual pursuit in that context meant the normal exercise of the profession in the state of origin, regardless of in which capacity – employed or self-employed, for which employer, for-profit or not, or in which regulatory framework. The activity need not have covered the full range of activities, but was not to consist just in research or assistance of students (paras 31-9).

Mosconi II, 2013 concerned the recognition of diplomas of architects in Italy. The Court entered the case to allow the national court to exclude reverse discrimination – apparently in contrast to *Mosconi, 2004*, an unpublished case in which the same issue had been at stake, but the Court had rejected the case for the situation having been purely internal to Italy. The question referred had been worded differently, though, in *Mosconi, 2004*. The Court reiterated that architects from other member states benefitted from automatic mutual recognition under Directive 85/384 on recognition in architecture. Hence, they could not lawfully be excluded from projects on certain classified heritage buildings, which were part of the regular profession of architects in the host state, or be asked to pass additional examinations to prove their qualification (paras 49-51).

3 Social security

Scope and definitions

The scope of the social security rules of the Union was clarified in a few decisions at the beginning of the 2010s. In *Borger, 2011*, the Court had the occasion to explain the personal scope of Regulation 1408/71, viz. the term 'employed person'. Ms Borger was an Austrian national who had been employed in Austria when she took statutory leave to take care of her child. During the two years she technically remained in employment. She then extended the leave for another six months in order to benefit from a children allowance. During her leave of absence she joined her husband who worked in Switzerland. The Court reiterated that the only point that mattered for the applicability of Regulation 1408/71 was that she was subject to a general or special scheme, be it on a compulsory or a voluntary basis, a scheme which insured here against at least one of the risks listed in article 1(a) Regulation 1408/71 (para. 26). Were thus irrelevant whether her employment was suspended during the additional six months; any personal motives for the suspension; and whether the additional six months would be taken into account for her claims when she would retire (paras 28-32). In a sense, the Court previously had clarified the personal scope also in *Baesen, 2010*. The Court explained that it was up to national law to define the terms ‘civil servants’ and ‘persons treated as such’ in article 13(2)(d) Regulation 1408/71. National law was free to establish that a person who was in some respects subject to a scheme for civil servants fell within the purview of that article (paras 25-30).

In *Salemink, 2012* the Court shed light on the territorial scope of Regulation 1408/71. After the Netherlands had exercised its sovereignty on the continental shelf adjacent to its territory by allowing the exploitation of gas through a rig, it could not lawfully claim that the free movement of workers was not applicable to a person employed by a Dutch company for work on that rig (para. 36). Consequently, Regulation 1408/71 applied to such a person, resulting in Dutch legislation remaining applicable pursuant to article 13(2)(a) Regulation 1408/71 when that person moved residence from the Netherlands to Spain. In such a situation, it was contrary to that article and the freedom of workers for the Netherlands to deny that person an incapacity benefit normally due under Dutch compulsory insurance on the sole ground that the person concerned did not have residence in the Netherlands. Moreover, to refer such a person to optional continued insurance was not an alternative, since it was less favourable (paras 37-44). In *Commission v. Netherlands (rigs), 2012* the Court was seized with a similar allegation with regard to Portuguese workers on platforms on the ‘Dutch shelf’, but the procedure was inadmissible, because the Commission had failed to explain in detail which benefits were withheld from those workers. *Bakker, 2012* concerned a similar constellation as *Salemink, 2012*. When a worker was employed for work aboard a ship flying the Dutch flag the connection established to the Netherlands was sufficiently close to warrant application of Dutch law, even if the ship regularly operated in the territorial waters of China or the United Arab Emirates (paras 27-30). Pursuant to article 13(2)(c) Regulation 1408/71 Dutch law was applicable. The connecting factor was the work aboard the ship. Hence, residence in the Netherlands could not lawfully be required for compulsory insurance with the Netherlands’ social security system (paras 32-5).

Special non-contributory benefits

Bartlett, 2011 again concerned the United Kingdom's disability living allowance, one part of which, the care component, had been the subject of *Commission v. Parliament (special benefits), 2007*. In *Bartlett, 2011* the focus was on the other part, the mobility component. The Court confirmed that it was a special non-contributory cash benefit which was listed in the annex to Regulation 1408/71 (paras 21-32). As it was closely linked to the social environment the Union legislature could lawfully make the mobility component subject to a residence requirement by including it in the annex, thus rendering article 10a Regulation 1408/71 applicable, without violating the free movement of workers (paras 38-40). (In the absence of precise facts the Court chose to focus on the free movement of workers, rather than Union citizenship.) *Commission v. Germany (benefits for the blind), 2011* also was a follow-up to *Commission v. Parliament (special benefits), 2007*. In the light of this judgment, Germany no longer contested that certain benefits for the deaf, blind, and disabled constituted sickness benefits under Regulation 1408/71 which were not to be made subject to residence (paras 26-30). Apart from that, such benefits were social advantages within the meaning of article 7(2) Regulation 1612/68, too. Under that provision a residence requirement was equally precluded, because it resulted in indirect discrimination (paras 38-40).

Stewart, 2011 concerned a British benefit granted for a year in case of incapacity in youth. The benefit was non-contributory and depended, among other conditions, on the residence, the presence for 26 out of the 52 weeks preceding the application, and the presence on the date of application in the United Kingdom. Ms Stewart, a British national who suffered from Down's syndrome, was denied the benefit, because she had moved to another member state with her parents when they retired. The Court classified the benefit on the specifics of the case as an invalidity benefit rather than a sickness benefit, because after a year it was replaced by a long-term invalidity benefit with which it constituted a single benefit (paras 30-53). As such it was exportable, because article 10 Regulation 1408/71 caught not just the retention but also the acquisition of benefits and because it was not listed as a benefit coming within the ambit of article 10a Regulation 1408/71 (paras 59-69). The residence condition was therefore not permissible. The requirement to be present for 26 weeks during the year preceding the application, moreover, in so far as it did not in any event amount to a residence requirement, constituted a restriction for it deterred Union citizens from exercising their freedom to move within the Union (paras 72-86). The needs for a genuine link with the member state granting the benefit and to maintain the financial balance of that state's social security system constituted grounds to justify such a restriction, in particular for a non-contributory benefit. However, the criterion was too exclusive. Other circumstances equally established such a genuine link, e. g. the facts that Ms Stewart had lived most of her live in the United Kingdom and received a disability allowance there thus establishing a relationship with the British system; that she was credited national insurance contributions in the United Kingdom; and that her parents on whom she depended had worked or received benefits there before moving abroad after retirement. Hence, the criterion went beyond what those aims required (paras 88-103). The requirement to be actually present on the day of application, in turn, was not suitable to achieve those aims (paras 106-8).

Discrimination

In *Landtová, 2011* the Court partially invalidated a judgment by the Czech constitutional court. That court had decided in essence that a pension calculated under Czech law alone had to be granted, when it was higher than a pension calculated pursuant to the Agreement between the Czech Republic and the Slovak Republic which allocated the competence to take into account periods of insurance completed before the dissolution of the Czech and Slovak Federal Republic. The Court found issue exclusively with the granting of the more advantageous pension to Czech nationals resident in the Czech Republic only. Both those requirements were precluded by articles 39 Treaty and 3(1) Regulation 1408/71, for amounting to direct and indirect discrimination, respectively (paras 42-8). Apart from that, the judgment of the supreme court merely granted a more advantageous benefit under national law. That did not affect the allocation of competences between the Czech Republic and the Slovak Republic, which had been preserved by article 7(1)(c) in conjunction with point 6 of annex III(A) Regulation 1408/71. As such it was compatible with Regulation 1408/71 (paras 32-9). In line with *Terhoeve, 1999*, until the Czech Republic had remedied the discrimination found – possibly by removing the advantage – the persons disadvantaged had to benefit from the more advantageous solution which Czech nationals had enjoyed hitherto (paras 51-3).

Applicable legislation

The Court also elaborated on the provisions determining the applicable legislation in a few decisions. In *Hudzinski, 2012* the Court was called upon to clarify *Bosmann, 2008*. In two separate cases, two Polish nationals claimed child benefits in Germany for their children who were resident in Poland. In both cases, Poland, rather than Germany, was the competent state pursuant to Regulation 1408/71. In one case pursuant to article 14a(1)(a), because Mr Hudzinski, a self-employed farmer in Poland, had come to Germany as a seasonal worker and had been employed for three months in Germany; in the other pursuant to article 14(1)(a), because Mr Wawrzyniak had been posted to Germany, while remaining employed in Poland. Both workers had lawfully become, by application, subject to unlimited income taxation in Germany. That was why German law granted an entitlement to child benefits, if it had not been for the national rule against overlapping which fully excluded German child benefits in the amount of 154 Euro per child in the light of the Polish benefits being paid in the amount of 12 Euro per child. The Court stuck to *Bosmann, 2008*. Germany had the power to grant child benefits in such circumstances, although Germany was not the competent state pursuant to Regulation 1408/71. In spite of the principle that only one legislation could be applied at a time, the aim of the free movement of persons required that Germany had that power (paras 41-9). That the persons concerned had not suffered a disadvantage in contrast to *Bosmann, 2008* was irrelevant (paras 51-7). That the workers were not resident in Germany was irrelevant, too, because being subject to unlimited taxation in Germany established a similarly close connection to Germany as the children's residence (paras 58-67). For the case of Mr Wawrzyniak, the posted worker, the Court further decided that when Germany subjected him to unlimited taxation and he thus basically contributed to the financing of child benefits Germany could not lawfully apply a national rule against overlapping. Migrant workers were disadvantaged, in particular when the amounts of the benefits diverged strongly and German law did not reduce the benefit by the amount granted in Poland, but rather denied a benefit altogether (paras 70-84).

In *Partena, 2012* Belgian law established an irrebuttable presumption that those who managed a Belgian company from abroad in fact pursued a self-employed activity and, by reason of that activity, were subject to social security contributions in Belgium. After having pointed out that the case concerned the situation where the agent of a Belgian company was either employed in Portugal or did not pursue an activity at all in Portugal while being resident there, the Court held that 'the location' of an activity was the general criterion which allowed the determination of the applicable legislation. Hence, first the location was to be established, then the law of the member state which applied in that location determined whether an activity amounted to 'employment' or 'self-employment' (paras 42-54). In contrast to the latter terms, the term 'location' was a term of Union law. It meant the 'place where, in practical terms, the person carrie[d] out the actions connected with that activity' (para. 57). The irrebuttable presumption Belgium applied ran the risk of frustrating that definition. It was not justified by the need to combat social security fraud, because it went beyond what was required by that aim. The person concerned notably had to have the possibility to prove that he in actual fact carried out the actions connected with an activity in another member state (paras 58-60).

Format, 2012 clarified what it meant to work normally in several member states as required by article 14(2)(b) Regulation 1408/71. The authorities issuing certificate E 101, according to the Court, had to base their finding in this regard first on the contract concluded between the employer and the employee and the foreseeable place of work, but also on the circumstances, such as previous contracts concluded with that employee or the practice of the employer concerned in general. If the employee did not in actual fact work in several member states, but only in one, the certificate E 101 previously issued had to be withdrawn. Article 13(2)(a) Regulation 1408/71 then typically became applicable (paras 43-50).

Sickness

Elchinov, 2010 was one of a few cases dealing with sickness benefits. It concerned treatment for sickness received abroad under article 22 Regulation 1408/71 and the freedom of services. Mr Elchinov, a Bulgarian national who was insured in Bulgaria, suffered from an eye sickness for which an advanced treatment was only available in Germany. Obviously, Bulgarian law did not specifically include the treatment method, but it broadly included a category within which the treatment could fall. Mr Elchinov applied in Bulgaria for the authorization to receive that treatment in Germany, but underwent treatment there before the authorization was refused. After having reiterated the case-law established under article 22 Regulation 1408/71 and article 49 Treaty, the Court held that reimbursement could not lawfully be excluded in all cases in which the authorization had not been granted before the treatment was administered, including urgent cases, even though all other conditions had been met (paras 45-50). Whether the treatment method to be applied abroad corresponded to a treatment available under national legislation which determined only broad categories of what it covered, was for the national court to decide in the light of the lists of treatments national law had established (paras 58-62). If the treatment method was covered, article 22 Regulation 1408/71 applied and the authorization had to be granted, if the same or equally effective treatment was not available in the competent state (paras 64-67). In any event, an assessment on a case-by-case basis was required. Hence, a general presumption that national legislation did not cover a treatment method when it was not available in Bulgaria could not lawfully be applied under article 22 Regulation 1408/71 or article 49 Treaty (paras 69-72). If treatment abroad was provided under article 22 Regulation 1408/71, the amount to be reimbursed was basically determined by host state legislation, with the modifications established by the case-law. If treatment was provided under article 49 Treaty, 'home' state legislation was pertinent. In any case, form E 112 was normally not needed any longer when treatment had been sought before authorization was granted. Direct reimbursement was then required (paras 74-80).

Van Delft, 2010 dealt with the sickness insurance of pensioners. The Netherlands had reformed their sickness insurance system to introduce general compulsory insurance for residents. That reform had some effects on those receiving pensions in the Netherlands while being resident abroad. Those pensioners had under the previous system taken out voluntary insurance with companies in the Netherlands or in other member states. The switch to the compulsory system arguably had the effect of rendering articles 28 and 28a Regulation 1408/71 applicable, entitling those pensioners after registration in the host state to sickness insurance there as if they were ensured there at the expense of the state paying the pension, i. e. the Netherlands. Accordingly, the Netherlands authorities deducted contributions from the pensions. In addition, the Netherlands legislation provided that the voluntary insurance contracts of such pensioners be terminated automatically. According to the Court, the pensioners concerned could not lawfully elude the new Dutch system and hence Regulation 1408/71 by not registering in the host state. In spite of the appearance created in *Van der Duin, 2003*, such an option or right to choose was not inherent in the system of Regulation 1408/71. That system relied on solidarity and applied regardless of whether the persons subject to contributions in fact received benefits. Moreover, when articles 28 and 28a were applicable, article 13(f) was not. The deductions the Netherlands made were therefore lawful (paras 38-79). The free movement of workers, moreover, was not applicable to pensioners who had moved residence after having ceased all occupational activities (paras 88-93). Rather, Union citizenship applied. The introduction of the new system and the resulting effects on pensioners abroad were compatible with Union citizenship, in particular since it contained a mechanism to adapt the contributions to the cost of living in the state of residence (para. 104). However, Union citizenship required that the consequences of the automatic termination of insurance contracts were not discriminatory of the pensioners concerned, notably because of their lack of residence. Subject to the national court's assessment, discrimination could notably reside in the less advantageous conditions granted to non-residents by insurance companies for new contracts for supplementary insurance, which had become necessary because the old contracts had been terminated by law. Even a practice by insurance companies that implemented a political agreement was caught by the prohibition of discrimination of Union citizens (paras 94-128).

Da Silva Martins, 2011 further developed the *Molenaar, 1998*-line of case-law which had qualified benefits granted to address the risk of reliance on care as sickness benefits. In the case at issue, a Portuguese national received old-age pensions in both Germany and Portugal. When he moved his residence from Germany to Portugal after retirement the benefits he received under his German care insurance were discontinued. Basically, German law would have allowed him to remain subject to care insurance on an optional continued basis, but it was unclear whether that was possible under Regulation 1408/71. The Court first recounted the *Molenaar, 1998*-case-law and emphasized that the reason why benefits granted to counter the risk of reliance on care had been qualified as sickness benefits was that that risk had only recently been addressed by the laws of the member states and was, hence, not covered by Regulation 1408/71. The Court then answered very much on the specifics of the case. Given that German law did not a priori preclude optional continued insurance, Regulation 1408/71 was not opposed to such continuation. The principle that only the social security legislation of a single member state was applicable did not apply to care benefits when they had to be qualified as sickness benefits while they addressed a risk different from sickness, i. e. the risk of becoming reliant on care (paras 37-59). Hence, basically sickness benefits were to be provided by Portugal as the state of residence paying a pension, while Germany had to provide care benefits. If it turned out that Portugal's social security system provided cash benefits to address the risk of reliance on care, Germany would have to top-up those benefits, else contributions the pensioner had paid would be lost without return (paras 60-87). (For the case-law regarding care insurance under the freedom of services see below.)

Aggregation

The aggregation of insurance periods also came back to the Court in the 2010s. In *Tomaszewska, 2011* Polish law required the completion of a minimum period of contribution of 30 years for the acquisition of a pension. To the periods of contribution actually completed a maximum of a third of those periods could be added as periods of non-contribution. The Court found that periods of contribution completed in other member states had to be taken into account not only to determine the actual number of periods completed, but also to determine the number of periods of non-contribution capable of being added, otherwise a restriction of the free movement of persons arose (paras 32-7). Migrant workers would have been treated less favourably. Such a disadvantage was not justified by administrative difficulties, because only the grounds mentioned in article 39(3) Treaty, namely public policy, security, or health, were capable of justifying such a restriction (para. 38).

Salgado González, 2013 next dealt with the calculation of the theoretical amount for aggregation in Spain. In the case at issue, the Spanish authorities had, according to the Court, correctly taken into account periods of insurance completed in Portugal for the qualifying period of 15 years required by Spanish law (para. 45). However, when establishing the average contribution basis, which served to determine the pension to be paid in Spain, the authorities had to adjust the divisor used so that it reflected the periods completed in Spain only, when they calculated the theoretical amount under article 46(2)(a) Regulation 1408/71. If the same divisor was used as in situations where a person had not made use of the freedom to move, i. e. the divisor 210, migrant workers would be disadvantaged for the theoretical amount resulting for them would be lower (paras 46-51).

After that, in *Van den Booren, 2013* the Court reiterated that benefits were not of the same kind for the purpose of the calculation under article 46(2) Regulation 1408/71 when they were based on the insurance careers of two different persons. Hence, the Belgian rule against the overlapping of benefits was lawfully applied, when a person's survivor's benefit in Belgium was reduced in the light of an increase in that person's own old-age benefit due in the Netherlands (paras 28-36). While the considerations that decided *Van Munster, 1994* and *Engelbrecht, 2000* were not transposable to the case at issue, the national court had to make sure that no unjustified obstacle to the free movement of persons arose (paras 38-46).

Unemployment

Unemployment benefits occupied the Court in *Jeltes, 2013*. The Court emphasized the amendments the new Regulation 883/2004 had made to the scheme governing unemployment benefits and found, as a consequence, that the *Miethe, 1986*-case-law as to the atypical frontier worker did no longer apply. The Union legislature had taken the decision that all wholly unemployed frontier workers were to receive unemployment benefits where they resided, even if they retained strong links in the member state where they used to work. Pursuant to article 65 Regulation 883/2004, frontier workers in addition benefitted from the employment services of the state of their last employment (paras 24-35). The Netherlands could therefore lawfully rely on a residence condition to refuse unemployment benefits to wholly unemployed frontier workers residing in Germany or Belgium even if they were Dutch nationals. Such a condition had the same effect as article 65(2) (paras 39-40). The fact that unemployment benefits were in general higher in the Netherlands in such circumstances did not amount to a restriction of the free movement of persons (paras 41-45). The transitional regime of article 87(8) Regulation 883/2004, which allowed the maintenance of benefits paid under Regulation 1408/71, applied in principle by analogy to unemployment benefits pursuant to article 71 (paras 51-6). However, whether the situation of the person concerned had not changed since the entry into force of Regulation 883/2004, a further condition for article 87(8) of that Regulation to apply, was for the national court to assess under national law (paras 57-60).

Family benefits

A number of decisions then concerned family benefits. *Schwemmer, 2010* specifically addressed article 76 Regulation 1408/71 and article 10 Regulation 574/72. Ms Schwemmer, a German national who was in minor employment in Germany not subject to mandatory social security, was married to a worker who was employed in Switzerland. She took care of their children, after they had divorced. Her application for child benefits in Germany based on her residence there was only partially granted, because her former husband could have applied, but did not apply for child benefits in Switzerland. The German authorities suspended the benefit as far as it 'overlapped' with the Swiss benefit and merely granted her the top-up amount. After having reiterated that Regulation 1408/71 applied pursuant to the Agreement on Free Movement with Switzerland (paras 31-2), the Court found that the Regulation applied *ratione personae*, since the children's father was an employed person in Switzerland. The divorce was irrelevant and so was the fact that the annex to the Regulation had the effect of excluding the mother from the scope of the Regulation (paras 34-8). Article 76 Regulation 1408/71, though basically applicable to situations of overlapping benefits, was not to be applied, since the right to child benefits in Germany was not based on the mother carrying on an occupation in Germany as required by that article, but based on her residence. That was why the article, including its amendment in the second paragraph requiring that any lack of application for a benefit be disregarded, was not applicable (paras 40-6). Article 10 Regulation 574/72 addressing the overlapping of family benefits was pertinent, though. Under that article, all formal and substantive conditions of national law for the award of benefits had to be met for overlapping of benefits to occur. Hence, in the absence of the husband's application for benefits in Switzerland, overlapping did not occur under article 10 Regulation 574/72. The amended article 76(2) Regulation 1408/71 was not to be applied by analogy to article 10 Regulation 574/72 (paras 49-58). Germany, thus had to award the full child benefit.

Xhymshiti, 2010 also concerned family benefits under the Agreement with Switzerland. In this case, a Kosovar worked in Switzerland, while he was resident in Germany with his wife who was also a Kosovar. Both their children were German nationals. The German authorities refused to top-up the child allowance Ms Xhymshiti was paid in Switzerland. The Court ruled that Regulation 859/2003, which had amended Regulation 1408/71 to include third country nationals within its scope, was not applicable under the Agreement with Switzerland. The relevant annex of the Agreement had to be amended for that purpose. In absence of such an amendment, Switzerland had to be considered a third country for the purposes of Regulation 859/2003. The Xhymshitis' situation therefore only concerned one member state and a third country, which was why Regulation 859/2003 was not applicable (paras 30-39). The Union citizenship of the two children did not change that assessment in any way. Hence, German law was applicable exclusively. The refusal to top-up the allowance was lawful (paras 41-4).

In *Bergström, 2011* again family benefits under the Agreement with Switzerland were at issue. A Swedish national had worked in Switzerland. After having given birth to a child she stopped working and then went back to Sweden where her husband had found employment. Her application for the Swedish parental benefit was rejected, because she had not completed the prerequisite 240 days of employment in Sweden. In fact, she had not completed a single day of employment in Sweden, but all of them in Switzerland. The Court found, based on the wording, the aim, and the equality of treatment clause of the Agreement, that the Agreement and with it Regulation 1408/71 applied to a returner, a person who came back to the state of which she was a national, after having worked in another state party to the Agreement (paras 28-34). With the parental benefit being a family benefit, periods of employment as qualifying periods had to be aggregated. More specifically, Sweden's authorities had to aggregate periods completed in Switzerland, even if *all* periods had been completed in Switzerland. The Agreement and Regulation 1408/71 were entirely unambiguous in that regard (paras 36-44). For the income determining the amount of the parental benefit, the provisions of the Regulation 1408/71 on sickness benefits were pertinent. Since she had never earned income in Sweden, the income of a person in a comparable situation in Sweden had to be the yardstick, rather than the income she had gained in Switzerland (paras 47-52).

Perez Garcia, 2011 dealt with family allowances of pensioners who were receiving pensions in two member states, namely Germany and Spain, and who had moved residence from Germany to Spain. The Court ruled that a right to such an allowance was not to be considered to be 'acquired' under articles 77(2) (b)(i) and 78(2)(b)(i) when a pensioner had lawfully opted for a benefit in Spain which did not qualify as a family allowance and the exercise of that option excluded the grant of a Spanish family allowance which would have been due but for the option exercised. In such a situation, Germany could not lawfully refuse to grant a full family allowance to the pensioner whose pension was due under German law alone. In particular, article 76(2) Regulation 1408/71, which had been amended to guarantee that the option to a right was to be considered a right acquired, was not applicable by analogy under articles 77 and 78, for lack of a specific amendment of those articles. That interpretation was imperative, else the migrant worker was deprived of benefits due under national law alone (paras 42-55).

Aggregation more broadly

Reichel, 2012 was about child-raising periods to be taken into account for the calculation of an old-age benefit. Since Regulation 1408/71 did not address that question and Regulation 987/2009 implementing the new Regulation 883/2004 did not yet apply, the applicable legislation in the case at issue was determined by the closest connection to a member state. For Ms Reichel, this was Germany, because she had resided and worked in Germany before she gave birth to two children and worked there again after the period during which she had resided with her husband in Belgium and raised her children, without however ever working in Belgium (paras 26-30 and 32-6). In those circumstances, the freedom of Union citizens to move required Germany to take into account the periods of child-raising in Belgium in the calculation of the old-age benefits due. German law could not lawfully refuse to take into account those periods completed abroad, solely because more than a month had passed between the completion of the last period of insurance by virtue of work and the birth of the child. Otherwise Union citizens who had exercised their freedom were disadvantaged (paras 37-44).

In *Dumont, 2013* benefits for orphans were at issue, more specifically aggregation for the purpose of acquisition of such benefits. The Court made it clear that articles 78(2) and 79(1) Regulation 1408/71 only determined the applicable legislation. Beyond that, the applicable national law provided for the conditions for the acquisition of benefits. When pursuant to Belgian law it was required to take into account not just the periods the deceased person completed but also those of the surviving parent, aggregation had to be applied to the latter periods as well (paras 37-47). Moreover, that applied irrespective of whether periods had been completed in Belgium at all before the death of the deceased parent, since Belgian law was applicable pursuant to Regulation 1408/71 (paras 49-60).

Ankara

Akdas, 2011 concerned a Dutch special non-contributory supplement to invalidity benefits which was intended to bring up invalidity pensions to the level of the Dutch minimum wage. For this supplement an amendment of Regulation

1408/71 had deleted the residence clause waiver. However, a corresponding amendment of article 6(1) Decision 3/80 under the Ankara Agreement had not been adopted. Hence, the Court found, the Netherlands could not refuse to continue to grant the supplement to a Turkish national lawfully receiving Dutch invalidity benefits, just because he had moved his residence to Turkey. Since Decision 3/80 had not been amended, Union citizens were not treated less favourably than Turkish nationals which would have been at odds with article 59 Additional Protocol to the Ankara Agreement (paras 76-95). Apart from that, the Court found that article 6(1) Decision 3/80 had direct effect (paras 68-73).

For completeness, three more decisions must be mentioned. In *Reinke, 2010* the Court ordered the case closed, because the main claim before the national court had been met in the meantime. In essence, it had concerned the claim of a pensioner insured in Germany for reimbursement of the cost caused by an emergency hospital treatment in Spain. She had been admitted to a private hospital to have a stroke treated, because no bed in the public hospital had been available. In *United Kingdom v. Council, 2012* the United Kingdom sought interim relief. The Council had granted the mandate to renegotiate the Agreement with Switzerland on free movement of persons pursuing the aim of replacing Regulation 1408/71 with Regulation 883/2004. The United Kingdom claimed that the legal basis of the Council's decision was wrong and that it would suffer irreparable harm if the Joint Committee under the Agreement decided to replace Regulation 1408/71 before the Court ruled on the merits of the action. The Court rejected that argument, holding that the Union would have to renegotiate the replacement in the Joint Committee if it turned out that the Council had relied on the wrong legal basis (paras 37-8). Moreover, rights acquired by Swiss nationals in the United Kingdom in the meanwhile were not necessarily acquired, but could be limited in several regards (para. 45). Damage would be pecuniary in nature anyway (para. 41). Finally, the case brought by the Commission in *Commission v. Belgium (indexation), 2013* was rejected on procedural grounds. The Commission had failed to state coherently how Belgium had infringed Union law by abolishing a condition for indexation of pensions as per 2004 and not for the time period before that. The condition had been to have residence within the Union or in a country with which Belgium had concluded a convention guaranteeing reciprocity only.

4 Services

Posted workers

With *Commission v. Germany (posted workers), 2010* posted workers came back to the Court. The Court confirmed the allegation of the Commission that Germany had to extend the advantages contained in a bilateral convention between Poland and Germany, from the moment on that Poland had acceded to the Union, to other member states. More specifically, companies from other member states than Germany which posted Polish workers to Germany had to be able to benefit from the quota allocated in the convention to such workers, else they suffered direct discrimination contrary to the freedom of services, because they were forced to establish themselves in Germany (paras 40-1). Only the grounds expressly mentioned in the Treaty could possibly justify such discrimination. Economic considerations and practical difficulties, such as the effective monitoring of posting and the recovery of social security debts, apart from not being express grounds, were not admitted by the case-law to justify discriminations that were not direct (paras 47-51). Besides, the need to maintain the balance and reciprocity of bilateral agreements, a ground established by *Gottardo, 2002*, was not a ground that could be argued for relationships between the member states (paras 42-6). As a further point the Court ruled that the standstill clause in the Act of Accession of Poland covered a labour market protection clause of Germany which had existed at the time of accession and was updated depending on the circumstances. Germany was therefore allowed, depending on the prevailing situation, to add or remove to a list districts in which a 30 per cent-ceiling of unemployment was reached and for which the restrictions for Polish workers contained in the convention with Germany, which the Act of Accession covered, applied as a consequence (paras 64-6).

In *Rani, 2010* the Court confirmed that the posting of workers was not to be made subject to a company being established in the host state. For lack of transitional provisions in the Act of Accession, Hungary was not allowed to maintain in force a provision that reserved the activities of temporary work agencies to national companies (paras 37-9 and 48). *Santos Palhota, 2010* declared Belgium's formalities applying to companies posting workers to Belgium incompatible with the freedom of services. Directive 96/71 did not regulate the measures imposed to control compliance with the Directive (paras 25-7). However, the need to declare the posting of workers five days ahead of the beginning of the works in fact constituted an authorization requirement, because the workers posted were not allowed to begin their work during those five days. As such, the requirement did not comply with the case-law which allowed only a simple declaration (paras 33-41 and 51-2). The documents to be furnished by the company posting workers were in line with that case-law, though (paras 55).

In *Vicoplus, 2011* the Court spelled out two points. On the one hand, the old member states, such as the Netherlands, could lawfully require Polish posted workers to have a work permit during the transitional phase after accession, although the transitional measures in the Act of Accession of Poland technically only concerned workers and not employees posted as part of service provision. However, that kind of service provision possibly had the same impact on the labour market which the transitional measures intended to prevent (paras 26-40). On the other hand, a 'hiring out' of a worker pursuant to article 1(3)(c) Directive 96/71 presented three characteristics, namely the worker concerned was employed by the agency posting him; the making available of an employee was the main purpose of the service provision, in contrast to a 'posting' where it was a secondary part of a broader service provided; and the employee concerned was working under the control and direction of the user undertaking in the host state. The return to the member state of origin, however, was not a necessary characteristic of 'hiring out' a worker (paras 44-50).

In *Commission v. Belgium (employment agencies), 2011* the Court confirmed that Belgium had infringed the freedom of services by requiring that temporary employment agencies in Brussels met certain requirements. According to Belgian law, they namely had to have the exclusive purpose of providing services as temporary employment agencies and they had to have a particular form of company. In both cases it was difficult for the Court to imagine how such serious restrictions could be justified (paras 15 and 21). (Belgium had not contested the infringement.)

Games of chance

In *Santa Casa, 2010*, one of a long series of gambling cases of the 2010s, the Court ruled that it did not have jurisdiction. The national court decided to maintain its question despite the ruling in *Liga Portuguesa and Bwin, 2009*, but failed to explain the facts and national law sufficiently to allow the Court to answer the question referred. *Ladbrokes, 2010* and *Sporting Exchange, 2010* then again concerned a gambling and betting monopoly. In *Ladbrokes, 2010* the Netherlands had entrusted a single licence to one national operator of certain games of chance. A British company that lawfully offered games of chance in the United Kingdom was prohibited from offering them in the Netherlands via internet. The Court left the application of the criteria developed in the gambling case-law to the referring court. In particular, that court had to verify the consistency and systematics of the national measure. In that regard, it was not inconsistent with the aims of preventing fraud and addiction, which were both part of consumer protection, to expand games of chance in a controlled way in order to draw gambling away from clandestine to legal activities. For that purpose, ads, a range of games, and new distribution channels were all necessary. Even the generation of profits was not inconsistent, provided that it was incidental and not the main aim of the measure. The national court had to verify, though, whether unlawful gambling constituted a real and significant problem in the Netherlands, taking into account the conditions of the licence issued and the code of conduct enacted (paras 26-36). Assuming that the national legislation was compatible with the freedom of services, any measures implementing it, including actions brought by private individuals, did not constitute additional restrictions warranting a separate examination (paras 42-9). If the circumstances discussed by the Court were all found by the national court to be present, the Netherlands authorities were not obliged to recognize the licence issued in the United Kingdom or in general tolerate games of chance offered via internet even in the absence of any advertising (paras 54-7).

In *Sporting Exchange, 2010*, handed down on the same day as *Ladbrokes, 2010*, the single licence issued by the Netherlands for sports and horse race betting were also challenged by a British company offering services via internet. The Court ruled in the same way as for games of chance via internet and for justification on the grounds of preventing fraud and addiction (paras 26-36). The Court added, though, that the obligation of transparency, which had been developed under the freedom of services for public service concessions, had to be respected, too, with all the implications when the single licence available in the Netherlands was issued, irrespective of whether it was a service concession or not. The grounds justifying the restriction that consisted in the availability of only one licence, did not justify the lack of a sufficient degree of advertising of the licence to be awarded, since the award as such did not have an impact on the proliferation of gambling. Justification of the lack of transparency was only possible, if the licensed operator was subject to direct state supervision or strict control (paras 42-60).

Sjöberg, 2010 also dealt with gambling legislation. Sweden reserved all activities relating to games of chance to a public non-profit entity. Accordingly, a private for-profit operator, be it established in Sweden or other member states, could not lawfully offer or advertise gambling services in Sweden. In the case at issue, two editors of magazines in Sweden had advertised the services of private for-profit operators established in other member states where they were licensed to offer games of chance. The editors were prosecuted. The Court held that the restriction of the freedom of service recipients in Sweden as well as of providers established abroad which resulted from the prohibition for private for-profit operators to offer games of chance in Sweden could be justified by the aim of imposing strict limits on for-profit gambling. A member state was entitled to see it as unacceptable that private entities exploited social evils or the weaknesses and misfortune of gamblers. Along with the prohibition of the services as such, a ban on advertisements of the services prohibited was equally justified (paras 41-5). The national court had to take care, though, that purely domestic violations of ad bans were not subject to lighter penalties or subject to less diligent prosecution than in the case of cross-border ads, else discrimination contrary to the service freedom arose (paras 55-6).

The next wave of gambling cases was overcome by the Court on 8 September 2010. In *Stoß, 2010* the monopoly created by some German Länder to offer sports betting and lotteries was at issue in the light of the freedom of services and establishment. The Court confirmed first that it was possible, based on the member states' discretion, to establish public monopolies for gambling, although authorizations of private persons combined with appropriate controls, as practised in other member states, were possibly less restrictive (paras 74-82). Having confirmed that the transnational gambling possibilities the internet offered were not such as to jeopardize by themselves the consistency and systematics of regional monopolies (paras 85-7), the Court focused on the circumstances prevailing in Germany. While each game of chance needed to be assessed on its own in terms of restrictions, it was nevertheless inconsistent with the aims of preventing money squandering and addiction, in the view of the Court, that highly addictive gambling machines were only subject to authorization and the corresponding policy had been substantially expanded, while there was a monopoly for betting and lotteries. Moreover, some of the proceeds from lotteries which were aggressively marketed fed the public purse, which in turn was at risk of becoming an end in itself. In those circumstances, the referring court could find that a monopoly in betting on sports competitions was not any longer justified (paras 91-105). In spite of that, Germany was not under a duty to recognize authorizations to offer gambling services issued in other member states, but could require that providers obtain a new authorization in Germany (paras 111-4). Besides, the Court clarified that a study as to the risks inherent in gambling was not necessarily needed before adoption of a national measure. A measure could be proven proportionate without such a study (paras 71-2).

Carmen Media, 2010 also concerned the regulatory framework for gambling, as amended, in Germany. The Court added that the fact that the authorization to offer gambling services granted by Gibraltar in the case at issue exclusively covered services provided via internet to recipients established abroad was not such as to render the freedom of services inapplicable. Any possible tax avoidance was not the topic of the preliminary ruling procedure, though (paras 42-50). Moreover, the Court confirmed that the specifics of gambling services offered via internet were such that a prohibition to offer them in Germany was not inappropriate (paras 98-105). A transitional period of one year, combined with certain conditions, that allowed those who had offered lotteries lawfully via internet under the previous legislation to convert their businesses did not render the German measure inconsistent, either (paras 106-10). *Winner Wetten, 2010* then also related to the German gambling legislation, but concerned the freedom of services and establishment only indirectly. Rather, a problem of the primacy of Union law was raised, namely whether the German constitutional court could lawfully grant a transitional period during which the legislation of a Land had to be adapted. (For the gambling judgments that were decided primarily on the basis of the freedom of establishment, see above.)

Next, in *Zeturf, 2011* the Court mainly left it to the national court to assess the public monopoly in France on the organisation of horse races and horse race-betting in the light of the established case-law. The Court reiterated though the applicable case-law as to (i) the objectives a system of exclusive rights for betting could lawfully pursue, confirming that generating revenues for social policy aims, such as the rural development of horse breeding, did not in itself constitute a reason justifying a restriction on gambling services (para. 53); (ii) the strict control to be exercised over the body holding exclusive rights to organize horse race betting, pointing out that even a public non-profit body could be tempted to expand betting so as to raise more revenues and be able to accomplish its public policy task more effectively, which possibly resulted in an inconsistency with the aims pursued (paras 59-62); (iii) the controlled expansion of gambling activities by a dynamic commercial policy pursued by the holder of exclusive rights. In a similar vein, the Court left it to the referring court in *Dickinger, 2011* to assess the monopoly of a private licence holder in Austria to organize casino games via internet. Yet the Court clarified a number of points. First, a mere computer server in Austria supporting internet services provided from Malta did not render the freedom of establishment applicable, for lack of a stable and continuous basis in the host state. Rather, the freedom of services was exclusively applicable (paras 34-7). Second, the monopoly of a private company as a licence holder had to be assessed in the light of the criteria developed in the case-law. However, the aim stated in the relevant act of maximising revenue for the state could not alone justify the restriction of services inherent in a private monopoly (para. 55). Third, a substantial increase in the activities of the holder of an exclusive licence and the corresponding increase in income called for particular attention by the referring court when assessing whether an aim justifying a restriction was pursued in a systematic way, despite an expansive commercial policy for games of chance (para. 61). Hence, a distinction had to be made in cases of monopolies between a restrained commercial policy which channelled gamblers towards lawful offers and an expansionist policy which in reality aimed at increasing revenues (para. 69). Fourth, the requirement of a certain legal form and financial capacity of the holder of the exclusive licence was in accordance with the freedom of services, provided the requirements were not excessive (para. 77). Fifth, the need for the registered office to be located in the state where the exclusive licence was granted was only susceptible of justification by grounds mentioned explicitly in the Treaty. Under the public order ground an exclusive licence combined with an establishment requirement was in any case not justified by the aim of maximizing public revenue (para. 81). Sixth, the prohibition for the exclusive licence holder to set up branches abroad was a restriction for which no justification had been put forward; the freedom of a member state to regulate games of chance in its territory was not a ground suitable for justification in that regard (para. 87). Finally, the requirement established by the services case-law to take into account 'home' state regulation, controls, and supervision did not apply to games of chance. For lack of harmonisation a member state need not have trusted the checks undertaken by other member states which were possibly based on different choices and means. Those checks did not necessarily provide sufficient guarantees for consumer protection (paras 96-9).

In *HIT, 2012*, the Court next assessed Austria's requirement to have a permit to advertise in Austria games of chance lawfully offered in another member state. The permit was only granted, if the level of protection of the consumers in the member state where the games of chance were offered corresponded to the level of protection guaranteed in Austria. The Court found that requirement to be a justified restriction of the freedom to provide services, given that it was up to each member state to set the level necessary to protect consumers. However, it was only to be required that the level of protection in the other member state was equivalent, rather than identical to the level in Austria, else the Austrian rule went beyond what was necessary to protect consumers (paras 23-32).

In *Garkalns, 2012* the Latvian legislation prohibited games of chance in a list of locations, but conferred local authorities wide discretion to assess the situation and grant permits. In the case of Garkalns, a Latvian company that wanted to open an amusement arcade in a shopping centre in Riga, the local authorities refused the permit, because the centre was heavily frequented and within the vicinity of a school. The inhabitants of the neighbourhood allegedly had to be protected from disturbances. The Court addressed the question to allow the referring court to exclude reverse discrimination and because it was 'far from inconceivable' that companies in other member states wanted to open amusement arcades in Latvia (paras 20-1). Examining only the freedom of services, as the national court had only asked about services, although the freedom of establishment was possibly concerned as well (paras 24-32), the Court again left the ultimate assessment to the national court. However, the Court stated that a broad discretion was not, in principle, excluded under the freedom of services. The national court had to make sure, though, that the protection of consumers and residents was genuinely pursued and that the requirements of the authorization case-law were met, i. e. objective, non-discriminatory criteria known in advance were to be applied and reasons had to be given in the decision (paras 40-7).

Finally, in *Stanleybet, 2013* the monopoly in games of chance in Greece came to the Court. Greek legislation granted exclusive rights to a company the Greek state controlled. However, some of the control over the company was released and private shareholder were allowed to hold the majority of shares in the company. The company benefitted from preferential treatment in terms of advertising. It expanded its activities and offered games of chance *inter alia* in Cyprus. Yet the Greek authorities rejected the request for permits by British companies that lawfully offered games of chance in the United Kingdom. The Court reiterated the established case-law on state monopolies in games of chance and again left the assessment to the national court, pointing out though that the activities of the Greek monopolist seemed inconsistent with the aim to combat crime (para. 35). If the national court found that the freedom of services and establishment were violated, a transitional period was not to be granted, as the Court had already held. That did not necessarily imply, though, that the Greek authorities were obliged to grant the British companies any permits. Liberalization of the market of games of chance was not the only possibility. Other reforms could be undertaken (paras 38 and 44-7).

Medical services

The Court addressed medical services in several decisions in the 2010s. In *Commission v. Spain (Chollet), 2010* the Court refused to extend the reasoning in *Vanbraekel, 2001* to unscheduled medical treatment in a hospital abroad which (the treatment) had become necessary during a temporary stay. The Court ruled that a person insured for sickness in Spain was not deterred from seeking medical services in France when the treatment in France had not been planned, but became necessary e. g. during a tourist visit. The restrictive effect on the freedom to seek services in other member states was too uncertain and indirect. Hence, the cost to be born regularly by the insured person herself under the French system, which was equally imposed on the person who had been treated in France and was insured under the Spanish system, need not have been reimbursed to the latter person owing to the freedom of services, even though it would have been covered had the treatment taken place in Spain where treatment was generally free of charge. In coming to that conclusion the Court relied on a number of factors, chief among them (i) that the member states lacked control over the increasing number of unscheduled treatments abroad; (ii) the uncertainty of whether treatment in the host state would be required at all; and (iii) that the very fabric of the system established by Regulation 1408/71, which consisted in an overall compensation of risks, would have been undermined in case of full reimbursement (paras 58-79).

The judgment in *Elchinov, 2010* as to the prior authorization to receive medical treatment for sickness abroad concerned the freedom of services as well as article 22 Regulation 1408/71 (see above, under social security). In *Commission v. France (Vanbraekel), 2010* the Court reiterated that a prior authorization scheme for *extra muros* treatment abroad was not justified under the freedom of services. However, the Court qualified that ruling in that planned *extra muros* treatment involving major medical equipment which national law listed exhaustively could lawfully be likened to hospital treatment. The same considerations as with hospital treatment, notably the need for proper planning, justified a prior authorization scheme in such cases (paras 34-44). Moreover, the Court found that the French legal provisions and administrative practice were such as to allow for respect of the *Vanbraekel, 2001*-line of authority (paras 57-68).

In *Commission v. Luxembourg (lab analyses), 2011* reimbursement of the cost arising from analyses conducted in laboratories abroad was excluded by Luxembourg's social security system, unless an agreement to that effect existed. According to the Court, an obstacle to the freedom of movement of medical services existed in that it was unlikely that foreign laboratories concluded agreements under Luxembourg's social security system (paras 37-41). Luxembourg had failed to show that medical services as such and the balance of the social security system would have been put at risk, if reimbursement had been granted in the case of foreign laboratories. Luxembourg's conditions and limits for reimbursement were applicable though, as long as they were objective, non-discriminatory, and transparent (paras 44-6).

In *Commission v. Portugal (medical treatment), 2011* the Court did not add much to the existing medical services case-law, but simply applied it to Portugal's system. Portugal had failed to comply with the freedom of services in that it required a triple prior authorization for *extra muros* specialist medical treatment abroad for the cost caused to be reimbursable. (Portugal required that authorization only outside the scope of article 22 Regulation 1408/71; paras 60-87).

Moreover, in other cases of such treatment, e. g. by general practitioners or dentists, the service freedom was *a fortiori* violated, because provision was not made at all for reimbursement in Portuguese law (para. 92).

In *Commission v. Germany (care insurance), 2012* the Commission challenged under the freedom of services the limited exportability of benefits under the German care insurance. However, the Court ruled that the medical services case-law was not transposable to benefits provided under care insurance (paras 50 and 52). Such benefits were akin to sickness benefits, as the case-law under social security had established (see above), and articles 22 and 32 Regulation 1408/71 applied to them. Given that particular regime for receiving care benefits in kind and cash abroad, the Commission had failed to show how the German rules on care insurance restricted the free movement of services (paras 51-8).

Taxes

Taxes occupied the Court repeatedly under the freedom of services during the beginning of the 2010s. *Zanotti, 2010*, a case referred by an Italian court, concerned the tax deductibility of tuition fees paid for university courses at educational establishments abroad. The Court reiterated that the freedom of services was applicable when public education was not concerned because the services provided were mainly financed by private funds (paras 26-34). Tax deductibility could not lawfully be refused for courses attended abroad, if it was permitted for similar courses attended in Italy, else a higher tax burden resulted (paras 40-4). However, Italy was allowed to limit the deductible amount in general to 19 per cent of the fees paid and subject it to the limit of the tuition fees paid at the universities which were closest to the tax residence of the person concerned, because then a deterrent effect did not result (paras 45-62). A possibly less restrictive measure proposed by the Commission was irrelevant, given that a restriction did not arise (paras 63-5). The same analysis was applicable under Union citizenship, if the freedom of services for some reason did not apply (paras 68-77).

In *Commission v. Portugal (tax on interest), 2010* the Court rejected the Commission's allegations that the freedom of services and capital was violated. The Commission's example of calculation had failed to establish that the tax-burden on interest on loans taken out by non-resident companies was heavier in Portugal than in case of loans taken out by resident companies (paras 27-30).

In *VAV-Autovermietung, 2010* the Court ordered that the amendments the Netherlands had made to its law on the taxation of cars used in the Netherlands, since the Court had handed down *Van de Coevering, 2006* and *Ilhan, 2008*, did not live up to the freedom of services. The amount of tax on leased cars levied at the occasion of the car's first use in the Netherlands had to reflect the duration of the lease contract as well as the actual use made of the car in the Netherlands. It was not sufficient to reimburse proportionately, without interest, the amount that was initially levied in full, after it had turned out that the car was no longer used in the Netherlands (paras 27-8).

In *Schmelz, 2010* the Sixth VAT Directive 77/388 itself was scrutinized by the Court on compatibility with the free movement of services. The Directive allowed the member states to exempt small undertakings established in their territory from value added tax with loss of the right of deduction, while they were precluded from exempting such undertakings established abroad. Ms Schmelz was resident in Germany and rented out an apartment she owned in Austria. The German authorities claimed value added tax on the rent generated, while Austria would have exempted her as a small undertaking from such tax in application of the authorization in the Directive. The Court found that the freedom of services applied to the lease of the apartment pursuant to *Hengartner, 2010* (see below), although she had rented it out for several years. The freedom of establishment, in contrast, only applied in case of a permanent presence in real estate that was actively managed (paras 39-43). The Directive, in allowing the member states to exempt only locally established undertakings from tax, established a restriction to freedom of services. Undertakings established in Austria were in a position to offer more attractive services owing to the exemption (paras 51-4). However, the need to ensure effective fiscal supervision justified the restriction. The Directive provided for a simplified scheme for small undertakings which exempted them from most formalities in order to reduce the administrative burden they had to shoulder. That was why the 'home' member state of a small undertaking, in this case Germany, did not have any data to communicate to the host state, viz. Austria. Such data was necessary, though, to supervise those undertakings fiscally and to ascertain that the conditions for the exemption to apply were in fact met. Thus, to extend the exemption from value added tax to undertakings established abroad would mean to undo the simplified scheme, because only then was it possible to prevent tax evasion. For the same reason the state where a small undertaking was established was justified in taking account only of the turnover generated in its territory for the purpose of the exemption (paras 59-73).

In *Tankreederei, 2010* Luxembourg refused to grant tax credits for investments used abroad, notably in the case of the Luxembourg company Tankreederei on the ground that the vessels it operated from Luxembourg provided refuelling services to ships in the Netherlands and Belgium. The Court found the freedom of services to be restricted by the selective tax deductibility (paras 17-8). Luxembourg had not argued any justification, but the Court pointed out nonetheless that the refusal was not justified. Were rejected in particular the balanced allocation of powers of taxation, for all of Tankreederei's activities were taxable in Luxembourg, the cohesion of the tax system, for lack of a direct link to the taxation of income of service recipients, and the prevention of abuse for wholly artificial arrangement were not specifically targeted (paras 21-9). Finally, while the choice of interests to be promoted by means of tax benefits was up to the member states and in that regard a degree of connection with society could be required, the general refusal for investments made abroad lacked any connection to a social objective (paras 30-2).

In *Waypoint, 2011* the Court invalidated a tax credit Belgian law granted in so far as it relied on the establishment of a contractor in Belgium. The tax credit was granted based on the income from a loan which (the loan) served to finance the acquisition of an asset, but only when that asset was used by a company established in Belgium. Waypoint had leased an aircraft and then subleased it to a company established in France. It was refused the tax credit for the initial lease. The Court decided that the tax credit hindered the conclusion of contracts serving to finance the acquisition of assets which were ultimately used by companies established outside Belgium (paras 23-5). The freedom of services was thus restricted. A justification had not been put forward. In *SIAT, 2012* the Court also invalidated a Belgian tax rule, at least partly. Belgian law drew a distinction in terms of tax deductibility of business expenditures, namely expenditures that arose in connection with service contracts concluded with parties established in Belgium were presumed to be necessary and hence deductible, if the taxpayer demonstrated the authenticity and the amount paid; expenses that arose from contracts concluded with parties established in other MS in which the party to the contract was not subject to tax on income or was subject to a regime which was considerably more advantageous than the Belgian regime were presumed not to be deductible, unless the taxpayer proved that the payments related to a genuine and proper transaction and did not exceed what was normally paid for such transactions. According to the Court, there was a restriction of the freedom of services in the presumption and the substantive conditions to rebut it. In addition, uncertainty was created, because it was unclear which tax regimes were considerably more advantageous. In fact the Belgian authorities determined that on a case-by-case basis (paras 20-9). Comparability was not an issue, because in both cases the person concerned was resident in Belgium and subject to the conditions imposed by Belgian tax law as well as to the supervision in Belgium (paras 30-3). Justification was in principle possible by a combination of the needs to ensure fiscal supervision, to prevent tax evasion and avoidance, and to guarantee a proper allocation of powers of taxation. In particular, the Belgian regime did not exclude deductibility categorically, but rather allowed the taxpayer to bring proof. Moreover, it facilitated the allocation of powers of taxation (paras 36-48). However, the measure went beyond what those grounds required. The uncertainty created by the notion of a tax regime being considerably more advantageous and the fact that the tax authority need not have brought any prima facie proof as to tax avoidance had the effect that the only criterion applied to pinpoint tax avoidance was the level of taxation in the other member state. In that regard, the measure was not proportionate to the aim pursued (paras 54-9).

Next, in *X NV, 2012* a Dutch semi-professional football club invited some British peers for friendly matches and paid them a certain amount of money. The Dutch authorities ordered the Dutch club to pay directly wage tax on the remuneration paid to the British clubs, since the Dutch club had failed to withhold wage tax on the payments. The Court found the obligation to withhold wage tax at source to amount to a restriction of the freedom of service recipients. A recipient was deterred from receiving services by providers in other member states, given that the obligation to withhold tax did not apply in cases of resident service providers. The restriction arose regardless of whether the tax burden was greater than in purely domestic situations, because the administrative formalities and the risk of liability as such amounted to a burden for the service recipient. It was irrelevant that the burden was probably negligible or that it was possibly set off by other advantages. The case was not comparable to *Truck Center, 2008*, because the service provider and the recipient were different entities (paras 20-33). Yet the restriction was justified by the need to collect taxes effectively, given that only occasional services of short duration were concerned. To require the service provider to submit a tax declaration instead, would have simply shifted the burden on the provider. In addition, the tax authorities would have faced an increasing burden (paras 39-52). That the Netherlands had in the meanwhile abolished the obligation to withhold wage tax did not have an impact on the assessment, because the system of protection of a member state had to be assessed on its own, even if it was amended later on (paras 37-8). Moreover, the tax treatment of the service provider in the state where it was established did not have an impact on the question whether the service recipient in the state where it was established faced a restriction due to the obligation to withhold wage tax (paras 55-6).

Telecommunication and broadcasting

The Court addressed telecommunication services in numerous decisions in the 2010s. In *Telekomunikacja Polska, 2010* the Court clarified that the Framework Directive 2002/21 and the Universal Service Directive 2002/22 left enough room for the national legislature to prohibit the bundling of several telecommunication services certain providers offered to the consumer. According to *Commission v. Poland (broadband internet), 2010*, Poland had violated the same Directives by fixing the prices of broadband internet access services without having analysed the market first. The transitory provision in the Framework Directive that maintained the measures enacted under the previous telecommunication regime pursuant to Directive 98/10, which it had repealed, was not to be interpreted to cover the Polish measure. According to *Polska Telefonia, 2010*, the national authority had to take into account under the Universal Service Directive the cost caused by the transfer of a phone number to another service provider and balance it with the possible disincentives for a user to make use of number portability. The authority could then impose a maximum limit to the fee chargeable to the consumer for the transfer of a number.

Commission v. Portugal (universal service), 2010 ruled that Portugal violated the Universal Service Directive by not conducting an objective and transparent procedure to determine the universal service provider; instead Portugal had just maintained the licence of the national telecommunication service provider. *Base, 2010* established that it was not *per se* excluded that the national legislature exercised the functions of the national regulatory authority under Directives

2002/21 and 2002/22, provided though that it met the requirements as to competence, independence, impartiality, and transparency. Moreover, the questions whether a universal service provider bore an 'unfair burden' and which compensation was due as a result had to be answered on a case-by-case basis. The latter ruling was the same as in *Commission v. Belgium (universal service), 2010* which was handed on the same day as *Base, 2010*. In addition, the Court established in *Commission v. Belgium (universal service), 2010* how the net cost of the provision of universal services was to be calculated, while particularly taking account of intangible benefits.

In *Esposito, 2010* the Court decided in an order that the Framework Directive 2002/21 and the Authorization Directive 2002/20 did not deal with a tax that was levied from a consumer who had concluded a mobile phone contract with a telecommunication service provider. *The Number, 2011* established that article 8(1) Universal Service Directive only covered services provided by the universal service provider itself to the end-user. Provision of data on directories by the universal service provider to competitors was not part of the universal service.

In *Commission v. Belgium (must-carry), 2011* the Court held that Belgian law did not clearly state the criteria for selecting the television broadcasters benefitting from must-carry status, as required by *United Pan-Europe, 2007* and henceforth article 31(1) Universal Service Directive. It remained unclear whether the selected broadcasters offered content which in its entirety met cultural policy objectives. Hence, the freedom of services and the Directive were infringed (paras 49-55). Moreover, the applicable criteria were not transparent and non-discriminatory, either (paras 59-70), and the criterion of a sufficient number of end-users was disregarded (paras 71-5).

In *Deutsche Telekom, 2011* the Court established that 'external data', i. e. data a telecommunication company obtained through the conclusion of contracts with other companies assigning phone numbers to subscribers rather than when it assigned phone numbers itself, was not covered by article 25(2) Universal Service Directive. Consequently, an obligation to pass on that data to competitors offering directory services did not exist under Union law. Yet as the Directive only partially harmonised the law with regard to consumer protection, the member states remained free to impose such an obligation (paras 29-46). In *Vodafone España, 2012* the Court decided that article 13 Authorisation Directive 2002/20 allowed only the levying of charges from the holder of rights who was also the proprietor of telecommunication facilities installed on, above or under ground. That article, moreover, had direct effect. According to *Belgacom, 2013* a renewal of the authorization for mobile telecommunication service providers to use certain bandwidths had to be subject to the same rules under the Authorisation Directive 2002/20 as the first award of such an authorization, in particular with regard to one-off fees. Amendments with regard to fees had to respect the first paragraph of article 14, rather than the second.

In *Eleftheri tileorasi, 2011* the Court ruled that a programme aired could be qualified as intentional 'surreptitious advertising', which was prohibited pursuant to article 1(d) of the television without frontiers directive 89/552, even when a payment for consideration had not been made. In *Mesopotamia, 2011* Germany prohibited all activities of a Danish broadcaster in Germany, because it retransmitted television content that was biased towards the terrorist group PKK, inter alia by portraying the PKK's fighters as heroes and martyrs. Denmark, in contrast, did not find any issue with the content broadcast. According to the Court, under Directive 89/552 it was up to the state having jurisdiction, in this case Denmark, to address public order concerns raised by programmes. Thus, Denmark had to decide whether to apply the clause in article 22a which *inter alia* allowed a prohibition on the ground of inciting hatred based on nationality and thus included 'principles of international understanding' as they were at issue in the case at hand (paras 39-45). However, based on its general legislation on associations and in accordance with the logic of *De Agostini, 1997*, Germany was free to prohibit any activity of the company concerned in Germany, such as productions, screenings, etc., provided that the retransmission of programmes which Denmark had not prohibited was not hindered (paras 50-3).

In *Premier League, 2011* the association that filmed the premier league football games in the United Kingdom and marketed the television broadcasting of the games granted licences to broadcasters. Those licences were always by contract territorially bound, i. e. each licence granted the right to broadcast in one member state. The signal was encrypted. The end-user used a decoder to decrypt the signal. Some owners of public houses in the United Kingdom concluded contracts with the exclusive broadcaster in Greece under false names and addresses in Greece and used the decoder thus received in the United Kingdom to decrypt the 'Greek' signal and broadcast the game in the public houses in the United Kingdom. They were prosecuted, because British law prohibited importing decoders that served to decrypt a signal unlawfully. After having found that the Conditional Access Directive 98/84 did not apply, for the decoders brought from Greece were not illicit devices given that they had been obtained with the authorization of the Greek broadcaster, the Court found that the freedom of services was unlawfully restricted. That freedom was exclusively applicable, because the goods imported, i. e. the decoders, only served to receive the services (paras 78-82). It was restricted, because the British legislation conferred protection on the contractual arrangements that provided for territorial exclusivity (paras 86-9). While the United Kingdom was free to protect the football matches in a way akin to intellectual property rights and thus create a ground of justification, the restriction went beyond what that protection required. The remuneration paid for the licence reflected the territorial exclusivity, which in turn entrenched the division of the markets along the borders of the member states. It was precisely that division which was to be abolished by the common market (paras 115-6 and 94-119). The aim of making crowds go to the stadiums in the United Kingdom could justify a restriction, though not the territorial exclusivity, because the closed times in the United Kingdom during which the games were not to be broadcast, could also be agreed upon in the licence agreements with the Greek licence holder (paras 122-4). The facts that false names and addresses had been used to receive 'Greek' decoders and that the games were shown for commercial purposes in the United Kingdom did not change that assessment (paras 126-31). (The rest of the judgment dealt with competition law, which was violated as well, and the copyrights directive 2001/29, which essentially precluded the broadcasting of the games in such circumstances in public.)

In *Commission v. Spain (TV ads), 2011* the Court confirmed that any type of advertisement broadcast between or during programmes was to be qualified as advertisement spots, unless it was clear that the limits Directive 89/552 set to their duration were such that those broadcasts were disadvantaged. Spain had therefore failed to fulfil its obligations by regularly classifying a set of advertisements as 'other advertisements' to which the limits applicable to advertisement spots did not apply.

In *Sky Österreich, 2013* the public broadcaster in Austria, ORF, requested Sky Österreich, the holder of the contractual exclusive right to broadcast Europa League football matches in Austria, to provide access to footage free of charge for the purpose of short news reports. Sky challenged the validity of article 15(3) Directive 2010/13, on which ORF based its claim, in the light of the fundamental rights to property and to conduct business freely. (Directive 2010/13 had replaced the television without frontier Directive 89/552.) The Court found that the right to property in article 17 Charter of Fundamental Rights was not affected, because Sky did not hold an established right. Its exclusive right had always been subject to the obligation to provide footage for short news reports, since Directive 2007/65 had amended Directive 89/552 (paras 33-9). However, the freedom to conduct business pursuant to article 16 Charter was affected, because under article 15(3) Directive 2010/13 only the cost directly arising from the access to the material could be charged and the contract could not lawfully be refused for events of high public interest. The core of that right was not affected, though. Further, the restriction of that right was justified by the need to guarantee the right to access information and media pluralism pursuant to article 11 Charter. If cost proportionate to what the holder of the exclusive right had paid could be charged, broadcasters would be prevented from reporting on events of high public interest. The Union legislature had struck a proper balance between the fundamental rights at issue. It had precisely defined what could be broadcast, namely only reports on high interest events which (the reports) were not longer than 90 seconds; only reports in news broadcast were allowed; if possible the logo of the exclusive rights holder had to be shown (paras 42-67).

Public service concession

Wall, 2010 was one of several public service concession cases. The Court elaborated in this case on the obligation of transparency derived from the freedom of services and establishment. After having held that the substitution of a subcontractor could exceptionally amount to a substantial amendment of essential provisions of the concession contract so that the award of the contract had to be reopened for competition, notably when the subcontractor had been a decisive factor in the conclusion of the contract (paras 37-42), the Court explained why the awardee concerned was not itself, as a public authority, bound by the obligation of transparency. Inspired by Directive 92/50, the Court found that the awardee was not effectively controlled by a public authority solely because it appointed four out of 16 board members and held 51 per cent of the shares when a three quarter majority was needed to adopt decisions. Moreover, the awardee also pursued other business in competition on the market (paras 47-57).

In *Loutraki, 2010*, Greece partially privatised a casino business it owned via call for tenders. The Court found that the contract concluded based on the tender constituted a mixed contract, an indivisible whole made up of inseparably linked parts, the main object of which determined which rules, namely the public contracts directives or the market freedoms, were applicable. In the case at issue the main object was the sale of shares, while the works and services aspects were ancillary. As such a sale of shares was not within the purview of the public contracts directives, the market freedoms applied exclusively (paras 46-63).

Commission v. Ireland (award criteria), 2010 was a case in which Directive 2004/18 did not apply, because according to its annex the translation services for which Ireland publicly called for tenders were not within its scope. Instead, transparency and equal treatment applied on the basis of the freedom of services and establishment, given that the contract had a certain cross-border interest (paras 29-33). Those principles did not require that the criteria that had been published and on the basis of which the contract was awarded were not attributed certain weightings at the date when the call was closed (paras 40-9). However, they did require that the criteria and the way they were weighted were not changed after the persons in charge of deciding on the award of the contract had examined the offers. From that moment on, the criteria and the weightings had to remain the same and had to be interpreted in the same way throughout the procedure (paras 57-64).

In *Stadler, 2011* the Court clearly distinguished the public service contracts to which Directive 2004/18 did apply from public service concessions to which only the fundamental rules of the Treaty were applicable. The award of a contract in Bavaria for ambulance transports constituted a service concession, for the contractor was not remunerated by the contracting authority, but rather by a third entity which collected part of the fees on behalf of the contractor. In addition, the contractor bore a minimal part of the risk of the economic activity which sufficed in particular in cases of public service utilities (paras 27-49). In contrast, in *Norma-A, 2011* a bus transport service provider did not bear a significant part of the risk. The contract concluded was thus a public service contract (paras 39-58). In *Strong Segurança, 2011* the Court confirmed that the 'non-priority' services included in annex II B Directive 2004/18, to which not all provisions of the Directive applied, remained subject to the requirements of transparency and equal treatment flowing from the freedom of services in cases of cross-border interest. However, from those principles an obligation analogous to article 47(2) Directive 2004/18, viz. the obligation to prove the necessary resources when relying on the capacities of other entities in a tender, could not be derived for non-priority services (paras 35-45).

Econord, 2012 further developed the in-house exception to the obligation to tender contracts publicly. The Court first reiterated that for that exception to apply *inter alia* the degree of control over an entity had to be similar as in the case of a department of the controlling authority itself. Joint control by several public authorities was an option. The Court then clarified that joint control over an entity was not given when only the public authority holding the majority of the shares in an entity had control over it, while the position of the other shareholding public authorities was purely formal. If the in-house exception had applied even when the possibility for the minor partner to participate in the control over the entity had been slight, the way to circumvent the obligation to tender contracts publicly would have been open. The national court thus had to verify whether a shareholders' agreement allowing for consultation, the appointment of a member of the supervisory council, and the joint nomination of one member of the managing board provided a possibility to contribute effectively to the control over the entity concerned so as to warrant application of the in-house exception (paras 30-2).

In *Azienda Sanitaria, 2012* the Court decided that a contract between a public authority and a university based on which a study of the seismic vulnerability of hospitals was to be conducted could not escape the rules on public procurement, be it Directive 2004/18 or transparency and equal treatment on the basis of the market freedoms, depending *inter alia* on the volume of the contract. The study was not about the pursuit of a public aim by two entities. Private undertakings, engineers and architects normally provided such services as those inherent in the study. Private operators could possibly gain an advantage from the conduct of the study (paras 34-8).

Non-discrimination

Non-discrimination in services in general occupied the Court in quite a few decisions. In *Commission v. Portugal (construction sector), 2010* Portugal imposed all requirements which companies established in Portugal and operating in the construction industry had to meet on foreign companies wishing to provide construction services in Portugal. That notably included a prior authorization from the Portuguese authorities, but also stringent requirements as to the company structure, police records, etc. The Court found that Portugal's approach restricted the freedom of services (para. 86). The services Directive 2006/123 was not yet applicable. In any event, it incorporated the principles on market access based on non-discrimination and objective justification which flowed from the freedom of services (paras 87-8). The arguments Portugal put forward in justification of the restriction, namely consumer protection, the safety of building, and the protection of the environment, were already sufficiently addressed by Directive 2005/36 on recognition of professional qualifications. It was irrelevant that Portugal's approach aimed at the entire economic activity of construction companies, while the Directive only concerned professional qualifications. Moreover, Portugal's requirements duplicated the conditions companies met in the 'home' state already (paras 89-107).

Josemans, 2010 dealt with a Dutch local measure that allowed only residents of the Netherlands to have access to so-called coffee shops where, in addition to non-alcoholic drinks and food, cannabis was lawfully offered for consumption. A proprietor of a coffee shop had admitted non-resident Union citizens and was sanctioned. For the Court, the proprietor could not lawfully rely on the freedom of services with regard to the sale of cannabis, because that substance was not lawfully tradable in all member states, except for medical purposes. That purpose, however, was not at issue in the case at hand (paras 41-3). Yet, since he was incidentally prevented from offering other regular restaurant services to nationals of other member states, the freedom of services was affected nonetheless (paras 30-49). The restriction imposed by the residence condition (paras 57-9) was justified, though, by the aim of combating drug tourism which was related to public order and health concerns. That aim was pursued in a consistent and systematic way as well. The consumption of soft drugs could not be likened to prostitution, as the latter was tolerated in most member states. The reasoning in *Adoui, 1982* was therefore not transposable. The discriminatory nature of the measure on its own did not imply that the aim was pursued in an inconsistent way. Moreover, other means had been tested and proven ineffective previously and measures had to be easily manageable and controllable (paras 66-83).

In *Peñarroja Fa, 2011* a translator established in Spain who had worked for courts there sought to become enrolled in the registers of expert translators the French courts kept. The French judges had recourse to those registers when they needed expert translators. The requirements imposed for registration mainly related to professional experience. In particular, for the register with the *cour de cassation*, three years of experience in translating for the French lower courts was required. According to the Court, those translators provided services within the scope of the freedom of services, although the consideration was set by a public authority and the work was carried out under the direction of the judges (paras 38-9). The existence of registers resulted in a restriction of the service freedom, as courts were inclined to appoint translators from the registers, although they were in principle free to appoint any translator (paras 51-3). The restriction was justified by the need to protect litigants and to administer justice soundly. However, experience acquired abroad had to be taken into account and a reasoned decision in that regard was to be given which was subject to judicial review (paras 55-64). In particular for the highest courts, the member states had the discretion to set the level of experience required with the lower courts to three years. However, professional experience acquired abroad in working with courts, particularly the highest courts, had to be factored in (paras 69-77).

In *Commission v. Portugal (real estate agents), 2011* the Court rejected a series of conditions Portugal imposed on companies and natural persons applying for a licence to pursue the activity of real estate agency. Were namely incompatible with the freedom of services the requirements (i) to be established in Portugal, as it embodied the very negation of the freedom of services and a convincing argument in favour of justification on grounds of public order or consumer protection had not been put forward (paras 71-5); (ii) to be fully registered in Portugal, to have full insurance coverage in Portugal, to have capital within the meaning of Portugal's regulation, and to submit fully to disciplinary control in Portugal, because 'home' state regulation was not taken into account (paras 77-84); (iii) to pursue exclusively the activity of real estate agency (para. 85). The latter requirement (iii) was also incompatible with the freedom of establishment. In a similar vein, the Court in *Commission v. Austria (fiscal representative), 2011* rejected Austria's requirement of fiscal representatives to be established or at least present in Austria. The case concerned proofs to be delivered for the purpose of taxation of certain distributions made by funds. The Court rejected the requirement as amounting to the very negation of the freedom of services (paras 23-5). It was not justified by the need to ensure that fiscal representatives had the professional qualifications required or to protect consumers, since an establishment in Austria did not guarantee that a fiscal representative had the knowledge of Austrian law required (paras 27-32).

Duomo, 2012 concerned an amendment in Italian law that required companies to have a minimum paid-up share capital of ten million Euro to be admitted as a service provider for the collection of local taxes on behalf of Italian municipalities. Some Italian companies that had provided that service previously were excluded from certain public tenders for the services after the threshold had been introduced. The Court entered the merits although the situation was confined to Italy, because it was 'far from inconceivable' (para. 27) that the legislation would apply to companies established in other member states and because reverse discrimination would possibly have to be excluded. Moreover, the national court had indicated that compliance with Union law was required for national legislation to be lawful (para. 28). The measure restricted the freedom of services and establishment, although it was indistinctly applicable. It required entities to incorporate and to increase their paid-up share capital (paras 37-8). Justification by the need to protect the public authorities against non-performance by the concession holder given the considerable sums involved – if admissible at all as a ground for justification – did not succeed. Less restrictive measures were available. Italian law already required compliance with the conditions in the public tender as to the technical and financial capacity and solidity and the threshold of paid-up capital could possibly be adapted in the light of the volume of the contract to be awarded (paras 40-4).

In *Volksbank România, 2012* Romanian legislation prohibited certain charges in the context of consumer credits secured by mortgages. As a consequence, Volksbank România adapted its contracts by re-labelling the 'risk charge' levied of 0.2 per cent per month to 'administrative charge'. The Romanian authorities intervened. According to the Court, Romania was not prevented by Directive 2008/48 on consumer credits from adopting such a measure, because the Directive did not apply to such contracts. The freedom of services did not preclude the measure, either. While the freedom of services did apply, because cross-border credit contracts were concerned, the measure did not establish a restriction. It was applicable indistinctly and foreign banks did not have to adapt their commercial policy to gain access to the Romanian market or to compete in it. The measure did not concern the approval of foreign banks in Romania. The foreign banks' freedom to contract was not affected, either. The amounts chargeable or the interest rates in general were not restricted. The measure was, in sum, too uncertain and indirect to hinder the freedom to provide cross-border services (paras 76-81).

In *Commission v. Beligum (Limosa), 2012* Belgium introduced a one-stop shop system pursuant to which self-employed persons established abroad who intended to provide services in Belgium had to file a prior electronic declaration containing information as to the date, duration, place, and nature of the service as well as the identity of the service recipient. It had to be made each time a new service was provided. Failure to comply resulted in penalties. Such a system, according to the Court, established a restriction of the freedom to provide services (paras 39-42). For justification it did not matter that the obligation was only imposed on service providers abroad, for those providers were not in a situation that was objectively comparable to resident service providers. It was not necessary to impose entirely equivalent requirements. The information exchange mechanisms were either limited in scope under Directive 2006/123 or not yet in place regarding Directive 883/2004. While the prevention of social security fraud and social dumping as well as the protection of workers were valid grounds, a general presumption of fraud was not to be applied. Belgium had, in particular, failed to show why it needed information on so many details (paras 45-55).

In *DKV, 2013* the Court screened Belgium's system to manage certain insurance premiums. In Belgium, premiums once they were set when the contract was concluded could only be increased based on several indices, save when the authorities granted an authorization because losses were looming for the insurance undertaking concerned. In the case at issue, an increase of premiums for certain contracts insuring hospitalization was at stake. While Belgium's system was in keeping with the freedom to set premiums under the third non-life insurance Directive 92/49, it constituted a restriction of the freedom of services and establishment. It required foreign insurers to adapt their commercial policies and premium structures to be able to offer services in Belgium (paras 34-6). Hence, they were dissuaded from offering their services. The protection of consumers, however, justified the restriction. Consumers were protected from sharp and unexpected premium increases, in particular when they became older and the risk of hospitalization was more likely to realize itself. The possibility to carry out an authorized increase in extraordinary circumstances also took the edge off the system (paras 40-7).

Maritime transport

Maritime services came to the Court again in some cases in the 2010s. In *Commission v. Spain (port charge), 2010* the Court confirmed Spain's infringement of the freedom of services and Regulation 4055/86 on maritime cabotage. Spain had not contested that the charges levied at its ports, the amount of which varied based on the origin or destination of the goods in archipelagos, member states, or third countries, were unlawful. The Court then rejected the Commission's case in *Commission v. Malta (ferry), 2010*. Malta had concluded a contract right before accession concerning ferry services within Malta without having called for tenders or demonstrated a real public service need. The Court, however, was not in a position to address a potential effect of Regulation 3577/92 before accession, for lack of the Commission having argued the point, or the maintenance of the contract in force after accession, as the Commission had not raised the point in the reasoned opinion.

In *Navtiliaki Etairia Thasou, 2011* two companies submitted ferry schedules they intended to operate on different routes between Greek islands, but the authorities amended their schedules and allocated them different time slots for certain ports. The Court found that approach to amount to a prior authorization procedure which restricted the freedom of services (paras 41 and 44). As such it had to abide by the authorization case-law, i. e. it had to be based on objective, non-discriminatory criteria known in advance which circumscribed the authorities discretion. Apart from that, though, the allocation of certain time slots was a suitable and necessary means of ensuring port safety and avoiding the presence of several ships at the same time (paras 45-50). In addition, as for public service obligations, article 4(2) Regulation 3577/92 exhaustively listed the public service requirements. The authorities could only rely on that article once it was shown that the services for each route would be inadequate without the imposition of a public service obligation (paras 52-62).

Air transport

Air transport was raised only in one case, namely *Neukirchinger, 2011*. It concerned air transport of passengers by hot-air balloon. Austria fined a German national, who held the necessary licence in Germany, for transporting passengers in Austria in a balloon without having an Austrian licence. That licence was subject to residence/seat in Austria as well as the same substantive requirements as the German licence. The Court reiterated that the freedom of services was not applicable as such in the transport sector. However, the Union legislature had adopted a common air transport policy. That policy did not cover passenger transport via hot-air balloons. Yet the objectives of that policy applied nonetheless. Hence, the general principle of non-discrimination pursuant to article 12 Treaty was applicable (paras 22-9). The residence requirement amounted to discrimination based on nationality and was thus precluded. The need to obtain a new licence in Austria for the granting of which the same conditions as in Germany applied came down to discrimination, too, which moreover was not justified by the need to protect the health of passengers, because it was disproportionate not to take account of 'home' state regulation (paras 32-43).

The Services Directive

The services Directive 2006/123 was at issue in *Société fiduciaire, 2011*. The case was about a prohibition in French law of canvassing for certified accountants. Canvassing was not defined by the Directive, but under French law it involved the accountant seeking contact to potential customers, who had not solicited the contact, with a view to providing services. The Court qualified canvassing as a commercial communication within the meaning of the Directive, as it was a method of direct marketing (paras 32-8). Given the objective of the Directive, which was to abolish restrictions to service provision, and the aim of article 24(1), which required the member states to abolish all total prohibitions of commercial communications by members of the regulated professions (paras 26-30), the French prohibition fell foul of that article. The prohibition was 'total' within the meaning of that article, since it deprived service providers of an effective means of penetrating the national market as established in *Alpine Investments, 1995* and thus constituted a restriction (paras 40-3). Since article 24(1) was violated, the total prohibition could not be justified, on the basis of overriding reasons relating to public interests and proportionality, by the possibilities contained in article 24(2) for the member states to regulate the content and methods of commercial communications by members of regulated professions, even though the French prohibition was indistinctly applicable (paras 44-5).

Switzerland

In *Hengartner, 2010* the Court dealt with services under the Agreement on free movement of persons with Switzerland. Two Swiss citizens leased a right to hunt on a ground in Austria for leisurely purposes. They were charged taxes at the rate applying to third country nationals for leases of hunting-grounds in Austria, while the rate for Union citizens and Austrian nationals was lower. According to the Court, a lease of a right to hunt was a service. The hunters did not establish themselves in Austria. In any event, they were not entitled to rely on the internal market freedom of establishment as third country nationals (paras 25-6). Accordingly, the question referred concerned the free movement of services under the Agreement with Switzerland (paras 31-4). However, the Agreement only provided for a limited liberalization of short-term services. It did not contain a provision that allowed service receivers to benefit from fiscal non-discrimination (paras 37-43). Hence, the higher tax rate was in accordance with the Agreement.

Secondary law

The Court also decided some cases on the basis of other secondary law designed to implement the freedom of services in the 2010s. In *Commission v. Belgium (funds), 2010* the Court confirmed that the third non-life insurance directive, i. e. Directives 73/239 and 92/49, applied to the Belgian funds called *mutualités* as far as they offered supplementary sickness insurance. Belgium had not contested that it had not yet adopted the implementing provisions. In *Commission v. Ireland (direct insurance), 2011* the Court ruled that an exemption from the first non-life insurance Directive 73/239 did not apply any longer, because the functions of the insurance body concerned had been expanded by Irish legislation. In *Commission v. Slovenia (direct insurance), 2012* it was held that Slovenia violated the first non-life insurance Directive and the third non-life insurance directive 92/49 by requiring prior authorization for the general conditions of supplementary sickness insurance and systematic notification in case they were amended, as well as by insisting on a confirmation in case premiums were increased. A further plea that the freedom of services was violated, because an agent had to be appointed in Slovenia, was not addressed for procedural reasons.

In *Commission v. Greece (postal services), 2010* the Court confirmed that a new ministerial decision violated Directive 97/67 on postal services in that it required certain express postal service providers to reconstitute themselves as independent providers and in that it prevented them from using trucks beyond a certain size for their services. Greece had not contested the infringement. In *Nilas, 2012* the Court held that a market run by an operator that merged with a market operator running a 'regulated market' within the meaning of Directive 2004/39 on markets in financial instruments did not become (the market) a 'regulated market' itself by reason of the merger. Rather, a separate authorization was required. However, inclusion in the list of 'regulated markets' was not a constitutive element for being such a market. In *Grilc, 2013* the Court ruled that the victim of a car accident was entitled to bring a claim, in court if necessary, against the body established pursuant to article 6 of the fourth Directive 2000/26 on car insurance, after the claim had not been met by the insurer. In *RVS, 2013* the Court gave preference to a dynamic interpretation of article 50 Directive 2002/83 on direct life assurance. Accordingly, the state having the power to levy indirect charges on life assurance contracts was the state where the person assured had actual residence, rather than where she had had residence at the time the contract had been concluded.

Purely internal situations

Two more cases concerned purely internal situations in the 2010s. In *Sbarigia, 2010* the owner of a pharmacy situated in the pedestrian zone in Rome sought exemption from the opening hours and holidays the law imposed. The Court declared the question inadmissible, because the situation was confined in all aspects to Italy and reverse discrimination of service providers was not at issue. The freedom of establishment was not concerned, either (paras 23-8). In *Omalet,*

2010 the Court for the same reasons, namely the situation being purely internal and a lack of reverse discrimination, declined to enter the merits of the case. Omalet, a Belgian company had failed to withhold social security contributions and was held liable jointly and severally, after its Belgian subcontractor had gone out of business.

Further cases

For completeness, two more cases must be mentioned. In *Dijkman, 2010* the Court only examined the free movement of capital. A heavier tax burden on foreign-sourced than on domestic dividends could in that case only be avoided by appointing a domestic intermediary who channelled the foreign-sourced dividends to the domestic recipient. The restriction of the free movement of services that consisted in the disadvantage foreign intermediaries suffered was entirely secondary to the restriction of the freedom of capital. In *Commission v. Belgium (OPCVM), 2012* the Court declined to enter the freedom of services under the European Economic Area Agreement, because the free movement of capital was violated by a distinction Belgian law drew in investments in fund-like entities based on their place of establishment (para. 21).

C The evolution of interpretive formulas

In the following three chapters, the evolution of a set of interpretive formulas is traced, beginning with broad and restrictive formulas, followed by formulas that rely on the ideas of coordination and on a notion being fundamental.[26] The chapters on 'broad' and 'coordinated' are structured according to four time periods, each of roughly 15 years. These time periods were chosen, to reflect the broader development of case-law described in the part on 'the case-law'. An initial phase of about 15 years, 'the early days', was generally marked by the first steps of the Court, mostly in social security in which Regulation 3 applied. The next 15 years leading up to the 'Maastricht moment' saw the surge of the free movement of workers case-law, while social security shifted mostly to Regulation 1408/71. Then came the Maastricht period which was marked by many sweeping judgments in the freedoms of workers, establishment, and services. It is hard to determine an end to that period, but it seems that 'the present' has begun around the year 2007 – though this terminology should not be given too much weight. This chronological structure is admittedly to some extent random. But a direct, chronologically unstructured examination of formulas throughout almost 60 years of case-law would simply be impractical. For each of the time periods thus identified, first the occurrences and then the power – the 'spin' – of interpretive formulas are examined. The chapter on 'fundamental' is structured slightly differently due to its focus on a more recent interpretive formula. It begins with the roots of the formula, moves on to the occurrences and then examines the power/spin of the formula.

I 'Broad'

In this chapter, broad and restrictive interpretive formulas are examined: When have such formulas occurred in the Court's case-law and when did they spin the Court's decisions? The chapter begins with the time span during which the case-law of the Court on persons and services began to establish itself, i. e. the period leading up to the mid-1970s, and then proceeds by time spans of roughly 15 years.

26 For an answer to the question why these three types of formulas are examined see the introduction to this book.

1 In the early days: until the mid-1970s

Three branches of broad interpretation

The Court tackled the first serious wave of free movement of workers cases in the years 1974 and 1975. In some of these cases the Court applied two interpretation techniques that are of interest. On the one hand, in *Cristini, 1975* the Court stated that the right of workers to the same social advantages pursuant to article 7(2) Regulation 1612/68 was not to be interpreted restrictively (para. 12).[27] On the other hand, the Court decided in *Bonsignore, 1975* that a migrant worker was not to be expelled from the host country based on general preventive grounds. The Court arrived at this conclusion in *Bonsignore, 1975*, because the public policy and security derogations from the freedom of workers, as exceptions from the principle, had to be interpreted strictly (para. 6). A few months before that, the Court in *Van Duyn, 1974* had stated in a similar vein that public policy restrictions of the freedom of workers had to be interpreted narrowly, because they derogated from a fundamental principle. The member states were not to determine the scope of the restrictions unilaterally without being subject to Community control (para. 18). A similar approach was applied in *Rutili, 1975.* According to that judgment, public policy restrictions of the fundamental principle of equal treatment and the free movement of workers had to be interpreted strictly, so that the member states could not determine their scope unilaterally without control by the institutions of the Community (para. 27). Hence the need for a genuine and sufficiently serious threat to public policy. Similarly, the Court had previously put forward in *Sotgiu, 1974* that the public service exception was not to have a scope beyond the aim for which it had been included in the Treaty, given the fundamental nature of the freedom to move (para. 4).

However, the above judgments from the wave of worker cases of the mid-1970s did not mark the first time that the Court applied those two types of broad interpretation. Indeed, those broad interpretations had become so rich by then that the notion of 'branches' of a broad interpretation is in order, namely (i) a first branch of the broad or restrictive interpretation of terms as such and (ii) a second branch of the strict interpretation of exceptions to broad rules. In addition, a third branch of broad interpretation (iii) had grown by the mid-1970s. Let us examine how these three branches had established themselves before the Court overcame the first wave of worker cases in the way described above. The exclusive focus, obviously, is on the judgments within the scope of this book.

27 Some of the footnotes of this chapter mention cases in which the text of the Court's decision proves that the parties or the Advocate General had argued on the basis of broad interpretation, while the Court ultimately did not include that broad interpretation in its reasoning. For instance, the Commission in *Alaimo, 1975*, at p. 112, argued a broad interpretation of the right under article 12 Regulation 1612/68. The Court did not address that argument as such, but recognized it in substance by confirming the interpretation given in *Casagrande, 1974*.

First branch: broad interpretation of notions

After having adopted a strict interpretation of an essential procedural requirement for the validity of a decision, viz. unanimous assent by the Council, in three Coal and Steel Community cases[28] and having interpreted the procedural term 'another person' in the 'broadest' sense in *Plaumann, 1963*[29], the Court began to clarify the scope *ratione personae* of Regulation 3 and lay down the details of what the term worker meant in social security. In *Hoekstra, 1964* the Court reasoned that 'workers' within the scope of Regulation 3 were not limited to employed persons but included those who had once been employed and could be employed again (para. 3). Similarly in *Bertholet, 1965* and *Van Dijk, 1965* the Court did not see a reason to restrict the scope *ratione personae* of Regulation 3 to those who had been employed in several states or who had been employed in one state while they had resided in another or to exclude frontier workers (pages 87 and 104, respectively).[30] Next, the Court reasoned in *De Cicco, 1968* that Regulation 3 was based on a wide conception of persons to whom it applied. The Regulation covered not just wage-earners but also assimilated persons and thereby it followed a tendency of the member states to extend the benefits of their social security schemes to new categories of persons by reason of identical risks. Regulation 3 thus had to be applied to a special scheme for craftsmen (p. 480). In *Compagnie belge, 1969* the Court then saw Regulation 3 as applicable whenever a wage-earner was in a situation involving international elements. The subrogation article, i. e. article 52, hence applied in case an employed person was injured in a traffic accident during a private journey abroad (paras 4-6). Based on the same expansive reasoning as in *De Cicco, 1968*, the Court afterward ruled in *Janssen, 1971* that a person treated as a self-employed helper under national legislation was a person assimilated to a wage-earner within the meaning of Regulation 3 (paras 5-9).

Apart from that wide approach to the personal scope of Regulation 3, the Court also dealt with the idea of broad notions in several other social security cases. In *De Moor, 1967*, the Court discarded a 'liberal interpretation' of article 28 Regulation 3 which would have led to proportional calculation independently of whether article 27 on aggregation of insurance periods had been applied previously (p. 207).[31] In *Torrekens, 1969* the Court reasoned that the periods that were assimilated to insurance periods pursuant to article 1(r) Regulation 3 were

28 *Lemmerz, 1965*, at p. 699; *Mannesmann II, 1965*, at p. 741; and *Aciéries du Temple, 1965*, at pp. 772-3. Obviously, these cases are not within the domain of case-law this book covers. They are mentioned to complete the picture of the beginning of the case-law, which is, obviously, of great importance.

29 *Plaumann, 1963*, at pp. 106-7: '[...] provisions [...] regarding the right of interested parties to bring an action must not be interpreted restrictively'. The case concerns custom duties and admissibility in annulment procedures. It is also merely mentioned to complete the picture.

30 Advocate General Gand in the joint opinion in these cases advocated the same wide interpretation of the scope *ratione personae* as the Court had applied in *Hoekstra, 1964*. See p. 93 of the opinion.

31 In *Molkerei Zentrale, 1968*, at p. 155, moreover, the Court reasoned that the term 'directly' and 'indirectly' in article 95 Treaty had to be interpreted widely. This decision is merely mentioned for completeness. It is not within the body of case-law investigated by this book.

to be understood widely so that a French non-contributory scheme was covered and aggregation had to be applied (para. 17). In *Frilli, 1972*, the Court used expansive rhetoric with regard to the distinction of social security and assistance. It found – though very much on the facts of the case and with much caution – that Belgium's guaranteed income for elderly persons was covered by Regulation 3, *inter alia* because article 1(s) addressed benefits 'in the widest sense' (para. 17). In *Callemeyn, 1974* again certain benefits meeting both objectives of social security and assistance were drawn within the scope of Regulation 1408/71, once more by means of a notion of benefits in the 'widest possible sense' (para. 10). That formula also served the Court to justify in *Biason, 1974* that a supplementary allowance to an invalidity pension under French law was covered by Regulation 1408/71 (para. 14) and that a benefit for handicapped persons was covered by Regulation 3 in *Mazzier, 1974* (para. 10).[32]

Second branch: narrow exceptions from rules

The second branch of broad interpretation already established itself in some of the first cases concerning the Coal and Steel Community. In those cases, the Court strongly relied on the argument that an exception from a rule had to be construed narrowly.[33] In some early free movement of goods cases the Court applied this approach, too.[34] In *Ugliola, 1969*, the very first judgment in the free

32 In *Anselmetti, 1975*, at p. 784, Italy argued on the basis of *Frilli, 1972*, and *Biason, 1974*, that 'benefits' and 'pensions' in article 1(s) Regulation 3 had to be understood in the 'widest possible sense', but the Court did not reflect that argument in the judgment, while it followed the Italian argument in substance.

33 See notably the early cases dealing with ferrous scrap and the equalization scheme: *Safe, 1959*, at p. 195, and *Snupat I, 1959*, at p. 143 – in both cases the Court stated that equalization did not apply to own resources and that this constituted an exception to the rule; *Snupat II, 1961*, at p. 85 – the Court argued that 'bought scrap' rather than 'own resources' was to be interpreted widely, because the latter constituted an exception to the rule of equalization; *Klöckner, 1962*, at p. 340, and *Mannesmann I, 1962*, at p. 371, confirmed the approach in *Snupat II, 1961*; *Espérance-Longdoz, 1965*, at p. 1079, and *Hainaut-Sambre, 1965*, at p. 1109, confirmed that the obligation to contribute to the scheme is the rule, while the exemption from the obligation is the exception which was to be interpreted strictly. These cases are outside the scope of this book and are mentioned for the sake of completeness.

34 Already in *Commission v. Luxembourg and Belgium (gingerbread), 1962*, at p. 432, the Court concluded that the prohibition of new custom duties together with the free movement of goods constituted an 'essential rule' any exception to which had to be clearly stipulated and narrowly interpreted; in addition, the concept of charges having equivalent effect complemented the rule rather than the exception. This was confirmed in *Commission v. Luxembourg and Belgium (milk products), 1964*, at p. 633. Moreover, the Court in *Commission v. Luxembourg and Belgium (gingerbread), 1962*, at p. 434, explained that the derogations in agriculture from the common market rules were exceptional in nature and had to be narrowly interpreted; to extend them would transform the exception into the rule. That narrow interpretation of the rules on agriculture as exceptions to the free movement in the common market was confirmed in *Commission v. Italy (potable alcohol), 1969*, at para. 6. In *Germany v. Commission (sheep), 1966*, at p. 169, the Court again found that the prohibition of charges having an equivalent effect to custom duties was a fundamental provision for the free movement of goods, an essential legal principle. Hence, only those exceptions that could clearly be allowed based on a narrow interpretation were admissible. In *Commission v. Italy (artistic objects), 1968*, at p. 430, the Court ruled that the derogations from the free movement of goods in article 36 of the Treaty could only be applied to quantitative restrictions and equivalent measures and not to the prohibition to levy export duties, because as an exception to the fundamental rule of free movement the article had to be construed strictly. In *Salgoil, 1968*, at p. 463, the Court reasoned that articles 36, 224 and 226 of the Treaty dealt with clearly defined exceptional cases which were not susceptible to a wide interpretation. In *Bock, 1971*, at para. 14, the Court argued that article 115 Treaty had to be narrowly construed

movement of workers, the Court did not apply the technique with full force though. The Court merely stated that exceptions to the free movement of workers had to be strictly construed and that the restrictions were limited to those mentioned explicitly by article 48(3) Treaty (para. 6). In *Marsman, 1972* the Court more openly stated that article 48 was only subject to the conditions which were laid down restrictively in article 48(3) (para. 4). In the coordination of social security, in contrast, the narrow interpretation of restrictions did not gain any foothold at all, despite the flood of cases the Court dealt with in that domain. *Bentzinger, 1973* would have lent itself to such an interpretation, as it concerned the relationship between article 12 Regulation 3, i. e. the rule that the legislation of the state of employment is applicable, and article 13(1)(c), i. e. the exception that the legislation of the state of residence applies when employment is carried on in several states one of which is the state of residence. The Court did not reason on the basis of a narrow interpretation of the exception though, perhaps because it would not have yielded the result the Court had in mind.[35]

Third branch: the greatest possible freedom

A third branch of broad interpretation had established itself before the first wave of workers cases in the mid-1970s. The Commission in *Guerra, 1967* (page 222) argued expansively in favour of migrant workers in case of doubt, which the Court had allegedly established in *Nonnenmacher, 1964*. While the Court had indeed ruled along these lines in *Nonnenmacher, 1964* (para. 1(B)), finding that two social security legislations could under certain circumstances be applied simultaneously, the Commission's argument was not reflected in the judgment in *Guerra, 1967*. The Commission put forward the same expansive argument in *Merola, 1972* (pages 1258-9), but again to no avail. Yet, indisputably, the Court in the earliest social security cases relied on the rather disruptive idea that article 51 aimed at the establishment of 'as complete a freedom of movement for workers as possible' forming part of the 'foundations' of the Community (*Hoekstra, 1964*, para. 1). *Nonnenmacher, 1964* used similar language, namely the 'greatest possible freedom of movement for workers' (para. 1(B)), though leaving aside the 'foundations of the Community', to substantiate what the Commission later on in *Guerra, 1967* in vain tried to promote as a principle of interpretation in favour of the migrant worker. Despite the failure of the Commission's argument

---

and applied, because derogations from the free movement of goods were authorized which created obstacles to the implementation of the common commercial policy. Moreover, in *Marimex, 1972*, at para. 4, the Court again stated that article 36 of the Treaty had to be interpreted strictly, because it derogated from the basic rule of the free movement of goods. It was therefore not to cover rules of a different nature than those within the scope of article 30 to 34 of the Treaty. (Again, these cases are mentioned for completeness only.).

35 For completeness, the Commission advocated a strict interpretation of article 36 Treaty in the famous goods case *Dassonville, 1974* (see p. 847), based on the ruling mentioned above in *Commission v. Italy (artistic objects), 1968*. The Court did not reflect that argument in its decision, though, because it found that the measure at issue constituted a means of arbitrary discrimination or a disguised restriction (paras 7-8).

in *Guerra, 1967*, the *Hoekstra, 1964*-formula was born to last.[36] In *Singer, 1965* the Court essentially reiterated the same solution it had found in *Van Dijk, 1965*, as to the scope of the term 'worker' in the context of subrogation, but in addition underpinned it with the *Hoekstra, 1964*-formula, including the foundational aspect which *Nonnenmacher, 1964* had omitted. In substance the Court affirmed in *Singer, 1965* that the solution complied with article 51 of the Treaty (p. 971).

In a sense, *Heinze, 1972* was an offspring of that interpretive branch. The Court distinguished social security from assistance with regard to a benefit designed to prevent the spread of tuberculosis by stating that Regulation 3 had to be interpreted in the light of the 'fundamental aim' of article 51 Treaty which was to establish 'the most favourable conditions' for achieving the free movement of workers (para. 4). The same formula was obviously used in *Ortskrankenkasse Hamburg, 1972* (para. 4) and *Land Niedersachsen, 1972* (para. 4). (The judgments came down on the same day and concerned the same issue.)[37]

So, by the time the Court tackled the first wave of free movement of workers cases – and Hans Kutscher by the way famously established the canon of interpretation of Community law in 1976 in his 'Methods of Interpretation'[38] – we can discern three branches of broad interpretation. (i) The broad or restrictive interpretation of notions as such – this was predominantly applied in social security, viz. secondary law cases, but also in one free movement of workers case, namely *Cristini, 1975*. (ii) The idea that a rule is to be construed broadly, while the exception thereto narrowly. The Court applied this technique in the free movement of workers, interpreting mostly primary law. In particular in the mid-1970s worker cases, the Court mixed the idea of narrowly construing ex-

36 The differences in the wordings of the passages in *Hoekstra, 1964*, speaking of 'as complete a freedom as possible' and in *Nonnenmacher, 1964*, using the term 'the greatest possible freedom', are due to diverging translations. In the judgments in French the two passages are identical: 'l'établissement d'une liberté aussi complète que possible de la circulation des travailleurs'. (Yet the foundation-part of the *Hoekstra, 1964*,-formula was absent in the *Nonnenmacher, 1964*-passage in French, too.) The true source of the formula is thus *Hoekstra, 1964*. That is why we designate it as the *Hoekstra, 1964*-formula.

37 A number of further cases that were decided before the first wave of worker cases are to be mentioned. (i) Probably the most disruptive judgment of that period, *Costa v. ENEL, 1964*, came down without any of the broad rhetoric that is of interest to this book. (The disruption, of course, was not caused by the establishment dimension of the judgment. That dimension was rather unspectacular.) (ii) The limits of what can be argued on the basis of a broad interpretation were shown in *Murru, 1972*. Mr Murru argued vaguely on the basis of the spirit and principles of Regulation 3 together with the need for a broad interpretation (see Advocate General Römer, p. 342, and p. 335), but the Court refused even to address those arguments in the judgment. (iii) Probably the most famous judgment in social security, *Petroni, 1975*, interestingly, was drafted without any of the expansive rhetoric one would expect from such a judgment. The 'if workers were to lose advantages guaranteed by the laws of a single member state'-formula (para. 13) broke free though and developed a life of its own; see by way of examples the cases *Ten Holder, 1986* (para. 22), and among the latest *Da Silva Martins, 2011* (paras 74-5). Note also that *Petroni, 1975* did not come out of the blue. Its theme was already subliminally present in the very early social security cases, such as *Kalsbeek, 1964*, and *Nonnenmacher, 1964*, but also more obviously in *Keller, 1971* and, of course, *Niemann, 1974*.

38 Kutscher, 'Methods of Interpretation as Seen by a Judge at the Court of Justice'. Kutscher did not in his contribution distinguish the interpretive formulas examined in this chapter. See the brief discussion in the introduction.

ceptions to rules with a hierarchical, structural approach. The freedom is fundamental, whereas the derogation therefrom is not; hence the first must be broadly, the second narrowly understood. (iii) The 'greatest possible freedom'-approach, which was confined to social security.

The spin exerted by interpretive formulas

Within those three branches, the judgments in which a broad interpretation spun the decision into a specific direction are of particular interest. When was a broad notion, a narrow exception, or the 'greatest possible freedom' instrumental in the Court's reaching a specific result? Of course, the answer to this question can never be straightforward. The spin that an interpretive formula provides may vary in force. It can be strong or weak. Moreover, everything the Court says in a decision is instrumental to some extent, else it would not, or at least should not, be said. Nevertheless, a number of judgments stand out, among them most clearly those of the third branch.

The 'greatest possible freedom'-passage was clearly spinning the case towards the finding that Dutch legislation could be applied simultaneously in *Nonnenmacher, 1964*. The broad reading of the 'worker'-notion in *Hoekstra, 1964* pivoted on that formula. And the offspring of the *Hoekstra, 1964*-formula was also clearly instrumental in the Court's finding in the tuberculosis judgments that the benefit at issue was a social security benefit (*Heinze, 1972*; *Ortskrankenkasse Hamburg, 1972*; and *Land Niedersachsen, 1972*). In the first branch, a broad 'worker'-notion spun the decision to some degree in *Bertholet, 1965*, while spin was less obvious in *Van Dijk, 1965*. In *De Cicco, 1968* a wide approach to the scope *ratione personae* of Regulation 3 was pivotal in the Court's reasoning and so was it in *Janssen, 1971*. In the judgments in the second branch, the narrow interpretation of exceptions exerted less spin on the decisions.

2 From the mid-1970s until the 'Maastricht moment'

By the time Joseph Weiler announced the 'Transformation of Europe'[39] in 1991 and the Maastricht treaty came around, the Court had handed down scores of judgments in which formulas of broad interpretation were applied and further refined. Let us therefore take a closer look at this development, beginning with the first branch, i. e. broad notions.

a) First branch: broad notions

In *Bozzone, 1977* the Court interpreted the term 'legislation of a member state' in articles 1(j) and 2(1) Regulation 1408/71 widely: 'The term is remarkable for its breadth' (para. 10). This formula was reiterated in *Commission v. Belgium (Congo), 1980* (para. 4) and additional arguments against the applicability of the

39 Weiler, 'The Transformation of Europe'.

same Belgian legislation that had been at issue in *Bozzone, 1977* were rejected. (The cases dealt with Belgian benefits acquired during work in the former Belgian Congo which were subject to residence in Belgium or Belgian nationality.) In *Blottner, 1977* the term 'legislation' in article 45(3) in conjunction with article 1(j) Regulation 1408/71 was also interpreted 'widely', so as to cover legislation that had been in force at the time when an individual was subject to it, but not any longer when the Regulation entered into force, as well as legislation that is in force when the risk materializes (para. 17).

In *Brack, 1976* the Court came back to the scope *ratione personae* of the social security provisions. It fell back on the passage stated in *De Cicco, 1968* and *Janssen, 1971* with regard to Regulation 3 and the tendency of member states to expand the applicability of their social security schemes, but in doing so dropped any reference to a wide conception of the persons covered (para. 20). Nonetheless, the Court concluded very much on the specifics of the case that the person concerned was an 'employed person' within the scope of Regulation 1408/71, although national law had refused to grant that status in the case at issue. In *Walsh, 1980* the Court again refused to interpret the personal scope of Regulation 1408/71 restrictively. Thus, a 'person who is compulsorily insured' pursuant to article 1(a)(ii) included those who did not pay contributions at the time the risk materialized but were still insured owing to compulsory contributions paid as an employed person at an earlier period (para. 6).[40]

In *Levin, 1982*, the Court then ruled more explicitly as to the terms 'worker' and 'activity as an employed person' in the free movement of workers. Those terms defined the scope of application of a fundamental freedom and as such they were not to be interpreted restrictively (para. 13). *Forcheri, 1983* took it a step further. Seized with the question of whether the fees for vocational training payable by the spouse of a person employed by the Community could be higher than for a spouse of a regular migrant worker, the Court first extended the benefit of free movement to workers employed by the Community and then stated that the right to free movement was not to be interpreted narrowly according to the legislative practice of the Community and established case-law of the Court (para. 11). Hence vocational training came within the ambit of the Treaty.

In *Robards, 1983* the Court accepted a wide interpretation of the term 'spouse' in article 10(1)(a) Regulation 574/72 in the light of the purpose of that provision. Consequently, it included a divorced spouse (paras 15-9). The Court used the conclusion reached in that case – no restrictive interpretation of article 10(1)(a) – to underpin the solution it found in *Kromhout, 1985*, namely the application of the rule against overlapping, although Regulation 1408/71 was not technically applicable to one specific parent (para. 16).

40 *Pierik II, 1979*, in a sense also interpreted the personal scope of Regulation 1408/71 extensively, though without using any of the characteristic wording. The Court merely stated that the definition of a 'worker' in article 1(a) Regulation 1408/71 had 'a general scope' (para. 4); article 22(1)(c) Regulation 1408/71 was therefore not to be interpreted so as to include only active workers. Pensioners were entitled to rely on that article, too.

Next, on a more general level, the Court rejected a challenge to the *Laterza, 1980*-supplement[41] in *Patteri, 1984*. It had been argued that article 51 Treaty had to be interpreted restrictively allowing the Council only to regulate aggregation and residence. However, the Court turned down that restrictive interpretation. Referring to the very first three social security cases, *Hoekstra, 1964*; *Nonnenmacher, 1964*; and *Kalsbeek, 1964*, the Court ruled that aggregation and residence were just two among other topics which the Council could lawfully address to implement the fundamental freedom of movement (paras 7-8).

In *Diatta, 1985* the Court held that article 10 Regulation 1612/68, having regard to its context and objectives, was not to be interpreted restrictively (para. 17). The article therefore did not require spouses to live under the same roof permanently and the marriage had to be dissolved formally for the rights to expire under that article. In *Reed, 1986* the Court, however, rejected an even broader interpretation of article 10 Regulation 1612/68. In the absence of a general social development in the Community, unmarried partners could not be considered as spouses within the sense of that article (para. 15). However, article 7(2) Regulation 1612/68, in turn, was not to be narrowly construed pursuant to *Cristini, 1975* (para. 25 of *Reed, 1986*). Hence, social advantages included the possibility to live together with an unmarried partner. Nationals of other member states had to benefit from the same advantage in that regard as Dutch nationals.[42]

With *Hoeckx, 1985* the Court returned to the distinction between social security and assistance. Yet the *Frilli, 1972*-formula which had spoken of benefits 'in the widest sense', did not find an echo in the case of Belgium's minimex. Instead, the Court found, minimex amounted to social assistance. Yet it fell within the purview of article 7(2) Regulation 1612/68. The Court thus in substance fol-

41 *Laterza, 1980*, is an interesting case. The Court established a right to a supplement under article 77(2)(b)(1) in order to guarantee the higher benefit previously awarded by a member state other than the state where the person concerned resided. However, the Court handed down this expansive ruling without any of the characteristic broad reasoning; it merely referred to the 'greatest amount' (para. 9). The Court, of course, proceeded in a similar way in *Gravina, 1980* (para. 7).

42 *Even, 1979*, is noteworthy in this context. The national court had enquired about a broad or restrictive interpretation of Regulation 1408/71 with regard to an exemption from the reduction of pensions in case of early retirement of soldiers who had been injured in war and suffered from invalidity. The Court eschewed Regulation 1408/71 which it held inapplicable to victims of war (article 4(4)). It also considered article 7(2) Regulation 1612/68 inapplicable, for the article was not concerned with benefits offered as a reward for the service offered to a country during wartime and as a recompense for hardship suffered during that service. The Court thus in substance rejected a broad application of article 7(2) Regulation 1612/68. In some contrast to *Even, 1979*, the Court in *Reina, 1982*, read article 7(2) rather expansively and included a childbirth loan despite the aim of demographic policy it pursued. The Court used none of the language typical of such expansive rulings though.

lowed the Commission which had argued that article 7(2) was not to be interpreted restrictively (para. 8).[43] The ruling in *Scrivner, 1985* was identical.[44]

The first and the second branch connecting

In *Kempf, 1986*, the Court again was seized in the context of Belgium's social assistance. In that context, the Court reminded the national court of the fact that the term 'worker' had to be broadly construed pursuant to *Levin, 1982*, after that court had found that the work of a music teacher of 12 lessons per week was genuine and effective. Interestingly, in this case the first and second branch of broad interpretation, i. e. the broad interpretation of terms as such and the narrow construction of exceptions, connected. The free movement of workers as one of the foundations of the Community, and in particular the terms 'worker' and 'activity as an employed person' were to be interpreted broadly, while derogations and exceptions were to be construed narrowly (para. 13). It followed that where the work pursued was genuine, it did not have an impact on the rights as a worker that the income was supplemented by assistance originating from the public purse. In a similar, though less immediate way the two branches came into contact in *Lawrie-Blum, 1986*. A trainee teacher was a worker, for the term determined the scope of a fundamental freedom and as a consequence was to be understood broadly (para. 16). The public service exception derogated from a fundamental freedom and hence had to be limited to what was strictly necessary to protect the interests which that article deemed worthy of protection (para. 26). The post of a trainee teacher did not meet those very strict requirements (para. 28).

The first and the third branch connecting

In *Van Roosmalen, 1986* again two of the branches of broad interpretation connected, this time the first – broad interpretation of terms – and the third, the 'greatest possible freedom'. The Court reiterated that before the amendment of

43 *Piscitello, 1983*, *Giletti, 1987*, and *Newton, 1991* all concerned the distinction between social security and social assistance as well. In *Piscitello, 1983* an Italian social aid pension, in *Giletti, 1987* a French supplementary allowance for pensioners, and in *Newton, 1991* a British mobility allowance were at issue. In all cases the *Frilli, 1972*-formula – benefits 'in the widest sense' – cannot be found. Interestingly – or perhaps accordingly – the Court in *Newton, 1991* found that the benefit was only part of social security, if the person concerned had worked in the member state concerned before. In *Piscitello, 1983* and *Giletti, 1987*, the Court found that the benefits concerned were to be categorized as social security, despite the absence of the *Frilli, 1972*-formula.

44 *Gravier, 1985*, is obviously an important decision in this regard. The Court decided that non-discrimination pursuant to article 7 Treaty directly applied to access to vocational training. Consequently, students from other member states could not lawfully be subject to higher fees for vocational training. The Court handed down this disruptive ruling without using any broad language, probably out of respect for the member states' sensitivities in educational matters. *Brown, 1988* set some limits to *Gravier, 1985*, with regard to maintenance grants for students, again without applying any typical language. Interestingly, the Court in *Brown, 1988* considered as a worker a prospective student who found employment before the beginning of his studies because of the perspective of those studies. Again the Court refrained from using any of the broad reasoning that is typical for other judgments expanding the worker notion. Equally in *Lair, 1988*, handed down on the same day as *Brown, 1988*, the Court refrained from reasoning in expansive terms, even with regard to article 7(2) Regulation 1612/68 and the definition of a 'worker', though again the substance was rather far-reaching.

Regulation 1408/71, which extended the scope to cover self-employed persons, the scope *ratione personae* of the Regulation had to be construed broadly, given the aim of article 51 which was to contribute to the greatest possible freedom of workers, one of the foundations of the Community (para. 18). That was valid also after the amendment, i. e. for self-employed persons (para. 19). Factoring in the qualification with regard to the Netherlands in the annex, a priest who was maintained by his parishioners thus was a self-employed person (para. 22). In a second step the Court then restated the *Bozzone, 1977*-formula – 'the term [legislation of a member state] is remarkable for its breadth' (para. 28) – to find that a priest who had worked in a third state while being affiliated to a Dutch social security scheme had enough of a link to that scheme so that Regulation 1408/71 was applicable.[45] That second step was confirmed in *Laborero, 1987*, again with reference to *Bozzone, 1977* (para. 23). The formula used was slightly different, the Court namely stated: 'the term 'legislation' is very broad'.[46]

Lebon expanding Kempf

In *Lebon, 1987* the Court interpreted the notion of a 'dependant' of a migrant worker as a factual circumstance in which a person depended on a worker, irrespective of the reason for the dependency or the capacity of the person herself to pursue a gainful activity, and underpinned that interpretation by the *Kempf, 1986*-approach requiring a broad construction of the free movement of workers as one of the foundations of the Community (para. 23). The Court thus detached the *Kempf, 1986*-formula from the worker-notion and applied it in a broader context. In contrast, the Court in *Bettray, 1989* restated the need for a broad notion of a 'worker' given that it defined the scope of one of the fundamental freedoms (para. 11), but conversely concluded, after having applied the criteria developed to determine whether an activity constituted genuine 'work', that a rehabilitation programme which allowed former drug addicts to pursue a remunerated activity with the aim of reintegration did not amount to 'work'. In *Lopes da Veiga, 1989* the Court reiterated the *Kempf, 1986*–approach – this time again with regard to the term 'worker' calling for a broad interpretation (para. 13) – to lay the foundation for the argument why a mariner working on board a ship flying the flag of a member state was entitled to rely on articles 6 to 8 Regulation 1612/68.[47]

45 In 1986, the Court also delivered the bold judgment in *Ten Holder, 1986*, according to which in essence the legislation of the member state of former employment continued to apply, if the person concerned did not take up employment again after she had stopped working. The judgment obviously led to the introduction of article 13(2)(f) Regulation 1408/71. Note that one party feared an excessively broad application of article 13(2)(a) (para. 11), but that fear was not reflected in the wording of the Court's decision.

46 The Commission in *De Jong, 1986*, had argued in the written submissions that a broad interpretation of point 2(c) of part I of Annex VI to Regulation 1408/71 was necessary, but abandoned the argument in the oral submissions (paras 11-2). This argument was not reflected literally in the Court's reasoning, in contrast to the third branch of broad interpretation (see below).

47 In *Agegate, 1989* in contrast, the Court elaborated on the term 'worker' in the Act of Accession of Spain and Portugal – where it was to be understood in the same way as in the free movement of workers – with regard to fishermen, without having recourse to a broad understanding of the term (see

With *Antonissen, 1991* the Court expanded the possibilities for job seekers to stay in the host state. From the outset, the Court in this judgment made it clear again that the free movement of workers in general had to be interpreted broadly in keeping with the *Kempf, 1986/Lebon, 1987*-approach (para. 11). Hence, the Court rejected a strict interpretation which would have threatened to render article 48(3) Treaty ineffective. In *Giagounidis, 1991* the Court then reiterated the broad approach in *Kempf, 1986/Lebon, 1987* to free movement, while referring to *Antonissen, 1991*, in order to disregard the relatively clear wording of Directive 68/360. It was not necessary for identification to produce the specific document used when immigrating to the host state.

Further broad interpretation

In *ASTI, 1991* the Court refused to interpret the notion of 'trade-union organizations' in article 8(1) Regulation 1612/68 restrictively (para. 16). As a consequence, participation in the elections to occupational guilds in Luxembourg had to be open for migrant workers. In keeping with *Lawrie-Blum, 1986* the Court in *Bleis, 1991* decided that the 'very strict' conditions of the public service derogation were not fulfilled in the case of secondary teachers, either (para. 7).[48]

In the entire period leading up to the 'Maastricht moment' the Court applied broad interpretation, in a literal sense, in only two cases concerning the freedom of establishment. One of them was *Knoors, 1979* and concerned secondary legislation implementing the freedom of establishment. The Court held that Directive 64/427 on self-employed persons in manufacturing and processing industries was based on 'a broad definition of the beneficiaries' (para. 17), so that a state's own nationals who returned from abroad were entitled to rely on it in principle vis-à-vis that state. The other case was *Steinhauser, 1985*. In that case both the plaintiff and the Commission had argued a broad interpretation of the freedom of establishment so as to include not just the taking up, but also the pursuit of business in the host state (paras 9-10). The Court followed them on the merits and rejected the nationality condition applied in certain offers for the allocation of premises (para. 16).

b) Second branch: narrow exceptions from rules

Let us now see how the second branch of broad interpretation, in which rules – broad rules – are combined with narrow exceptions, developed up to the 'Maastricht moment'. In *Di Paolo, 1977* the strict interpretation of an exception appeared for the first time in a social security judgment. The Court explained that the rule in article 67 Regulation 1408/71, which declared the state of employment as competent for unemployment benefits, suffered an exception in article

paras 34-6). In a similar vein, the Court in *Le Manoir, 1991*, did not employ any broad language when qualifying a trainee as a worker.

48 In *Faux, 1991* one of the parties argued on the basis of a wide interpretation of the notion of a frontier worker pursuing an occupation, thus including workers who were partially or intermittently, but not wholly unemployed (para. 8). The Court did not follow that argument by deciding that even a wholly unemployed frontier worker came within the scope of Regulation 36/63 (see para. 11).

71, that is that the state of residence was competent in some circumstances, such as in the cases of frontier workers and weekly commuters. From that the Court deduced that the concept of residence in another state than the state of employment was not to be given an 'excessively wide interpretation'. Indeed it had to be interpreted strictly (paras 12-3).

With *Bouchereau, 1977* the Court then returned to the free movement of workers. It reiterated the approach applied in *Van Duyn, 1974* and *Rutili, 1975* to the public policy derogation in article 48(3), namely as an exception to the fundamental rule of the free movement of workers it had to be construed strictly, precluding any unilateral determination of its scope by the member states. The Court then circumscribed the remaining discretion further by adding the need for a 'genuine and sufficiently serious threat to the requirements of public policy affecting one of the fundamental interests of society' (para. 35).

The second branch of broad interpretation was then left dormant for more than five years, before being revived by *Peskeloglou, 1983*. The Act of Accession of Greece contained a permission for the member states and Greece to maintain existing immigration authorization schemes for a number of years. According to the Court, that permission constituted an exception to the free movement of workers and consequently had to be interpreted restrictively (para. 12). The conditions for taking up and pursuing employment could therefore not lawfully be made more stringent during the transitional period.

In *Kempf, 1986* and *Lawrie-Blum, 1986* the second branch connected with the first branch, as already mentioned above.[49] *Commission v. Italy (research council), 1987* further confirmed the approach taken in *Lawrie-Blum, 1986*. As a derogation from the fundamental principle of free movement, the public service exception had to be construed in such a way as to limit its scope to what was strictly necessary for safeguarding the interests which that provision allowed the member states to protect (para. 7).[50] The posts in the Italian national research council were not be considered as coming within the public service derogation.

The second branch in establishment and services

In *Commission v. Greece (vocational schools), 1988* the second branch for the first time bore fruit under the freedom of establishment. The Court, obviously inspired by the workers case-law, decided that the official authority exception in article 55 Treaty derogated from the fundamental principle of the freedom of es-

49 Note that the Court in the famous case *Johnston, 1986* – a case that is outside the scope of this book – relied on the narrow interpretation of the public safety derogation from an individual right in article 2(2) Directive 76/207 on equal treatment for men and women (para. 36).

50 Before, *Commission v. Belgium (public service), 1980* had elaborated extensively on the public service derogation, which Belgium had understood institutionally so as to allow exemption of all public service posts from free movement. The Court rejected that understanding and opted for a narrow exception, without however using any language typical of the second branch or, more specifically, the wording used in *Sotgiu, 1974*. Similarly, the public service exception had been at stake in *Commission v. France (nurses), 1986*. The Commission in that case had argued a narrow interpretation of the exception (para. 5). Yet none of the typical language made it into the Court's own reasoning, either.

tablishment and therefore was to be interpreted in a manner which limited its scope to what was strictly necessary to safeguard the interests which it allowed the member states to protect (para. 7). The setting up of a private school and a vocational training school or the activity of teaching at home were not in that sense connected to the exercise of official authority.

Next, in *Bond, 1988* the second branch – and 'broad' interpretation in general – for the first time truly reached into the nascent realm of the free movement of services. The public policy derogation in article 56 Treaty, to which article 66 referred, was at issue. The Court stated: '[T]he measures taken by virtue of that article must not be disproportionate to the intended objective. As an exception to a fundamental principle of the Treaty, Article 56 of the Treaty must be interpreted in such a way that its effects are limited to that which is necessary in order to protect the interests which it seeks to safeguard.' (Para. 36) One cannot help but notice the difference to the public policy derogation under the free movement of workers and establishment: the word 'strict' (or 'strictly', etc.) is absent from the *Bond, 1988*-passage. This might be explained by the context of audiovisual services in which *Bond, 1988* was set, a context that has always been particularly sensitive for the member states. It could also be due to services more generally, which is a domain in which economies traditionally have been more structured and infused by the state as an actor in its own right. *ERT AE, 1991*, the next services case in which the second branch played a role, did not provide any clue in this regard. It was also set in a context of audiovisual services. Moreover, the Court in this case tersely stated that article 56 Treaty, to which article 66 Treaty referred, had to be interpreted strictly (para. 24), thus bringing the second branch closer to the first.

Weakness of the second branch in social security

In between these two judgments in services, the Court built on the second branch in two more cases. The first, *Rebmann, 1988*, in a sense, both confirmed the weakness of this branch in social security but also in a way strengthened it. Faced with the question of which state had to take account of periods of unemployment for pension purposes in the situation of frontier workers, the Court reiterated that the member state of employment was as a rule the competent state for frontier workers pursuant to article 13(2)(a) Regulation 1408/71, a rule which suffered exceptions though, in particular in the case of unemployed frontier workers, for reasons of practicality and policy. The Court acknowledged that those exceptions as derogations were in principle susceptible of application by analogy, thus defying on the face of it the narrow interpretation of an exception. However, application by analogy was only possible when the situation which the exception did not govern expressly was closely connected to the situations it covered explicitly and identical grounds that had led to the exception being established in the first place applied *in concreto* (para. 16). That was not the case for periods of unemployment with regard to pension rights. Indeed the member state of employment was in a more regular and better position to take those periods into account. On the merits the Court thus strengthened the second branch by rejecting on the facts of the case reasoning *per analogiam* for an exception, while at the same time confirming its weakness in social security by basically allowing the extension of an exception – and by not mentioning the rule–broad/exception–narrow interpretation in the first place.[51] The second case was *Agegate, 1989*. In this case, the Court transposed the approach taken in *Peskeloglou, 1983* from the Act of Accession of Greece to that of Spain and Portugal. The authorization for states to take exception from the freedom of movement, as a derogation, equally had to be interpreted restrictively, precluding states from making conditions more stringent (para. 39).

c) The third branch: the greatest possible freedom

In the third branch, which is dominated by the *Hoekstra, 1964*-formula of the 'greatest possible freedom', we witnessed two outbursts of broad interpretation as it had been applied before, one in the years 1986/87 and another in the years 1990/91, after an isolated appearance in 1978. The latter appearance occurred in *Belbouab, 1978* where the Court began by stating the *Hoekstra, 1964*-formula – the aim of article 51 Treaty was the 'greatest possible freedom' for workers which was one of the foundations of the Community (para. 5) – and thus set the tone for the decision to take. Was relevant to determine the nationality of a person the time period during which insurance periods were completed rather than the point in time at which a person applied for a pension.

The third branch's outburst in the mid-1980s

After this one isolated appearance, the third branch disappeared from view for some time – a busy time notably with the Court handing down 70 social security judgments – only to come back to prominence in six judgments in the mid 1980s. In *Spruyt, 1986*, the *Hoekstra, 1964*-formula (in para. 18) introduced, together with other passages, the Court's reasoning on the complex transitory provisions of the Netherlands for spouses which (the reasoning) ultimately led to the finding that the provisions were discriminatory. In contrast, in *De Jong, 1986*, handed down on the same day, the Court did not find any discrimination, because the spouse had not resided in the Netherlands at the relevant time. However, the Court also introduced its reasoning in *De Jong, 1986* by the *Hoekstra,*

51 In *Fellinger, 1980* the Court addressed the situation of a wholly unemployed frontier worker, who claimed that the salary last gained in the state of employment was relevant to determine the amount of unemployment benefits he had a right to in the state of residence – in relatively clear contradiction to the rule in article 68 Regulation 1408/71. In essence, the Court acceded to the claim and decided that the rule in article 68, including the exception contained therein, could not be applied to wholly unemployed frontier workers, for it would mean to make the rule the exception. If the rule, including the exception, was applied to them, they would never receive benefits on the basis of the salary they in fact had gained. Indeed the rule implicit in Regulation 1408/71 was that the benefits normally had to be calculated on the basis of the actual last salary, rather than a notional salary. Hence, for fully unemployed frontier workers the actual last salary was relevant. The Court did not discuss the logic the second branch would have implied, possibly because it would not have yielded the result the Court had in view, but possibly also because it would just have added an additional, unnecessary layer of complexity to an already complex train of thought.

1964-formula (para. 14). *Van Roosmalen, 1986*, in which the first and the third branch of broad interpretation connected was already discussed above.

In *Rijke, 1987*, the Court again reiterated the formula as a preliminary remark (para. 13) before answering the question asked by rejecting that a one-year time period to file an application for voluntary continued insurance in national law was precluded under Regulation 1408/71. In *Rindone, 1987* the Court next underpinned with the *Hoekstra, 1964*-formula – dubbed '*Spruyt, 1986*' by the Court – the decision that an institution of the competent state had to accept the findings of the medical officer of the institution at the place where the person concerned was resident (para. 13). The Court concluded the outburst of the third branch of the mid-1980s in *Campana, 1987*. Interestingly, the Court in this case reverted to the formula used in *Heinze, 1972*, which we called the 'offspring', rather than the *Hoekstra, 1964*-formula, to include certain German benefits into 'unemployment benefits' under Regulation 1408/71. Most probably the Court did so, because benefits with preventive functions were at issue both in *Heinze, 1972* and *Campana, 1987*. With this outburst of the third branch in the mid-1980s it is in particular noteworthy that the Court in three judgments, namely *Spruyt, 1986*; *De Jong, 1986*; and *Rijke, 1987*, placed the *Hoekstra, 1964*-formula ahead of the reasoning on the specifics of the case and hand in hand it with other 'principles' from the case-law, such as the *Petroni, 1975*-formula.

The third branch's outburst at the beginning of the 1990s

After that, the third branch did not make an appearance in the next 35 social security judgments. Then the second outburst came with *Winter-Lutzins, 1990* and four more judgments belonging to the third branch within less than a year. *Winter-Lutzins, 1990* again concerned the Netherlands' transitional arrangement which had already been at issue in *Spruyt, 1986* and *De Jong, 1986*. The Court again began with the *Hoekstra, 1964*-formula (para. 13), together with other case-law, before entering the specifics of the case, essentially confirming the sufficient-link requirement, evidenced e. g. by residence, in order to benefit from notional years. In *Buhari Haji, 1990* the Court was faced with a similar context as in *Belbouab, 1978*. Hence the Court first mentioned the ruling in this case before reiterating the *Hoekstra, 1964*-formula, though without the foundational part (para. 20), as it had done in *Belbouab, 1978*. In contrast to the latter case though, the person concerned in *Buhari Haji, 1990* did not succeed, because at the relevant time he had been a British national, and thus the national of a non-member state. (At the relevant time, the United Kingdom had not yet joined the Community.)

In *Rönfeldt, 1991* the Court then used the *Hoekstra, 1964*-formula, in a slightly different wording, namely 'the greatest possible measure of freedom' (para. 24), together with the *Petroni, 1975*-approach, to justify why the benefit of a convention between member states which had been in force before Regulation 1408/71 became applicable had to be maintained. Next, in *Noij, 1991*, the

Court took recourse *inter alia* to the *Hoekstra, 1964*-formula, again in a somewhat different form mentioning 'the fullest possible freedom' (para. 13), to found a more general principle that pensioners could not lawfully be required to contribute to the social security scheme of the state where they were resident for benefits which were payable by another member state that paid their pensions. Finally, in *Masgio, 1991*, one of the relatively rare social security cases in which the principle of non-discrimination was applied, the Court found that non-discrimination had to be interpreted in the light of its objective, namely to contribute to the greatest possible freedom of movement, one of the foundations of the Community (para. 16). Again combining this *Hoekstra, 1964*-logic with the *Petroni, 1975*-approach, the Court found that Germany's way of determining, and notably reducing a pension, was discriminatory.

'Conditions most favourable'

In addition to the *Hoekstra, 1964*-formula, which was generally consolidated during the 15 years up to the 'Maastricht moment', another offspring of the third branch of broad interpretation developed. In *Mouthaan, 1976* the Court stated that article 71(1)(b)(ii) Regulation 1408/71 aimed at granting unemployment benefits to the worker 'in conditions most favourable to the search for new employment' (para. 13). The term 'conditions most favourable' is, of course, reminiscent of the formula initially used in *Heinze, 1972* which we named the 'offspring', i. e. 'the most favourable conditions'-passage (para. 4). Indeed, in the French versions of the two judgments the terms are identical ('les conditions les plus favorables'). Witness therefore the sprouting in *Mouthaan, 1976* of a second offspring of the third branch of broad interpretation. In *Mouthaan, 1976* the passage was used to explain why the legislation of the state of residence was applicable under article 71 Regulation 1408/71 to a frontier worker. While the passage was then curiously absent from *Di Paolo, 1977* where the Court explained the logic of article 71, it came back in *Aubin, 1982* (para. 12). In this judgment, the Court cited the *Mouthaan, 1976*-formula again to explain the reasoning underlying article 71, before coming to the conclusion that Belgium's legislation was applicable in the case at issue, irrespective of whether the person concerned was a frontier worker or not.

In *Miethe, 1986* the Court was next faced with a 'false frontier worker' (para. 15). Mr Miethe, a German national, had moved to Belgium for family reasons, while retaining all business and ties in Germany. Formally, he would have been entitled to unemployment benefits only in Belgium rather than in Germany as a frontier worker under article 71(1)(a)(ii). Yet the Court cited the *Mouthaan, 1976*-formula to justify why Mr Miethe was not a frontier worker properly speaking, although he returned to Belgium on a daily basis. Since he maintained all his ties in Germany and found the most favourable conditions to seek work there, he was a worker other than a frontier worker who benefitted from the choice available under article 71(1)(b) to receive benefits either in the state of employment or the state of residence. In *Bergemann, 1988* the *Mouthaan, 1976*-

formula was again and for the last time applied during the period up to the beginning of the 1990s. It served to found the right under article 71(1)(b) of a person who had worked in the Netherlands, but while she was on leave moved her residence to Germany to live with her husband and child; she did not return to the Netherlands anymore. For the Court, with her not being a frontier worker, she found the most favourable conditions for new employment in Germany (para. 21), resulting in article 71(1)(b) being applicable.

d) Spin – in the second branch

Among the judgments examined within the three branches of broad interpretation those in which this interpretation was decisive – a phenomenon we named 'spin' – are again of particular interest. In the *second* branch, broad interpretation for the first time in *Bouchereau, 1977* began to provide spin and help the Court steer the decision in a specific direction. In *Bouchereau, 1977* the Court initiated the relevant part of the judgment with the need for a strict interpretation of the public policy exception. This spin continued throughout the period in a similar way for the exception in *Peskeloglou, 1983* as well as with the connection of the two branches in *Kempf, 1986* and with *Lawrie-Blum, 1986*. In *Commission v. Italy (research council), 1987* second branch logic also provided spin, but it was blurred by other arguments. In *Commission v. Greece (vocational schools), 1988*, that logic provided spin for the establishment and services aspects of the case and was carried through to the worker aspect of the judgment. In *Bond, 1988*, again interpretation belonging to the second branch provided some, but not the only spin. Perhaps typically, the only cases within the second branch in which a broad interpretation-formula was used, but failed to provide spin were the two social security cases, *Di Paolo, 1977*, and *Rebmann, 1988* with their inconclusive reasoning, and the services case *ERT AE, 1991*, which again bears witness to the weakness of the second branch in social security and services.[52] This means, conversely, that whenever the broad rule/narrow exception-formula was used in *worker* cases, it was pivotal.

Spin in the third branch – evolving into empty spin

The third branch is equally interesting with regard to spin. In eight judgments during the period the greatest possible freedom formula spun the decisions, namely *Belbouab, 1978*; *Spruyt, 1986*; *Van Roosmalen, 1986*; *Campana, 1987* with the offspring formula; *Masgio, 1991*; *Noij, 1991*; and to a more limited extent *Rönfeldt, 1991*. In one judgment, *Rindone, 1987*, the formula played a minor role as an ex post confirmation of the decision reached before in the judgment.

However, in early 1986 an entirely new phenomenon of spin appeared in a third branch judgment: empty spin. In *De Jong, 1986*, the Court for the first time did mention the formula of the 'greatest possible freedom', but in substance

52 *Agegate, 1989*, is an exception in this regard. This can be explained by the fact that it essentially just restated *Peskeloglou, 1983*.

decided against those who were supposed to enjoy that greatest possible freedom. It was the first judgment in the third branch in which an unbiased reader encountered the formula and thus caught a glimpse of the result to come – only to see the decision being turned around, the result being in fact the inverse of what the use of the formula had implied.[53] This empty spin in *De Jong, 1986* finds an explanation in its twin judgment, *Spruyt, 1986*, which was identical in most parts, except for a decisive aspect of the facts, namely non-residence. This aspect led the Court in *De Jong, 1986* to adopt a decision in clear opposition to that it had taken in *Spruyt, 1986*.

Soon, however, empty spin became somewhat more common in the third branch. In *Rijke, 1987*, *Winter-Lutzins, 1990*, and *Buhari Haji, 1990* the 'greatest possible freedom' was stated, the outcome thus 'announced' – but the Court then backed out, ruling in the inverse sense. Admittedly, the explanation for empty spin given in *De Jong, 1986* is also valid in *Rijke, 1987* and *Winter-Lutzins, 1990* which were both connected to the same legislation that had been at issue in *Spruyt, 1986*. *Buhari Haji, 1990*, moreover, to some extent mirrored *Belbouab, 1978* in that the facts were quite alike while the formula had been used with genuine spin in *Belbouab, 1978*. Despite that, it cannot be overlooked that the formula of the 'greatest possible freedom' lost some of its power and magic when empty spin emerged. The formula sorts weakened from the period leading up to the 'Maastricht moment'.

In contrast, the second offspring of the third branch, the *Mouthaan, 1976*-formula, remained untainted by empty spin. The formula served to spin the decisions in *Miethe, 1986* and *Bergemann, 1988* and thus to grant a not quite obvious right to unemployment benefits. Within the second offspring the formula was never used in the sense of empty spin.

Why empty spin?

Beyond what was said above the deeper causes for the emergence of empty spin within the third branch are hard to pin down. Why would the Court want to state a formula such as the *Hoekstra, 1964*-formula, which typically spins a decision, only then to decide against the direction of that spin? There is no obvious explanation from within the case-law. An examination of extraneous factors would have to investigate a number of points. Perhaps the emergence of empty spin correlates with – or is even caused by – Hjalte Rasmussen's serious and profound critique of the Court's activism.[54] While Rasmussen did not directly attack the Court for being formulaic, his critical study might have prompted some rethinking in general within the Court. That could have resulted in a more trans-

53 'Empty spin' needs to be distinguished from 'no spin'. In both cases the same formula is used, but with empty spin the formula creates a certain expectation which is then frustrated, while with 'no spin' an expectation is not created in the first place. Obviously, the distinction is partly connected to the position of the formula within the reasoning of the Court. The distinction is probably best understood, when a no spin-case, such as *Rindone, 1987* is read together and compared with an empty spin-case, such as *De Jong, 1986*.

54 Rasmussen, *On Law and Policy in the European Court of Justice*.

parent approach to taking a decision, notably one that involved stating an established formula not just when it fitted the outcome desired, but also when that outcome went against the grain of a formula. However, the external perspective on the case-law is not the concern of this book.

Spin in the first branch

In the first branch – broad interpretation as such – spin is less obvious. In *Bozzone, 1977* the formula used – '[t]his definition is remarkable for its breadth' – spun the decision, as much as in *Commission v. Belgium (Congo), 1980*. In *Levin, 1982* the non-restrictive interpretation of the personal scope provided some spin and so it did with the substantive scope in *Forcheri, 1983*. In *Robards, 1983*, the wide interpretation of article 10(1)(a) Regulation 574/72 produced some limited spin; in *Diatta, 1985* it was the non-restrictive interpretation of article 10 Regulation 1612/68. In *Lawrie-Blum, 1986* the broad understanding of a 'worker' spun the first part of the judgment; in *Kempf, 1986* it did so, too. In the second part of *Reed, 1986*, the broad reading of article 7(2) Regulation 1612/68 contributed some spin. In *Van Roosmalen, 1986* broad interpretation provided spin twice, once the broad term 'self-employed person' did and once the *Bozzone, 1977*-formula did. In *Lopes da Veiga, 1989* again the broad 'worker'-notion spun the decision to some extent. The broad understanding of the freedom as such spun the decision strongly in *Antonissen, 1991* and in *Giagounidis, 1991* in the second question.

In only one single judgment the new phenomenon of empty spin emerged: *Bettray, 1989*. In this case the Court set out with the need for a broad understanding of the term 'worker', but ended up with the finding that a former drug addict in rehabilitation could not be a worker. That the judgment was handed down at the end of the 1980s fits well with the emergence of empty spin in the third branch. Finally, it remains to be observed that the phenomenon of spin in general, including empty spin, has become much more common during the period leading up to the 'Maastricht moment', though only in absolute terms. In 30 out of 318 judgments in our domain spin occurred during that period, while it appeared in 8 out of 99 judgments handed down during the period up to the mid-1970s.

e) Some conclusions from the period

During the period leading up to the 'Maastricht moment' it has become obvious that the three branches of broad interpretation we initially identified further established themselves. In keeping with the generally expanding case-law in the free movement of workers and social security the branches grew broader in these domains. In the free movement of services and establishment though the branches remained very weak. The first branch involving broad notions as such encompassed two and the second branch concerning narrow exceptions from rules three judgments. Obviously, this weakness reflects the general state of the case-law in those domains: Free movement of services and establishment was still only moderately developed at that time. Each one of those five judgments, moreover, remained rather inconclusive from the point of view of broad interpretation.

Beyond these general observations things become more complicated. One could perhaps discern a tendency towards wide scopes in the freedom of workers and secondary legislation based on it. At least the practice under the first branch comprising broad notions indicates so. The 'perhaps' remains a must though, as it is hard to factor in the cases in which broad interpretation did not occur at all. That is the vast majority of the judgments within our domain, namely 318 in the period from 1977 to 1991, out of which 64 were discussed above, one way or another, under broad interpretation. Negative proof is, as always, difficult.

On a more specific level, one evolution is striking, namely the evolution from the notion of a 'worker' being in need of a broad interpretation in *Levin, 1982* to the imperative of interpreting the fundamental freedom of workers as such broadly in *Forcheri, 1983* and *Kempf, 1986*. These judgments, therefore, are of key importance with regard to broad interpretation. The evolution was then completed in *Lebon, 1987* when the link to the 'worker' notion was dropped altogether. Of course, the broad interpretation of the free movement of workers has been 'negatively' present from early on. From the worker cases in the mid-1970s onwards, the second branch was mostly applied to derogations from the free movement of workers, resulting in an imperative to read restrictions narrowly. Conversely, this implies a broad understanding of the freedom itself.

While the first branch spanned both worker and social security cases and the occasional establishment case, something like a rift existed between the domains in the second and the third branch. The second branch has almost exclusively been applied in worker cases, if we ignore for a moment the two services cases, *Bond, 1988* and *ERT AE, 1991*. The Court remained strangely reluctant to reason along broad rules and narrow exceptions in the coordination of social security. Conversely, the third branch involving the greatest possible freedom, with all its curious wave-like comings and goings, has been applied exclusively in social security. There has not been a single judgment in the free movement of workers in which the 'greatest possible freedom' appeared, although intuitively the logic of that notion would chime with the broad approach to the free movement of workers proclaimed in *Kempf, 1986*. While from the point of view of the second branch this rift remains a mystery, it can tentatively be explained from the perspective of the third branch. The Court has probably been reluctant to uproot bluntly the idea of the 'greatest possible freedom' with all its implications in social security and to transpose it to the different field of the free movement of workers. Perhaps rightly so. Obviously, the *Kempf, 1986/Lebon, 1987*-formula has risen up to the challenges in equal measure. And the harmony which could be attained by marrying the *Hoekstra, 1964*- and the *Kempf, 1986/Lebon, 1987*-formulas is expendable, for the Court at least.

Besides, a further feature of both the second and the third branch during the period leading up to the 'Maastricht moment' strikes us as odd. In both branches, the Court has almost consistently combined the idea – the rule is to be broad, the exception narrow and the freedom is to be the greatest possible – with structural, almost hierarchical logic: the rule is *fundamental*, hence broad; the freedom is part of the *foundations* of the Community, hence it has to be the greatest possible.[55] This hierarchical aspect remains an enigma. Obviously, the derogations from the fundamental freedom are equally part of primary law and therefore 'fundamental' in nature. So, what does this hierarchy within primary law mean? Is it necessary in addition to the duet of rule-exception? Is that duet too weak and hence in need of hierarchical crutches?[56] And where do the 'foundations of the Community' come to an end?

To come to a conclusion with regard to the *power* of the interpretive formulas, i. e. their 'spin', is more difficult. The power of the interpretive formula has been most evident in the second branch, which includes narrow restrictions from broad rules. In free movement of *worker* decisions, whenever the formula was used it usually spun the decision, which is another way of saying that the formula was pivotal. In the freedom of establishment and services the same cannot be confirmed. In the third branch, 'the greatest possible freedom' also usually spun the decisions. It is in this third branch that empty spin occurred for the first time. This is the phenomenon where a formula is stated, thus giving rise to a certain expectation of the outcome, only to be frustrated, because the outcome is counter to this expectation. Empty spin clearly weakened 'The greatest possible freedom'. For the first branch – broad notions more generally – spin is harder to observe, because it encompasses a more diverse, less consolidated range of notions. Nonetheless, spin is clearly observable in the first branch, too (see above).

3 During the age of Maastricht

Let us take a closer look at how broad interpretation evolved over the next fifteen years, from 1992 to 2006 – a period that is best called the 'age of Maastricht', for obvious reasons. Expect an inundating flood, for the number of judgments in general in our domain more than doubled during that period.

a) First branch: broad notions – 'worker'

In the first branch – the broad, or restrictive, interpretation of terms in general – the evolution in the notion of the 'worker' first attracts attention. In *Raulin, 1992* the Court reiterated that that notion was not to be interpreted restrictively (para. 10). That was why a person employed by means of an on-call contract was not *per se* excluded from being a worker. It was up to the national court to

55 To some extent, this type of hierarchical reasoning is also present in the first branch. See only the development towards the broad interpretation of the *fundamental* freedom of workers, which was complete with *Lebon, 1987*.

56 *Commission v. Luxembourg and Belgium (gingerbread), 1962*, at least seems to imply so, in the confusion created over which provision constituted the rule and which the exception (p. 434).

qualify the specific aspects of such a contract under the Court's case-law.[57] In *Twomey, 1992* the Court then addressed the concept of a worker in article 19 Regulation 1408/71 and concluded based on *Pierik II, 1979* that it was not to be interpreted restrictively (paras 13 and 17). The concept included a person who had stopped working in one state, moved to another and then fell ill, before beginning the new employment there.

Next, the Court dealt with the 'worker'-notion in *Krid, 1995* in the context of the Algiers Agreement with Algeria. The understanding of who was a worker had to be broad in the same way as under the Rabat Agreement with Morocco.[58] At least in part as a consequence of that, the widow of an Algerian national could lawfully claim the *Giletti, 1987*-allowance in France.[59] In *Birden, 1998* the Court was called upon to interpret the notion of a worker under the Ankara Agreement with Turkey, namely Decision 1/80. The person concerned had been employed by a social institution within the framework of a social programme financed entirely by the state. According to the Court, under the Ankara Agreement also a broad interpretation of the term 'worker' was required in keeping with the internal market case-law (para. 25), notwithstanding the judgment in *Bettray, 1989* which went against the grain of the general trend in the case-law of the Court towards broad interpretation (para. 31).

With *Meeusen, 1999* the Court further clarified the worker notion of the free movement of workers. Given that it was not to be construed restrictively it could not be excluded in principle that the wife who had been employed by her husband's company in which he was the sole shareholder and director was a worker (para. 13). In *Lehtonen, 2000* the Court accepted that professional basketball players were workers, partly because the notion was not to be interpreted restrictively in view of a fundamental freedom being at stake (para. 42).[60] Returning to

57 *Bernini, 1992* which was handed down on the same day as *Raulin, 1992* dealt with the notion of a 'worker', too. One of the questions was whether a trainee in the context of occupational training was a worker. The Court began its answer by the very same definition of a worker as in *Raulin, 1992* but omitted the passage as to non-restrictive interpretation. More specifically, in *Raulin, 1992* and *Bernini, 1992* the beginnings of the definition diverged as follows (divergences are in italics): 'It *must/should* be recalled at the outset that the Court has consistently held that the concept of worker *within the meaning of article 48 EEC Treaty* has a *specific* Community meaning *and must not be interpreted in a restrictive manner*.' (para. 10 and 14, respectively; in *Bernini, 1992* the Court left the qualification to the national court.) In French the two passages are identical: 'Il convient de rappeler à titre liminaire qu'il est de jurisprudence constante que la notion de travailleur revêt une portée communautaire et ne doit pas être interprétée de manière restrictive.'.

58 The Court in *Kziber, 1991* and *Yousfi, 1994* had established that a 'worker' under the Rabat Agreement was not just a person who was actively working, but also a pensioner or a person who did not work any longer because a risk had materialized against which the person had been insured. The Court decided so without applying any literal broad interpretation.

59 In *Megner, 1995* the Court interpreted the personal scope of Directive 79/7 on equal treatment of men and women in social security partly by adopting the notion of a 'worker' from the free movement of persons. The Court held, in particular, that the concept of the 'working population' was very broad (para. 16) and referred to *Levin, 1982*, and *Kempf, 1986*. The definition of a 'worker' had been in the Community sphere since *Hoekstra, 1964* (para. 20). Hence, the Court concluded, persons in minor employment were part of the 'working population' within the meaning of the Directive. (*Nolte, 1995* was identical.).

60 In *Leclere, 2001* some parties had argued a broad interpretation of the 'worker'-notion in order for article 7(2) Regulation 1612/68 to encompass pensioners and certain rights to benefits (para. 54). The

the Ankara Agreement, the Court in *Kurz, 2002* included an apprentice in the 'worker'-notion of Decision 1/80, partly owing to the need for a broad interpretation (para. 32). In *Ninni-Orasche, 2003* the Court again stated that the term 'worker' as in free movement of *workers* was not subject to a narrow interpretation (para. 23). Hence, a short period of employment – 2.5 months in the case at issue – did not in itself disqualify a person from being a worker. The Court then proceeded to qualify a number of other factors as irrelevant for the question whether the person concerned was a worker (paras 28-31). *Collins, 2004* raised the question of how a long absence from the host state of employment affected the status of a worker. In the case at issue the Court found, despite the need for a broad interpretation (para. 26), that a connection did not exist between casual work and the search for a job in the host state 17 years later. (The more famous part of *Collins, 2004* evidently concerned the right of a job-seeker to an allowance in the light of equal treatment and Union citizenship.) In *Trojani, 2004* the Court reiterated the credo of a broad notion of a 'worker' (para. 15), but left it to the national court to assess whether 'work' in a rehabilitation programme of the salvation army for pocket money and certain benefits constituted genuine work. The Court again, as in *Birden, 1998*, carefully delimited the implications of *Bettray, 1989* (para. 19). (Again it is the Union citizenship dimension for which *Trojani, 2004* is known.) According to *Kranemann, 2005*, German trainee lawyers were workers, in part again due to broad interpretation (para. 12). *Mattern and Cikotic, 2006* re-stated that with regard to professional training as a health care assistant (para. 18).

Broad free movement of workers

The Court not only interpreted the concept of a 'worker' broadly, but also the free movement of workers as such, in keeping with the *Kempf, 1986/Lebon, 1987*-approach. In *Commission v. Belgium (residence permits), 1997* the Court reiterated the imperative of interpreting broadly the free movement of workers as one of the foundations of the Community so as to include job seekers, as established in *Antonissen, 1991* (para. 14). In *Yiadom, 2000* this approach in the first branch of broad interpretation connected with the second branch involving narrow exceptions to broad rules. The Court was called upon to determine the procedural rights of a person temporarily admitted to the United Kingdom in the light of Directive 64/221. The Court answered with the need for a broad interpretation of the free movement of persons and the corresponding imperative of construing exceptions therefrom narrowly (para. 24). With regard to the procedural provisions which ensure the protection of that freedom the Court then went on to state that they had to be interpreted in favour of the migrant worker (para. 25) – a line that is, somewhat strangely, reminiscent of the *Nonnenmacher, 1964*-argument the Commission had proposed in *Guerra, 1967* and which

Court rejected that approach, without using any broad or restrictive language. Putting *Meints, 1997* into perspective, the Court required a link between the previous employment and the benefit for article 7(2) Regulation 1612/68 to apply, excluding 'new' benefits (para. 59).

the Court had rejected at that time. The Court concluded in *Yiadom, 2000* that the same procedural rights had to be available in case of temporary admission as when the person was regularly present. In a similar vein, though much less expansively, the Court in *MRAX, 2002* ruled that article 9 Directive 64/221 had to be construed broadly with regard to the persons to whom it applied (para. 101). Consequently, the procedural rights of spouses could not lawfully be made dependent on the possession of an identity document or a valid visa. In *Zhu and Chen, 2004* the Court next held that the sufficient resources of a child Union citizen required by Directive 90/364 did not have to stem from personal resources of the child, but could be provided by her parent. The Court justified that conclusion by the need for a broad interpretation of provisions laying down a fundamental principle like the free movement of persons (para. 31). In *Commission v. Belgium (own resources), 2006* the Court reiterated that very consideration with reference to *Zhu and Chen, 2004* (para. 40) when it invalidated Belgium's approach to personal resources.

Broad interpretation in services

In *Deliège, 2000* the Court in a similar way applied broad interpretation in the free movement of services. Faced with the question whether the sport activities of a judoka amounted to economic activities and provision of services, the Court took recourse to *Levin, 1982* and stated that the terms defined the scope of a fundamental freedom. That was why they were not to be interpreted restrictively (para. 52). After having analysed the activities of judokas in detail, the Court concluded that they indeed offered and received services and enabled others to provide services.

In *Oulane, 2005* the Court took it a step further. Having been asked whether the right of residence of a service recipient under Directive 73/148 on restrictions regarding establishment and services depended on production of an identity document, the Court started out by saying that the free movement of persons was one of the foundations of the Community and that provisions enshrining it were to be construed broadly, referring to paragraph 24 of *Yiadom, 2000* (para. 16). From that the Court concluded that unequivocal proof of the identity of a service recipient other than an identity card or passport had to be admitted.

Further broad interpretation

Apart from the worker notion and the free movement of persons and services as such, the Court also applied broad interpretation in a number of other judgements. In *Imbernon Martínez, 1995* the Court ruled that article 73 Regulation 1408/71 was not to be interpreted restrictively (para. 27). The article broadly applied to all members of the family of a migrant worker. As a consequence, it also precluded the factoring out of the spouse of a migrant worker for the entitlement to and the amount of a family allowance on the ground that the spouse was not resident in the host state.[61] In *Naruschawicus, 1996* the Court decided that the concept of an employed person in Regulation 1408/71, and hence article 71(1)(b)(i), was wider than the concept of a civil servant in article 13(2)(d) Regulation 1408/71 (para. 21). That was why the special scheme for wholly unemployed frontier workers and other workers having residence abroad applied also to civil servants.[62] With *Meints, 1997* the Court came back to the social advantages in article 7(2) Regulation 1612/68. Since those advantages were not to be interpreted restrictively (para. 39), they included a lay-off benefit granted to those who had worked on a farm the arable land of which was temporarily set aside.

Connection of the first and third branch

In *Stöber and Pereira, 1997*, again two branches of broad interpretation connected, as in *Van Roosmalen, 1986*, i. e. the first and the third branch. Indeed the question raised in *Stöber and Pereira, 1997* was quite similar to that answered in *Van Roosmalen, 1986*. Despite the need for a broad interpretation of the term self-employed persons in order to contribute to the greatest possible freedom of migrant workers, one of the foundations of the Community (para. 30), the limitation of self-employed persons in the annex to Regulation 1408/71 for Germany to those who were compulsorily insured prevailed. (The principle of non-discrimination had to be observed nonetheless.)

More broad interpretation

In *Akman, 1998* the Court concluded in the context of the Ankara Agreement that article 7(2) Decision 1/80 was not to be interpreted strictly (para. 39). Hence, a worker did not necessarily have to be employed in the host state at the time his descendant sought access to the employment market.[63] In *Stallone, 2001*

61 In *Baglieri, 1993* the national court had harboured doubts with regard to a restrictive interpretation of article 9(2) Regulation 1408/71 (paras 7-8). The Court did not share those doubts, but refrained from using any broad language (see para 14-8). In *El-Yassini, 1999* the referring court wondered whether article 40 of the Rabat Agreement with Morocco could be interpreted broadly in the same way as its homologues in article 7(1) Regulation 1612/68 and article 6(1) Decision 1/80 (para. 14). The Court opted against such a broad interpretation, but refrained from using any of the typical language. On a different note, interestingly, the judgment in *Bosman, 1995*, despite its disruptive effect on sports law and the market access approach, was handed down without the use of any broad interpretation at all.

62 In *Naruschawicus, 1996* the Court referred to *Van Poucke, 1994* for the wide concept of an 'employed person'. In *Van Poucke, 1994* the Court had ruled that an employed civil servant to which Regulation 1408/71 applied came within the purview of article 14c Regulation 1408/71 as an employed person. But the Court did not make use of any broad interpretation. In *De Jaeck, 1997* the reference in *Van Poucke, 1994* to the Community definition of a worker made the Court clarify that the terms 'employed' and 'self-employed persons' in title II of Regulation 1408/71 were to be defined by the relevant national law (see para. 33). The Court again did not apply any broad interpretation. On a different note, one party in *Vougioukas, 1995* argued a strict interpretation of the term 'special scheme for civil servants' in article 4(4) Regulation 1408/71 (paras 8 and 24). The Court did not follow that argument. Nor did it address broad interpretation. However, the Court delivered the ruling that aggregation had to be applied to civil servants subject to a special scheme directly on the basis of article 51 ECT, because the failure of the Community legislature to coordinate such schemes violated this article (see para. 36). The Court delivered that rather disruptive ruling without applying any broad interpretation.

63 In *Kulzer, 1998* the Court interpreted the scope of Regulation 1408/71 so as to include Mr Kulzer, a retired civil servant, although he himself had never made use of his freedom to move. In essence, the movement of his daughter rendered Regulation 1408/71 applicable. The Court interpreted the scope

the Court rejected a restrictive reading of article 68(2) Regulation 1408/71 which would have excluded from the scope of that article a Belgian unemployment benefit that was increased not on the basis of the 'number of members of the family' as mentioned in article 68(2), but depending on whether the unemployed person lived alone or with *one* family member (para. 18).[64] In *Baumbast, 2002*, the Court three times rejected a restrictive interpretation. The Court first ruled that the right of a former migrant worker's children to continue their education pursuant to article 12 Regulation 1612/68 could not be interpreted restrictively (para. 55); next, that right was not to be interpreted so restrictively as to include exclusively common children of the migrant worker and his spouse (para. 57); finally, again given that that article could not be read restrictively, it granted a right of residence to the primary carer of children attending educational courses who (the children) had a right of residence (para. 74).[65] In *Mediakabel, 2005* the Court rejected a narrow interpretation of the term 'broadcasting services' in Directive 89/552, as it would jeopardize the aims of the Directive (para. 49). Hence, the pay-per-view services offered by Mediakabel had to be categorized as broadcasting services.

'Aim and broad logic'

In *Kurz, 2002* – in which the Court also broadly construed the worker-notion under the Ankara Agreement – the Court opened a new line of authority of broad interpretation. Ruling on whether a regular apprentice belonged to the duly registered labour force within the meaning of article 6(1) Decision 1/80 the Court answered in the affirmative and added that that conclusion was consistent with the aim and broad logic of Decision 1/80, which was to promote the integration of Turkish workers in the host state (para. 45). In *Wählergruppe Gemeinsam, 2003* that same approach under the first branch then connected with more broad interpretation under the first branch and with the second

---

of Regulation 1408/71 that expansively without using any of the language typical for broad interpretation, apart from the passage from *Pierik II, 1979* according to which 'the term 'worker' was general in its scope [...]' (para. 24). On a different note, the Court in *Kuusijärvi, 1998* applied something like a broad interpretation. It held that article 13(2)(f) Regulation 1408/71, which had been inserted into the Regulation following *Ten Holder, 1986*, was 'couched in general terms' (para. 40) so that it included any person who had ceased for whatever reason an economic activity, be it temporarily or definitely. Partly as a result of that, a residence clause in Swedish legislation was not precluded.

64 In *Commission v. Belgium (insurance), 2000* Belgium argued a restrictive interpretation of article 55 Directive 92/49 so as to exclude insurance for accidents at work offered (the insurance) by private for-profit undertakings as part of Belgium's compulsory social security scheme (para. 37). The Court rejected that argument, but in doing so did not apply any broad language.

65 In *Schilling, 2003* the referring court very much reasoned in terms of broad/narrow interpretation of article 14 of the Protocol on the Privileges and Immunities of the European Communities (para. 13 and 14), but the Court refused to answer the question asked in those terms (para. 31) and put the emphasis on the free movement of workers. On a different note, in *Öztürk, 2004* Austria had argued that the concept of indirect discrimination adopted by the Court in *Taflan-Met, 1996* was not so broad as to require the taking into account of periods during which unemployment benefits were received in another member state for the qualifying period of an early retirement pension (para. 42). The Court did not address broad interpretation, but in substance rejected Austria's argument (paras 62-5). Finally, in *Commission v. Belgium (CESS), 2004* the Commission had argued that it followed from *Gravier, 1985* that the term 'vocational training' had to be construed very widely (para. 12). The Court accepted that argument, though only implicitly.

branch. The aim and broad logic of Decision 1/80 justified transposing the ruling in *ASTI, 1991* and *Commission v. Luxemburg (ASTI II), 1994* as to representation in chambers of workers to article 10 Decision 1/80 (para. 79), against any argument for a narrow interpretation (para. 80). That finding was underpinned by article 48(2) Treaty, which was a general principle, giving expression to non-discrimination, and hence the term 'conditions of work' had to be interpreted broadly (para. 85). Moreover, participation in chambers of workers did not constitute an exercise of powers conferred by public law. That exception to the freedom of movement had to be confined to what was strictly necessary to protect the interests of member states (para. 92).

The 'aim and broad logic' approach first used in *Kurz, 2002* was then taken out of the context of the Ankara Agreement in *Commission v. Austria (trade unions), 2004* and transposed to other Association Agreements the Community had concluded, i. e. the European Economic Area and the Agreements with central and Eastern European and Maghreb countries (para. 8). More specifically, the Court transposed the solution found in *Wählergruppe Gemeinsam, 2003* regarding worker councils, including the narrow interpretation of the derogation, under the Ankara Agreement to the other Association Agreements and stated that interpretation to be 'the only one consistent with the aim and broad logic of the agreements concerned' (para. 53). Hence, the connection between the first and the second branch of broad interpretation was maintained in *Commission v. Austria (trade unions), 2004*.

In *Sedef, 2006* the Court came back to the Ankara Agreement and applied a slightly modified version of the *Kurz, 2002*-formula. Faced with the issue of whether the three indents of article 6(1) Decision 1/80 had to be fulfilled progressively, i. e. the second after the first and the third after the second, the Court stated that the 'broad logic and practical effect' of gradual integration of workers into the host state's labour force required it to be so (para. 37).

The concept of establishment is 'a very broad one'

In the freedom of establishment, an important development in terms of broad interpretation was initiated in *Gebhard, 1995*. The judgment is well known for establishing the test to be applied to restrictions of the establishment freedom (in para. 37), but the judgment also made it clear that the concept of establishment was 'a very *broad* one, allowing a Community national to participate, on a stable and continuous basis, in the economic life of a Member State other than his State of origin and to profit therefrom, so contributing to economic and social interpenetration within the Community in the sphere of activities of self-employed persons […]' (para. 25; emphasis added). The Court used this broad definition to delineate establishment from services, which were subordinate (para. 22). As a consequence, Mr Gebhard's activities as a lawyer in Italy came within the reach of the freedom of establishment. This broad concept of establishment was applied in two more establishment cases in the age of Maastricht. In *Reisebüro Broede, 1996* the Court came back to the formula in a situation in which it was unclear whether debt collection on behalf of companies by a French company in Germany came within establishment or services. Having stated that the concept of establishment was broad (para. 20), the Court directed the national court to determine whether the freedom of services or the freedom of establishment was applicable and proceeded itself to examine the freedom of services, while ending up applying the *Gebhard, 1995*-test. Almost ten years later,[66] the Court reiterated the broad approach to establishment in *N, 2006* (para. 26) to justify why the freedom of establishment applied when a person who held all the shares in a company moved his residence to another member state.[67]

b) Second branch: narrow exceptions from rules – second branch connecting with third

Knoch, 1992 was the first judgment in the age of Maastricht in which broad interpretation within the meaning of the second branch, involving narrow restrictions from broad rules, was applied. In addition, in this judgment the second branch became entangled with the second offspring of the third branch relying on 'conditions most favourable' stemming from *Mouthaan, 1976*. Faced with the situation of Ms Knoch, a German national who had worked in the United Kingdom as a university language assistant for two years and then claimed unemployment benefits in the United Kingdom before going back to Germany where she again claimed unemployment benefits, the Court began by reiterating the rulings in *Bergemann, 1988* concerning the most favourable conditions under article 71, i. e. third branch logic (para. 14) and in *Di Paolo, 1977* that article 71 Regulation 1408/71 was a derogation from the general rule in article 67(3) which (the derogation) was to be interpreted strictly, at least with regard to 'residence' thus relying on second branch logic (para. 20). In spite of that second ruling, Ms Knoch's situation in the United Kingdom was not, according to the Court, stable enough to amount to residence in the United Kingdom where she had worked (para. 25). Hence, she had to benefit from the choice in article 71(1)(b)(ii) of where to claim benefits, in Germany or the United Kingdom. Moreover, that included the possibility to receive benefits first in the United Kingdom under British law and then to continue receiving benefits under German law in Ger-

66 It remains unclear why the Court did not make use of the broad conception of establishment laid down in *Gebhard, 1995* in the meantime. In *Commission v. Belgium (associations), 1999* Advocate General Cosmas had at least proposed a broad interpretation of 'profit-making' entities (para. 12), but the Court refused to address that proposition, instead ruling vaguely that the right to form associations in Belgian law applied to nationals of other member states and therefore one of the fundamental freedoms was affected. Hence, Belgium's rules were within the scope of the Treaty (para. 12). The Court concluded that article 6 Treaty precluded the nationality requirements. *Baars, 2000* could have been another case in point, but the Court failed to mention establishment as a broad concept, although a situation not unlike that in *N, 2006* was at issue. Possibly the Court preferred not to delimit the freedom of capital, which was being discussed in *Baars, 2000*, from establishment by giving an undue weight to establishment, as the Court had done it in relation to services in *Gebhard, 1995*.

67 In *Stauffer, 2006* the Court reiterated that the concept of establishment was broad (para. 18), but went on to examine the free movement of capital, because the case concerned immovable property that was not actively managed (para. 19).

many, viz. an 'entitlement to successive benefits' (para. 31), else she would not receive benefits under article 71 in 'the most favourable conditions' (para. 33).

Second branch and recognition

Almost three years later the Court came back to the second branch in *Commission v. Italy (dentists), 1995* in the context of Directives 78/686 and 687 on mutual recognition in dentistry, i. e. of secondary legislation essentially implementing the freedom of establishment. This was the very first time that broad interpretation in general was applied in the rules on recognition of professional qualifications. The Court rejected Italy's transitional creation of a special category of dentists. It argued that the derogations from the rule requiring dentists to have one of the formal qualifications in article 2 Directive 78/687, which (the derogations) were laid down in articles 7 and 19 Directive 78/686 and 1(4) Directive 78/687, had to be narrowly construed. In the words of the Court, any derogation from a rule 'intended to guarantee the effectiveness of rights recognized by the Treaty must be interpreted strictly' (para. 23), citing as proof *Bonsignore, 1975*, *Peskeloglou, 1983*, and *Agegate, 1989*. Interestingly, the Court added that 'only derogations expressly provided for in the Treaty or the relevant directives [we]re allowed' (para. 23).

Derogations

In *Commission v. Luxembourg (public service), 1996* the Court next addressed Luxembourg's reservation of entire domains of public service to Luxembourg nationals. In keeping with case-law, the Court rejected Luxembourg's institutional approach to article 48(4) ECT. With regard to primary school teachers the Court in particular confirmed that the 'very strict conditions' for posts to come within the exception in article 48(4) were not fulfilled (para. 33). In a similar vein the Court in *Commission v. Spain (private security guards), 1998* rejected Spain's argument in favour of certain nationality requirements for the provision of private security services. Taking recourse to *Commission v. Greece (vocational schools), 1988*, the Court reiterated that the official authority derogation in articles 55 and 66 Treaty, as a derogation from the fundamental freedom of establishment, was to be interpreted so that it strictly limited the scope to what was necessary for the member states to safeguard their interests (para. 34). The Court then proceeded to refute Spain's arguments as to the connection of the activities of private security guards to the exercise of official authority.

Second branch in social security

In *Bastos Moriana, 1997* the Court dealt with the *Laterza, 1980*/*Gravina, 1980*-supplement in cases when the pension paid was not based on national law alone, but instead on aggregation pursuant to Regulation 1408/71. The Court decided that that supplement-case-law constituted an exception that could not be widened in order to apply in cases of aggregation (para. 19). In those cases the person concerned was not deprived of a benefit due under national law alone.[68] *Stinco, 1998* next[69] concerned the calculation of the theoretical amount under article 46(2)(a) Regulation 1408/71. It was unclear whether an Italian pension supplement had to be taken into account when the theoretical amount was calculated. The Court replied that that was the case in accordance with established case-law. The newly introduced article 10a Regulation 1408/71 addressed only the non-exportability of certain benefits. It did not change the obligation to factor in statutory minimum benefits when determining the theoretical amount. As a derogation from a rule that was intended to improve the situation of migrant workers, article 10a was to be interpreted strictly (para. 16).[70]

Second branch in services

In *Calfa, 1999* the Court essentially applied the expulsion case-law under the freedom of services. Faced with an expulsion for life for drug possession for personal use in Greece, the Court acknowledged that the use of drugs constituted a danger for the society within sense of the public policy derogation. That exception though, 'like all exceptions from a fundamental principle of the Treaty', had to be interpreted restrictively (para. 23). The Court then went on to find that the expulsion requirements were not met, in particular because of the automatism that applied.[71] Still within the freedom of services, the Court applied second branch logic to secondary legislation in *ARD, 1999*. The Court ruled that the gross rather than the net principle was applicable to television ads under Directive 89/552. Restrictions of the provision of services as a fundamental freedom, such as broadcasting services, had to be expressed in clear terms (para. 29); in the absence of unequivocal and clear terms restrictions had to be interpreted restrictively (para. 30). In the case of article 11(3) Directive that meant an interpretation in the 'strictest possible sense' (para. 31).

In *Cura Anlagen, 2002*, faced with certain restrictions of the freedom to provide services in car leasing, the Court reverted to the *Bond, 1988*-formula: 'As an

68 In *Gómez Rodríguez, 1998* the Court confirmed the approach in *Bastos Moriana, 1997* holding essentially that when the age limit for orphan benefits was reached in Spain, a consecutive benefit need not have been granted in Germany, if the benefit was not payable pursuant to German law alone. The Court reached that conclusion without relying on the broad interpretation it applied in *Bastos Moriana, 1997*.

69 In *Spataro, 1996* France had argued a restrictive interpretation of the exception for Belgium in article 69(4) Regulation 1408/71 and Advocate General Lenz had seconded that argument (see paras 20 and 28 of the Opinion). However, while the Court in substance conceded the point – article 69(4) only applied to the requalification for Belgian unemployment benefits by a returning job seeker – the Court did not argue on the basis of broad interpretation.

70 In *Plum, 2000* the Court reasoned that article 14(1)(a) Regulation 1408/71, which determined the legislation applicable in case of posted workers, was an exception from the rule in article 13(2)(a) Regulation 1408/71 that the legislation of the state of employment was applicable (para. 14). Although the Court in the following interpreted article 14(1)(a) narrowly in fact, broad logic under the second branch was not applied explicitly.

71 In *Commission v. Spain (VAT), 1999*, a value added tax case, the Court addressed the public safety derogations *inter alia* in articles 48 and 56 and ruled that '[b]ecause of their limited character, those articles do not lend themselves to a wide interpretation' (para. 21). In this judgment, the Court also voiced the following with regard to a specific provision of a value added tax directive: '[...] it must be observed that this exemption, being an exception, is to be interpreted strictly' (para. 31).

exception to a fundamental principle of the Treaty, Article 46 [of the] Treaty must be interpreted in such a way that its effects are limited to that which is necessary in order to protect the interests which it seeks to safeguard.' (Para. 31) The Court put that formula ahead of the considerations of the restrictions which it then assessed separately.

Further derogations

In *Nazli, 2000* the Court transposed to Decision 1/80 the expulsion case-law as interpreted in *Calfa, 1999*, including the full passage as to the restrictive interpretation of the public policy exception as well as all other exceptions from fundamental freedoms (para. 58).[72] On the basis of the same passage from *Calfa, 1999* the Court in *Commission v. Belgium (security firms), 2000* rejected Belgium's requirement for private security undertakings to be established in Belgium and the justificatory argument based on public policy (para. 28).[73] In *Yiadom, 2000*, it was already mentioned, the first and the second branch of broad interpretation connected (see above).[74]

Second branch connecting with the third in social security, sometimes

In *Jauch, 2001* the second branch of broad interpretation entwined with the 'greatest possible freedom' of the third branch. The Court was asked to qualify the Austrian care allowance, which was listed in the annex to Regulation 1408/71 as a benefit exempted from exportability. The Court began with the 'greatest possible freedom'-passage from *Hoekstra, 1964*, dubbed *Spruyt, 1986*, and continued that, while the Community legislature could derogate from the exportability of benefits, as it did in article 10a Regulation 1408/71 for special non-contributory benefits, such derogations were to be interpreted strictly (paras 20-1) – a fact the Court had already hinted at in *Stinco, 1998*. The Court therefore had the task to examine whether benefits listed in annex IIa fulfilled the requirements of article 4(2a), which were that a benefit was both 'special' and 'non-contributory'. That turned out not to be the case for Austria's care allowance.

In *Skalka, 2004* the Court confirmed the approach elaborated in *Jauch, 2001*, stating that article 10a Regulation 1408/71 was an exception from the principle of exportability which had to be interpreted restrictively (para. 19). The Court omitted third branch interpretation, merely recounting *Jauch, 2001*. In keeping

72 In *Wijsenbeek, 1999* the Commission argued that the freedom of *Union citizens* to move freely within the Union pursuant to article 8a Treaty had to be interpreted broadly, while limitations of that freedom were to be construed narrowly (para. 36). The Court did not include that argument in its decision.

73 In *Commission v. Italy (temporary labour), 2002* the Commission, faced with Italy's requirement for companies to be established in Italy in order to be authorized to provide temporary labour services, argued that the public policy exception was to be interpreted narrowly (para. 13). The Court did not address that argument expressly, but rejected Italy's requirement, because it was a restriction that was not necessary for the protection of workers.

74 In *Commission v. United Kingdom (open skies), 2002* the Commission had argued a narrow interpretation of the public policy derogation (para. 56). The Court did not accept the justification put forward, but did not apply any second branch logic.

with that judgment the Court went on to examine whether the Austrian compensatory supplement to pensions was special and non-contributory. The supplement met both requirements. In *Hosse, 2006* the Court reiterated the exact same approach to articles 4(2a) and 10a, this time not just reiterating the interpretation under the second branch but also that under the third branch (paras 24 and 25). The Court then continued to reject the special nature of the Austrian care allowance at issue. In *Kersbergen, 2006* the Court again scrutinized a benefit under articles 4(2a) and 10a and the case-law, this time the Dutch disability allowance for young people. The Court just cited the second branch interpretation – omitting the 'greatest possible freedom' – and found the benefit to meet both requirements, being special and non-contributory.

Second branch and recognition again

In *Klett, 2002* the Court for the second time applied broad interpretation in recognition of professional qualifications.[75] The Court held that article 19b Directive 78/686 on qualifications in dentistry as a derogation, like the other exceptions in this directive as held in *Commission v. Italy (dentists), 1995*, was to be interpreted strictly (para. 31). A postdoctoral course in dentistry which was merely offered as a transitory measure for those who had already begun it before accession of Austria therefore need not have been opened for doctors from member states other than Austria.

In *Beuttenmüller, 2004* broad interpretation under the second branch was again applied in recognition of qualifications. A German land had argued that the training for teachers in the land consisted of four years of training: three years of courses and 18 months of practical experience through teaching. That would have rendered applicable the derogation from the requirement to recognize foreign qualifications contained in the final subparagraph of article 3 Directive 92/51. However, the Court underpinned the conclusion reached on other grounds by finding that the exception from the general rule that a regulated profession could be exercised in the host state by those qualified to exercise it in the 'home' state had to be interpreted strictly (para. 64). Periods of probationary practice of teachers could therefore not be factored into the four years of post-secondary course in article 3.[76]

More derogations

The connection between the first and the second branch in *Wählergruppe Gemeinsam, 2003* was already discussed (see above). The *Kurz, 2002*-approach

75 On a more general note, in *Luxembourg v. Parliament (lawyer directive), 2000* the Parliament and the Council had argued in favour of a strict interpretation of the procedural rule in article 57(2) Treaty requiring unanimous adoption for Directive 98/5, because it was an exception derogating from the general procedure applicable with regard to article 57(1) (para. 52). The Court did not adopt that argument, but ruled that article 57(1) was the right legal basis.

76 In *Colegio, 2006*, the Court stopped just short of second branch interpretation: dealing with compensatory measures for recognition of qualifications within the purview of Directive 89/48 the Court stated that 'the scope of article 4(1) of the Directive, which expressly authorises compensatory measures, must be restricted to those cases where they are proportionate to the objective pursued.' (Para. 24.).

involving the 'aim and broad logic' and broad interpretation of 'conditions of work' in article 48(2) Treaty namely came together with the narrow interpretation of the public authority derogation, which goes back as far as *Sotgiu, 1974.* In *Commission v. Austria (trade unions), 2004* that connection was maintained (see above). In *Anker, 2003* and *Marina Mercante, 2003* the Court again applied the strict interpretation of the public service derogation in article 39(4) Treaty (paras 60 and 63 and paras 41 and 44, respectively). Consequently, while ship masters had some powers of public authority, they were typically exercised only sporadically, e. g. on small ships. Hence, the application of the derogation was not justified.

Second branch and secondary law

In *Commission v. Italy (direct insurance), 2003* the Court interpreted secondary legislation. Italy had claimed to be entitled to freeze certain insurance premium rates on the basis of the exception from the freedom to set rates contained in the fourth direct insurance Directive 92/49. The Court rejected that claim, because the exception had to be interpreted strictly (para. 34). Italy's approach to price control was not general, binding, and homogenous within the meaning of the exception.

Union citizenship implying a particularly restrictive interpretation of derogations

In *Orfanopoulos, 2004*, the first of seven judgments in 2004 in our domain applying second branch interpretation, the Court was again seized with the expulsion of nationals of other member states. More specifically, the obligation compulsory by law to expel foreigners who had committed certain offences was at issue. The Court first reiterated the need for a broad interpretation of the free movement of workers and a restrictive construction of the corresponding derogations, in particular the public policy derogation (paras 64 and 67). Then the Court added that a 'particularly restrictive interpretation' of derogations from the freedom of workers was called for in the light of the Union citizenship of the person concerned (para. 65). The Court thus added another ring of constraint around derogations from the freedom of workers. The Court then ruled that the duty to expel a national of a member state without that the personal conduct or the concrete danger were taken account of violated article 3 Directive 64/221. Again referring to the narrow interpretation of the public policy derogation, the Court found that the threat posed by the individual had to be present at the time of his or her expulsion (para. 79).

In *Omega, 2004* the public policy derogation was applied again, this time in the context of a restriction of the freedom of services, namely to operate a laserdrome. The Court rehearsed the narrow interpretation required for the public policy derogation from the fundamental freedom of services with the aim of preventing states from determining its scope unilaterally without control by Community institutions (para. 30). Yet the Court did not add the passage from *Or-*

fanopoulos, 2004 as to a particularly restrictive interpretation owing to Union citizenship, preferring to cite *Van Duyn, 1974* and *Bouchereau, 1977*. That can partly be explained by services being at issue, rather than the freedom of workers, which (services) are less directly related to the free movement of Union citizens. As is well known the Court then went on to accept the justification of the restriction by human dignity, in spite of the restrictive interpretation of the public policy derogation endorsed earlier in the judgment.

In *Commission v. Germany (expulsion), 2006*, one out of ten judgments in 2006 that applied second branch broad interpretation, the Court came back to the public policy derogation in the context of the expulsion of nationals of other member states. Faced with several complaints by the Commission, the Court first called again for a narrow interpretation of the public policy derogation as an exception from the fundamental freedom of movement of persons, so as to avoid member states' unilaterally determining its scope (para. 34). But once more the Court omitted the *Orfanopoulos, 2004*-passage requiring a particularly restrictive interpretation by reason of Union citizenship. The Court in the following rejected all the Commission's complaints, bar one relating to the seriousness of the threat, while most complaints centered on the existence of an administrative practice. In *Commission v. Spain (Schengen alert), 2006* the Court found that the Schengen alert violated Directive 64/221, essentially because not sufficient information was made available to verify the threat emanating from a person having rights under the Directive, such as third country national spouses of nationals of member states. Part of the Court's examination was a recital of internal market expulsion case-law, among which was the passage as to the strict interpretation of the public policy derogation (para. 45). The Court again did not recite the *Orfanopoulos, 2004*-passage as to citizenship.

Narrow exception from recognition of driving licences

In *Kapper, 2004* the Court referred to *Beuttenmüller, 2004* to justify that the exception contained in article 8(4) Directive 91/439 on driving licences was to be interpreted strictly (para. 72). The principle required mutual recognition of driving licences, an exception was possible if a driver was subject to a measure affecting his right to drive in the host state. According to the Court, the strict interpretation of an exception from a rule in a directive applied *a fortiori* if the rule intended to enable the exercise of a fundamental freedom (para. 72). Given that, it was not to be refused indefinitely to recognize a licence issued subsequently in another state (para. 76). In *Halbritter, 2006* the Court confirmed that approach under the second branch (para. 26). A member state could therefore not negate the validity of a licence issued in another member state after the blocking period it had ordered had passed. The same second branch logic, moreover, made it impossible to check the ability to drive when a driver officially requested recognition of the licence issued in a state other than the state in which his previous licence had been withdrawn and the blocking period had passed (para. 35). In addition the same logic led the Court in *Kremer, 2006* (para. 28) to decide that the ruling applied *a fortiori* when a blocking period had not been ordered in the first place.

Narrow derogation from freedom of maritime services

In *Commission v. Greece (cabotage), 2004* the Court applied broad interpretation for the first time to maritime services. Article 6(3) Regulation 3577/92 on maritime cabotage extended for Greece the exception in article 6(2) concerning island cabotage in the Mediterranean. Greece applied that exception with regard to the Peloponnese. However, the Court rejected that interpretation. It underpinned its finding by reasoning that that article was a derogation from the general rules on the freedom to provide maritime services within a member state and, consequently, had to be interpreted strictly (para. 48).

Restrictive interpretation of the in-house exception

In *Parking Brixen, 2005* the Court transposed to public service concessions the distinction between the public authority performing certain activities in-house, i. e. via the departments it controlled, and it entrusting those activities to a third party. The Court ruled so on the basis of equal treatment, the freedom of services and establishment, and the consequent obligation to ensure transparency. Those principles did not apply when the public authority controlled the entity performing the activities and when the essential part of the entity's activities were carried out with the controlling authority. However, given that a derogation from the general rules of Community law was at issue, those two criteria, viz. control and an essential part of activities, were to be interpreted restrictively and the burden of proof was to be shouldered by those who relied on them (para. 63). Ultimately, the Court concluded that the necessary degree of control was not given in the case at issue. In *ANAV, 2006* the Court restated the same approach again in a public service concession case. As a derogation from the general rules of Community law, the in-house exception had to be interpreted strictly and the proof was to be brought by those seeking the benefit of the exception (para. 26). The Court left it to the referring court to assess whether the entity at issue fulfilled the requirements of the in-house exception.

Derogations again

In *Servizi ausiliari, 2006* the Court came back to the official authority derogation as applied in *Commission v. Spain (private security guards), 1998*. Having stated that articles 45 and 55 Treaty were derogations from fundamental freedoms the scope of which had to be limited to what was strictly necessary to protect the legitimate interests of the member states (para. 45), the Court found that the derogation did not apply for lack of a connection to official authority. The auxiliary tax services the entities at issue provided did not let them partake in official authority. In *Commission v. Austria (boilers), 2006*, the Court then reiterated the narrow interpretation of the public security derogation as an exception from the freedom of services (para. 25). Partly due to that, the requirement for inspectors of boilers to be established in Austria was not justified.

Finally, in *Honyvem, 2006* the Court applied second branch interpretation to a case concerning Directive 86/653 on commercial agents. The possibility in article 19 for member states to derogate from the indemnification due to the commercial agent pursuant to article 17(2) had to be interpreted strictly: 'the terms used to establish exceptions to a general principle laid down by Community law [...] are to be interpreted strictly' (para. 24). Whether a derogation was favourable to the agent, as article 19 required, therefore either was to be determined essentially when the contract ended or it had to be clear *ex ante* that a derogation never worked to the disadvantage of the agent.

c) Third branch: the greatest possible freedom

The third branch, which is dominated by the *Hoekstra, 1964*-formula of the 'greatest possible freedom', developed only modestly in the age of Maastricht. Broad interpretation within that sense cropped up only in ten judgments during those fifteen years. The first of them was *Paletta, 1992*. In this case, the Court ruled that the employer of a worker who (the worker) had fallen ill could be considered as the 'competent institution' to which article 18 Regulation 547/72 applied with regard to sickness benefits. Referring to *Rindone, 1987*, the Court found this conclusion to be in accordance with the aim of promoting 'the greatest possible freedom of movement for workers, which [wa]s one of the fundamental principles of the Community' (para. 24). It was already discussed that in *Knoch, 1992* the second offspring of the third branch, the 'most favourable conditions' pursuant to *Mouthaan, 1976*, connected with the second branch (see above).

Two branches connecting

In *De Wit, 1993* again a question came up with regard to the transitional mechanism of the Netherlands which had already been at issue in *Spruyt, 1986* and *De Jong, 1986*. As in those judgments, the Court began by reiterating the *Hoekstra, 1964*-formula (para. 16) and combined it with other case-law, notably the *Petroni, 1975*-line of authority. The Court then reasoned that the annex to Regulation 1408/71 aimed at removing obstacles for migrant workers and hence deserved a broad interpretation, thereby connecting the third with the first branch (para. 20). From this the Court concluded that years in employment of a Dutch person of public law which had been completed under the Dutch social security scheme while residing abroad established a link comparable to residence in the Netherlands. Thus, the transitional mechanism had to be applied according to the relevant annex.

In *Stöber and Pereira, 1997*, the first and the third branch connected but the definition in the annex concerning Germany prevailed, as it was mentioned above. In *Jauch, 2001*, the second and the third branch connected and the connection was maintained in *Hosse, 2006*, but not in *Skalka, 2004* and *Kersbergen, 2006*. This was discussed above.

'The most favourable conditions'

Next, in *Van Gestel, 1995*, the Court again resorted to the *Mouthaan, 1976*-formula, i. e. the second offspring of the third branch involving 'the most favourable conditions', this time to justify that article 71(1)(b) Regulation 1408/71 was also applicable to a person who worked and resided in the same state, but to whom the legislation of another state continued to apply owing to an agreement to that effect between the authorities of the two states (para. 20). Then in *Drake, 1994* the question came up whether the amendment of the annex to Regulation 1408/71 which concerned the Netherlands was valid in the light of articles 48 to 51 Treaty given that it had in essence introduced the condition that a person had to have an income during a period to be eligible for benefits under the relevant Dutch scheme. The Court found that a hierarchy between the annexes and the 'regular' provisions of Regulation 1408/71 did not exist. All provisions were adopted pursuant to article 51 Treaty and hence aimed at the greatest possible freedom of movement in the light of which they were to be interpreted (para. 20). The annex, however, was compatible with that purpose and with *Petroni, 1975*-logic. The reason for the person concerned not receiving any benefits was not the use he had made of the freedom to move, but that he had not worked before he became incapacitated.

In *De Laat, 2001* the *Mouthaan, 1976*-offspring again came to prominence. Faced with the question which member state was competent for unemployment benefits when a frontier worker's employment with the same company was reduced from full-time to part-time work, the Court had recourse to *Mouthaan, 1976*, since such a worker, too, deserved unemployment benefits in the most favourable conditions for finding work again (para. 32). Those conditions were, according to the Court, given in the state of employment, since any additional work that was compatible with the existing part-time employment of the frontier worker would in all probability be located in that state. Hence, the state of employment was competent under article 71(1)(a)(i) Regulation 1408/71, unless a frontier worker became fully unemployed and lost all links with that state.

The greatest possible freedom again

Finally,[77] in *Khalil, 2001* the Court went back to *Singer, 1965*, in which the power of the Community legislature to regulate certain social security aspects of the situation of persons who were not migrant workers had been confirmed on the basis of the *Hoekstra, 1964*-formula. Together with the historical context of the adoption of Regulation 1408/71, the *Hoekstra, 1964*-formula in the *Singer,*

77 The Netherlands and the Commission in *Commission v. Netherlands (frontier worker), 2003* argued on the basis of third branch logic (paras 16 and 25), but the Court found that the possibility to export unemployment benefits for three months applied to frontier workers without using any third branch broad interpretation.

1965-judgment served the Court to explain in *Khalil, 2001* why article 51 Treaty had been the right legal basis to regulate the coordination of the social security issues of stateless persons and refugees at the time the Regulation had been adopted (para. 54).[78]

d) Spin – and advance statement of case-law

In which judgments did broad interpretation spin the decision? In the age of Maastricht, spin in general has become a little harder to observe, in particular in the first branch of broad interpretation. This is due to the Court's practice beginning in that period to re-state entire parts of case-law 'in abstract', i. e. before addressing the case at issue. The practice has been in flux, blending in and out of the more traditional structure of judgments. It is therefore not consistently applied. Generally, it can be said that the Court has resorted to this advance statement of case-law in the interest of clarity, in particular when the case-law has reached a certain complexity. It is evident in *Kurz, 2002*, and even more so in *Ninni-Orasche, 2003*, to some extent also in *Kranemann, 2005* and *Mattern and Cikotic, 2006*.

This advance statement of practice should be distinguished from 'empty spin' which had come up before the age of Maastricht. In 'empty spin', an expectation is raised by the use of a specific formula, but it is then not met, because the decision is taken against the grain of the formula. In an advance statement of practice, case-law is stated in a preliminary fashion, in a similar though not quite as detached way as the Court puts the relevant positive law ahead of the consideration of the case at issue. But obviously the two phenomena overlap.

Spin in the first branch: 'worker'

Spin can be observed at work in a series of judgments in which the Court interpreted the worker-notion under the first branch. In *Krid, 1995* the broad interpretation of the personal scope of the Algier Agreement spun the decision towards the obligation to grant the *Giletti, 1987*-allowance, at least to some degree. In *Birden, 1998* spin was a little stronger with regard to the broad interpretation of the scope of Decision 1/80 under the Ankara Agreement, resulting in the qualification of a position in a social programme as 'work'. In *Meeusen, 1999* broad interpretation of the term 'worker' had a clear impact on the classification of the spouse employed by the company of which her husband was the sole shareholder and director as a worker. In *Kurz, 2002* spin by the broad interpretation of the worker-notion was partly obscured by an advance statement of case-law, but it contributed some momentum toward the qualification of an apprentice as a 'worker'. The same is valid for *Ninni-Orasche, 2003* where very short employment was at issue, *Trojani, 2004* which concerned a personal reha-

78 Advocate General Jacobs added the additional argument, based on case-law, that the personal scope of Regulation 3 and article 51 Treaty had traditionally been interpreted widely – which is in fact an argument under the first branch of broad interpretation – concluding that the inclusion of stateless persons and refugees within Regulation 1408/71 was in keeping with the Court's case-law (paras 40-56).

bilitation programme, *Kranemann, 2005* which dealt with a mandatory legal traineeship, and *Mattern and Cikotic, 2006* which concerned professional training as a care assistant.

Spin in other parts of the first branch

Besides the worker-notion spin is discernible in a number of judgments within the first branch. In *Imbernon Martínez, 1995* the broad interpretation of article 73 Regulation 1408/71 was instrumental in including all family members with regard to residence. In *Meints, 1997* the broad interpretation of article 7(2) Regulation 1612/68 was at least partly relevant in reaching the conclusion that the special lay-off benefit at issue constituted a social advantage. In *Yiadom, 2000* the broad interpretation of the free movement of workers – together with the interpretation in their favour – and the corresponding narrow understanding of derogations spun the decision to some extent towards granting the same rights to a temporarily admitted person as to a regularly admitted person.

In *Deliège, 2000* the broad understanding of the scope of the freedom of services was decisive in including the activities of judokas; the spin did not carry through to the end of the judgment, though, since the Court did not find a restriction. The initial spin hence turned 'empty' in a certain sense. In *MRAX, 2002* a broad understanding of article 9 Directive 64/221 made it possible to apply procedural minimum guarantees regardless of whether specific documents could be produced. In *Wählergruppe Gemeinsam, 2003* several instances of broad interpretation under the first and the second branch provided strong spin, resulting in the imperative to include Turkish workers in elections to a body representing workers. In *Oulane, 2005* the broad construction of provisions implementing the free movement of persons was instrumental to admitting other evidence than identity cards or passports to establish identity. The spin also subliminally carried through to the answers to the further questions.

In *Sedef, 2006* the *Kurz, 2002*-formula provided some spin for the decision that the three indents of article 6(1) Decision 1/80 were to be fulfilled progressively. Yet other arguments also fed that decision. The broad interpretation of establishment as a term hardly provided any spin, except in *N, 2006* where it brought the situation at issue within the scope of the freedom of establishment.

Spin in the second branch

In the second branch of broad interpretation, spin was a very regular occurrence in the age of Maastricht. In *Commission v. Italy (dentists), 1995* the decision hinged strongly on the narrow interpretation of the derogation in Directive 78/686 and 78/687, resulting in the rejection of the additional category of dentists Italian law had created. In *Stinco, 1998* the strict interpretation of the derogation from the rule of exportability of benefits in article 10a Regulation 1408/71 was an important factor in the finding that the calculation of the theoretical amount was not altered by that article. In *Commission v. Spain (private security guards), 1998* the narrow interpretation of the official authority derogation partly spun the decision towards the rejection of the nationality requirement. In *Calfa, 1999* a restrictive reading of the public policy derogation played a strong part in the rejection of the automatism in expulsion. In *ARD, 1999* the strict understanding of a derogation in the absence of clear wording in secondary legislation clearly spun the decision towards the gross principle under Directive 89/552. In *Jauch, 2001* the strict reading of article 10a Regulation 1408/71 together with third branch logic clearly enabled the decision of the Court to examine the properties of the benefits at issue despite their listing in the relevant annex. In *Klett, 2002* the narrow interpretation of the exception in article 19b Dir. 78/686, compiled with other arguments, allowed the Court to decide that the course concerned did not have to be accessible to migrant doctors.

In *Cura Anlagen, 2002*, in contrast, spin was very limited. The *Bond, 1988*-formula was part of an advance statement of case-law. Consequently, any possible spin was hidden beneath the other case-law put ahead. Yet some spin can still be discerned in that the Court rejected several of the restrictions of the freedom to provide car leasing services.

In *Anker, 2003* and *Marina Mercante, 2003* the strict reading of the public service derogation was partly responsible for the restriction not being justified when the public powers were exercised only occasionally, notably on small ships. In *Commission v. Italy (direct insurance), 2003* the Court's strict construction of the exception in Directive 92/49 spun the decision against Italy's freezing of insurance premium rates. In *Orfanopoulos, 2004* second branch logic provided strong spin towards the conclusion that the legal duty to expel a person and not to assess the threat at the time the expulsion was executed was unlawful. In *Kapper, 2004* the narrow understanding of an exception was instrumental in the conclusion that the recognition of a driving licence issued in another member state could not be refused indefinitely.

In *Parking Brixen, 2005* there was clear spin. After having applied second branch interpretation, the Court went on to interpret the facts very strictly, making it plain that a large degree of control was needed for the in-house exception to apply – a degree of control that was not given in the case at issue. In *Commission v. Spain (Schengen alert), 2006* spin by second branch logic is hard to detect, as broad interpretation was part of an advance statement of case-law. Yet the logic appears softly to have carried through to the Court's decision that the Schengen alert did not live up to the requirements of the internal market. In *Servizi ausiliari, 2006* interpretation under the second branch spun a minor part of the judgment in which the Court found that the provision of auxiliary tax services was not a part of the exercise of official authority. In *Commission v. Austria (boilers), 2006* the narrow understanding of the public security exception mildly spun the decision to find unlawful the requirement of being established in Austria. Furthermore, in *Honyvem, 2006* second branch logic provided strong spin, leading the Court to the conclusion that a derogation in a contract with an agent always had to work in favour of the agent.

Spin in third branch-combinations

In the third branch of broad interpretation, the *Hoekstra, 1964*-branch, spin continued to be a regular occurrence. *Knoch, 1992*, the first judgment in the third branch in which spin occurred during the age of Maastricht, was particularly interesting, because the connection between the third branch of broad interpretation and the second combined with spin. The 'conditions most favourable'-passage, i. e. the offspring stemming from *Mouthaan, 1976*, first spun the decision in one direction, then second branch-logic in the form of the strict interpretation of article 71 Regulation 1408/71 as a derogation from the rule, provided counter-spin. In spite of that counter-spin, the Court found that Ms Knoch had not had residence in the United Kingdom. The third branch then came back (para. 33) as a justification why consecutive unemployment benefits had to be granted in Germany. From the perspective of the second branch, the judgment can therefore be seen as a rare example of empty spin.

In *De Wit, 1993* spin can also be observed in a combination of two branches of broad interpretation, namely the third and first branch. This time both branches, viz. the 'greatest possible freedom' and a broad interpretation of the annex, provided combined spin for the Court to find that the years of employment completed abroad in the case at issue had to be taken into account under the Dutch transitional mechanism.

Spin in the third branch

In *De Laat, 2001* the *Mouthaan, 1976*-formula, that is the 'most favourable conditions', clearly spun the decision of the Court to find the member state of employment competent for unemployment benefits in case of a reduction of employment. In *Khalil, 2001* the *Hoekstra, 1964*-formula supplemented the interpretation of the historical context of the adoption of Regulation 1408/71. In that function it provided some, albeit limited, spin to the Court's decision that Regulation 1408/71 had been validly adopted on the basis of article 48 and 51 Treaty.

Spin at its clearest in third branch

Finally, the judgment in *Jauch, 2001* created an interesting phenomenon with regard to spin. In *Jauch, 2001* broad interpretation under the third branch, i. e. the 'greatest possible freedom', combined with second branch logic, i. e. the strict understanding of exceptions from the exportability of benefits, to create the necessary spin for the Court to found its power to review the properties of certain benefits, namely the properties of being special and non-contributory, despite their listing in the annex to Regulation 1408/71. The result of the following review was that Austria's care allowance did not meet the requirements.

Skalka, 2004 stands in stark contrast to *Jauch, 2001* in this regard. In *Skalka, 2004* the Court reiterated the power it had founded in *Jauch, 2001* to review the properties of benefits in spite of the listing in the annex, citing the strict interpretation of the exception from exportability, while *omitting* the 'greatest possible freedom'. The benefit at issue, Austria's special supplement, was then found to be both 'special' and 'non-contributory' and hence exempted from exportability.

Conversely, *Hosse, 2006* was again in harmony with *Jauch, 2001*. First, the Court rehearsed both the strict interpretation of the exception from exportability and the 'greatest possible freedom'. Owing to the spin thus created, the Court then found the benefit at stake, an Austrian care allowance, not to meet the requirement of being 'special' to be exempted from exportability. Hence, the allowance was exportable.

Again in stark contrast to *Hosse, 2006* – and thus *Jauch, 2001* – in *Kersbergen, 2006* the Court only recounted second branch logic with the strict understanding of the exception from exportability, but left aside 'the greatest possible freedom'. It then considered the benefit at issue, the Dutch disability allowance for young people, to be exempted from exportability, because it was both 'special' and 'non-contributory'. To sum it up, the Court seemingly added the 'greatest possible freedom' to the narrow understanding of the exception from exportability if – and only if – the benefit concerned was to be exportable (*Jauch, 2001* and *Hosse, 2006*); in contrast, the Court left aside the 'greatest possible freedom', citing merely the strict interpretation of the exception, when the benefit at stake was *not* to be exportable (*Skalka, 2004* and *Kersbergen, 2006*). It appears unlikely that this was a coincidence.

The logical consequence would have to be that *Skalka, 2004* and *Kersbergen, 2006* were cases of empty spin. This indeed is so, but only to a limited extent. In both cases the broad interpretation pursuant to the second branch was part of a sort of an advance statement of case-law, which preceded the examination of the properties of the benefits. Hence, the contrast between the spin created in the advance statement and the following decision against the direction of that spin was softened in both judgments.

Empty spin

Apart from this occurrence, 'empty spin' remained very rare in the age of Maastricht. The empty spin in the second branch in *Knoch, 1992* was already mentioned above. It was the first time that empty spin occurred to some extent in the second branch of broad interpretation. *Stöber and Pereira, 1997* was a case of empty spin only on the face of it. The Court cited the 'greatest possible freedom' based on *Hoekstra, 1964* together with broad interpretation which created spin, but then gave preference to the definition of self-employed persons in the annex which concerned Germany, thus counteracting the spin. However, the 'greatest possible freedom' ultimately prevailed, if only from a substantive point of view, owing to non-discrimination, which struck down the residence requirement. Non-discrimination, therefore, in a sense restored the power of the spin.

In only two more cases empty spin appeared during the age of Maastricht, namely *Collins, 2004* and *Omega, 2004*. In the first question of *Collins, 2004* the broad notion of a 'worker' seemed to create momentum, but the Court decided against that momentum right away. For Mr Collins the connection with the labour market had been lost by reason of the time that had passed. The following questions then were disconnected from the first. From the perspective of empty spin, *Collins, 2004* therefore belongs in the same row as *Bettray, 1989*. Finally, in *Omega, 2004* the Court first advised a strict interpretation of the public policy derogation from the freedom of services, creating certain spin, but then decided against its own advice that Germany had enough leeway to outlaw simulated killing games by reason of the protection of human dignity. *Omega, 2004*, thus, was the first case of empty spin in the free movement of services.

e) Some conclusions from the period

Broad interpretation evolved in all three branches during the age of Maastricht, albeit to varying extents. In the first branch comprising broad notions as such, we had noted the development in the free movement of workers from the broad interpretation of terms as such, notably in *Levin, 1982*, towards the broad interpretation of the freedom itself, in particular from *Kempf, 1986* and *Lebon, 1987*, during the previous period leading up to the 'Maastricht moment'. It has further evolved during the age of Maastricht, with a culmination in the expansive ruling in *Yiadom, 2000* positing an interpretation in favour of the migrant worker. Yet that interpretation was put forward only with regard to the procedural rights of migrant workers.

It is interesting to see in that context that during the age of Maastricht this development in the free movement of workers was retraced in the other freedoms. The delay in this retracing is due to the case-law on those freedoms taking off only in the late 1980s. In the free movement of services, we have already noted the interpretation of a derogation so that its effects were limited to what was necessary, rather than *strictly* necessary, in *Bond, 1988*. After this modest beginning, the Court became more assertive in the age of Maastricht in *Deliège, 2000* interpreting more generally the terms defining the scope of the freedom of services broadly. In *Oulane, 2005* the Court then continued even more expansively, in the context of receiving services, that provisions enshrining the free movement of persons were to be construed broadly. The second branch underpinned this evolution in services in *Calfa, 1999* where the public policy derogation was said not to be susceptible of a broad interpretation, and in *ARD, 1999* where the Court advocated a strict interpretation of exceptions from the freedom of services as laid down in secondary legislation, indeed an interpretation in the 'strictest possible sense' (para. 31). Again the second branch complemented the first in a specific development, which is a testimony of their common root of broad interpretation. *Calfa, 1999* in addition, in a certain sense, harmonised the second branch across the various freedoms by holding that all exceptions from a fundamental principle of the Treaty had to be interpreted restrictively.[79]

In the freedom of establishment, *Gebhard, 1995* certainly triggered a larger evolution in establishment. It also initiated the concept of establishment as being

79 Yet the Court reverted to the relatively timid *Bond, 1988*-approach in *Cura Anlagen, 2002*.

a very broad one, literally. In the same year, the Court in *Commission v. Italy (dentists), 1995* had already propounded under the second branch that any derogation from a rule guaranteeing Treaty rights was subject to a strict interpretation, and even limited the derogations to those expressly stated. Yet in the age of Maastricht clear textual evidence of a broad interpretation of the freedom of establishment *as such* was missing – that is, evidence which would be comparable to the *Kempf, 1986*, *Lebon, 1987*, *Yiadom, 2000*-line of authority for workers or to the *Calfa, 1999*, *Deliège, 2000*, *Oulane, 2005*-line for services. That observation also applies to Union citizenship. While in *Zhu and Chen, 2004* Union citizenship was at issue, the Court mostly interpreted Directive 90/364 and in that context underpinned its finding by the statement that provisions laying down a fundamental principle like the free movement of persons were to be interpreted broadly. Even before that judgment, *Orfanopoulos, 2004* had put forward that Union citizenship called for a 'particularly restrictive interpretation' of derogations from the worker freedom. Undoubtedly though, at least a nucleus of a more general broad interpretation of Union citizenship was obviously there.

In the second branch comprising narrow exceptions from rules, one point attracts attention. In both *Commission v. Italy (dentists), 1995* and *ARD, 1999* the Court combined second branch-logic with the explicitness of the exception. Both cases concerned second branch interpretation in secondary legislation. In *Commission v. Italy (dentists), 1995* the Court admitted 'only derogations expressly provided for in the Treaty or the relevant directives' (para. 23); in *ARD, 1999* the Court required restrictions of the freedom of services to be expressed in unequivocal and clear terms, else a restrictive interpretation was to be applied. This may have appeared like the beginning of a new approach in case-law, urging not just a restrictive interpretation of exceptions from rules in secondary legislation but in addition requiring them to be clear, an approach that could potentially even replace second branch-logic. However, the ensuing case-law in the second branch failed to confirm that approach. The following cases – *Klett, 2002*; *Commission v. Italy (direct insurance), 2003*; *Beuttenmüller, 2004*; *Kapper, 2004*; *Halbritter, 2006*; *Commission v. Greece (cabotage), 2004*; and *Honyvem, 2006* – all are at odds with the idea of a new beginning.

The rift we observed for the time before the age of Maastricht between the second branch concerning narrow exceptions, which (the branch) had never been applied in social security judgments, and the third branch relying on the greatest possible freedom, which (the branch) had been confined to social security, was finally bridged in the age of Maastricht. *Jauch, 2001* applied second branch logic in social security, notably to the new article 10a Regulation 1408/71. Interestingly, the Court accomplished this transposition by taking recourse to third branch logic. The combination of the second and the third branch in *Jauch, 2001* is not entirely surprising, given the disruptive nature of the judgment. The judgments following after *Jauch, 2001* further rooted the second branch in social security. Yet it remained confined to the context of article 10a Regulation 1408/71.

Apart from that, it is noteworthy that the Court strongly relied on second branch interpretation when it made the requirement of transparency prosper in public procurement outside the relevant directives, notably for the in-house exception beginning in *Parking Brixen, 2005*. This again can be seen as indicative of the disruptive nature of this line of judgments.

Besides those developments in the age of Maastricht we also note that some formulas have phased out. In the first branch, the *Bozzone, 1977*-formula describing 'legislation of a member state' in Regulation 1408/71 as being 'remarkable for its breadth' is one such phrase. It had been used repeatedly before the age of Maastricht, but then did not crop up again. Possibly, this is due to the term having been clarified early on and thus no longer being in need of further explanation. The *Frilli, 1972*-formula involving benefits 'in the widest sense' under Regulation 1408/71 was no longer used, either, perhaps because the distinction between social security and social assistance had undergone legislative transformation. In the third branch, the first offspring brought into being in *Heinze, 1972*, i. e. 'the most favourable conditions' for achieving the free movement of workers, also went out of use during the age of Maastricht.

For the *power* of the interpretive formulas of the three branches – i. e. their spin – it is again hard to come to general conclusions. Their power is best understood by reading the above passages concerning spin. Generally, it can be said though that the practice of the Court to state case-law in advance, that is to say before speaking to the facts of the case – a practice begun during the age of Maastricht – made spin harder to detect. When a formula is grouped together with other formulas and case-law before the law is applied to the facts, it becomes harder to say which formula had how much impact. This advance statement of case-law is not identical to the phenomenon of empty spin which was observed first some time before the age of Maastricht. An advance statement of case-law does not raise any expectations, or at least raises them to a lower level.

Apart from that, the analysis of spin revealed for all three branches of broad interpretation – broad notions, narrow exceptions, and the greatest possible freedom – that the formulas were powerful. In each branch the formulas frequently, though not always, spun decisions. While the analysis above should be considered for the more elaborate details, two more points are noteworthy. First, empty spin occurred for the first time in freedom of services during the age of Maastricht. Second, the clearest manifestation of the spin a formula of broad interpretation can exert is found in the four cases *Jauch, 2001*, *Skalka, 2004*, *Hosse, 2006*, *Kersbergen, 2006*. A holistic perspective on these four cases reveals that the Court added 'the greatest possible freedom' to the narrow understanding of an exception from the exportability of certain benefits if – and only if – the Court wanted the benefit concerned to be exportable. The spin, the power of formulas has never come clearer than this.

4 The present

Finally, we come to the last seven years, a period which is obviously best referred to as 'the present'. Let us examine how broad interpretation has fared in the present, beginning with the first branch, i. e. broad interpretation of notions as such, and moving along to the second and third branch. Again, expect broad interpretation to grow commensurately with the case-law having increased considerably in our domain.

a) *First branch: broad notions – 'worker'*

The broad interpretation of the worker-notion, one aspect of the first branch of broad interpretation, has been strongly consolidated in the present. *El Youssfi, 2007* was the first out of ten judgment in which the notion of a 'worker' played a role. In the context of the Association Agreement with Morocco it was questionable whether Ms Youssfi could claim rights. The Court stated that the personal scope of article 65(1) Agreement, i. e. the notion of a worker, had to be understood broadly (para. 64). The Court left it to the national court to assess the particulars, but indicated that the person concerned possibly was entitled to claim rights herself as a former worker, or owing to her late husband having been or her descendants being workers.

Next, in *Alevizos, 2007* the Court reiterated that the worker-notion in article 39 Treaty was not to be construed narrowly (para. 67). The Court then elaborated further case-law, among which second branch case-law to the effect of the public service exception not being applicable (para. 69), and found that Mr Alevizos enjoyed the rights as a worker because he had been posted with the North Atlantic Treaty Organization. In *Raccanelli, 2008*, the Court re-stated the broad interpretation of the notion as part of the definition of a 'worker' (para. 33), but then left it to the national court to assess whether a doctoral student who was receiving a grant under a contract was to be qualified as a worker fulfilling the criteria of subordination and remuneration. In *Petersen, 2008* the Court recalled the broad understanding of the worker-notion to justify why a person who was receiving an advance benefit akin to an unemployment benefit in Austria still qualified as a worker for the purposes of the free movement of workers (para. 45). The Court then went on to strike down the residence clause contained in Austrian law by reason of non-discrimination.

In *Vatsouras, 2009* the broad understanding of who was a worker was part of a passage in which the Court reminded the national court that it had to assess carefully and in keeping with case-law whether the persons concerned were 'workers' under article 39 Treaty, despite their short and limited economic activity (para. 26). Next, in *Von Chamier-Glisczinski, 2009* the Court again reiterated the broad interpretation of the term 'worker' right before stating the definition of the term (para. 69). The facts remained inconclusive, though, as to whether the spouse of the person in care had in fact sought work in the host state. With that being unclear the Court refused to apply the free movement of workers. In *Genc, 2010* the Court then applied broad interpretation within the context of the Ankara Agreement, to which the free movement of workers was to be transposed so far as possible. The broad understanding and the definition of a worker (para. 19) was applied together with internal market case-law to the effect that very limited work was still capable of conferring the status of a worker. In *Van Delft, 2010* the Court also had recourse to broad interpretation along with the worker definition (para. 89). However, the Court found that the freedom of workers was inapplicable, because the persons concerned had all moved residence after they had stopped working. In *Commission v. Netherlands (portable funding), 2012* the broad understanding of who was a worker served the Court to reject the Netherlands' argument that a risk existed that persons resident abroad abusively claimed portable funding in the Netherlands to finance studies abroad (para. 68). Furthermore, in *L.N., 2013* the Court, after having argued on the basis of second branch logic (see below), relied on the broad interpretation of 'worker' (para. 39) to explain why a person who had come to Denmark and worked there, while knowing that he would begin a course of studies in Denmark, still was capable of qualifying as a worker.

Other broad notions

Broad interpretation in general also came to be applied outside the context of the worker-notion in the present, though in a relatively limited number of cases. In *Jia, 2007* the Court first restated *Lebon, 1987* as to the concept of 'dependence' of a relative on a self-employed person. In that context the Court recalled that the free movement of persons, one of the foundations of the Community, was to be understood broadly (para. 36). That led the Court to conclude that the situation of dependence could exist in the state of origin or the state from which the relative concerned had come.

In *Eind, 2007* the Court refused to interpret secondary legislation on movement and residence of migrant workers restrictively (para. 43). Partly as a result of that refusal, the daughter of a migrant worker returning to his home state who (the daughter) was a third country national could not lawfully be refused a right of residence, merely because she could not have benefitted from such a right before her father had moved to work in another member state. In *Commission v. Netherlands (automatic expulsion), 2007* the Court argued that the safeguards in Directive 64/221 required a broad interpretation (para. 35). From that the Court concluded that the safeguards had to be available even to those who were not lawfully resident in the host state. (As to the broad interpretation under the second branch see below.)

In *Geven, 2007*, the Court came back to article 7(2) Regulation 1612/68. The term 'social advantages' in that article was not to be interpreted restrictively (para. 12). As had been held in *Martínez Sala, 1998*, it included the German child-raising allowance.[80] Next, in *Derin, 2007* the Court was seized with the question of treatment of Turkish nationals which was more favourable under the Ankara Agreement than the treatment Union citizens enjoyed under Union law. In that context, the Court restated *Wählergruppe Gemeinsam, 2003* as part of an advance statement of case-law, including the declaration made in that case that the aim and broad logic of Decision 1/80 was the gradual integration in the host state (para. 53).

In *Metock, 2008* the Court then addressed the question whether the family consisting of a Union citizen and a third country national had had to be founded before the citizen's exercise of the right to free movement or whether it was sufficient when the founding of the family had occurred *after* the citizen's movement for the provisions on family reunification pursuant to the Union citizenship Directive 2004/38 to apply. The Court answered sweepingly that the provisions of the citizenship Directive were not to be interpreted restrictively and be deprived of their effectiveness (para. 84). Hence it was sufficient for the family to have been founded after the citizen had moved to the host state. Owing to the same logic it was irrelevant whether the third country national had entered the host state before or after the Union citizen (para. 93).[81]

In *Bekleyen, 2010* the Court again applied broad interpretation, this time within the context of the Ankara Agreement. The Court re-stated what had already been established in *Akman, 1998*, namely that article 7(2) Decision 1/80 was not to be interpreted restrictively (para. 23). Hence, a need for temporal concomitance between the worker's presence in the host state and the child beginning vocational training there could not be read into that article. The result was an autonomous right of the child to access the employment market in the host state. In *Teixeira, 2010* and in *Ibrahim, 2010* the question came up whether article 12 Regulation 1612/68 required the primary carer of a child in education to have sufficient resources as a condition for the right of residence based on that article. The Court had recourse to *Baumbast, 2002* where it had ruled that article 12 was not to be interpreted restrictively (para. 67 and para. 52, respective-

80 Interestingly, in a judgment of the same day, *Hartmann, 2007*, which also dealt with article 7(2) Regulation 1612/68 in a constellation that was only slightly different, the Court did not mention the broad interpretation of that article at all.

81 In *Chakroun, 2010* the Court transposed broad interpretation to the context of Directive 2003/86 on family reunification by third country nationals on the basis of *Metock, 2008*. The Court refused to interpret the provisions of this Directive restrictively, too (para. 64). This led to the conclusion that for the purpose of applying the income requirement in article 7(1)(c) Directive 2003/86 a distinction was not to be drawn based on when the family concerned had been constituted. The Court also applied some broad interpretation akin to second branch logic in para. 43, ruling that article 7(1)(c) was to be interpreted strictly, because the general rule was that family reunification was to be authorized. That interpretation was put forward based on effectiveness and without any reference to internal market law. On a different note, in *Bosmann, 2008* the national court enquired whether article 13(2)(a) Regulation 1408/71 had to be interpreted restrictively (para. 13). The Court did not formulate its answer in terms of broad or narrow interpretation, but ruled that that article did not preclude German legislation from applying in addition to the legislation of the state of employment, thus essentially validating the narrow interpretation the national Court had alluded to. Moreover, the Court also sanctioned a restrictive interpretation of article 10(1)(a) Regulation 574/72 at which the referring Court had hinted, too (para. 13). But again the Court refrained from using any terms of broad interpretation.

ly). Based on that argument the Court rejected the need for self-sufficiency under article 12 Regulation 1612/68.

In *Lassal, 2010* the Court drew on the broad interpretation of the provisions of Directive 2004/38 posited in *Metock, 2008* (para. 31). Given that broad interpretation, it did not matter whether the five year-period of residence required for the right to permanent residence to arise had been completed before the date for transposition of the Directive or after.

Very broad establishment

The 'very broad' interpretation of the concept of establishment put forward in *Gebhard, 1995* for the first time has become a regular occurrence in the present. In *Commission v. Austria (self-employment), 2008* the Court made reference to that broad concept (para. 24) to find that self-employed workers in Austria came within the freedom of establishment in spite of Austria's claim that those self-employed persons circumvented the limitations of the free movement of workers applicable to the new member states. (As to the broad interpretation under the second branch applied in this case see below.)[82] In *Filipiak, 2009* the Court again reiterated that 'very broad' understanding of establishment (para. 52). However, the Court could not rule out that the freedom of services was applicable at the same time, because it was unclear whether the person concerned, in addition to being part of a partnership, also provided services. The Court therefore proceeded to examine both freedoms. In *Stoß, 2010* and *Winner Wetten, 2010* the Court proceeded in the same way, after having referred to the broad concept of establishment (para. 59 and 46, respectively). It was for the national court to decide which freedom, freedom of services or freedom of establishment, was in fact applicable. The Court then went on to examine both freedoms.

In *Attanasio, 2010* the Court again delimited the freedom of establishment from the freedom of services. It began by reiterating the very broad concept of establishment (para. 36). In the following the Court analysed only the freedom of establishment, because the operation of a gas station implied a stable and continuous basis. In *Bejan, 2010*, the Court proceeded in exactly the same way as in *Attanasio, 2010*, after having made reference to the very broad concept of establishment (para. 41). The Court then again examined exclusively the freedom of establishment, as the establishment in Romania of an insurer established in another member state was concerned. In contrast, in *Schmelz, 2010* the Court rehearsed the very broad concept of establishment (para. 37), but found that the freedom of services was to be applied exclusively, because the apartment Ms Schmelz owned in Austria was not actively managed.

82 *Elisa, 2007* was a free movement of capital case in which the Court distinguished that freedom from the freedom of establishment. It referred to the broad concept of establishment (para. 63), but found that free movement of capital applied, because the real estate concerned typically was not actively managed. In a similar vein, the Court in *Glaxo, 2009* found, after having declared the concept of establishment as being very broad (para. 46), that the freedom of capital was applicable, in essence because the capital aspects prevailed in the case at issue.

In *Commission v. Austria (notaries), 2011* the Court recited the very broad concept of establishment again (para. 77) to find that the freedom of establishment applied to notaries.[83] (For the broad interpretation under the second branch in the notaries-cases, see below.) Finally, in *A Oy, 2012* the Court transposed the broad interpretation of the concept of establishment to the freedom of establishment under the European Economic Area Agreement. The Court did not cite the broad concept to justify the application of the freedom of establishment rather than the freedom of capital to an exchange of shares involving a Norwegian company; instead, the Court referred to it when explaining the meaning of the freedom of establishment as it was to be transposed to the European Economic Area.

b) Second branch: narrow exceptions from rules

The second branch of broad interpretation – understanding the rule broadly and the exception narrowly – has grown disproportionately in the present. A long series of judgments had recourse to second branch logic. In the year 2007 alone, nine judgments were relevant under the second branch. First, in *Perez Naranjo, 2007* the Court put forward the strict interpretation of the exception in articles 4(2)a and 10a Regulation 1408/71 (para. 29), thus tying in with the *Jauch, 2001*-line. The Court abstained from mentioning third branch logic, though, and held article 10a applicable after a thorough examination of the properties of the French supplementary allowance at issue. As a result, the benefit was not any longer exportable. *Commission v. France (supplementary allowance), 1990* was thus overruled as a consequence of the amendments in articles 4(2)a and 10a Regulation 1408/71.

Derogations, connecting with first branch

Next, in *Commission v. Netherlands (automatic expulsion), 2007* the Court returned to the public policy exception, confirming that it was to be interpreted strictly for it derogated from the fundamental freedom of movement. Its scope was not to be determined unilaterally by a member state (para. 42). The Court then ruled that an automatism in expulsion was not entirely excluded by the Dutch legislation. That legislation was therefore not in accordance with Directive 64/221. In this judgment, broad interpretation under the first branch, i. e. the broad understanding of the safeguards contained in Directive 64/221 (see above) therefore was combined with second branch logic to reach the conclusion that the Netherlands had infringed Union law. In *Polat, 2007* the Court applied the very same passage as to the strict view of the public policy derogation within the context of the Ankara Agreement, namely article 14(1) Decision 1/80 (para. 33). In combination with other expulsion case-law the Court then found that the

83 In the other notaries-judgements, the very broad concept of establishment was applied in the same way: *Commission v. Belgium (notaries), 2011*, para. 78; *Commission v. France (notaries), 2011*, para. 68; *Commission v. Luxembourg (notaries), 2011*, para. 78; *Commission v. Germany (notaries), 2011*, para. 79; *Commission v. Greece (notaries), 2011*, para. 70; and *Commission v. Netherlands (notaries), 2011*, para. 51.

existence of several minor offences as such was irrelevant for the prospects of the offender committing other crimes.

Second branch and posted workers

In *Commission v. Germany (posted workers), 2007* the Court applied second branch interpretation within the context of the freedom of services, more specifically, the posting of workers. The Court found that the requirement imposed exclusively on foreign employment agencies to communicate any change of the place where the posted workers worked was discriminatory. As such it could only be justified by the express grounds contained in article 46 Treaty, which had to be interpreted strictly (para. 86). None of those express grounds had been argued. The same argument prevailed in *Laval, 2007*. In essence, the leaving out of account of foreign collective agreements in Swedish law amounted to discrimination in *Laval, 2007*. According to the Court, that discrimination was not justified, for the grounds argued did not come within the scope of those mentioned by article 46 Treaty, which had to be interpreted strictly (para. 117).

Further narrow derogations

In *Commission v. Austria (bio inspections), 2007* and *Commission v. Germany (bio inspections), 2007* the Court again, after *Servizi ausiliari, 2006*, reiterated that the official authority derogation was to be limited to what was strictly necessary to protect the legitimate interests of the member states (paras 35 and 44, paras 37 and 46, respectively). Accordingly, the Court found, after extensive examination of the powers of the private entities charged with tasks pursuant to Regulation 2092/91, that their connection to the exercise of official authority was not sufficient to justify application of the exception. In *Commission v. Italy (private security), 2007* the public order exception was said to be subject to a narrow interpretation, '[l]ike all derogations from a fundamental principle of the Treaty' (para. 49). Consequently the threat posed by foreign private security undertakings employing guards who had not sworn allegiance to the Italian Republic was not such as to warrant application of the exception. Interestingly, in that judgment the Court did not refer to a narrow construal of the official authority derogation when it held that the derogation did not apply for lack of a direct connection to the official authority.[84]

---

84 In *Jundt, 2007* one party had argued that the justificatory ground of the cohesion of the tax system, i. e. the *Bachmann, 1992*-ground, was subject to a strict interpretation (para. 46). The Court acceded to that argument in substance, but failed to frame its answer in terms of second branch logic. The Court ruled that the direct link required was missing between the contribution of taxpayers in general by reason of the tax they paid and the exemption from tax of expense allowances paid by universities (para. 69). Apart from that, the Court in that judgment did not expressly apply second branch logic to the official authority derogation, either. Instead, the Court reasoned on the basis of an abbreviated formula which in substance also amounted to a strict interpretation: '[T]hat derogation must, however, be restricted to activities which in themselves are directly and specifically connected with the exercise of official authority [...]' (para. 37).

Strict interpretation of non-exportability

In *Habelt, 2007* the Court next modified the consideration put forward in *Hosse, 2006*. In *Hosse, 2006* the Court had ruled that the Community legislature could validly derogate from the exportability of benefits, but that such derogations were subject to strict interpretation. In *Habelt, 2007*, the Court ruled along the same lines for the exclusion of benefits for victims of war from the scope of the Regulation in article 4(4). While the Community legislature could validly exclude certain benefits from the scope of the Regulation, such exclusions, like article 4(4), had to be interpreted strictly (para. 65).[85] Accordingly, that article did not apply to Germany's benefit of taking account of certain periods of contribution completed during the Third Reich. The benefit was granted not because of the war, but because contributions had been paid under German legislation. Hence, Regulation 1408/71 applied to the benefit at issue. With the same argument the Court included within the scope of Regulation 1408/71 the benefit that certain period completed under a foreign state's social security scheme were taken account of under German law (para. 108).[86]

Narrow derogations again

In the year 2008, broad interpretation under the second branch was again applied in numerous cases. In *Commission v. Luxembourg (posted workers), 2008* the Court dealt with Luxembourg's qualification of various national provisions as public policy under article 3(10) Directive 96/71, thus rendering them applicable to workers posted to Luxembourg. The Court answered that public policy provisions derogated from the free movement of services. As such they were to be interpreted strictly. Their scope was not to be determined unilaterally by a member state (para. 30). More specifically, the derogation in article 3(10) was an exception from the exhaustive list in article 3(1) that enumerated matters in which the host state could impose its law on the undertaking posting workers. That exception, hence, had to be construed strictly (para. 31). The Court then proceeded to reject every single obligation Luxembourg law had imposed under the heading of public policy. The Court moreover repeated the same second branch logic (in paras 49 and 50) when it rejected Luxembourg's automatic adjustment of remuneration.

In *Jipa, 2008* the Court repeated the imperative to interpret the public policy and security derogations from the free movement of persons restrictively in order to avoid that the member states defined their scope unilaterally (para. 23). That and arguments based on case-law led the Court to the conclusion that only the situation in the state ordering a measure against a person was decisive. It was that situation which determined whether the threat emanating from a person

85 The Court's reference to paragraph 37 of *Hosse, 2006* was in all likelihood meant to refer to paragraph 25.

86 In *Habelt, 2007*, the Court also invalidated the exception from exportability contained in an annex to Regulation 1408/71 for certain German benefits. In doing so, the Court did not apply any second branch broad interpretation.

was such as to justify a measure against him, rather than the situation in another state. In *Commission v. Italy (ship officers), 2008* the Court applied *Marina Mercante, 2003* and *Anker, 2003* to Italy's requirement that ship captains be of Italian nationality. The Court referred to the strict interpretation of the public service derogation from free movement in article 39(4) Treaty (para. 15). In contrast, in *Commission v. France (ship officers), 2008*, a decision of the same date with the same content, the Court did not refer to second branch logic. Later on, *Commission v. Greece (ship officers), 2009* applied the very same logic as *Commission v. Italy (ship officers), 2008* (para. 29).

In *Commission v. Austria (self-employment), 2008*, in which the Court had already applied interpretation under the first branch as to the broad concept of establishment, the Court also stated that the public policy derogation from free movement was subject to a narrow interpretation (para. 35), thus bringing together the first and the second branch, though only very loosely. Together with a lack of a serious, present threat this made the Court reject Austria's argument in favour of a restriction of the freedom of establishment because of a vaguely alleged phenomenon of bogus self-employment.

Narrow exceptions from recognition of driving licences

In a series of judgments the Court in 2008 came back to the strict interpretation of the exception from mutual recognition of driving licences in case of sanctions, which (the strict interpretation) had first been advanced in *Kapper, 2004*. In *Wiedemann, 2008* and *Zerche, 2008* that strict interpretation was routinely reiterated as part of a block of case-law (paras 60 and 57, respectively). The Court ultimately concluded that recognition need not have been granted when the residence requirement had not been satisfied. In *Möginger, 2008* the Court then confirmed that a licence issued abroad need not have been recognized when it had been issued during the blocking period a state had ordered. This was valid even if the licence had only been *used* after the blocking period had expired. The Court came to that conclusion after having re-cited the second branch logic applied in the preceding cases (para. 37). In *Weber, 2008*, in turn, the Court again rehearsed the same second branch logic (para. 29). It then found that the authorities did not have to recognize a licence which was issued abroad while the authorities were in the course of adopting sanctions.

The second branch logic with regard to the withdrawal of driving licences was continued in 2009 in *Schwarz, 2009*. In that case the Court routinely recapitulated the restrictive interpretation of the exception from mutual recognition (para. 84). Yet the Court sanctioned the refusal to recognize the Austrian licence at stake, because it had been issued before the German licence which had been withdrawn and a test of the fitness to drive had not been passed after the withdrawal.

In *Wierer, 2009* the Court then slightly modified and expanded broad interpretation. Before this decision, second branch logic had always been applied with regard to the refusal to recognize a driving licence issued abroad in the light of a domestic withdrawal of a licence, in particular pursuant to article 8(4) Regulation 91/439. In *Wierer, 2009* the Court then applied second branch interpretation to the authorization established in *Wiedemann, 2008* and *Zerche, 2008* to take exception from mutual recognition if it was evident from the foreign licence itself or other irrefutable evidence stemming from the state that had issued the licence that the residence condition had been disregarded. That exception, according to the Court, was not to be understood broadly, else mutual recognition became nugatory (para. 52). Hence, the sources indicating that the residence requirement had been disregarded were exhaustively enumerated in *Wiedemann, 2008* and *Zerche, 2008*.

Later on, in *Scheffler, 2010*, the Court again rehearsed the narrow interpretation of the exception from mutual recognition of driving licences (paras 62-3), but ultimately left it to the national court to decide whether a report issued after a new licence had been granted abroad – a report that related to conduct having taken place before the new licence was issued abroad – cast doubt on the present fitness of the driver concerned to drive. The Court only indicated that that appeared not to have been the case.

Exception from the free choice of one's lawyer

In *Eschig, 2009* the Court next applied second branch interpretation to Directive 87/344 on legal expenses insurance. The Court ruled that the authorization in article 5 to take exception from the rule of free choice of one's legal representative was subject to narrow interpretation and hence could not be applied by analogy (para. 59). Therefore, the exception was not applicable outside the specific cases to which it applied pursuant to the wording of the article, i. e. cases arising from the use of road vehicles.

Derogations, again

In *Commission v. Portugal (vehicle inspection), 2009* the public authority exception pursuant to article 45 Treaty was again applied. The Court stated the usual second branch approach limiting the derogation from the freedom to what was strictly necessary to protect the legitimate interests of the member states (para. 34). However, before that, the Court made it clear that the public authority derogation was applicable not just to discriminatory measures, but also to mere restrictions (para. 33).[87] After having examined the facts the Court then rejected application of the derogation for lack of a direct connection between the bodies taking roadworthiness tests for vehicles and official authority.[88]

87 On the face of it, this second point (in para. 33) could be considered a refusal by the Court to apply the exception restrictively. Yet another perspective seems equally valid, namely that the Court in essence applied *a maiore ad minus*-logic in ruling that measures which were less restrictive of the freedom – mere restrictions – were susceptible to justification on an equal level as more restrictive measures, viz. discriminatory measures.

88 In a series of cases involving imported military goods, the Court ruled that the public safety derogations pursuant to *inter alia* articles 39, 46, and 58 Treaty, were not to be read so as to remove public security issues from the scope of Community law. In addition, articles 296 and 297 Treaty, as derogations from fundamental freedoms, were to be interpreted restrictively (*Commission v. Finland (mili-*

In *Commission v. Germany (posted workers), 2010* the Court applied the derogations in article 46 Treaty relating to public policy, security, and health in the same way as in *Commission v. Germany (posted workers), 2007* and *Laval, 2007*. The grounds mentioned were the only derogations that could lawfully be relied upon to justify discriminatory measures and they (the derogations) had to be interpreted strictly (para. 48). The arguments Germany put forward in justification of the refusal to extend the benefits of the Germano-Polish convention to undertakings established in other member states did not come within the scope of those express derogations. Hence, they were inadmissible.

Further second branch interpretation

After that, two more judgments applied broad interpretation under the second branch in secondary legislation. In *Commission v. Poland (broadband internet), 2010* article 27 Framework Directive 2002/21, a transitory provision, was at issue. It constituted a derogation from the general rule that the preceding Directive 98/10 was abolished in that the article authorized that certain measures adopted under the preceding Directive remained valid. As such it was to be interpreted strictly (paras 50 and 65) and did not include measures concerning high-speed internet, because the preceding Directive did not apply to those measures in the first place. *Volvo, 2010* was about the exception in article 18 Directive 86/653 from the commercial agent's right to indemnity in case of the agent's default which led to the contract being terminated. For the Court, that exception from the right to indemnity was not, as an exception from the rule, to be extended to become applicable in situations when the contract had already been terminated and the agent's default came to light only subsequently. Else an additional ground to deprive the agent from the indemnity was added, whereas no such ground was expressly provided for by the directive (para. 42).[89]

Back to derogations

Sayn-Wittgenstein, 2010 again concerned public policy, which as a derogation from a fundamental rule was to be interpreted strictly (para. 86). The prerequisite threat to a fundamental interest of society was, however, considered to be present in the case at issue, in part owing to the discretion member states had in adopting public policy measures. Austria could lawfully rely on equal treatment of Austrian citizens before the law to abolish titles of nobility, even if that resulted in a Union citizen being hindered in the exercise of her freedom. *Metin*

---

tary equipment), 2009 paras 45-6; *Commission v. Sweden (military equipment), 2009* paras 43-4; *Commission v. Germany (military equipment), 2009* paras 68-9; *Commission v. Italy (dual use equipment), 2009* paras 45-6; *Commission v. Greece (military equipment), 2009* paras 50-1; *Commission v. Denmark (military equipment), 2009* paras 51-2; *Commission v. Italy (military equipment), 2009* paras 46-7; and *Commission v. Portugal (military equipment), 2010* paras 62-3).

89 In diploma recognition the Court stuck to the formula used in *Colegio, 2006*, which is alike but not quite the same as second branch logic (see above). In *Van Leuken, 2008*, the Court employed the very same formula – 'the scope of article 4(1) of the Directive [89/48], which expressly authorises compensatory measures, must be restricted to those cases where they are proportionate to the objective pursued,' para. 24 – to develop its differentiated approach allowing partial recognition.

Bozkurt, 2010 dealt with the public security derogation under the Ankara Agreement, namely article 14 Decision 1/80. That derogation was subject to strict interpretation and its scope was not be determined unilaterally by the states concerned (para. 56). The derogation and other related case-law was to be applied by the national court to the facts of the case.

Second branch in universal service

In the year 2011, the Court first applied broad interpretation under the second branch within the context of the Universal Service Directive 2002/21. According to the Court, article 8(1) was an exception to the rule prohibiting the imposition of specific obligations on operators individually. As such it was to be interpreted strictly (para. 31). Hence, essentially, only those specific obligations could be imposed on a designated universal service provider that related to the elements of universal service provision mentioned in articles 4 to 7 and 9(2). In particular, only the specific service provision by such a provider itself to the end-user was covered.

Further derogations

In *Commission v. Austria (notaries), 2011* and the other notaries-judgments the Court had applied the very broad concept of establishment (see above). The Court then connected this first branch interpretation with the second branch. It ordered the usual narrow interpretation of the public authority derogation so that its scope was limited to what was strictly necessary for the legitimate interests of the member states to be safeguarded (para. 83[90]). The Court then proceeded to examine and reject the direct connection to official authority for every single aspect of the activities of notaries. (That rejection, to be sure, concerned only the nationality requirement.)

Commission v. Portugal (real estate agents), 2011 again concerned *inter alia* the public authority derogation with regard to which the Court stated the usual second branch logic amid a long advance statement of case-law. In the following the Court struck down all restrictions Portugal imposed on real estate service providers.

In a series of cases in 2011, the public policy derogation was applied. In *Dickinger, 2011*, a gambling case, the public policy exception was again said to be subject to a narrow interpretation, because it derogated from a fundamental freedom (para. 82). The Court then left it to the national court to decide whether the effective supervision of those offering games of chance necessarily required them to be established in Austria.

In *Graf, 2011* the narrow understanding of the public policy derogation was transposed to the Agreement on Free Movement with Switzerland. The Court

90 Para. 84 of *Commission v. Belgium (notaries), 2011*; para. 74 of *Commission v. France (notaries), 2011*; para. 84 of *Commission v. Luxembourg (notaries), 2011*; para. 85 of *Commission v. Germany (notaries), 2011*; para. 76 of *Commission v. Greece (notaries), 2011*; and para. 57 of *Commission v. Netherlands (notaries), 2011*.

conceded with reference to internal market case-law that public policy within the meaning of the derogation in article 5(1) annex I of the Agreement could vary from state to state and be subject to variation in time. Yet its scope was not to be determined unilaterally by a state and it was subject to strict interpretation when it constituted a justification for a derogation from a fundamental rule such as equal treatment (paras 32-3). Germany's approach of not authorising a land lease by a Swiss farmer on the ground that it would have distorted competition and led to an unsound distribution of land did not possibly fit within that concept of public policy. Hence, it was rejected as incompatible with the equal treatment clause in the Agreement.

In *Aladzhov, 2011* the public policy derogation was, in turn, applied in a Union citizenship case, more specifically based on article 27 Directive 2004/38 on Union citizenship. The Court rehearsed the narrow understanding of the derogation to avoid unilateralism by the member states (para. 34) when faced with the question whether the home state of a Union citizen could impose a prohibition to leave the state as long as tax liabilities remained unsettled or unsecured. Yet the assessment of the facts, including the question whether the risk that the tax owed could not be recovered amounted to a threat to public policy meeting the standards of the case-law, was left for the national court to decide. The same is true for *Gaydarov, 2011*, which was handed down on the same day as *Aladzhov, 2011* and concerned almost the same constellation in Bulgaria (para. 32).

In *Ziebell, 2011*, the public policy derogation under the Ankara Agreement with Turkey was at issue. The Court refused to apply the guarantees contained in article 28(3)(a) Directive 2004/38 by analogy under article 14(1) Decision 1/80. Instead, article 12 Directive 2003/109 which addressed the status of third country nationals in the Union was the right frame of reference. In that context, the narrow understanding of the public policy clause as a derogation from a fundamental freedom which excluded unilateralism by the states concerned had to be applied to the expulsion of a Turkish second generation immigrant (para. 81). After having restated the rest of the expulsion case-law the Court appeared to indicate that the expulsion of the Turkish national concerned was not in accordance with the case-law. But the Court left the ultimate assessment to the national court.

In *P. I., 2012* the Court interpreted the concept of imperative grounds of public security in article 28(3) citizenship Directive. In this context the Court stated that the public policy and security derogation took exception from free movement and as such was to be interpreted restrictively and in a way that avoided unilateralism (para. 23). Accordingly, the Court directed the national court to apply the established expulsion case-law also with regard to article 28(3), while conceding that certain particularly serious crimes committed by an individual against a child could come within the scope of 'imperative grounds'.[91]

Second branch in secondary law

A few cases of broad interpretation also concerned secondary legislation in the year 2011, among them *Commission v. Ireland (direct insurance), 2011*. The first non-life insurance Directive 73/239 contained an exemption from the requirements of the directive which (the exemption) had covered a specific Irish insurance body when it entered into force. Thereafter, the Irish legislature repeatedly changed the law governing that body, expanding its functions. The Court found that the exemption from the obligations in the Directive had to be interpreted restrictively, since 'derogations or exceptions to a general rule must be interpreted narrowly' (para. 44). As a consequence, the exemption no longer covered the Irish body since its role and functions had been expanded by law. Another case in which second branch logic was applied in secondary legislation was *Commission v. Spain (TV ads), 2011*, in which the duration of certain television spots that were akin to advertisements and the corresponding qualification under Directive 89/552 were at issue. The Court admitted that the derogations from the freedom of services in the Directive were subject to strict interpretation when they were not expressed in clear and unequivocal terms pursuant to *ARD, 1999* (para. 48). However, the restriction on broadcasting time of advertisements was to be applied to any form of advertisements broadcast between programmes or during breaks, unless some other forms of advertisements were clearly disadvantaged. Hence, the time-wise restriction had to be applied to other forms of advertisements that were only slightly longer than the usual ad spot.

More second branch and driving licences

In the year 2012, broad interpretation under the second branch began with recognition of driving licences in *Akyüz, 2012*. The Court took recourse to the narrow interpretation of the exception from mutual recognition allowing the refusal to recognize a licence in case of sanctions. First, the Court restated that interpretation as part of an advance statement of case-law (paras 45-6) leading it to a refusal to equal a first issue of a licence with the situation when a licence was withdrawn. Then the Court reiterated that narrow interpretation to justify the limitation of information sources that testified the lack of residence of the person concerned in the issuing state (para. 65). In that regard, the transmission of such evidence via the diplomatic representation of the host state was valid. In *Hofmann, 2012* the Court next confirmed that the second branch interpretation applied to article 8(4) Directive 91/439 remained valid with regard to article 11(4) of the new Directive 2006/126 (para. 71) – as did the rest of the case-law

91 Interestingly, in *Tsakouridis, 2010* the Court refrained from applying any broad interpretation of the second branch when construing the ten year-period of residence in the host state required for enhanced protection and when interpreting the notions of 'serious grounds of public policy or public security' in article 28(2) Directive 2004/38 and 'imperative grounds of public security' in article 28(3), although it set a very high threshold for the application of these articles in expulsion contexts.

regarding mutual recognition – despite the transformation of the option not to recognize a driving licence into an obligation.

Narrow student loans

In *Commission v. Austria (transport fare), 2012*, the Court established that article 24(2) citizenship Directive was to be interpreted narrowly as a derogation from equal treatment (para. 54). Consequently, the article only covered student loans and grants, in contrast to general maintenance aid by means of reduced transport fares for students. The final result was that the criterion requiring a genuine link with the host state society was not complied with in that Austria relied on the need to receive an allowance in Austria. The judgment in *Commission v. Austria (transport fare), 2012* was followed up and clarified by *L.N., 2013*. In this judgment – it was mentioned above – the Court applied first branch logic to construe the notion of a 'worker' broadly. The Court combined that interpretation with the narrow reading of article 24(2) citizenship Directive under the second branch, bringing the two branches together. That article released states from the obligation to offer migrant students maintenance grants on an equal basis. As a derogation from equal treatment it was subject to a narrow interpretation which had to be in accordance with the free movement of workers (para. 33). Hence, the Court concluded, the right of a migrant worker to equal treatment with regard to maintenance aid prevailed in case a student who was a Union citizen was working in the host state.

c) *Third branch: the greatest possible freedom – moving beyond social security*

In the third branch of broad interpretation, in which the *Hoekstra, 1964*-formula has been most prominent up to the present, only a few judgments have been relevant. *Hendrix, 2007* was the first. In this case, the same Dutch benefit was at issue as in *Kersbergen, 2006* and the Court first briefly confirmed the assessment made in that judgment of the lawfulness of the Dutch residence condition under articles 4(2)a and 10a Regulation 1408/71. However, the Court thereafter referred to the *Hoekstra, 1964*-formula – 'the greatest possible freedom', by now re-named '*Jauch, 2001*' by the Court (para. 52) – in order to establish a link to the free movement of workers in article 39 Treaty and Regulation 1612/68. This marked the first time that the greatest possible freedom-formula played a role outside the context of the measures coordinating social security. The Court cited the need to ensure the greatest possible freedom for workers to justify why article 7(2) Regulation 1612/68 and non-discrimination had to be applied alongside with articles 4(2)a and 10a Regulation 1408/71. The consequence was that the residence condition the Netherlands imposed had to comply with non-discrimination and, in particular, had to be justified in the traditional sense, viz. beyond the mere special and non-contributory character laid down in article 4(2)a Regulation 1408/71. Ultimately, the Court considered the residence requirement lawful, but only because its effect was cushioned by a hardship clause in Dutch law.

Obviously, it would have been hard to fit the need for such a clause within the criteria applicable pursuant to article 4(2)a Regulation 1408/71, i. e. 'special' and 'non-contributory'. Hence, the Court preferred to apply article 7(2) Regulation 1612/68 over distorting article 4(2)a Regulation 1408/71 further. From the perspective of the third branch, this preference of the Court brought the *Hoekstra, 1964*-formula in contact with the free movement of workers, which was a novel development.[92]

After *Hendrix, 2007*, 'the greatest possible freedom' was next applied outside the context of article 4(2)a Regulation 1408/71. In *Chuck, 2008* the Court had to answer the question whether aggregation of insurance periods completed in Denmark and the Netherlands had to be applied pursuant to Regulation 1408/71 when the national of a member state concerned resided outside the Union, in the United States. In the absence of any clear indication in the Regulation the Court cited the aim of 'the greatest possible freedom' for migrant workers to give an affirmative answer (para. 28). Suitably the Court referred to *Belbouab, 1978* and *Buhari Haji, 1990*, which dealt with similar situations as *Chuck, 2008*, rather than to the latest third branch case-law which was tailored to a considerable extent to article 4(2)a Regulation 1408/71. The third branch then went still for more than three years.

Revival of third branch

The third branch was, however, revived with *Da Silva Martins, 2011*. In this case the Court availed itself of the 'greatest possible freedom' as a part of its justification of why the German care allowance had to be exportable in the specific context (para. 70). In *Hudzinski, 2012* the Court next had recourse to the *Hoekstra, 1964*-formula (para. 53) to underpin its decision that Regulation 1408/71 did not preclude Germany from granting child benefits, although Germany was not the competent state pursuant to the Regulation. In *Partena, 2012* the Court began the merits with 'the greatest possible freedom' for migrants workers as the aim of article 48 Treaty (para. 46). That led the Court to claim the power for the Union to define the term 'location' in the context of self-employment.

In *Dumont, 2013* the Court then confirmed Belgium's power – and obligation – to take into account for the purpose of an orphan's benefit certain periods of insurance the spouse of the deceased person had completed abroad. In coming to that conclusion the Court repudiated one of Belgium's arguments by reference to the *Hoekstra, 1964*-formula (para. 53). Finally, *Jeltes, 2013* concluded the Court's case-law under the third branch for the present. In *Jeltes, 2013* the Court

92 In *Perez Naranjo, 2007* the Court applied second branch logic when qualifying a benefit under article 4(2)a Regulation 1408/71 (see above). Yet the Court failed to mention third branch logic, viz. the 'greatest possible freedom'. Since the Court reached the conclusion that the benefit met the requirements of that article and therefore was exempt from exportability, this judgment fits with *Skalka, 2004* and *Kersbergen, 2006*. *Commission v. Parliament (special benefits), 2007* also categorized certain benefits under article 4(2)a. Interestingly, the Court reached the conclusion that none of the benefits – except one part of a British benefit, potentially – could lawfully be exempted from exportability without applying either second or third branch logic.

made it plain that *Miethe, 1986* was not good law any longer under the new Regulation 883/2004. The new regulation of unemployment benefits, which made it mandatory for unemployed frontier workers to seek pecuniary benefits exclusively where they resided, overrode the authority of *Miethe, 1986* and the logic of the second offspring of the third branch, i. e. the *Mouthaan, 1976*-formula of the 'conditions most favourable', which had been at the heart of *Miethe, 1986*. In coming to the end of the case-law on broad interpretation for the time being, we witness what is very likely to be the end of the second offspring of broad interpretation.

d) *Spin – in the first branch*

The judgments in which broad interpretation spun the decisions are again of interest. While spin occurred regularly in the first and third branch, the second branch stands out with the most manifestations of spin. Let us briefly go through each branch individually to see where broad interpretation was effective. In the first branch, spin first manifested itself in the present in *Jia, 2007*. The broad interpretation of the free movement of persons provided some spin for the Court to define 'dependence'. However, the first branch-logic was part of a restatement of *Lebon, 1987*, which as a whole inspired the Court's conclusion. In *Alevizos, 2007* the broad worker notion stood at the beginning of the Court's reasoning, providing some momentum towards the final conclusion. Yet the spin was very limited, as the personal scope of article 39 Treaty was not the main issue the case had raised. In *Commission v. Netherlands (automatic expulsion), 2007* a broad interpretation of the safeguards contained in Directive 64/221 was instrumental for the Court's finding that those safeguards had to apply to unlawfully resident Union citizens, too. In addition, a milder sort of spin applied in that the narrow understanding of the public policy exception in part led the Court to the finding that under the Netherlands' legislation an unlawful automatism in expulsion was not entirely excluded.

In 2008, first, the broad interpretation of the provisions of the citizenship Directive 2004/38 was pivotal in *Metock, 2008* in reaching the conclusion that direct family reunification with third country nationals was possible, thus reversing *Akrich, 2003*. However, effectiveness, the wording of the relevant provisions, and the viability of the internal market also underpinned that conclusion. In *Petersen, 2008* the broad worker-formula mildly spun the decision. It was responsible, to a very limited extent, for including an unemployed person who had applied for an invalidity benefit within the scope of article 39 Treaty. In *Commission v. Austria (self-employment), 2008* spin was applied twice. First, the broad understanding of establishment provided certain spin. After having re-stated that understanding, the Court found that the self-employed persons concerned were within the purview of the freedom of establishment, irrespective of whether they circumvented the limitations of the freedom of workers. Second, the narrow interpretation of the public policy derogation was partly responsible for the Court not hearing Austria's argument that countering bogus self-employment was a public policy imperative. In *Von Chamier-Glisczinski, 2009* spin seemed empty on the face of it. After having put forward the broad understanding of the term 'worker', the Court found the free movement of workers not to apply. Yet that non-applicability was due to the facts having been unclear rather than the Court's unwillingness to extend the worker-notion. Hence, true empty spin did not occur.

In *Genc, 2010* the broad worker-notion in the free movement of workers provided some momentum for the finding that very limited work amounted to 'work' within the meaning of the Ankara Agreement. Yet, in this judgment we clearly see that the broad understanding of 'worker' increasingly becomes part of a ritualistic restatement of the definition, blotting out possible spin. The broad understanding of 'worker' thus more and more becomes akin to an advance statement of practice. In *Van Delft, 2010*, in contrast, there was an element of empty spin. Despite the professed broad interpretation of 'worker' the Court refused to classify the persons concerned as 'workers'. However, the empty spin is put into perspective by the Court having established long before that such persons, viz. mainly pensioners, were not to be considered as workers. The point therefore hardly raised any doubts. Hence, the passage, like in *Genc, 2010*, should be seen more like a ritualistic statement which served to indicate that Union citizenship rather than the free movement of workers had to be addressed. In *Bekleyen, 2010* the refusal to interpret article 7(2) Decision 1/80 narrowly provided the Court with some of the impetus necessary to found a right of the child of former Turkish workers to access the employment market in the host state autonomously. In *Teixeira, 2010* broad interpretation of article 12 Regulation 1612/68 contributed some spin to the answer to question 2(b). It was part of the rationale explaining why self-sufficiency was not required under article 12 for the primary carer of a child in education. The same is obviously valid for *Ibrahim, 2010*. In *Lassal, 2010* the broad interpretation of Directive 2004/38 established in *Metock, 2008* stood at the beginning of the Court's reasoning on why periods of residence in the host state completed before the citizenship Directive became fully applicable counted towards the five year-period needed for the right to permanent residence. It spun the decision to a considerable degree. In *L.N., 2013* the combination of the broad worker notion under the first branch with a narrow reading of the exception in article 24(2) citizenship Directive produced strong spin for the Court to decide that student workers in the host state could rely on equal treatment with regard to maintenance aid.

Spin by very broad establishment

The 'very broad concept of establishment', put forward for the first time in *Gebhard, 1995*, also exerted spin. *Commission v. Austria (self-employment), 2008* was already mentioned. Further, *Filipiak, 2009* was interesting. The Court first put forward the broad understanding of establishment, but then found that the freedom of services could be applicable, too. Hence, *Filipiak, 2009* could be read as a case of empty spin. However, this is the point where the broad construal of establishment is about to become part of a ritualistic, formulaic statement of what establishment is, a statement that does not play any role whatsoever in the decision – in this case whether services or establishment was at issue – like the broad understanding of 'worker'. Like the latter, it is immediately followed in the pertinent passage by the other elements defining the notion. The 'very broad concept' of establishment thus turned into a sort of advance statement of case-law. This was confirmed by *Attanasio, 2010*. In this judgment the Court used the broad understanding of establishment to begin the delimitation of freedom of services from freedom of establishment. However, broad interpretation was again more part of a definition ritualistically put forward than a formula that truly spun the decision. The same is valid for *Stoß, 2010*; *Winner Wetten, 2010*; *Bejan, 2010*; and *Schmelz, 2010*. In *Commission v. Austria (notaries), 2011* and the other notaries judgments the very broad concept of establishment was part of an advance statement of practice in an even more patent way. Apart from that, the second branch logic in the notaries judgments provided some momentum allowing the Court to reject the public authority derogation as not pertinent. In *A Oy, 2012*, in contrast, the 'very broad concept of establishment' was referred to in order to explain the meaning of establishment within the internal market and then to transpose the concept to the European Economic Area. In this context, broad interpretation provided no spin whatsoever, though.

Spin in the second branch

In the second branch of broad interpretation where broad rules combine with narrow exceptions spin occurred in many other cases besides those already mentioned in connection with the first branch. In *Polat, 2007* the narrow view of the public policy derogation contributed some spin, together with other case-law, for the decision of the Court to declare several minor offences in themselves as irrelevant. In *Commission v. Austria (bio inspections), 2007* and *Commission v. Germany (bio inspections), 2007* the narrow interpretation of the official authority derogation provided spin for the Court to ignore the connection between the activities of private supervisory entities and the exercise of authority. In *Commission v. Italy (private security), 2007* the narrow construal of the public order exception was instrumental in the Court's rejection of the oath of allegiance private security guards were required to take. The narrow understanding of provisions excluding certain benefits from the scope of Regulation 1408/71 in *Habelt, 2007* spun the decision towards applying the Regulation to the German benefits at issue.

In *Commission v. Luxembourg (posted workers), 2008* the strict interpretation of the public policy derogation came first and patently directed the decision towards a rejection of the requirements Luxembourg imposed on undertakings posting workers to Luxembourg. In *Jipa, 2008* some spin was applied by the Court's narrow interpretation of the public policy and security derogation. It made the Court focus on the situation in the state ordering a measure against a Union citizen rather than the situation in other member states.

In *Eschig, 2009* second branch logic provided spin against the extension of the exception Directive 87/344 contained. However, that potential extension was only one minor aspect of the question asked. In *Commission v. Portugal (vehicle inspection), 2009* the narrow interpretation of the public authority derogation imparted some spin. In part due to second branch logic the Court refused the connection of bodies testing the roadworthiness of vehicles with official authority.

Spin and driving licences

In *Wiedemann, 2008* and *Zerche, 2008* second branch interpretation was stated as part of an advance statement of case-law. Had it not been for that advance statement, empty spin would have occurred, since the Court had in fact broadened the exception by sanctioning non-recognition in case the residence requirement had been disregarded by the state issuing the driving licence. In *Weber, 2008* empty spin was somewhat clearer. The Court first hinted at the narrow interpretation of the exception allowing refusal of recognition of a driving licence issued abroad. Yet it then validated the refusal *in concreto*, because the licence had been issued abroad while the authorities were in the course of adopting sanctions. *Schwarz, 2009* also would have been a case of empty spin, but the second branch logic was encapsulated in an advance statement of case-law which slowed down the spin. The Court thus did not counteract spin by sanctioning Germany's refusal to recognize the Austrian licence issued previously. In contrast, in *Wierer, 2009* spin was strong. The narrow construal of the exception from the obligation to recognize driving licences issued abroad was instrumental in the Court's finding that certain evidence was inadmissible for the proof that the residence requirement had been disregarded.

Further spin in the second branch

In 2010, in *Commission v. Germany (posted workers), 2010* the narrow understanding of the derogations in article 46 Treaty spun the decision to some extent. Yet it was more the fact that Germany's arguments failed to fit within the grounds expressly mentioned in that article which was decisive, rather than the strict interpretation of the justificatory grounds as such. In *Commission v. Poland (broadband internet), 2010* the narrow interpretation of the transitory measure in article 27 Directive 2002/21 spun the decision. It was the foundation for the Court to reject the extension of the preceding Directive 98/10 to cover measures concerning high-speed internet.

Sayn-Wittgenstein, 2010 was a case of empty spin. The Court first pushed for a narrow interpretation of the public policy exception, but then turned against that spin. The margin of discretion of member states took precedence over the freedom of Union citizens. The effects of Austria's abolishing of titles of nobility on that freedom hence were lawful. In contrast, in *Gaydarov, 2011*, second branch logic as to the public policy and security derogations provided some limited spin towards indicating that the Bulgarian approach was unlawful. The ultimate assessment was left to the national court, though.

In 2011, in *The Number, 2011* the narrow construal of the exception in article 8(1) Universal Service Directive 2002/21 provided the initial spin. From that spin, at least partly, resulted the Court's finding limiting the obligations of universal service providers. In *Commission v. Portugal (real estate agents), 2011* the long advance statement of case-law extinguished most of the spin the second branch logic with regard to the public order derogation could have exerted. The public order derogation did not figure very prominently, either, among the grounds Portugal put forward to justify the restrictions it imposed on real estate agents established abroad. Some spin was provided by second branch logic in *Commission v. Ireland (direct insurance), 2011*. The narrow understanding of the exemption in the first non-life insurance Directive 73/239 led the Court to a close examination of the additional functions of the Irish insurance body, with the final result that the exemption no longer covered it. In *Graf, 2011* the narrow understanding of the public policy derogation in the Agreement with Switzerland clearly spun the decision against Germany's argument alleging distortion of competition and unsound land distribution.

Commission v. Spain (TV ads), 2011 was a clear case of empty spin. The Court conceded that the restriction of the freedom of services had to be construed restrictively, but then went on to interpret the limitation on broadcasting time for advertisements contained in Directive 89/552 – which was a restriction of free services – broadly, so that it included all forms of advertisement broadcast between programmes or during breaks, including those Spain had exempted time-wise from the restrictions by qualifying them as other ads not subject to the limitation in broadcasting time. In *Ziebell, 2011* the restrictive reading of the public policy derogation produced the slightest spin, although it was deeply imbedded in a longer statement of case-law. The Court seemed to edge the national court toward the finding that the expulsion of Mr Ziebell was unlawful under the expulsion case-law.

In the year 2012, spin occurred in three more cases in the second branch. In *Akyüz, 2012* the narrow derogation from the mutual recognition of driving licences had an impact two times. First, the spin was stronger in the refusal to equal the issuing of a licence for the first time with a withdrawal; second, the spin was weaker, becoming almost empty, in that the Court admitted an intermediary who transmitted the information from the 'home' state regarding non-residence. In *P. I., 2012* second branch logic made the Court apply the expulsion case-law also under article 28(3) citizenship Directive. In that sense the narrow interpretation of the public policy derogation spun the decision. However, that spin was neutralized to a large extent, even emptied, by the Court's broad understanding of what constituted an imperative ground. Crimes committed by an individual against another individual could possibly amount to such a ground. Yet this approach of the Court must certainly be seen on the facts of the case, i. e. in the light of the crime at issue having been the extraordinarily heavy abuse of a child. Finally, in *Commission v. Austria (transport fare), 2012* the narrow construal of the derogation from equal treatment in article 24(2) citizenship Directive tipped the balance against the inclusion of more general maintenance aid in the exception. In relation to the requirement of a general link with the host state society the narrow interpretation of article 24(2) was a minor point, though.

Spin in the third branch

In the third branch of broad interpretation, *Perez Naranjo, 2007* is the first judgment to be mentioned as regards spin. It fits in with the remarks made with regard to *Skalka, 2004* and *Kersbergen, 2006*. *Perez Naranjo, 2007* was again a case in which second branch logic could be considered to have provided spin, but then the Court decided in the opposite sense, likening it to a case of empty spin. Yet, the narrow understanding of the exception in this judgment occurs more like an advance statement of case-law which puts spin into perspective. Apart from that, the judgment confirms what we have observed for the other judgments with regard to article 4(2)a Regulation 1408/71, namely *Jauch, 2001; Skalka, 2004*; *Kersbergen, 2006*; and *Hosse, 2006*: The Court simply omits the 'greatest possible freedom' when the benefit at issue is not supposed to be exportable.

In *Hendrix, 2007* the *Hoekstra, 1964*-formula was again clearly instrumental in the Court's disruptive finding that a hardship clause was required to soften the effects of the residence requirement that articles 4(2)a and 10a Regulation 1408/71 allowed the Netherlands to impose. The formula also provided the spin necessary to build a bridge from social security to the free movement of workers. We already noted above that in that regard *Hendrix, 2007* was clearly a novel judgment, for before that, the Court had always avoided bringing the *Hoekstra, 1964*-formula into contact with the free movement of workers. Interestingly, *Hendrix, 2007* can also be read as announcing a new approach that breaks with the spinning practice mentioning third branch logic only with regard to articles 4(2)a and 10a Regulation 1408/71, when the benefit concerned was, in the eyes of the Court, supposed to be exportable. That new approach was implemented in *Commission v. Parliament (special benefits), 2007*. In that judgment the Court essentially eliminated several benefits from the annex of Regulation 1408/71 for they failed to meet the criteria in article 4(2)a. However, in doing so the Court did not apply any second or third branch logic at all. Hence, *Commission v. Parliament (special benefits), 2007* can be understood as announcing that third branch logic would not any longer be applied functionally, with spin, when it came to the qualification of a benefit under article 4(2)a. Indeed, it seemed that broad interpretation altogether would not any longer be applied in relation to that article. This take is confirmed to some extent by the fact that the third branch then went quiet for more than three years. The only judgment that followed until mid-2011 was *Chuck, 2008* which concerned a different context, though. *Chuck, 2008* dealt with the aggregation of insurance periods for Union citizens residing outside the Union. The 'greatest possible freedom' provided the necessary spin for the decision by the Court to apply the aggregation of periods of insurance completed in several member states even when the Union citizen was resident outside the Union at the moment when he applied for a pension. The third branch then went quiet for more than three years and with it, obviously, the phenomenon of spin.

Then, however, the 'greatest possible freedom' came back. In *Da Silva Martins, 2011* the formula was part of a broader advance statement of case-law concerning the aims of article 42 Treaty. Despite that, the formula can be seen to have provided some spin towards the decision enabling the exportability of a care allowance. In *Hudzinski, 2012* the *Hoekstra, 1964*-formula was again applied outside the context of article 4(2)a Regulation 1408/71. It served to bolster the decision of the Court, reached on the basis of other case-law, to allow the state which was not competent pursuant to Regulation 1408/71 to grant child benefits. In that function, however, the formula did not exert any spin. Next, in *Partena, 2012* the Court began with the *Hoekstra, 1964*-formula and thereby spun the decision to deny the member states the power to define the location where a self-employed activity took place. The formula was thus applied in the context of determining the applicable legislation. In *Dumont, 2013* the Court applied the 'greatest possible freedom'-formula to create some spin to reject the arguments Belgium had put forward to justify why a period needed to have been completed in Belgium for aggregation of periods completed abroad to become mandatory in case of orphan's benefits. Finally, we have already noted *Jeltes, 2013*. The judgment effectively declared *Miethe, 1986* dead under the new Regulation 883/2004, thus indirectly neutralizing any spin of the *Mouthaan, 1976*-formula, the second off-spring of broad interpretation, for the future.

e) Some conclusions from the present

In the present we observed the continuation of broad interpretation in all three branches. The broad interpretation of the worker notion in the first branch has become part of a routine. The Court has regularly cited it as part of the definition of the term 'worker'. In a similar vein, the 'very broad concept' of establishment stemming from *Gebhard, 1995* has become part of the Court's routine when explaining establishment, in particular to delimit it from the freedom of services. As a consequence of these routines, the broad interpretation of the two notions has become more like an advance statement of practice, though not being 'advance' in a localized sense. Consequently broad interpretation has lost some of its power here and spin cannot be discerned. In contrast, second branch logic has its heyday in the present. The use of a narrow interpretation of the exception from a rule has become much more frequent. The cases relevant under broad interpretation within the second branch have become relatively more numerous. Second branch logic has been routinely applied in secondary legislation, too.

At the end of the age of Maastricht, we observed that Union citizenship and the freedom of establishment possibly stood on the threshold of a development mirroring the evolution in the free movement of workers and services. To recapitulate briefly, in the age of Maastricht and before, the freedom of workers and services was widened first by broad notions, narrow exceptions were added in, and a climax was reached by a sweeping broad understanding of the freedom itself, notably through the *Kempf, 1986*, *Lebon, 1987*, *Yiadom, 2000*-line of authority for workers and through the *Calfa, 1999*, *Deliège, 2000*, *Oulane, 2005*-line for services. Speaking broadly, those developments have been confirmed for workers and services in the present. More strikingly, in the present, Union citizenship has clearly crossed the threshold mentioned. The Court sweepingly declared secondary legislation implementing citizenship as worthy of broad interpretation in *Commission v. Netherlands (automatic expulsion), 2007* and even more clearly in *Metock, 2008* and *Lassal, 2010*. That first branch logic was seconded by interpretation under the second branch in *Commission v. Austria (transport fare), 2012* and *L.N., 2013*. Only *Sayn-Wittgenstein, 2010* ran counter to this trend. In the freedom of establishment, in contrast, corresponding clear evidence is not there. While 'the very broad concept' of establishment has become a regular occurrence, it has also been turned into a sort of advance statement of case-law which merely serves to delimit the freedom of services from the freedom of establishment. Perhaps this lack of evidence of the freedom of establishment crossing the threshold in the same way as the other freedoms is due to the interlinking between the freedom of services and the freedom of establishment. Frequently, services and establishment overlap. What the Court says of the one is valid for the other, at least sometimes. That might equally hold true for the broad interpretation applied to the freedom of services. Perhaps the freedom of establishment has sneaked across the threshold along with services. *Calfa, 1999*, for instance, is in all likelihood transposable from services to establishment for our concerns. Yet some uncertainty remains.

Apart from those broader trends, some more specific points are noteworthy. *Eschig, 2009* seems to have linked second branch logic involving narrow exceptions with a prohibition to reason by analogy, at least in secondary legislation. This approach relatively clearly conflicts with *Rebmann, 1988* where the Court had admitted reasoning by analogy for exceptions under certain circumstances. The situation not covered by the exception namely had to be closely connected to the situation it covered and the same grounds that had led to the establishment of the exception had to justify its application. The Court has so far not applied the approach in *Eschig, 2009* again. On a different, though related note the idea put forward in the age of Maastricht that second branch logic was connected to the explicitness of an exception seems to live on, though on a rather subliminal level. Remember that the idea had been posited in *Commission v. Italy (dentists), 1995* and *ARD, 1999*. The following judgments, *Klett, 2002*; *Commission v. Italy (direct insurance), 2003*; *Beuttenmüller, 2004*; *Kapper, 2004*; *Halbritter, 2006*; *Commission v. Greece (cabotage), 2004*; and *Honyvem, 2006*, all had failed to corroborate that approach though. Yet in the present, *Volvo, 2010* seems to have revived it. The Court ruled that additional exceptions to the rule establishing the commercial agent's right to indemnity could not be created. The exceptions were limited to those explicitly mentioned. The revival was short-lived, though, if a revival it was. *Commission v. Spain (TV ads), 2011* intervened and revoked the limitation *ARD, 1999* seemed to have laid down. The Court admitted that *ARD, 1999* had made second branch logic authoritative in the absence of clear and unequivocal terms in secondary legislation. Nonetheless the Court proceeded to interpret the exception broadly in *Commission v. Spain (TV ads), 2011*. For lack of any further case-law in the present *Commission v. Spain (TV ads), 2011* for now must be read as a renunciation of the approach linking second branch logic with the explicitness of terms.

In the present the public policy exception has been quite dominant. The derogation was frequently applied. Conversely, second branch interpretation of the derogation lost some of its power, notably in the following judgments. In *Sayn-Wittgenstein, 2010* Austria's public policy concerns prevailed over the freedom of Union citizens, despite a professed narrow understanding of the freedom. In *Tsakouridis, 2010* the strict interpretation of the public policy and public security derogations was not even mentioned. *Dickinger, 2011* and *Aladzhov, 2011* both left the application of the derogation to the national court, although the Court saw a need for narrow interpretation. *Gaydarov, 2011* proceeded in a similar way. Arguably though, the Court stated more explicitly that the situation was not in accordance with the derogation. Yet ultimately the Court left the decision to the national court. *Graf, 2011* could be seen as counter-indicative in this regard. However, it only transposed second branch logic for the public policy derogation to the Agreement on Free Movement with Switzerland. *Ziebell, 2011*, in a sense, positioned itself in the middle of this case-law. The Court hinted at a narrow understanding of the public policy exception and implied that it might have been violated, but left the assessment under the Ankara Agreement to the referring court. In sum, it seems that a less aggressive understanding of the public policy derogation, playing down the effect of second branch logic, seems to be a trend of the day. Note, however, that some public policy decisions fall out with this trend (see above under spin).

In the third branch, *Hendrix, 2007* stands out for it finally connected the 'greatest possible freedom', the *Hoekstra, 1964*-formula which had been applied exclusively under social security, to the free movement of workers. The formula served to justify why the residence condition lawfully imposed pursuant to articles 4(2)a and 10a Regulation 1408/71 had to be assessed in addition under article 7(2) Regulation 1612/68, increasing the need for justification beyond the mere special and non-contributory character of the benefits. Has the bridge thus established been confirmed? The answer is not in the affirmative, at least for the moment. However, in the decisions following after *Hendrix, 2007* the 'greatest possible freedom' was applied outside the articles it had hitherto been typically applied to. The formula no longer turned around article 4(2)a Regulation 1408/71, or the Dutch transition (*De Jong, 1986* and *Spruyt, 1986*). The formula rather unlocked new fields, like the division of powers in *Hudzinski, 2012*, aggregation in *Dumont, 2013*, the export of a care-allowance in *Da Silva Martins, 2011*, or the definition of Union terms like 'location' in *Partena, 2012*. Hence 'the greatest possible freedom' has broken free and begun to take wider influence in the case-law of the Court. Overall, we observe a movement from relatively obscure, highly specific constellations into the 'light'. That movement can be traced from the beginnings with *Hoekstra, 1964/Nonnenmacher, 1964* over *De Jong, 1986/Spruyt, 1986* to *Jauch, 2001* and, finally, the case-law initiated by *Hendrix, 2007*. That the latter case-law is new is evidenced also by *Commission v. Parliament (special benefits), 2007*. That judgment, it seems at least for the moment, has killed off third and second branch logic on broad notions and restrictive exceptions with regard to articles 4(2)a and 10a Regulation 1408/71. All the judgments following after *Commission v. Parliament (special benefits), 2007* that applied the 'greatest possible freedom' did so in the contexts of other articles (see above). Besides those profound developments in the third branch of broad interpretation, it appears that the first offspring of this branch, the case-law having begun with *Heinze, 1972* has continued to lay low in the present. Not a single judgment has tied in with that tradition. More drastically, the second offspring of the third branch, the *Mouthaan, 1976*-line of broad interpretation, was expressly cut off by the Court in *Jeltes, 2013*. Legislative amendment had explicitly revoked *Miethe, 1986*.

Beyond that, it is difficult to find a pattern or come to simple conclusions on the *power* of broad interpretive formulas. The above passages on 'spin' stand on their own. Having said that, spin occurred most regularly and strongly in the second branch on narrow exceptions, while it was quite frequent in the first and third branch on broad notions and the greatest possible freedom, too. In the first branch, two broad notions have lost some of their power in the present, namely the 'worker' and the 'establishment'. The idea that they must be interpreted broadly has become part of a standard statement which is put forward ritualistically. Hence, the notions no longer have any discernible effect. The situation here is similar as with advance statements of case-law. Besides, empty spin continued to occur with some regularity, as in fact have advance statements of case-law.

We conclude with the likely coming to an end of the extraordinary spinning phenomenon with regard to articles 4(2)a and 10a Regulation 1408/71. Remember that the Court in the past only mentioned the 'greatest possible freedom' in the context of these articles when a benefit was to be exportable. After this clearest form of spin by the 'greatest possible freedom' had first been confirmed in the present, it now seems to have come to an end with *Hendrix, 2007* and *Commission v. Parliament (special benefits), 2007*. However, although this clear form of spin seems to have vanished, it is not the end of the 'greatest possible freedom' as such. After *Commission v. Parliament (special benefits), 2007* the formula has found new application outside the context of article 4(2)a and 10a Regulation 1408/71. Yet in the new context – or rather the new contexts – in which the *Hoekstra, 1964*-formula was applied after *Commission v. Parliament (special benefits), 2007* the formula proves more alive than ever. The 'greatest possible freedom' continues to exert power and spin decisions in a broader field than ever.

II 'Coordinated'

In this chapter, the evolution of formulas of coordination is traced in the same way as with broad interpretation in the previous chapter, beginning with the early days of the case-law. The entire body of case-law of free movement of persons and services uncovered in the first part is scrutinized for the idea of coordination and for interpretive formulas that rely on it. After it is established where such formulas occur, their power – in other words the 'spin' they exert in the Court's decisions – is examined. What is meant by 'coordinated' and 'coordination' should become clear in the following section.

1 In the early days: until the mid-1970s

The origin of 'simply coordinated'

In the year 1971, the Court handed down the judgment in *Keller, 1971*. In this case, the French authority had applied aggregation and apportionment pursuant to Regulation 3 to calculate an old age pension. Yet the amount of the pension calculated on the sole basis of national law would have been higher, if periods of insurance completed exclusively in France would have been taken account of. The Court ruled that the pension had to be awarded on the basis of national law. As a consequence, Mr Keller was treated more favourably than a worker who had spent his entire career in France. In brief, Mr Keller in addition to the French pension received a pension in Germany. As a result, the overall amount of his pension was higher than a French pension could possibly be. The Court justified this more favourable treatment in the last paragraph. According to the Court, it was not due to Community law, but due to the inexistence of a common social security scheme. The Community approach 'depend[ed] on a simple coordination of national legislative systems which ha[d] not been harmonized' (para. 13).

The idea inherent in this passage of the national social security schemes being 'simply coordinated' was to make a strong career in the Court's social security case-law. However, it did not come out of the void. In 1967, the idea was already present in two judgments: *Colditz, 1967* and *De Moor, 1967*. In *Colditz, 1967* the Court was faced with the question whether all pensions needed to be fixed necessarily at the same time in the states concerned, viz. at the time the worker first applied for a pension in one state. The Court gave a negative answer, leaving the worker the more favourable option to continue to acquire pension rights in one state while in another a pension was already being paid. The answer of the Court began with the fact that Regulations 3 and 4 had not set up a 'common system of social security'. 'Separate systems' were allowed to continue to exist 'creating separate claims against separate institutions against which the recipient ha[d] direct rights either under national law or national law supplemented, if necessary, by Community law' (all on p. 234).[93] In a judgment handed down on the same day, *De Moor, 1967*, the Court made use of this consideration in a slight variation to underpin the conclusion that proportional calculation pursuant to article 28(1) Regulation 3 could not lawfully be applied, if a benefit was due solely on the basis of national law, i. e. without the need to aggregate periods first. According to the Court, a common system did not exist under which the migrant worker held a single entitlement which was simply apportioned between the states. Rather, separate claims arose against separate institutions under separate systems (p. 207). The Court then continued to find that an improper plurality of benefits did not result from this reading, hence ruling in favour of the migrant worker. Thus, the idea of 'simple coordination' according to *Keller, 1971* was implied by the 'separate systems' remaining in existence according to *Colditz, 1967* and *De Moor, 1967*.

The passage from *Keller, 1971*, in turn, was reapplied in the exact same words – at least in the French text – in *Mancuso, 1973*. It served the Court to underpin its finding, which was obviously related to that in *Keller, 1971*, that an invalidity pension awarded solely on the basis of national law without prior aggregation of periods was not to be reduced, either, based on apportionment pursuant to article 28(1) Regulation 3, like an old age pension. Any resulting cumulation of benefits awarded in several member states favouring migrant workers was the consequence of 'simple coordination' of national legislations which had not been harmonized (para. 17).

From justifying advantages to distributing powers ...

Next, *Rzepa, 1974* applied the passage from *Keller, 1971* in a shortened version. Belgium wanted to apply article 34(4) Regulation 4, which concerned the advance payment of pensions, to a benefit awarded solely on the basis of national law. In particular, the statute of limitation for a re-claim of benefits paid in advance was at issue. The Court answered that article 34(4) was not to be applied to a benefit that had been due by reason of national law only, i. e. without previous aggregation of periods completed in several states. In any event, the Court continued, had the benefit been based on aggregation, even then the statute of limitation would have been governed by national law, since the 'system embodied in Regulation [...] 3 and 4 rest[ed] on mere coordination' (para. 12; 'simple coordination' in French as in *Keller, 1971*). Any benefit paid in application of Community law was based on both national and Community law, with national law always governing the statute of limitation. Hence, Community law need not have laid down such a limitation. Thus, whereas the 'simple coordination'-passage in *Keller, 1971* and *Mancuso, 1973* had served to explain why a cumulation of benefits in favour of migrant workers was lawful, in *Rzepa, 1974* 'simple co-

93 The Court then continued that the Community system could not, in the absence of an express provision, be interpreted in a way that a worker was deprived of the benefit of part of the legislation of a member state (p. 234). That approach later on fed into the judgment in *Petroni, 1975*, under the name of which it became known. Interesting as it may be, this formula is not in the focus of this chapter.

ordination' in a shortened version moved away from justifying an advantage for migrant workers. It rather served to distribute powers between the Community and the member states.

... and back to justifying advantages

In *Massonet, 1975*, the Court returned to the more favourable treatment of migrant workers as put into practice by *Keller, 1971* by means of the 'simple coordination'-passage. The case concerned the situation where a widow received a pension based solely on Luxembourg law which (the pension) was increased by reason of her having raised her children. Simultaneously she received a pension in Germany into which certain notional periods were factored, again owing to her having raising children, but which (the German pension) finally came about as a result of aggregation and apportionment. The Court again sided with the migrant worker, or rather his surviving wife, holding that the Luxembourg pension due solely pursuant to national law could not lawfully be reduced by applying aggregation pursuant to Community law. The notional periods were not truly overlapping. Any advantage drawn exclusively by migrant workers was due to 'simple coordination' within the sense of *Keller, 1971* (para. 27).

The complexity of coordination

Besides the above six judgments, coordination played an important role in two more judgments in the narrative of social security during the early years.[94] Firstly, in *Guissart, 1967*, shortly after the Court had laid the foundation for the *Keller, 1971*-ruling in *Colditz, 1967* and *De Moor, 1967*, the Court dealt with the question whether insurance periods completed in another member state were to be taken into account as notional years in Belgium. In keeping with *De Moor, 1967* the Court stated that aggregation applied only in specific cases determined by Community law. If the aim of Community law was achieved on the basis of national law alone, there was no room for aggregation. Yet, 'the complexity of the problems posed by the co-ordination of national legislative systems prevent[ed] this interpretation from becoming an absolute principle' (p. 434). This meant, in particular, that periods completed in one state, which gave rise to benefits in that state, were not to be considered as notional periods in another.

94 In this chapter, the footnotes at least in part serve to complete the picture of coordination in the case-law of the Court. The judgments in which coordination (or 'coordinated', etc.) is mentioned, though without attributing any argumentative function to the notion, are briefly noted in roughly chronological order. In this regard several judgments must be mentioned now. In *Bonsignore, 1975*, para. 5, the Court stated that the objective of Directive 64/221 on public policy, security, and health measures was to coordinate those measures in order to reconcile them with the free movement of persons and the prohibition of discrimination. However, that those measures were *coordinated* was not subject to further consideration. In *Petroni, 1975*, para. 20, the Court also referred to coordination, though only for the powers of the Council to coordinate national social security systems pursuant to article 51 Treaty. The role of the term was thus wholly inconsequential in this judgment. The same is valid for *Triches, 1976*, para. 17. The Court only mentioned the 'system for co-ordinating family allowances'. In *Reyners, 1974* the Court used the term 'coordination of laws' in the context of the measures to be adopted to implement the freedom of establishment (para. 20). However, the term was only mentioned in passing and no argument was developed on the basis of it. The same is valid for *Van Binsbergen, 1974*, para. 21, with regard to the freedom of services.

By this ruling the Court conceded that Community law was unable, because of complexity, to foresee the consequences it had for all social security situations. Beyond that, 'the complexity of [...] coordination' served to qualify aggregation and render it less cogent. In this case the aspect prevailed that, with an approach relying on coordination, periods of insurance were not to be taken account of twice.[95]

The shift of Regulation 1408/71

The other judgment in which coordination played a certain role was *Kunz, 1973*. This judgment, in a sense, was symbolic of the change Regulation 1408/71 was about to bring in terms of coordination. The Court ruled that article 22(1) Regulation 3 was not to be interpreted against the grain of the wording in the sense that the pensioner concerned was to receive sickness benefits in kind in the Netherlands, although he did not have an entitlement under Dutch law to such benefits. In particular, an argument could not be drawn from the new Regulation 1408/71 which established just such an entitlement. The reason for that argument being inadmissible was that Regulation 1408/71 extended 'the Community's social law, which until then was limited to coordinating national laws regarding social security' (para. 5). This dictum, in turn, implied that the reason why article 22(1) Regulation 3 did not create an entitlement to benefits in kind in the Netherlands was that it merely coordinated the national laws.[96]

Spin

What about the power of 'coordinated'? In all the above judgments we can observe the spin of the interpretive formula, as we did with broad interpretation in the previous chapter. Spin in that sense first occurred in the two precursors to *Keller, 1971*. In *Colditz, 1967* the idea that later crystallized in *Keller, 1971* spun the decision to a considerable extent. The 'separate claims ...'-passage was instrumental in the Court's finding that an application for a pension in one state

95 On a different note, a statement in Advocate General Dutheillet Lamothe's common opinion to *Keller, 1971*, *Gross, 1971*, and *Höhn, 1971*, is confusing. In the original version in French the third point the Advocate General made begins as follows: 'Jusqu'à la coordination, qui apparaît de plus en plus nécessaire, des différents régimes nationaux de sécurité sociale [...]'. The German version also reads: 'Bis zur Koordinierung der verschiedenen nationalen Systeme der sozialen Sicherheit, die sich immer mehr als notwendig erweist [...]'; the Italian version: 'Fino al coordinamento, che s'impone sempre più, dei regimi previdenziali nazionali [...]'; and the Dutch version: 'Zolang het niet is gekomen tot de met de dag urgenter wordende coördinatie van de verschillende nationale regelingen inzake de social zekerheid [...]' (each passage is on p. 883). Obviously, when the opinion was translated into English the faux pas was corrected. It reads: 'Until such time as the different national social security systems are *harmonized*, which appears increasingly necessary [...]' (p. 882, emphasis added).

96 This reading is supported by Advocate General Roemer's opinion which gives the following reason why the relevant article in Regulation 3 did not create any entitlement to benefits in the Netherlands: 'First, it is material that the object of Regulation No 3 is only to coordinate national insurance schemes. From this it follows that where there is any doubt one cannot proceed from the assumption that basic changes in national law were intended; at least one cannot bring about such changes by way of analogy or filling of omissions.' (P. 1037) While the Court in result followed the Advocate General, the Court failed to include the argument put forward by the Advocate General. Indeed, the Court expressly accepted only the second point of the Advocate General – which is not in the above quote – namely that only article 28 Regulation 1408/71 created a direct claim to benefits based on Community law.

did not necessarily trigger the award of a pension in another state. In *De Moor, 1967*, in contrast, spin was relatively limited. The 'separate claims ...'-passage followed upon the Court's point that apportionment was not of general application, which is indicative of an absence of spin. Yet, the passage exerted some spin, in particular with regard to the rejection that an improper plurality of benefits occurred. In *Guissart, 1967* 'the complexity of [...] coordination' was instrumental in the Court's decision to eschew the consequences of a strict application of aggregation. It turned aggregation into a relative principle, one that could be overruled by the need to avoid situations where an insurance period gave rise to rights under the national schemes of two states. In contrast, in *Keller, 1971*, the judgment that crystallized 'simple coordination', that passage did not exert any spin on the Court's decision. Rather, it served to justify at the end of the judgment why the more favourable treatment of migrant workers in contrast to workers who had spent their entire career in one member state was justified. The same is true of *Mancuso, 1973*. In *Kunz, 1973*, spin cannot be discerned, either. In *Rzepa, 1974* 'simple coordination' in an abbreviated version provided the spin needed to answer *eventualiter* that national law, in any case, governed the statute of limitation of claims aiming at repayment of benefits advanced. Finally, in *Massonet, 1975* in a similar vein as in *Keller, 1971* the 'simple coordination'-passage functioned as an *ex post* justification underpinning the Court's conclusion. We conclude that only in *Colditz, 1967*; *Guissart, 1967* and to a limited extent in *De Moor, 1967* and *Rzepa, 1974* the relevant passages spun the decision.

Some conclusions from the period

During the foundational period of the Court's case-law, *Keller, 1971* crystallized an interpretation which had been inherent in *Colditz, 1967* and *De Moor, 1967*. It drew on the 'simple coordination' of national social security schemes. 'Simple coordination' served the Court to underpin its conclusions, notably to justify why the favourable treatment migrant workers enjoyed in contrast to purely domestic workers, namely the possibility to cumulate benefits under various national systems, was lawful. This was explicit in *Keller, 1971*, *Mancuso, 1973*, and *Massonet, 1975* and implicit in *Colditz, 1967* and *De Moor, 1967*. In *Rzepa, 1974*, moreover, 'simple coordination' served to divide the powers between the Community and the member states, awarding to the latter the power to regulate the statute of limitation of repayments of benefits advanced. In two more judgments, *Guissart, 1967* and *Kunz, 1973*, the idea of coordination was applied in two slightly different contexts, namely in the sense of the 'complexity of [...] coordination' and as a criterion allowing to draw a distinction between Regulation 3 and Regulation 1408/71. As to the power of the passages concerned – 'spin' – the conclusion from the early days is that it was rather limited. Only in two decisions spin was clearly discernible, while in two more decisions spin was there to a lesser degree.

2 From the mid-1970s until the 'Maastricht moment'

a) Occurrence of 'coordinated' – 'simple coordination' under Regulation 1408/71

'Simple coordination' appeared for the first time during the next 15 years in *Mura, 1977*.[97] This judgment is crucial, because it transposed the idea of 'simple coordination' to the new Regulation 1408/71. This was not self-evident, in particular in the light of the distinction drawn in *Kunz, 1973* between Regulation 3 and Regulation 1408/71, with the latter extending the Community's social law beyond the coordination of national laws.[98] The Court in *Mura, 1977* began with the simple coordination-passage from *Keller, 1971*[99] to explain why a more favourable treatment of migrant workers in contrast to purely domestic workers needed to be accepted (para. 10). However, the Court continued, if a benefit was based on national law alone, that law could be applied in its entirety. The benefit could notably be reduced on the basis of purely national rules against the overlapping of benefits pursuant to article 12 Regulation 1408/71. The only condition was that the Community rules on aggregation and apportionment of benefits would have been applied, if they had been more favourable for the migrant worker.

97 A number of further decisions deserve to be mentioned at this point. In *Hirardin, 1976* Advocate General Trabucchi had argued that the Court would better not ground its decision in acquired rights, because that risked creating a substantive norm, whereas the Community provision in Regulation 3 merely coordinated the national schemes (pp. 566-7). The Court reflected none of these concerns in its judgment and based it on the idea of acquired rights. In *Kermaschek, 1976* the Court mentioned that article 67 to 70 Regulation 1408/71 pursued only one purpose, namely that of coordinating rights to unemployment benefits based on national law for employed persons who were nationals of a member state (para. 9). However, that statement was made not in the context of *coordination*, but rather to explain why family members of migrant workers were not entitled to claim unemployment benefits under the Regulation, while the migrant workers concerned themselves were. In *Strehl, 1977*, para. 14, the Court again, like in *Petroni, 1975*, mentioned the powers of the Council pursuant to article 51 Treaty to lay down provisions to coordinate the national social security systems. Further consequence was not attached to the notion of coordination, though. The same is true of the identical reference in *Manzoni, 1977*, para. 11. In *Kuyken, 1977*, para. 11, the Court merely mentioned that Regulation 1408/71 concerned the coordination of the laws of the member states as to unemployment benefits. In *Thieffry, 1977*, para. 11, the Court referred to coordination in a similar, unobtrusive way as in *Reyners, 1974*: the Council had the duty under article 57 Treaty to issue directives to coordinate national provisions on self-employment. Later on, the reference to coordination in *Klopp, 1984*, para. 9, was similar. In *Bouchereau, 1977*, para. 15, the Court again, after *Bonsignore, 1975*, inconspicuously referred to coordination with regard to Directive 64/221.

98 This extension becomes more than evident in *Blottner, 1977* which was handed down more than four months before *Mura, 1977*. In *Blottner, 1977* the Court held that article 45(3) Regulation 1408/71 had to be applied, even though a migrant worker had not been subject to type A legislation, because she had moved away before the relevant legislation was changed from type A to type B. The Court justified that interpretation *contra legem* as follows: 'The structure of the system of harmonization of national legislation established by the regulation is based upon the principle that a worker must not be deprived of the right to benefits merely because of an alteration in the type of legislation in force in a Member State.' (para. 16) Obviously, *Blottner, 1977*, must be seen as an antagonist to the continuing line of authority relying on 'mere coordination'. Interestingly, the Court only referred to *Blottner, 1977*, once, in *Derks, 1984*. However, the reference did not involve the harmonization-passage in any way.

99 The relevant passage in *Mura, 1977* in French was worded slightly differently, though the content was identical to the passage in *Keller, 1971*. The English version further altered the wording, in particular it mentioned 'mere co-ordination', instead of 'simple coordination' as in *Keller, 1971*.

Coordination to the disadvantage of migrant workers

The year 1979 then produced two unexpected developments. First, in *Brunori, 1979* the Court acceded to the Commission's argument alleging that the aggregation of periods of insurance was not to be applied in the context of the obligation provided by German law for stonemasons to remain compulsorily insured under a special insurance scheme for 216 months, since the exclusive aim of Regulation 1408/71 was to coordinate national legal systems (para. 5). It was for national law to determine the conditions of affiliation. This ruling comes as a surprise, at least to some extent, as it marked the first time that the idea of mere/simple coordination had the effect of disadvantaging migrant workers. Previously, the 'simple coordination'-passage had consistently been cited to the effect of favouring migrant workers, in particular over purely domestic workers. Perhaps this was the reason why the Court in *Brunori, 1979* refrained from referring to the characteristic wording of the 'simple coordination'-passage, preferring to state the Commission's argument instead and acceding to it.

'Separate claims'

The second unexpected development took place in *Rossi, 1979*. This judgment went back to the origin of the *Keller, 1971*-passage, namely *Colditz, 1967* and *De Moor, 1967*. The Court had recourse to the 'separate claims'- rather than the 'simple coordination'-phrase, thus at the same time reviving 'separate claims' after almost twelve years and transposing it to Regulation 1408/71 (para. 13).[100] The Court then adduced *Petroni, 1975*-logic and went on to create the supplement to be paid by the state the social security scheme of which awarded a higher benefit under article 79(3) Regulation 1408/71. The tale of the 'separate claims'-phrase continued with *Laterza, 1980* and *Gravina, 1980*. In these cases, the Court expanded and generalized the conclusion drawn in *Rossi, 1979* as to the payment of a supplement. As in *Rossi, 1979*, the Court justified this approach by the argument of coordination in the disguise of the 'separate claims'-phrase (para. 8 and 7, respectively) in combination with *Petroni, 1975*-logic.

Inversing simple coordination

The Court in *Testa, 1980*, in a sense, inversed the 'simple coordination'-logic, thus epitomising the novelty of Regulation 1408/71. The Court ruled that article 69 Regulation 1408/71 was not 'simply a measure to co-ordinate national laws' (para. 5). Rather, the article created an autonomous entitlement rooted in Community law to export unemployment benefits for three months. As a consequence, after those three months had passed, falling back on national law was not an option, irrespective of what national law provided. A migrant job seeker who failed to return in time to the state providing the benefits forfeited the right to continue to receive benefits, except in the circumstances provided by article

100 The relevant passages in *Colditz, 1967*, and *Rossi, 1979*, in the French versions are identical, apart from a minor specification related to the facts of *Colditz, 1967*.

69(2). Thus, the antagonist of 'simple coordination', harmonization, worked to the disadvantage of the migrant job seeker concerned.

Simple coordination, in effect a (dis)advantage for migrant workers

'Simple coordination' then disappeared from view for more than five years.[101] It came back prominently in *Pinna, 1986* in which the Court declared void the special regime article 73(2) Regulation 1408/71 had established for the benefit of France. That article had exempted French family benefits – and only French family benefits – from the exportability laid down in article 73(1). The Court began by stating that article 51 Treaty provided for 'the coordination, not the harmonization' of national law (para. 20). Consequently, differences in the national schemes and the rights granted thereunder remained unaffected. Nonetheless, the Court continued, a high degree of similarity in social security rules was beneficial for the free movement of workers. Hence, Community law had to refrain from adding to the disparities that already existed between the member states' schemes – which was exactly what article 73(2) had done. Non-discrimination fed into this consideration and the Court struck down the second paragraph of article 73. The formula used in *Pinna, 1986* can be considered to have amalgamated the previously used 'simple coordination'-passage with the 'separate claims'-phrase. Moreover, 'coordination, not harmonization' was put forward in a case that ultimately turned out, by making French benefits exportable, to the advantage of the migrant worker, like it had been initially the case when the coordination-passages had been applied. Yet the situation was not the same. The Court in *Pinna, 1986* ruled to the advantage of the migrant worker, *despite* the mere coordination of national schemes, rather than *because of* it.[102] That twist

101 Some more decisions need to be discussed briefly. In *Galinsky, 1981*, p. 952, the Commission had argued against considering a self-employed person who had been compulsorily insured in that capacity in the United Kingdom as a worker under article 1(a) Regulation 1408/71 for the purposes of British benefits merely because he had been subsequently insured as a worker in the Netherlands. The Commission had argued that Regulation 1408/71 was by nature an 'exercise in coordination'. To treat such a person as a worker in the United Kingdom would mean to harmonise the legislations of the member states (p. 952). The Court tacitly rejected that argument and considered the person concerned a worker under article 1(a), while ignoring the argument based on coordination. The Court dismissed the claim based on another ground, though. (The Court referred to coordination in passing in para. 12 by mentioning 'the rules on the coordination of national legislative systems relating to social security'.) In *Baccini, 1982* the Commission had argued that the Community rules as to social security pursued three aims, one of which was the fundamental principle that migrant workers were not to suffer a disadvantage by reason of the national social security schemes being merely coordinated and not yet harmonized (p. 1073). The Commission made this statement nota bene with regard to Regulation 1408/71. The Court only implicitly included those considerations (paras 13-4). In *Castelli, 1984* the Commission had argued that to recognize Ms Castelli's right under Regulation 1408/71 to a minimum pension available in Belgium for the elderly would mean to create a right under the Regulation, thus bidding farewell to the Regulation's approach of mere coordination (p. 3207). The Court eschewed that problem by recognizing a right under article 7(2) Regulation 1612/68.

102 Again, some further cases deserve to be mentioned in the interest of completeness. In *De Jong, 1986*, on p. 674, Advocate General Mancini in a preliminary remark recalled the basis of 'mere coordination' of the Community rules and the consequent power of the member states to determine conditions of insurance affiliation. The Court in the judgment itself only referred to this power of the member states as reiterated in *Coonan, 1980* (para. 13). Nonetheless, it cannot be denied that a certain affinity exists between the *Coonan, 1980*-line of authority granting member states the power to

was, however, counteracted in *Burchell, 1987* in which the Court advanced the 'coordination, not harmonization' formula from *Pinna, 1986* (para. 17 of *Burchell, 1987*) to come to the conclusion that the rule against the overlapping of benefits in article 10(1)(a) Regulation 574/72 was not to be applied when a family benefit was due in any event on the basis of national law, notably without recourse to article 73 Regulation 1408/71. Quite the contrary, because of mere coordination article 10(1)(a) was only applicable to benefits awarded on the basis of article 73. 'Coordination' thus went back to working for, rather than against migrant workers.

Lenoir, 1988 tied in with *Pinna, 1986*. The non-exportability of certain benefits, including some French benefits, pursuant to article 77 Regulation 1408/71 was challenged in that case in a similar way as in *Pinna, 1986*. The Court reiterated 'coordination, not harmonization' as established in *Pinna, 1986* (para. 13 of *Lenoir, 1988*), but in contrast to *Pinna, 1986* did not put the formula into perspective subsequently. More specifically, the Court refused to invalidate the article of the Regulation, because it did not add to the disparities between the schemes of the member states. Rather, those disparities had already been in existence. The article applied according to objective criteria. The French benefits at issue, moreover, were tied to the social environment. It thus became evident from *Lenoir, 1988* that 'coordination' also functioned to the disadvantage of migrant workers, in this case pensioners. What could have already been suspected from *Brunori, 1979* and *Pinna, 1986*, hence became certain with *Lenoir, 1988*, namely that 'coordination' was not a one-dimensional driver of advantages for free movers. It was also liable to turn against them.

---

determine conditions of affiliation and the 'coordination'-case-law. Note therefore that *Kits van Heijningen, 1990* and *De Paep, 1991* later on limited the power of the member states in this regard to a certain extent. On a different note, the Court in *Miethe, 1986* denied a wholly unemployed frontier worker the option to choose where to receive unemployment benefits solely because the national law of the state not competent pursuant to Regulation 1408/71 would have granted such benefits. To grant such an option would run counter the scope of the Regulation which intended to coordinate the national social security schemes (para. 11). The same passage was later on reiterated in *Rebmann, 1988*, para. 9, and 'the rules relating to coordination' were also mentioned in para. 12. In both judgments coordination was mentioned only in passing. Apart from that, the Court in a series of judgments dealing with (co-)insurance mentioned coordination. The direct applicability of the freedom of services did not depend on coordination or harmonization of the laws of the member states (para. 25 of *Commission v. Germany (insurance), 1986*); the relevant directives were the 'coordination directives' (*inter alia* para. 40), which had established 'minimum coordination' (para. 65). However, all these references to coordination did not serve the Court to build an argument on the basis of that term. The same is true for the three other judgments delivered on the same day, namely *Commission v. France (co-insurance), 1986*; *Commission v. Ireland (co-insurance), 1986*; *Commission v. Denmark (co-insurance), 1986*, though for the latter to a lesser extent. In *Bertini, 1986*, para. 11, the Court held that the obligation for a member state to modify the regulation of the medical profession exercised by its own nationals could only arise from directives to coordinate the national rules. Further consequences was not attached to the term coordination. Finally, in *Van Roosmalen, 1986*, para. 19, the Court referred to the preamble of Regulation 1390/81 according to which the coordination of the national social security schemes was necessary for self-employed persons. Coordination was only mentioned en passant, though.

Obfuscation of the origins of 'simple coordination'

Borowitz, 1988, in contrast, followed up on *Brunori, 1979*; *Laterza, 1980*; and *Gravina, 1980*. Seized with the question of whether the calculation pursuant to article 46(1) Regulation 1408/71 allowed Germany to take account of periods of insurance in accordance with a bilateral social security convention with Poland, the Court answered with the 'sole objective of coordination' of the Community rules (para. 23). Hence, Germany was free to take heed of such periods. Yet other member states were not required to do so. That integrated approach happened to secure an advantage for the migrant worker concerned. It is noteworthy, furthermore, that the Court referred to *Brunori, 1979*, in which the wording of the coordination-passage could not be attributed with full certainty to the characteristic *Keller, 1971*-passage, and to *Laterza, 1980* and *Gravina, 1980* which had used the separate claims-phrase. Moreover, *Pinna, 1986* was not cited at all. We thus observe in *Borowitz, 1988* what had been adumbrated in preceding judgments, namely that the origins of 'coordination' have been obfuscated. 'Simple coordination' was being dissociated from specific judgments to become something like an abstract idea without a root that is clearly attributable to a specific judgment.[103]

Further simple coordination cases

In *Jordan, 1989* French legislation had limited a newly introduced benefit. It only applied to pensions calculated after a certain date, thus excluding recalculation of benefits awarded before that date. The Court referred to *Pinna, 1986* to underscore the argument that article 51 Treaty only provided for coordination, while leaving differences in the national schemes unaffected (para. 13). Accordingly, it was for the member states to decide when a change in the criteria for the award of a benefit would take effect. Article 51 Regulation 1408/71 was not applicable, which was a result to the detriment of the migrant worker concerned.[104] Next, *Cabras, 1990* referred to mere coordination without, however, citing any case-law. Thus, 'coordination' as an idea justified the inconveniences that arose for a migrant worker because a pension was split between two states, i. e. because two bodies concurrently paid benefits, which could be subject to separate readjustment, while the total amount of the benefit was subject to the ceiling in article 46(3) (para. 31). The Court expressly accepted the disadvantage that migrant workers suffered relative to purely domestic workers in this regard (para. 30). In *Rönfeldt, 1991* 'coordination' by reference to *Pinna, 1986* and

103 For completeness: In *Roviello, 1988*, para. 17, the Court incidentally used the term coordination: 'Point 15 is not of such a nature as to guarantee the equal treatment required by Article 48 of the Treaty and therefore has no place in the coordination of national laws provided for in Article 51 of the Treaty [...]'.

104 For the sake of completeness it must be mentioned that *Pinna II, 1989* reiterated the ruling in *Pinna, 1986* and in that context mentioned coordination, too (para. 12). Moreover, in *Echternach, 1989*, para. 21, the Court mentioned that there was no coordination of school diplomas in the specific case, but did not attach any further consequence to the notion of coordination. In *Van de Bijl, 1989*, para. 14, the Court also referred incidentally to the coordination of national laws in the context of recognition of professional qualifications.

Borowitz, 1988 dispatched the preliminary point that the different schemes of the member states relied on different age limits for retirement (para. 12). 'Coordination' implied that this difference was to be accepted.

'Coordination' and the 'stability of the system'

In *Newton, 1991* the idea of coordination served in a new capacity. The Court ruled that a British benefit for handicapped persons was not to be exportable for handicapped persons who had previously been subject exclusively to the social security scheme of a member state other than the United Kingdom. For them, the relevant allowance constituted social assistance which was not subject to Community rules. To rule otherwise would have meant to interpret the Community rules which merely coordinated national social security schemes in a way that would have upset schemes such as the British (para. 18). 'Mere coordination' thus served as a reason why 'the stability of the system instituted by national legislation' (para. 17) was not to be upset, to the disadvantage of the person concerned *nota bene*.

For and against migrant workers

In *Paraschi, 1991* the Court ruled that the extension of a reference period relevant for the acquisition of an invalidity benefit could not lawfully be granted only for sickness that occurred in the state concerned, else migrant workers who tended to return home when sick were disadvantaged. The Court arrived at this conclusion despite the mere coordination of national schemes (para. 22). *Paraschi, 1991* thus was a decision to the advantage of migrant workers, but on a close reading of the text it had that effect *in spite of* 'coordination'. *Paraschi, 1991*, therefore, added further weight to the argument that the idea of coordination, in principle, worked to the detriment of migrant workers. In *Durighello, 1991*, 'coordination' finally came back to the aid of migrant workers. The Court conceded that Regulation 1408/71 did not address benefits for dependent spouses of pensioners. That was why Italy had refused a pensioner drawing a pension in application of the Regulation such a benefit. However, the Court countered, national schemes were merely coordinated, as ruled in *Rossi, 1979* in the context of family benefits (para. 14). Adding in *Petroni, 1975*-logic, the Court decided that national law had to be applied fully even when a pension was drawn on the basis of Regulation 1408/71. Hence, the Italian benefit was due to the person concerned.[105]

b) Spin

In which judgments did 'mere coordination' spin the Court's decisions? To be again clear, this question is not the same as the question whether 'simple/mere

105 Again for the sake of completeness, in *Les Assurances du crédit, 1991* the Court referred repeatedly to coordination in the context of the direct insurance Directive 73/239. However, none of these references made use of coordination as an argument or a substantial concept. That is equally true for *Karella, 1991* in which the Court mentioned the coordination of safeguards under Directive 77/91 on, to put it briefly, shareholder protection (para. 25).

coordination' works in favour of migrant workers. 'Spin' asks whether a formula or an idea was instrumental in the Court having reached a specific decision; the question of the benefit of a decision for migrant workers is interested in the substantive outcome, the result of the use of a formula or an idea for a specific group.

In *Mura, 1977*, the first judgment in the period in which the 'simple coordination'-passage was used, it is subject to doubt whether spin occurred. Arguably, the Court began its judgment with the passage, but this was owed to the way the national court had asked the question. Besides the Court also had to clarify that a more favourable treatment of migrant workers was still not unlawful, in spite of the new Regulation 1408/71 having become applicable. The Court did this by reference to 'simple coordination' and the fact that the situations of migrant and purely domestic workers were not comparable. However, the hard issue to be solved was then to some extent disconnected from the 'simple coordination'-passage, with the Court ruling that national law could be applied in its entirety, viz. including national rules against overlapping. Perhaps this disconnection occurred, because the Court first professed the more favourable treatment of migrant workers underpinned by 'mere coordination', but then in substance ruled against that more favourable treatment by allowing the reduction of benefits on the basis of national rules against overlapping. One can therefore validly consider that an element of empty spin was inherent in *Mura, 1977*, though it was not very patent.

In *Rossi, 1979* the revived *Colditz, 1967/De Moor, 1967*-phrase of 'separate claims' together with *Petroni, 1975*-logic spun the Court's decision towards the disruptive finding that the higher benefit pursuant to national law had to be safeguarded, resulting in the obligation of the state that provided for the higher amount of benefit to pay a supplement. In *Brunori, 1979* 'coordination' in the Commission's argument, which was accepted in brief by the Court, provided the necessary spin to come to the conclusion that the requirement to be affiliated for 216 months to a specific insurance scheme constituted a condition of affiliation to which aggregation of periods was not applicable. In *Laterza, 1980* and *Gravina, 1980* the 'separate claims'-phrase exerted strong spin. It functioned as the main argument together with *Petroni, 1975*-logic to establish a right to receive the greatest amount of benefit the law of one of the member state involved provided.

Negative spin

Testa, 1980 was an interesting case from the perspective of 'coordination' spinning the Court's decision. In that judgment harmonization- rather than coordination-logic provided the spin for the Court to sanction a job seeker returning late to the state sponsoring his unemployment benefits. Seen from the inverse point of view, it could thus be said that 'simple coordination' negatively exerted spin.

Empty spin

Next, in the disruptive ruling *Pinna, 1986* 'coordination, not harmonization' led the way. However, in spite of what the formula would have indicated – i. e. that article 73(2) simply recorded disparities that existed anyway by reason of mere coordination – the Court ruled that the article was invalid, because it added to the disparities and violated non-discrimination. Hence, *Pinna, 1986* must be regarded as the first clear case of empty spin of 'coordination'. Remember that empty spin occurred for the first time in *broad* interpretation in *De Jong, 1986*, i. e. a little more than one month after *Pinna, 1986* had been handed down. This can be seen as a testimony to the verity of empty spin. In *Paraschi, 1991* the Court's decision that certain events taking place abroad had to be taken into account for the purpose of extending the reference period was heavily influenced by non-discrimination. The idea of 'mere coordination' was stated, but the Court chose to ignore it. Hence, *Paraschi, 1991* can be seen as the second clear case of empty spin in 'coordination'.

More 'un-empty' spin

In *Burchell, 1987* spin was very strong. The *Pinna, 1986*-formula was the only argument the Court advanced to come to the conclusion that article 10(1)(a) Regulation 574/72 could not lawfully be applied in the context of the case. In *Borowitz, 1988* 'coordination' was again instrumental for the Court to allow an integrated approach to the calculation pursuant to article 46(1) Regulation 1408/71 including periods of insurance recognized as such by a German-Polish convention. In *Lenoir, 1988* 'coordination, not harmonization' again spun the Court's decision. It legitimized the finding that article 77 Regulation 1408/71 was in accordance with article 51 Treaty and, implicitly, that France's residence requirement for the family benefits at issue was lawful. In *Jordan, 1989* the reference to 'coordination' in *Pinna, 1986* catalyzed the decision to enable the member states to determine the point in time from which an amendment to a benefit would apply and thus to influence which pensions had to be recalculated. In *Rönfeldt, 1991* the idea of coordination spurred the Court's decision towards acceptance of the different age limits for retirement existing in the member states. Arguably though, this was a minor and quite evident point in the judgment. Finally, in *Durighello, 1991* 'mere coordination' led the Court to direct the national authorities to apply national law fully, although the person concerned received a pension on the basis of Regulation 1408/71. The spin of 'coordination' was, however, soft, since *Petroni, 1975*-logic provided most of the momentum needed to arrive at this conclusion.

c) Some conclusions from the period

Three interesting aspects should be mentioned with regard to the period from 1976 to 1991. First, 'coordination' grew from two passages firmly rooted in two origins, namely 'sole coordination' stemming from *Keller, 1971*, and 'separate claims' from *Colditz, 1967* and *De Moor, 1967*, into a more abstract idea of which the root in case-law was no longer evident. *Pinna, 1986* certainly played a key role in this regard juxtaposing 'coordination' and 'harmonization'. The judgment which was disruptive also in other respects, namely by invalidating article 73(2) Regulation 1408/71, dissociated 'coordination' from its origins and made it less context-dependent. The following judgments then relied more on this abstract idea. Some of them, in particular *Borowitz, 1988*, cited a seemingly random collection of judgments, or no source at all, namely *Cabras, 1990* and *Newton, 1991*. Again others, namely *Jordan, 1989* and *Rönfeldt, 1991*, simply referred to *Pinna, 1986*. *Paraschi, 1991* in turn referred to just the latest judgments. *Durighello, 1991* referred to a judgment in which 'coordination' was relevant in a similar context.

Second, the function of the idea of coordination changed. It turned from a reason to rule in favour of migrant workers into an excuse for some disadvantages they suffered. This evolution was not entirely linear, but it was definitely there. The first judgment in this new twist of 'coordination' was *Brunori, 1979*. *Pinna, 1986* was also a key judgment in this regard, with the Court ruling in favour of migrant workers *despite* 'mere coordination'. *Pinna, 1986* marked the turning point. After *Pinna, 1986*, in five out of nine judgments the idea of 'coordination' had a detrimental effect on migrant workers, namely *Lenoir, 1988*, *Jordan, 1989*, *Cabras, 1990*, *Rönfeldt, 1991*, and *Newton, 1991*, with *Cabras, 1990* being the most illustrative case. In *Cabras, 1990*, like in the early social security judgments such as *Keller, 1971* and *Mancuso, 1973*, the Court underpinned at the very end of the judgment the conclusion it had reached by the idea of 'mere coordination'. Yet the idea in *Cabras, 1990* functioned in a way that was diametrically opposed to the way the same idea had worked in *Keller, 1971* and *Mancuso, 1973*. In *Cabras, 1990* the reference to 'mere coordination' served to explain why migrant workers had to accept that they were put in a less advantageous position vis-à-vis purely domestic workers, while in *Keller, 1971* and *Mancuso, 1973* it had served to explain the inverse, viz. why migrant workers deserved to be treated more favourably. In *Newton, 1991* the evolution was also relatively patent. 'Mere coordination' was used as a ground to prop up the British system which would have been put in jeopardy had the Court ruled in favour of the migrant worker concerned.[106] After *Pinna, 1986* only *Burchell, 1987*; *Borowitz, 1988*; and *Durighello, 1991* came down in favour of migrant workers. In *Paraschi, 1991* the Court, moreover, ruled to the advantage of migrant workers, but did so in spite of coordination like in *Pinna, 1986*. The evolution of 'mere coordination' from a force working for the good of migrant workers into a power they had to struggle with seems almost ironic in view of the Commission having floated the idea in *Baccini, 1982* that one of three principles governing the Community's social security law was that migrant workers were

106 Interestingly, the Court had already reserved the stability of the national system in *Frilli, 1972* (para. 21). Yet *Frilli, 1972* was not discussed under this aspect in *Newton, 1991*. Advocate General Darmon mentioned the judgment, but only to explain that the difference between social security and social assistance was not clear-cut (para. 11).

not to suffer a disadvantage by reason of the national social security schemes being merely coordinated and not yet harmonized (see footnote 101 above). Apart from that, the evolution was probably related, to a certain extent, to the shift from Regulation 3 which had only coordinated national schemes to Regulation 1408/71 which had harmonized some limited aspects of them. To be sure though, the new use of 'mere coordination' contra migrant workers was clearly not limited to domains which Regulation 1408/71 had harmonised. On a different note, it can be remarked that the evolution, interestingly, developed largely in parallel with the abstraction of 'coordination' into an idea. Perhaps 'coordination' was abstracted to mask the functional change.

Third, though one should be prudent with simple conclusions as to the power of 'coordination', spin definitely occurred on a very regular basis with 'coordination'. The idea of 'mere coordination' clearly spun a large number of the Court's decision. At the same time 'empty spin' emerged. Apart from the debatable precursor in *Mura, 1977*, empty spin became very clear in *Pinna, 1986* and *Paraschi, 1991*. The occurrence therefore largely coincided with the first appearance of empty spin in broad interpretation in *De Jong, 1986*. Lastly, it is also noteworthy that 'coordination' in *Testa, 1980* again shifted its form in terms of spin and occurred in a new variant: negative spin.

3 During the age of Maastricht

a) Occurrence of 'coordinated' – the beginning of the age

At the beginning of the age of Maastricht the idea of 'coordination' figured prominently in a series of judgments. *Levatino, 1993* was the first in it.[107] 'Coordination' occurred in two parts of the judgment. Asked to clarify whether article 51(1) or (2) Regulation 1408/71 was to be applied to adjust a benefit that was granted in Belgium to bring the combined pensions paid in Belgium and Italy up to the Belgian minimum income, the Court answered with *Rönfeldt, 1991* that mere coordination was the aim of Regulation 1408/71; the rights granted to migrant workers were not to lead to the disruption of a national system as held in *Frilli, 1972* (paras 30-1). That was not the case, however, since article 51(2) was applicable for the purposes of the Belgian benefit whenever the pension paid in Italy was increased. Consequently, the Belgian authorities always had to recalculate the benefit that guaranteed a minimum income as soon as a pension paid abroad was increased. As a result, migrant workers were not treated more

107 Strictly speaking, *Levatino, 1993* was not the first judgment to mention coordination in the age of Maastricht. In *Commission v. Belgium (insurance taxation), 1992*, para. 19, and in *Bachmann, 1992*, para. 26, the Court in essence stated that 'coordinating or harmonising measures' would have been necessary to match contributions and the advantages they yielded in terms of taxation. However, the Court did not use coordination as a substantive argument. Moreover, in *Sindesmos Melon, 1992*, para. 32, like in *Karella, 1991*, the Court referred to the aim of coordination of Directive 77/91 on shareholder protection, without turning it into an argument though.

favourably than purely domestic workers. If that had been the case, in any event, it would have been the result of mere coordination of national schemes as held in *Mura, 1977* (para. 49 of *Levatino, 1993*). Despite this last passage, 'mere coordination' in combination with the need to prevent the disruption of a national scheme ended up working against migrant workers.

Next, in *Lepore, 1993* the Court answered the third – and least contentious – question by reference to 'mere coordination' (para. 34). In the light of that, Community rules did not contain any provision which precluded national authorities from applying the same method of calculation for notional periods as for the previously awarded invalidity pension – a result that proved disadvantageous for the migrant worker.[108]

In *McLachlan, 1994* 'coordination' loomed large. According to the Court, the 'separate claims'-phrase in *Rossi, 1979* (para. 29) justified that periods completed abroad were only taken into account to determine the acquisition and the rate of a benefit, but not for its calculation, even when differences in the age limit for retirement existed between national schemes. Eventual disadvantages for migrant workers were inherent in the system which relied on separate claims against separate institutions. As such they were the consequence of mere coordination and the lack of a common system (paras 37-8).

In *Van Munster, 1994* the Court shortened the passage used in *Rönfeldt, 1991*, leaving out the word 'coordination', but conveying the same message (para. 18). The Court used this passage to explain why Belgium's application of a household rate to pensions, while the Netherlands had abolished that system, was in accordance with article 51. The Court then also juxtaposed the idea of 'mere coordination' with *Petroni, 1975*-logic (para. 27), and adduced the aim of creating a unified pension career for the migrant worker based on coordination, rather than harmonisation (para. 29). Then the Court ruled that the Belgian authorities would have been obliged to take into account the fact that the overall amount of pension the married couple received had not changed by reason of the award in the Netherlands of a separate pension to the spouse who had never worked. While the judgment was, obviously, strongly beneficial for migrant workers, this was the case more *despite* 'mere coordination', than owing to it; in essence, it was *Petroni, 1975*-logic that proved advantageous for migrant workers.[109]

108 Two further decisions need to be mentioned here. In *Baglieri, 1993* the Court rejected the claim that compulsory insurance affiliation in the host state necessarily had to result in the right of a national returning to her home state to be affiliated to a voluntary insurance scheme in the home state. According to the Court, such a right presupposed the harmonization of national schemes, which had not yet taken place (para. 17). In *Grana-Novoa, 1993*, para. 22, the Court en passant referred to the coordination of national social security schemes by Regulation 1408/71, but did not attribute any significance to the term.

109 For the sake of completeness, some further cases need to be mentioned. In *Haim, 1994*, para. 3, the Court in passing used the notion of coordination. It stated that the coordination of provisions concerning the activities of dental practitioners was ensured by Directive 78/687. The same passage was included in *Tawil-Albertini, 1994*, para. 3. In this judgment, the Court also used the term coordination incidentally in para. 12. Moreover, in *Commission v. Spain (doctors), 1994* the Court repeatedly referred to coordination with regard to the 'coordination directive' 75/363 concerning doctors. Yet

Coordination and derived rights

The Court put the derived rights approach into perspective in *Cabanis-Issarte, 1996*.[110] Non-discrimination prevented the Netherlands from applying a different rate for the spouse of a migrant worker to determine the amount payable to buy in certain insurance periods. In that context, the Court confirmed that the sole aim of the provisions on unemployment benefits in articles 67 to 70 Regulation 1408/71 was the coordination of the national schemes relating to unemployment benefits of workers (para. 23). This meant that the spouse of a migrant worker could not lawfully rely on those articles. Yet, the emphasis in this passage was clearly on opposing workers to family members, rather than on mere coordination in contrast to harmonization (The part restricting that approach for other benefits did not rely on 'coordination'.)[111]

Six decisions in 1997

In the year 1997, the Court had recourse to 'coordination' in six decisions. In *De Jaeck, 1997* the Court granted the member states the power to define both the terms 'employed/self-employed person' and 'person who is employed/self-employed', with the latter being used only in title II of Regulation 1408/71. The Court justified this by the 'coordination, not harmonization'-formula stemming from *Pinna, 1986* (paras 18 and 28) – which ultimately worked to the detriment of at least the migrant worker concerned. In *Hervein I, 1997* the *Pinna, 1986*-formula was used in an identical way and for an identical purpose (para. 16). Next, in *Stöber and Pereira, 1997*, after having declared the definition of 'self-employed person' in the annex relevant for German law, the Court stated that Germany was entitled to restrict a benefit to those who belonged to a solidarity system of old age insurance, since Regulation 1408/71 merely coordinated national laws (para. 36). Despite that, Germany could not lawfully rely on the resi-

---

coordination was never substantively used as an argument, not even in para. 13. In *Vougioukas, 1995* the Court in a similar way used the word 'coordination' a number of times, as in para. 19: 'Article 4(4) of Regulation No 1408/71 excludes, in general terms, special schemes for civil servants and persons treated as such from the coordination of social security schemes under that regulation.' (See also paras. 13, 26, 31, 32, 33, 34, 35, and 36.) Moreover, *Drake, 1994*, in para. 12, fleetingly referred to the primary purpose of Regulation 1408/71 and Regulation 574/72 of coordinating the various national laws.

110 In the year 1995, the Court referred to coordination in a number of judgments without however attributing the concept any argumentative significance. In *Leclerc-Siplec, 1995* 'the fields coordinated' by the television without frontiers Directive 89/552 were mentioned twice (paras 30 and 32); in *Moscato, 1995*, para. 28, the Court referred to the 'Community coordination of social security schemes in the Member States'; and in *Gebhard, 1995*, para. 36, the Court again referred to the duty of the Council to issue directives coordinating national provisions concerning self-employed activities.

111 In *Pafitis, 1996*, para. 38, and *Siemens, 1996*, para. 13, the Court again employed the term coordination with regard to Directive 77/91 on shareholder protection, but without attributing any substance to it. The same is valid for coordination in *Tomberger, 1996*, para. 17, with regard to Directive 78/660 on annual accounts; and for coordination as used several times in *Commission v. Belgium (TV broadcasting), 1996* with regard to Directive 89/552 on television without frontiers. In *Taflan-Met, 1996* the Court mentioned the term 'coordinate' a number of times with regard to Decision 3/80 and Regulation 1408/71, but again no substance was behind the use of the term (paras 3, 5, 26, and 27).

dence of the children of a migrant self-employed person, because that would mean to discriminate that person. While 'mere coordination' would have negatively affected migrant workers, non-discrimination ensured that the outcome was to their benefit. In *Merino García, 1997* the Court was seized with the same German legislation. However, the Court left out the solidarity-consideration and 'coordination' stated in that context in *Stöber and Pereira, 1997*. Instead, 'coordination, not harmonization' (*Pinna, 1986*) was put forward to justify the compatibility of the solution in the annex for Germany with the Treaty provisions (para. 27). In *Cirotti, 1997* the Court was seized with a situation akin to that at issue in *Levatino, 1993*. However, this time a straightforward Belgian pension was at issue, to which article 51(1) rather than (2) Regulation 1408/71 had to be applied. Any possible advantage for migrant workers was justified by a lack of comparability with non-migrant workers and the idea of 'mere coordination' combined with the lack of a common system as held in *Mura, 1977* (para. 33). Finally, in *Snares, 1997* the Court justified the newly introduced article 10a Regulation 1408/71, which exempted certain benefits from the waiver of residence requirements, by reference to 'coordination'. That a benefit, such as the British benefit at issue, could be made subject to a residence requirement was the consequence of a lack of harmonization (para. 45) as was the resulting reduction in means for the migrant worker concerned (para. 51). Thus, the absence of harmonization, i. e. the negative equivalent of 'coordination', in essence worked at least against the migrant worker concerned.[112]

112 The Court in *Snares, 1997* in addition mentioned the term 'coordination' several times in the judgment. However, in these parts the term was used inconspicuously in a descriptive way, like to describe 'the system of coordination established by the said article 10a' Regulation 1408/71 (para. 27; similarly in paras 29, 32, 33, 37, 40, 46, and 49). The same is valid for *Partridge, 1998*, which dealt with the same British benefit, but included transitional issues (see paras 28, 30, 33, and 34). In a similar vein, in *France v. Commission (pension funds), 1997*, para. 24, the Court held that the Council was exclusively competent to issue directives for the coordination of the member states' law concerning self-employed activities. Coordination, hence, was again inconspicuous. It was so, too, in: *Germany v. Parliament and Council (deposit guarantee), 1997* in which the Court mentioned coordination several times with regard to Directive 94/19 on deposit guarantee schemes; *Futura, 1997*, paras 34 and 35, with regard to article 54(3)(g) Treaty and potential coordinating rules for annual accounts; *Saldanha, 1997*, para. 23, *Daihatsu, 1997*, paras 15 and 18, and *Rabobank, 1997*, paras 19, 22, and 25, with regard to article 54(3)(g) Treaty and the powers of the Council and the directives to coordinate shareholder protection; and *Denuit, 1997*, para. 33, with regard to the fields coordinated by the television without frontiers Directive 89/552. In some contrast, the Court in *De Agostini, 1997* mentioned the coordination by this directive in several paragraphs (paras 24, 25, 27, and 32) and, based on the idea that coordination was only partial, found that the member state in which a programme from another member state was retransmitted could lawfully take some measures to protect consumers. In the year 1999, the Court also mentioned coordination in several judgments without attributing the term a proper argumentative dimension. In *Swaddling, 1999* the coordination rules in article 10a Regulation 1408/71 were mentioned several times (paras 23, 24, and 32). In *Nijhuis, 1999* Community coordination measures and techniques were mentioned repeatedly (paras 29-32). The same is true of *Sürül, 1999* with regard to Decision 3/80 under the Ankara Agreement with Turkey (paras 53-55, and 58). In *Romanelli, 1999*, para. 12, the Court referred to the 'measures taken to coordinate credit institutions' (para. 12) in the context of Directives 77/780 and 89/646 on banks. In *Carbonari, 1999* the Court interpreted the 'coordination directive' 75/363 on activities of doctors. The Court used the term 'coordination directive' throughout the judgment. However, coordination as a concept did not play a role, even in the Court's statement that the coordination directive introduced some harmonisation (para. 38).

Come-back in 2000

The idea of 'coordination' then disappeared from view for almost three years.[113] It came back in *Movrin, 2000*. In this judgment, the Court qualified a German supplementary allowance as an old age benefit which was exportable. In response to the German argument alleging that the former migrant worker, now pensioner concerned was better off in terms of the amount of sickness insurance contributions he had to pay than non-migrant workers turned pensioners, the Court simply referred to the idea of 'mere coordination' of national schemes which had not been harmonised as ruled in *Keller, 1971* and *Mura, 1977*. Any advantages migrant workers possibly drew were a consequence of the lack of a common system (para. 51). *Movrin, 2000* thus clearly ended up favouring migrant workers. In *Engelbrecht, 2000*, essentially the same constellation as in *Van Munster, 1994* was at issue in almost identical legal circumstances. The Court ruled in the same ways as in *Van Munster, 1994*, making use of the same shortened coordination-passage in the same way (para. 37). The judgment in spite of that passage, but owing to *Petroni, 1975*-logic, again was strongly beneficial for migrant workers.[114]

113 A number of decisions should also be mentioned. In *Kohll, 1998* the Court in para. 47 only referred to 'several coordinating or harmonising directives' that had been adopted in the context of recognition of professional medical qualifications. That statement served to weaken the argument of public health put forward as a justification, but coordination hardly played an argumentative role in it. On a different note, in *Decker, 1998* the 'absence of harmonisation' led the Court to reiterate that the member states had the power to determine the conditions of insurance as well as entitlement (para. 23). Yet that did not remove the national provisions relating thereto from the scope of the free movement of goods. In *Decker, 1998* the Court *inter alia* referred to *Coonan, 1980*, to underline the passage including the 'absence of harmonization'. Thus the note made above, in footnote 102, equally applies to *Decker, 1998*. *Terhoeve, 1999* tied in with *Decker, 1998* in this regard and expressly so (para. 34). Moreover, in *Terhoeve, 1999*, the Court referred to coordination ('coordinating' in para. 44), but it seems that this occurred in relation to the power of a member state to coordinate the levying of social security contributions and taxes within its own national legal system. Moreover, the Court in passing referred to coordination in social security in *Kulzer, 1998*, para. 30, and *Grajera Rodríguez, 1998*, para. 26. In *Bellone, 1998*, para. 10, the Court simply mentioned the intention of Directive 86/653 to coordinate national laws on agency contracts. In *Gemeente Arnhem, 1998*, para. 41, the Court with regard to Directive 92/50 on public service contracts referred to the purpose of coordinating at the Community level the national award procedures, which (the purpose) was to eliminate barriers to the freedom of services and thereby protect the interests of economic operators established in other member states. However, it was the freedom of services upon which the Court built its argument rather than the fact of coordination. The same is true of *University of Cambridge, 2000*, para. 16, in which the same passage was reiterated.

114 Four more decisions of the year 2000 need to be discussed briefly with regard to coordination. In *Hocsman, 2000* the Court also referred to 'harmonisation or coordination', if only in an inconspicuous way: 'While that principle [i. e. the principle of recognition stemming from *Vlassopoulou, 1991*] was indeed applied in cases concerning professions for the practice of which there were no harmonisation or coordination measures in existence at the time, its legal ambit cannot be reduced as a result of the adoption of directives on mutual recognition of diplomas.' (Para. 31.) Later on, the Court in *Tennah-Durez, 2003* also explained the system put in place for professional qualifications of medical doctors in terms of coordination and harmonisation in a preliminary remark: 'Hence, Community law makes the award of a doctor's diploma by Member States subject to certain specific requirements, in order that the diploma is capable of being recognised automatically and unconditionally in all the Member States. Those requirements entail a degree of harmonisation and coordination at Community level of both basic and specialist medical training (the harmonisation aspect) and of the rules for taking up and pursuing the activities of a doctor in the Member States (the coordination aspect).' (Para. 31) In the answer to the questions, the Court also relied on the idea of harmonisation, namely in order to hold that a member state could not lawfully award a doctor diploma which

Two judgments in 2001

In *Commission v. Germany (artists' contribution), 2001* the Court declared Germany's legislation compatible with the principle that only one legislation was to be applied to one and the same worker. Germany required German undertakings to levy certain contributions on the services provided by artists and journalists, be they established in Germany or abroad. The Court began by the objectives of Regulation 1408/71 and the fact that it established 'only a system of coordination' (para. 22). The Court then went on to validate the German legislation based on other arguments, notably the prohibition for German undertakings to pass on the levy to the artists. The Court in particular sanctioned that the ultimate level of contributions artists and journalists bore could differ, even depending on the system they were insured with. For the Court that was 'inherent in the mechanism of straightforward co-ordination' (para. 29). Thus, in a sense, *Commission v. Germany (artists' contribution), 2001* again was a judgment in which 'coordination' had a disadvantageous effect on migrant workers. In *Ruhr, 2001* the Court confirmed the ruling in *Cabanis-Issarte, 1996*. The main aim of article 67 to 71a Regulation 1408/71 was solely to coordinate unemployment benefits for workers, not for their family members.[115]

Inverse 'mere coordination'

Next, in *Rydergård, 2002* the Court came back to *Testa, 1980* where it had turned around 'mere coordination'. The Court reiterated that article 69 Regulation 1408/71, which regulated the export of unemployment benefits, did not merely coordinate national laws, but set up an 'independent body of rules' which allowed migrant jobseekers to claim benefits independently of national law. That body of rules had to be interpreted uniformly (para. 18). In spite of that, nation-

---

did not comply with the requirements of Directive 93/16 (in para. 54); and in order to hold that the degree of harmonisation this Directive achieved was not such as to make unnecessary all verification of the training in case of transfer from one institution to another (para. 59). The preliminary remark also justified the rejection of reasoning *per analogiam* with Directive 89/48 and 92/51 (para. 65) and the binding effect of a diploma on the authorities of other member states (para. 75). On a different note, one party in *Vogler, 2000* argued that the Community had the power 'only to coordinate, but not harmonise, the social security systems of the member states' (para. 14). The Court reflected none of that argument in its order rejecting the challenge of the validity of articles 13(1) and 14a(2) Regulation 1408/71. (The mentioning of 'coordinate' in para. 23 was inconspicuous.) In *Luxembourg v. Parliament (lawyer directive), 2000*, para. 32, the Court referred to a situation of 'absence of coordination' which entitled the member states to adopt certain measures. The term coordination, however, did not serve as a basis for an argument.

115 For completeness: In *Khalil, 2001* the Court in passing referred to coordination. The Court ruled that article 51 Treaty had been the right legal basis for the adoption of Regulation 1408/71 and that third country nationals who came directly from a third state to a member state were not entitled to rely on that Regulation. In ruling so, the Court referred to coordination twice. First, article 51 Treaty provided for the technique of coordination to achieve the aim of establishing as complete a freedom as possible, which (the technique) would be ineffective if it applied solely to migrant workers moving within the Community (para. 55). Second, the Court recalled the aim of article 51 Treaty, which was to coordinate national regimes, in order to begin the passage refusing third country nationals who remained in one member state the benefit of Regulation 1408/71 (para. 66). Besides, the Court in *SIAC, 2001*, para. 32, and *HI, 2002*, para. 43, reiterated the passage including the term coordination which had been stated in *Gemeente Arnhem, 1998*. In *Leclere, 2001*, para. 29, the Court en passant mentioned the coordination provisions of Regulation 1408/71.

al law played a certain role, notably, by determining whether a migrant jobseeker had been available for four weeks as article 69(1)(a) required. That solution turned out to the disadvantage of Ms Rydergård, because she had not received unemployment benefits for four straight weeks after she had drawn a benefit available pursuant to Swedish law, because her child had fallen sick.

The 'return' of 'complexity'

After that, in *Hervein II, 2002* the situation at issue in *Hervein I, 1997* returned to the Court, this time for an assessment of the validity under the Treaty of the application of two national legislations at the same time when a person was simultaneously employed in one state while being self-employed in another. The Court repeatedly relied on 'coordination'. It first drew on 'coordination, not harmonisation' in *Pinna, 1986* (para. 50) and deduced from that that Community law did not offer a guarantee that activities pursued in several states were neutral in terms of social security contributions (para. 51). Hence, any resulting disadvantage in comparison to purely domestic workers was acceptable under articles 48 and 52 Treaty, provided in essence that contributions were not paid without any potential return. The Court then reiterated 'mere coordination' which had the consequence that different levels of contributions existed depending on where an activity was pursued (para. 52). From that the Court inferred that the validity of article 14c(b) could only be assessed *in abstracto*. That assessment, essentially, yielded that it could sometimes be more complicated to be subject to two legislations simultaneously. However, in the absence of harmonisation Community law did not guarantee 'neutrality as regards [...] complexity' (para. 58), either. The Court concluded that the Council fulfilled its function to establish a working system, in particular it made sure that equality of treatment for migrant workers was ensured, in spite of mere coordination (para. 60). Thus article 14c(b) was valid. But the states concerned had to make sure that contributions paid resulted in additional social security cover and that the benefit of previous conventions were safeguarded. In essence, the Court relied on 'coordination' several times to justify a solution, which was at least cumbersome for migrant workers.[116]

The two decisions relying on 'coordination' that followed were less spectacular. The Court began *Pasquini, 2003* with 'mere coordination' of national laws, referring somewhat inexplicably to *Lenoir, 1988* (para. 52). As a consequence, national law governed the statute of limitation applicable to claims seeking repayment of pensions paid in excess of what had been due. Ultimately though, the procedural principles of equivalence and effectiveness came to the aid of the migrant worker by, in essence, limiting the period of recovery of sums paid in ex-

116 The Court in a further decision used the term coordination, while not attributing any significant substance to it, namely in *Axa Royale*, 2002, para. 20. The Court pointed at the aim of the third life assurance Directive 92/96 of coordinating minimum provisions.

cess to one year.[117] After that came *Adanez-Vega, 2004*. In that judgment the Court decided a minor point by reference to 'coordination'. Owing to the idea of mere coordination, it was up to national law to determine the concept of 'employment' in article 71(1) Regulation 1408/71 (para. 33).[118]

Advance statement of case-law

Finally, two judgments made use of the idea of coordination in the year 2006. First, *Piatkowski, 2006* was the first clear case in which the idea of 'mere coordination' was part of an advance statement of case-law. The occurrence of that phenomenon by and large corresponds to the advance statements of case-law that emerged in broad interpretation, notably first in *Kurz, 2002* and *Ninni-Orasche, 2003*. The Court in *Piatkowski, 2006* reiterated as part of a preliminary statement that Regulation 1408/71 put in place merely a system of coordination as held in *Hervein II, 2002* (para. 20). The decision itself was then only loosely connected to that and other ideas advanced preliminarily. The Court later on in the judgment concluded that the Netherlands had the power to subject a certain amount paid to meet a debt to social security contributions as income of the person concerned. The second case, *Nikula, 2006*, did not involve an advance statement. Mere coordination with reference to *Piatkowski, 2006* (para. 20 of *Nikula, 2006*) set the tone for the judgment, while it was not directly linked to the first point at issue which was rather decided by articles 27 and 33(1) Regulation 1408/71. Those articles determined that the state of residence was competent to levy contributions from resident pensioners and to grant them benefits in kind. However, 'in the absence of harmonisation' (para. 24) the member state concerned also had the power, within certain confines, to determine the income subject to contributions.[119]

117 In *BIAO, 2003*, paras 69 and 73, the Court in the context of Directive 78/660 on annual accounts referred in passing to the coordination of national provisions and valuation methods.

118 Several judgments in the years 2004 and 2005 referred to coordination, while not relying on it as a substantive concept. In *Paul, 2004*, para. 43, the Court in the context of the banking directives 77/780, 89/299, and 89/646 and article 57(2) Treaty stated as follows: 'However, the coordination of the national rules on the liability of national authorities in respect of depositors in the event of defective supervision does not appear to be necessary to secure the results described in the preceding paragraph.' Although it may seem so from the pure wording of that passage, the Court did not argue on the basis of coordination. This is obvious from the preceding paragraph in the judgment. In *Bacardi, 2004*, para. 25, the Court again mentioned the 'fields coordinated' by the television without frontier directive 89/552 as in *Leclerc-Siplec, 1995*. In *Skalka, 2004*, para. 31, again the coordinating provisions laid down in article 10a Regulation 1408/71 were mentioned like in *Swaddling, 1999*. In *Epikouriko Kefalaio, 2004*, paras 24 and 25, the Court mentioned the coordinating rules and the coordination of national provisions in the context of Directive 73/239 and 79/267 on direct insurance and life assurance. In *Salgado, 2005*, para. 29, the Court mentioned the 'Community coordination of social security schemes'. In *Commission v. Austria (dentists), 2005* the Court again repeatedly used the term 'coordination directive' for Directive 78/687 on dental practitioners.

119 In *Honyvem, 2006* relating to Directive 86/653 on commercial agents the Court mentioned the aim of the Directive of coordinating the laws of the member states as regarded agency contracts (para. 18), as in *Bellone, 1998*. In *Centrosteel, 2000* the Court had stated the same passage, except that it said that the Directive intended to *harmonise* the laws of the Member States (para. 13). In the French versions of the judgments the Court consistently used the word 'harmoniser'. In any case the Court used the term(s) in an inconspicuous way. In *Commission v. France (performing artists), 2006*, para. 48, the Court again mentioned en passant the coordination of social security. In *Kersbergen, 2006*,

b) Spin – and advance statement of case-law

When did 'coordination' spin the decision? Before addressing this question, a remark on the advance statement of case-law is in order. It is noteworthy that the advance statement of case-law observed in broad interpretation also came in use for 'mere coordination' late in the age of Maastricht, notably in *Piatkowski, 2006*. This judgment, however, remained the only occurrence of an advance statement of case-law within 'coordination'. Obviously, the advance statement of case-law neutralised any spin 'coordination' could have had in *Piatkowski, 2006*.

Apart from that, though, spin regularly occurred with 'mere coordination'. In *Levatino, 1993* the idea of 'the sole purpose being to secure coordination' when it first occurred in the judgment was combined with the need to avoid disruption of the national scheme. This led to the conclusion that the Belgian benefit guaranteeing a minimum income had to be recalculated whenever the pension paid abroad had been adjusted. Spin was thus strong, in particular since it enabled an interpretation which, judged by the wording of article 51 Regulation 1408/71, was quite counter-intuitive. In *Lepore, 1993* 'mere coordination' spun the decision in the – minor – question of how to calculate remuneration for notional periods under national law. In *McLachlan, 1994* the 'separate claims'-phrase which had re-emerged provided spin to justify why periods completed abroad were not factored into the calculation of a benefit. The second reiteration of the phrase together with 'mere coordination', however, merely explained the resulting disadvantages *ex post*. However, in aggregate, although 'coordination' loomed large in this judgment, spin was soft at best, because the real argument put forward by Mr McLachlan was one of consistency between unemployment and old age benefits. That argument, in a way, was eschewed by the Court pointing out the obvious on the basis of 'coordination'. In *Van Munster, 1994* the Court repeatedly relied on 'mere coordination'. While in the first question spin could not be ascertained, in the second question 'mere coordination' could have created some spin. Yet the 'mere coordination'-passage was preceded by the negative qualifier '[w]hile it is true...', which *ab initio* cancelled any spin possible. *Petroni, 1975*-logic followed to become the essential reason why national authorities were obliged to interpret national law in view of the implications of another member state's law with regard to household pensions. The same is true for *Engelbrecht, 2000*. In *De Jaeck, 1997* the *Pinna, 1986*-formula framed the Court's consideration. It was mentioned both at the beginning and towards the middle of the judgment. The formula spun the Court's decision in the direction of granting member states the power to define the terms at issue, namely employed/self-employed persons. In *Hervein I, 1997*, the formula was used only once, but for an identical purpose and with the same spin.

---

para. 23, again the Court simply referred to the coordinating regime established by article 10a Regulation 1408/71.

The return of empty spin

Then came *Stöber and Pereira, 1997* and with it empty spin returned. 'Mere coordination' seemed to spin the Court's decision towards validating Germany's approach relying on the residence of a migrant self-employed person's children. However, non-discrimination intervened and cancelled out the momentum 'mere coordination' had provided. The spin given did not, therefore, prevail in the end. In *Merino García, 1997*, in the same legal context as in *Stöber and Pereira, 1997*, 'coordination, not harmonization' provided the momentum to clear the annex regarding Germany of any suspicion of incompatibility with the Treaty. However, the element of empty spin present in *Stöber and Pereira, 1997* did not occur in *Merino García, 1997*. I took until 2002 for the next case of empty spin to occur with *Rydergård, 2002*, with the inverse of 'mere coordination' nota bene. Although article 69 Regulation 1408/71 had not merely coordinated national laws as to unemployment benefits – an idea that exerted spin – national law determined when a jobseeker had been available for four weeks within the meaning of article 69(1)(a). Next, in *Pasquini, 2003* 'mere coordination' initially spun the decision towards awarding the power to regulate the statute of limitation applicable to the recovery of sums overpaid to the member states. That spin was cancelled though by the principles of equivalence and effectiveness which had the effect of fixing the statute of limitation to one year. Hence, it was just an element of empty spin that occurred in *Pasquini, 2003*.

Regular spin

In the meanwhile regular spin continued to occur. In *Snares, 1997* the 'absence of harmonization', when it was mentioned for the first time, was part of a whole number of considerations that led the Court to the decision to sanction the exemption from the waiver of residence clauses in article 10a and the British residence requirement. Hence, spin was very mild at best. In *Commission v. Germany (artists' contribution), 2001* the idea of mere coordination then again clearly spun the Court's decision. The Court put 'coordination' forward right at the beginning of the judgment and thus set the tone to validate Germany's contributions levied on artists and journalists. Moreover, 'coordination' also served to validate the differing levels of contributions that resulted.

Hervein II, 2002 certainly was the pinnacle in terms of spin by 'mere coordination'. The Court repeatedly referred to the idea of coordination to justify the simultaneous application of two national legislations to one and the same person, because he was at the same time employed in one state and self-employed in another. More specifically, 'mere coordination' spun the decision towards accepting that no neutrality as to contributions and their levels could exist when activities were pursued in two states at the same time. It also spurred the decision on to accept a lack of neutrality in terms of complexity. 'Coordination' thus drove the entire decision.

In *Adanez-Vega, 2004* 'mere coordination' spun a minor part of the decision. It motivated the Court to leave it to national law to determine the concept of 'employment' in article 71(1) Regulation 1408/71. Finally, in *Nikula, 2006* 'mere coordination' and the 'absence of harmonisation' provided some spin, at least for the Court to grant Finland the power to determine the income of resident pensioners relevant for social security contributions.

c) Some conclusions from the period

The idea of 'mere coordination' was applied in a wide variety of cases and circumstances during the age of Maastricht. The abstraction of the idea we noted in the previous period was confirmed in the age of Maastricht. A single root in case-law has no longer been discernible. The Court referred to the latest judgment applying the idea of 'mere coordination' or to the last judgment deploying the idea in a similar legal context.

We also note that the turn 'mere coordination' had taken during the preceding period was confirmed in the age of Maastricht. 'Mere coordination' in the majority of cases worked to the detriment of migrant workers. *Levatino, 1993*, *Lepore, 1993*, and *McLachlan, 1994* were clear in this regard; *Cabanis-Issarte, 1996* and *De Jaeck, 1997* less obviously so, but still migrant workers did not emerge unscathed from those judgments. In *Stöber and Pereira, 1997* 'coordination' seemed to work to the detriment of migrant workers, but the resulting judgment was largely advantageous *qua* non-discrimination. *Merino García, 1997* is difficult to classify in this regard, while in *Snares, 1997* 'coordination' was clearly detrimental to workers. In *Pasquini, 2003* 'coordination' functioned disadvantageously, but equivalence and effectiveness cancelled the effect. The detrimental role of 'coordination' was rather clear in *Hervein II, 2002*. In *Van Munster, 1994* and the related *Engelbrecht, 2000* 'coordination' seemed to work to the detriment of migrant workers, but *Petroni, 1975*-logic intervened and gave the judgments the strongly advantageous twist for migrant workers. In some contrast, the inverse was the case in *Rydergård, 2002*: the decision worked to the disadvantage of migrant workers although 'no mere coordination', viz. harmonisation, had been achieved by article 69 Regulation 1408/71. Thus, *Rydergård, 2002* with some imagination could be read inversely, so that 'mere coordination' would have advantaged migrant workers. Despite that, the initial function which 'mere coordination' had of supporting migrant workers by securing them an advantage over purely domestic workers – a function it had fulfilled most prominently in the earliest case-law – almost vanished. It was only apparent in two judgments, namely *Cirotti, 1997* and *Movrin, 2000*.[120] Hence, in the vast majority of cases in which the Court applied the idea of 'mere coordination' that idea had a negative effect on migrant workers.

Again, the question whether 'mere coordination' favours or disfavours migrant workers needs to be distinguished from the power, the spin of the interpretive formula. 'Mere coordination' continued to spin the Court's decisions regu-

120 Two judgments can be considered to be neutral with regard to the effect of 'coordination' on migrant workers, namely *Adanez-Vega, 2004* and *Piatkowski, 2006*.

larly during the 'age of Maastricht' – sometimes even strongly – while empty spin remained rather rare. Moreover, a clear advance statement of case-law, which almost by nature neutralizes any possible spin, occurred only in one case for 'mere coordination'. Beyond those rather general conclusions, the above examination offers further details.

4 The present

a) Occurrence of 'coordinated' – frequent use

The present again witnessed regular use of the idea of mere coordination. The first judgment in the present in which 'coordination' played a role was *Derouin, 2008*. Seized with the question whether the competent state pursuant to Regulation 1408/71 was free or obliged to levy certain contributions on income gained abroad, the Court *inter alia* answered with 'mere coordination' (paras 20 and 26). As a consequence, the member state concerned was free to determine the tax base relevant for such contributions and thus to include or forgo the income concerned, provided that the insured person enjoyed all of the benefits under that state's legislation. The member state enjoyed that freedom to the detriment of the migrant worker concerned.[121] In contrast, *Chuck, 2008* was largely beneficial for migrant workers. The Court began with strong 'mere coordination'-logic (paras 26-7), but counteracted it with broad interpretation on the 'greatest possible freedom'. Based on the objectives of article 51 Treaty, the

121 In the context of the posted workers Directive 96/71 several judgments referred to coordination. After the Court had referred to coordination already in *Arblade, 1999* – the 'Community directives providing for coordination or a minimum degree of harmonisation in respect of the information necessary for the protection of workers' (para. 67) – the Court in *Commission v. Germany (posted workers), 2007* stated: 'Directive 96/71 seeks to coordinate the laws of the Member States by establishing a list of national rules that a member state must apply [...].' (Para. 17) In *Laval, 2007* the Court held: 'It follows from recital 13 to Directive 96/71 that the laws of the Member States must be coordinated in order to lay down a nucleus of mandatory rules for minimum protection to be observed in the host country by employers who post workers there.' (Para. 59) The Court then went on to state that nonetheless the material content of those rules was not harmonised and could be freely determined by the member states (para. 60). This has been the only situation in the context of Directive 96/71 in which the Court actually used coordination to some limited extent as an argument rather than mentioning it as a mere fact without attaching any consequences to it. In *Commission v. Luxembourg (posted workers), 2008* the Court in a preliminary observation in para. 24 reiterated para. 59 of *Laval, 2007*, when assessing Luxembourg's public policy provisions. However, that reference to coordination was of little significance. Rather, the reasoning based on public policy and broad interpretation drove the Court's considerations. In *Santos Palhota, 2010*, para. 26, the Court again in passing cited coordination: 'Directive 96/71 seeks to coordinate the substantive national rules on the terms and conditions of employment of posted workers, independently of the ancillary administrative rules designed to enable compliance with those terms and conditions to be monitored.' From that the Court concluded that the member states were free to lay down those latter rules, provided they complied with the Treaty. On a different note, the Court also mentioned coordination en passant in a few other judgments in 2007. In *El Youssfi, 2007*, para. 39, the Court mentioned the coordination of social security systems; in *Hendrix, 2007*, the coordinating provision of article 10a Regulation 1408/71 (para. 38) and 'a coordinating regulation such as Regulation 1408/71' (para. 51). In *Commission v. Ireland (An Post), 2007*, para. 27, finally, the Court rehearsed the passage from *Gemeente Arnhem, 1998*, including 'coordinating'.

Court found that residence outside the territory of the Union did not prevent aggregation of insurance periods completed within the Union pursuant to Regulation 1408/71. In *Baesen, 2010* the Court applied 'mere coordination' in what had by then become the standard way: It reiterated 'mere coordination' to lead up to the finding that national law determined who was a 'civil servant' for the purpose of article 13(2)(d) Regulation 1408/71 (paras 22 and 25). At least for the migrant worker concerned, this finding constituted a disadvantage.[122]

Absence of harmonisation as a proxy

The Court in *Klöppel, 2008* referred to the 'absence of harmonisation' in social security and inferred from that the power of the member states to determine the conditions of social security benefits, subject to compliance with the Treaty (para. 16). In this context,[123] 'absence of harmonisation' stood in for 'mere coordination' and fulfilled the same role. However, the Court resorted to non-discrimination in article 3(1) Regulation 1408/71 to make Austria include periods during which a partner had drawn a childcare allowance abroad for the purpose of an allowance in Austria. Hence, despite 'coordination' in the form of 'no harmonisation', a result in favour of migrant workers was reached. In *Elchinov, 2010* the Court again resorted to 'absence of harmonisation' as a proxy for 'mere coordination', like in *Klöppel, 2008*, this time in the context of article 22 Regulation 1408/71 (para. 57). 'Mere coordination' in this case served the Court to hand on the task to the national court to determine whether a specific treatment was listed pursuant to national legislation and thus covered.

'Coordination' v. free movement

The Court in *Petersen, 2008* rehearsed 'mere coordination' (para. 41) after having qualified the Austrian benefit at issue as an unemployment benefit. 'Mere coordination' was then juxtaposed with *Petroni, 1975*-logic. From that logic the Court concluded that the compatibility of the Austrian legislation with the free movement of workers had to be examined. That examination yielded that Austria's residence requirement was not in accordance with the free movement of workers. Obviously, that result was to the advantage of migrant workers, though it was so *despite* coordination rather than owing to it. In *Leyman, 2009* the Court applied almost the same approach. After having found that Belgium's way of calculating an invalidity benefit as per the end of a one-year period of incapacity complied technically with article 40 Regulation 1408/71, the Court examined the free movement of workers. That examination began with the shortened version of 'mere coordination' based on *Rönfeldt, 1991* and *Van Munster,*

122 The Court mentioned coordination in some other decisions, too, though without attributing any significance to the term. In *Commission v. Spain (hospital pharmacists), 2008*, para. 42, the Court mentioned coordination in the context of article 47(3) Treaty and Directive 89/48 on diploma recognition. In *Bosmann, 2008*, para. 30, the Court referred to the coordination of national social security legislations. In *Commission v. Spain, 2008*, para. 23, the Court mentioned coordination with regard to Directive 77/91 on shareholder protection, like in *Siemens, 1996*.

123 See below the note in footnote 127.

1994 (para. 40) and *Petroni, 1975*-logic immediately followed. That logic was disregarded in that Belgian law had the effect that the person concerned had paid contributions for a year, but failed to receive any return. The resulting disadvantage was contrary to the freedom of workers, although no guarantee existed for a move to another state to be neutral in terms of social security. Thus, *Petroni, 1975*-logic again intervened in favour of the migrant worker, although 'mere coordination' had suggested the contrary.[124]

No guarantee of neutrality

In *Von Chamier-Glisczinski, 2009* the Court also relied on 'mere coordination' (para. 84). It served to put into perspective the less favourable treatment the Union citizen concerned suffered, because sickness insurance pursuant to German legislation and in accordance with Regulation 1408/71 did not cover the care allowance in kind provided in Austria. That disadvantage was the consequence of 'mere coordination'. A guarantee that a move to another state would be neutral in terms of social security did not exist (para. 85). Hence, article 18 Treaty did not render the relevant German legislation invalid, to the obvious distress of migrant workers. In quite a similar way the Court in *Van Delft, 2010* came back to 'mere coordination' (para. 99) combined with the no neutrality-guarantee. Again that approach held out against the challenges put forward by the migrant pensioners on the basis of Union citizenship. They, in particular, had to accept that a change in Dutch legislation had the effect of entitling them, as pensioners receiving a pension in the Netherlands, to draw benefits in the host state where they resided, while the voluntary Dutch sickness insurance contracts they had concluded under the old Dutch scheme were *eo ipso* terminated. The only condition was that the new insurance contracts that all pensioners had to conclude in that context were not less advantageous for them than for pensioners residing in the Netherlands.

'Coordination' under medical services

The Court in *Commission v. Spain (Chollet), 2010* used 'mere coordination' again together with 'no neutrality' to distinguish the case of unplanned hospital treatment in the host state from the *Vanbraekel, 2001*-constellation of planned hospital treatment abroad. Interestingly, the Court applied 'mere coordination'-logic within the context of the freedom of medical services which was the only provision at issue, while article 22 Regulation 1408/71 was not directly involved.

124 In *Eschig, 2009*, the Court dealt with Directive 87/344 on the coordination of legal expenses insurance. In the context of a contractual restriction to choose the lawyer representing the insured in proceeding involving group claims the Court added that the Directive did 'not seek to completely harmonise' the national rules on legal expenses insurance, but that the member states remained free to determine the applicable rules, while respecting Community law (paras 65-6). However, a further consequence was not drawn from that. In *Semen, 2009*, para. 14, the Court again stated simply that Directive 86/653 sought to coordinate the laws of the member states on agency contracts, like in *Honyvem, 2006*. In *Rüffler, 2009*, moreover, the Court mentioned the 'coordination of social security schemes' (para. 79) and 'rules of secondary legislation coordinating the social security systems' (para. 81). However, coordination was inconsequential in those passages.

The Court relied on 'mere coordination' (para. 61) to explain why the 'home' state did not have to provide supplementary cover to help the service receiver meet the cost encountered by reason of unplanned medical treatment in the host state where the sickness insurance scheme provided less coverage than in the 'home state'. Again the judgment worked to the disadvantage of migrant workers.[125]

Advance statement

The Court again referred to 'mere coordination' in *Tomaszewska, 2011*. The reference was part of an advance statement of practice (para. 25), after which the Court found that Poland was required to take account of periods of insurance completed abroad when determining the maximum number of periods of non-contribution allowed to count towards the thirty years of contribution needed to acquire a pension in Poland.[126] Next, in *Da Silva Martins, 2011* 'mere coordination' (para. 71) and the no neutrality-clause joined the broad interpretation of the 'greatest possible freedom', again in an advance statement of case-law. From this the Court concluded that the German care allowance was to be exportable in the circumstances of the case. That decision was very much informed by the free movement of workers and the idea that contributions paid were not to remain without return. Both judgments, *Tomaszewska, 2011* and *Da Silva Martins, 2011* were favourable for migrant workers. In *Stewart, 2011* the Court again recited 'mere coordination' as part of an advance statement of case-law (para. 75)[127] when examining the compatibility of the condition to have been

125 The Court in *Pérez and Gómez, 2010*, para. 50, stated the following: 'That finding is supported, furthermore, by recital 26 in the preamble to Directive 2005/36 [on professional qualifications], pursuant to which the directive does not coordinate all the conditions for access to activities in the field of pharmacy, so that the territorial distribution of pharmacies, in particular, remains a matter for the Member States.' Although it was not very explicit, the Court in this passage relied on the coordination of only certain conditions in Directive 2005/36 to justify in part why certain powers remained with the member states. Besides, in *Rani, 2010*, para. 34, the Court mentioned the direct applicability of article 49 Treaty without that any harmonising or coordinating provisions were necessary, like in *Commission v. Germany (insurance), 1986*. No further consequences were attached to the notion 'coordinating provisions'. In *Idrima Tipou, 2010*, para. 38, article 50(2)(g) Treaty was mentioned according to which the Union legislature was to adopt directives to coordinate the protection of the interests of certain members of companies; accordingly, Directive 68/161 pursued the aim of coordinating national provisions in this regard (para. 39). In both passages coordination did not have any further significance. Finally, in *Commission v. Ireland (award criteria), 2010*, para. 30, the Court again reiterated the passage stemming from *Gemeente Arnhem, 1998*, including 'coordinating'.

126 In *Stark, 2011* the Court again applied Directive 87/344 on the coordination of legal expenses insurance. Referring to *Eschig, 2009* the Court deduced from the lack of complete harmonisation (para. 31) that the parties to an insurance contract were free within certain limits to determine what the contract covered.

127 In *Stewart, 2011* 'mere coordination' was immediately followed by the following passage: 'Therefore, in the absence of harmonisation at EU level, it is for the legislation of each Member State to determine, first, the conditions concerning the right or duty to be insured with a social security scheme and, second, the conditions for entitlement to benefits', followed by a reference to *Kohll, 1998*. The Court has routinely put that passage, or one that is similar, forward at the beginning of medical services judgments, see *Smits, 2001*, para. 45, or *Commission v. France (Vanbraekel), 2010*, para. 29. It also appeared in some form or another in social security judgments (see footnote 102 above). In *Stöber and Pereira, 1997*, which was discussed above under 'mere coordination', the member states' power to determine the conditions for entitlement was explained by the merely coordinating role that Regulation 1408/71 played (para. 36). Thus, there is an obvious affinity between

present for 26 out of 52 weeks to be entitled to a benefit in the United Kingdom. The Court ultimately accepted the argument that the criterion was not representative of a genuine link with the British society. Thus it fell afoul of the requirements of Union citizenship.[128]

'No neutrality' and 'coordination', again

In *Hudzinski, 2012* the Court also reiterated 'mere coordination' together with the resulting power of member states to determine the criteria for social security

---

'mere coordination' and 'in the absence of harmonisation', as is also evidenced above in *Rydergård, 2002*, and *Nikula, 2006*. However, 'absence of harmonisation' can only be treated as a substitute for 'mere coordination', if there *are* coordinating provisions, i. e. typically in social security (see *Klöppel, 2008*, para. 16). Thus, the use of 'absence of harmonisation' in medical services judgments which were handed down exclusively on the basis of the freedom of services is of little interest for this chapter. 'Absence of harmonisation' in those cases merely stands for 'there are no Community rules' and hence the member states retain the corresponding power. See para. 100 of *Müller-Fauré, 2003*; para. 17 of *Inizan, 2003*; para 92 of *Watts, 2006*; para. 23 of *Stamatelaki, 2007*; para. 29 of *Commission v. France (Vanbraekel), 2010*; para. 53 of *Commission v. Spain (Chollet), 2010*; para. 47 of *Commission v. Portugal (medical treatment), 2011*; or para. 49 of *Commission v. Germany (care insurance), 2012*. Admittedly though, it was not always obvious whether the Court reasoned on the basis of the freedom of medical services or the provisions of social security: see *Kohll, 1998* (para. 18), and *Elchinov, 2010*, para. 40. *Xhymshiti, 2010*, was a borderline case in that regard. The Court ruled that Regulation 1408/71 was not applicable, essentially because only Germany was concerned and Switzerland could not be considered a member state, since the extension of the scope of Regulation 1408/71 to cover third country nationals had not been transposed under the Agreement on Free Movement with Switzerland. Hence the reference of the Court in para. 43 to the 'absence of harmonisation' could not be understood to stand for 'mere coordination', for there was no coordination in that situation for third country nationals. The difference becomes much clearer in *tax* judgments such as *Gilly, 1998*. In this judgment the Court repeatedly pointed to the absence of harmonisation: 'no unifying or harmonising measure for the elimination of double taxation has yet been adopted at Community level' (para 23); 'in the absence of any Community legislation in the field, the determination of those [tax] scales is a matter for the Member States' (para. 47). It is obvious that those passages cannot be read inversely so as to substitute for 'mere coordination'. Hence, such passages in tax judgments are of little interest for 'coordination' as an interpretive formula, which is the subject of this chapter. Nonetheless, it would certainly be interesting to examine the narrative of the idea of 'absence of harmonisation' in the medical services and tax case-law, in particular through the prism of 'spin'.

128 In *Commission v. Ireland (direct insurance), 2011* the Court applied Directive 73/239 on direct insurance. The Court began the judgment by referring to coordination: '[T]he First Directive is intended to facilitate the taking-up and pursuit of direct insurance other than life insurance by removing variations between national laws on controls and by coordinating, in particular, legal provisions on the financial guarantees required of the insurance undertakings.' (Para. 2) However, the Court did not draw any apparent conclusion from that reference to coordination, in contrast to the broad interpretation that came to be applied in the same judgment. In *Perez Garcia, 2011*, para. 51, the Court also mentioned coordination unobtrusively in the context of the social security rules. Similarly, in *Commission v. Portugal (medical treatment), 2011*, para. 81, coordination was mentioned inconspicuously in the context of an argument on the quality of medical services ('several coordinating or harmonising directives'). In *Bergström, 2011*, para. 33, the Court ruled that the Agreement on Free Movement with Switzerland had to be applicable to a Swedish national who had worked in Switzerland, but then returned to Sweden, else the coordination between the Swiss system and the system of Sweden as a member state would be precluded in 'a not insignificant number of situations'. Coordination did not play an argumentative role in that context, though. In a similar way, the Court in *Akdas, 2011*, para. 70, referred to the 'technical provisions for the coordination of the different national laws on social security'. In *Mesopotamia, 2011*, moreover, the Court again referred a number of times to the 'fields coordinated' by Directive 89/552 on television without frontiers. In para. 32, in addition, the Court stated that the fields coordinated by the Directive were only coordinated in so far as television broadcasting was concerned. In none of these references did coordination as a concept play a role of any significance. In a similar vein, the Court in *Premier League, 2011* mentioned several times the 'fields coordinated' by the Conditional Access Directive 98/84 (paras 69-74).

benefits (para. 42). The 'no neutrality-guarantee' fed into this consideration for the Court to reach the preliminary result that the workers concerned were in principle entitled exclusively to family benefits in Poland. However, the Court then put that result into perspective, partly based on broad interpretation. Regulation 1408/71 was not to be understood so as to deprive a migrant worker of child benefits national law conferred. Moreover a national rule against the overlapping of benefits was not to be applied, either, in the circumstances of one of the cases at issue. Thus, in *Hudzinski, 2012* again 'mere coordination' would have resulted in a disadvantage for migrant workers, but the freedom of workers neutralised its push. Hence the outcome strongly benefitted migrant workers. Next, in *Commission v. Germany (care insurance), 2012* the Court resorted to 'mere coordination' pursuant to article 48 Treaty (para. 57) and the resulting 'no neutrality-guarantee' for movements in application of the freedom of medical services. The passage, however, was only one argument in many which led the Court to refuse to transpose in general the medical services case-law under the free movement of services to the reliance on care. Nonetheless, 'mere coordination' contributed to a decision that was detrimental for migrant workers.

The latest cases

In *Commission v. Austria (transport fare), 2012* the Court rejected Austria's argument drawn from the fact that the reduced transport fare constituted a family benefit subject to Regulation 1408/71. The Court held that non-discrimination was to be complied with irrespective of whether Regulation 1408/71 applied. In that context the Court reiterated that Regulation 1408/71 merely coordinated national schemes (para. 46) and the member states remained at liberty to determine the conditions for entitlement and the right or duty to be insured, provided they complied with the Treaty freedoms.[129]

In *Dumont, 2013* the Court made use of 'mere coordination' together with the 'different claims…'-passage (read: 'separate claims', para. 41), and combined it with the power of the states to lay down the conditions of benefits to explain why articles 78(2) and 79(1) Regulation 1408/71 merely determined the applicable legislation rather than the conditions of social security benefits. As a consequence, if the applicable national law provided for orphan's benefits, those benefits had to be granted, if necessary after aggregation of periods. The result of the application of 'mere coordination' was thus favourable for migrant workers. Next, in *Salgado González, 2013* 'mere coordination' (para. 35) again together with the member states' power to define the conditions for entitlement to benefits was part of a short advance statement of case-law. Ultimately, the Court

129 In the action for interim relief in *United Kingdom v. Council, 2012* the Court in para. 41 referred to coordination: 'With regard to the damage alleged by the United Kingdom resulting from rights definitively acquired by individuals in the area of coordination of social security over the course of the period during which the decision of the Joint Committee applying the contested decision remains in force, it must be held that this is damage which is essentially pecuniary in nature.' Obviously, the idea of coordination did not have any impact on the reasoning of the Court. The same is valid for the reference to coordination in para. 29 of *Reichel, 2012*.

concluded that the Spanish average contribution basis had to be calculated by reference to the periods completed in Spain only, but that conclusion favouring migrant workers was strongly based on an interpretation of the relevant articles of Regulation 1408/71.

Finally, in *Jeltes, 2013* 'mere coordination' appeared twice. First, it served to explain why the new regime for unemployment benefits of frontier workers under Regulation 883/2004, which broke with *Miethe, 1986*, was in accordance with the free movement of workers. Arguably, the amount of unemployment benefits the state of employment would have awarded would have been higher in the case at issue than the amount granted in application of the new regime by the state of residence. However, that was the consequence of 'mere coordination' together with the 'no neutrality-guarantee' (para. 43) and the lack of harmonisation (para. 45). Second, 'mere coordination' implied that the term 'unchanged situation' in article 87(8) Regulation 883/2004 was to be determined by national law (para. 59). In both occurrences, the migrant workers concerned had to accept a disadvantage owing to 'mere coordination', though in the first occurrence the disadvantage was clearer.

b) Spin

When was the idea of 'mere coordination' instrumental for the Court's decision? In which judgments did it exert spin? In *Derouin, 2008* 'mere coordination' clearly provided the spin needed to arrive at the conclusion that the competent member state pursuant to Regulation 1408/71 was free to include or ignore certain income gained abroad when levying social security contributions. In *Commission v. Spain (Chollet), 2010* 'mere coordination' to some limited extent spun the decision not to oblige the 'home' state to meet the cost that host state legislation did not cover in cases of unplanned treatment, while such cost would have been covered had the treatment been provided in the 'home' state. Curiously, 'mere coordination' served as justification in the context of the freedom to receive services.

In *Elchinov, 2010* the 'absence of harmonisation' substituted for 'mere coordination' in the context of article 22 Regulation 1408/71. It provided the spin necessary to hand on the decision whether a specific treatment was covered to the national court. In *Van Delft, 2010* coordination-logic spun the Court's decision very strongly. It provided the momentum for the Court to find that the effects of the change in Dutch legislation on pensioners living abroad were in accordance with Union citizenship. The only proviso was that the national court did not find any discriminatory treatment in the conclusion of the new insurance contracts which had become necessary as a consequence of the change in legislation. In *Baesen, 2010* 'mere coordination' prompted the Court to grant the power to fill the notion 'civil servant' with content to the member states.

In *Commission v. Austria (transport fare), 2012* 'mere coordination' provided some limited spin to decide the minor issue that non-discrimination applied even though a benefit was possibly within the scope of Regulation 1408/71. In *Du-*

mont, 2013 'mere coordination' spun the Court's decision towards ignoring the wording of article 78(2)(b) Regulation 1408/71. The Court held that the norm merely identified the applicable legislation by means of connecting factors, while the national law thus identified determined the substantive conditions. The rest of the judgment, however, did not result from 'coordination', but was largely unrelated to it. In that part the spin exerted by broad interpretation in the form of the 'greatest possible freedom' was more dominant. In *Jeltes, 2013*, finally, the second occurrence of 'mere coordination' clearly spun the decision towards accepting the power of the member states to define the term 'unchanged situation'. In the first occurrence, in contrast, it merely served to explain why the consequence of the new regime established by Regulation 883/2004 – that the amount of unemployment benefits paid *in concreto* was lower than under the old regime of Regulation 1408/71 – was in accordance with free movement of workers. In that regard 'mere coordination' could only be considered to have exerted very limited spin.

Empty spin

In a quite surprising number of decisions the phenomenon of empty spin occurred in the present. In *Klöppel, 2008* 'absence of harmonisation' as a proxy for 'mere coordination' initially seemed to spin the decision. It seemed that the Court would accept that Austria would not take account of periods during which a childcare allowance was paid abroad. However, non-discrimination stepped in and turned around the decision, emptying the spin the 'absence of harmonisation' had created. *Chuck, 2008* again was a case of empty spin of 'mere coordination'. The Court first referred to 'mere coordination', implying that aggregation was subject to the laws of the member states in case the person concerned resided outside the Union. However, that spin was countered by the broad interpretation formula of the 'greatest possible freedom'. Hence, the spin of 'mere coordination' was counter-spun by broad interpretation. In *Petersen, 2008* 'mere coordination' in a similar way spun emptily. 'Mere coordination' would have implied that Austria's residence requirement was lawful, but *Petroni, 1975*-logic intervened to justify the examination under article 39 Treaty. The outcome of that examination was that the residence requirement was not in accordance with the free movement of workers. The spin 'mere coordination' had initially provided was thus cancelled. The same can be said of *Leyman, 2009*. 'Mere coordination' would have indicated that the disadvantage resulting from Belgian legislation would have been acceptable. However, the free movement of workers stepped in to neutralize that spin. In the perspective of the freedom of workers, the disadvantage that would have resulted was unacceptable, since social security contributions would have been paid in vain. As a result, the spin provided by 'mere coordination' did not prevail, but became empty. *Hudzinski, 2012* again was a clear case of empty spin. The Court first reached the preliminary conclusion that Poland was competent for the family benefits of the persons concerned based on 'mere coordination', but then this conclusion was neutralized. It did not mean that German law could not under any circumstances award benefits. Moreover, despite the preliminary conclusion, the national rule against overlapping could not be applied, either. Thus, the clear spin 'mere coordination' had initially brought to bear ran empty. The final decision went against the grain of what 'mere coordination' had indicated.

Advance statement cancelling out spin

In *Tomaszewska, 2011* 'mere coordination' could possibly have exerted spin, but it was part of a long advance statement of practice which made spin impossible to detect. The same is valid for *Da Silva Martins, 2011*, in which 'mere coordination' together with the 'greatest possible freedom'-formula was part of an advance statement of practice. This made it difficult to determine any spin, including empty spin. In *Stewart, 2011* 'mere coordination' was again part of an advance statement of case-law. Hence, any spin 'coordination' might have exerted was shrouded.

Compliance with the Treaty freedoms obscuring spin

In *Salgado González, 2013* 'mere coordination' was again enveloped in an advance statement of case-law, though it was a short statement. However, a tendency of the Court which has been discernible in the latest judgments in the present became certain in *Salgado González, 2013*, namely that the Court has moved to combine 'mere coordination' with the member states' power to determine the conditions of entitlement to social security and then to put those two considerations into perspective right away by emphasizing the need to comply with the Treaty freedoms. This firm combination of three partly conflicting elements – 'mere coordination', the power of the member states, the Treaty freedoms – has further worked to obscure the spin 'mere coordination' potentially could have.

c) Some conclusions from the period

In the present, the idea of 'mere coordination' regularly occurred in the judgments of the Court. The negative twist it had taken in the period leading up to the 'Maastricht moment' has broadly been confirmed. In most judgments, 'mere coordination' erected an obstacle for migrant workers, though in some it succumbed to other arguments. In *Derouin, 2008*, *Von Chamier-Glisczinski, 2009*, *Van Delft, 2010*, *Baesen, 2010*, *Commission v. Germany (care insurance), 2012*, and *Jeltes, 2013* 'mere coordination' rather patently worked to the disadvantage of migrant workers. *Klöppel, 2008*, *Petersen, 2008*, *Leyman, 2009* and *Hudzinski, 2012* all worked to the advantage of migrant workers, but the decisions did so *in spite of* 'mere coordination'. Hence, these judgments confirm the role of 'mere coordination' as an obstacle migrant workers have to overcome. *Chuck, 2008*, *Tomaszewska, 2011*, *Da Silva Martins, 2011*, *Stewart, 2011*, and *Salgado González, 2013* were counter-indicative of that trend in that they broadly turned out in favour of migrant workers. At the same time, the idea of 'mere coordination' played a very limited role in those judgments. *Dumont, 2013* thus remains as the only judgment in which the use of 'mere coordination' clearly resulted in an advantage for migrant workers.[130] Apart from that, the present confirmed the abstraction of 'mere coordination'. The idea has been used as an abstract concept a clear root of which is no longer discernible.

From the way the Court has handled 'coordination' and from the spin it exerted in the present we see that various factors continue to attenuate spin. Certainly, 'mere coordination' has lost some of its power because of the practice of advance statement of case-law. That practice had already emerged during the age of Maastricht, but it has become more frequent in the present, though being far from omnipresent. The practice has come along with the recent tendency of the Court to encapsulate 'mere coordination' in a fixed set of considerations with the power of the member states to define conditions of benefits and the need to respect the Treaty. That tendency together with the practice of advance statement of case-law has buried spin in a number of cases. Moreover, empty spin of 'mere coordination' has become a more regular occurrence in the present than in the previous age of Maastricht, numbering five out of about 50 judgments handed down in total on the basis of social security in the six and a half years of the present. That empty spin has become frequent is perhaps best explained by the Court's relatively liberal admission, in the present, of arguments based on the fundamental freedoms, in particular Union citizenship, in social security. Overall, the conclusion emerges – if a conclusion in one sentence is admissible at all given the complexity of the topic – that the idea of 'mere coordination' has lost some of the power it had in earlier cases to spin social security decisions.

It remains to be added that outside social security the idea of 'mere coordination' has never had any power in the first place. This chapter has clearly shown this, notably in the footnotes. The only non-social security judgments in which the idea of coordination played a role were *De Agostini, 1997*; *Laval, 2007*; and *Pérez and Gómez, 2010*. Even in those judgments the use of 'coordination' never came close to exerting spin like in the social security judgments. This comes as quite a surprise, given that several other Union measures in our domain have coordinated national laws. Think only of directive 64/221 on the *coordination* of measures justified on grounds of public policy, security, or health measures, directive 86/653 on the *coordination* of laws relating to self-employed commercial agents, or directive 89/552 on the *coordination* of laws relating to the pursuit of television broadcasting activities.

130 *Elchinov, 2010* and *Commission v. Austria (transport fare), 2012* defy any categorization in this regard.

III 'Fundamental'

In the judgment in *Grzelczyk, 2001* the Court in paragraph 31 famously came up with the idea that Union citizenship was 'destined to be the fundamental status of nationals of the member states'. This chapter looks at the career this idea of the 'fundamental status' made in the Court's case-law. Like in the previous chapters on 'broad' and 'coordinated' the questions to be answered are: What was the role the formula of the 'fundamental status' played in the case-law? When did the formula crop up? When was it crucial for the Court's decisions, when did it spin decisions?

Despite the similar investigative thrust, the following chapter is structured somewhat differently than the previous two. Given that the 'fundamental status' of Union citizenship only emerged after the turn of the millennium, the newer case-law of the Court obviously is most relevant. However, hierarchical approaches such as that inherent in the notion of the 'fundamental status' are as old as the Court's case-law. Hence, this chapter first looks at other terms the Court had identified as 'fundamental' (section 1) and as a 'status' (section 2) before arriving at the 'fundamental status'. A more complete picture thus emerges of what the Court implies when it qualifies a notion, such as a status, as 'fundamental'. The details of spin need not be explored in this regard though.[131] The chapter then moves on to the 'fundamental status' as such and explores the occurrences of the term in case-law and the power it wields ('spin') (sections 3 and 4).

1 Previously existing 'fundamental' notions

The 'fundamental' freedoms and non-discrimination

When looking for precursors of the 'fundamental status' in terms of hierarchy, the 'fundamental' freedoms and, closely linked to them, the 'fundamental' principles of non-discrimination or equality of treatment are the obvious candidates. In the case-law under scrutiny in this book, the *Court* – as in the Court's reasoning, not in the parties' arguments – qualified one of the market freedoms or non-discrimination with the adjective 'fundamental' in more than three hundred judgments.[132] Occasionally the Court used the word 'basic' rather than 'funda-

131 The sheer number of times the Court made use of such hierarchical terms makes a qualitative analysis of the spin they brought to bear impossible, at least for this book.

132 *Frilli, 1972*, para. 19; *Van Duyn, 1974*, para. 13 and 18; *Reyners, 1974*, paras 24 and 43; *Sotgiu, 1974*, paras 4 and 11; *Walrave, 1974*, para. 18; *F., 1975*, para. 15; *Rutili, 1975*, para. 27; *Watson and Belmann, 1976*, para. 16; *Inzirillo, 1976*, para. 14; *Patrick, 1977*, para. 9; *Bouchereau, 1977*, paras 30 and 33; *Knoors, 1979*, para. 20; *Webb, 1981*, para. 17; *Beeck, 1981*, para. 12; *Broekmeulen, 1981*, para. 20; *Levin, 1982*, para. 13; *Forcheri, 1983*, para. 11; *Auer II, 1983*, para. 19; *Rienks, 1983*, para. 9; *Fearon, 1984*, para. 7; *Hoeckx, 1985*, para. 23; *Frascogna, 1985*, para. 23; *Kromhout, 1985*, para. 21; *Steinhauser, 1985*, para. 14; *Kempf, 1986*, para. 13; *Lawrie-Blum, 1986*, paras 16 and 26; *Spruyt, 1986*, para. 25; *Commission v. France (tax credit), 1986*, para. 13 and 25;

Gül, 1986, para. 14; *Segers, 1986*, para. 12; *Commission v. Germany (insurance), 1986*, paras 27 and 54; *Commission v. France (co-insurance), 1986*, para. 17; *Commission v. Denmark (co-insurance), 1986*, para. 17; *Commission v. Ireland (co-insurance), 1986*, para. 17; *Commission v. Italy (research council), 1987*, para. 7; *Frascogna II, 1987*, para. 6; *Heylens, 1987*, paras 8, 12, 14, and 15; *Commission v. Italy (social housing), 1988*, para. 19; *Gullung, 1988*, para. 12; *Commission v. Germany (lawyers), 1988*, para. 12; *Commission v. Greece (vocational schools), 1988*, para. 7; *Lair, 1988*, paras 18 and 19; *Ledoux, 1988*, para. 11; *Cowan, 1989*, para. 19; *Commission v. Belgium (border control), 1989*, para. 15; *Commission v. Greece (real estate), 1989*, para. 26; *Bettray, 1989*, para. 11; *Groener, 1989*, para. 19; *Corsica Ferries, 1989*, para. 8; *Noij, 1991*, para. 13; *Commission v. France (tourist guides), 1991*, para. 14; *Commission v. Italy (tourist guides), 1991*, para. 17; *Commission v. Greece (tourist guides), 1991*, para. 18; *ASTI, 1991*, para. 11; *Säger, 1991*, para. 15; *Micheletti, 1992*, para. 10; *Singh, 1992*, para. 15; *Kus, 1992*, para. 34; *Konstantinidis, 1993*, para. 12; *Kraus, 1993*, paras 16, 28, 29, 32, 35, 40, and 41; *Ramrath, 1993*, para. 29; *Commission v. Greece (vehicles), 1993*, para. 31; *Vander Elst, 1994*, para. 16; *Vougioukas, 1995*, para. 42; *Gebhard, 1995*, para. 37; *Esso, 1995*, para. 12; *Bosman, 1995*, paras 78, 93, and 129; *Guiot, 1996*, para. 11; *Cabanis-Issarte, 1996*, paras 26 and 34; *O'Flynn, 1996*, para. 21; *Commission v. Italy (securities dealing), 1996*, para. 12; *Data Delecta, 1996*, paras 12 and 22; *France v. Commission (pension funds), 1997*, paras 8 and 9; *Hayes, 1997*, paras 13 and 25; *Futura, 1997*, para. 31; *SETTG, 1997*, paras 21 and 23; *Shingara, 1997*, para. 40; *Sodemare, 1997*, para. 19; *Parodi, 1997*, para. 21; *Iurlaro, 1997*, para. 30; *Saldanha, 1997*, paras 17, 19, and 21; *Schöning, 1998*, para. 12; *Decker, 1998*, 19 and 39; *Kohll, 1998*, paras 15, 20, 41 and 46; *ICI, 1998*, para. 29; *Commission v. Spain (private security guards), 1998*, para. 34; *De Castro, 1998*, para. 34; *Bickel, 1998*, para. 17; *Calfa, 1999*, paras 16, 17, 18, and 23; *Terhoeve, 1999*, paras 36, 44, and 45; *El-Yassini, 1999*, para. 45; *Centros, 1999*, paras 34 and 37; *Royal Bank of Scotland, 1999*, para. 22; *Sürül, 1999*, para. 68; *Gómez Rivero, 1999*, para. 26; *Commission v. Belgium (associations), 1999*, para. 12; *De Bobadilla, 1999*, para. 11; *Baxter, 1999*, para. 18; *Saint-Gobain, 1999*, para. 34; *ARD, 1999*, para. 29; *Vestergaard, 1999*, para. 23; *Arblade, 1999*, paras 34 and 37; *Nazli, 2000*, para. 58; *Commission v. France (social debt repayment), 2000*, para. 49; *Commission v. France (general social contribution), 2000*, para. 46; *Commission v. Belgium (security firms), 2000*, para. 28 and 37; *Deliège, 2000*, para. 52; *Lehtonen, 2000*, para. 42; *Baars, 2000*, paras 27 and 37; *Angonese, 2000*, para. 35; *Sehrer, 2000*, para. 31; *Haim II, 2000*, para. 57; *Centrosteel, 2000*, para. 13; *Hocsman, 2000*, para. 24 (it is unclear whether the Court speaks itself or merely restates a party's argument); *Erpelding, 2000*, para. 30; *Commission v. France (public tender), 2000*, para. 50; *Corsten, 2000*, paras 35 and 42; *Ferlini, 2000*, para. 50; *Luxembourg v. Parliament (lawyer directive), 2000*, paras 23 and 43; *Yiadom, 2000*, para. 25; *Mac Quen, 2001*, para. 26; *Analir, 2001*, paras 25, 37, and 38; *Metallgesellschaft, 2001*, para. 41, 59, and 67; *Mazzoleni, 2001*, para. 25; *Fahmi and Amado, 2001*, para. 51; *Commission v. Italy (transport consultants), 2001*, para. 23; *Commission v. Italy (language assistants), 2001*, para. 28; *Smits, 2001*, para. 54 and 90; *Vanbraekel, 2001*, para. 42; *Grzelczyk, 2001*, para. 33; *Finalarte, 2001*, para. 31; *Commission v. Germany (contract labour), 2001*, para. 19; *Jany, 2001*, para. 64; *Gottardo, 2002*, para. 34; *Canal Satélite, 2002*, paras 28, 31, 34, 35, and 41; *Dreessen II, 2002*, para. 25; *Commission v. Italy (temporary labour), 2002*, paras 18 and 33; *Cura Anlagen, 2002*, para. 31; *Sea-Land, 2002*, para. 39; *HI, 2002*, paras 42 and 47; *D'Hoop, 2002*, para. 29; *Carpenter, 2002*, paras 38 and 39; *Paracelsus, 2002*, paras 39 and 55; *MRAX, 2002*, para. 53; *Mertens, 2002*, para. 26 and 37; *Payroll, 2002*, para. 31; *X and Y, 2002*, paras 51, 52, and 62; *Olazabal, 2002*, para. 43; *Lankhorst, 2002*, para. 36; *De Groot, 2002*, paras 97, 103, 106, 114, and 115; *Commission v. Italy (local museums), 2003*, paras 22 and 23; *Commission v. Italy (patent services), 2003*, para. 28; *Wählergruppe Gemeinsam, 2003*, paras 75, 85, 86, 87, and 92; *Müller-Fauré, 2003*, paras 72, 84, 85, 92, 95, and 102; *Pasquini, 2003*, para. 70; *Commission v. Netherlands (driving licence), 2003*, para. 67; *Burbaud, 2003*, para. 95; *Anomar, 2003*, para. 39; *Bosal, 2003*, para. 26; *Inspire Art, 2003*, para. 133; *Köbler, 2003*, para. 102; *Marina Mercante, 2003*, para. 41; *Anker, 2003*, para. 60; *Garcia Avello, 2003*, paras 24 and 28; *Abatay, 2003*, para. 111; *Inizan, 2003*, para. 57; *Schilling, 2003*, paras 40 and 41; *Neri, 2003*, paras 40 and 46; *Commission v. France (fixed levy), 2004*, para. 27; *De Lasteyrie du Saillant, 2004*, paras 40, 51, 60; *Collins, 2004*, para. 63; *Kapper, 2004*, para. 72; *Orfanopoulos, 2004*, para. 96 and 98; *Pusa, 2004*, para. 17; *Trojani, 2004*, para. 40; *Commission v. Austria (trade unions), 2004*, para. 39; *Springer, 2004*, para. 66; *Caixa-Bank, 2004*, para. 21; *Wolff & Müller, 2004*, para. 30; *Omega, 2004*, paras 23, 26, 30, and 35; *Zhu and Chen, 2004*, paras 31, 33, 39, and 40; *Commission v. Greece (cabotage), 2004*, para. 32; *Fournier, 2005*, paras 20 and 24; *Bidar, 2005*, paras 33 and 46; *Kranemann, 2005*, paras 27 and 34; *Commission v. Spain (visa prior to entry), 2005*, para. 26; *Commission v. Greece (opticians), 2005*, para. 34; *Burmanjer, 2005*, para. 35; *Allard, 2005*, paras 30 and 32; *Commission v. Austria (university), 2005*, para. 63; *Schempp, 2005*, para. 18; *Coname, 2005*, paras 16 and 20; *Commission v. Denmark (car registration), 2005*, paras 80 and 81; *Parking Brixen, 2005*, para. 46; *Commission v. France (project delegation), 2005*, para. 32; *Contse, 2005*, paras 23, 24, 25, and 26; *Marks & Spencer, 2005*, para. 44; *Colegio, 2006*, para. 21; *Commission v. Spain (Schengen alert), 2006*, paras 41 and 45; *Rockler, 2006*, para. 22; *Öberg, 2006*, para. 19; *CLT-UFA, 2006*, para. 12; *Keller Holding, 2006*, paras 24, 40, and 45; *Commission v. Spain (Vigo), 2006*, para. 45; *Commission v. Belgium (own resources), 2006*, paras 40 and 41; *Servizi ausiliari, 2006*, para. 45; *ANAV, 2006*, para. 18; *Commission v. Germany (expulsion), 2006*, paras 34, 108, and 109; *Watts, 2006*, paras 115, 116, and 121; *N, 2006*, paras 40, 49, and 51; *Cadbury Schweppes, 2006*, para. 50; *Wilson, 2006*, para. 69; *Commission v. Luxembourg (lawyers), 2006*, para. 39; *Fidium Finanz, 2006*, para. 33; *Commission v. Greece (gaming), 2006*, para. 49; *Commission v. Portugal (capital gains deduction), 2006*, paras 24 and 29; *Commission v. Belgium (contractors), 2006*, para. 35; *Turpeinen, 2006*, para. 19; *FII Group, 2006*, para. 46; *ITC, 2007*, paras 40 and 41; *Commission v. Sweden (tax deferral), 2007*, paras 25 and 26; *Commission v. Denmark (insurance taxation), 2007*, paras 46, 51, and 58; *Placanica, 2007*, para. 68; *Thin Cap, 2007*, paras 68 and 73; *Rewe, 2007*, para. 62; *Talotta, 2007*, para. 35; *Alevizos, 2007*, para. 69; *Commission v. Netherlands (automatic expulsion), 2007*, para. 42; *Commission v. Belgium (tax matters), 2007*, para. 47; *Commission v. Germany (posted workers), 2007*, para. 64 (and para. 21); *Geven, 2007*, para. 27; *Lakebrink, 2007*, para. 24; *Gootjes-Schwarz, 2007*, para. 87; *Commission v. Germany (private schools), 2007*, paras 120 and 126; *Commission v. Italy (horse races), 2007*, paras 22 and 35; *Polat, 2007*, para. 33; *Morgan, 2007*, para. 23; *Geurts, 2007*, para. 14; *Commission v. Ireland (An Post), 2007*, para. 26; *Commission v. Austria (bio inspections), 2007*, para. 35; *Commission v. Germany (bio inspections), 2007*, para. 37; *Commission v. Germany (psychotherapists), 2007*, paras 49 and 70; *Eind, 2007*, para. 44; *Viking, 2007*, paras 45, 51, 52, 58, 59, 68, and 77; *Commission v. Italy (private security), 2007*, paras 18 and 49; *United Pan-Europe, 2007*, paras 39 and 45; *Laval, 2007*, paras 93, 101, and 103; *Asociación Profesional, 2007*, para. 71; *Jundt, 2007*, paras 61 and 67; *Commission v. Germany (housing subsidy), 2008*, para. 26; *Lammers, 2008*, para. 27; *Commission v. Italy (public works), 2008*, paras 69 and 81; *Deutsche Shell, 2008*, para. 37; *French Community, 2008*, paras 35, 45, 52, and 55; *Rüffert, 2008*, para. 36; *Commission v. Spain (hospital pharmacists), 2008*, para. 37; *Secap, 2008*, paras 18, 20, 21, 29, and 35; *Delay, 2008*, para. 29; *Nerkowska, 2008*, para. 26; *Commission v. Luxembourg (posted workers), 2008*, paras 30, 43, 49, and 50; *Jipa, 2008*, paras 18, 23, and 24; *Commission v. France (insemination), 2008*, paras 56 and 93; *Brescia, 2008*, para. 58; *Raccanelli, 2008*, para. 45; *Metock, 2008*, para. 56; *Bauer Verlag, 2008*, paras 37 and 40; *Renneberg, 2008*, para. 81; *Commission v. Spain (diploma), 2008*, para. 72; *Coditel, 2008*, para. 25; *Förster, 2008*, paras 37 and 43; *Papillon, 2008*, para. 41; *Khatzithanasis, 2008*, para. 32; *Zablocka-Weyhermüller, 2008*, para. 29; *Jobra, 2008*, paras 18 and 37; *Cartesio, 2008*, para. 109; *Huber, 2008*, para. 71; *Commission v. Austria (self-employment), 2008*, para. 35; *Commission v. Spain (R&D), 2008*, paras 32 and 34; *Commission v. Italy (ship officers), 2008*, para. 15; *Uteca, 2009*, para. 18, 20, 21, 22, 24, 25, and 33; *Hartlauer, 2009*, para. 64; *Rüffler, 2009*, para. 63; *Aberdeen Alpha, 2009*; *Liga Portuguesa and Bwin, 2009*, para. 47; *Sea, 2009*, para. 38; *Eurawasser, 2009*, para. 44; *Acoset, 2009*, para. 46; *Commission v. Portugal (vehicle inspection), 2009*, para. 34; *Presidente, 2009*, paras 42 and 47; *Filipiak, 2009*, para. 72; *Pesla, 2009*, paras 35, 36, 38, and 51; *Rubino, 2009*, para. 34; *Serrantoni, 2009*, paras 22, 23, and 24; *Mariano, 2009*, para. 21 *Commission v. Austria (patent lawyers), 2009*, para. 31; *Commission v. Austria (bank account), 2009*, para. 46; *Commission v. Greece (ship officers), 2009*, para. 29; *Commission v. Germany (posted workers), 2010*, para. 51; *Attanasio, 2010*, paras 23, 50, 51, and 55; *Wall, 2010*, para. 33; *Ciba, 2010*, para. 45; *Metin Bozkurt, 2010*, para. 56; *Zanotti, 2010*, para. 69; *Pérez and Gómez, 2010*, paras 40, 43, 45, 63, and 68; *Sporting Exchange, 2010*, paras 39, 49, 50, and 59; *Ladbrokes, 2010*, para. 40; *Sjöberg, 2010*, para. 49; *Carmen Media, 2010*, paras 86 and 87; *Engelmann, 2010*, paras 47, 49, 54, and 55; *Lassal, 2010*, para. 29; *Commission v. Portugal (construction sector), 2010*, para. 107; *Commission v. Ireland (award criteria), 2010*, para. 29; *Vandorou, 2010*, para. 66; *Josemans, 2010*, paras 50 and 66; *Sayn-Wittgenstein, 2010*, paras 86 and 90; *Yellow Cab, 2010*, paras 51 and 53; *Rani, 2010*, para. 53; *Bejan, 2010*, para. 41; *Commission v. Greece (transfer tax), 2011*, paras 14 and 51; *Commission v. Luxembourg (lab analyses), 2011*, para. 45; *Commission v. Belgium (must-carry), 2011*, para. 43; *Stadler, 2011*, para. 49; *Casteels, 2011*, para. 22; *Navtiliaki Etairia Thasou, 2011*, para. 48; *McCarthy, 2011*, para. 27; *Runevič-Vardyn, 2011*, paras 62, 88, and 90; *Commission v. Belgium (notaries), 2011*, paras 77 and 84; *Commission v. France (notaries), 2011*, paras 67 and 74; *Commission v. Luxembourg (notaries), 2011*, paras 77 and 84; *Commission v. Austria (notaries), 2011*, paras 76 and 83; *Commission v. Germany (notaries), 2011*, paras 78 and 85; *Commission v. Greece (notaries), 2011*, paras 69 and 76; *Zeturf, 2011*, para. 48; *Commission v. Portugal (real estate agents), 2011*, paras 64, 66, 67, and 72; *Stewart, 2011*, para. 81; *Dickinger, 2011*, paras 30, 31, 33, 82, and 87; *National Grid, 2011*, paras 26 and 84; *Premier League, 2011*, paras 78, 79, 93, and 123; *Graf, 2011*, para. 33; *Commission v. Portugal (medical treatment), 2011*, paras 76 and 80; *Aladzhov, 2011*, paras 25 and 34; *Gaydarov, 2011*, paras 25 and 32; *Commission v. Hungary (proper-*

mental'.[133] (In the French versions of these judgments the Court consistently used the adjective 'fondamentale', except in one of them.[134]) In the domain this book analyses the Court used the qualifier 'fundamental' for the market freedoms or non-discrimination/equality of treatment altogether 610 times.

'Fundamental' rights

While the qualification of one of the market freedoms or non-discrimination as 'fundamental' manifestly serves to put the freedom inherent in the Treaty in a hierarchical position vis-à-vis other norms of primary or secondary law, the qualification of a *right* as 'fundamental' is somewhat different. The term 'fundamental rights' is more or less synonymous with 'human rights', while perhaps emphasizing more the constitutional, domestic quality of the norm. Fundamental rights were not intrinsic to the Treaty, in contrast to the market freedoms. They joined the Treaty by judicial fiat in *Internationale Handelsgesellschaft, 1970*, after indications to that effect in *Stauder, 1969*. Obviously, to qualify a right as fundamental, as with the *fundamental* right to property or the *fundamental* right not to be tortured, means to rank the right and put it into a hierarchical position vis-à-vis other norms. In that aspect fundamental rights are at least similar to the fundamental market freedoms. In the case-law this book examines, fundamental rights were mentioned for the first time in *Rutili, 1975* (para. 32). From then on 'fundamental human rights', as the Court called them in *Belbouab, 1978* (para. 10), played a role in numerous decisions by the Court in our domain. If we disregard procedural fundamental rights for the sake of simplicity, fundamental rights played a more or less significant role in 66 of the Court's decisions in this book's

ty tax), 2011, paras 69, 71, and 87; *Commission v. Netherlands (notaries), 2011*, paras 50 and 57; *Ziebell, 2011*, para. 81; *Costa and Cifone, 2012*, paras 54, 59, and 61; *Duomo, 2012*, paras 26 and 42; *P. I., 2012*, para. 23; *Hudzinski, 2012*, para. 82; *Commission v. Netherlands (portable funding), 2012*, para. 58 and 73; *Susisalo, 2012*, paras 27 and 37; *SIAT, 2012*, para. 38; *Commission v. Spain (income tax), 2012*, paras 62, 64, 72, 84, and 91; *Vale, 2012*, para. 28; *Volksbank România, 2012*, para. 70; *Garkalns, 2012*, para. 21; *A Oy, 2012*, para. 32; *DIVI, 2012*, para. 50; *Byankov, 2012*, para. 31; *Prete, 2012*, para. 25; *X NV, 2012*, para. 30 and 31; *Caves Krier, 2012*, para. 52; *Azienda Sanitaria, 2012*, paras 23 and 24; *Stanleybet, 2013*, paras 25 and 47; *L.N., 2013*, para. 28; *Petersen, 2013*, para. 28; *Van den Booren, 2013*, para. 43 and 44; *Las, 2013*, paras 20, 23 and 28.

133 *Commission v. France (maritime worker quota), 1974*, para. 21; *Bonsignore, 1975*, para. 5; *Bouchereau, 1977*, para. 15; *De Castro, 1998*, para. 23; *Commission v. Italy (resources), 2000*, para. 35; *Corsten, 2000*, para. 31; *Mac Quen, 2001*, para. 24; *Paracelsus, 2002*, para. 26; *Commission v. France (bio-medical labs), 2004*, para. 55; *Colegio, 2006*, para. 29; *Commission v. Spain (private security), 2006*, para. 23; *Commission v. Greece (gaming), 2006*, para. 47; *Commission v. Austria (boilers), 2006*, para. 18 (not available in English, but with reference to *Commission v. Spain (private security), 2006*, para. 23); *Jia, 2007*, para. 40; *Commission v. Austria (bio inspections), 2007*, para. 29; *Commission v. Germany (bio inspections), 2007*, para. 31; *Commission v. Germany (psychotherapists), 2007*, para. 48; *Commission v. Italy (private security), 2007*, para. 16; *Dermoestética, 2008*, paras 31 and 34; *Commission v. Portugal (vehicle inspection), 2009*, para. 27; *Serrantoni, 2009*, para. 23; *Loutraki, 2010*, para. 63; *Commission v. Luxembourg (lab analyses), 2011*, para. 36; *Commission v. Portugal (medical treatment), 2011*, para. 50.

134 In the French version of *Serrantoni, 2009*, para. 23, the Court mentioned 'les règles de base du traité' rather than 'les règles fondamentales du traité'.

domain.[135] The Charter of Fundamental Rights brought fundamental market freedoms and fundamental human rights together, at least to some extent.[136]

'Fundamental interests of society' and other 'fundamental' notions

There are two more varieties of fundamental logic. Firstly, the Court required that certain public interests needed to touch on the 'fundamental interests' of society to justify a derogation from the market freedoms. In the case-law under scrutiny, this variety is principally, but not exclusively, connected to the expulsion of migrant persons from the host state. The term 'fundamental interests' obviously serves to qualify certain interests of states vis-à-vis other such interests. However, the assessment needed to distinguish between 'fundamental interests' and other interests is usually left to the national court. This variety of fundamental logic appeared for the first time in our domain in *Bouchereau, 1977* where the Court stated in para. 35: 'the concept of public policy presupposes, in any event, the existence, in addition to the perturbation of the social order which any infringement of the law involves, of a genuine and sufficiently serious threat to the requirements of public policy affecting one of the fundamental interests of society'.[137] After that, the Court had recourse to this variety of fundamental logic in 36 cases in the case-law this book examines.[138] In those cases, the Court

135 This number does not include decisions in which only the parties or the referring courts argued on the basis of fundamental rights. The 66 decisions were the following: *Rutili, 1975*, para. 32; *Belbouab, 1978*, para. 10; *Testa, 1980*, paras 18-22; *Demirel, 1987*, para. 28; *Bond, 1988*. Paras 40-1; *Commission v. Germany (adequate housing), 1989*, para. 10; *ERT AE, 1991*, paras 41-6; *Gouda, 1991*, para. 23; *Commission v. Netherlands (broadcasting), 1991*, para. 30; *Grogan, 1991*, paras 26 and 30-1; *Singh, 1992*, para. 22; *Veronica, 1993*, para. 9; *TV10, 1994*, paras 23-6; *Bosman, 1995*, paras 79-80; *Commission v. Belgium (TV broadcasting), 1996*, paras 43-5; *Kremzow, 1997*, paras 14-9; *Gloszczuk, 2001*, para. 85; *Kondova, 2001*, para. 90; *Carpenter, 2002*, paras 40-5; *Baumbast, 2002*, para. 72; *Rinke, 2003*, paras 25-8 and 32-42; *Akrich, 2003*, paras 58-60; *RTL, 2003*, paras 67-73; *Orfanopoulos, 2004*, paras 97-99; *Springer, 2004*, paras 47-58; *Omega, 2004*, paras 33-40; *Berlusconi, 2005*, paras 66-78; *Commission v. Spain (Schengen alert), 2006*, para. 47; *Commission v. Germany (expulsion), 2006*, para. 107-113; *Echouikh, 2006*, paras 64-5; *Derin, 2007*, para. 64; *Spain v. United Kingdom (Gibraltar), 2006*, para. 60, 64, 90, and 94-6; *Eman and Sevinger, 2006*, para. 48 and 54; *El Youssfi, 2007*, para. 75; *Viking, 2007*, paras 43-7 and 86; *United Pan-Europe, 2007*, paras 41-2; *Laval, 2007*, paras 90-5; *Centro Europa 7, 2008*, paras 117-21; *Metock, 2008*, para. 79; *Kabel Deuschland, 2008*, paras 33-8; *Mariano, 2009*, para. 29; *Pignataro, 2009*, paras 21-3; *Bressol, 2010*, paras 83-8; *Metin Bozkurt, 2010*, para. 60; *Pérez and Gómez, 2010*, para. 65; *Lassal, 2010*, para. 29; *Tsakouridis, 2010*, para. 52; *Sayn-Wittgenstein, 2010*, paras 52 and 89-91; *Commission v. Belgium (must-carry), 2011*, paras 53-5; *McCarthy, 2011*, paras 27 and 29; *Runevič-Vardyn, 2011*, paras 66 and 89; *Deutsche Telekom, 2011*, paras 49-66; *Mesopotamia, 2011*, para. 33; *Dereci, 2011*, paras 69-74; *Köppl, 2011*, para. 53; *Ziebell, 2011*, para. 82; *Costa and Cifone, 2012*, para. 86; *Kahveci, 2012*, para. 40; *Kamberaj, 2012*, para. 92; *P. I., 2012*, para. 26; *Susisalo, 2012*, para. 37; *Erny, 2012*, para. 50; *Dülger, 2012*, paras 53 and 62; *Byankov, 2012*, para. 46-7; *Iida, 2012*, paras 78-81; *O and S, 2012*, paras 59 and 75-80; *Las, 2013*, para. 26; *Sky Österreich, 2013*, paras 31-67.

136 See *Lassal, 2010*, para. 29, discussing article 45 of the Charter.

137 In *Rutili, 1975*, para. 28, the term 'fundamental interests' had not yet been used.

138 *Adoui, 1982*, para. 8; *Commission v. Germany (adequate housing), 1989*, para. 17; *Clean Car, 1998*, para. 40; *Commission v. Spain (private security guards), 1998*, para. 46; *Calfa, 1999*, paras 21 and 25; *Nazli, 2000*, para. 57; *Commission v. Belgium (security firms), 2000*, para. 28; *Jany, 2001*, para. 59; *Commission v. United Kingdom (open skies), 2002*, para. 57; *Commission v. Denmark (open skies), 2002*, para. 135; *Commission v. Germany (open skies), 2002*, para. 157; *Olazabal, 2002*, para. 39; *Orfanopoulos, 2004*, para. 66; *Omega, 2004*, para. 30; *Commission v. Spain (Schengen alert), 2006*, paras 46, 52, 53, 55, and 59; *Commission v. Germany (expulsion), 2006*, paras 35, 54, 70, 74, and 100; *Commission v. Austria (posted workers), 2006*, para. 64; *Gattoussi,*

mentioned the 'fundamental interests' 67 times. Secondly, there is a pool of cases including decisions in which the Court used the qualifier 'fundamental' – or in a similar vein 'basic' – in largely heterogeneous circumstances. Another 42 decisions belong to this pool.[139]

2006, para. 41; *Commission v. Austria (boilers), 2006*, paras 25-6; *Commission v. Netherlands (automatic expulsion), 2007*, para. 43; *Polat, 2007*, paras 28, 34, and 39; *Commission v. Italy (private security), 2007*, paras 49 and 50; *Commission v. Luxembourg (posted workers), 2008*, para. 50; *Jipa, 2008*, paras 23, 26, and 30; *Commission v. Austria (self-employment), 2008*, paras 35 and 37; *Commission v. Germany (posted workers), 2010*, paras 49 and 51; *Tsakouridis, 2010*, para. 48; *Metin Bozkurt, 2010*, paras 57 and 61; *Sayn-Wittgenstein, 2010*, para. 86; *Commission v. Portugal (real estate agents), 2011*, paras 67 and 73; *Dickinger, 2011*, para. 82; *Aladzhov, 2011*, paras 35, 37, 40, 42, and 47; *Gaydarov, 2011*, paras 33, 38, and 42; *Ziebell, 2011*, paras 82, 84, 85, and 86; *P. I., 2012*, paras 28, 30, 33, and 34; *Byankov, 2012*, paras 40 and 42.

139 *Torrekens, 1969*, para. 10: the 'fundamental principles' laid down in article 51 Treaty; *Heinze, 1972*, para. 4: the 'fundamental aim' of article 51 Treaty (the same in *Land Niedersachsen, 1972*, para. 4, and *Ortskrankenkasse Hamburg, 1972*, para. 4); *Mancuso, 1973*, para. 14: a 'fundamental difference' between system of old-age pension and invalidity pensions; *Commission v. France (maritime worker quota), 1974*, paras 24 ('fundamental provisions') and 25 ('fundamental rules'); *Balsamo, 1976*, para. 12: the 'fundamental conditions' necessary to be able to claim the advantage of the benefit; *Laterza, 1980*, para. 8: the 'fundamental principle that the rules of coordination must guarantee to migrant workers all the benefits which have accrued to them in different member states (the same in *Gravina, 1980*, para. 7); *Commission v. Belgium (public service), 1980*, para. 19: the rule of unity and efficacy of Community law 'which is fundamental to the existence of the Community must also apply in determining the scope and bounds of article 48(4)' Treaty; *Piscitello, 1983*, para. 11: lack of means as the 'fundamental criterion'; *Forcheri, 1983*, para. 16: certain 'fundamental objectives' of the common vocational training policy; *Patteri, 1984*, and *Campana, 1987*, para. 8, respectively: the 'fundamental aim' of article 51 Treaty; *Commission v. Italy (lottery machinery interim I), 1992*, para. 28: breach of 'fundamental rules' in the Treaties; *Paletta, 1992*, para. 16: the 'fundamental characteristics' of a benefit, and para. 24: the greatest possible freedom of movement for workers as one of the 'fundamental principles' of the Community; *Cabanis-Issarte, 1996*, para. 31: the 'fundamental Community law requirement' that rules should be applied uniformly; *Taflan-Met, 1996*, para. 31: the 'fundamental principle' of aggregation of periods; *Germany v. Parliament and Council (deposit guarantee), 1997*, para. 41: the 'fundamental differences' between deposit guarantee schemes in the member states; *Sürül, 1999*, para. 54, again the 'fundamental principle' of aggregation; *Konle, 1999*, para. 38: article 222 does not exempt a state's system of property from the 'fundamental rules' of the Treaty; *Movrin, 2000*, para. 38: the 'fundamental characteristics' of a benefit; *BIAO, 2003*, para. 72: the 'fundamental principle' that annual accounts must be given a true and fair view; *Givane, 2003*, para. 29: the 'fundamental condition' for the right to remain in the host state; *Commission v. Netherlands (frontier worker), 2003*, para. 32: the 'fundamental competence' of a member state; *Commission v. Greece (architects), 2004*, para. 18: the 'fundamental obligation' in a national decree; *Berlusconi, 2005*, para. 54: the 'fundamental principle' of true and fair view, and para. 62: the fundamental role played by the publication of annual accounts; *Sedef, 2006*, para. 45: the 'fundamental distinction' between the phases when rights are being acquired and when they have already been acquired; *Commission v. France (performing artists), 2006*, para. 51: one of the 'most fundamental characteristic rights' of salaried employment; *Perez Naranjo, 2007*, para. 34: the 'fundamental importance' of personal needs; *Habelt, 2007*, para. 82: the 'fundamental objective' of the Union to encourage movement of persons and their integration in the host state; *Metock, 2008*, para. 89: the 'fundamental right of residence' of Union citizens; *Gaz de France, 2009*, para. 38: the 'fundamental principle of legal certainty'; *Sayn-Wittgenstein, 2010*, para. 93: the 'fundamental constitutional objective' pursued by Austria; *Premier League, 2011*, para. 115: the 'fundamental aim' of the Treaty of completion of the internal market; *Kahveci, 2012*, para. 33: the 'fundamental objective' of consolidating the position of a family member; *Commission v. Estonia (tax allowance), 2012*, para. 64: the 'fundamental principles' of the Treaty; *Dülger, 2012*, para. 40: the 'fundamental objective' of consolidating the position of a family member. The Court referred to the 'basic principles' in article 48 to 51 Treaty in *Villano, 1979*, para. 9; and to the rule of aggregation of periods as one of the 'basic principles' of social security coordination in *Moscato, 1995*, para. 28, and the same in *Salgado, 2005*, para. 29, and *Tomaszewska, 2011*, para. 30.

Conclusions

The idea of a 'fundamental status' put forward in *Grzelczyk, 2001* did not come out of the blue. The Court's case-law this book examines shows a strong tradition of reasoning in terms of hierarchy. The market freedoms and non-discrimination are routinely qualified as 'fundamental' by the Court. Fundamental (human) rights, of which the origin is in the Court's case-law (at least for the Union), also embody a hierarchical approach that is similar to the approach inherent in the 'fundamental status'. Finally, a number of other notions have emerged from the Court's case-law as 'fundamental'. Most prominent among them are the 'fundamental interests of society'.

2 The 'status', linking to Union citizenship

The fundamental status-formula used for the first time in *Grzelczyk, 2001* is invariably linked to Union citizenship. The Court had never mentioned a fundamental status *expressis verbis* before the advent of Union citizenship with the Maastricht Treaty. However, it would be wrong to think that Union citizenship and with it the 'fundamental status' started on a blank page with the statement in *Grzelczyk, 2001*, even if we ignore the other hierarchical approaches described above. Indeed, several precursors of the status of Union citizenship manifested themselves in the Court's case-law, long before Union citizenship arrived.

The origins: the 'Community national' …

The most prominent of the precursors of the 'Union citizen' is the notion of a 'Community national'. In the case-law this book focuses on this term made its first appearance in *Fiege, 1973* where the Court stated with regard to pensions in the context of the independence of Algeria: 'Such a worker was assimilated to the persons of French nationality mentioned in Annex A to Regulation no 3, placed in similar circumstances, and is thus a Community national subject to a French institution' (para. 26). The term then disappeared for some time, only to come back in *Choquet, 1978* where the Court in the paragraph introducing the judgment mentioned the mutual recognition of 'driving licences for the benefit of Community nationals' (para. 1). In *Pieck, 1980*, the Court in a similar vein mentioned an 'EEC national' in the 'whether' (para. 11).[140] In *Prodest, 1984* the Court referred to the 'advantages enjoyed by Community nationals' pursuant to article 7(2) Regulation 1612/68 (para. 8). In *Commission v. Belgium (pension deductions I), 1985* the Court mentioned 'Community nationals residing in another Member State' in the declaration for failure to have fulfilled Community obligations (para. 11).

140 In French: 'ressortissant communautaire'.

… And the 'Community citizen'

During the same time span it can be observed that the Court used a similar term in the English versions of the judgments: the term 'Community citizen'. In the case-law on persons and services, the Court mentioned that term for the first time in the 'whether' in *Hirardin, 1976* (para. 3).[141] Similarly, the Court referred to 'citizens of the EEC' in the 'whether' in *Jansen, 1977* (para. 11). *Sagulo 1977* mentioned the right of residence for 'Community citizens' in the terms right at the beginning of the entry of the judgment in the Court reports, so did *Pieck, 1980.* In point 2 of the ruling in *Adoui, 1982* the Court mentioned 'citizens of the Community', while in the corresponding summary of the ruling the term 'citizens of member states of the Community' was mentioned.

In *Commission v. Germany (nurses), 1985*, paras 4 and 6, the Court summarized articles 4, 11, and 12 Directive 77/452 on nurses and in doing so 'reverted' to 'Community nationals', although those articles of the Directive, in fact the entire Directive, knew no such term.[142] In *Gül, 1986* the Court recounted the facts and mentioned 'Community national' (para. 6). In *Commission v. Italy (tourism), 1986*, para. 14, the Court then again mentioned 'Community citizens' twice. In the French version of the judgment the Court in this paragraph used the term 'citoyen communautaire', while in the French versions of all the above judgments which mentioned 'Community citizen' in English – or some variation of it – the Court consistently used the terms 'ressortissant(s) de la Communauté' or 'ressortissant(s) communautaire(s)' in French.

The parties/national courts driving the 'Community national'

It thus becomes evident that by the time the Single European Act came into force the term 'Community national' had already crept into the vocabulary of the Court. This was no coincidence. Whereas the Court used the term sparingly and perhaps somewhat reluctantly – as the above references show – the parties and the referring courts much more liberally spoke of 'Community nationals' and 'Community citizens' (in French 'ressortissants communautaires' or 'ressortissants de la Communauté' if not indicated otherwise below). This is evident in the Court's citing of their arguments/questions. In *Bonsignore, 1975* the national Court mentioned an 'EEC national, who ha[d] been convicted of an offence' (para. 4, in the second question).[143] In *Hirardin, 1976* the parties referred to

141 To complete the picture two judgments should be briefly mentioned, although they are not part of the free movement of persons and services. In the German version of the agriculture judgment *Balkan-Import-Export, 1976*, para. 14, the Court used the term 'Marktbürger'. The English version used the word 'trader', the French 'opérateurs économiques'. In *Rewe, 1976*, a goods case, the Court used the term 'Community citizen' in the 'whether' (para. 3); the German version again used 'Marktbürger', the French 'justiciable de la Communauté'.

142 The French version of the judgment mentioned 'ressortissants communautaires', but only in para. 4.

143 Yet in the French version the same term reads: 'ressortissant d'un État membre de la Communauté'. In *Mazzier, 1974*, the referring court also mentioned 'Community nationals', as is evident from the 'Facts' (p. 1253; 'ressortissants de la Communauté' in French). In the famous judgment in *Dassonville, 1974*, para. 5, the Court also mentioned 'all Community nationals' ('tous leur ressortissants' in French). The case is obviously outside of persons and services.

'Community citizen[s]' (p. 556) and 'Community nationals' (p. 557) and the referring court to 'Community citizen' (p. 555).[144] In *Jansen, 1977* the referring court questioned about 'citizens of the EEC' (p. 832); in *Choquet, 1978* about 'citizens of the Community' (para. 3).[145] In *Auer, 1979*, the Commission referred to 'Community nationals' (p. 443). In *Mialocq, 1983*, the French government mentioned '[a]ny Community national' (p. 2068). In *Rienks, 1983* the referring court mentioned 'Community national' three times in its questions (p. 4236 and para. 5). In *Luisi and Carbone, 1984* the referring court mentioned 'Community nationals' (p. 384 and para. 7),[146] so did one party in *Prodest, 1984* (para. 3). In *Meade, 1984* the Commission put forward the 'status of Community nationals' and suggested an answer that referred to 'Community nationals' (pp. 2634 and 2635, respectively). It again referred to 'Community nationals' in *Fearon, 1984* (p. 3682). In *Hoeckx, 1985*, the referring court mentioned 'Community nationals' (para. 5). In *Commission v. Belgium (pension deductions I), 1985* the subject of the application mentioned 'Community nationals' (p. 1100). In *Mutsch, 1985*, the referring court's question referred to a 'German-speaking EEC national' (para. 5).[147] In *Commission v. Belgium (vocational training, interim), 1985*, the Commission argued on the basis of the term 'Community nationals' (para. 13). In *Reed, 1986* the Netherlands' argument mentioned 'EEC nationals' (para. 19).[148] In *Lawrie-Blum, 1986* the applicant referred to 'Community citizens' (para. 12). In *Commission v. Italy (tourism), 1986* the Italian government argued on the basis of the terms 'Community nationals' (para. 8) and 'citizen of the Community' (para. 9).[149]

It were therefore for a very large part the parties – individuals and the Commission, sometimes the member states – and the referring courts that pushed the term 'Community national' onto the agenda of the Court. This is evident from the eleven decision mentioned above in which it was exclusively them who spoke of 'Community nationals' and not the Court. Moreover, it is evident from the decisions in *Hirardin, 1976*; *Jansen, 1977*; *Choquet, 1978*; *Prodest, 1984*; *Commission v. Belgium (pension deductions I), 1985*; and *Commission v. Italy (tourism), 1986*. In these judgments the Court itself only mentioned the term, after either a party or the referring court had done so. The Court mentioned the term on its own initiative only in *Fiege, 1973*; *Sagulo 1977*; *Pieck, 1980*; *Adoui, 1982*, *Commission v. Germany (nurses), 1985*; and *Gül, 1986*. Indeed, of those six decisions only in *Fiege, 1973* the term was properly part of the reasoning of the Court. In *Sagulo 1977* the term was mentioned in the introductory terms; in *Pieck, 1980* it was mentioned in the introductory terms, too, and in the 'whether'; in *Adoui, 1982* it popped up in the final ruling; in *Commission v.*

144 'Ressortissants communautaires' or 'ressortissants de la Communauté' in French.
145 'Ressortissants de la Communauté' and 'ressortissants communautaires' in French.
146 In French: 'sujets de l'ordre communautaire' in para. 7.
147 In French: 'un individu s'exprimant en langue allemande, ressortissant de la CEE'.
148 In French: 'ressortissants de la CEE'.
149 In para. 9 the French version used the term 'citoyen communautaire'.

Germany (nurses), 1985 it was part of an advance statement of the law, and in *Gül, 1986* of the description of the facts. We can thus conclude that the term 'Community national' was driven by those who came to the Court rather than by the Court itself. It was them who pushed the term from the 1970s to the mid-1980s.

The 'Community national' becoming current

From the advent of the Single European Act on, the term 'Community national', or its equivalents, came to appear much more regularly in the Court's own reasoning. Until the Maastricht Treaty went into force, the Court itself, in its reasoning or at least the summary or the ruling, mentioned the term in many judgments.[150] The decisions in which the parties or the referring court exclusively spoke of 'Community nationals' and the Court implicitly refused to use the term became comparatively rare.[151] So by the time the Maastricht Treaty came around and with it true 'Community nationality', viz. Union citizenship, the term 'Community national' had become current at the Court. It was not any longer shy about using it.

Interestingly, the Court continued to use the term 'Community national' despite the advent of Union citizenship with the Maastricht Treaty. Indeed, it fur-

150 *Commission v. Italy (social housing), 1988*: in the summary; *Pesca Valentia, 1988*: 'EEC national' in para. 11, but also in the facts in para. 3, in the questions in paras 5 and 16; 'Community nationals' in two answers in paras 15 and 21, and the ruling; *Stanton, 1988*: 'Community citizens' in para. 11 and the summary; *Wolf, 1988*: 'Community citizens' in para. 13 and the summary; *Daily Mail, 1988* in para. 15; *Steymann, 1988*: 'EEC national' though only in the description of the facts in para. 5; *Echternach, 1989* in para. 11; *Commission v. Belgium (border control), 1989* in the description of the facts in para. 4; *Lopes da Veiga, 1989* 'EEC national' in explaining national law in para. 3; *Groener, 1989*, para. 13; *Agegate, 1989* in para. 20 and 'Community citizen' in the keywords and 'EEC national' in the re-statement of British law and the question asked; *Dzodzi, 1990* in paras 12, 13, 24, 26, and 44 and in the questions in para. 7, the 'whether' in para. 11, the Commission's argument in para. 16, 'Community citizen' also in the questions asked; *Roux, 1991* in summary 4, question 4 in para. 6, the 'whether' in para. 25, in paras 27 and 32, and ruling 4; *Antonissen, 1991* in paras 14 and 21, but also in the parties' arguments in paras 4 and 9; *Giagounidis, 1991*: 'Community subject' in para. 20, 'ressortissant communautaire' in French; *Vlassopoulou, 1991* again the same term 'Community subject' in paras 22, 23, the summary and the ruling, and 'Community national' in the question asked in para. 5; *Barr and Montrose, 1991* in paras 18, 19, 20 and in the keywords, summary, the 'whether' in para. 15, as well as the second 'whether' in para. 21, the second answer in para. 24 and the ruling; *Commission v. Belgium (pension deductions II), 1992* in the summary, in the application, and the facts in para. 3; *Gray, 1992* in para. 10 and the summary; *Borrell, 1992* in paras 15, 18, and 19; *Micheletti, 1992* in para. 11 and the facts in para. 4; *Singh, 1992* in para. 23, the question in para. 9, and the United Kingdom's argument in para. 14, and 'Community citizen' in para. 16 and the summary; *Koua Poirrez, 1992* in the reply in para. 15 and the ruling, and 'EEC national' in the question in para. 8; *Kus, 1992* in para. 35 and in Germany's argument in para. 32; *Kraus, 1993* in paras 23, 32, and 40, as well as in the summary and the facts in para. 4; *Ramrath, 1993* in paras 28, 29, and 31; *Schmid, 1993* in para. 20; *Grana-Novoa, 1993* in para. 22. 'Community nationals' was mentioned just in the introductory terms of the decision in *Bettray, 1989*.

151 *Zaoui, 1987* in para. 5, 'Community citizen' was used in the introductory terms though; *Commission v. Belgium (vocational training), 1988* in para. 2; *Commission v. Germany (adequate housing), 1989* in the Commission's translation of the title of the German act in para. 2; *Nino, 1990* in question 2 in para. 5; *Commission v. France (allowance), 1991* in para. 12; *ERT AE, 1991* with 'Community citizens' in the second question in para. 5; *Bachmann, 1992* in para. 12; *Bauer, 1992* in para. 5; *Di Crescenzo, 1992* in para. 9; *Commission v. United Kingdom (fishing licences), 1992* with 'EEC nationals' in para. 6; *Werner, 1993* with 'EEC nationals' in para. 8; and *Acciardi, 1993* in paras 8 and 20.

ther ballooned until the 'fundamental status' was first mentioned in *Grzelczyk, 2001*. The Court, moreover, narrowed it down to the term 'Community national', dropping 'EEC national' and 'Community citizen' almost completely.[152]

Three decades of 'Community nationality' – and more

So, when *Grzelczyk, 2001* arrived and declared Union citizenship as the 'fundamental status', the unofficial status of 'Community nationality' had been leading a covert life in the case-law of the Court for almost three decades. For the sake of completeness it is worth mentioning that the Court continued to refer to 'Community nationals' after *Grzelczyk, 2001*. Indeed in *Grzelczyk, 2001* itself it was mentioned (para. 28).[153] Thereafter, the Court mentioned it in its reasoning in 99 judgments.[154] In addition the parties or the descriptions of the facts or the

---

152 The Court in its own reasoning referred to 'Community nationals' in the following judgments: *Haim, 1994* in paras 12, 16, 25; *Scholz, 1994* in paras 9 and 12; *Commission v. Spain (museum admission), 1994* in para. 10; *Commission v. Spain (tourist guides), 1994* in paras 9 and 14; *Commission v. Belgium (minerval), 1994* in paras 12 and 19 and in the law in para. 2; *Van Munster, 1994* in para. 23; *Eroglu, 1994* in para. 21; *Schumacker, 1995* in paras 46, 49, and 58; *Vougioukas, 1995* in paras 38 and 39; *Gebhard, 1995* in paras 20 and 25; *Bosman, 1995* with 'Community citizen' in para. 94; *Cabanis-Issarte, 1996* in para. 21; *Reisebüro Broede, 1996* in para. 20; *Commission v. Belgium (residence permits), 1997* in para. 17; *Merino García, 1997* in para. 30; *Shingara, 1997* in paras 39, 40, and 41; *Dafeki, 1997* in paras 8 and 21; *Pereira Roque, 1998* in para. 36; *De Castro, 1998* in paras 18 and 35; *Awoyemi, 1998* in para. 30; *Calfa, 1999* in para. 25; *Terhoeve, 1999* in para. 27 and 37; *Centros, 1999* in para. 19; *Commission v. Belgium (aircraft registration), 1999* in para. 12; *Commission v. France (social debt repayment), 2000* in para. 32; *Commission v. France (general social contribution), 2000* in para. 30; *Commission v. Italy (register), 2000* in paras 12 and 14; *Sehrer, 2000* in para. 32; *Hocsman, 2000* in paras 23, 35, and 40; *Erpelding, 2000* in paras 24 and 26; *Borawitz, 2000* in paras 18 and 35; *Ferlini, 2000* in para. 42; *Yiadom, 2000* in paras 25, 27, 33, 36, 40, and 43; and *Elsen, 2000* in para. 34. In these judgments the references to 'Community national' in the introductory terms, keywords, summaries, rulings or by the parties or referring courts are not mentioned; in other words, only the paragraphs in which the Court itself speaks to the audience are listed. In the following decisions just the parties or the referring court mentioned 'Community nationals' or the term was only mentioned in the facts or national legislation: *Krid, 1995* with 'EEC national' in paras 13 and 14; *Gaal, 1995* in para. 5; *Commission v. France (ship registration), 1996* in para. 29; *Asscher, 1996* in the 'whether' in para. 35; *Commission v. Belgium (unemployment), 1996* in para. 22 and 32; *Commission v. Germany (directives), 1997* in para. 10; *Commission v. Ireland (ship registration), 1997* in para. 8 and 9; *Commission v. Germany (ID checks), 1998* in para. 2; *Commission v. Greece (large families), 1998* in paras 9, 14, 22, and 31; *Gschwind, 1999* with 'Community citizen' in para. 12; and *Graf, 2000* in para. 21. 'Community national' was mentioned only in the keywords and the summary in *Gallagher, 1995*; and merely in the introductory terms in *Uecker and Jacquet, 1997*.

153 The nexus between the terms 'Community national' and 'Union citizen' is further illustrated in Advocate General Jacobs' opinion in *Khalil, 2001*, para. 19, where he stated: '[...] it is settled law that that provision [article 48 Treaty] guarantees free movement only to Community nationals (now citizens of the Union)'.

154 *Kondova, 2001* (para. 80); *Gloszczuk, 2001* (para. 75); *Khalil, 2001* (para. 40); *Ruhr, 2001* (para. 19); *Dreessen II, 2002* (paras 24, 27, and 31); *Kauer, 2002* (para. 44); *Hervein II, 2002* ('Community citizens' in para. 47); *Commission v. Spain (doctors), 2002* (paras 18, 24, 26, and 54); *Mertens, 2002* (paras 26 and 37); *Ueberseering, 2002* (para. 56); *De Groot, 2002* (paras 76 and 77); *Commission v. Italy (patent services), 2003* (para. 22); *Commission v. Netherlands (driving licence), 2003* (para. 66); *Burbaud, 2003* (para. 108); *Van Lent, 2003* (paras 14 and 15); *Ninni-Orasche, 2003* (paras 33 and 48); *Schilling, 2003* (paras 23, 24, and 28); *Commission v. France (bio-medical labs), 2004* (para. 58); *Collins, 2004* (paras 37 and 39); *Weigel, 2004* ('Community citizens' in para. 52); *Kapper, 2004* (para. 27); *Orfanopoulos, 2004* (paras 83 and 98); *Beuttenmüller, 2004* (para. 53 and 'Community citizens' in paras 36 and 63); *Commission v. Netherlands (ships), 2004* (paras 15, 16, and 32); *Commission v. Luxembourg (posted workers), 2004* (para. 43); *My, 2004* (para. 37 and 'Community citizen' in para. 49); *Laurin Effing, 2005* (para. 52); *Oulane, 2005* (para. 24 and 49); *Kranemann, 2005* (para. 25); *Commission v. Spain (visa prior to entry), 2005* (paras 35, 37, 38, and

law, though not the Court in its reasoning, mentioned the term in four more decisions.[155]

The end of the 'Community national'

After the Lisbon Treaty abolished the pillar structure by merging the Community with the Union the terms 'Community national' or 'Community citizen' were no longer used, except at one occasion.[156] Instead, the Court preferred the term 'European Union national', mentioning it in its reasoning in a few decisions.[157]

Conclusions

By the time *Grzelczyk, 2001* came around to pinpoint Union citizenship as the 'fundamental status', the Court – driven by the referring national courts as well as the parties – established a routine of referring to the 'Community national'.

46); *Commission v. Greece (opticians), 2005* (para. 27 and 34); *Commission v. Italy (teaching experience), 2005* (paras 13, 14, 16, 17, and 21); *Aslanidou, 2005* ('Community citizens' in para. 35); *Commission v. Denmark (car registration), 2005* (para. 34); *Marks & Spencer, 2005* (para. 30); *Nadin and Durré, 2005* (para. 34); *Rockler, 2006* (paras 14 and 15 and 'Community citizens' in para. 17); *Öberg, 2006* (paras 11 and 12 and 'Community citizens' in para. 14); *Ritter-Coulais, 2006* (paras 31 and 33); *Keller Holding, 2006* (para. 29); *Commission v. Finland (car registration), 2006* (para. 38); *Commission v. Spain (work experience), 2006* (para. 14, 16, and 19); *Mattern and Cikotic, 2006* (paras 17, 24, and 28); *Commission v. Germany (expulsion), 2006* (paras 36, 38, 72, 84, 95, and 109); *N, 2006* (paras 26, 27, 28 and 30); *Spain v. United Kingdom (Gibraltar), 2006* (para. 80); *Cadbury Schweppes, 2006* (paras 36, 41, and 53); *Commission v. Italy (work experience), 2006* (paras 16, 18, 19, and 21); *Commission v. Portugal (capital gains deduction), 2006* ('Community citizens' in para. 15); *Turpeinen, 2006* (para. 14); *Chateignier, 2006* (para. 26); *ACT Group, 2006* (para. 42); *FII Group, 2006* (para. 39); *Denkavit, 2006* (para. 20); *Jia, 2007* (para. 25, 30, 33, 35, 37, 42, and 43); *Lyyski, 2007* (para. 31 and 35); *ITC, 2007* (para. 31); *Commission v. Sweden (tax deferral), 2007* (para. 17); *Thin Cap, 2007* (para. 36); *Rewe, 2007* (para. 25); *Alevizos, 2007* (para. 65, 72, and 74); *A and B, 2007* (para. 23); *Commission v. Netherlands (automatic expulsion), 2007* (para. 36); *Oy AA, 2007* (para. 29); *Derin, 2007* (para. 67); *Lakebrink, 2007* (paras 12, 15, 17, and 36); *Commission v. Germany (private schools), 2007* (para. 114); *Viking, 2007* (para. 68); *Geurts, 2007* (para. 14); *Commission v. Germany (psychotherapists), 2007* (para. 49); *Commission v. Germany (housing subsidy), 2008* (para. 21); *Lammers, 2008*; *Mayeur, 2008* (paras 19 and 20); *French Community, 2008* (paras 44 and 45); *Commission v. Spain (hospital pharmacists), 2008* (para. 41); *Burda, 2008* (para. 76); *Jipa, 2008* (para. 25); *Commission v. France (insemination), 2008* (para. 56); *Renneberg, 2008* (paras 33, 36, 37, 43, 44, 84, and 'Community citizens' in para. 44); *Zablocka-Weyhermüller, 2008* (paras 35, 36, and 37); *Commission v. Austria (self-employment), 2008* (paras 24, 27, and 30); *Truck Center, 2008* (para. 31); *Soysal, 2009* (paras 55 and 61); *Hartlauer, 2009* (para. 33); *Commission v. Greece (dividends), 2009* (para. 36); *Rüffler, 2009* (para. 66); *Apothekerkammer, 2009* (para. 22); *Commission v. Italy (pharmacies), 2009* (para. 43); *Aberdeen Alpha, 2009* (para. 37); *Sahin, 2009* (paras 47, 67, 69, 71, 72, 73, and 75); *Glaxo, 2009* (paras 45 and 46); *Wolzenburg, 2009* (para. 68); *Filipiak, 2009* (para. 52, 58, and 59); *Serrantoni, 2009* (para. 41); *SGI, 2010* (para. 38); *X Holding, 2010* (para. 17); *Winner Wetten, 2010* (para. 46); and *Stoß, 2010* (para. 59). The paragraphs in which in addition the Court merely mentioned the terms 'Community national' or 'Community citizen' as part of the summary or the introductory terms, keywords, or ruling or in which the parties referred to the terms are not mentioned in the list in this footnote.

155 *D'Hoop, 2002* (para. 22); *Baumbast, 2002* (paras 23 and 66); *Commission v. Greece (architects), 2004* (paras 1 and 8 and the Court in the ruling); and *Eman and Sevinger, 2006* (para. 6). In addition, 'Community nationals' was mentioned in the summary in *Metock, 2008*.

156 *Serrantoni, 2009*, para. 41, was the only decision in persons and services in which the Court used the term 'Community nationals' after the Lisbon Treaty had entered into force on 1 December 2009.

157 *Bejan, 2010* in para. 41; *Akdas, 2011* in paras 87, 88, and 95; *Commission v. Netherlands (notaries), 2011* in para. 51; *Notermans, 2012* in paras 23 and 24; *A Oy, 2012* in para. 24; and *Petersen, 2013* in paras 35 and 37. In addition, the referring court mentioned the term European Union national in *Rahman, 2012* (see para. 17) and *Prete, 2012* (see para. 13).

This notion thrived in the case-law of the Court for almost three decades. While obviously no direct connection can be drawn to the 'fundamental status', the existence in case-law of an 'unofficial' status delivers at least some explanation for the Court's ease in *Grzelczyk, 2001* in declaring Union citizenship as the 'fundamental status'.

3 The evolution of the 'fundamental status'

After this separate, but largely parallel evolution of 'fundamental' and status-based notions, the 'fundamental status' of Union citizens finally made its first appearance in *Grzelczyk, 2001*. In the following, the evolution of this 'fundamental status' after its first appearance is explored.

a) Occurrence – in the 2000s

The Court again referred to the fundamental status in *D'Hoop, 2002* (para. 28). Belgium had refused the tideover allowance to a Belgian national who had studied in Belgium, because she had passed her secondary education in France. The Court rejected that criterion as discriminatory of Union citizens who had made use of their freedom to move. Only a real link to a state's society could lawfully be required. Next, in *Baumbast, 2002* the fundamental status (para. 82) preceded the Court's conferring a direct right of residence of Union citizens on the basis of article 18 Treaty. This time the Court omitted the consideration on equal treatment which had followed the fundamental status-passage in *Grzelczyk, 2001* and *D'Hoop, 2002*.

In *Garcia Avello, 2003* the Court began its reasoning on the refusal in Belgian law to admit Spanish double-barrelled surnames by the fundamental status formula (para. 22), which it supplemented in the following paragraph by considerations on equal treatment. Ultimately, this led the Court to reject the serious inconvenience caused for Union citizens, because it amounted to discrimination.

In *Collins, 2004* the fundamental status-formula was again referred to (para. 61). In the following the Court ruled that a jobseeker's allowance was not to be withheld any longer from Union citizens who had genuinely sought work in the host state for a reasonable period. Next, the Court cited the fundamental status-formula in *Orfanopoulos, 2004* (para. 65). The Court left aside the aspect of equal treatment, though. Rather, the formula in this case underpinned the Court's reasoning that a very strict interpretation of derogations from the free movement of workers was required. Ultimately, the Court rejected any automatism in the expulsion of nationals of other member states who benefitted from the free movement of persons or services. In *Pusa, 2004* the Court put the fundamental status-formula including the equal treatment passage right at the beginning of the judgment (para. 16). The Court then rejected Finland's refusal to take into account taxes due in another member state in the calculation of the attachable part of a pension paid in Finland. In *Zhu and Chen, 2004* the Court mentioned the 'fundamental status' – without any hint at equal treatment – when it found that a minor child who was a Union citizen had a right of residence based on the Treaty subject to certain conditions (para. 25).

In *Bidar, 2005* the Court then mentioned the fundamental status-formula together with equal treatment at the beginning of the reasoning (para. 31). The ultimate consequence was that the member states could not any longer withhold maintenance grants from migrant Union citizen students as such. They were only allowed to require a real link with the host state's society. In *Commission v. Austria (university), 2005* the Court found that Austria's requirement for access to university education, i. e. proof of access in the 'home' state, amounted to indirect discrimination and underpinned this finding with the 'fundamental status' and equal treatment (para. 45). Thereafter, the Court mentioned the 'fundamental status' together with equal treatment in *Schempp, 2005* (para. 15). The Court then ruled that it did not violate non-discrimination or the rights of Union citizens to move freely that maintenance payments to a recipient abroad were not tax deductible in Germany.

Next, Spain argued on the basis of the fundamental status-formula in *Spain v. United Kingdom (Gibraltar), 2006*. However, the Court rejected the argument that the fundamental status-formula implied that only Union citizens could vote and stand in the elections of the European Parliament (para. 74). Hence, the United Kingdom was free to include certain persons who were closely affiliated with the United Kingdom in the electorate. In *Turpeinen, 2006* the Court began its consideration of article 18 Treaty with the fundamental status-formula including equal treatment (para. 18). Ultimately, this led the Court to find that a Finnish pensioner who had moved to Spain was treated less favourably in terms of taxation than a pensioner who had remained in Finland.

Then in *Commission v. Netherlands (automatic expulsion), 2007* the Court began to address the issue whether Union citizens who were not lawfully resident in the host state could rely nonetheless on Directive 64/221 by referring to the fundamental status of Union citizenship (para. 32). The Court left aside equal treatment, though. It concluded that such Union citizens could indeed rely on the Directive. In *Gootjes-Schwarz, 2007* the Court again began the part on Union citizenship by the fundamental status-formula including the passage on equal treatment (para. 86), after having found that Germany's refusal to allow the deduction of private school fees paid abroad violated the free provision of services. Under citizenship the same conclusion was then reached as under services. The same is true of *Commission v. Germany (private schools), 2007*, which concerned the same German provisions. The fundamental status-formula was referred to in the same way (para. 125). Thereafter the Court mentioned the fundamental status-formula in *Eind, 2007* (para. 32) when it awarded the third country national daughter of a returning migrant worker, who was a Union citizen, the right to reside with her father although he was not economically active.[158]

In *Huber, 2008* the Court opened its considerations on Germany's register of foreigners in relation to the purpose of fighting crime by the fundamental status-formula including equal treatment (para. 69). In the following the Court found that the situations of German nationals and other Union citizens did not differ with regard to fighting crime. Hence, it was not justified to keep a separate data register just for Union citizens who were not German nationals.

Mariano, 2009 was the next case in which the 'fundamental status' including equal treatment was mentioned (para. 18). The Court then refused to enter the substance of the argument put forward, because all aspects of the situation were confined to Italy. After that, the fundamental status-formula including equal treatment came up in *Rüffler, 2009* (para. 62). In this case the Court then found that Poland had to allow a pensioner to deduct sickness insurance contributions made in Germany for the purposes of direct taxation in Poland. The next case in which the fundamental status-formula was mentioned together with equal treatment was *Gottwald, 2009* (para. 23). The Court introduced its reasoning by the formula. In the end, it found lawful Austria's relying on residence or regular presence of disabled persons for them to receive a toll disc allowing free use of highways.

Occurrence in the early 2010s

In *Rottmann, 2010* the Court again put forward the fundamental status-formula, though without mentioning equal treatment (para. 43). The formula in part justified why the withdrawal of national citizenship came within the scope of Union law and why a member state was not at complete liberty to withdraw the nationality from one of 'its' nationals. The next case was *Zanotti, 2010*. The fundamental status-formula was mentioned in para. 68 together with equal treatment. The Court then reproduced for Union citizenship the considerations put forward in the first part of the judgment as to services. Ultimately, this meant that a discriminatory approach to tax deductibility of tuition fees was precluded, while a purely territorial or quantitative approach was lawful.

In *Ruiz Zambrano, 2011* the Court also had recourse to the fundamental status-formula without mentioning the equal treatment aspect (para. 41). The Court concluded that a father who was a third country national could lawfully derive a right of residence from his minor children who were Union citizens, even in the state of which the children were nationals. In *McCarthy, 2011* the fundamental status-formula was also mentioned, again without the phrase concerning equal treatment (para. 47). In some contrast to *Ruiz Zambrano, 2011*,

---

158 In *Metock, 2008*, para. 4, the Court recounted the legal context which included the preambular clause of the citizenship Directive 2004/38 stating that 'Union citizenship should be the fundamental status of nationals of the Member states [...]'. The same is valid for *Ibrahim, 2010*, para. 8; *Teixeira, 2010*, para. 8; *Bressol, 2010*, para. 5; *Lassal, 2010*, para. 4; *Tsakouridis, 2010*, para. 3; and *Ziolkowski, 2011*, para. 3.

however, a right of residence could not be derived from the Union citizen in her 'home' state for the benefit of her husband who was a third country national. No link was established with any situation governed by Union law. The fundamental status-formula was used next in *Runevič-Vardyn, 2011* (para. 60) again together with equal treatment. The Court then basically left it to the national court to decide whether a serious inconvenience was caused for the Union citizens concerned. In *Stewart, 2011* the Court then mentioned the fundamental status-formula together with the equal treatment aspect (para. 80) and in the following invalidated the United Kingdom's requirement for the award of an invalidity benefit to have been present in the country in the past. In *Dereci, 2011* the Court then clarified that a Union citizen in his 'home' state could not require family reunification with a third country national on the pure basis of Union citizenship, despite the fact that Union citizenship was the 'fundamental status' (para. 62). The Court next mentioned the fundamental status-formula in *Ziebell, 2011* in the context of the Ankara Agreement with Turkey (para. 73). However, the Court refused to interpret Decision 1/80 in the same way as the Union's provisions on expulsion of Union citizens.

Thereafter, the fundamental status-formula was used again in *Commission v. Austria (transport fare), 2012* in combination with the passage on equal treatment (para. 38 and indirectly para. 51). Ultimately, the Court rejected Austria's relying on parents' receiving income allowance in Austria for their descendants to benefit from reduced student transport fares. The receipt of income allowance was not necessarily representative of a genuine link with Austria. The fundamental status-formula, excluding the equal treatment aspect, was also mentioned in *Hungary v. Slovakia, 2012* (para. 40). The Court eventually decided that the visit of a head of state who was a Union citizen was not governed by the rules on Union citizenship, but by international law. *Prete, 2012* was next. The Court mentioned the 'fundamental status' including equal treatment in para. 24. It then went on to find that a period of six years of studies in the host state was not to be considered as solely representative of a real link to the employment market in the host state. Then, the fundamental status-formula was mentioned, without the part on equal treatment, in *O and S, 2012* (para. 44). The Court ruled that, subject to the referring court's assessment, the effectiveness of Union citizenship was not hampered by the refusal to grant a third country national a residence permit.

Finally, in *L.N., 2013* the Court referred to the 'fundamental status', too, including the equal treatment clause (para. 27). Following that reference, the Court in essence rejected the idea that the Union citizen concerned could not rely on his rights as a worker, because he had intended to study in the host state from the outset.

The blessings of the 'fundamental status'

Almost all of the above decisions in which the Court took recourse to the fundamental status-formula turned out favourably for Union citizens. This is certainly valid for *Grzelczyk, 2001*; *D'Hoop, 2002*; *Baumbast, 2002*; *Garcia Avello,*

2003; *Collins, 2004*; *Orfanopoulos, 2004*, at least for the part in which the fundamental status-formula was mentioned; *Pusa, 2004* in that the Court essentially required Finland's authorities to factor in tax due in Spain; *Zhu and Chen, 2004*; *Bidar, 2005*; *Commission v. Austria (university), 2005*; *Turpeinen, 2006*; *Commission v. Netherlands (automatic expulsion), 2007*; *Gootjes-Schwarz, 2007*; *Commission v. Germany (private schools), 2007*; *Eind, 2007*; *Huber, 2008*; *Rüffler, 2009*; *Rottmann, 2010* in that the formula served to limit the power to withdraw citizenship; *Ruiz Zambrano, 2011* in that the Union citizens did not have to leave the Union with their father; *Stewart, 2011*; *Prete, 2012*; and *L.N., 2013*.

In only a handful of the cases in which the fundamental status-formula was mentioned Union citizens ended up with a less favourable position. That is certainly true for *Schempp, 2005*; *Mariano, 2009* in that the Court refused to extend Union citizenship to cover purely internal situation; *Gottwald, 2009*; *Hungary v. Slovakia, 2012* in that the provisions on Union citizenship were overruled by international law; and *O and S, 2012* though only to a certain extent, since the Court left most of the assessment to the national court.

Besides these clear decisions, a small number of decisions defy categorization in terms of how favourable or unfavourable they were for Union citizens. In *Spain v. United Kingdom (Gibraltar), 2006*, Spain had argued that the fundamental status-formula implied that only Union citizens were to have a right to vote in the elections to the European Parliament, but the Court rejected that argument. In *Zanotti, 2010* the Court drew a factual distinction between quantitative/territorial limitations to the deductible amount and discriminatory limitations and left it to the national court to categorize the case at hand. In *McCarthy, 2011* and *Dereci, 2011* the Court refused generally to class the situation of a Union citizen in his or her 'home' state as purely internal, though it turned out that the cases at issue *were* purely internal to a member state. In *Runevič-Vardyn, 2011* the decision was unclear in that the issue to be resolved was left to the referring court. Finally, in *Ziebell, 2011* the Court refused to extend the case-law on the expulsion of Union citizens to Turkish nationals, so that Union citizenship was not truly concerned by the decision.

b) Spin

That so many decisions mentioning the fundamental status-formula turned out favourably for Union citizens is an indication of the strength of the formula. However, did the formula in these cases indeed spin the Court's decisions? How instrumental was it in the Court's decisions? Spin is examined in the following.

In *Grzelczyk, 2001* itself, which was the origin of the fundamental status-formula, that formula contributed some spin for the Court to reach the decision that the Belgian benefit could not lawfully be refused in situations such as that at issue. The formula set the tune for the Court to reach its disruptive decision. Then, in *D'Hoop, 2002* the 'fundamental status' of Union citizenship, followed by the equal treatment clause, clearly spun the decision, bringing the Court to the conclusion that Belgium's requirement to have passed secondary education in Belgium fell foul of the Treaty. In *Baumbast, 2002* the fundamental status-formula provided the justification for the Court to reject the idea that article 18 Treaty did not confer a direct right of residence.

In *Collins, 2004* the fundamental status-formula served the Court to put into perspective some established case-law. That case-law had held that those seeking employment in the host state could have benefitted from equal treatment exclusively with regard to access to employment. The formula provided the spin needed to reduce the criterion allowed as a condition for a jobseeker's allowance to a genuine link with the host state's employment market. In *Orfanopoulos, 2004* the fundamental status-formula provided some decisive spin. It was instrumental at least in part for the rejection of any automatism forcing a national authority to order the expulsion of a national of a member state. In *Zhu and Chen, 2004* again the 'fundamental status' commenced the Court's consideration of the right of residence of a minor Union citizen. It provided the impetus necessary for the Court to reject arguments based on the source of the means to support the minor and on abuse of rights.

In *Bidar, 2005* the fundamental status-formula at the beginning of the decision created the momentum for the Court to include maintenance grants within the scope of the Treaty and, more specifically, Union citizenship. Together with other case-law it notably led the Court to rescind *Brown, 1988* and *Lair, 1988*. In *Turpeinen, 2006* spin by the 'fundamental status' was obvious. It initiated the Court's rejection of Finland's difference in tax treatment of pensioners depending on whether they lived in Finland or abroad.

In *Commission v. Netherlands (automatic expulsion), 2007* the fundamental status-formula again clearly spun the Court's decision. It was put forward right at the beginning of the Court's reasoning and led it towards the conclusion that even Union citizens who were unlawfully resident in the host state could rely on Directive 64/221. In *Gootjes-Schwarz, 2007* the fundamental status-formula exerted some spin. The spin was limited, though, because the Court essentially transposed the assessment made previously under the free movement of services to citizenship. The same is true for *Commission v. Germany (private schools), 2007* which concerned the very same German rules.

In *Huber, 2008* the fundamental status-formula delivered the thrust necessary to reject Germany's separate register for Union citizens who were not German nationals. Then, in *Rottmann, 2010* the fundamental status-formula served to limit the power of the member states to withdraw nationality from a Union citizen. In this function it exerted considerable spin.

In *Ruiz Zambrano, 2011* the spin of the fundamental status-formula was again very strong. It drove the Court towards the decision of granting the third country national concerned a right of residence derived from his children. In *Stewart, 2011* the fundamental status-formula exerted some spin, although it was embedded in other case-law. In part, it made room for the Court to invalidate the United Kingdom's condition for the award of a benefit which consisted in the need to have been present in the United Kingdom in the past.

In *Commission v. Austria (transport fare), 2012* merely some limited spin can be discerned. The Court included the fundamental status-formula in the beginning of its considerations and embedded it in other case-law. Moreover, the final result to reject the income allowance as not representative of a connection with Austria appeared quite removed from the formula. Finally, in *L.N., 2013* the fundamental status-formula was mentioned at the beginning of the judgment. It noticeably spun the Court's decision towards considering a student as a worker.

Empty spin

While the 'fundamental status' regularly spun decisions, empty spin – a phenomenon that was also observed in the previous chapters with 'broad' and 'coordinated' interpretation – also occurred, notably in the following four, or five, decisions. *Schempp, 2005* was the first case with an element of empty spin. The Court started out with the 'fundamental status', embedded it in other case-law, and then found that the relevant tax situations in Austria and Germany were not comparable. The 'fundamental status' thus ran empty. Neither non-discrimination nor the right of Union citizens to move were violated by Germany's refusal to allow the deductibility of maintenance payments to a recipient established in Austria. *Mariano, 2009* was the second case in which the fundamental status-formula spun empty. The Court first mentioned the 'fundamental status'. Yet it turned against the thrust of the formula to hold that Union citizenship could not extend the scope of the Treaty. Hence, the 'fundamental status' fizzled and Ms Mariano's claim that she was discriminated on the ground that she had not been married went unheard. In *Gottwald, 2009* again the fundamental status-formula's spin was empty. The Court introduced its considerations with the formula, but then found Austria's restriction of the freedom of Union citizens to be justified. In *Dereci, 2011* empty spin could, with some imagination, be considered to have occurred. However, the decision merely clarified what the Court had laid out in *Ruiz Zambrano, 2011* and *McCarthy, 2011*, which the Court routinely reiterated. Finally, in *Hungary v. Slovakia, 2012* spin was again empty. The Court began its considerations with the fundamental status-formula, but then turned against the moment of the formula and decided against the thrust of Union citizenship. The visits of heads of state were governed by international law rather than Union citizenship.

No spin, advance statement

In some cases no spin occurred. In some of them this was because the 'fundamental status' was included in an advance statement of case-law. These are the following decisions. In *Pusa, 2004* the Court put the fundamental status-formula right at the beginning of the judgment, thus setting the tone for the decision. However, other case-law followed upon the formula in an advance statement of case-law, thus obscuring the formula's potential spin. In *Commission v. Austria (university), 2005* the fundamental status formula did not exactly spin the Court's decision. It rather just underpinned the finding that Austria's approach amounted to indirect discrimination.

In *Spain v. United Kingdom (Gibraltar), 2006* the fundamental status-formula did not exert any spin at all. Spain attempted to inject some spin by relying on the formula and thereby prompt the Court to exclude certain persons who were not Union citizens from the electorate for the European Parliament. But the Court expressly rejected that idea. In *Eind, 2007* the fundamental status-formula hardly provided any spin at all. It was merely mentioned to supplement the complex argument of the Court on why a national returning from a member state to his home state conferred a right of residence to his third country national daughter, although he was not working in his home state.

In *Zanotti, 2010* the fundamental status-formula did not spin the Court's decision, either. The Court's decision in the first part on the freedom of services was simply transposed to the freedom of Union citizens for cases in which the courses offered did not amount to services. In that process, the fundamental status-formula was mentioned merely as a matter of routine. In *Ziebell, 2011* spin again did not occur. The Court mentioned the fundamental status-formula, but only to explain the interpretation it had given to Union citizenship with regard to the member states. For Turkish nationals that interpretation could not apply. Hence, Union citizenship – and with it the 'fundamental status' – was not truly concerned in *Ziebell, 2011*.

In *Prete, 2012* the fundamental status-formula was part of an advance statement of case-law concerning the applicability of the free movement of workers. The Court then discussed the facts with regard to the need to interpret the freedom of workers in the light of Union citizenship. In that discussion the judgments in *Collins, 2004* and *Ioannidis, 2005* informed the Court's decision more than the fundamental status-formula. Consequently, the formula did not exert any spin. In *O and S, 2012* the fundamental status-formula was again part of an advance statement of case-law. Moreover, the Court left the assessment to the referring court, providing it merely with directions. These directions hardly disclose any spin carried over from the advance statement of case-law.

Spin uncertain

In some decisions, it is hard to decide whether the 'fundamental status' exerted any spin. In *Garcia Avello, 2003* the fundamental status appeared at the beginning of the decision and created the mood in which the Court was able to require Belgium to accept Spanish double-barrelled surnames. Yet spin is not obvious in this judgment, since the 'fundamental status' was part of a small advance statement of case-law. In *Rüffler, 2009* the spin the fundamental status-formula could have exerted was tempered by other case-law which was recited. Thus, the short advance statement of case-law obscured most of the spin.

In *McCarthy, 2011* spin is difficult to ascertain. On the one hand, the fundamental status-formula served the Court to rule that the situation of a Union citizen who had never made use of her freedom to move, but rather remained in her home country was not necessarily removed from the grasp of Union law. On the other hand, the Court ruled that Ms McCarthy *was* removed from the grasp of Union law, because she had not been deprived of the substance of her rights as a Union citizen. This second aspect emptied the spin of the fundamental status formula to a certain extent. In *Runevič-Vardyn, 2011* it is again not easy to determine spin. The Court mentioned the fundamental status-formula, but it was in a sort of advance statement of case-law put forward before the Court addressed the restriction and the corresponding justification. Moreover, the Court left it mainly to the national court to assess the degree of inconvenience caused to the Union citizens concerned. Thus, for lack of a clear result of the judgment, spin cannot be determined with certainty.

c) Conclusions

The decisions in which the fundamental status-formula materialized turned out in the vast majority of cases in favour of Union citizens. Moreover, when the fundamental status-formula was used it was regularly decisive in the Court's decisions. It very often exerted spin. The cases in which spin was empty were rather rare, though they have become more frequent recently. In some cases spin was buried in an advance statement of case-law. Overall, the essence is that the 'fundamental status' is a formula of great, almost eerie power.

4 Counterfactual evidence

The power the 'fundamental status' exerted in the decisions above, in which it was mentioned, can be cross-checked with the decisions in which the formula was *not* mentioned although Union citizenship was at issue. Such counterfactual check is possible for the 'fundamental status', because only a limited number of judgments deal with Union citizenship, with which the 'fundamental status' is inextricably linked. It would obviously not make much sense to check non-citizenship cases on the absence of the 'fundamental status'.

Before Grzelczyk

In the judgments that were handed down before *Grzelczyk, 2001*, the fundamental status-formula was not used, although Union citizenship played a role in them. The first of these was *Martínez Sala, 1998*;[159] then came *Bickel, 1998*;[160] *Wijsenbeek, 1999*; *Kaba, 2000*; and *Kaur, 2001*. In the latter three decisions, the

159 In *Skanavi, 1996*, the Court refused to address Union citizenship, because the freedom of establishment gave specific expression to article 8a Treaty (para. 22). In *Uecker and Jacquet, 1997*, the Court found that Union citizenship did not extend the scope of Union law to cover purely internal situations. The ruling in *Kremzow, 1997*, was similar. One could consider *in extremis* that these were unfavourable decisions for Union citizens.

160 In *Bickel, 1998*, the Court merely supplemented the reasoning on the free movement of services with the free movement of Union citizens (para. 15).

outcome tended to be unfavourable for Union citizens. Yet it would stretch logic quite a bit to draw an *e contrario* argument from that. After all, the fundamental status-formula at that time had not existed.

After Grzelczyk, non-occurrence in the 2000s

After the Court had established the formula in *Grzelczyk, 2001*, the situation was as follows. In *Olazabal, 2002* the Court refused to address Union citizenship, because the free movement of workers was a specific expression of the freedom of Union citizens (para. 26). In *Stylianakis, 2003* the Court ruled in the same way for freedom of services (paras 18-20). In *Baldinger, 2004* the Court did not mention Union citizenship at all, although Advocate General Ruiz-Jarabo Colomer discussed the 'fundamental status' (in para. 26 of the opinion). According to the Court, the benefit concerned was available only for victims of war and as such not covered by Regulations 1408/71, 1612/68 or article 39(2) Treaty. In *Gaumain-Cerri, 2004* the Court struck down Germany's residence condition for third parties providing care in Germany directly on the basis of Union citizenship. The Court did not use the term 'fundamental status', although it mentioned the 'status of Union citizenship' (para. 34) with reference to paragraph 28 of *D'Hoop, 2002* where the fundamental status-formula had been expressly referred to. Next, in *Lindfors, 2004* the Court under Union citizenship in essence validated Finland's tax on cars imported in connection with a change of residence. Yet the Court left the assessment of whether a disadvantage resulted for Union citizens to the national court.

In *Trojani, 2004* the Court made it clear that the right of residence of Union citizens was conditional on the citizen concerned having sufficient resources. However, when the Union citizen was lawfully resident in the host state, he was not to be denied the benefit of non-discrimination with regard to social assistance. In *Ioannidis, 2005* the Court applied the free movement of workers, but read it in the light of Union citizenship (para. 22) so as to preclude the place where secondary education was passed as a condition for a tideover allowance. Then the Court refused to address Union citizenship on its own. In *Commission v. Belgium (own resources), 2006* the Court struck down Belgium's requirements relating to the sufficient means a Union citizen was to have and the deportation order that was automatically served if he did not have those means. In *De Cuyper, 2006* the Court found a residence requirement for unemployment benefits justified under the freedom of Union citizens to move.[161] In *Eman and Sevinger, 2006* the Court found it discriminatory that Dutch nationals in third states were allowed to stand and vote in the elections to the European Parliament, while Dutch nationals resident in Aruba were not. The Court reached this result on the basis of equal treatment. The same approach was not precluded by Union citizenship as such. In *Tas-Hagen, 2006* the Court found that residence at

161 In *Hosse, 2006*, para. 19, the national court also asked about the compatibility of the residence requirement in Austrian law with Union citizenship. The Court did not address the question, because the residence requirement fell foul of article 19(2) Regulation 1408/71.

the time an application was submitted was not an appropriate criterion to establish a link with a state's society for the purpose of entitlement to a benefit for victims of war. The freedom of Union citizens to move thus precluded it. In *Commission v. Portugal (capital gains deduction), 2006* the Court invalidated Portugal's provisions on the basis of the freedom of workers and establishment and then transposed that finding to Union citizenship (para. 37). The same is true for *Commission v. Sweden (tax deferral), 2007* (para. 30).[162]

In *Commission v. Belgium (tax matters), 2007* the Court rendered invalid certain Belgian rules concerning insurances and pension funds. The Court first ruled on the basis of the free movement of persons and then transposed the ruling to the freedom of Union citizens (para. 72). In *Morgan, 2007* the Court applied the freedom of Union citizens and invalidated Germany's condition for a grant, which was to have studied for at least a year in Germany and to pursue the same studies abroad.[163]

In *Commission v. Germany (housing subsidy), 2008* the Court again just transposed the ruling concerning the free movement of workers and the freedom of establishment to Union citizenship (para. 30). In *Commission v. Netherlands (own means), 2008* the Court declared unlawful the proof the Netherlands required for 'sufficient means'. In *Nerkowska, 2008* the Court on the basis of Union citizenship invalidated Poland's criterion of continuous residence for a benefit for victims of deportation. In *Jipa, 2008* the Court found that the determination by the host state that a Union citizen had been illegally resident was not sufficient in itself for the 'home' state lawfully to order that citizen not to leave the 'home' state. In *Metock, 2008* the Court enabled direct family reunification with third country nationals on the basis of the citizenship Directive 2004/38. That was confirmed in the order in *Sahin, 2008*. In *Grunkin, 2008* the Court found that a child who was a Union citizen had to be registered under the double-barrelled surname in its 'home' state, when it was so registered lawfully in the state of residence. In *Förster, 2008* the Court sanctioned a requirement of five years of residence for entitlement to maintenance grants. In *Zablocka-Weyhermüller, 2008* the Court struck down Germany's residence requirement for a benefit for victims of war, because it disproportionately interfered with the freedom of Union citizens.[164]

In *Vatsouras, 2009* the Court refused to declare invalid article 24(2) Directive 2004/38, but required that it be interpreted in accordance with the freedom of

162 In *N, 2006*, the Court did not address Union citizenship, because the freedom of establishment was applicable (para. 23).

163 In *ITC, 2007* the Court refused to address Union citizenship given that Germany's approach was at odds with the freedoms of workers and services. In *Alevizos, 2007* the Court also assessed the situation under the free movement of workers and then declined to address Union citizenship (para. 80). The same is true for *Hendrix, 2007* (para. 62). In *Jundt, 2007* Union citizenship only supplemented the assessment made under the freedom of services (para. 62).

164 In *Mayeur, 2008* the Court refused to deal with the substance of the case, because all elements were confined to one member state. The citizenship Directive 2004/38 was thus not applied. The same is valid for *Pignataro, 2009*. In *French Community, 2008* the Court did not discuss Union citizenship, because the rules at issue were contrary to the freedom of workers and establishment (para. 59).

Union citizens and the freedom of workers. In *Von Chamier-Glisczinski, 2009* the Court protected Germany's refusal to export a care allowance. In *Commission v. Germany (savings-pension bonus), 2009* the Court struck down certain German rules on the basis of the free movement of workers and then transposed that ruling to Union citizenship for those who were not economically active (para. 115). In *Wolzenburg, 2009* the Court sanctioned the criterion the Netherlands applied to refuse to surrender persons for the execution of a judgment. It was compatible with Union citizenship to require in that regard a period of five years of residence in the Netherlands.[165]

Non-occurrence in the early 2010s

In *Teixeira, 2010* and *Ibrahim, 2010* the Court confirmed the right of residence of the child in education and its primary carer based on article 12 Regulation 1612/68, although the citizenship Directive 2004/38 had repealed articles 10 and 11 Regulation 1612/68. The Court also rejected restrictions on the basis of the age of the dependant and the resources of the carer. In *Bressol, 2010* the Court essentially sent back the case to the national court to assess the proportionality of Belgium's restriction of access to studies in medicine under Union citizenship. In *Lassal, 2010* the Court interpreted Directive 2004/38 liberally so that a Union citizen who had completed five years of residence in the host state before the Directive was to be implemented could be considered to have permanent residence. In *Van Delft, 2010* the Court basically validated the effects a change in the Dutch insurance system had on Union citizens living abroad. In *Tsakouridis, 2010*, the Court essentially left the assessment of the period of presence of ten years and the imperative grounds of public security to the national court, requiring only an overall assessment of the situation and very good reasons for expulsion. In *Sayn-Wittgenstein, 2010*, the Court found it compatible with Union citizenship that the Austrian authorities deleted from their registers a certain part of the surname of a Union citizen to give effect to an amendment of Austria's constitutional law. The Court did not mention the 'fundamental status', although the Commission had used it as an argument (para. 51).

In *Commission v. Greece (transfer tax), 2011* the Court disallowed Greece's taxation of real estate under the free movement of workers and establishment and then transposed that ruling to Union citizenship (para. 60). In *Dias, 2011* the Court held that periods during which insufficient resources were available to a Union citizen in the host state did not constitute periods of legal residence, even if she held a residence permit. Such periods were capable of extinguishing her right to permanent residence. In *Aladzhov, 2011* and *Gaydarov, 2011* the Court left it to the national court to determine whether unsettled tax liabilities of a Union citizen amounted to a threat to public policy within the meaning of the Court's case-law. In *Commission v. Hungary (property tax), 2011* the Court

165 In *Leyman, 2009* the Court did not address Union citizenship, but the free movement of workers (para. 20). In *Josemans, 2010* the Court discussed the free movement of services rather than Union citizenship (para. 53).

found Hungary's way of taxing real property in accordance with the freedom of workers and establishment and then transposed that finding to Union citizenship (para. 89). In *Ziolkowski, 2011*, the Court found that the period of lawful residence in the host state, which was necessary to achieve permanent residence in the sense of Directive 2004/38, implied that the persons concerned had sufficient resources and sickness insurance during that period. Periods completed before accession of a member state basically counted towards the five year-period.[166]

In *P. I., 2012* the Court admitted serious crimes against minors as an imperative ground of public security capable of justifying expulsion of a Union citizen. In *Commission v. Spain (income tax), 2012* the Court found it incompatible with the free movement of workers and establishment that taxes became payable upon leaving Spain. The Court then transposed that finding to Union citizenship (para. 93). In *Reichel, 2012* the Court on the basis of Union citizenship required Germany to factor into the calculation of a benefit certain periods during which a Union citizen raised a child abroad. In *Rahman, 2012* the Court granted the member states wide discretion for reunification with third country nationals not belonging to the core family of a Union citizen. In *Czop, 2012* the Court confirmed that pre-accession periods counted toward the five year-period of permanent residence under Directive 2004/38. In *Byankov, 2012* the Court ruled that a prohibition for a Union citizen to leave the country had to be amenable to review after a certain time. Finally, in *Iida, 2012* the Court refused to accede to a claim of a third country national on the basis that he was married to a Union citizen. The Union citizen was not deprived of the genuine enjoyment of her rights.

No non-spin, the blessings of the absence of 'fundamental status'

Logic excludes the possibility to determine the 'non-spin' of the fundamental status-formula in the above decisions where the 'fundamental status' was not mentioned. More specifically, it cannot be gauged how the absence of the formula spun the Court's decision. What can be gauged, though, is whether the above decisions turned out in favour of Union citizens, while spin and favour are obviously not the same.

The picture that emerges with regard to favour is mixed. On the one hand, many decisions proved to be favourable to Union citizens, although the fundamental status-formula was not mentioned, namely the following decisions: *Gaumain-Cerri, 2004*, which was a case in which it seems almost bizarre that the Court did not mention the fundamental status-formula, since the paragraph in

166 In *Commission v. Portugal (tax representative), 2011* the Court found it unnecessary to address Union citizenship after having found a violation of the free movement of capital (para. 60). The same is true for *van Putten, 2012* (para. 55). In *Bartlett, 2011*, *Schulz-Delzers, 2011*, and *Caves Krier, 2012* the Court did not discuss Union citizenship, because it found specific expression in the free movement of workers (para. 41, para. 30, and para. 30, respectively), while the same was true for *Commission v. Belgium (registration duties), 2011* with regard to the freedom of capital (para. 30). In *Kamberaj, 2012* the Court found the questions concerning Union citizenship inadmissible. In *Commission v. Netherlands (certain charges), 2012* the Court found it unnecessary to compare charges imposed on third country nationals with those imposed on Union citizens.

D'Hoop, 2002 to which the Court referred *did* mention it and the decision was in harmony with the typical thrust of the 'fundamental status'; *Ioannidis, 2005* though technically it was a freedom of workers case; *Commission v. Belgium (own resources), 2006*; *Tas-Hagen, 2006*; *Morgan, 2007*; *Commission v. Netherlands (own means), 2008* though directives 68/360, 90/364, and 90/365 were applied rather than article 18 Treaty; *Nerkowska, 2008*; *Jipa, 2008* even though it was left to the 'home' state to assess the grounds of public order justifying a prohibition to leave; *Metock, 2008* and *Sahin, 2008*; *Grunkin, 2008*; *Zablocka-Weyhermüller, 2008*; *Teixeira, 2010* and *Ibrahim, 2010* although the two decisions were based on the free movement of workers; *Bressol, 2010* though the assessment was left to the national court; *Lassal, 2010*; *Tsakouridis, 2010*, though again the assessment was passed back to the national court; *Reichel, 2012*; and *Byankov, 2012*.

A number of further decisions can be considered to belong to this category, though with less certitude. These are decisions that turned out favourably for Union citizens, but the case was less involved with Union citizenship, given that the Court simply transposed the assessment made previously in the same decision under one market freedom to Union citizenship: *Commission v. Belgium (tax matters), 2007*; *Commission v. Sweden (tax deferral), 2007*; *Commission v. Germany (housing subsidy), 2008*; *Commission v. Germany (savings-pension bonus), 2009*; *Commission v. Greece (transfer tax), 2011*; and *Commission v. Spain (income tax), 2012*.

Of all those decisions that were generally favourable for Union citizens, while the Court in its reasoning did not mention the 'fundamental status', six are relative, namely *Metock, 2008*; *Teixeira, 2010* and *Ibrahim, 2010*; *Bressol, 2010*; *Lassal, 2010*; and *Tsakouridis, 2010*. In each one of those the Court in the 'legal context' recited preambular clause 3 of the citizenship Directive 2004/38 which mentions the 'fundamental status'. Therefore, the Court perhaps found it unnecessary to cite the 'fundamental status' again in the reasoning.

The curse of the absence of 'fundamental status'

On the other hand, a series of decisions in which the 'fundamental status' was not mentioned turned out rather unfavourably for Union citizens. The following decisions belong to this category: *Baldinger, 2004*; *Lindfors, 2004* though it was subject to the national court's assessment; *De Cuyper, 2006*; *Mayeur, 2008* and *Pignataro, 2009*, because the Court refused to address purely internal situations; *Förster, 2008*; *Vatsouras, 2009* in a sense because the Court refused to declare invalid article 24(2) Directive 2004/38; *Von Chamier-Glisczinski, 2009* in that the Court protected Germany's refusal to allow a benefit to be exported; *Van Delft, 2010*; *Sayn-Wittgenstein, 2010*; *Dias, 2011*; *Aladzhov, 2011* and *Gaydarov, 2011* though the assessment *in concreto* was left to the national court; *Ziolkowski, 2011* although only with regard to the first and less obvious answer, while the second answer turned out rather favourably for Union citizens; *P. I., 2012*, though only in that a settled, but highly criminal Union citizen was lawfully ordered to leave the 'host' state with the result that the threat the citizen posed was passed on to another member state to whom the citizen did not have any connection bar nationality; *Rahman, 2012* because of the large discretion to assess reunification with certain third country nationals; *Iida, 2012* while the constellation in this case was special, because an application under Directive 2003/109 had not been submitted. Again, to these decisions the judgment in *Commission v. Hungary (property tax), 2011* must be added, because the Court simply transposed the conclusion from the free movement of workers to Union citizenship. Moreover, of these decisions *Ziolkowski, 2011* seems quite particular, because the clause of the preamble of Directive 2004/38 containing the 'fundamental status' was cited under 'legal context'.[167]

Conclusions

The conclusion from the appraisal of the decisions in which the Court did *not* mention the fundamental status-formula – the counterfactual evidence, so to speak – is not very clear. The blueprint is not simple. A decision does not always turn out unfavourably for Union citizens if the 'fundamental status' is not mentioned. That, however, hardly invalidates the 'positive' power of the fundamental status-formula. Thus, the outcome for once is quite simple. If the Court mentions the 'fundamental status', the decision tends to favour Union citizens – and the 'fundamental status' usually spins the decision.

167 A number of decisions defy categorization in the above terms, notably the decisions in which the Court expressly refused to discuss Union citizenship (*Olazabal, 2002*; *Stylianakis, 2003*; and the decisions mentioned in the footnotes above); *Trojani, 2004*, which is as hard to categorize as it is to read; *Eman and Sevinger, 2006*, because the Netherlands' way of determining the franchise was compatible with Union citizenship, but not equal treatment; *Wolzenburg, 2009*; and *Czop, 2012*, for merely confirming *Ziolkowski, 2011*.

D Conclusion

This book pursues two goals. On the one hand, all decisions the Court of Justice of the European Union has ever handed down in the free movement of persons and services are unearthed. Roughly 1400 decisions come to light. The thick description in the first part of this book contains them all. This part of the book is helpful for practitioners who want to have a complete picture of the case-law and for scholars whom it allows further to build and deepen their own work.

On the other hand, a more scholarly goal is pursued. The evolution of certain interpretive formulas in the body of case-law unlocked in the first part is traced. The account of this enquiry as such has certain value, which again draws to a large measure on the completeness and comprehensiveness of the enquiry. Every single instance within the 1400 decisions in which the interpretive formulas concerned were applied is considered. There is no decision within the large body of case-law examined in which one of the interpretive formulas is applied, but which goes undiscussed in the second part of this book. While this part of the book allows practitioners to hone their argument based on the interpretive formulas concerned for future cases, broader developments and useful conclusions for scholarly purposes also emerge from the enquiry undertaken. They are summarized below.

That the amount of decisions by the Court of Justice involved in one way or another with the free movement of persons and services is so large may come as something of a surprise.[168] The large number of decisions in turn conditions the number of comprehensively traceable interpretive formulas. Three important strands of interpretive formulas are mapped out within the body of case-law: those operationalizing either a broad or restrictive interpretation, an interpretation based on the idea of 'coordination', or an interpretation relying on concepts that are fundamental. Further evidence can thus be found in this book of the Court's structuralism and activism, although the latter notion, which is politically loaded, is clearly not the central concern of this book.

I Spin and emptiness

Apart from the individual conclusions drawn for each of the interpretive formulas (see below), some general developments and patterns emerge from this book. First, the impact an interpretive formula has in a decision can be assessed. An attempt is made in this book to determine qualitatively the 'spin' a formula exerts

168 At the outset when the enquiry was begun, the expectation had been that no more than 200 decisions would come to light. Yet, after the enquiry is launched, scientific rigour binds the scholar. Hence, once it turned out that the case-law has grown exponentially, a great effort had to be invested to tackle and come to grips with the unexpected number of 1400 decisions. This, in turn, has limited the number of interpretive formulas that could be traced comprehensively in the body of case-law thus established to three.

in each specific decision of the Court. What is meant by 'spin' is best understood by reading a concrete judgment where spin is evident, e. g. *Burchell, 1987* for 'coordinated' or *D'Hoop, 2002* for the 'fundamental status'. 'Spin' is certainly gradual. All three of the interpretive formulas examined sometimes spin decisions, while at other times they fail to do so. Unsurprisingly for case-lawyers, no clear observable overall pattern emerges of when they do and when they do not. It is all the more important to know the specific cases of spin by interpretive formulas, for it improves distinguishing.

'Spin' is more complex though. In the late 1980s, the phenomenon of 'empty spin' emerged with all three interpretive formulas. 'Empty spin' occurs when an interpretive formula is applied in a decision – e. g. that nationals of the member states are to enjoy the greatest possible freedom, that national social security systems are merely coordinated, or that the status of Union citizenship is fundamental. This raises certain expectations of the outcome of the decision. The expectations are then immediately frustrated, because the decision goes against the grain of the formula – the other way round so to speak. Again, 'empty spin' is best understood by reading decisions in which it occurred, such as *De Jong, 1986*, the first case where the 'greatest possible freedom' spun empty, *Pinna, 1986*, the first case of 'empty spin' concerning 'coordinated', or *Schempp, 2005*, the first 'fundamental status' case with an element of 'empty spin'. Clearly, cases of 'empty spin' are important, for they put into perspective the powers of interpretive formulas.

There is more to 'empty spin', though. It is also a sign of a broader evolution in the Court's drafting of decisions. Another such sign is the emergence of advance statements of case-law in the early 2000s, with the first case being *Kurz, 2002*. Advance statements of case-law occur with all three interpretive formulas. The Court puts the formula ahead of the actual reasoning on the merits of the case, normally together with other case-law, not unlike it does with statutory law which it often cites before addressing the merits of the case. Obviously, when an interpretive formula is part of an advance statement, spin is obfuscated, the power of the interpretive formula is diminished.

The emergence of 'empty spin' and advance statements of case-law can be seen in two perspectives. One portrays the Court in a favourable, the other in a less favourable light. The first sees the occurrence of advance statements of case-law as being partly due to the growing complexity and density of the case-law. Frequently, the case-law needs to be cited – the cases and the relevant rulings listed – before that case-law can be applied to the facts. Given the complexity of the case-law, a more integrated approach would risk rendering decisions incomprehensible. 'Empty spin' is seen in this perspective as a sign of transparency. A formula is not just cited when needed to steer a decision in a specific direction, but also when the Court decides against what the formula implies. The emergence of 'empty spin' and advance statements of case-law are thus part of an evolution towards more clarity and perhaps honesty in case-law. In the second perspective the feeling dominates that the advent of 'empty spin' and advance statements of case-law signal a step towards formulaic, boilerplate text. Since, say, a decade, it seems that standardized pieces of text are fed into decisions whenever they fit – often just approximately. Pursuing other goals, this book obviously does not provide compelling proof of the verity of that second perspective. It can only be stated that the way the three interpretive formulas evolved in the last ten to twenty years reveals clear marks of boilerplate statements. Sometimes the use of standardized formulas seems unreflected in the light of the thrust and the outcome of the decision concerned. The feeling is hard to dispel that we have already moved quite deeply into legal automation.

II Breadth

In the free movement of persons and services the Court interprets certain notions broadly, while others restrictively. It also applies certain inherently expansive concepts. This is the story of the first interpretive formula which is narrated in this book. In truth we are looking at a set of interpretive formulas, encompassing in a first branch, *inter alia*, the early broad notion of 'worker', the later 'very broad' notion of establishment, and a broad notion of free movement in general; in a second branch narrow exceptions from rules; and in a third branch the apogee of broad interpretation, the 'greatest possible freedom'. These three branches can be clearly distinguished, but sometimes they 'touch' each other in a specific decision. Only the 'greatest possible freedom' has been confined to social security decisions, at least until very recently.

While the occurrences and the development of formulas of broad interpretation through the three branches and the impact they have can be read up in detail in the second part of this book – especially the crystal clear 'spin' and power of 'the greatest possible freedom' in a series of cases – a more general pattern of evolution in the case-law deserves mention. Early on, the Court of Justice posited a broad notion of 'worker' backed up soon by a restrictive reading of derogations from the free movement of workers. 'Worker' broadly understood subsequently evolved into a broad understanding of the free movement of workers more generally, an evolution that was largely complete by the time the Maastricht treaty came around. This might not be terribly surprising and may all be well known (though solid evidence for well-known facts is, of course, still scientifically valuable). Yet what is interesting is that this evolution was eventually mirrored for the freedom of services, once the services case-law took off. The evolution went from restrictive exceptions to the freedom of services over the broadly interpreted scope of the freedom to broadly construed provisions enshrining the free movement of services in general. In addition, a similar evolution can later be witnessed for Union citizenship. The Court began with some broad language both for workers and *citizens*, underpinned by a particularly restrictive interpretation of derogations from the freedom of *workers*, given *Union citizen-*

ship. Soon the sweeping ruling was added that secondary legislation implementing citizenship in general was worthy of broad interpretation and the narrow understanding of restrictions of the freedom of citizens was fed in.

Relatively speaking, the freedom of establishment was held back in this regard, at least to some extent. The Court seemed to embark on a new course in terms of broad interpretation with the 'very broad' notion of establishment after Maastricht – this being one of the lesser well known aspects of *Gebhard, 1995* – but the interpretive evolution stopped there. The 'very broad' notion did not morph into a broad freedom of establishment in general, nor was it backed up by a narrow understanding of restrictions. It is possible though that the corresponding developments in the free movement of services cover the freedom of establishment, too, since the two freedoms are strongly entwined. Yet no clear evidence has emerged in this regard.

Possibly, the above pattern of evolution, which is now established clearly for the freedoms of workers, services, and Union citizens, is a mere technicality at risk of being over-interpreted. But a broader point should stick: 'broad notions' sometimes herald a more general expansive approach. Hence, scholars and practitioners should be alert when the Court sorts a seemingly innocent broad notion.

III Coordination

In contrast to the frequent, manifold, and relatively complex occurrences of broad and restrictive interpretation, interpretation on the basis of 'mere coordination' is quite straightforward. Again, the details of the formula and its 'spin' can be studied in the relevant chapter, but certain points deserve to be mentioned here. Although other instruments also coordinate national law within the free movement of persons and services, 'mere coordination' is employed as an interpretive formula, as an argument with a certain impact in decisions, only in social security. In the coordination of social security 'mere coordination', however, performed a surprising and noteworthy volte-face. Initially, under the reign of Regulation 3, the idea that the national social security systems were 'merely coordinated' served as a justification for the Court to allow migrant workers to retain certain advantages. With the advent of the successor, Regulation 1408/71, which remained coordinative save in certain clearly circumscribed situations, the function of 'mere coordination' changed. In the subsequent decisions applying Regulation 1408/71 'mere coordination' served as an excuse for certain *dis*advantages migrant workers suffered. This reversal becomes very clear in *Cabras, 1990*, in particular when the case is contrasted to *Keller, 1971* and *Mancuso, 1973*. The formula's volte-face is truly remarkable given that *both* Regulations 3 and 1408/71 rested on the idea of coordination rather than harmonization of national social security system. The little case-law we have so far under the new Regulation 883/2004 shows no sign of such a spectacular turn.

What is furthermore interesting with 'mere coordination' – apart from its frequent application and power which can be verified in the relevant chapter of this book – is the way the formula was uprooted and became abstract. Originally, the roots of the formula of 'mere coordination' in certain decisions was quite clear, but the Court in the mid-1980s detached it from these origins and turned it into an abstract concept for which soon an almost random assembly of decisions was referenced. This is probably just one case of many in which the Court's referencing practice lacks clarity. Often the Court merely refers back to the latest case(s) in which an interpretive formula was applied. Apart from that it is worth noting that this abstraction of 'mere coordination' occurred largely in parallel with the volte-face described above. For both, *Pinna, 1986* can be identified as a turning point. However, to suspect a causal connection between the two developments – implying that the abstraction was made in order to conceal the volte-face – would probably stretch things too far. There are some natural limits to the consistency and interpretability of the Court's case-law. Perhaps the volte-face and abstraction of 'mere coordination' are just signs of the fact that *Pinna, 1986* is a leading case, in more than one regard.

IV Fundamentality

The interpretive formula designating Union citizenship as the 'fundamental status' is by nature relatively young. Yet the idea of treating some notions as fundamental whereas others remain something less than fundamental is as old as the 'broad' formulas and the formula of coordination. Hence, the 'fundamental status' can be seen to rely on two traditions in the Court's case-law. On the one hand, there is a hierarchical, structural tradition in case-law which has notably come to fruition with the *fundamental* rights and, of course, the *fundamental* freedoms. On the other hand, the case-law also includes a status tradition, at least from an informal perspective. Thus, Union citizenship – the 'fundamental status' – was preceded informally in case-law by the notion of the Community national. The establishment of the tradition of the Community national in case-law goes back to the push and drive of the parties to cases and the referring courts. Detailed evidence of the two traditions – 'fundamental' and 'status' – is included in the chapter on 'fundamental'.

While the 'fundamental status' is obviously kin to the 'broad' formulas – it having supplemented the application of broad interpretation to the freedom of Union citizens (see above) – the 'fundamental status' has a clear dimension of its own. Despite its short period of existence, it has acquired an almost eerie power. When the 'fundamental status' is mentioned in a decision, it usually spins it and, further, the result turns out almost consistently in favour of the Union citizen concerned or Union citizens more generally. This is most evident in the early citizenship decisions. However, the results from a counterfactual check – which this book can make for the 'fundamental status' due to the limited number of Union citizenship decisions, while it proves impracticable for the other interpretive formulas – remain inconclusive. Thus, when the 'fundamental status' goes unmentioned in a Union citizenship decision, the decision is still capable of going either way, pro or contra Union citizen. The 'negative power' of the 'fundamental status', i. e. the power to impair through absence, is weak. Its absence has no consistent effect on decisions. Yet this does not at all curtail the 'positive power' of the formula.

E Table of Cases

F Bibliography

Adams, Maurice; de Waele, Henri; Meeusen, Johan; Straetmans, Gert (eds), *Judging Europe's Judges – The Legitimacy of the Case Law of the European Court of Justice*, Oxford, Hart, 2013.

Arnull, Anthony, 'The Americanization of EU Law Scholarship', in Arnull, Anthony; Eeckhout, Piet; and Tridimas, Takis (eds), Continuity and Change in EU Law, Oxford, OUP, 2006, p. 415-431.

Arnull, Anthony, *The European Union and its Court of Justice*, Oxford, OUP, 2006.

Aust, Helmut Philipp, 'Von Unionsbürgern und anderen Wählern – Der Europäische Gerichtshof und das Wahlrecht zum Europäischen Parlament', (2008) 11 Zeitschrift für europarechtliche Studien (2) 221-242.

Barceló, John J., 'Precedent in European Community Law', in Maccormick, Neil; and Summers, Robert (eds), Interpreting Precedents – A Comparative Study, Aldershot, Dartmouth, 1997, p. 407-422.

Beck, Gunnar, *The Legal Reasoning of the Court of Justice of the EU*, Oxford, Hart, 2012.

Bengoetxea, Joxerramon, *The Legal Reasoning of the European Court of Justice: Towards a European Jurisprudence*, Oxford, Clarendon, 1993.

Biondi, Andrea, 'Recurring Cycles in the Internal Market: Some Reflections on the Free Movement of Services', in Arnull, Anthony; Eeckhout, Piet; and Tridimas, Takis (eds), Continuity and Change in EU Law, Oxford, OUP, 2006, p. 228-259.

Bredimas, Anna, *Methods of Interpretation and Community Law*, Amsterdam, North Holland, 1978.

Calliess, Christian, 'The Dynamics of European Citizenship: From Bourgeois to Citoyen', in ECJ (ed.), The Court of Justice and the Construction of Europe: Analyses and Perspectives on Sixty Years of Case-law, The Hague, Asser, 2013, p. 425-441.

Cappelletti, Mauro, *The Judicial Process in Comparative Perspective*, Oxford, Clarendon, 1989.

Chevalier, Roger-Michel, 'Methods and Reasoning of the European Court in Its Interpretations of Community Law', (1964) 2 Common Market Law Review 21-35.

Colneric, Ninon, 'Entwicklungslinien in der Rechtsprechung des Gerichtshofes der Europäischen Gemeinschaften zum Status von Ausländern', in Barwig, Klaus; Beichel-Benedetti, Stephan; and Brinkmann, Gisbert (eds), Perspektivwechsel im Ausländerrecht, Baden-Baden, Nomos, 2007, p. 49-60.

Dawson, Jack, *The Oracles of the Law*, Ann Arbor, University of Michigan Press, 1968.

Dawson, Mark; De Witte, Bruno; Muir, Elise (eds), *Judicial Activism at the European Court of Justice*, Cheltenham, Edward Elgar, 2013.

de Búrca, Gráinne; Weiler, Joseph (eds), *The European Court of Justice*, Oxford, Oxford University Press, 2001.

Eichenhofer, Eberhard, *Sozialrecht der Europäischen Union*, 5. edition, Berlin, Schmidt, 2013.

Epiney, Astrid, *Umgekehrte Diskriminierungen*, Köln, Heymanns, 1995.

Everson, Michelle, 'The Legacy of the Market Citizen', in Shaw, Jo; and More, Gillian (eds), New Legal Dynamics of European Union, Oxford, Clarendon, 1995, p. 73-90.

Garth, Bryan G., 'Migrant Workers and Rights of Mobility in the European Community and the United States: A Study of Law, Community, and Citizenship in the Welfare State', in Cappelletti, Mauro; Seccombe, Monica; and Weiler, Joseph (eds), Integration Through Law: Europe and the American Federal Experience, vol. 3, Berlin, De Gruyter, 1985, p. 85-163.

Gerken, Lüder; Rieble, Volker; Roth, Günter H.; Stein, Torsten; Streinz, Rudolf, *"Mangold" als ausbrechender Rechtsakt*, München, Sellier, 2009.

Grimmel, Andreas, 'Judicial Interpretation or Judicial Activism? The Legacy of Rationalism in the Studies of the European Court of Justice', (2012) 18 European Law Journal (4) 518-535.

Habermas, Jürgen, 'Bringing the Integration of Citizens into Line with the Integration of States', (2012) 18 European Law Journal (4) 485-488.

Hakenberg, Waltraud, 'Der Europäische Gerichtshof – 59 Jahre Gestaltung von Europa durch Recht', in Meng, Werner; Ress, Georg; and Stein, Torsten (eds), Europäische Integration und Globalisierung, Baden-Baden, Nomos, 2011, p. 233-247.

Haltern, Ulrich; Bergmann, Andreas (eds), *Der EuGH in der Kritik*, Tübingen, Mohr Siebeck, 2012.

Hanf, Dominik, 'Le développement de la citoyenneté de l'Union européenne', in Hanf, Dominik; and Muñoz, Rodolphe (eds), La libre circulation des personnes – Etats des lieux et perspectives, Brussels, Peter Lang, 2007, p. 15-28.

Hufeld, Ulrich, 'Vom Wesen der Verfassung Europas – die Freiheit der Unionsbürger als europäisches Legitimationsfundament', (2011) 59 Jahrbuch des öffentlichen Rechts der Gegenwart 457-475.

Hunnings, Neville March, *The European Courts*, London, Cartermill, 1996.

Ipsen, Hans Peter; Nicolaysen, Gert, 'Haager Kongress für Europarecht und Bericht über die aktuelle Entwicklung des Gemeinschaftsrechts', (1964) 17 Neue Juristische Wochenschrift (8) 339-344.

Jorens, Yves; Schulte, Bernd (eds), *European Social Security Law and Third Country Nationals*, Bruxelles, La Charte, 1998.

Kahil-Wolff, Bettina; Greber, Pierre-Yves, *Sécurité sociale: aspects de droit national, international et européen*, Basel, Helbing, 2006.

Kutscher, Hans, 'Methods of Interpretation as Seen by a Judge at the Court of Justice', in European Court of Justice (ed.), Judicial and Academic Conference, Luxembourg, 1976, p. I-1-51.

Lasser, Mitchel de S.-O.-L.'E., *Judicial Deliberations – A Comparative Analysis of Judicial Transparency and Legitimacy*, Oxford, Oxford University Press, 2009.

Lecourt, R., *L'Europe des Juges*, Brussels, Bruylant, 1976.

Maduro, Miguel Poiares, *We, the Court*, Oxford, Hart, 1998.

Mann, C. J., *The Function of Judicial Decision in European Economic Integration*, The Hague, Nijhoff, 1972.

Mertens de Wilmar, J., 'Reflexions sur les méthodes d'interprétation de la Cour de Justice des Communautés Européennes', (1986) 22 Cahiers du Droit Européen (1) 5-20.

O'Leary, Siofra, 'Free Movement of Persons and Services', in Craig, Paul; and de Búrca, Gráinne (eds), The Evolution of EU Law, 2nd edition, Oxford, Oxford University Press, 2011, p. 499-545.

Paskalia, Vicki, 'Co-ordination of Social Security in the European Union: An Overview of Recent Case Law', (2009) 46 Common Market Law Review (4) 1177-1218.

Pennings, Frans, *European Social Security Law*, Antwerpen, Intersentia, 2010.

Plender, Richard, 'The Interpretation of Community Acts by Reference to the Intentions of the Authors', (1982) 2 Yearbook of European Law 57-105.

Rasmussen, Hjalte, *On Law and Policy in the European Court of Justice*, Dordrecht, Martinus Nijhoff, 1986.

Rogers, Nicola; Scannell, Rick, *Free Movement of Persons in the Enlarged European Union*, London, Sweet & Maxwell, 2005.

Sankari, Suvi, *European Court of Justice Legal Reasoning in Context*, Groningen, Europa Law Publishing, 2013.

Schermers, Henry G.; Flinterman, Cees; Kellermann, Alfred E.; von Haersolte, Johan C.; van de Meent, Gert-Wim A. (eds), *Free Movement of Persons in Europe*, Dordrecht, Nijhoff, 1993.

Shaw, Jo, 'A View of the Citizenship Classics: Martínez Sala and Subsequent Cases on Citizenship of the Union', in Maduro, Miguel Poiares; and Azoulai, Loïc (eds), The Past and Future of EU Law – The Classics of EU Law Revisited on the 50th Anniversary of the Rome Treaty, Oxford, Hart, 2010, p. 356-362.

Snyder, Francis, *New Directions in European Community Law*, London, Weidenfeld, 1990.

Spaventa, Eleanor, *Free Movement of Persons in the European Union – Barriers to Movement in their Constitutional Context*, Kluwer, Alphenn aan den Rijn, 2007.

Stone Sweet, Alec, 'The European Court of Justice', in Craig, Paul; and de Búrca, Gráinne (eds), The Evolution of EU Law, 2nd edition, Oxford, Oxford University Press, 2011, p. 121-153.

Stone Sweet, Alec, *Governing with Judges – Constitutional Politics in Europe*, Oxford, Oxford University Press, 2000.

Thürer, Daniel, 'Die Worte des Richters – Gedanken rund um die Verfassungsgerichtsbarkeit', in Hammer, Stefan; Somek, Alexander; Stelzer, Manfred; and Weichselbaum, Barbara (eds), Demokratie und sozialer Rechtsstaat in Europa – Festschrift für Theo Öhlinger, Wien, WUV, 2004, p. 272-297.

Thym, Daniel, 'Toward 'Real' Citizenship? The Judicial Construction of Union Citizenship and Its Limits', in Adams, Maurice; de Waele, Henri; Meeusen, Johan; and Straetmans, Gert (eds), Judging Europe's Judges, Oxford, Hart, 2013, p. 155-174.

Tobler, Christa, *Indirect Discrimination: A Case Study into the Development of the Legal Concept of Indirect Discrimination under EC Law* Antwerpen, Intersentia, 2005.

Tryfonidou, Alina, 'In Search of the Aim of the EC Free Movement of Persons Provisions: Has the Court of Justice Missed the Point?', (2009) 46 CMLR (5) 1591-1620.

Van der Mei, Anne Pieter, *Free Movement of Persons Within the European Community – Cross-border Access to Public Benefits*, Oxford, Hart, 2003.

Vauchez, Antoine, 'The transnational politics of judicialization. Van Gend en Loos and the making of EU polity', (2010) 16 European Law Journal (1) 1-28.

Waelbroeck, Michel, 'Le Rôle de la Cour de justice dans la mise en oeuvre du Traité CEE', (1982) 18 Cahiers du Droit Européen (4) 347-380.

Weiler, Joseph, *The Constitution of Europe*, Cambridge, Cambridge University Press, 1999.

Weiler, Joseph H. H., 'The Transformation of Europe', (1991) 100 The Yale Law Journal (1990-1991) 2403-2484.

Weiss, Friedl; Wooldridge, Frank, *Free Movement of Persons within the European Community*, 2. edition, Kluwer, Alphenn aan den Rijn, 2007.

White, Robin C. A., *EC Social Security Law*, Harlow, Longman, 1999.

White, Robin C. A., 'Social Solidarity and Social Security', in Arnull, Anthony; Barnard, Catherine; Dougan, Michael; and Spaventa, Eleanor (eds), A Constitutional Order of States?, Oxford, Hart, 2011, p. 301-319.

White, Robin C. A., *Workers, Establishment, and Services in the European Union* Oxford, Oxford University Press, 2004.

Wollenschläger, Ferdinand, *Grundfreiheit ohne Markt*, Tübingen, Mohr Siebeck, 2007.

G Acknowledgments

My sincere thanks go to Prof. Bardo Fassbender who not only delivered the first expert opinion (*Erstgutachten*) but also proved a constant source of inspiration and encouragement. To him I owe more than he probably realizes. I am also deeply grateful to Prof. Astrid Epiney and Prof. Daniel Thym for having provided the other two expert opinions.

A journey of more than five years concludes with this book. It is up to the reader to judge whether the effort made to come to the end of this journey brings 'the greatest possible freedom' any closer. It is, however, subject to no doubt whatsoever that this book could not have been realized without the steady support and enouragement of a number of persons. To them go my heartfelt thanks. In roughly chronological order they are: Prof. em. Daniel Thürer, who had supervised my doctoral thesis, for encouraging me to continue with a *Habilitation* and continuously supporting me during the time; Prof. Oliver Diggelmann for his open eyes and ears, generous support, and frank advice at critical junctures; Prof. Thomas Gächter for supporting my grant applications; Prof. Hans-Peter Folz for welcoming me spontaneously when I one day wandered into the offices of the international lawyers at LMU Munich; Prof. Peter M. Huber and Prof. Rudolf Streinz for generous hospitality at LMU; Prof. Christian Walter for generously hosting me for a number of years at his chair and institute at LMU, for offering motivation, inspiration, intellectual discourse, and a quiet place to work without ever asking for anything in return; Dr. Helmut Aust, Dr. Benedikt Pirker, Prof. Sebastian Unger, and Dr. Antje von Ungern-Sternberg for the friendship and support without which it is impossible to go through a *Habilitation*; the many dear colleagues at LMU, including Prof. Ino Augsberg, Dr. Gebhard Bücheler, Ute Freitas, Dr. Daniel Fröhlich, Franka Fruhstorfer, Dr. Martin Heidebach, Dr. Albert Ingold, Prof. Daniel Kahn, Carolin König, Prof. Sophie Lensky, Stephan Lorentz, Dr. Walther Michl, Prof. Florian Möslein, Dr. Laura Münkeler, Ingeborg Neber-Germeier, Dr. Donald Riznik, Dr. Meinhard Schröder, Christine Schuhbeck-Schmidt, Prof. em. Bruno Simma, Paulus Suh, Markus Vordermayer, Prof. Ferdinand Wollenschläger, Quirin Weinzierl, and Dr. Markus Zöckler; Prof. Christoph Frei and Prof. Dirk Lehmkuhl for introducing me to University of St. Gallen (HSG) and for continuous support and friendship; Prof. Bernhard Ehrenzeller, Prof. Roland Kley, Prof. Markus Müller-Chen, and Prof. Benjamin Schindler for invaluable advice and encouragement at the right moment; Dr. Andrew Walton, Dr. Michael Waibel, and Dr. Oliver Westerwinter for support and friendship; the many dear colleagues and friends at HSG, including Prof. Carl Baudenbacher, Prof. Christine Benesch, Dr. Andreas Böhm, Samuel Cobbi, Prof. James Davis, Dr. Daniela Engelmann, Martina Flockerzi, Sabine Greiser, Prof. Lukas Gschwend, Silvio Hänsenberger, Prof. Peter Hettich, Michèle Klarer, Dr. Katrin Krehan, Theresia Langosz, Moritz Meyer, Dr. Simon Planzer, Dr. Roland Portmann, Anita Samyn, Prof. Mark Schelker,

Gabriela Schmid, and Prof. Isabelle Wildhaber; Dr. Jenö und Irène Stähelin for generously supporting my stay at Harvard and for generously offering the best quiet place to write a book; Prof. William Alford for generously hosting me at Harvard; and Prof. Florent Thouvenin for a great time at Harvard and elsewhere. I am also deeply grateful to Dr. Valentin Zellweger, Marianne Pfister, Dr. Malcolm Mac-Laren, and Fredrik von Bothmer who have continuously encouraged and motivated me for a number of years now – sometimes perhaps without noticing it themselves.

Anybody who has ever been involved in a *Habilitation* knows that it cannot be done without the steady support, patience, understanding, and encouragement of family and friends. Barbara, Lotti, Kaspar, Sue, and Mike generously provided all this and more than anyone could ever ask for; so did Martin, Anna, Leonhard, and in particular Jonathan. It is to them I am most grateful.

Finally, my thanks go to the Swiss National Science Foundation and the University of Zurich for supporting me with generous grants and to Emil-Zaugg-Fonds at HSG for supporting the publication of this book with a generous contribution.